English Legal System

English Legal System

Steve Wilson

Helen Rutherford

Tony Storey

Natalie Wortley

OXFORD
UNIVERSITY PRESS

OXFORD
UNIVERSITY PRESS

Great Clarendon Street, Oxford, OX2 6DP,
United Kingdom

Oxford University Press is a department of the University of Oxford.
It furthers the University's objective of excellence in research, scholarship,
and education by publishing worldwide. Oxford is a registered trade mark of
Oxford University Press in the UK and in certain other countries

First edition 2014
Impression: 1

Published in the United States of America by Oxford University Press
198 Madison Avenue, New York, NY 10016, United States of America

British Library Cataloguing in Publication Data
Data available

ISBN 978-0-19-966992-9

Printed in Great Britain by
Ashford Colour Press Ltd, Gosport, Hampshire

Preface

In many ways the English legal system is the most challenging first year subject a law student will encounter. A brief survey of the contents of a book on the subject will reveal that it encompasses the nature of law, the sources of law, the institutions and personnel of the law, and the civil and criminal justice systems. In studying the English legal system students are expected, amongst other things, to find and interpret source materials, to demonstrate an understanding of diverse topics, such as judges as law-makers and the operation of juries, and to be able to analyse and evaluate the operation of institutions such as Parliament as a law-making body and the effectiveness of the courts. When this is added to the constant changes being made to aspects of the English legal system, the volume and diversity of material to be studied can begin to feel overwhelming.

This book has been designed and written to help students focus on the essential points that they need to understand in navigating their way through the study of the English legal system. Its main purpose is to provide an explanation of essential information concerning the English legal system and then to guide students to the significant debates which underpin the system. The text is not intended to be an exhaustive account of the law in this area, but rather it is intended to direct students to important concepts, principles, themes, and issues found within the English legal system syllabus and then to suggest further sources that may be profitably explored. The primary sources of the information are indicated in the text and students are encouraged to consult these so as to develop an appreciation of how such source materials are to be found and interpreted. In the text you will encounter legislation which has not yet fully come into force e.g. Crime and Courts Act 2013. Where appropriate the law has been stated as it currently stands but an indication has also been given of the impact of the prospective change.

The features used in the book aid a structured approach to the study of the English legal system, making clear key points and identifying major themes, thus providing a focus for such legal studies. As the English legal system is a dynamic subject touching on many aspects of life each chapter begins with a Talking Point, which seeks to contextualise the material covered in that chapter. These Talking Points raise issues that can be further explored as understanding of the chapter content develops. This understanding is further assisted with the aims of chapters clearly signposted at the beginning and the significant points summarised at the end of each chapter. Understanding of material may be tested by Thinking Points in the text and then extended by the Critical Debate features which are present in the chapters. The inclusion of further reading lists allows students to continue their research independently; these lists outline the significance of the reading identified. The book is complemented by an Online Resource Centre which will be used to inform readers of important changes and developments in the law. The Online Resource Centre also includes a bank of multiple-choice questions allowing students to further test their knowledge and understanding of the content of the subject.

Another purpose of this book is to aid the development of study skills in this subject area. Unlike substantive areas of law which tend to be based upon the study of legislation and case law and take, in large part, a problem-based approach, the English legal system module tends to take a more evaluative and discussion-based approach. Chapter 1 gives advice, for example, on how to prepare for tutorials and how to write essays. Sample examination and coursework questions and answers are also to be found at the end of appropriate chapters. This feature gives guidance on how to structure answers, choose relevant content, and relate such material to the requirements of the question.

The authors would like to acknowledge the work done on earlier incarnations of this book by Michael Stockdale and Rebecca Mitchell. We would like to thank the late Alan Davenport, our much-missed friend and colleague. Thanks also go to the following for their much-appreciated comments and advice: Gavin Doig, Richard Glancey, Nicola Hyam, Kirsty Swann, Chris Rogers, and Leslie Rutherford. Thanks should also go to the anonymous reviewers, both academics and students, for their helpful and insightful comments and encouraging words. Finally, our thanks go to Helen Davis and Sarah Viner for their help, guidance, and patience in managing the project and keeping the authors on track!

Guide to the features in *English Legal System*

🎯 Learning objectives

By the end of this chapter you should:

- appreciate the characteristics of law;
- be able to identify sources of law and explain the differe processes of law-making;
- understand the various meanings of the term common l

Learning objectives

Each chapter begins with a bulleted outline of the main concepts and ideas you will encounter. These provide a helpful signpost to what you can expect to learn from the chapter.

🕐 Talking point

Operation Yewtree was set up to investigate hundreds of claims came to light following the death of Jimmy Savile in 2011. As par sixteen suspects have been arrested, the majority of whom have be To date, charges have only been brought against five men. This h about whether those accused of sexual offences, particularly ra

Talking points

After the learning objectives, each chapter continues with an outline of a particularly interesting or controversial matter in the subject to capture your interest and to provide a real-world context for the overview which follows.

Thinking point

Trial in the Crown Court is more time-consuming and courts. The classification of offences determines wher reclassifying offences as summary, trial costs may be s A reclassification of an offence as summary would dep be tried by jury. Is this important?

Thinking points

Throughout each chapter there are numerous thinking points which ask you to pause and consider questions around whether the legal system is effective and where reforms are proposed or needed.

⚠ Critical debate

The 'right to die' issue was highlighted in the cases of *R Ministry of Justice* and *R (on the application of AM) v DF* the interplay of law and morality, the limits of judge-m the courts and Parliament. Read the cases and conside

(a) The arguments concerning assisted dying raise issu

Critical debates

Each chapter has its own critical debate where you are asked to consider a controversial or thought-provoking topic and encouraged to develop your own views on it.

particulars of claim: *The particulars of claim is*
the basis of the case against the defendant. It wi
facts relied upon in support of those allegations.
Part 16 and the associated practice direction.

In the context of a personal injury claim, th
claimant's date of birth and details of his inj

Definitions

Key terms are clearly and concisely
explained in definition boxes.

 Example

After having a few pints of beer, Joe decides to see how fast his new Porsc
car can go. He drives it at high speed around a blind bend and crashes int
driven by Anne. Anne is injured in the collision and her car is written off.

Joe could be prosecuted in the criminal courts for offences such as drivin
alcohol above the prescribed limit and driving dangerously. The criminal
determined in either the magistrates' court or the Crown Court.

Examples

Numerous examples can be found in each
chapter to illustrate the system in practice
and provide everyday examples of the
procedures being outlined.

Key point

The Parliament Act procedure allows for a Bill to be
the monarch without the consent of the House of Lc
allowing for a Bill to be passed by the House of Lords
the House of Commons.

Key points

Key points are highlighted to draw your
attention to the essential matters in each
chapter.

 Alternative
dispute resolution
is considered in
chapter 17.

Prior to commencing pr
solicitor will take statem
expert witnesses). Decisi
obtained. Evidence to su
as accident reports from
an accident: medical no

Cross references

Frequent cross referencing between
chapters highlights where topics overlap
and helps you direct your studies.

Summary

- The role of a judge in interpreting a statute is t
  tention of Parliament. The concept of intentio
  lems.
- The principles of statutory interpretation are no
  tools that courts may use to find the intention

Chapter summaries

The central points and concepts covered
are distilled into a summary at the end of
each chapter.

? Questions

1 Explain public legislation; private legislation; an

2 Explain the differences between government b

3 What are the conditions that must be satisfie
money bill) can be passed under the terms of t

4 Explain the differences between the affirmativ

End-of-chapter questions

The self-test questions at the end of each chapter encourage you to test your understanding of the topic as a whole to develop your analytical skills.

✳ Sample question and outline answer

Question

The changes to the composition of the House of
last 60 years mean that the procedure for passi
Act 1911 (as amended) is no longer justified. Exp
the *Parliament Act 1911* (as amended) and consi
twenty-first century.

Sample questions and outline answers

At the end of each chapter is a sample question which is accompanied by an outline answer. This provides an example of how this topic might be assessed and gives you an insight into how to approach your answer using the information provided in the chapter you have just read.

N Further reading

To understand how the rules of statutory interpre
to read the leading cases. In reading such cases pa
ments raised by lawyers before the courts.

· Beatson J. 'Common Law, Statute Law, and Con
This article explores the relationship between comm

Further reading

Selected further reading is included at the end of each chapter to provide a reliable platform for further study.

OXFORD
UNIVERSITY PRESS

online
resource
centres

Search

Home > Law > English Legal System (ELS) > Wilson et al: English Legal System

Resources

Multiple choice questions

Updates

Sample Act of Parliament

Browse:

All subjects

Law

Wilson et al: English Legal System

Resources

Multiple choice questions
A bank of 150 questions with answers and feedback to support your learning
understanding

Updates
Regular updates on key cases and areas of reform

Online Resource Centre

An Online Resource Centre provides a bank of 150 multiple-choice questions with immediate answers and feedback to support your learning and test your understanding. It also provides regular updates on key cases and areas of reform.

www.oxfordtextbooks.co.uk/orc/wilson_els/

Outline contents

Detailed contents

5 The doctrine of judicial precedent

6 The law and institutions of the European Union

7 Human rights and fundamental freedoms

Table of cases

Table of statutes

Table of European treaties, directives, and conventions

Table of statutory instruments

1 Studying English legal system

Introduction

The subject 'English legal system' has always occupied an uneasy position on under-graduate degrees. The content encompassed in a module entitled 'English legal system', depends very much upon the university at which law is being studied. Indeed, the group of topics taught might not even be referred to by that name, instead being called Legal Process or Legal System and Method. Syllabuses are varied and different approaches to the study of the English legal system may be discerned. At one level, there is the explanation of the making and operation of laws and the institutions of the law; at another level there is an evaluation of processes and institutions. Some programmes may emphasise the socio-legal nature of law.

One feature, however, which is common to the teaching of the English legal system, is that it is almost uniformly, and for good reason, taught on year one of law degree programmes. The good reason is that a student needs to know much about the op-eration of laws and the legal system to make sense of the substantive subjects, such as criminal law, contract, and tort. However, in many ways English legal system, or at least aspects of it, would be more profitably studied in the final year of a degree once a student has been exposed to the substantive subjects, the common issues that surround them, and acquired a significant body of legal knowledge. In essence, the study of English legal system requires this solid knowledge base before any attempt may be made to complete the exercises that your tutors are likely to set. A first year student has, therefore, an initial task of absorbing much basic information concerning the personnel, principles, and institutions of the English legal system. Only once this knowledge has been acquired can the evaluation or criticism of the institutions and operation of the legal system be usefully attempted.

You will find that the subject area of the English legal system is dynamic, in the sense that it is subject to considerable change and there are always different ways of achieving desired outcomes. For example, the passing of the Legal Aid, Sentencing and Punishment of Offenders Act 2012 represented a major change to the funding of civil legal services, the consequences of which will take a number of years to be fully evaluated. Another example of the dynamic nature of the subject matter is the constant amendment of the criminal justice system; the past decade has seen numerous statutes dealing with crime, police, and justice passed by Parliament. Significant changes have also been made to the English legal system by the Constitutional Reform Act 2005, which saw the introduction of the Supreme Court in 2009 as a replacement for the Appellate Committee of the House of Lords, and by the Tribunals, Courts and Enforcement Act 2007, which in part was intended to create a new simplified structure for tribunals. It is important to be aware of change and from where such change originates. To this end it is very important to watch developments in Parliament and to read a quality newspaper to keep abreast of developments.

1.1 From 'A' level to degree study

The jump from 'A' level study to that at degree level may not be that obvious. After all if you have studied 'A' level Law you might already be familiar with aspects of the English legal system and criminal law, tort, or contract. The subject matter may be the same, for example, the legislation and significant case law in relation to murder will be the same whether studied at 'A' level or as an undergraduate. Indeed you may feel that the notes given at 'A' level are superior to the more sketchy notes given at university, where you might receive fewer hours of tuition. As for assessment you again might form the view that more help was forthcoming at 'A' level, by way of feedback on essays in advance of submission, than during your degree studies. The similarities and differences outlined here mask the important differences between 'A' level and degree study.

The first important point to recognise is that at degree level the emphasis is placed upon the process of study. By this is meant the collection, reading, and use of source materials. While 'A' level study may have consisted of teacher-led collection of information and its interpretation, once at university the emphasis will be placed upon you to become, eventually, an independent learner. Of course this will not happen overnight, but the course set by tutors will be that of a journey towards educational self-sufficiency. So lectures may be used to direct you towards particular source materials or to focus on a particular issue, assuming that you will explore the factual background for yourself when you leave the lecture theatre. The phrase used to describe degree level study is that a student is 'reading' a subject, be it history, economics, or law. This sets what is expected of an undergraduate student; that the student will, under the direction of tutors, read the source materials of the law.

A second point to appreciate is that the directed reading will be to various sources but most significantly to the primary sources of law. The material to be accessed is the same material as will be used by judges and lawyers. It is essential in the early days of study at university that you recognise that there is a hierarchy of materials that you need to be able to find, read, and use. While at 'A' level you may have worked predominantly from worksheets, pre-prepared notes, or textbooks, at first year degree level onwards you will be expected to consult primary legal materials, i.e. legislation, case law, and other supporting documents. This is not to say that secondary sources, such as textbooks, have no role to play – they do, but they are very much to be used as a guide to finding, reading, and understanding the primary sources of law.

If you appreciate the differences between 'A' level and degree study from the outset of your legal studies you will find the transition easier to achieve as you will understand what is expected of you and what you can expect of your tutors. Indeed in the first few weeks at university you should take the opportunity to understand where law is to be found and the significance of the source you seek to access. This process will be started in the induction course which often precedes the start of the modules you will study throughout your first year.

1.2 Advice on studying the English legal system

English legal system is usually a core first year subject on law degrees. Indeed those of you who have studied law at 'A' level will be familiar with some of the content of this area of study. Generally speaking a full English legal system syllabus will cover the following areas:

- **Legal method**. This includes an exploration of the sources of law and the framework for how law is to be read and used. Legal method encompasses statutory interpretation and the doctrine of judicial precedent;

- **The institutions of the English legal system**. This will involve a description and evaluation of institutions, such as Parliament's role as a law-making body, and the composition, jurisdiction, and structure of the courts and other methods of dispute resolution; and

● **The personnel of the law**. Here the role and organisation of solicitors, barristers, and judges will be considered.

While there is a basic core of material to learn, the approach to the study of this material may differ from syllabus to syllabus. For example, some modules on the English legal system may seek to emphasise the operation of law in an economic and social context; others may emphasise what the law is and how the law is to be interpreted.

Studying any module on a law degree requires the use and development of a range of skills and approaches. As has already been seen, there is a shift from 'A' level, where reliance to a great extent is placed upon the tutor for the material and its interpretation, to degree level where reliance is to be on your own efforts, guided by the teaching staff. This shift needs to be appreciated early in your degree programme as this impacts upon the way you are to approach legal studies. One of the first important early tasks to undertake, on a law degree programme, is to determine 'what are the expectations of me'? Once you identify these expectations it is possible to focus your studies accordingly.

1.2.1 Aims and outcomes

It is always important to study with a purpose, to understand what the module is trying to achieve. A small amount of time spent reading the aims and outcomes of the English legal system module will give you an insight into what is expected of you by the end of the year. Use the aims and outcomes as a check list, as the year progresses, to monitor your development on the module. Also be aware that it is the aims and outcomes that will be tested in the assessment process. Bearing this in mind will aid your preparation for the assessment process and allow you to concentrate your efforts effectively.

1.2.2 Syllabus

Equally a perusal of the syllabus will give further guidance. Identifying the syllabus content of the English legal system module on *your* programme of study is particularly important as English legal system modules differ greatly from law school to law school. Look to see what is encompassed in the module. The module might focus on, for example, legal method, or on the institutions. It should be apparent also from your lecture and seminar programme where emphasis is being placed within the syllabus.

1.2.3 Reading

Another early task you should undertake is to acquaint yourself with the range and types of materials you will have to access while studying the English legal system. Reading your textbook, *English Legal System*, is a starting point but, as with reading other textbooks, this will not be sufficient within itself. Reliance on a textbook alone will not help you to develop the understanding and skills necessary to become a good law student and ultimately a good lawyer. It is necessary go to the original authorities, legislation, cases, journal articles, and other materials that underpin the subject. Increasingly invaluable material is to be found on the internet; particularly in relation to the institutions you are studying, e.g. **www.parliament.uk** and **www.lawsociety.org.uk**. Another invaluable site relates to legislation, **www.legislation.gov.uk**. This site contains legislation in its original form and also supporting materials, such as Explanatory Notes (for an explanation of the significance of Explanatory Notes see Chapter 4, 4.4.2). At your university you will also have access to databases, such as Westlaw or LexisLibrary, which contain in electronic form many sources available in hardcopy form in a law library. However, not all material on the internet, for example material which provides commentary or even basic information, will have been peer reviewed or checked, so it must be treated with caution. Check the authenticity of material before relying upon it or citing it in submitted work.

1.3 **Lectures**

It is argued that, as lectures may be a very passive experience for students, they are of less value in this interactive age. They are, however, still relied upon as the principal means of teaching on many degree programmes. On any module lectures may be used to serve a variety of purposes. The lecture may be used to explain how to undertake analysis of an issue; it may concentrate on a small point of law or on a difficult legal area; or be used to give an explanation of trends or themes. It is important for you to determine what it is that the lecturer is seeking to achieve; put another way you need to be aware of what purpose the lecture is intended to serve. This may be made plain by the lecturer or it may be that this is something that you have to deduce for yourself from the content of the lecture. Some students believe that lectures are there solely to provide a set of notes which when learned will be the basis for examination success. The lecture, or lecturer, will soon disabuse you of this notion. It is unlikely that your lecturer will seek to provide an exhaustive set of notes on the English legal system. Indeed you might feel that the notes given at 'A' level (should you have studied Law at 'A' level) were more comprehensive. Notes are not the issue; you might, however, find more comprehensive notes provided by your lecturer on your institution's e-Learning website or virtual learning environment. The purpose of the lecture should be to give focus to your study of an area of law, to explain and to direct you to sources of further study. A lecturer may also present different points of view and give guidance on the evaluation of the information supplied. A degree education is designed to prepare you to become an independent learner. By this is meant that you will be expected eventually to find source materials, read the source materials, and then use the materials. The module tutors' roles will be to support you as you develop this new approach to learning. The expectation of the lecturer is that you will use the guidance given to undertake core reading and further research. Irrespective of the content the lecture will provide a selection of sources which should be carefully noted along with the key points of explanation. The lecturer will be indicating where you should direct your efforts in your studies after the lecture.

In the early days of your study of law you should familiarise yourself with the materials to which you will be directed and where these may be found. The main materials you will need to access on a regular basis are:

1. Legislation – This comprises primary legislation in the form of Acts of Parliament and secondary legislation in the form of delegated legislation, such as statutory instruments;

2. Law reports – Law reports record the decisions of the courts;

3. Journal articles – The law library will house series of journals such as the *Law Quarterly Review* (LQR), the *Modern Law Review* (MLR), *Cambridge Law Journal* (CLJ), and the *Oxford Journal of Legal Studies* (OJLS). These contain, for example, articles where academics explore issues raised by the law or explain the impact of recent legislation or case law; and

4. Reports – You may be referred to Royal Commission reports or reports of the Law Commission or other government publications.

There are two methods that may be used to locate these sources: first, the university library; and, second, the databases available on the internet. You will be introduced to both of these resources during your law degree induction course. Particularly note where these sources are located in the library. It will be evident that internet access is more convenient and has certain advantages. For example, note that in using commercial legal databases such as Westlaw or LexisLibrary, the legislation you access is in its amended form. Also on accessing a case you will find much information to put the case in context, not least what has happened to the case since it was decided, e.g. has it been reversed on appeal or has it been overruled by a later court?

1.3.1 **Note taking**

A lecturer may begin by outlining what is to be covered in a lecture and highlight the main points that are to be explored. Indeed you should actively look for the structure of the session. This might be made clear in the introductory comments made by the lecturer or in PowerPoint slides, which accompany the lecturer's comments. Such a structure then can form the skeleton for your notes; sub-headings are a useful way to organise your notes. Under these sub-headings key points and important sources should be recorded. These notes are a starting point for your post-lecture study.

Do not attempt to capture every word of the lecturer. As well as outlining the issues to be covered in a lecture, lecturers will often repeat themselves in summarising what has been explained or in explaining the same point in several ways. Note the main points of the lecture and, of course, the sources of law.

A word of warning – it is essential to later check your notes. Cases or statutes may be misspelt or the names of concepts phonetically reproduced in notes, for example 'obita dicter' instead of the correct 'obiter dicta'. Should such errors find their way into essays or exam answers it becomes immediately apparent to the marker that a student has done little beyond reading the notes made in a lecture.

To save time you may wish to develop a system of abbreviations. For example, court could be abbreviated to c/t, Parliament to Parl't, Senior Courts Act 1981 to SCA1981, Court of Appeal to CA and so on. For further illustrations of this process see Wilson and Kenny, *The Law Students' Handbook*.

In summary, it is important to appreciate what it is that the lecture seeks to achieve and what your expectations should be of a lecture. The lecture is there to guide you as to the significant issues and/or arguments on a particular topic, to point you in the direction of relevant source materials, and to expose you to the methods of the law. At the end of a lecture there may be time for questions to be answered, but if not, a note should be kept and any queries followed up in general reading or in a tutorial or seminar. The lecture is not designed to give you a complete set of notes or to exhaustively consider all the points on a particular subject. Think of the lecture as the starting, not the end, point of a process. What comes next is at the heart of the learning process.

1.3.2 **After the lecture**

As soon as possible after the lecture you should have a period of consolidation, where you ensure that the notes you have taken are accurate and that you understand the contents. Such a process is likely to fix the material in your mind and promote long-term retention. Reading a textbook at this point will help you retain and develop your understanding of your area of study. Further to this you should compile a list of sources that you need to read. The next step is perhaps the most important in the learning process. Following the direction given by the lecturer, and supplemented by your own research, you should read the source materials.

An early skill to develop is how to first find and then read the cases, legislation, journal articles, and reports cited in the lecture. This is an essential part of academic study and effort spent in year 1 developing such ability will reward you throughout your degree level studies and beyond. When reading and making notes on source materials always make a note of the reference for the source, e.g. case, journal article, or book; this is a good habit and will in the long run save you time.

1.4 **Preparing for seminars or tutorials**

Two obvious points should be made. First, in order to develop an understanding of an area and to appreciate how to tackle questions it is essential that you attend the seminar or tutorial. Some students view the lecture as the most important teaching session and avoid attendance at seminars. However, this misses the point of each session. Lectures and seminars serve different, but complementary, purposes. Lectures give direction and guidance, but seminars provide an opportunity for deeper exploration of issues and allow students to engage with the learning process. Understanding of an area or point may be confirmed by a seminar or tutorial or misapprehensions corrected. To have confirmed that your understanding of a legal area and approach to reading and using source materials are correct means that you can continue your future studies with confidence. Second, to maximise the benefit to be gained from the seminar you need to be in a position to understand the issues raised by the material; failure to undertake the reading means that you will find it difficult, if not impossible, to take part in the seminar discussions. So, attendance at the seminar is not enough, you must be fully prepared.

Seminars or tutorials may be based on the content of a lecture or some aspect of the lecture. Your work after the lecture will have started the preparation for the seminar. Consideration will have to be given to any further reading needed to answer the question or task set. Indeed there may a reading list attached to the question or task. As a minimum this reading should be undertaken. Thought must then be given to what the question or task requires you to do and how the information you have collected may be used in satisfying such requirements.

You may be asked a question on a problem area in the law. For example:

Example

'The creation of the Judicial Appointments Commission (JAC) in April 2006 was a positive development. However, although Parliament got it right with the issue of the composition of the JAC, it got it wrong with the issue of its powers. The JAC should have had power to directly appoint judges, rather than simply act as a recommending body.'

Discuss.

The difficulty you will have in answering a question of this type is, first, identifying and analysing the requirements of the question and then, second, structuring the material. By addressing the following questions this will help you analyse and structure material:

- Why and how did the problem in the law arise?
- What is the nature of the problem – give an explanation of it.
- How was, or is, the problem to be dealt with?
- Has the solution to the problem worked?

So the question on the Judicial Appointments Commission could be tackled in the following way:

(a) the perception of the judiciary as government appointees lacking independence; and the criticism that judges came from a narrow social background and failed to proportionately mirror the gender and ethnicity composition of society;

(b) an overview of the system for the appointment of judges prior to the creation of the Judicial Appointments Commission, including identification of problems such as a lack of transparency in the appointments process;

(c) the creation of the Judicial Appointments Commission by the Constitutional Reform Act 2005;

(d) an explanation of the composition of the Judicial Appointments Commission and whether as the question suggests the composition is satisfactory given the problems that were to be addressed by its creation;

(e) what powers the Judicial Appointments Commission has and the role of the Lord Chancellor in the process of appointment;

(f) finally, consideration should be given to what has been the effect of the operation of the Judicial Appointments Commission on the appointment of judges; recourse to statistics on judicial appointments in terms of gender and ethnicity would be essential.

1.5 Assessment

One of the first matters you will want to establish is how your module is to be assessed. This might be by an assignment or by an end of semester or end-of-year examination or both. Getting to grips with the content of the module is one thing, demonstrating that you understand that content is another. You will have learned in your previous studies how to answer questions; this ability must be further developed and with some adaptation will serve you in answering law questions.

1.5.1 Assignments (forming part of the assessment for English legal system)

Before you begin, ensure that you know the requirements of the assignment, e.g. word limits (are footnotes and bibliography included in the word count?), hand-in dates etc. Follow the requirements carefully. For example, do not exceed the word limit; at some universities exceeding the word limit will be an automatic failure. Guidance on this point may be found in the assessment regulations of your university.

A difference from 'A' level that will be immediately apparent is that your tutor will not be prepared to discuss the assignment with you. This extends to not commenting upon drafts of your answer. The expectation is that you will research and write the essay by yourself. This is a further reason for taking all the opportunities that your module provides, such as attending lectures and seminars and submitting non-assessed work for helpful comments on your understanding of an area of law and style of answer.

1.5.2 Importance of assessment criteria

The piece of work set should indicate the criteria against which your assignment is to be assessed. For example, such criteria may include: ability to research and awareness of sources; analysis; relevance of subject matter; clarity of expression; accuracy; presentation; and appropriate citation of authority, referencing, and inclusion of a bibliography. Use these criteria as a check list so as to ensure that you have done all the things expected of you by the examiner.

1.5.3 Writing an assignment

The starting point is to determine what it is that you have been asked to complete. As many English legal system assignments are in the form of essays, pay particular attention to the instruction. Usual instructions are 'explain', 'comment', 'discuss', or 'evaluate'.

- **Explain**. In providing an explanation it is expected that you will give reasons for the matter raised by the question.
- **Comment**. This instruction expects you to comment upon a proposition or state of affairs raised in a quotation or statement. You may need to place the event in context or to demonstrate the impact that it has had.
- **Discuss**. Where 'discuss' is used you are given the opportunity of assessing the strengths and weaknesses of, for example, a particular position, argument, or rule of law. This may be done in the form of debate or argument.
- **Evaluate**. This is an invitation to appraise the worth of an argument or topic.

The purpose of a written answer is to show that you understand an area of law as it applies to a question. In writing your answer you should list the issues raised by the question and then select material relevant to the issues. The process of selection of material is important as this, in part, demonstrates to the examiner that you understand what the question concerns. It can be seen that relevance depends upon the terms of the question. A question is not usually an invitation to write all you know about a topic area; material must be selected by you and its link to the question made plain.

For example, consider the following question:

> ### ⊜ Example
>
> In the interpretation of legislation the role of judges is to give effect to the intention of Parliament. This process is not without its difficulties.
>
> **Discuss.**

(Note – You might want to come back to this question after you have read the chapter on statutory interpretation.)

The central issue in the issue question concerns the role of judges in the process of statutory interpretation. So immediately the limits of your answer are set, you are to explore the judicial role in interpreting legislation, not consideration of judicial law-making generally, e.g. through development of the common law. Within the limits set you must then identify what the question requires you to consider; the question asks for an exploration of the relationship between judges and Parliament in relation to legislation. The constitutional position is that Parliament makes law and the judges interpret and apply the law so made. However, therein lies the problem – the process assumes that the intention of Parliament is first, clear and, second, clearly expressed in the language used in the legislation. The case law reveals that the problems inherent in the open textured nature of language coupled with few clues as to what Parliament's intention might be lead to the need for the judges to determine the meaning of the legislation. How do the judges do this and what are the difficulties in this process? In order to explore further the role of the judges you must now evaluate the interpretative process by explaining the rules of statutory interpretation and the uncertainties accompanying the process. Traditionally, the courts in seeking to ascertain the intention of Parliament have employed the literal, golden, and mischief rules. The nature and content of these rules need to be explained together with the intrinsic and extrinsic aids to construction – the use of the debates of Parliament as found in Hansard as an aid to finding the intention of Parliament must be considered. The recent case law indicates that the courts should favour a purposive construction of legislation, e.g. *R (Quintaville) v Secretary of State for Health*. The purposive approach needs to be explained and any difficulties associated with the approach identified. Additionally, you can make the point that where there are rights under the European Convention on Human Rights then by s.3 of the Human Rights Act 1998 the courts are under a duty to read and give effect to primary legislation and subordinate legislation in a way which is compatible with the Convention rights 'in so far as it is possible to do so'. The difficulties encountered in interpreting and applying s.3 should be explored.

Once you have collected the information you want to use in answer to the question asked the next part of the process is to structure the information.

The material selected must then be structured. An answer should have an introduction, a middle section, and a conclusion. It is the middle section where the issues raised by the question should be considered. This will itself need to be structured to ensure that the issues are dealt with appropriately. This particular question requires:

- an exploration of the relationship between Parliament and the courts and the search for the intention of Parliament;
- the process of statutory interpretation;
- the rules of statutory interpretation and the difficulties with the approaches, including the purposive approach and the aids to construction;
- section 3 Human Rights Act 1998.

The introduction and conclusion should be written after you are satisfied with the middle section. An introduction should outline the issues to be considered in the middle section and a conclusion should draw together what has been said in the middle section. Importantly, a conclusion should not introduce new material; a conclusion draws from material already discussed in the body of the text. On reviewing your essay should you find new material in your conclusion then you must revise your conclusion or amend your middle section.

In displaying your understanding explanations must relate to the issues raised by the question. If a question mentions a concept, for example the doctrine of judicial precedent, then some explanation of the concept must be given. If a question asks you to discuss a statement, such as the following, 'The doctrine of judicial precedent is inflexible and unjust', then it is not enough to merely explain the doctrine of judicial precedent. The main thrust of the question concerns an exploration of the advantages and disadvantages of the doctrine of precedent and whether the former outweigh the latter. Emphasis needs to be placed on the perception that the doctrine is inflexible and unjust. The issue of certainty in the law created by the doctrine must be carefully considered. It must also be noted that the doctrine operates in different ways in different courts so that there may be an opportunity for a court to overrule an unjust precedent. Avoidance of precedents, for example by distinguishing, may also be explored.

Remember you should make explicit reference in your essay to source material and include appropriate references. References may be included in footnotes.

1.5.4 **Referencing**

An important part of scholarship is appropriate and effective referencing. The idea behind referencing is that the reader is able easily to locate the sources upon which you rely. Referencing also ensures that credit is given to the originator of the work; without referencing the ideas of another person may appear to be those of the writer of the assignment. Failure to acknowledge the work of another by an appropriate reference may infringe your university's plagiarism regulations and lead to sanctions been taken against the offending student.

There are various ways in which references may be presented. In the first instance, establish if your Law school specifies a particular referencing system; if so use it. If not you may want to consider the guidance given in the Oxford Standard for Citation of Legal Authorities (OSCOLA), which may be accessed at **http://denning.law.ox.ac. uk/published/oscola.shtml**. The important point is to include all information necessary for the marker to find the source and to be consistent in the presentation of such information.

1.5.5 **Finally...**

Before submitting your assignment, check for obvious mistakes of presentation, grammar, punctuation, and typographical errors.

1.5.6 **What to do after the return of your assignment**

While an assignment may count towards your final mark for this module, it should also be viewed as a further learning experience. There is an important feedback opportunity to be taken. Feedback may be given orally in a lecture, in written form dealing with general issues, and/or in specific comments on your assignment. Reflect on the comments and seek to discover where extra marks may have been gained by identifying any weaknesses in your understanding of the question set, the relevant law, or your essay technique. Should you be unclear on any of these matters make an appointment to see your tutor for further advice and guidance.

1.6 **A note about group work**

Teamwork is an important feature of everyday working life so it is possible that you may be asked to submit a group assignment or undertake a group presentation. The issue here is one of organisation and management. Clear identification of roles and responsibilities within the group is vital to the success of such an undertaking.

1.7 **Oral presentations**

With the increasing emphasis upon the development of skills, you may be asked to give a presentation either individually or as part of a team. In doing so certain basic points should be borne in mind. First, the key to a successful presentation is structure. Always make sure that your audience knows where the presentation is going. Use PowerPoint or a flip chart to highlight the main points you wish to make. At the conclusion of your presentation summarise what you have said. Second, try to pace your presentation; delivered too fast you will lose your audience, too slow and their attention will wander. Third, it is best to deliver the material as if you are talking naturally, rather than reading a prepared speech. This is difficult if you are not confident of remembering your material. It is possible to use postcards for the main points you wish to make and hold these in your hand as an aide memoire. By not over-relying on notes you can maintain eye contact, which makes your presentation more interesting for your audience and allows you to gauge if your explanation is being understood. Attempt to vary the pace of your delivery and add emphasis where appropriate. Fourth, do not make your explanations too detailed; sometimes less is more. Rather than go for detail try to extract some general points and supporting examples. Of course, this approach depends on the subject matter of the presentation. Fifth, use PowerPoint for the presentation of tables, statistics, or diagrams.

1.8 **Examinations**

Examinations are an opportunity to demonstrate what you know but more importantly what you understand. Knowledge is a prerequisite for examination success but it not the only or most important element. What an examiner is looking for in a script is an understanding of an area of the law as it applies to the question asked. An ability to analyse the questions set, choosing and explaining relevant law, and then demonstrating how such law relates to the requirements of the questions is needed.

Your examination may take the form of a closed-book or open-book examination. The difference is that in a wholly closed-book exam no materials, such as notes and textbooks, are allowed in the exam room, whereas an open-book examination allows materials to be taken into the examination. A halfway house occurs where a statutes book only may be taken into the examination. The type of exam will determine your approach to preparing for the examination. The difference from a marker's perspective is that with a closed-book exam *some* credit may be given for knowledge of the law, whereas with an open-book exam credit will not be given for knowledge alone, the emphasis is on analysis and use of the law.

1.8.1 **Preparing for examinations**

An obvious key to examination success in law, which applies to all subject areas, is that you must know the relevant law and that this must be apparent in your answers. Unless you are possessed of a photographic memory, there is no avoiding the difficult process of committing large bodies of legal material to memory (of course, the approach for open-book exams is different). The process is made easier if you adopt good working practices throughout your study of the English legal system module, such as carrying out post-lecture consolidation of your notes as described earlier and spending some time each week or fortnight refreshing your knowledge by re-reading your notes. Nonetheless, it is probably unavoidable, in the weeks leading up to the examinations, that you will have to spend a significant amount of time reading and re-reading your notes to ensure that you have instant recall of the concepts, detail, and sources of several topic areas in the examination room. Don't think that an open-book exam is a passport to a revision-free run-up to the exam. While there is no need to have a flawless recall of the detail of the law you must understand your material and be able to locate material readily. The trap for the unwary is that sifting through notes or books looking for a source or trying to understand a point relevant to a question set takes time and open-book exams will be subject to a time limit. Again some mastery of your materials is needed which, in turn, depends upon effective revision.

Try to be systematic in your revision by drawing up a revision schedule which allows you to cover all your modules equally and allows time for consideration of examination technique, i.e. how to answer the potential questions.

There are a number of simple matters that may be dealt with prior to the examination which will take some of the stress out of the examination situation:

- First, ensure that you know where the examination is to be held; if you are unfamiliar with the location visit it before the date of the examination.

- Second, be aware of the requirements of the examination, e.g. how many questions must be attempted; what is the duration of the examination; and is there a compulsory question or is there a free choice of questions to answer?

- Third, calculate what length of time you may spend attempting an answer to each question required.

- Fourth, check to see if the examination is a closed-book exam or one where materials are permitted in the examination. Is it possible to take a statutes book into the examination?

Students often spend an inordinate amount of time seeking to question spot. While it is unrealistic to recommend that you should not do this, it should be approached with caution. Some guidance on the likely content of the English legal system paper may be found by looking at where emphasis has been placed in the lecture and seminar programmes during the course of the year. It would be an unusual approach to teach certain areas but then to examine different ones. Past exam papers may give some indication of likely question areas, but remember that the emphasis of the module might have been different in previous years. However, some topics are so important that it is highly likely that there will be an exam question on this subject. For example, if the English legal system syllabus includes legal method it would be improbable that no question on statutory interpretation or on the doctrine of judicial precedent would feature in the exam. If you are to question spot be aware that you need to revise a sufficient number of areas to allow you to attempt answers to all the questions required.

If four answers are to be written it is a risky strategy to revise only four areas. Not all of the areas may feature in the examination paper. Even if the four areas appear in the questions asked they might not be in a form that you can answer. In consequence, if you do question spot and tailor your revision accordingly, build in a margin for the 'unexpected'.

1.8.2 **The examination**

Effective preparation should ensure that you can concentrate your efforts on writing the requisite number of answers. You must use the time available effectively. Practising writing essays under exam conditions prior to the exam should alert you to what it is possible to write within the allotted time. Obviously, effective time management will avoid the trap of failing to attempt all the questions required by the instructions. Success or failure in an exam may rest on a last answer; remember in a four answer exam paper it is easier to get 40 per cent out of 100 per cent than out of 75 per cent. Should you be running out of time then, as a last resort, at least indicate your understanding of the final question in note form. You will not achieve full marks but may do enough to make a difference to your final result.

Another aspect of time management is directing your effort according to the weighting of marks within the exam paper and/or within questions. Should the exam paper contain a compulsory question this may carry, say, 40 per cent of the marks; in which case you should use 40 per cent of the allotted time in producing an answer. Equally, if a question is in two parts and the marks split is part (a) 60 per cent and part (b) 40 per cent obviously a larger proportion of time should be spent on part (a).

1.8.3 **Post-examination**

Once you have finished your examination, try to forget about it. Unless this is your last examination do not be tempted to hold a post-mortem with your friends and fellow students. There is nothing to be gained from this process; indeed the opposite is quite true. In general, students are not in the best position to assess their performance in the heat of the examination room and discussion of such may unnerve and divert the further effort required for forthcoming exams. Put thoughts of the examination to one side and concentrate on your remaining exams.

Once you have received your results, whether you have, hopefully, passed or failed there will always be something to learn about your performance. You should receive some form, or forms, of feedback on your paper; it is important to reflect on what the good points of your examination performance are and where you could improve. Generic feedback on the content of answers may be given to you in written form or otherwise be available on the e-Learning website for your module; you may get your exam paper returned to you. Whatever form the feedback takes seek to learn from it and to carry forward this guidance into the next year of study. If you feel unclear, make an appointment to see your module tutor who will be able to analyse your examination performance and provide advice on what needs to be done to improve.

Further reading

- **Strong, S.I.** *How to Write Law Essays and Exams*, 3rd edn, Oxford University Press (2010)
  Contains much advice on how to structure answers to essay and problem questions and on how to develop a good legal writing style.

- **Wilson, S.** and **Kenny, P.** *The Law Student's Handbook*, 2nd edn, Oxford University Press (2010)
  Contains practical advice on lectures, seminars, the use of sources of law, and how to prepare, write, and reference law assessments.

2 English legal system – an overview

⊙ Learning objectives

By the end of this chapter you should:

- appreciate the characteristics of law;
- be able to identify sources of law and explain the different processes of law-making;
- understand the various meanings of the term common law;
- know in outline the structure, composition, and jurisdiction of the courts;
- be able to explain the impact of membership of the European Union and the European Convention on Human Rights; and
- have an overview of the bodies and personnel of the law.

🔴 Talking point

The foreword to a report entitled When Laws Become Too Complex states:

> The volume of legislation, its piecemeal structure, its level of detail and frequent amendments, and the interaction with common law and European law, mean that even professional users can find law complex, hard to understand and difficult to comply with…Excessive complexity hinders economic activity, creating burdens for individuals, businesses and communities. It obstructs good government. It undermines the rule of law.

To be effective a legal system must consist of laws that are clear and accessible. Without clarity and accessibility citizens will not know of the extent of their rights and duties or indeed where to find such law in the first place. In making sense of the English legal system this quote raises a range of matters that will be addressed in this chapter and form the basis of further study:

- What is law and where is it to be found?
- What is legislation and how can it be changed or amended?
- Why is legislation amended?
- What is the common law?
- How does the common law and legislation interact?
- What is European law and what impact does it have on English law?
- Why is law complex?

The other side to having rights and duties is the process for the resolution of disputes over such rights and duties and their enforcement. In the English legal system the courts determine disputes and enforce the law. The main questions that arise are:

- What is a court?
- How are the courts organised?
- If a party disagrees with the decision of a court what may be done?
- How are cases before the courts funded?

Introduction

The study of the English legal system involves two different, but related processes. First, as a law student, you must learn a large body of factual material about the fundamental concepts of law, the sources of English law, and the institutions and the personnel of the law. You will encounter the material in this chapter during your study of the English legal system but you will find that the material also underpins an understanding of other substantive modules, such as contract, tort, and criminal law. This information contains the 'basic tools' that a law student needs to start to understand law and how it operates.

Second, such knowledge is essential to the next process which involves a critical evaluation of the operation of law and its institutions; it is one thing to say what the law is, but quite another to explain if the law or an institution is operating effectively. A sound knowledge base is needed to found critical studies of the legal system or of the 'law in action'.

This chapter seeks to provide an overview of the law and the English legal system, introducing fundamental legal concepts and the terminology of law, which can seem somewhat mysterious in the early days of legal study. Some general themes or issues arising out of the basic information are outlined in this chapter preparatory to a more detailed discussion in later chapters.

....

2.1 **What is law? – some basic ideas**

Much of law is concerned with definitions: who is an employee, what is a public place, or what is a business?

See chapter 7, 'Human rights and fundamental freedoms' and the difficulties caused by the meaning of 'public authority' under the Human Rights Act 1998.

Many disputes coming before the courts require determination of such an issue. For example, in s.6 of the Caravan Sites Act 1968, a duty was placed on county councils to provide gypsies with adequate accommodation (note that this provision of the Caravan Sites Act 1968 has now been repealed). Immediately it must be determined who falls within the term 'gypsies'. In its ordinary meaning, 'gypsies' refers to people of Hindu descent, alternatively known as Romanies. However, s.16 defined 'gypsies' as 'persons of nomadic habit of life, whatever their race or origin'. It may be seen that the definition in the 1968 Act raises a further definitional issue of what is meant by 'nomadic'. Originally, the word 'nomadic' meant tribes moving from place to place to find pastures for the purposes of grazing livestock. How does the word apply to modern travellers; must they be moving from place to place for an economic purpose or merely be travelling for any purpose? Can an individual be a nomad or must there be a group?

Such questions exercised the Court of Appeal in *Regina v South Hams District Council and Another, ex parte Gibb* [1994] 3 WLR 1151 and further see Lord Millett's comments in 'Construing Statutes' (1999) 20 Stat LR 107. The important point is that problems of definition are common in law. As seen earlier, there are various meanings that may be given to a particular word. In a statute, Parliament may leave a word undefined or indeed may provide a definition which may be narrower or broader than the meaning of a word in its everyday usage. It is for lawyers to interpret words and if such is not clear then to argue the point before a court.

Indeed, the meaning of many of the terms we are to consider in this chapter depends upon the context in which the term is used. For example, see later the variable meaning of the term common law.

A definition of law itself has proved elusive and much academic comment exists on the problems of devising a complete definition. Rather than exploring these sometimes esoteric arguments, by way of introduction a number of features associated with law are identified to highlight some of the characteristics of law in a practical sense.

See chapter 4, 'The interpretation of statutes'.

- The features associated with law are: a basis for recognising what is law, as opposed to, for example, the rules of a game or a moral code;
- a defined area where the law applies, such as in a state or other defined geographical area, and when law comes into operation; and
- the content of the law in terms of doctrine, principles, and rules.

2.1.1 **Recognised as being law**

The law of England and Wales primarily comes from two sources: Parliament and the courts. In relation to law made by Parliament, as long as a bill is passed by the House of Commons and the House of Lords and receives the royal assent, the resulting Act of Parliament is recognised as law. Equally, cases decided by the courts which interpret Acts of Parliament or develop the common law are recognised as a source of law. Originally, the law made by judges through case law was the most important source of law, as Parliament met infrequently. However, with the ascendancy of Parliament as the law-maker, legislation increasingly became the main source of law.

Morality and the law may coincide, but not necessarily. Using morality as a guide to what should be subject to legal intervention is problematic. The difficulty, of course, lies in defining what is immoral. Religion may give guidance, but not all members of a society will necessarily agree on what is, or what is not, immoral. Attempts have been made to identify criteria against which to judge whether conduct should attract legal intervention. For example, John Stuart Mill in *On Liberty* said, '[t]he only purpose for which power can be rightfully exercised over any member of a civilised community against his will is to prevent harm to others. His own good, either physical or moral, is not a sufficient warrant.' But this principle in itself calls for judgements as to what constitutes harm and who falls within the category of 'others'.

Morality may underpin law, for example, the law of contract may be seen as based upon the moral principle that a person should fulfil his promises. Theft is considered immoral and is also illegal, being a criminal offence under the Theft Act 1968. However, not every immoral act will constitute a criminal offence or a civil wrong. For example, prostitution may be considered immoral but being a prostitute is not a crime in itself; however, many activities associated with prostitution are criminal, e.g. soliciting. It is arguable that morality is not the key for recognising law. Indeed, a law which is considered to be immoral may nonetheless be law. On this view morality does not, therefore, determine what is to be considered law. This may be labelled as a positivist approach.

However, it should be noted that some legal scholars, the natural lawyers, argue that a law-making process which fails to recognise a moral dimension to law is fundamentally flawed. Lord Steyn in a lecture identified the tyrannies of Nazi Germany, apartheid in South Africa, and Chile under General Pinochet as demonstrating 'that majority rule by itself, and legality on its own, are insufficient to guarantee a civil and just society. Even totalitarian states mostly act according to the laws of their countries.' In Europe, the European Convention on Human Rights seeks to ensure that the laws of signatory states protect human rights and fundamental freedoms, thus giving a moral core to laws. Further discussion of the positivist/natural law debate goes beyond the ambit of this book and these important issues may be further pursued in a course on jurisprudence.

For our present limited purposes, and taking a positivist approach, what is, or what is not law, depends upon the source from which it emanates; as will be seen the passing of the Human Rights Act 1998 means there is a domestic mechanism for ensuring that the law of the United Kingdom is compatible with the European Convention on Human Rights. A doctrine, principle, or rule is a law if it comes from a recognised validating source, such as Parliament or the courts. So, for a bill (a draft Act of Parliament) to become law, it must be passed by Parliament and receive the royal assent of the monarch. This is the recognised way in which an Act of Parliament is made. Equally, decisions made by the courts are recognised as part of the law of England and Wales.

2.1.2 **Geographical area and commencement**

Laws apply to a defined geographical area usually corresponding to the territorial limits of a state. The United Kingdom, comprising England, Wales, Scotland, and Northern Ireland, is a state. However, in the United Kingdom there is not a single legal system. English law and the English legal system apply in England and Wales. Many aspects of the law and legal system of Scotland are markedly different from those of England and Wales; to some extent, the same is true of Northern Ireland. In relation to an Act of Parliament it will apply to the whole of the United Kingdom unless the Act indicates otherwise. Some statutes may be arranged in parts, with one part applying to England and Wales, another part applying to Scotland, and yet another applying to Northern Ireland.

Generally, in interpreting statutes the courts presume that an Act of Parliament only applies to the United Kingdom, unless extra-territorial operation of the Act is expressly or impliedly provided for by the Act in question. It is possible for Parliament to pass laws which apply to acts committed outside the United Kingdom. For example, murder is triable in England and Wales wherever the offence is committed by a British subject, see s.9 of the Offences Against the Person Act 1861. This provision does not extend to Scotland. Legislation has been specifically enacted to allow the courts of the United Kingdom to try homicides committed abroad by non-British subjects under the War Crimes Act 1991.

Another major source of law is the law created by judges; this, too, is only applicable within England and Wales. The common law, that is judge-made law, does not operate in Scotland. Indeed, Scotland has a separate criminal law and procedure and areas of civil law, such as contract and tort, are different from those laws applying in England and Wales.

2.1.3 **The commencement of Acts of Parliament**

An Act of Parliament comes into force at the start of the day on which the Act receives the royal assent (see s.4 of the Interpretation Act 1978), unless the Act provides otherwise. If an Act is not to come into force on the day of the royal assent then it is necessary to look at the Commencement section of the Act, which will specify when the Act is to come into force. This may be done by: (a) stipulating a date when the Act becomes operative; or (b) stating that an Act is to be brought into force, or parts of it are to be brought into force, by statutory instrument to be made by a minister.

Generally, Acts of Parliament operate from the day they come into force and in this way only affect the future. This is not to say that Parliament cannot pass an Act which has retrospective effect, applying to past conduct; Parliament may do so if such an intention is made clear in an Act of Parliament. However, retrospective effect is considered to be objectionable as rights already accrued may be affected and previously lawful behaviour may become criminal and subject to a penalty. In the interpretation of Acts of Parliament by the courts it is presumed, in the absence of a clear intention to the contrary, that a statute is not to have retrospective effect. It may be noted that by Article 7 of the European Convention on Human Rights retrospective criminal law is prohibited. However, judge-made law does operate retrospectively. As to how judge-made law operates in England and Wales see at 5.2.

2.1.4 **The content of law**

Criminal offences and civil wrongs

Glanville Williams, in *Learning the Law*, said that:

> the distinction between a crime and civil wrong cannot be stated as depending upon *what is done*, because what is done may be the same in each case. The true distinction resides, therefore, not in the nature of the wrongful act but in the legal *consequences that may follow it.*

> ### ☰ Example
>
> If a person punches another then the legal consequences that may follow are twofold: first, the crime of, at least, battery may have been committed; and second the tort of battery may have been committed. In this way one act may lead to two separate legal consequences, being prosecution for a crime in the criminal courts and punishment if convicted and civil proceedings where the injured party may seek to obtain remedies in respect of a civil wrong.

It is important to note that the criminal law and civil law serve different purposes. The criminal law provides a system for the punishment of wrongdoers by the state. Under such a system the purpose is to maintain social order by deterring behaviour which violates other members of society's personal security and property rights. The focus is on the wrongdoer, or defendant, and once convicted questions arise as to how to deal with the wrongdoer. In essence, the criminal justice system is punitive; a wrongdoer may be punished by the infliction of a fine or a period of imprisonment. However, the courts have a wide array of sentencing powers and elements of sentencing are designed to have a rehabilitative effect on the wrongdoer, so it is not a wholly punitive system.

While the person who has been subjected to a battery may derive some comfort from an assailant being punished, he or she may have suffered losses in the form of pain, suffering, possible medical or dental costs, and time off work. The civil law provides a system for the compensation of such losses; in this case, the tort of battery would provide a remedy. So losses suffered owing to the commission of the tort of battery would be compensated by the award of a remedy of damages. Under the civil law the focus is upon the person who has suffered loss and damages are intended, as far as money can, to put the person in the position they would have been in had the wrong not been committed: i.e. put the innocent party financially in the position they would have been in had the wrong not been committed.

The great branches of English law are the civil law and the criminal law. The civil law creates a system of rights and remedies for regulating interaction between members of society. Historically, the main areas of the civil law were the laws of contract and tort. These areas provide examples of how the system of rights and remedies operate. Treitel, in *The Law of Contract*, defines a contract as 'an agreement giving rise to obligations which are enforced or recognised by law'. Thus, obligations may be created by the parties' agreement and should a party fail to perform their side of the agreement the other will have remedies for this failure. The main remedy is that of damages, which are designed to compensate for the loss caused to the innocent party.

The law of tort encompasses a number of situations where the law imposes a duty to act in accordance with a certain standard. The duty does not depend upon there being a contract. Examples of torts are negligence, nuisance, assault and battery, trespass, and defamation. Law may be classified in various other ways, for example, public law and private law or substantive and procedural law.

> ### 🔑 Key point
>
> The same set of facts may give rise to various legal consequences, sometimes both criminal and civil in nature.

2.2 Common law and equity

Another important classification of law that will be encountered in the early stages of a law course is that of common law and equity.

2.2.1 Common law

The term common law gives rise to difficulty as it has several meanings, so any meaning depends upon the context in which the term is used: Common law may mean the law created by the common law courts in contrast to the law created by the Court of Chancery, which was called equity.

- Common law may mean all the law created by the courts, including the law of equity, as opposed to the law created by Parliament, that is legislation. In this sense, common law may be also termed 'judge-made' law.
- Common law may refer to a legal tradition which defines the English legal system and other derivative legal systems as opposed to the civilian legal tradition exemplified by the systems of mainland Europe. Apart from England and Wales other examples of a common law tradition are to be found in the legal systems of the states of the United States (with the exception of Louisiana), Canada, and Australia. Common law in this sense refers to forms of law-making, particularly judge-made law, which is governed by the doctrine of judicial precedent. The characteristic feature of the civilian systems is that law is to be found in codes made by the legislature. The civilian tradition is seen in the legal systems of France and Germany. While the French law of contract is codified and to be found in legislative form, the English law of contract is to be found mainly in the decisions of judges as reported in the law reports. As will be seen, a first issue when reading cases is to determine what the law is, as judges will not usually clearly state the rule upon which a decision is based.

It is not suggested that codification is unknown to English law; the Sale of Goods Act 1893 was an example of codification. Many areas of English law are a mix of legislation and case law.

2.2.2 Equity

The first point to note about equity is that it is a body of law developed by the judges, subject to the doctrine of precedent and in this sense is the same as other judge-made law. However, the origins, development, and the substance of equity are very different to those of the common law. Equity developed because of the rigidity of the common law; the price of certainty is sometimes injustice. To remedy injustices, it was possible to petition the Chancellor as 'keeper of the King's conscience', acting on behalf of the king as the fountain of justice. At first, equity was merely the Chancellor acting according to conscience. There was no system and therefore no certainty; it was said that equity depended upon the 'length of the Chancellor's foot', meaning that who was Chancellor determined the type of justice dispensed. Eventually from this process developed the Court of Chancery to administer equity. This court may be contrasted with the common law courts – Common Pleas, Exchequer, and King's Bench – which administered the common law.

The Chancellor was commonly an ecclesiastic and equity was based upon moral principles which eventually crystallised as a body of law governed by the doctrine of precedent. Equitable jurisdiction encompassed 'fraud, accident and breach of confidence'. Fraud in equity included many instances of sharp practice, whereas the common law concept of fraud was based on intent to deceive. Accident referred to mistakes, for example, in relation to written documents which equity could correct. Breach of confidence contained the main equitable jurisdiction relating to trusts as well as issues relating to the abuse of trust and confidence.

Having two jurisdictions, one common law and one equitable, administered by separate courts, operating side by side inevitably led to conflict. Ultimately it was determined that where common law rules and equitable rules conflicted then the rules of equity were to prevail.

> ### ⬚ Example
>
> In the law of property and the law of contract you will see the operation of the common law rules and those of equity. At common law merely part-paying a debt does not discharge the full debt, even if coupled with a promise by the creditor that the part-payment does discharge the full debt. (You will discover in contract that the reason why there is no discharge is that the debtor gives no consideration for the promise, i.e. gives nothing in return as they are doing less than they are bound to do.) However, a principle of equity, that of estoppel, was used to prevent a creditor going back on a promise to accept less in circumstances where a debtor had relied upon the promise, even though no consideration had been provided. See *Hughes v Metropolitan Railways* (1877) 2 App Cas 439 and *Central London Property Trust v High Trees House Ltd* [1947] KB 130.

By the 1800s, equity was beset by major problems (Dickens' novel, *Bleak House*, gives a flavour of the operation of equity at this time). Amongst these problems was an unduly complex and extremely slow procedure and where a party sought both common law and equitable remedies, it was necessary to commence proceedings in both the common law courts and the Court of Chancery. The Judicature Acts

1873–75 reformed this situation by fusing the administration of law and equity, so that both legal and equitable remedies could be awarded by the same court. The old common law courts and the Court of Chancery were replaced by the High Court (see later).

2.2.3 **Common law – in the sense of judge-made law**

The decisions of judges in cases brought before the courts are a major source of law. Such decisions are recorded in law reports and are used by lawyers in determining what is the law. Judges in deciding cases must look to the relevant previous case law. In doing so judges have to operate within the doctrine of binding precedent, which means that like cases must be decided alike. Courts are arranged hierarchically and a judge in a lower court must follow the law as laid down by the higher courts. There are two elements to the doctrine of precedent:

- the search for a principle of law on which a previous case was decided and application of the principle to the instant case if the facts of the cases are sufficiently similar; and
- the doctrine of *stare decisis*, indicating when one court is bound by a principle of law coming from another court.

This system promotes certainty and allows lawyers to consult case law in the knowledge that, for example, principles stated in the Supreme Court must be applied by the lower courts, such as the Court of Appeal or the High Court. Under this system, when a principle of law is established it operates both retrospectively and prospectively, in the sense of applying to the future.

Judge-made law is different in form to the law made by Parliament. As W. Twining and D. Miers note in *How to Do Things with Rules*, statute law is in a fixed verbal form whereas judge-made law is in a non-fixed verbal form. This means that the text in a statute is fixed, unless amended by a subsequent Act of Parliament, whereas judge-made law has first to be ascertained from a case and may be clarified or developed in later cases. This leads to a difference in approach to the interpretation of the law. Lord Reid, commenting on the nature of case law in *Broome v Cassell & Co Ltd* [1972] AC 1027, said (at p.1085):

> experience has shown that those who have to apply the decision to other cases and still more those who wish to criticise it seem to find it difficult to avoid treating sentences and phrases in a single speech as if they were provisions in an Act of Parliament. They do not seem to realise that it is not the function of...judges to frame definitions or to lay down hard and fast rules. It is their function to enunciate principles and much that they say is intended to be illustrative or explanatory and not to be definitive.

See 5.2, 'Nature of judge-made law'.

Most of English law comes from legislation and case law, in the sense of judge-made law. The judicial role is to interpret legislation and to develop the common law.

While legislation and case law are the main sources of law it should be noted that you may encounter some historical sources of law that in some instances predate legislation and case law. These are custom, Roman law, and authoritative texts, such as *Blackstone's Commentaries* and *Coke's Institutes*. Custom as a source of law comprises rules that have their origin not in legislation or judge-made law but, amongst other matters, in long usage. The common law in its development drew on customary law. Indeed the same may be said, but to a lesser extent, of Roman law. The courts have in certain instances drawn upon Roman law to deal with situations where there was a lack of decided case law. See, for example, in the law of contract *Taylor v Caldwell* (1863) 3 B & S 826 where Blackburn J referred to Roman law in creating a general rule of discharge of contract, frustration. Finally, authoritative texts, the legal writings of judges and academic lawyers, again have played a small role in the development of the common law. Such writings may also be consulted by the courts when seeking to interpret a statute see, for example, *R v JTB* [2009] UKHL 20. An example of the limits of these texts may be seen in *R v R* [1992] 1 AC 599.

Also note that the courts may take into account relevant academic literature, text-books, and journal articles in deciding cases; see *R v Shivpuri* [1987] AC 1 later in the chapter for an illustration of this point.

2.3 **Parliament and legislation**

Legally, Parliament is the supreme law-making body and may make laws on any subject it chooses. To become an Act of Parliament a bill must pass through the House of Commons and the House of Lords (subject to the Parliament Acts 1911–49) and then receive the royal assent.

Sir Ivor Jennings, in *The Law and the Constitution*, wrote that Parliament could legislate to outlaw the smoking of cigarettes on the streets of Paris. While legally this is possible as a consequence of the doctrine of parliamentary supremacy, politically and practically Parliament would be ill-advised to do so, not least because there would be no means of enforcing such a law.

Treaties may be entered into by the government of the UK in the name of the Crown. Examples of treaties entered into by the UK are the Treaty of Rome 1957, which established the European Economic Community, and the European Convention on Human Rights 1950. However, while such treaties bind the UK in international law, they form no part of domestic law unless incorporated by Act of Parliament. Obligations under the treaties mentioned earlier have been incorporated into domestic law by the European Communities Act 1972 and the Human Rights Act 1998, respectively. That is not to say the international treaties that remain unincorporated into English law have no effect. There is a presumption of statutory interpretation that Parliament does not intend to legislate in contravention of an international treaty to which the UK is a signatory. Of course, this is only a presumption and should Parliament by clear words

Chapter 4, 'The interpretation of statutes' and chapter 7, 'Human rights and fundamental freedoms'.

indicate an intention not to comply with a treaty obligation then the courts must give effect to this intention.

In making laws Parliament is supreme; in the United Kingdom there is no higher law-making body than Parliament. This is called the doctrine of parliamentary sovereignty or supremacy. Under this doctrine Parliament is not bound by past parliaments nor may it bind future parliaments. This means that no Act of Parliament may be entrenched, i.e. made impossible to repeal. To amend or repeal any Act of Parliament, no special procedure is required; the amending or repealing Act must, as already stated, pass through both Houses of Parliament and receive the royal assent. However, it may be the case that for a future Parliament to repeal or amend some statutes, for example, the European Communities Act 1972 and the Human Rights Act 1998, very clear legislative words would be required.

Once an Act of Parliament has been made then its validity may not be questioned in the courts or by other bodies, see *British Railways Board v Pickin* [1974] AC 765.

Example

An example of an attempt to challenge the validity of an Act of Parliament was seen in *Jackson v Attorney General* [2006] 1 AC 262. This case concerned the Hunting Act 2004 which made it an offence to hunt wild animals with dogs, except in limited circumstances. The Act was passed using the Parliament Acts 1911–49 when the House of Lords failed to pass the bill. In *Jackson v Attorney General* a challenge to the validity of the Act was mounted. The argument in essence concerned the procedure for the making of the Hunting Act 2004. The Parliament Act 1911, which allows a bill to become an Act without the assent of the House of Lords after a delay, was passed by the House of Commons and the House of Lords and then received the royal assent. The Parliament Act 1949, which shortened the time that a bill may be delayed, was passed using the Parliament Act 1911. It was argued that the Parliament Act 1911 delegated power to the House of Commons to pass legislation without the assent of the Lords, but by passing the Parliament Act of 1949 the Commons had sought to enlarge its powers. This was in contravention of the established principle that powers conferred on a body by an enabling Act (i.e. here the Parliament Act 1911) may not be enlarged or modified by that body unless there are express words authorising such enlargement or modification. In other words, the argument was that the Parliament Act 1949 should have been assented to by the House of Lords, without such assent it was not valid and any legislation made under it was likewise invalid.

This was rejected by the House of Lords. Lord Bingham said (at p.280) that 'the overall object of the 1911 Act was not to delegate power: it was to restrict, subject to compliance with the specified statutory conditions, the power of the Lords to defeat measures supported by a majority of the Commons…' The Hunting Act 2004 was validly enacted.

Note the challenge was not on the substantive ground that the Hunting Act 2004 was bad legislation. Such a challenge would also fail as English law does not recognise such a ground of challenge.

Should statute law and case law conflict then statute law will prevail. Case law cannot repeal an Act of Parliament, whereas it is clear that an Act of Parliament may alter, in whole or part, case law.

The effect of legislation may be outlined in the long title to an Act.

An Act of Parliament may create new law or may affect existing law. You may find references in the long title to an Act that the Act is intended to repeal legislation, amend existing legislation or case law, consolidate legislative provisions, or codify an area of law. Table 2.1 explains and gives examples of the types of legislation.

Table 2.1 Table of legislation – explanation and examples

Types of legislation or legislative provision	Explanation	Examples
Repealing	An Act of Parliament does not cease to be law due to the passage of time or by falling into disuse. For a statute or a statutory provision to cease to be law it must be repealed by a further Act of Parliament. A schedule of repeals is a usual feature of an Act of Parliament. Additionally, the Law Commission (see later) keeps statutes under review and will seek to repeal obsolete Acts of Parliament	The Larceny Act 1916 was repealed by the Theft Act 1968 A provision of the Caravans Sites Act 1968, s.6, was repealed by the Criminal Justice and Public Order Act 1994 See the Statute Law (Repeals) Act 2004
Amending	An Act may seek to amend existing statutes or alter the common law	The Law Reform (Frustrated Contracts) Act 1943 amended the existing common law on the frustration of contracts
Consolidating	Consolidating legislation brings together in one Act of Parliament all the statutory provisions on a particular subject area. It is designed to make the law easier to find	The long title to the Employment Rights Act 1996 simply states that it is 'An Act to consolidate enactments relating to employment rights'
Codifying	Whereas consolidation concerns bringing together statutory provisions, codification is designed to bring all law, statutory and case law, together in a single statute. Such Acts make the law easier to find	The Sale of Goods Act 1893 was a codifying measure. Subsequently, the Act was amended and the Act and amendments were consolidated in the Sale of Goods Act 1979. Many areas of English law are not codified, e.g. criminal law, contract, and tort

The volume and complexity of legislation give cause for concern and have done so for many years. In 2013 the Office of Parliamentary Counsel (made up of lawyers specialising in drafting government bills) published a report *When Laws Become Too Complex – A review into the causes of complex legislation*. The report indicates a number of issues: that the average length of bills introduced into Parliament has increased significantly; multi-purpose bills (bills covering more than one legal area) are more common than they were; and between 1983 and 2009 Parliament passed into law 100 criminal justice bills creating over 4,000 new criminal offences. The causes of legislative complexity are considered in the report which may be found at **www.gov.uk/ government/publications/when-laws-become-too-complex**.

The role of judges in relation to Acts of Parliament is to give effect to the intention of Parliament which is to be collected from the words used in the statute. As Lord Diplock said in *Duport Steel v Sirs* [1980] 1 WLR 142, at p.157:

> ...Parliament makes the laws, the judiciary interpret them. When Parliament legislates to remedy what the majority of its members at the time perceive to be a defect or a lacuna in the existing law (whether it be the written law enacted by existing statutes or the unwritten common law as it has been expounded by the judges in decided cases), the role of the judiciary is confined to ascertaining from the words that Parliament has approved as expressing its intention what that intention was, and to giving effect to it. Where the meaning of the statutory words is plain and unambiguous it is not for the judges to invent fancied ambiguities as an excuse for failing to give effect to its plain meaning because they themselves consider that the consequences of doing so would be inexpedient, or even unjust or immoral.

Lord Diplock is emphasising the separation of powers between Parliament and the courts. The role of judges is to interpret law made by Parliament and they must be careful not to encroach on this law-making function. But although the language used by Parliament to express its legislative intention is paramount, as will be seen later, the judges are able to use other aids to interpretation in establishing the purpose of Parliament.

See 4.4.1, 'Aids to construction found within an Act of Parliament'.

Parliament may empower other persons or bodies to make law on its behalf. Examples of such include government ministers, government departments, and local authorities. This is an important source of law as it allows Parliament to concentrate on principles and leave details to be supplied by delegated legislation. The power to make delegated legislation is given in an Act of Parliament (which is referred to as the parent or enabling Act). Unlike primary legislation, the validity of delegated or secondary legislation may be challenged in the courts if the maker has acted ultra vires, which is beyond the powers given by the parent Act.

The inputs involved in the process of parliamentary law-making are neatly summed up in the following quotation of Lord Hailsham in *R v Shivpuri* [1987] AC 1, at p.11 (a case which is further discussed in chapter 5 on judicial precedent):

> ...as one of the authors of the decision in *Reg. v. Smith (Roger)* [1975] A.C. 476 I must say that I had hoped that my opinion in that case would be read by Parliament as a

cri de coeur, at least on my part, that Parliament should use its legislative power to rescue the law of criminal attempts from the subtleties and absurdities to which I felt that, on existing premises, it was doomed to reduce itself, and, after long discussions with the late Lord Reid, I had reached the conclusion that the key to the anomalies arose from the various kinds of circumstance to which the word 'attempt' can be legitimately applied, and that the road to freedom lay in making an inchoate crime of this nature depend on a prohibited act (the so called, but ineptly called, 'actus reus') amounting to something more than a purely preparatory act plus an intent (as distinct from an attempt) to carry the act through to completion. When the Criminal Attempts Act 1981 was carried into law, and I read section 6 which abolished altogether the common law offence except as regards acts done before the commencement of the Act, I was happily under the impression that my hopes had been realised, and that my carefully prepared speech in *Reg. v. Smith* would henceforth be relegated to the limbo reserved for the discussions of medieval schoolmen. It was therefore with something like dismay that I learned that the ghost of my speech had risen from what I had supposed to be its tomb and was still clanking its philosophical chains about the field, and that the new Act had formed a tilting yard for a joust of almost unexampled ferocity between two of the most distinguished professors of English criminal law in the United Kingdom.

In a nutshell, Lord Hailsham felt that the common law had reached an impasse and it was for Parliament to remedy this difficulty. Parliament passed the Criminal Attempts Act 1981, abolishing the common law offence. However, the House of Lords in *Anderton v Ryan* [1985] AC 560 interpreted the Criminal Attempts Act 1981 in such a way that it resurrected the approach in *R v Smith (Roger)*. This interpretation was then the subject of academic criticism by, amongst others, Professor Glanville Williams in an article entitled, 'The Lords and Impossible Attempts, or *Quis Custodiet Ipsos Custodes?*' (1986) CLJ 33. The House of Lords usually follows its previous decisions but in *R v Shivpuri* it departed from its decision in *Anderton v Ryan* as it considered it to be wrong. Diagram 2.1 shows the law-making bodies and the forms that law may take.

2.3.1 **Relationship between the law of the UK and the law of the European Union**

When the UK government signed the treaties giving membership of the European Communities for the treaty obligations thereby undertaken to have effect under UK law, it was necessary for an Act of Parliament to be passed incorporating such obligations. The law-making institutions of the European Community (EC) were empowered to make laws for the UK by reason of the European Communities Act 1972. The effect of this Act is that in areas of law affected by the European Community there is interaction between two legal systems, that of the domestic system of the UK and that of the European Community. It was decided by the European Court of Justice that in instances of conflict between national law and Community law, Community law was supreme, *Costa v ENEL* [1964] ECR 1125. The European Community has been subsequently renamed the European Union, see chapter 6.

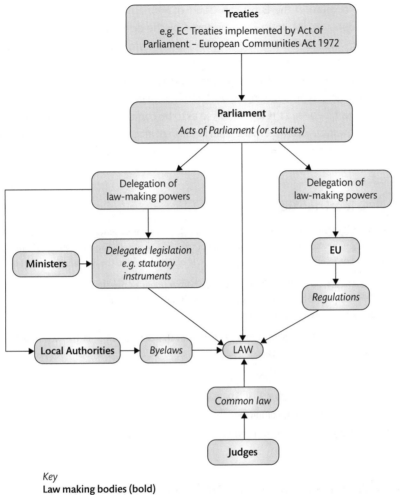

Key
Law making bodies (bold)
Forms of law (italics)

Diagram 2.1 Law-making bodies and forms of law

2.3.2 Relationship between the law of the UK and the European Convention on Human Rights

The Convention on Human Rights operates under the Council of Europe. The political element is the Committee of Ministers, consisting of a representative from each signatory state and the judicial body is the European Court of Human Rights. A key point to note is that the Council of Europe is distinct from the institutions of the European Union. The jurisdictions of the Court of Justice of the European Union and the European Court of Human Rights are distinct and must not be confused.

The Human Rights Act 1998 incorporated Convention rights into English law. By the 1998 Act the English courts must take into account any judgment, decision, declaration, or advisory opinion of the European Court of Human Rights; note that while such judgment, decision, etc. must be considered by the domestic courts, they need not be followed. The Human Rights Act 1998 does not provide a yardstick by which to strike down legislation which is not in conformity with the Convention. Instead, the Act requires that the courts seek to interpret and apply primary legislation and subordinate legislation, as far as is possible, in a way which is compatible with the Convention rights. If it is not possible to read the legislation so as to be compatible with Convention rights then the domestic court must make a declaration of incompatibility, throwing the onus upon the government to introduce amending legislation in Parliament.

> ### ! Critical debate
>
> The concept of the rule of law is frequently mentioned by parliamentarians, lawyers, and political commentators. It is a difficult concept to define precisely. The late Tom Bingham (a former Lord Chief Justice) in his book *The Rule of Law* provided the following description:
>
> > all persons and authorities within the state, whether public or private, should be bound by and entitled to the benefits of laws publicly made, taking effect (generally) in the future and publicly administered in the courts.
>
> One of the principles which is to be derived from this description is, in the words of Tom Bingham, that 'the law must be accessible and so far as possible intelligible, clear and predictable'.
>
> Consider the following questions:
>
> (a) Why must the law comply with this principle?
>
> (b) Does English law wholly comply with this principle?
>
> (c) What changes could be made to ensure further compliance with the principle?

2.4 Criminal law and civil law – terminology, differences, and themes

2.4.1 Criminal

In criminal trials the burden of proof is upon the prosecution to prove the defendant's guilt. This means that the onus falls on the prosecution to prove all the ingredients of a crime with which a defendant is charged; a defendant is innocent until proven guilty. The standard of proof is that the prosecution must prove the defendant's guilt beyond reasonable doubt. Note that in certain instances the burden of proof is placed upon a defendant, for example, if the defendant raises a defence of insanity or diminished responsibility. However, the standard of proof, when a defendant has the burden of proof, is the lesser civil standard of balance of probabilities.

The criminal courts of trial are the magistrates' courts and the Crown Court. In the former courts, questions of fact are determined by the magistrates or district judge whereas in the Crown Court, findings of fact are made by a jury, consisting of twelve people.

A characteristic of the criminal process is that it is said to be adversarial. The process is not a process to necessarily discover the truth of what happened but one to test the strength of the case against an accused. It is important to understand how the rules of criminal procedure and evidence govern this process and to consider if it is fair to both sides. An issue that needs to be borne in mind is the relative resources of the state, as prosecutor, on one side and the defendant on the other: are the parties on a level playing field?

The adversarial process is often compared with the inquisitorial process practised in mainland European criminal justice systems, where responsibility for a criminal case is assumed by an investigating magistrate. The magistrate plays a much more active role in a case, unlike under the English model where the judge is largely passive, relying on the parties to present a case and certainly has no role in the investigation of a case. It is a matter of some debate as to which system is fairer to a defendant, with greater safeguards built into the adversarial model. Of course, whatever the rules it must always be borne in mind how they operate in practice.

See further chapter 13, 'The criminal process: pre-trial and trial'.

The criminal justice system in recent years has been the subject of major changes. As well as being somewhat of a political battlefield there is a constant drive to make the process more efficient and thereby save costs.

2.4.2 Civil

In civil trials the burden of proof is placed upon a party who makes an allegation of fact. Usually a claimant will have the burden of proof and the standard of proof is that of the balance of probabilities, i.e. the facts alleged must be more likely to be true than not. It is important in studying substantive subjects, such as contract and tort, to note any special rules relating to burden of proof.

> ### ⊜ Example
>
> In the law of contract, note the following situation where the ordinary burden of proof is reversed: s.11(5) of the Unfair Contract Terms Act 1977 provides that where an exemption clause is subject to the test of reasonableness under the Act then it is for the person who relies on the clause to show that it is reasonable.

The adversarial model was also seen as the basis for civil justice but this has been weakened following introduction of the Civil Procedure Rules which allow a judge to manage a case, rather than to leave such to the parties.

Thinking point

It can be readily understood that a major concern in the drive for efficiency in criminal justice is to save costs. Are there dangers, and if so what, in diverting criminal cases from proceeding to court?

2.4.3 **Terminology**

In civil cases, a person commencing proceedings against another is called the claimant (in the older cases you will encounter the term plaintiff), while the person against whom proceedings are brought is termed a defendant.

In criminal cases, a prosecution will be undertaken by the state in the name of the monarch (Regina or Rex) against a defendant or accused. Note that in some older cases a prosecution before a magistrates' court would be made in the name of a police officer involved in the case. Often such cases were appealed to the Divisional Court of the Queen's Bench Division of the High Court and are reported under the names of defendant and prosecutor, e.g. *Brutus v Cozens* [1972] 1 WLR 484.

It is to be noted that the terminology is not interchangeable, so in a civil trial a defendant is not prosecuted for a breach of contract or commission of a tort; equally if a judge finds that a defendant has committed a breach of contract or a tort the defendant is said to be liable as opposed to criminal trials where a defendant may be guilty.

2.5 **Classification of the courts**

Courts are divided into superior courts and inferior courts.

A superior court is one with unlimited jurisdiction, both in a geographical and monetary sense. An inferior court has limited jurisdiction. The superior courts are the Supreme Court (previously the House of Lords), Court of Appeal, High Court, Crown Court, Privy Council, and Employment Appeal Tribunal; the inferior courts include the magistrates' courts and the county courts. The major differences between the courts relates to their powers in relation to contempt of court and to the supervision of the inferior courts by a superior court, i.e. the High Court.

2.5.1 **Constitutional Reform Act 2005**

On 1 October 2009 the House of Lords was replaced by the Supreme Court of the United Kingdom. In the English legal system there was already a Supreme Court, which consisted of the Court of Appeal, the High Court, and the Crown Court; these courts are now collectively termed the Senior Courts of England and Wales (the Supreme

Court Act 1981 which governed the Court of Appeal, the High Court, and the Crown Court was renamed the Senior Courts Act 1981). The then current judges of the House of Lords, the Lords of Appeal in Ordinary, also known as the 'law lords', were retitled Justices of the Supreme Court.

2.5.2 Overview of the composition and jurisdiction of the courts

It is evident in studying the system of courts that it was not planned. The courts system has simply grown, quite often to meet specific needs. Note it is not possible to classify courts as criminal or civil courts as some courts exercise both criminal jurisdiction and civil jurisdiction. However, the organisation of the courts allows for some specialisation. When studying the courts, seek to identify:

- the courts where cases commence;
- the courts in which appeals are heard; and
- the courts that exercise both *first instance* and appellate jurisdiction.

   a court of first instance: *A case will commence in a court of first instance (i.e. a court of trial). This jurisdiction is also termed original jurisdiction. Decisions of courts may be challenged on appeal and erroneous decisions corrected. Courts hearing appeals are said to have appellate jurisdiction.*

In explaining the courts below a brief indication is also given of the judges who sit in particular courts.

Information on the judiciary may be found at **www.judiciary.gov.uk/**. This basic information on the courts and judges is necessary for an understanding of how the doctrine of judicial precedent operates and background for informing your understanding of the substantive areas of law.

See chapter 8 on 'The judiciary' and the chapters on criminal and civil procedure.

(Note – The following descriptions of the jurisdiction of the courts only deal with the courts of England and Wales and courts having an effect on the English legal system.)

2.5.3 Magistrates' courts

Magistrates' courts are presided over by Justices of the Peace (alternatively termed magistrates). Cases are normally heard before a bench of two or three Justices of the Peace, s.121 Magistrates' Court Act 1980. Justices of the Peace need not be legally qualified, so they may be advised about matters of law by a justices' clerk. District Judges (Magistrates' Court) also sit in magistrates' court and replaced stipendiary magistrates. Unlike lay justices, who are unsalaried, District Judges (Magistrates' Court) are legally qualified and salaried. A District Judge (Magistrates' Court) carries out the same criminal and civil work as that of a lay magistrate but may sit alone when hearing a case, s.26 Courts Act 2003.

The magistrates' courts have predominantly a criminal jurisdiction but also have an important civil jurisdiction.

Criminal jurisdiction

All criminal cases commence in the magistrates' courts, but not all cases are tried there. Where a defendant is charged with an indictable offence which is only triable on indictment a magistrates' court must send the defendant to the Crown Court for trial. If an indictable offence is triable either way then a magistrates' court must determine in which court the trial will be held, i.e. whether a defendant is to be tried in the Crown Court or a magistrates' court. If a defendant is charged with a summary offence (or the offence is triable either way and the case is suitable for summary trial and the defendant consents to such trial) the magistrates' court may try the defendant.

Where a magistrates' court's jurisdiction relates to offences committed by children and young persons it is referred to as a youth court.

Terminology

Criminal offences are classified as either indictable offences or summary offences, depending upon the seriousness of the offence. Schedule 1 to the Interpretation Act 1978 provides that:

(a) indictable offence means an offence which, if committed by an adult, is triable on indictment, whether it is exclusively so triable or triable either way;

(b) summary offence means an offence which, if committed by an adult, is triable only summarily.

The classification is an essential element in the process of deciding where an offence is to be tried, i.e. via a summary trial in a magistrates' court or a trial on indictment in the Crown Court.

All common law offences are indictable, as are offences created by statute if the statute specifies a penalty to be imposed following trial on indictment.

Example

Section 8(2) of the Theft Act 1968 provides, 'A person guilty of robbery, or of an assault with intent to rob, shall on conviction on indictment be liable to imprisonment for life.'

All summary offences are created by statute and are identified in a statute by specification of a maximum penalty which may be imposed following summary conviction.

> **Example**
>
> Section 12(2) of the Theft Act provides the following penalty for taking a motor vehicle: the guilty person 'shall…be liable on summary conviction to a fine not exceeding level 5 on the standard scale, to imprisonment for a term not exceeding six months, or to both'.

Finally, some indictable offences are triable either way, i.e. may be tried on indictment in the Crown Court or tried summarily in a magistrates' court. Such offences are readily identifiable. First, where a statute creates an offence, alternative penalties are specified, one following summary conviction and the other following conviction on indictment. Second, Sch.1 to the Magistrates' Courts Act 1980 lists offences which are triable either way.

See chapter 13, 'The criminal process: pre-trial and trial.

Indictable offences may be:

- triable only on indictment in the Crown Court; or
- triable either way in the Crown Court or magistrates' court.

Summary offences may only be tried in a magistrates' court, unless linked to a trial on indictment.

Civil jurisdiction

Jurisdiction is given by statute, and consists primarily of licensing, family proceedings, and the care and adoption of children. See 2.5.6 which deals with the creation of the Family Court. Certain civil debts, for example in relation to income tax, may be recovered in a magistrates' court.

> **Thinking point**
>
> Trial in the Crown Court is more time-consuming and costly than trial in the magistrates' courts. The classification of offences determines where a trial may take place. By reclassifying offences as summary, trial costs may be saved. Is such an approach defensible? A reclassification of an offence as summary would deprive a defendant of an opportunity to be tried by jury. Is this important?

2.5.4 **Crown Court**

The basic position in the Crown Court is that proceedings will be before a single judge. The judge may be a High Court judge, a circuit judge, a recorder, or a District Judge (Magistrates' Court). On hearing an appeal, a judge of the High Court or a circuit judge or a recorder shall sit with not less than two nor more than four Justices of the Peace, ss.8 and 74 Senior Courts Act 1981.

The Crown Court is part of the Senior Courts and has jurisdiction throughout England and Wales; it is one court that sits in various locations. While it is a superior court it is subject in certain instances to the supervisory jurisdiction of the High Court (see later).

Trial on indictment

The main jurisdiction of the Crown Court is to that of trial on indictment, before judge and jury, s.46 Senior Courts Act 1981. Following the Criminal Justice Act 2003, it is possible for a judge to sit without a jury where there is a danger of jury tampering, s.44.

Committals for sentence

The Crown Court deals with cases that have been committed by the magistrates' court for sentence where the magistrates' court is of the opinion that its sentencing powers are inadequate.

Appeals

There are various rights of appeal to the Crown Court from the magistrates' courts, including:

- against sentence where a defendant pleads guilty;
- against sentence or conviction where a defendant pleads not guilty; and
- against licensing decisions.

Additionally, in certain instances appeals to the Crown Court may come from the decisions of local authorities and other bodies.

2.5.5 County courts

The following judges may sit in a county court: every circuit judge, every judge of the Court of Appeal, every judge of the High Court, and every recorder, s.5 County Courts Act 1984, district judges and deputy district judges, ss.6 and 8 County Courts Act 1984. In practice, the day to day work of the court is generally carried out by district judges and deputy district judges.

The county courts are a creation of statute and, in consequence, jurisdiction is given by statute. The county courts are governed by the County Courts Act 1984 and deal exclusively with civil cases. Note that once the Crime and Courts Act 2013 is brought into force under the County Courts Act 1984 (as amended by s.17 Crime and Courts Act 2013) the county court is to be a single court and a court of record, in a similar way to the High Court.

While much of the jurisdiction of the county courts is the same as for the High Court there are limitations as to subject matter, financial limitations, and territorial limitations.

A county court has concurrent jurisdiction with the High Court, that is has jurisdiction over most of the civil claims which may be the subject of proceedings in the High Court. The jurisdiction of the county courts includes the following:

- subject to limited exceptions, a county court may hear and determine any action founded on contract or tort, s.15 County Courts Act 1984;

- provided the High Court has not been given exclusive jurisdiction, a county court may hear and determine an action for the recovery of a sum recoverable by virtue of any enactment, s.16 County Courts Act 1984;

- actions for recovery of land and actions where title is in question, s.21 County Courts Act 1984;

- equity jurisdiction, s.23 County Courts Act 1984. Note that this jurisdiction is subject to a £30,000 limit; and

- probate, s.32 County Courts Act 1984 again subject to a £30,000 limit.

Jurisdiction is also conferred on the county courts by other statutes, for example:

- by s.33 of the Matrimonial and Family Proceedings Act 1984 a county court may be designated as a divorce county court and such court shall have jurisdiction to hear and determine any matrimonial cause, but may only try such a cause if it is also designated as a court of trial. Every matrimonial cause must commence in a divorce county court and shall be heard and determined there unless it is transferred to the High Court. See 2.5.6 which deals with the creation of the Family Court.

Commencing proceedings – county courts or High Court

As was seen in criminal cases, the jurisdictional limits of the magistrates' courts and Crown Court separate cases involving serious crimes from less serious cases. This is done on the assumption that a fuller treatment should be given to serious cases. The position is similar in the trial of civil cases.

In the civil process, the two courts of trial are the county courts and the High Court. At one time, whether an action for contract or tort proceeded in a county court or the High Court was determined on the basis of the amount of the claim. This was seen as not being the best use of resources, especially where the claim was relatively straightforward. Moreover, this took no account of the difficulty of a case. Even cases with a relatively small monetary value may give rise to novel and complex points of law, which may have a significant impact on other cases. In consequence, the Lord Chancellor was given power to reallocate business between the High Court and county courts by s.1 of the Courts and Legal Services Act 1990. This reallocation was effected by the High Court and County Courts Jurisdiction Order 1991 (SI 1991/724).

The important point to note is that if a county court has jurisdiction, then by Article 4 of the 1991 Order, proceedings may be commenced in either a county court or the High Court. The 1991 Order abolished many restrictions on the jurisdiction of the county courts. For example, the county courts now have unlimited jurisdiction in relation to cases concerning tort and contract. So, in relation to such cases, a claimant has a choice of the court of trial but it is not a completely free choice. The basic principle in Article 4 is qualified in the following ways:

- a case should commence in the High Court taking into account, (i) the financial value of the claim or the amount in dispute; (ii) the complexity of the facts, legal issues, remedies, or procedures; (iii) the importance of the claim, e.g. does it involve a point of law of general public interest;

- a case cannot commence in the High Court unless the value of the claim is more than £25,000; and

- if a case concerns personal injuries it must not commence in the High Court unless the claim is worth £50,000 or more.

(See Practice Direction – How to Start Proceedings – The Claim Form (2000) PD 7A; Articles 4A and 5 High Court and County Courts Jurisdiction Order 1991 (SI 1991/724), as amended.)

Importantly, cases commenced in a county court or the High Court may be transferred from one court to the other where appropriate under ss.40–42 of the County Courts Act 1984.

Small claims jurisdiction

The county courts have an important jurisdiction in relation to small claims. This jurisdiction, for example, covers breach of contract, personal injuries claims, and some landlord and tenant disputes. A claim may be allocated to the small claims track by a district judge, depending upon the amount of the claim and the complexity of the case. In general, where a claim is for £10,000 or less it will be allocated to the small claims track, subject to the following: if it is a personal injury claim it will only be allocated to the small claims track if it is for £1,000 or less; and in a repairs claim against a landlord by a tenant it will only be allocated to the small claims track if it is for £1,000 or less. The procedure involved should allow litigants to appear without legal representation. The hearing is to be informal and the court may adopt a proceeding that it considers to be fair; the strict rules of evidence do not apply. The perceived advantages are that the small claims process is quicker, less costly and stressful, and is flexible. Nevertheless, litigants should consider alternatives to going to court such as seeking to negotiate or agreeing to an alternative dispute resolution method such as mediation. Note that the suggestion that a claimant should consider alternative ways of resolving a dispute, will not necessarily be costs free.

> **Thinking point**
>
> A significant point to consider is that if a whole class of case is disposed of by the small claims procedure in the county court with little or no opportunity of appeal, there is a danger that divergences may arise in the interpretation of the law in different parts of the country. Additionally, as these cases are unreported such 'law' will be unknown. This tendency is reinforced by the periodic raising of the small claims monetary limit, thus bringing more cases within the small claims jurisdiction. Do you think the significance of these points is outweighed by other factors such as the time and costs savings associated with the small claims jurisdiction?

Appellate jurisdiction

There is a limited appellate jurisdiction whereby circuit judges may hear appeals from the decisions of district judges.

2.5.6 **Family court**

(Note at the time of writing the sections of the Crime and Courts Act 2013 that establishes the family court had not been brought into force. It would appear that the court will commence in April 2014.)

The jurisdiction of the courts in relation to family law was exercised by Family Proceedings Courts, which were located in the magistrates' court, by the county courts, and by the High Court (Family Division). Inevitably issues of where a case was to commence arose, particularly for litigants in person. In consequence, following consultation and a review, s.31A Matrimonial and Family Proceedings Act 1984 (as amended by s.17 Crime and Courts Act 2013) establishes the family court as a single entry point in place of the three possible entry points just outlined. The court will be a national court, in this respect similar to the Crown Court. The jurisdiction of the court will be exercised by judiciary of all levels, which will allow for the allocation of proceedings to the appropriate level of judge depending upon the type and complexity of proceedings. The judges of the family court include High Court judges (puisne judges), Circuit judges, district judges, District Judges (Magistrates' Court), and justices of the peace (not being District Judges (Magistrates' Court). For a complete list of judges of the family court see s.31C Matrimonial and Family Proceedings Act 1984 (as amended by Sch. 10, Crime and Courts Act 2013). By s.31B 'sittings of the family court may be held ... at any place in England and Wales'. The creation of this court gives rise to issues concerning judicial precedent. This is explained in 5.5.7.

The jurisdiction of the High Court (Family Division) is preserved in respect of its inherent jurisdiction and international caseload. Indeed by s.31I(i) 'if the High Court, at any stage in proceedings in the family court, thinks it desirable that the proceedings, or any part of them, should be transferred to the High Court, it may order the transfer to the High Court of the proceedings or part.'

2.5.7 **High Court**

High Court judges, alternatively known as puisne judges, sit in the High Court. Judges are referred to as Mr Justice, or Mrs Justice, which may be abbreviated to J as in, for example, Smith J. The judges are attached to divisions of the High Court. As of 2013, there were eighteen High Court judges attached to the Chancery Division, seventy-three to the Queen's Bench Division, and nineteen to the Family Division. Each Division is headed by a senior judge: in the Chancery Division, the Chancellor of the High Court; in the Queen's Bench Division, the President of the Queen's Bench Division (note the Lord Chief Justice is also part of the Division); and in the Family Division, the President of the Family Division, s.5 Senior Courts Act 1981. At first instance one High Court judge sits to hear a case.

The High Court is mainly a civil court (note the important criminal jurisdiction exercised by the Queen's Bench Division). It is comprised of three divisions: the Queen's Bench Division; the Chancery Division; and the Family Division, s.5 Senior Courts Act 1981. The divisions allow for specialisation and this is further achieved by specialist courts within the Divisions. Within the Queen's Bench Division there are specialist courts: the Administrative Court; Admiralty Court; Commercial Court; Mercantile Court; and Technology and Construction Court. There are specialist courts also attached to the Chancery Division, for example, the Patents Court. It is particularly important to appreciate that the High Court has both first instance (original) and appellate jurisdiction. The main statute governing the High Court is the Senior Courts Act 1981. The jurisdiction of the High Court is based in part upon statute and is in part inherent, as the result of the development of the old common law courts; see s.19 of the Senior Courts Act 1981. At first instance the High Court has unlimited civil jurisdiction of a general nature. Table 2.2 gives an indication of the subject matter of the jurisdiction of each division (see s.61 of and Sch.1 to the Senior Courts Act 1981).

Appellate jurisdiction

Divisional Court
Divisional Courts consist of two or more judges, s.66(3) Senior Courts Act 1981.

The High Court also acts as a court of appeal in certain instances. A major appellate function in criminal cases is exercised by the **Divisional Court** of the Queen's Bench Division. Appeals are heard following summary trial before a magistrates' court by way of case stated where it is alleged that the decision is wrong in law or was given in excess of jurisdiction, s.111 Magistrates' Courts Act 1980. In addition, an appeal from a magistrates' court to the Crown Court following summary trial may be further appealed, by defence or prosecution, by way of case stated to the Divisional Court of the Queen's Bench Division, s.28 Senior Courts Act 1981. The grounds once again are that the decision is wrong in law or is in excess of jurisdiction.

Table 2.2 Jurisdiction of the High Court

Queen's Bench Division	Chancery Division	Family Division
Jurisdiction includes cases concerning contract and tort. Also, the following specialist courts fall within the Queen's Bench Division:	Jurisdiction includes cases concerning:	Jurisdiction includes cases concerning:
Administrative Court	property;	all matrimonial causes and matters;
Main jurisdiction is public and administrative law cases including, judicial review, statutory appeals, and habeas corpus	the execution of trusts; the administration of the estates; bankruptcy;	legitimacy; proceedings under the Children Act 1989; adoption;
Admiralty Court	partnerships; probate business, other than non-contentious business; and companies.	non-contentious probate business; s.30 of the Human Fertilisation and Embryology Act 1990;
Jurisdiction over cases concerning maritime issues, such as collision of ships		
Commercial Court	Patents Court	all proceedings under the Child Support Act 1991;
Jurisdiction includes cases concerning business documents or contracts; the export or import of goods; insurance; banking and financial services; and arbitration	Hears issues concerning patents; see Patents Act 1977 and Senior Courts Act 1981 s.6	all proceedings under ss.6 and 8 of the Gender Recognition Act 2004; and all civil partnership causes and matters
Technology and Construction Court		
Jurisdiction over technically complex cases, such as building cases		See 2.5.6 which deals with the creation of the Family Court

Supervisory jurisdiction

The Queen's Bench Division of the High Court exercises supervisory jurisdiction by means of judicial review. Judicial review is described in *Halsbury's Law of England* as 'the process by which the High Court exercises its supervisory jurisdiction over the proceedings and decisions of inferior courts, tribunals, and other bodies or persons who carry out quasi-judicial functions or who are charged with the performance of public acts and duties'. The process does not look at the merits of a case and in this sense is not an appeal; rather, it concentrates on the process by which a decision is made. A decision-making body must act within its powers and in accordance with the rules of natural justice.

2.5.8 **Court of Appeal**

Judges in the Court of Appeal are termed Lords Justices of Appeal (abbreviated to LJ singular or LJJ plural). In 2013 there were thirty-three Lords Justices of Appeal and five Lady Justices of Appeal: thirty-eight judges in total. Usually three Lords or Lady Justices of Appeal will hear an appeal, although in some instances a case may be heard by a two-judge Court of Appeal. When a difficult or important point of law is to be decided then a five-judge Court of Appeal may be convened. For example, see *R v James (Leslie)* [2006] QB 588 discussed in chapter 5 on 'The doctrine of judicial precedent'.

The Court of Appeal is, in most instances, an intermediate appeal court, i.e. not a final court of appeal.

Court of Appeal (Civil Division)

The jurisdiction of the Court of Appeal (Civil Division) is wholly appellate, in other words it only hears appeals from the decisions of other courts. The civil appeals process is somewhat complicated. Appeals from the county courts and the High Court are governed by Civil Procedure Rules 52 and Practice Direction 52 – Appeals.

The Practice Direction states clearly the routes of appeal in tabular form in paragraph 2A1. The principle for the destination of appeals is based upon the seniority of judges, the type of claim, and the nature of the decision reached by the court.

Court of Appeal (Criminal Division)

The Court of Appeal (Criminal Division) has appellate jurisdiction.

See chapter 16, 'Criminal and civil appeals'.

Appeal following conviction on indictment before the Crown Court

Such an appeal only lies: (a) with the leave of the Court of Appeal; or (b) if the judge of the court of trial grants a certificate that the case is fit for appeal (s.1 Criminal Appeal Act 1968). The Court of Appeal may allow an appeal and quash the conviction if it thinks that the conviction is unsafe. By s.7 of the Criminal Appeals Act 1968 where the Court of Appeal allows an appeal against conviction it may order that an appellant be retried if it appears to the Court that the interests of justice so require.

Appeal against sentence following conviction on indictment

An appeal may be made to the Court of Appeal against sentence (not being a sentence fixed by law). Such an appeal against sentence lies only with the leave of the Court of Appeal unless the judge passing sentence grants a certificate that the case is fit for appeal.

Other appeals

Under Part 1 of the Criminal Appeal Act 1968, appeals may be heard where a person has been found to be not guilty by reason of insanity or where there has been a finding that a defendant is unfit to stand trial. An appeal may be heard against any order or decision of the Crown Court made in respect of contempt of court.

In the past, following trial on indictment only a defendant had a right of appeal. However, this situation has changed significantly.

The Attorney General may refer a case to the Court of Appeal, with leave of the Court of Appeal, where he considers that the sentence is unduly lenient, ss.35 and 36 of Criminal Justice Act 1988. The court may quash any sentence passed and substitute such sentence as the Court of Appeal thinks appropriate for the case.

Should an accused be acquitted following trial on indictment, the Attorney General may refer a point of law to the Court of Appeal for the opinion of the court. Importantly, the opinion given does not affect the acquittal of the defendant. (Note the cases are named Attorney General's Reference and sequentially referenced according to number and year, for example, *Attorney General's Reference No.1 of 2006*.)

Under the Criminal Justice Act 2003 in relation to certain serious offences the prosecution may appeal to the Court of Appeal for an order quashing a defendant's acquittal following trial on indictment and ordering a retrial.

Should prosecutors have a general right of appeal against acquittal?

2.5.9 Supreme Court

On 1 October 2009 the Supreme Court of the United Kingdom replaced the Appellate Committee of the House of Lords as the highest court in the United Kingdom. This change was brought about by the Constitutional Reform Act 2005. By s.40(1) of the Act, the Supreme Court is a superior court of record. There was a seamless transition with the judges in the House of Lords, the 'law lords', becoming the first justices of the Supreme Court.

Reasons for its creation

The Appellate Committee of the House of Lords was located in the Palace of Westminster, alongside the legislature and the judges, the 'law lords', sat in the legislative chamber of the House of Lords. There was no physical or legal separation of the legislative and judicial functions and the doctrine of separation of powers was not clearly observed in the British constitution. While it was considered that there was not a problem, in that the integrity and independence of the 'law lords' was not questioned, this lack of separation gave the *appearance* that the House of Lords in its judicial capacity was not independent and gave rise to fears that there was a lack of compliance with Article 6 of the European Convention on Human Rights, the right to a fair trial.

The creation of the Supreme Court of the United Kingdom, addressed these concerns by (a) physically separating the court from the legislative chamber, the Supreme Court is located in the former Middlesex Guildhall in Parliament Square, Westminster, and (b) by removing the right of the 'law lords' to take part in the business of the House of Lords as a legislative chamber.

Membership and jurisdiction

The first Justices of the Supreme Court were the 'law lords' or Lords of Appeal in Ordinary from the House of Lords. They still carry their title of Lord or Lady. However, new appointments are not made Life Peers but are to be given the courtesy title of Lord or Lady; the first new appointment to the Supreme Court of the United Kingdom was Sir John Dyson (now Lord Dyson), who had previously sat in the Court of Appeal. By s.23 of the Constitutional Reform Act 2005 the court consists of twelve justices. (Section 23 has been amended by the Crime and Courts Act 2013 to provide that the court is to consist of no more than the equivalent of twelve full-time justices. This indicates that there could be more than twelve justices if there are part-time appointments. The amendment is not yet in force.)

The justices usually sit in panels of five but may also sit in panels of seven or nine. The panels of seven or nine are constituted when a previous decision is asked to be, or may be, departed from, the case raises an issue of constitutional significance, or the issue raised is one of great public importance. For an example of an issue of great public importance see *Granatino v Radmacher (formerly Granatino)* [2010] 2 WLR 1367. In this case the Supreme Court, consisting of nine justices, considered the legal effect of pre-nuptial agreements and decided that the rule that such agreements were contrary to public policy was obsolete and no longer of application.

The jurisdiction of the Supreme Court is as the ultimate court of appeal in the United Kingdom, hearing both civil and criminal appeals, together with the devolution jurisdiction of the Privy Council (see s.40(4)(b) of Constitutional Reform Act 2005).

A lecture by Lord Hope on the workings of the new Supreme Court of the United Kingdom may be found at **www.guardian.co.uk/law/2010/jun/24/uk-supreme-court**.

See generally **www.supremecourt.uk/**.

Civil appeals

An appeal lies to the Supreme Court from:

- any order or judgment of the Court of Appeal (Administration of Justice (Appeals) Act 1934, s1(1)); and
- the High Court under the 'leapfrog procedure' (Administration of Justice Act 1969, ss.12–15).

Criminal appeals

Either the defendant or the prosecutor may appeal from:

- any decision of the Court of Appeal (Criminal Division) (Criminal Appeal Act 1968 s.33); or

- any decision of the High Court in a criminal cause or matter (Administration of Justice Act 1960 s.1(1)(a)).

Leave to appeal is required from the court below or, if refused, by the Supreme Court. Leave to appeal will only be granted if the court below, that is the Court of Appeal (Criminal Division) or the High Court, has certified that the case raises a point of law of general public importance; and if it appears to that court or the Supreme Court that the point is one that ought to be considered by the Supreme Court.

> ### ⬟ Example
>
> For many years persons involved in law or the criminal justice system were barred from sitting on juries. In 2004, the law was amended to allow police officers, judges, lawyers, and others in the criminal justice system to sit on juries. In 2007, an appeal to the House of Lords was launched by defendants following conviction in the Crown Court on the ground that the involvement of jurors who were part of the prosecution system, i.e. a police officer and a Crown Prosecution Service lawyer, had denied them a fair trial under Article 6 of the European Convention on Human Rights. The Court of Appeal had decided that there was no breach of Article 6, but had certified that the cases raised a point of law of general public importance. See further chapter 10, 'The jury'.

2.5.10 Judicial Committee of the Privy Council

The membership of the Judicial Committee of the Privy Council is made up mainly of Justices of the Supreme Court and others who have held high judicial office, sometimes from commonwealth countries. The governing statute is the Judicial Committee Act 1833.

The Judicial Committee of the Privy Council acts as a court of appeal from commonwealth countries, overseas territories, and Crown dependencies, in relation to 'devolution issues' under the Government of Wales Act 1998, the Scotland Act 1998, and the Northern Ireland Act 1998, and in respect of certain admiralty and ecclesiastical appeals.

Decisions of the Judicial Committee of the Privy Council while not binding on the English courts are persuasive and can have an important impact upon the development of English law. See for example *Attorney General for Jersey v Holley* [2005] 2 AC 580 which is discussed in chapter 5.

More information can be found at **www.jcpc.uk**.

2.5.11 Court of Justice of the European Union

The Court of Justice of the European Union (CJEU) is composed of one judge from each of the Member States, together with a number of Advocates General. While the judges decide cases brought before the court, the Advocates General have an advisory role, assisting the court by providing a non-binding opinion on cases. The composition and jurisdiction of the court is governed by Articles 251–281 of the Treaty on the Functioning of the European Union.

The jurisdiction of the CJEU encompasses preliminary rulings and direct actions. Preliminary rulings result from requests by the national courts of Member States in relation to matters such as the interpretation of the Treaties or decisions on the validity and interpretation of acts of the institutions of the Union. Direct actions include proceedings taken against Member States for failures to fulfil obligations imposed by the Treaties.

Preliminary rulings are not to be confused with appeals. The court will rule on the legal point which will be referred back to the national court which must then give effect to the ruling by applying it to the facts of the case in question.

Due to a heavy caseload, the CJEU is assisted by the General Court. This court has a limited jurisdiction but includes preliminary rulings on specified matters. Decisions of the General Court may be appealed to the CJEU.

One of the roles of the CJEU is to ensure that Union law develops in a consistent way. The preliminary ruling procedure is a mechanism which enables national courts to establish that domestic law is compliant with Union law. Union law thus impacts upon the development of the laws of the UK.

2.5.12 **European Court of Human Rights**

This is a completely separate court to the CJEU and it is a common mistake for students to confuse the two courts. The Court of Human Rights has jurisdiction over all cases involving the interpretation or application of the Convention for the Protection of Human Rights and Fundamental Freedoms (1950). The composition of the Court is currently forty-seven judges with a judge from each Contracting State; judges are independent and are not appointed in a representative capacity. The Parliamentary Assembly of the Council of Europe elects judges from a list of three proposed by each state. The jurisdiction of the court covers 'all matters relating to the interpretation and application of the Convention and the protocols'. Protocol 14 (a protocol amends or adds to the European Convention on Human Rights) sought to improve the operation of the court, which has been subject to a considerable backlog of cases. Cases may be filtered out or dealt with by a single judge in clearly inadmissible cases and where cases are repetitive, dealing with the same defect in national law, they may be decided by a committee of three judges. Chambers of seven judges deal with the majority of cases, but a case may be referred to a Grand Chamber of seventeen judges where it raises 'a serious question affecting the interpretation or application of the Convention or the protocols thereto, or a serious issue of general importance'.

Further attempts to address the problems faced by the European Court of Human Rights are two additional Protocols. Protocol 15 (which at the time of writing was yet to be ratified by all member states) reduces the time-limit within which an application may be made to the Court of Human Rights after the final decision of domestic courts, from six months to four months. The Protocol also seeks to enhance the principle of subsidiarity and margin of appreciation (the principle of subsidiarity means that member states have the primary responsibility to secure the rights defined in the Convention). A draft Protocol 16 allows the 'highest courts and tribunals' of domestic jurisidictions to seek an opinion from the European Court of Human Rights on questions of principle regarding interpretation and application of the Convention in cases before the domestic courts. It is hoped that by creating a dialogue between the European Court and national courts that cases may be concluded in a domestic forum rather than untimately going to the European Court.

Information on the operation of the court may be found in Article 2 of the Convention for the Protection of Human Rights and Fundamental Freedoms. See **www.echr.coe.int/**.

The UK as a signatory of the Convention for the Protection of Human Rights and Fundamental Freedoms must comply with the obligations undertaken. The European Court of Human Rights may be asked to consider whether the UK has breached its obligations. Should the court decide that there is a contravention of the Convention, then English law will have to be amended.

Additionally, it will be seen in chapter 7, 'Human rights and fundamental freedoms', that the courts of the UK are obliged to consider the decisions of the European Court of Human Rights where relevant to the determination of Convention rights.

> ### 🔑 Key point
>
> It is important to know the organisation of the courts as there is a hierarchy and this is essential to understanding how the doctrine of binding precedent operates.

2.6 Legal personnel and bodies

Government and the English legal system – the Ministry of Justice

Responsibility for aspects of the legal system has vested in various government departments in the recent past; the Lord Chancellor's Department became in 2003 the Department for Constitutional Affairs, which in 2007 assumed certain responsibilities from the Home Office to become the Ministry of Justice. The Ministry of Justice has responsibility for the following areas:

- policy in relation to the criminal, civil, family, and administrative justice system, including the Law Commission;
- sentencing policy, probation, and prisons;
- the courts and tribunals;
- support for the judiciary;

- legal aid; and
- constitutional reform.

Further detail on the work of the Ministry of Justice is available at: **www.gov.uk/ government/organisations/ministry-of-justice**.

2.6.1 **Lord Chancellor**

See further chapter 8, 'The judiciary'.

For centuries the Lord Chancellor has played a pivotal role in the English legal system. The role of the Lord Chancellor encompassed membership of the government as a Cabinet minister, a law-making role as a member of the second legislative chamber the House of Lords, and as head of the judiciary, including sitting as a judge in the House of Lords. Additionally, the Lord Chancellor either appointed judges or recommended judges for appointment. The potential conflicts in the functions of the Lord Chancellor clearly ran counter to any concept of a separation of powers. In consequence, the role of the Lord Chancellor was greatly altered by the Constitutional Reform Act 2005.

2.6.2 **The Attorney General**

The Attorney General is a member of the government who advises the government on matters of law. The Attorney General and a deputy, the Solicitor General, are termed the Law Officers. In relation to criminal offences the Attorney General may prosecute, or take over the prosecution, in very important cases. By statute, the consent of the Attorney General is required for the prosecution of certain offences. The offences are ones which raise considerations of public policy, national security, or relations with other states. A list of the offences where consent of the Attorney General or the Director of Public Prosecutions is required may be found at **www.cps.gov.uk/ legal/a_to_c/consent_to_prosecute/**. The Attorney General is answerable for the Director of Public Prosecutions.

An important role of the Attorney General is to review 'lenient' sentences given by the Crown Court. Should the Attorney General take the view that the sentence is too low then it may be referred to the Court of Appeal for review.

The role of the Attorney General was identified in the White Paper on *The Governance of Britain* (Cm 7170, 2007) as one to be renewed to ensure public confidence. Critics have claimed that there is a conflict of interest in the Attorney General being a member of the government and also providing legal advice. The proposal to give the Attorney General power to block prosecutions in the national interest has attracted much critical comment.

2.6.3 **The Director of Public Prosecutions**

The Director of Public Prosecutions is head of the Crown Prosecution Service. The duties of the director, carried out through the Crown Prosecution Service, include: the taking over of all criminal proceedings (except for specified proceedings) instituted on behalf of a police force; the commencement and conduct of criminal proceedings in any case which 'appears to him to be of importance or difficulty' or 'it is otherwise appropriate for proceedings to be instituted by him'; and to take over a prosecution which has already commenced (including private prosecutions undertaken, for example, by a member of the public). See the Prosecution of Offences Act 1985. Note that by statute the consent of the director is needed for the prosecution of certain offences.

2.6.4 Crown Prosecution Service (CPS)

Prior to 1986 prosecutions were instituted by the police force investigating a crime. This situation led to a divergence in approaches to prosecution and a lack of objectivity in the decision to prosecute. It was decided that to promote consistency and to separate the investigative process from the decision to prosecute that a national Crown Prosecution Service should be created. The CPS was created by the Prosecution of Offences Act 1985. See generally **www.cps.gov.uk/**.

2.6.5 The Lord Chief Justice

The Lord Chief Justice under the Constitutional Reform Act 2005 has approximately 400 statutory duties. These include being the President of the courts of England and Wales, the head of the judiciary of England and Wales, and President of the Court of Appeal (Criminal Division).

2.6.6 Legal Aid Agency

The issue of access to justice is vital to the fair operation of a legal system. Rights may be established, but if unknown or unenforced then they become meaningless.

How disputes are resolved depends upon having access to advice and the mechanisms for dispute resolution. Inextricably bound up with this is the question of funding. It was once said that civil courts, like the Ritz hotel, were open to all; the point being, of course, that access is a question of cost. The government had expressed concerns over spiralling legal aid costs, particularly in relation to criminal cases. With the enactment of the Legal Aid, Sentencing and Punishment of Offenders Act 2012 (**www.legislation.gov.uk/ukpga/2012/10/contents**) the breadth of the civil legal aid system was significantly reduced. Part 1 deals with Legal Aid, both Civil and Criminal, while Part 2 deals with litigation funding and costs designed to implement reforms in line with the Jackson Review of Civil Legal Costs. The 2012 Act, in relation to legal aid, largely came into force on 1 April 2013.

The provision of legal aid, both civil and criminal, and advice in England and Wales is the responsibility of the Legal Aid Agency. This body came into being on 1 April 2013 and replaced the Legal Services Commission.

2.6.7 **Law reform**

As you will quickly discover, the law is dynamic, with new cases clarifying points of law and Parliament amending laws every year. The latter is the main method of law reform, with Parliament passing amending, consolidating, codifying, or repealing legislation.

The drivers of law reform are many. It has been seen that the judges may indicate the need for Parliament to pass legislation to resolve a problem in the common law. Pressure groups may campaign for a change to the law. Events may compel Parliament to legislate, for example, the successful appeals following miscarriages of justice in criminal trials in the 1990s led to the passing of the Criminal Appeal Act 1995. Two kinds of law reform agencies may be employed either to investigate or instigate changes in the law. First, there are ad hoc bodies such as royal commissions and departmental committees. For example, see the Royal Commission on Criminal Procedure 1981, Cmnd 8092, which criticised the process by which the decision to prosecute was taken. This led ultimately to the creation of the CPS. Second, there are permanent bodies, such as the Law Commissions established by the Law Commissions Act 1965. The 1965 Act established two Law Commissions, one for England and Wales and one for Scotland. By s.3 the duty of each is:

> to take and keep under review all the law with which they are respectively concerned with a view to its systematic development and reform, including in particular the codification of such law, the elimination of anomalies, the repeal of obsolete and unnecessary enactments, the reduction of the number of separate enactments and generally the simplification and modernisation of the law…

This is achieved by reviewing the existing law, preparing a consultation paper for circulation to lawyers and other interested parties or bodies, and finally the production of a report and if necessary a draft bill. While the Commission has been successful there are obstacles to the reform of the law, especially the securing of parliamentary time for the enactment of the proposals. Changes have been made to address the problem of non-implementation of Law Commission reports. These changes are reviewed in an article 'Reforming the Law (Commission): a crisis of identity' by Shona Wilson.

🖹 Example

In recent years, the Law Commission has produced reports on *Unfair Terms in Contracts*, Cmnd 6464; *Post-Legislative Scrutiny*, Cmnd 6945; and *Participating in Crime*, Cmnd 7084.

In 2008, the Law Commission considered the High Court's power to judicially review decisions in the Crown Court, except in 'matters relating to trial on indictment' as stated in s.29(3) of the Senior Courts Act 1981. As the extent of the exclusion is uncertain, this has given rise to expensive litigation. The Law Commission looked at how this problem could be resolved and 'how this review of jurisdiction [by the High Court] could be best transferred to the Court of Appeal (Criminal Division) to streamline procedures in criminal cases through a single line

of criminal courts'. In July 2010 it published a report, *The High Court's Jurisdiction in relation to Criminal Proceedings* LC324 recommending reform. It was recommended, inter alia, that appeal by way of case stated from the Crown Court to the High Court in criminal proceedings be abolished. This could ultimately alter the jurisdiction of the High Court.
Consider what has happened to the Law Commission reports?

Information on the Law Commissions and reports may found at: **www.lawcom.gov. uk/about.htm**.

2.6.8 Lawyers

In England and Wales, lawyers are divided into two professions: solicitors and barristers. Lawyers are involved in the provision of legal services, for example, advice, conveyancing, and representation before the courts, but they are not the only source of legal services. Indeed, the story of lawyers and the provision of legal services since the late 1980s has been one of increasing choice and because of competition lower costs but at the same time one of the protection of the quality of service. As will be seen, the reform of the legal professions and the efficient provision of legal services is ongoing. The way in which legal services are provided impacts upon access to justice, e.g. where disputes arise, particularly involving individuals; can legal advice be readily obtained?

Summary

- Defining law is problematic but it is important to recognise the sources from which law emanates, the geographical extent of law, and when law commences.

- The term common law has various meanings which depend upon the context in which the term is used.

- Law made by Parliament, on the one hand, and law made by judges, on the other, differ in a number of important respects.

- In the United Kingdom there is no higher law-making body than Parliament. Parliament is said to be supreme.

- The validity of an Act of Parliament may not be questioned in the courts or by other bodies.

- The role of the judges is to interpret statutes and to develop the common law through case law following the rules of judicial precedent.

- For treaty obligations, such as those relating to the European Communities and the European Convention on Human Rights, to become part of English law it is necessary for Parliament to pass legislation incorporating such obligations.

- The courts are arranged hierarchically and act as courts of first instance (or trial) or courts of appeal. The courts are not arranged as civil or criminal courts but exercise jurisdiction in relation to civil proceedings or criminal proceedings or both.
- Criminal and civil proceedings have different terminology, different rules relating to burden and standard of proof, and different outcomes.
- A feature of the English legal system is an adversarial approach to the determination of cases, rather than an inquisitorial approach.

? Questions

1 What is the difference between a crime and a civil wrong?

2 What is the meaning of the term 'common law' and what are the characteristics of a 'common law' legal system?

3 Explain the concept of parliamentary supremacy.

4 What is the significance for English law of the European Convention on Human Rights?

5 What are the differences between an adversarial and inquisitorial approach to adjudication?

6 What factors determine whether:
   (a) a criminal case commences in a magistrates' court or the Crown Court; and
   (b) a civil case commences in a county court or the High Court?

7 What are the functions of the:
   (a) Ministry of Justice;
   (b) Crown Prosecution Service; and the
   (c) Law Commission?

ℕ Further reading

You should aim to read as widely as possible to support your understanding of the dynamic nature of law and legal systems. Apart from books and articles get into the habit of reading heavyweight daily newspapers, as these report on current legal developments. There are also a number of useful websites you should access throughout your study of English legal system, some of which are identified in the text.

- **Bingham, T.** *The Rule of Law*, Penguin (2011)
  A short and readable book exploring the idea of the rule of law, see particularly chapter 10 on parliamentary sovereignty and the rule of law.

- **Malleson, K.** 'The Evolving Role of the Supreme Court' [2011] PL 724
  Considers the composition and role of the Supreme Court and whether the way in which the court exercises its role will change.

- **Pannick, D.** '"Better that a horse should have a voice in the House [of Lords] than that a judge should" (Jeremy Bentham): Replacing the Law Lords by a Supreme Court' [2009] PL 723
  Provides a historical view of the House of Lords and the arguments for the creation of the Supreme Court.

- **Steyn, Lord** 'Democracy, the Rule of Law and the Role of Judges' [2006] EHRLR 244
  A lecture considering the rule of law and its relationship with parliamentary supremacy and the consequences for the judiciary.

- **Twining, W.** and **Miers, D.** *How to Do Things with Rules*, 5th edn, Cambridge University Press (2010)
  An insightful exploration of rules, problems of interpretation, and their solution.

- **Williams, G.** 'The Definition of Crime' [1955] CLP 107
  An interesting exploration of the difficulties of definition in relation to the meaning of crime.

- **Wilson, S.** 'Reforming the Law (Commission): a crisis of identity' [2013] PL 20
  Reviews the operation of the Law Commission in the light of changes to parliamentary procedure and the passing of the Law Commission Act 2009.

Online Resource Centre

You should now attempt the supporting multiple choice questions available at **www.oxfordtextbooks.co.uk/orc/wilson_els/**.

3 Legislation and the law-making process

Learning objectives

By the end of this chapter you should:

- be able to describe the composition of the various bodies which form the UK Parliament;

- be able to understand the procedure by which primary legislation is produced in the UK, including derogations from it, in particular the Parliament Acts procedure;

- be able to assess the effectiveness of the parliamentary stages of law-making in the UK;

- be able to compare and contrast government bills and private members' bills, and evaluate their relative success rates;

- be able to identify and explain the different forms of secondary legislation; and

- be able to evaluate the need for secondary legislation and the effectiveness of Parliament's ability to prevent the abuse of delegated law-making powers.

🎙 Talking point

. . . .

In July 2013, the United Kingdom Parliament passed the Marriage (Same Sex Couples) Act 2013, which states in section 1 that 'marriage of same sex couples is lawful'. This marked a major extension to the previous definition of marriage in English law, which had been limited to opposite sex couples. (In Hyde v Hyde (1865–69) LR 1 P & D 130, Lord Penzance had said, 'I conceive that marriage, as understood in Christendom, may for this purpose be defined as the voluntary union for life of one man and one woman, to the exclusion of all others.')

The background to the passage of the 2013 Act can be traced to 'Equal Civil Marriage', the Coalition government's consultation paper on reforming the law in England and Wales in order to allow same sex couples to marry, which was published in March 2012. The government received over 228,000 responses to the consultation paper, making it the largest ever response to a government consultation (according to **www.legislation.gov. uk***). The Marriage (Same Sex Couples) Bill was introduced into Parliament in January 2013, passed by both Houses of Parliament, and received the Royal Assent in July, when it became the Act.*

*Outside of Parliament, the legislation has attracted support, such as from the lesbian, gay, and bisexual charity Stonewall (***www.stonewall.org.uk***) but has been criticised by others, such as the campaign group Coalition for Marriage (***http://c4m. org.uk/***).*

This chapter will examine the composition and powers of the UK Parliament, its relationship with the government, and the different forms of legislation that may be produced either by or on behalf of Parliament.

. . . .

Introduction

This chapter examines 'legislation', which is a very broad term describing all the law made by, or under powers granted by, the UK Parliament. Legislation made by Parliament itself, in the form of 'Acts of Parliament', is described as 'primary' legislation because it is the highest form of UK law. Legislation made by other bodies under powers granted to them by Parliament is known as 'secondary' or 'delegated' legislation. You should not assume, however, that primary legislation is automatically or necessarily more important than secondary legislation. For example, take the broad subject of 'prohibition of discrimination in the workplace'. Until recently, there were numerous pieces of legislation that prohibited discrimination at work, but whilst some forms of discrimination were prohibited by primary legislation, others were prohibited by secondary legislation. For example:

Example

Discrimination at work on grounds of sex, race, and disability was prohibited by primary legislation: the Sex Discrimination Act 1975, the Race Relations Act 1976, and the Disability Discrimination Act 1995, respectively; and discrimination at work on grounds of sexual orientation, religion or belief, and age were prohibited by secondary legislation, in the form of the Employment Equality (Sexual Orientation) Regulations 2003, the Employment Equality (Religion or Belief) Regulations 2003, and the Employment Equality (Age) Regulations 2006, respectively.

Is there any logical reason why this should have been? The answer appears to be 'no'. It makes perfect sense, therefore, that Parliament has now passed the Equality Act 2010, which consolidates all of the primary and secondary legislation above. Discrimination on grounds of age, disability, religion or belief, sex, and sexual orientation is now prohibited by primary legislation.

Moreover, very often the 'law' on a particular subject comprises a *combination* of primary and secondary legislation and it is necessary to be aware of both. Typically, where this does occur, primary legislation will lay down a framework of general principles and rules with the secondary legislation providing more details.

The most significant difference between primary and secondary legislation is that whilst the latter can be subject to 'judicial review' in the courts, Acts of Parliament are immune from challenge in the courts. This general principle was accepted by the judiciary in *British Railways Board v Pickin* [1974] AC 765, although it is subject to one important exception. When the provisions of an Act conflict with a 'directly effective' provision of European Union (EU) law, the latter has to be enforced instead – a concept known as the 'supremacy' or 'primacy' of EU law. This exception was confirmed to exist by the Judicial Committee of the House of Lords in *R v Secretary of State for Transport, ex parte Factortame Ltd & Others* [1991] 1 AC 603, a case involving a conflict between certain provisions of the Merchant Shipping Act 1988 and (what is now) Article 49 of the Treaty on the Functioning of the European Union. The House of Lords 'disapplied' the Act and applied Article 49 instead.

3.1 **Parliament**

3.1.1 **The nature and functions of Parliament**

The UK Parliament has three main functions: (1) to legislate – Parliament passes the laws by which the country operates; (2) to deal with public finance – the government raises money by Acts of Parliament; (3) to provide a forum in which the actions and policies of the government may be publicly scrutinised. This chapter will concentrate on the first of these functions, Parliament's legislative function.

The UK Parliament is actually composed of three bodies. These are the Queen in Parliament, the House of Lords, and the House of Commons. In theory, the most important of these bodies is the Queen; in practice, however, the real power lies with the House of Commons as the only directly elected body in Parliament. Most legislation originates from the government and is introduced first into the House of Commons, where it is known as a bill. In certain circumstances, the Commons has the power to legislate without the consent of the House of Lords – but the converse situation does not apply. The House of Lords used to have the power to veto any bills sent to it by the House of Commons. This power is now limited to a temporary veto following the enactment of the Parliament Acts (see 3.4). However, the Lords still plays an important role in the working of Parliament by suggesting amendments to bills introduced in the Commons and therefore providing an extra check on legislative proposals. In addition, bills can originate from the Lords. Such legislation tends to be of a non-contentious nature and initiation in the Lords can save valuable parliamentary time. (See 3.3 for an explanation of how a bill becomes an Act of Parliament.)

You should note that, following devolution, there is now a Scottish Parliament (under the Scotland Act 1998), and National Assemblies for Wales (under the Government of Wales Act 1998) and Northern Ireland (under the Northern Ireland Act 1998), each of which has (limited) law-making power within those jurisdictions. However, there is no English Parliament; the UK Parliament fulfils this function. This post-devolution situation is uneven and arguably unfair. For example, Scottish MPs can vote in the UK Parliament on matters that only or primarily affect England, but there is no such right for English MPs to vote in debates before the Scottish Parliament. As a result, there have been calls for the creation of a separate English Parliament.

'Parliament' should not be confused with 'government'. The UK government is, generally speaking, formed by the political party which secured the most seats in the House of Commons at the last general election. At the time of writing, that party is the Conservative Party. However, as they did not secure an outright majority, they were forced to enter into a coalition government alongside the Liberal Democrats. Many other political parties are represented in Parliament, including the Labour Party (the official opposition), the Democratic Unionist Party, the Scottish National Party, Plaid Cymru, and so on. There are also a small number of independents. The prime minister and all government ministers (the Cabinet) have to be members of one or other house of Parliament; in practice, most are members of the House of Commons.

The UK Parliament is relatively unusual in that members of the government also sit in Parliament. This may be contrasted with other countries such as the US, where the government, represented by the President, are chosen in an entirely separate process from the country's parliament, Congress.

3.1.2 **The House of Commons**

The House of Commons dates from the early thirteenth century. There are presently 650 seats in the House of Commons, each one representing a 'constituency'; the person elected to fill that seat is called a Member of Parliament (MP). The 650 constituencies cover the whole of the UK (England, Scotland, Wales, and Northern Ireland). All MPs are directly elected at a general election, through the system known as majoritarian vote (or more commonly first-past-the-post). The Parliamentary Voting System and Constituencies Act 2011 provided for the first-past-the-post system to be replaced with the 'alternative vote' system, although this was subject to ratification at a national referendum, which was held in May 2011. In the referendum (the first national referendum to be held in the UK since 1975), the result was a comprehensive rejection of the 'alternative vote' (68 per cent of voters said 'no'), meaning that the first-past-the-post system remains in place.

The Fixed-term Parliaments Act 2011 sets the date of the next general election as 7 May 2015, with subsequent elections to be held every five years, subject to a power vested in the prime minister to modify the date by up to two months.

Disqualification from membership of the House of Commons

There are no formal qualifications (educational, professional, or otherwise) required for MPs. However, a number of people are disqualified by law from being members of the House of Commons:

- persons under 18 years of age;
- aliens (that is, not British nationals);
- members of the House of Lords (peers);
- undischarged bankrupts;
- those convicted of 'corrupt or illegal practices';
- people listed in s.1 of the House of Commons Disqualification Act 1975, such as judges, civil servants, members of the Armed Forces, and members of any police force; and
- people currently serving a sentence of imprisonment of one year or more.

Clergy ordained in a number of churches (including the Church of England) used to be disqualified from membership. However, this was abolished by s.1 of the House of Commons (Removal of Clergy Disqualification) Act 2001. Until very recently, persons suffering from mental illness were disqualified from becoming MPs. The law was changed in this respect by s.1 of the Mental Health (Discrimination) Act 2013.

Thinking point

No formal qualifications (educational, professional, or otherwise) are required for MPs, yet they are responsible for producing legal rules to regulate a complex society with little outside help. Parliamentary time is constrained (in the Commons at least) by the need to balance other commitments, especially to constituencies. Short-term thinking is inevitable because of the recurring need for re-election. Party-political debates (especially in the Commons) often distract from the need to get the wording of the legislation right.

In light of this:

1. Consider whether, and if so how, the composition of the House of Commons should be changed.

2. What advantages, if any, are there in the adoption of fixed-term parliaments under the Fixed-term Parliaments Act 2011?

3.1.3 The House of Lords

The House of Lords is composed of two main groups, the Lords Temporal and the Lords Spiritual. The Lords Temporal consists of the hereditary peers, the life peers, and the judicial peers.

Hereditary peers

Until November 1999, over 750 hereditary peers were entitled to sit and vote in the House of Lords by virtue of birthright. There was much opposition to this hereditary principle, primarily on the basis that birthright alone should not justify a seat in Parliament. In 1999, therefore, the (then) Labour government introduced into Parliament a bill which duly became the House of Lords Act 1999. Section 1 of the 1999 Act removed the automatic right of all hereditary peers to seats in the House of Lords, although as a result of a compromise agreement during the progress of the bill, ninety-two hereditary peers were allowed to remain by virtue of s.2(2).

Life peers

Life peers are appointed under the Life Peerages Act 1958 by the Queen on the advice of the prime minister and, since 2000, with the approval of the House of Lords Appointments Commission (see later). The 1958 Act was intended to produce a more representative second chamber and to allow for people who had achieved a position of national prominence in their field to be recognised with a seat in Parliament. It also allowed for people other than 'professional' politicians to participate in the law-making process. The life peers include amongst their number former members of the Commons, former senior police officers, and people prominent in the professions and arts. In September 2013, there were 654 life peers (excluding those on leave of absence, suspended, or disqualified – see later for further discussion of disqualification).

Judicial peers

The UK's highest court, the Supreme Court, was established on 1 October 2009 by s.23 of the Constitutional Reform Act 2005, replacing the Judicial Committee of the House of Lords. When a judge was appointed to the Judicial Committee (under the Appellate Jurisdiction Act 1876) and made a 'law lord' (or rather, a 'Lord of Appeal in Ordinary', their official title), he was *also* made a judicial peer, a form of life peerage. This entitled the judge to sit in the House of Lords and participate in debates on proposed legislation and other matters. This presented a problem, as the law lords were simultaneously members of both the UK's legislature (Parliament) and its highest court (the Judicial Committee) – a clear breach of the doctrine of the 'separation of powers', according to which no-one should be simultaneously a member of more than one branch of government (the legislature, the executive, and the judiciary).

This problem has now been resolved. When the Supreme Court was established and the Judicial Committee was abolished, in October 2009, the existing 'law lords' at that time became the first judges of the Supreme Court. More significantly, however, all judges of the Supreme Court are disqualified from sitting in the House of Lords, which means that the 'separation of powers' is now respected. This disqualification does not apply to retired law lords. Furthermore, new judges appointed to the Supreme Court after 1 October 2009 will not be given peerages. Thus, for example, when Lord Dyson was promoted from the Court of Appeal to take up a seat in the Supreme Court in April 2010, he was not given a peerage.

The Lords Spiritual

This is a group of twenty-six Bishops of the Church of England. Uniquely among the present members of the House of Lords, the spiritual peers must retire on reaching the age of 70. The presence of the spiritual peers is controversial for several reasons. First, the very concept of 'spiritual peers' is debatable. The UK and Bhutan are the only countries in the world whose Parliaments automatically give seats to spiritual leaders. It has been argued that their continued presence is anachronistic, a throwback to the early years of the British Parliament when spiritual leadership was regarded as a far more important matter than it is today. Second, if the UK is to retain spiritual peers, why do they only represent one church (the Church of England)? In a multicultural, multi-faith nation, as the UK undoubtedly is today, why are no other churches officially represented?

The cross-benchers

The cross-benchers are those members of the Lords who are politically neutral. Their name derives from the fact that they literally sit in seats which 'cross' the Lords, rather than siding with the government benches or those of the opposition. Their number comprises some hereditary peers and some life peers and all the retired law lords. They are quite significant in terms of numbers and provide an important contrast with the Commons, where virtually every MP represents a political party.

The House of Lords Appointments Commission

This body was established in 2000. Despite its name, the Commission has no power to appoint life peers. Instead, it has two functions: to encourage members of the public to nominate non-party political life peers as so-called 'People's Peers' and to 'vet' nominees put forward by the prime minister and the political parties. In April 2001, the first 'People's Peers' were nominated by the Commission and duly recommended by the prime minister to the Queen. The list attracted severe criticism: there were seven knights and one lady, and three professors – ironically, just the sort of people who would in any event have been nominated by the prime minister.

In March 2006, the Commission refused to approve four prime ministerial nominees owing to certain alleged financial irregularities, sparking the 'cash for honours' scandal. It transpired that three people nominated by the then prime minister Tony Blair for life peerages had had their nominations blocked by the Commission on the basis that the nominees had made undisclosed loans to the Labour Party. Although the police investigated the allegations (which, if true, would have amounted to a criminal offence) no charges were ever brought. However, the scandal raised awareness of the potential for 'cronyism' inherent in the present system whereby life peerages are conferred by the prime minister.

Disqualification from membership of the House of Lords

These are as follows:

- aliens (not citizens of the UK);
- judges;
- members of the House of Commons or members of the European Parliament;
- persons under 21;
- undischarged bankrupts;

- persons convicted of treason; and
- members who have been expelled by the House.

3.1.4 **Reform of the House of Lords**

The House of Lords has been the subject of a great deal of criticism in recent years. Some of the major criticisms are as follows:

- the composition of the Lords is too restricted. The typical peer is male, middle-aged or older, based in the south of England, and comes from a middle-class or higher socio-economic background and is therefore unrepresentative of the general population;
- the Lords is an unelected body. This is obviously undemocratic, in the sense that the electorate have virtually no say in the composition of one of their parliamentary bodies;
- the presence of the spiritual peers is controversial.

Reform proposals to date

The removal of over 600 hereditary peers by the House of Lords Act 1999 (discussed previously) was intended to address the first criticism. However, the 1999 Act did not address the other criticisms and so debate continues as to the possibility of further reform. Since 2000, a number of reform proposals have come and gone, including no less than four government White Papers (see 3.3.1 for an explanation of White Papers). However, one option which has attracted support is a 'hybrid' of elected members (to ensure some democratic input and with it legitimacy) and appointed members (allowing for the retention of independent, non-political members and experts). However, there is disagreement over the exact proportion of the two groups. There is also disagreement over various other details, such as what form of electoral system should be used, how long the terms of office should be, whether the elected and/or appointed members should be entitled to stand for re-election or re-appointment, and whether or not the spiritual peers should be retained.

Following the general election in May 2010 and the formation of the Liberal-Democrat/Conservative coalition government, it was announced that the new government had reached an agreement that the House of Lords should be replaced by either a wholly or mostly elected body, with a system of proportional representation (PR) to be used in the election. In June 2012, the House of Lords Reform Bill was introduced into the House of Commons to put this agreement into effect. Specifically, the bill provided for a reformed House of Lords consisting of 360 elected members, ninety appointed members, twelve Lords Spiritual, and an unspecified number of 'ministerial members'. However, at the second reading stage in July, a significant number of Conservative MPs opposed the bill, forcing the government to abandon it.

The notion of replacing the House of Lords with an *entirely* elected upper chamber is particularly controversial. Although such a body exists in many other countries, such as Australia and the USA, it risks duplication of the House of Commons, and hence would put the two Houses on a possible collision course with both claiming equal democratic legitimacy. There is also the potential for deadlock during the legislative process if each House is dominated by a different political party, or alternatively 'rubber-stamping' of bills if both Houses are dominated by the same party.

! Critical debate

In February 2007, an editorial in *The Times* newspaper commented that '[t]he quest for Lords reform is akin to looking for the Goldilocks option. The Upper House has to have enough (electoral) legitimacy to be able to challenge a government but not so much that it leads regularly to gridlock'.

This comment reflects the twin imperatives for Lords reform of (a) legitimacy and (b) difference. The 'legitimacy' imperative is the need for the House of Lords to be taken seriously, not just by the government but by the general public. Replacing the presently unelected, primarily appointed House with a democratically elected body would go a long way to satisfying this. The 'difference' imperative is the need for the House of Lords to not simply replicate the House of Commons. The current House achieves this, but a democratically elected body may not do so. As *The Times* editorial points out, replacing the House of Lords with an elected body may lead to 'gridlock' involving the two Houses of Parliament, a situation which is particularly likely to happen if each House was controlled by a different political party. (This problem often afflicts the US Congress, with the House of Representatives often controlled by one party whilst the Senate is controlled by the other. As both House and Senate are directly elected, each can claim equal legitimacy and hence 'gridlock' often ensues.)

In the light of this, consider whether the present House of Lords should be replaced by a directly elected body. If you accept the arguments that (a) democratic legitimacy is essential, but that (b) simply replacing the House with a directly elected body creates too great a risk of 'gridlock', how might the composition of a reformed Lords be modified to avoid that risk?

3.2 **Primary legislation**

Primary legislation, in the form of Acts of Parliament, otherwise known as statutes, typically contains the fundamental principles of English law (other than those still regulated by the courts, known as the common law). As noted at the beginning of this chapter, there is also secondary legislation, which typically contains more detailed provisions. Secondary legislation will be dealt with in 3.5. The remainder of this section will concentrate on primary legislation.

There are literally thousands of Acts of Parliament in existence at any given time, covering just about any subject you care to name. There is no such thing as a 'typical' statute, although they do have various features in common. Statutes can range in size from a few lines to hundreds of pages. For example, at one extreme there is the Public Order (Amendment) Act 1996, which comprises a mere two sections. At the other extreme, is the Income Tax Act 2007 with 1,035 sections, while the Companies Act 2006 is so big that it is subdivided into forty-seven separate parts and contains a grand total of 1,300 sections.

3.2.1 Public, private, and hybrid legislation

Primary legislation may be either 'public', 'private', or 'hybrid'.

Public legislation

Public legislation affects the general law of the land, while private legislation is of a local or personal nature. The Human Rights Act 1998, the House of Lords Act 1999, and the Constitutional Reform Act 2005 are all examples of public Acts of Parliament from recent years.

Private (or local) legislation

Private (or local) legislation is designed to confer particular powers or benefits on any person(s) in excess of, or in conflict with, the general law. The promoters of such legislation are often local authorities, but private companies and occasionally individuals can also put forward proposals for such legislation, seeking special powers not available in the general law. Examples of private legislation from recent years include the HFC Bank Act 1999, the Leicester City Council Act 2006, the Transport for London Act 2008, and the Allhallows Staining Church Act 2010.

Hybrid legislation

Hybrid legislation refers to public legislation which affects a private person or interest in a particular way. The Channel Tunnel Act 1987 is a good example. It is public legislation in that, by allowing for the construction of a rail tunnel between the UK and France, it potentially affects everyone in the UK. However, it is also private as certain parts of the Act have very specific application. For example, Part IV of the Act is headed 'Construction and Improvement of Roads near Folkestone'. The most recent piece of hybrid legislation to be passed is the Crossrail Act 2008, which lays down the legal framework for the construction of new rail and underground links from Heathrow Airport in west London to Essex and Greenwich in east London.

3.2.2 'Constitutional' and 'ordinary' legislation?

There is a long-standing principle in English law that Parliament cannot bind itself. In other words, Parliament is free at any time to legislate on a subject and, to the extent that there is pre-existing, inconsistent legislation on the same subject, that earlier legislation is, either expressly or impliedly, repealed. This point was confirmed by the Divisional Court in *Thoburn v Sunderland City Council* [2002] EWHC 195 (Admin), [2003] QB 151. However, in the same case, the Divisional Court declared that there was an exception to the principle, which is when the pre-existing legislation is 'constitutional' in nature. Such legislation is, according to the Court, immune from implied repeal, albeit not express repeal. Laws LJ stated:

> We should recognise a hierarchy of Acts of Parliament: as it were 'ordinary' statutes and 'constitutional' statutes. The two categories must be distinguished on a principled basis. In my opinion a constitutional statute is one which (a) conditions the legal relationship between citizen and state in some general, overarching manner, or (b) enlarges or diminishes the scope of what we would now regard as fundamental constitutional rights.

Laws LJ listed several examples of 'constitutional' statutes: the Magna Carta 1297, the Bill of Rights 1689, the Union with Scotland Act 1706, the Representation of the People Acts 1832, 1867, and 1884, the European Communities Act 1972, the Human Rights Act 1998, the Scotland Act 1998, and the Government of Wales Act 1998. You should note that this development has not been addressed by either the Court of Appeal or the Supreme Court.

3.2.3 The origins of legislation

Government legislation

At the beginning of each parliamentary session, the monarch opens Parliament with a speech (the Queen's Speech) from the throne which outlines the government's main proposals for the session. Legislation is passed for various reasons.

- Most primary legislation is designed to implement government policy. For example, the Human Rights Act 1998 was a long-term objective of the Labour Party, even when in opposition, as was the House of Lords Act 1999. More recent examples of policy legislation include the Health Act 2006 (which prohibited smoking in enclosed public places in England) and the Child Poverty Act 2010.

- There are annual measures such as the Finance Act (which implements the government's Budget) and the Appropriation Act (which authorises public expenditure).

- Ad hoc measures arise in the course of every parliamentary session. Recent examples are:
  - o the Anti-terrorism, Crime and Security Act 2001, passed in the wake of the terrorist atrocities of September 11, 2001;
  - o the London Olympic Games and Paralympic Games Act 2006 (passed in response to the decision of the International Olympic Committee to award the

2012 Olympic Games to London – had the Games gone to Paris instead, there would have been no need for this statute);

o the Banking (Special Provisions) Act 2008, passed in order to allow the government to nationalise stricken banks (the first candidate being Northern Rock, which was in danger of collapse at the time).

- Some legislation is a response to decisions of the courts. For example:

  o the Contempt of Court Act 1981 was in part a response to the decision of the European Court of Human Rights in the *Attorney General v Times Newspapers Ltd* [1979] 2 EHRR 245 that the law of contempt of court as stated by the House of Lords in the case contravened the right to freedom of expression;

  o the Theft (Amendment) Act 1996 – a response to the House of Lords decision in *R v Preddy* [1996] AC 815;

  o the Sexual Offences (Amendment) Act 2000 – a response to the decision of the European Court of Human Rights in *Sutherland v United Kingdom* (1997); and

  o the Criminal Evidence (Witness Anonymity) Act 2008 – passed in response to the House of Lords' decision in *R v Davis* [2008] UKHL 36.

- Some legislation is required to give effect to the UK's international obligations, primarily under the various treaties that relate to membership of the EU. Thus, when the British government agreed to join what was then called the European Economic Community (EEC) by signing the European Community Treaty, legislation was needed to give effect to this, and Parliament duly passed the European Communities Act 1972. Since then, the government has agreed to sign a number of other EU Treaties and each time a new Act of Parliament has been passed in order to confirm this. For example, when the then Prime Minister John Major signed the Treaty of European Union in February 1992 (which created the European Union), Parliament duly passed the European Communities (Amendment) Act 1993. More recently, after the then Prime Minister Gordon Brown signed the Lisbon Treaty in December 2007, Parliament approved this action by passing the European Union (Amendment) Act 2008.

- Some legislation is required to implement EU directives (see next for more detail).

- Consolidation Acts are also passed from time to time. These bring various statutes which have been passed over the years on the same subject into one place, primarily for convenience. A good example is the Equality Act 2010, mentioned at the beginning of this chapter, which consolidates several earlier statutes.

- Codification Acts are similar to consolidation statutes, but with a broader scope. Codification statutes will bring together not just pre-existing statutes on one subject but also the case law that has built up on the subject. Good examples of such statutes are the Theft Act 1968 and the Police and Criminal Evidence Act 1984 (PACE).

- Once legislation has been passed by Parliament, it can only be repealed by Parliament itself. As a result, legislation is sometimes passed in order simply to repeal old statutes which would otherwise remain in force indefinitely, far beyond their useful life. The most recent example is the Statute Law (Repeals) Act 2013, which repeals dozens of old Acts of Parliament such as the Female Orphan Asylum Act 1800 and the Hospital for Poor French Protestants Act 1808.

Implementation of EU directives

A significant amount of UK legislation is passed in order to bring the UK into line with legislation produced by the EU's law-making bodies. There are various forms of EU legislation, discussed in detail in chapter 6, one of which is called a directive.

Directives are binding on the governments of the EU's Member States, including the UK, but only as to 'the result to be achieved', while leaving to the Member States the choice of 'form and methods' (according to Article 288 of the Treaty on the Functioning of the European Union). This means that a directive, on its own, has no legal force. The Member States must pass their *own* legislation, to achieve whatever 'result' the directive requires.

Example

Implementation of Directive 92/85 into UK law

Part VIII of the Employment Rights Act 1996 was passed in order to give effect to Directive 92/85 on the rights of pregnant workers. Article 8 of the directive states that 'Member States shall take the necessary measures to ensure that workers…are entitled to a continuous period of maternity leave of at least 14 weeks.' Section 73(1) of the 1996 Act (when first enacted) stated that 'an employee's maternity leave period continues for the period of 14 weeks from its commencement or until the birth of the child, if later'. Thus, the UK government had to achieve the 'result' stipulated in the directive of guaranteeing pregnant workers at least 14 weeks' maternity leave. The 1996 Act clearly achieved this result. (As it happens, s.73 was amended in 1999 in order to increase the minimum maternity leave period to 18 weeks, and again in 2006 to increase it to 26 weeks – an option provided for by the directive, which refers to a 'period of maternity leave of *at least* 14 weeks'.)

In practice, the majority of directives are given effect in the UK via secondary legislation, which will be discussed in detail later.

Private members' bills

During the course of the parliamentary session, there are limited opportunities for backbench MPs (in the Commons) and for members of the House of Lords to introduce proposals for legislation. These are called private members' bills. Often, the bill put forward has little chance of becoming law but is designed to draw attention to a particular issue and/or to try to embarrass the government into introducing a government bill. For example, between 1988 and 2002, no less than eight private members' bills were put forward relating to the control of high residential hedgerows. None of them became Acts; however, the then Labour government eventually responded and now ss.65–7 of the Anti-social Behaviour Act 2003 (which was a piece of government legislation) deals with the problems created by high hedges. Most often, private members' bills are either discontinued by the MP or peer who introduced it, or simply fail through lack of time.

However, that is not to suggest that backbench MPs have no chance of introducing important, and sometimes controversial, legislation. In fact, the government of the day may quietly provide assistance behind the scenes for such bills, although, politically, it may not wish to be too closely associated with them.

> ### 🔑 Key point
>
> The distinction between government bills and private members' bills is simply that the former are endorsed by the government whereas the latter are introduced into Parliament by individual MPs or peers. However, if/when a government or private members' bill becomes an Act of Parliament, the final legislation has exactly the same legal status.

Examples of private members' bills becoming important Acts of Parliament include the following:

- Abortion Act 1967 (which legalised abortions);
- Sexual Offences Act 1967 (which decriminalised homosexual acts between consenting male adults);
- Criminal Procedure (Insanity and Unfitness to Plead) Act 1991 (this Act abolished mandatory indefinite detention in a secure mental hospital following a verdict of insanity in a criminal trial, except in murder cases);
- Law Reform (Year and a Day Rule) Act 1996 (by this Act the ancient 'year and a day' rule in murder was abolished);
- Gangmasters (Licensing) Act 2004 (which created a Gangmasters Licensing Authority to regulate vulnerable workers in the agriculture and shellfish-gathering sectors);
- Presumption of Death Act 2013 (which provides that a person missing for seven years is presumed to have died).

Private members' bills take four forms:

1. **The Ballot.** At the beginning of each parliamentary session, those MPs who wish to do so enter a ballot. Twenty names are drawn out and those members, in order, have the opportunity to present their chosen bills to Parliament. The successful members are invariably lobbied from various sources to adopt their ideas for legislation, although typically less than half the bills introduced will become Acts of Parliament. Two recent Acts produced via this route are the Mental Health (Discrimination) Act 2013 and the Presumption of Death Act 2013.

2. **The 'Ten Minute Rule' procedure.** This is given its name because members are not permitted to make a full speech, but are allowed a 'brief explanatory statement' (i.e. about ten minutes) regarding the desirability of the bill. In reality, this procedure is used to gain publicity for a measure as there is rarely enough support, or time, to take the bill further. No Acts have been produced via this route since 2002.

3. **Standing Order 57 (Presentation Bills).** Under this procedure a member may present a bill when a gap in the Commons timetable occurs. As with Ten Minute Rule Bills, it is primarily a publicity opportunity rather than a serious attempt at introducing legislation. However, two Acts have recently been produced by this route – albeit for the first time since 1998 – the Driving Instruction (Suspension and Exemption Powers) Act 2009 and the Holocaust (Return of Cultural Objects) Act 2009.

4. **Peers' Bills.** This refers to bills introduced by peers in the Lords, some of which are subsequently adopted by a backbench MP and guided through the Commons. The most recent Act produced via this route is the Live Music Act 2012.

3.3 The passage of legislation through Parliament

In order to become an 'Act of Parliament', a legislative proposal – known as a 'bill' – must normally be passed by the House of Commons and the House of Lords and given the royal assent before it becomes law. As already indicated, most bills – whether government or private members' – originate in the House of Commons (and are known as 'Commons Bills'), whilst some bills may be introduced in the House of Lords (and are referred to as 'Lords Bills'). Generally speaking, bills relating to public finance, such as the annual Appropriation and Finance Bills, start in the Commons, while more technical bills typically start in the Lords.

3.3.1 Procedure for the passage of a public bill

All bills must pass through five stages in each House of Parliament before being sent for royal assent. However, there are certain steps that most bills go through before reaching that point.

Pre-legislative steps

Government bills are drafted by specialist lawyers in the Parliamentary Counsel Office (PCO), as instructed by the minister concerned. Even before that point, there may have been either a 'Green Paper' or 'White Paper', or both, prior to a government bill coming into existence. Green Papers are purely consultation papers on a particular subject, whereas White Papers set out the government's policy in more detail. Over the last ten years or so, it has become increasingly common for the government to publish draft bills and invite further comment and feedback. Sometimes, these draft bills are subjected to parliamentary scrutiny by Pre-legislation Committees.

Many government bills (and hence Acts) owe their existence to the work of the Law Commission. This body was established, by Parliament, in 1965, to review the law in England and Wales and to recommend proposals for law reform. Such reforms may be necessary for a variety of reasons: to modernise outdated law; to simplify overly complicated law; to make the law on a particular subject more accessible; and so on. The Law Commission works on a number of different proposals simultaneously. When it is ready to do so, it issues a Consultation Paper on an area of law, typically setting out the problems which it has identified with that area and proposing a range of options for reform. The paper will invite feedback on its proposals. This will typically be followed by a Report summarising the responses to the Consultation Paper and setting out the Law Commission's preferred option for reform. It is then up to the government to decide whether to translate the Law Commission's proposal into a government bill, although the government may well issue a Green and/or White Paper of its own first – especially if the government agrees with the Law Commission about the need for reform but not necessarily with the Law Commission's preferred option for reform.

For example, the law of voluntary manslaughter (the area of criminal law where the accused is charged with murder but invokes a special defence, reducing his or her liability to manslaughter), was completely overhauled by Parliament in the Coroners and Justice Act 2009. Briefly, this Act reformulated the defence of diminished responsibility, abolished the ancient common law defence of provocation, and introduced a new statutory defence of 'loss of control'. But how and why did this Act come into existence? The following chronology summarises the key steps:

- October 2003 – having taken the view that the law of voluntary manslaughter was out-of-date and overly complicated, the Law Commission published a Consultation Paper entitled *Partial Defences to Murder* inviting responses to its proposals to reform the area.

- August 2004 – following consultation, the Law Commission published a Report, also entitled *Partial Defences to Murder*, recommending how the law of voluntary manslaughter should be reformed.

- December 2005 – the Law Commission published a second Consultation Paper, entitled *A New Homicide Act for England and Wales?* This was more ambitious and wide-ranging than the 2003 Consulation Paper and 2004 Report, covering the whole range of homicide offences.

- November 2006 – following consultation, the Law Commission published another Report, also entitled '*A New Homicide Act for England and Wales?*', recommending how the law of murder (including all forms of manslaughter) should be reformed.

- July 2008 – the Labour government published its own Consulation Paper, entitled '*Murder, Manslaughter and Infanticide: Proposals for Reform of the Law*'. This adopted some, but by no means all, of the Law Commission's recommendations; it also amended some of the Law Commission's proposals for reform of the law of homicide. It included a draft Bill.

- January 2009 – following consultation, the Coroners and Justice Bill was introduced into Parliament. It closely resembled the government's draft Bill although there were some changes.

- November 2009 – the bill received Royal Assent and became the Coroners and Justice Act 2009.

The first reading

This is a purely formal stage. The title of the bill is read out, an order made for the bill to be published and a date fixed for the second reading. Before a government bill can progress to the next stage, s.19 of the Human Rights Act 1998 requires the minister to issue a statement, which must be to the effect that either:

- in his view, the provisions of the bill are compatible with the Convention rights ('a statement of compatibility'); or

- although he is unable to make a 'statement of compatibility', the government nevertheless wishes the House to proceed with the bill.

The reference to 'minister' and 'the government' in s.19 would seem to exclude both private and private members' bills from this requirement.

The second reading

At this stage, the House considers the principles and purposes of the bill. The minister or member will outline the bill's provisions and justifications. The opposition gives its views. This will not automatically or necessarily be negative, even for government bills. If the proposed legislation is uncontroversial or welcomed by all concerned, then it should attract 'cross-party' support. Backbenchers may draw attention to any weaknesses, particularly in regard to those they represent. For example, during the passage of the National Lotteries Bill in 1992/93, many backbench MPs from constituencies in which football pools companies' headquarters were based drew attention to the impact that the lottery would (and in fact did) have on employment.

Chapter 7, 'Human rights and fundamental freedoms'.

The bill is then voted on. If the bill is 'read' a second time, the House is deemed to have approved the bill in principle. If the second reading is defeated then that is the end of the bill. It is *extremely* unlikely that a government bill will fail a second reading. It may do so if the government has no overall majority and its opponents combine against it. This happened twice in the twentieth century – the Rent Restrictions Bill in 1923/24 and the Reduction of Redundancy Rebates Bill in 1976/77. In 1985/86, the Conservative government's Shops Bill was so unpopular that seventy-two of its own backbenchers voted against it at second reading and the bill was lost. So far this century, one government bill has already been lost – the House of Lords Reform Bill 2012 (discussed at 3.1.4).

Committee stage

In the Commons, the bill is typically next sent to a Public Bill Committee (formerly known as a Standing Committee) of between sixteen and fifty MPs (usually about eighteen). The composition of the Committee will reflect the political composition of the whole House. A new committee will be set up for each bill, and will be named after the bill – thus, for example, the committee dealing with Welfare Reform Bill was called the Welfare Reform Bill Committee. Each committee must consider the details of its bill (in theory, line by line). Amendments will usually be proposed and considered. Public Bill Committees have the power to take written and oral evidence regarding the contents of their bill from people and organisations outside of Parliament, the idea being that this will improve the scrutiny process.

The advantage of the committee stage is that it allows for several bills to progress through the House of Commons simultaneously, and it is also easier for detailed discussion to take place in a small committee room rather than on the floor of the House of Commons itself. However, some bills do have their 'committee stage' on the floor of the House of Commons, thus enabling all MPs to participate in the detailed debate if they wish to do so. This is known as a 'Committee of the Whole House'. This procedure may be used for the following:

- bills of constitutional importance (such as the bill which became the Human Rights Act 1998; and bills which are required to endorse the government's signing of international treaties, such as the bill which became the European Union (Amendment) Act 2008);
- bills which need to be passed quickly (such as the bill which became the Anti-terrorism, Crime and Security Act 2001, the bill which became the Banking (Special Provisions) Act 2008, and the bill which became the Criminal Evidence (Witness Anonymity) Act 2008);
- the major clauses of each year's Finance Bill(s); and
- non-controversial bills which go through 'on the nod'.

In the Lords, meanwhile, the committee stage will normally be taken on the floor of the House (potentially allowing all peers to participate).

Report stage

After detailed scrutiny by the Public Bill Committee, the bill is reported back to the House, allowing those MPs who were not on the Committee to participate in further scrutiny. Amendments made by the Committee will either be endorsed or reversed by the House. Occasionally, further amendments, usually government sponsored, may be made at this stage and new clauses added. Where a bill was considered by a committee of the Whole House, and not amended, then the bill progresses immediately to the third reading stage without a report stage.

Third reading

Once again, the whole House considers the proposals behind the legislation. In the Commons, there are strict limits on further amendments. Except for major bills, this stage is usually short.

The other House

These stages are then repeated in the other House. Each House has discretion to amend bills passed originally in the other House. Where this happens, the amended bill must return to its original House for consideration of the amendments. Thus, if a Commons bill is amended in the Lords, the amended bill must be returned to the Commons. If the Commons vote to agree to the amendments, then the bill can be presented for the royal assent (see later). If, however, the Commons rejects one or more of the Lords' amendments (or amends them) then the bill must go back to the Lords for them to decide whether to persist with their amendments.

If the Lords drop their amendments, then the bill can be presented for royal assent; however, if not, the bill must return to the Commons. This process can go on several times and is referred to as 'ping-pong', with a bill potentially shuttling back and forth several times between the two Houses. The process cannot go on indefinitely, however, because ultimately, if no agreement is reached before the end of the parliamentary session (when Parliament is 'prorogued'), then all outstanding bills are lost unless either agreement had been made to carry the bill over to the next session (about which, see later) or the provisions of the Parliament Act apply.

An example of the latter situation is the bill which became the Hunting Act 2004, which shuttled between the two Houses in November 2004. The bill passed by the Commons banned fox-hunting, but the Lords amended it to allow some form of licensed fox-hunting to continue. The Commons refused to accept these amendments, and the Lords refused to withdraw them, and eventually the 2003/04 session ended with no agreement. However, the bill was passed under the Parliament Act provisions.

Royal assent

Once the bill has been passed by both Houses of Parliament it receives the royal assent. This is now a purely formal stage, although governed by the Royal Assent Act 1967. The last monarch to refuse to grant the royal assent was Queen Anne in the 1706/07 session.

Commencement

On the date of the royal assent, a bill becomes an Act of Parliament. That does not necessarily mean that it has force of law, however. Unless otherwise provided in the Act of Parliament, the Act will come into force immediately but, very often, it is deemed to be desirable for commencement to be delayed, either for the whole Act or parts of it. The delay may be until a specified date or until such day as the relevant government minister 'may' prescribe. It follows that, sometimes, an Act – or at least part of it – never comes into force at all. An example is the Easter Act 1928, which aimed to set a fixed date for Easter, but is still not in force 85 years later.

A good example of an Act coming into force long after the royal assent is the Human Rights Act 1998. This received royal assent in November 1998, but did not come into force in England and Wales until 2 October 2000. The delay was quite deliberate – to give those persons and bodies affected by the Act (including judges and magistrates) time to adjust to it. The date of the Act coming into force was determined by the then Home Secretary Jack Straw in the Human Rights Act 1998 (Commencement No.2) Order 2000 (SI 2000/1851) (a form of secondary legislation called a 'commencement order' – see 3.5.1).

> ### ☰ Example
>
> The following is an example of a bill becoming an Act, the Racial and Religious Hatred Act 2006.
>
> The Racial and Religious Hatred Bill, a government bill, was designed to extend the racial hatred offences in the Public Order Act 1986 to cover stirring up hatred against persons on religious grounds. There were a variety of offences under the 1986 Act, each offence requiring that words, behaviour, written material, recordings, or programmes must be threatening, abusive, or insulting and intended or likely to stir up *racial hatred*. Under the new Bill, these offences would be amended so that each would apply to the stirring up of either racial *or religious* hatred, 'religious hatred' being defined as hatred against a group of persons defined by reference to religious belief or lack of religious belief.

Opponents of the bill argued strongly that the bill would, if enacted in its original form, inhibit freedom of speech. The Reverend James Jones, the Bishop of Liverpool, wrote in *The Telegraph* (24 October 2005) that:

> the probable consequences of this Bill will be not only unintended but also unaccepta-ble…bringing a person before the courts for their beliefs, however odious or innocuous, introduces to our society an element hitherto foreign and starts to shape our culture differ-ently. It makes people hesitant to express convictions which explicitly or implicitly criticise another faith. It begins to stifle and silence serious and robust debate about religion in a modern, pluralist and democratic culture…Sometimes religion needs to be criticised.

The Racial and Religious Hatred Bill was introduced into the Commons on 19 June 2005 and received its first reading that day. It received its second reading on 21 June and was then referred to Standing Committee A. It cleared that stage on 30 June 2005 and the Report and third reading were taken together on 11 July, when it was ready to go on to the Lords.

There it had its first reading on 12 July and a second reading on 11 October. However, after that it suffered a torrid time, especially at the Committee stage on 25 October, where the bill was significantly amended. In particular, the Lords deleted references to words that could be regarded as 'abusive or insulting', limiting the new offence to 'threatening' words. A second amendment deleted the word 'recklessness' from the new offence of inciting religious hatred, meaning that it could only be committed intentionally. The bill was reported on 8 November 2005 and the amended bill duly received its third reading on 24 January 2006 and thus cleared the Lords. The bill was returned to the Commons for consideration of the Lords' amendments on 31 January.

There, in a shock development, a Labour backbench rebellion led to the Lords' amendments being approved by the Commons, despite government opposition. With Prime Minister Tony Blair absent from the Commons, apparently satisfied that Labour's 65-seat Commons majority was big enough to overturn the Lords' amendments, the Commons instead approved the Lords' amendments on deleting the word 'recklessness' by 288 votes to 278 and on the deletion of the words 'abusive or insulting' by 283 votes to 282 – a difference of just one vote. These defeats constituted only the second and third times that Labour had lost votes in the Commons since being elected in June 1997.

The Bill – having had a version agreed by both Houses of Parliament – received the royal assent on 16 February 2006 and became the Racial and Religious Hatred Act 2006.

3.3.2 Carrying over bills from one parliamentary session to another

The long-standing rule that all public bills had to complete all their stages in both Houses and receive the royal assent within the same session of Parliament no longer applies. Instead, there is now an option to allow bills to carry over from one session to another. It was used for the first time when the bill which became the Financial Services and Markets Act 2000 was carried over from the 1998/99 session to the 1999/2000 session. Several more Acts have now been passed having been carried over, including the Constitutional Reform Act 2005 and the Corporate Manslaughter and Corporate Homicide Act 2007.

This brings the procedure for public bills into line with the procedure for passing private and hybrid bills, where carry-over has been accepted for some time. The Crossrail Act 2008, for example, was originally introduced as a hybrid bill in the 2004/05 session and was carried over three times before eventually becoming an Act of Parliament in the 2007/08 session.

The advantage of carry-over is that it avoids the hectic 'ping-pong' sessions which often occur at the end of every parliamentary session as the government desperately tries to get all of its bills through before Parliament is prorogued and all outstanding bills are lost. The danger of 'ping-pong' was that modifications and alterations to bills would be made in haste, and compromises made, without full consideration of their implications. However, there is a possible disadvantage of the new 'carry-over' facility: bills that are carried over may cause congestion in future parliamentary sessions with time having to be found for debate on them.

3.3.3 The effectiveness of parliamentary scrutiny of legislation

The effectiveness of Parliament in scrutinising legislation is limited by various factors.

The government's majority

The government can control its own supporters most of the time by relying on party loyalty and the whip system. Government bills are rarely lost in their entirety (but see the passage of the Racial and Religious Hatred Act 2006, described earlier, for the situation where the government failed to prevent one of its bills being amended).

The government's control of the timetable

The government has control of the parliamentary timetable and can normally ensure that there is time for its measures to be considered. It can use various procedural devices such as the 'closure' motion and the 'guillotine' to ensure that measures are voted on and not talked out. The 'guillotine' – officially known as an Allocation of Time Motion – is a procedure available in the House of Commons which sets a limit on the amount of time that may be spent on a particular stage(s) of a bill. It was first used in response to the delaying tactics known as 'filibustering' of certain MPs who were wasting huge amounts of time delaying the Criminal Law (Amendment) Bill in 1886/87. Some bills may be guillotined more than once, e.g.:

- Dangerous Dogs Bill 1990/91 – every stage, including consideration of Lords' amendments, was guillotined;
- Prevention of Terrorism (Additional Powers) Bill 1995/96 – second reading (three hours), Committee (two hours), Report and third reading (one hour); and the
- Human Reproductive Cloning Bill 2001 – every stage guillotined.

In recent years, however, guillotines have been deployed sparingly. In the whole of the 2006/07 session, for example, guillotine motions were used only twice, on the second reading of the bills which became the Investment Exchanges and Clearing Houses Act 2006 and the Northern Ireland (St Andrews Agreement) Act 2006.

Programme motions

In 1997/98, a trial was introduced to programme certain bills. The first programme was set down in January 1998 on the bill which became the Scotland Act 1998. Programme motions require a debate, which usually takes place immediately after the second reading. A programme motion (which is amendable) should state, amongst other things, the date by which the bill should be reported from Committee; the amount of time proposed for Report and third reading; and provisions for carrying over to a subsequent session (if any). It is evident that there has been a dramatic increase in the number of programme motions since their introduction in 1998. Over the same period, there has been a significant reduction in the use of guillotine motions, which suggests that programme motions have *effectively* replaced the guillotine as a means of controlling debate in the Commons.

Limited power of MPs

MPs have limited ability to scrutinise the activities of government effectively. This is caused by the following factors:

- lack of time: the amount of legislation being dealt with is extensive;
- lack of expertise: the complexity and technical nature of much legislation makes it difficult for the average MP to comment; and the
- lack of independent information: most information comes via the Whips.

The role of the opposition parties

There is a basic conflict between the need for technical scrutiny of legislation and the need for the opposition parties to be seen opposing government measures. It has been said that 'the purpose of many Opposition amendments is not to make the bill more generally acceptable but to make the government less generally acceptable'.

The role of the House of Lords

The power of the House of Lords to amend legislation has been limited by the Parliament Act procedure (described later) and by self-imposed limitations arising from its own concern about its lack of credibility. However, there are indications that the House of Lords, after the passage of the House of Lords Act 1999, regards itself as more 'legitimate' and more willing to exercise its powers to amend and even reject government legislation.

3.4 Resolving inter-House conflicts using the Parliament Act procedure

Prior to 1911, both Houses of Parliament had equal powers over legislation – in effect, both Houses enjoyed an absolute veto over bills and the agreement of both Houses was needed before a new Act of Parliament could be created. However, this was changed after the House of Lords refused to pass the Finance Bill in 1909, despite the fact that the bill had already cleared the Commons. The Liberal government at the time responded by introducing the Parliament Bill, which was duly passed by both Houses and became the Parliament Act 1911. Under the 1911 Act, the House of Commons is permitted to override the House of Lords' refusal to allow a bill to pass, provided that certain conditions are met (see later). Now, the House of Lords has merely a temporary veto over legislative measures. A 'money' bill must pass almost immediately, but other public bills may be delayed by a year.

You may be wondering why the House of Lords passed the Parliament Bill, given that, at the time, it still had its absolute veto over all bills. The reason is that the Lords was threatened with something far worse if it did not do so. Bear in mind that, at this time, the great majority of the Lords' membership were the hereditary peers, most of whom supported the Conservative Party. The Liberal government, therefore, made it known that King George V would be prepared, if necessary, to flood the Lords with hundreds of new Liberal-supporting hereditary peers. To the Conservative-supporting hereditary peers in the Lords, that was a much less attractive prospect than the loss of their veto, hence their support for the Parliament Act.

3.4.1 Money bills

A money bill is one which, in the opinion of the Speaker of the House of Commons, relates exclusively to central government expenditure, taxation, or loans. For money bills, s.1(1) of the Parliament Act 1911 (as amended), applies. The effect of this provision is that the bill may be presented for the royal assent and become an Act of Parliament – with or without the consent of the House of Lords – after one month. The bill must be sent to the Lords at least one month before the end of the session.

3.4.2 Other bills

For any other public bill (except a bill containing a provision to extend the maximum duration of Parliament beyond five years), s.2(1) of the Parliament Act 1911 (as amended) applies. When originally passed, s.2(1) of the 1911 Act required a bill to have been presented to the Lords in three successive parliamentary sessions. Only after three successive Lords' rejections would the Commons then have the authority to send the bill to the monarch for royal assent. This effectively allowed the Lords to delay by two years any bill of which it did not approve.

However, the 1911 Act was to be amended when the Parliament Act 1949 was passed. Controversially, the 1949 Act was itself passed under the 1911 Act provisions after the Lords rejected the bill three times. Section 2(1) of the 1911 Act (as amended) now provides that the Commons may submit a bill for royal assent after just two Lords' rejections. This effectively reduces the Lords' ability to delay any bill to one year.

The amended section provides, in full, as follows:

> Parliament Act 1911 (as amended – 1949 amendments in CAPITALS)
>
> 2(1) If any Public Bill is passed by the Commons in TWO SUCCESSIVE SESSIONS and having been sent to the Lords at least one month before the end of the session, is rejected by the Lords in each of these sessions, that Bill shall on the SECOND rejection by the Lords, unless the Commons directs to the contrary, be presented to the Sovereign for the royal assent and thereupon become an Act of Parliament without the Lords' consent. But the foregoing provision is not to take effect unless ONE year has elapsed between the date of the second reading in the first of the sessions in the Commons and the date of its passing the Commons in the second session.

Since 1911, the Parliament Act procedure has only been used seven times, as follows:

- Government of Ireland Act 1914;
- Welsh Church Act 1914;
- Parliament Act 1949;
- War Crimes Act 1991 – which allowed for the prosecution in the UK of suspected Nazi war criminals;
- European Parliamentary Elections Act 1999 – which introduced proportional representation for the 1999 UK elections to the European Parliament;
- Sexual Offences (Amendment) Act 2000 – which lowered the age of consent for homosexual sexual intercourse from 18 to 16;
- Hunting Act 2004 – which prohibits the hunting of wild mammals (particularly foxes) with dogs in England and Wales.

The *Jackson case: R (on the application of Jackson & Others) v Her Majesty's Attorney General* [2005] UKHL 56, [2006] 1 AC 262

After the Hunting Act 2004 was passed, various members of the Countryside Alliance brought a court case which involved not only a direct challenge to the Hunting Act 2004 but also an indirect challenge to the Parliament Act 1949. The Alliance alleged that, while the Parliament Act 1911 was valid, being an Act passed by both the

Commons and the Lords, the amendments made to it in the Parliament Act 1949 were invalid. That was because the 1949 Act was itself made under the 1911 Act powers – that is, it was passed by the Commons only. The Alliance argued that Parliament in 1911 never intended that the Parliament Act itself could be amended without the express agreement of the Lords. The Alliance further argued that all legislation passed under the amended Parliament Act procedures was invalid, too. Alternatively, it was suggested that the Hunting Act was a form of 'delegated' legislation, and therefore (unlike primary legislation) capable of being challenged judicially.

In February 2005, the Court of Appeal rejected these arguments. Lord Woolf CJ accepted that the Commons did have the power to amend the Parliament Act 1911, using the Parliament Act procedure itself. He said that once the 1911 Act had made the 'fundamental change' of allowing the consent of the House of Lords to bills to be dispensed with, the reduction of the two-year period in the original s.2(1) to the one-year period in the amended Act was a 'relatively modest and straightforward amendment'. A subsequent appeal to the Judicial Committee of the House of Lords was dismissed in October 2005, although the law lords rejected the suggestion that the 1911 Act permitted only 'relatively modest and straightforward' amendments. Lord Bingham (the senior law lord) stated:

> I agree with the appellants that the change made by the 1949 Act was not, as the Court of Appeal described it, 'relatively modest', but was substantial and significant. But I also agree with them and also the Attorney General that the breadth of the power to amend the 1911 Act in reliance on s.2(1) cannot depend on whether the amendment in question is or is not relatively modest…The 1949 Act and the 2004 Act are Acts of Parliament of full legal effect.

Lord Hope observed that 'each of the two main parties' had made use of the amended Parliament Act procedure (the War Crimes Act 1991 had been passed by a House of Commons under a Conservative government). He added that 'the political reality is that of a general acceptance by all the main parties and by both Houses of the amended timetable which the 1949 Act introduced. I do not think that it is open to a court of law to ignore that reality.' Lord Carswell hinted that there may be some limits to the uses that could be made of the 1911 Act's procedures, 'though the boundaries appear extremely difficult to define'. He noted that 'no government in the real political world' would attempt to use those powers for the purpose of 'fundamental constitutional change'.

Similarly, Baroness Hale pointed out that Parliament, in passing the Parliament Act 1911, had specifically excepted bills that would prolong the maximum life of Parliament beyond five years. She concluded that this meant that bills could be passed under the 1911 Act procedure, even where they amended the 1911 Act itself, except one to remove that exception. Baroness Hale said that Parliament had effectively 'disabled' itself from using the 1911 procedure to 'remove the exception'. This must be correct; otherwise a powerful government could effectively use the Commons to pass legislation extending the lifespan of Parliament indefinitely, removing the need for future elections and converting the UK into an elected dictatorship.

Lord Nicholls concentrated on the appellants' argument that the 1911 Act created a new delegated law-making body (comprising the Commons and the monarch) and that this body could not use its delegated powers to enlarge those powers. He stated:

> It would be inappropriate to liken the House of Commons to a 'delegate' or 'agent' when applying the 1911 Act procedure. The appropriate approach, rather, is to recognise that when it enacted s.2 the intention of Parliament was to create a second, parallel route by which…any public bill introduced in the Commons could become law as an Act of Parliament. It would be inconsistent with this intention to interpret s.2 as subject to an inherent, over-arching limitation comparable to that applicable in delegated legislation…The Bill to the Parliament Act 1949 was within the scope of s.2 of the 1911 Act. From this it follows that the legal challenge to the enactment of the Hunting Act 2004 also fails.

🔑 Key point

The Parliament Act procedure allows for a Bill to be passed by the House of Commons and the monarch without the consent of the House of Lords. There is no equivalent procedure allowing for a Bill to be passed by the House of Lords and the monarch without the consent of the House of Commons.

3.5 Secondary legislation

Not all legislation is made directly by Parliament. The sheer complexity of modern society means that Parliament has neither the time nor the detailed knowledge to enact all the various provisions that are required. Accordingly, power may be delegated by Act of Parliament (often called the 'parent' or 'enabling' Act) to the Privy Council, government ministers, local authorities, or other regulatory agencies to enable them to make 'secondary' or 'delegated' legislation.

🔑 Key point

Legislation can only be made by Parliament (primary legislation) or by other bodies on whom law-making power has been conferred by Parliament (secondary legislation). Other than Parliament itself, no body in the English legal system has independent law-making powers.

3.5.1 Forms of delegated legislation

Delegated legislation can be made in a variety of forms.

Statutory instruments

The most significant form of delegated legislation, numerically speaking, are those made by government ministers (and occasionally by other bodies) and called 'statutory instruments'. Typically, between three and four thousand SIs are produced every year. All statutory instruments are regulated by the Statutory Instruments Act 1946, which lays down certain procedural requirements for their making (see later). Statutory instruments are given titles, as well as reference numbers, known as the SI number. An SI number might appear as 2008/123, meaning that it is the 123rd statutory instrument produced in the year 2008. Here are some examples (note the variety of names):

- The Building (Electronic Communications) *Order* 2008 (SI 2008/2334);
- The Trade Marks (Amendment) *Rules* 2008 (SI 2008/2300);
- The Veterinary Medicines *Regulations* 2008 (SI 2008/2297);
- The Workmen's Compensation (Supplementation) (Amendment) *Scheme* 2008 (SI 2008/721).

Specific types of statutory instrument

'Commencement orders'

A number of statutory instruments are used to bring parts of pre-existing Acts of Parliament into effect. These are called 'commencement orders'. There may be more than one such order per Act, especially if the statute is large. A good example of a commencement order was given earlier in this chapter: the Human Rights Act 1998 (Commencement No.2) Order 2000 (SI 2000/1851), which brought the 1998 Act into effect on 2 October 2000.

'Remedial orders'

These are special statutory instruments made under s.10(2) of the Human Rights Act 1998, which applies 'if a provision of legislation has been declared under s.4 to be incompatible with a Convention right'. Although subject to certain preconditions, s.10(2) states that '[i]f a Minister of the Crown considers that there are compelling reasons for proceeding under this section, he may by order make such amendments to the legislation as he considers necessary to remove the incompatibility.' A case illustrating this procedure is *R (on the application of H) v Mental Health Review Tribunal for North & East London Region* [2001] EWCA Civ 415, [2002] QB 1. Here, the Court of Appeal declared an incompatibility between ss.72 and 73 of the Mental Health Act 1983 and Articles 5(1) and 5(4) of the European Convention (the right to liberty). Subsequently, the Health Secretary made a remedial order under s.10(2) of the 1998 Act – the Mental Health Act 1983 (Remedial) Order 2001 (SI 2001/3712) – which amended the 1983 Act.

'Regulatory reform orders'

The Legislative and Regulatory Reform Act 2006 had a controversial passage through Parliament before being enacted. This is not surprising, as s.1(1) of the Act states that a minister 'may by order under this section make any provision which he considers would serve the purpose in subsection (2)', while s.1(2) states that, '[t]hat purpose is removing or reducing any burden, or the overall burdens, resulting directly or indirectly for any person from any legislation.' Notice the reference to 'any provision' and 'any legislation'. The Labour government, which promoted the bill, was unapologetic: the explanatory notes to the Act published on the UK Legislation (**www.legislation.gov.uk**) website state that '[t]he power is a broad one, and it is intended to be so.' However, so sweeping are these powers that a number of special controls are placed on ministers seeking to exercise them. Section 3(2) lists a total of six conditions that must be met before a reform order can be made.

Orders in council

The highest form of delegated legislation is called an 'order in council'. Theoretically, these are made by the Privy Council, but in practice they are made by a government minister. Orders in council may (if made under statutory authority) be published as statutory instruments and subject to the provisions of the Statutory Instruments Act 1946. An example is provided by s.30(1) of the Civil Aviation Act 1980, which states that 'Her Majesty may by order in council direct that any of the provisions of this Act shall extend with such modifications (if any) as may be specified in the order to any relevant overseas territory'.

Byelaws

Local Authorities have power under a number of statutes to make 'byelaws' for the regulation, administration, and management of their affairs. Section 235(1) of the Local Government Act 1972, for example, allows a district council to make byelaws for the 'good rule and government of the whole or any part of the district and for the prevention and suppression and nuisance therein'. Other bodies have power under other statutes to make byelaws. The Strategic Rail Authority was, prior to its abolition, given power to create byelaws regulating rail transport under s.219 of the Transport Act 2000.

3.5.2 Why is delegated legislation necessary?

Time constraints

If all legislation took the form of primary legislation, Parliament would struggle to cope with the mass of detail required. Instead, an enabling (or 'parent') Act lays down broad principles leaving the details to be filled in by delegated legislation. For example, the primary legislation that deals with loans for students in higher education – originally the Education (Student Loans) Act 1990, subsequently repealed and replaced by Part II of the Teaching and Higher Education Act 1998 – confines itself to dealing with the question of students' eligibility to apply for a loan. Other matters, most importantly the maximum amount that can be borrowed per year, are dealt with by regulations, produced annually by the government. If Parliament had to deal with this amount of detail, the parliamentary timetable would soon be full as a new Act would be required every year.

Complexity

The subject matter of much legislation is technical and highly complex. It would be inappropriate to include this in an Act of Parliament. Not only would consideration of detailed, technical legislation in the contentious atmosphere of Parliament be ineffective, the principles of the resultant legislation would be difficult to comprehend. The procedure for making delegated legislation also makes it easier to consult experts during its formulation than in the case of primary legislation. Notable areas where this approach is adopted include health and safety regulations made under the Health and Safety at Work, etc. Act 1974 and the Food Safety Act 1990. Recent examples of complex, technical delegated legislation are the Waste Electrical and Electronic Equipment Regulations 2006 (SI 2006/3289) and the Horses (Zootechnical Standards) (England) Regulations 2006 (SI 2006/1757).

Flexibility

The use of delegated legislation can, for example, allow account to be taken of local conditions. For example, s.18(1) of the Clean Air Act 1993 provides that a local authority may, by order, declare the whole or any part of the district of the authority to be a smoke control area; and any order made under this section is referred to in this Act as a 'smoke control order'. This empowers local authorities to make smoke control orders in those areas where it is considered appropriate. An example of extremely specific delegated legislation is the A282 Trunk Road (Dartford-Thurrock Crossing Charging Scheme) Order 2008 (SI 2008/1951).

Emergencies

Use of regulations means emergency powers can be brought into effect very quickly to deal with outbreaks of disease, typically involving agricultural products. Examples of such 'emergency' legislation include the Food Protection (Emergency Prohibitions)

(Radioactivity in Sheep) Order 1991 (SI 1991/20) and the Food (Peanuts from China) (Emergency Control) (England) Regulations 2002 (SI 2002/774).

Incorporation of EU directives

As already indicated, most EU directives are implemented in the UK using delegated legislation. In this situation the 'parent' Act is usually the European Communities Act 1972, which lays down very broad law-making powers on government ministers to introduce delegated legislation as required to ensure that the UK complies with its obligations as a Member State of (what is now) the European Union by implementing directives. Although primary legislation is occasionally used to implement directives, if a separate Act of Parliament was required for every directive, Parliament would be so busy enacting those statutes that it would have little time doing anything else. Important examples include:

- The Health and Safety (Display Screen Equipment) Regulations 1992 (SI 1992/2792), which implement Directive 90/270;
- The Working Time Regulations 1998 (SI 1998/1833), which implement Directive 93/104;
- The Consumer Protection (Distance Selling) Regulations 2000 (SI 2000/2334), which implement Directive 97/7.

3.5.3 **Possible dangers inherent in secondary legislation**

Lack of accountability

Delegated legislation is not used simply to fill in details but is also used to establish matters of principle. In some instances, Parliament passes framework legislation which means little without the many regulations made under it. Ministers may be given sweeping powers to amend primary legislation (known as 'Henry VIII' clauses, on which see later). Yet, delegated legislation is rarely subject to the same level of scrutiny as primary legislation. The normal methods of scrutiny are avoided and, as is demonstrated later, the particular methods of scrutinising delegated legislation are patchy.

Potential for abuse

In many instances, the 'parent' Act will give the minister wide discretionary powers. A common formulation is to give the minister the power to 'make such regulations as he considers appropriate'. Where such wide discretion is given it can be extremely difficult to control the exercise of the power through the traditional operation of the ultra vires rule. (The ultra vires rule allows the courts to intervene if the minister making the regulations has gone beyond the limits of the powers granted to him by the enabling Act.)

There is also the risk that a minister might commit a constitutional impropriety, for example by creating regulations which operate retrospectively or attempt to impose a tax, without having express authority to do this under the parent Act.

'Henry VIII clauses'

There is a particular danger where a minister is given the power to amend primary legislation by delegated legislation. Any section in an Act by which this power is given is often referred to as a 'Henry VIII' clause. A good example is s.207 of the Equality Act 2010, which allows a minister to amend 'an enactment', including some provisions of the 2010 Act itself.

3.5.4 Control over delegated legislation

Widespread use of delegated legislation clearly has its dangers, particularly when it is used not simply for matters of a detailed or technical nature but to effect changes of substance in the law. Then it could be argued that too much power is concentrated in the hands of the executive, creating the opportunity for abuse. It is, therefore, considered important that the use of delegated powers is properly controlled. This control can be exercised in a number of ways.

The enabling Act

It is up to Parliament, when passing the enabling Act, to give the minister or other subsidiary body, powers, as wide or narrow as it chooses. If the resultant subordinate legislation goes beyond the limits of the parent Act, then it will be possible to challenge it in court as being ultra vires. The grant of wide discretionary power makes it much more difficult to control the exercise of power as the limits of the authority are not clearly stated. In the House of Lords, the Delegated Powers and Regulatory Reform Committee examines bills in the Lords and reports on any clauses that will give ministers powers to enact secondary legislation.

Laying before Parliament

Parliament can ensure greater control of delegated legislation by requiring that it should be laid before Parliament. It should be noted that:

● Not all delegated legislation is required to be laid before Parliament (in particular, commencement orders – which simply bring parts of pre-existing primary legislation into force – do not have to be laid).

- There are a number of different laying procedures. The enabling Act will specify which procedure applies. These range from a requirement to lay the delegated legislation before Parliament for information only, via a requirement that legislation be laid for a forty-day period during which it is subject to possible annulment (the negative procedure), to a requirement that the legislation will only come into effect after it has been approved by both Houses of Parliament (the affirmative procedure).

The negative procedure

The most common procedure is where delegated legislation is required to be laid before Parliament, usually for forty days, subject to a negative resolution. Here, the onus is on Parliament to pass a motion (called a 'prayer') to annul the legislation. An example is s.48(3) of the Food Safety Act 1990, which states that 'Any statutory instrument [made] under this Act…shall be subject to annulment in pursuance of a resolution of either House of Parliament.'

To bring a successful prayer to annul is difficult to achieve, certainly in the Commons, usually because the government can use its majority to defeat such a motion. The Commons last annulled a statutory instrument in October 1979, and the House of Lords last did so in February 2000, when a successful prayer was passed to annul the Greater London Authority Elections Rules 2000 (SI 2000/208).

The affirmative procedure

The most demanding form of laying procedure, at least in theory, is the affirmative procedure. This is where a piece of delegated legislation is laid, in draft, and has to be approved by *both* Houses of Parliament before it comes into effect. The government must therefore arrange for an appropriate motion of approval to be passed. However, this rarely poses problems for the government; indeed, the last occasion on which a draft statutory instrument failed to secure approval was in November 1969. In practice, the whole House of Commons never votes to approve a statutory instrument. Rather, they are referred to a Delegated Legislation Committee comprising around seventeen MPs. There are often debates about the SI leading up to the vote, but there is no power to amend the proposed legislation. The affirmative procedure is reserved only for the most important (about 10 per cent of all statutory instruments).

A good example of a delegated law-making power subject to the affirmative procedure is s.1(6) of the Education (Student Loans) Act 1990, which (prior to its repeal) stated that 'the power to make orders under [this section] shall be exercisable by statutory instrument and no such order shall be made unless a draft of it has been laid before and approved by a resolution of each House of Parliament'.

Thinking point

Which laying procedure would you prescribe to achieve the most effective parliamentary control over delegated legislation?

Failure to comply with laying arrangements

Failure to comply with any laying requirement will be a procedural irregularity, leaving the statutory instrument potentially open to challenge in the courts. However, the courts have never been entirely clear as to the effect of failure to comply with laying requirements. Would this invalidate the statutory instrument?

In the leading case on the subject, *R v Sheer Metalcraft Ltd* [1954] 1 QB 586, Streatfeild J said:

> I do not think that it can be said that to make a valid statutory instrument it is required that all these stages should be gone through, namely the making, the laying before Parliament, the printing and the certification of that part of it which it might be unnecessary to have printed. In my judgment the making of an instrument is complete when it is first of all made by the Minister concerned and after it has been laid before Parliament. When that has been done it then becomes a valid statutory instrument, totally made under the provisions of the Act.

This seems to suggest that a failure to comply would not invalidate a statutory instrument.

Scrutiny by parliamentary committee

There are two such committees, both of which check to see whether the attention of the Houses should be drawn to particular secondary legislation. The Parliamentary Joint Committee on Statutory Instruments (which consists of members from each House of Parliament), known as the Scrutiny Committee, considers whether the legal technicalities have been complied with. The Committee looks to see whether the legislation has been unduly delayed, purports to have retrospective effect, makes some 'unusual or unexpected' use of the powers conferred by the enabling Act, and so on. The Lords Secondary Legislation Scrutiny Committee, which was established in 2012, 'examines the policy merits of any statutory instruments or regulations laid before the House of Lords'.

Summary

- The UK Parliament is the body responsible for making all UK legislation. It is comprised of three constituent parts: the House of Commons, the House of Lords, and the monarch.

- The present House of Lords (non-elected) is complementary to the House of Commons (elected). The Commons has democratic legitimacy but is highly political and adversarial; MPs do not have the wealth of specialist knowledge and experience to be found in the Lords.

- Since the House of Lords Act 1999, there have been several reform proposals relating to the House of Lords. Most of these have recommended a 'hybrid' body comprising a combination of elected and appointed members.

- The legislative process in the UK Parliament (standard procedure) consists of a bill receiving, in each House: a first reading; second reading; committee stage; report stage; and third reading. If agreement is reached, the bill receives royal assent at which point the bill becomes an Act. If not, the bill fails, subject to the Parliament Act procedures.

- There are government bills and private members' bills. The latter take various forms – ballot, ten minute, presentation, and peers' bills. The success rate of private members' bills is low. Most private members' bills are really just designed to raise awareness.

- The Parliament Act 1911 procedure (as amended) is used to resolve inter-House conflicts. It allows the Commons and the monarch to pass bills without the consent of the Lords, provided certain conditions are satisfied.

- Secondary legislation is usually produced by government ministers in the form of statutory instruments. There are also byelaws, typically produced by local authorities. Statutory instruments may be subject either to a negative laying procedure or an affirmative laying procedure.

- Potential dangers of secondary legislation include the lack of parliamentary scrutiny and Henry VIII clauses (provisions within primary legislation conferring power on a government minister to amend that legislation by statutory instrument) which may be abused.

Questions

1 Explain public legislation; private legislation; and hybrid legislation.

2 Explain the differences between government bills and private members' bills.

3 What are the conditions that must be satisfied before a public bill (other than a money bill) can be passed under the terms of the Parliament Act procedure?

4 Explain the differences between the affirmative laying procedure and the negative laying procedure for statutory instruments.

5 Give three justifications for the existence of secondary legislation.

6 Give three possible dangers posed by the existence of secondary legislation.

Sample question and outline answer

Question

The changes to the composition of the House of Lords that have taken place over the last 60 years mean that the procedure for passing legislation under the *Parliament Act 1911* (as amended) is no longer justified. Explain the legislative procedure under the *Parliament Act 1911* (as amended) and consider whether it is still justified in the twenty-first century.

Outline answer

Answers should explain the (amended) Parliament Act procedure, which allows for bills to become Acts of Parliament without the consent of the House of Lords provided certain criteria satisfied (i.e. it must be a Commons bill, the bill must have been rejected twice in successive sessions, it must be substantially the same bill in each session, etc.). Give some examples of bills that have become Acts under the procedure, such as the War Crimes Act 1991 and the Hunting Act 2004.

Answers should explain the changes to the composition of the House of Lords 'over the last 60 years', i.e. since the early 1950s. This includes the creation of the first life peers under the Life Peerages Act 1958; the removal of most hereditary peers under the House of Lords Act 1999, the establishment of House of Lords Appointments Commission in 2000.

Answers should assess (a) whether the Parliament Act was justified in 1911, when it was originally enacted; and (b) whether it is justified in the twenty-first century. When the 1911 Act was passed the House of Lords was comprised primarily of hereditary peers, whereas the House of Commons was directly elected; the Commons could therefore make a strong claim to have significantly more democratic legitimacy than the Lords. It logically follows that an unelected body should not be able to thwart the wishes of an elected body and, therefore, the democratically elected Commons should get its way eventually. This fundamental position has not changed since 1911, despite the various reforms since 1958; the Lords is still unelected and hence should not be able to stop legislation which has been approved by the Commons.

This is especially true if the bill in question was designed to enact a proposal contained in the government's election manifesto, and which can therefore be taken to have attracted public support. These arguments can be countered by the fact that voter apathy means turnout at elections is often low, which undermines to some extent the Commons' claim to be more democratic. On the manifesto point, it is fanciful to suggest that all voters who voted for the eventual government supported (or were even aware of) every proposal in the party's manifesto. Moreover, the first-past-the-post electoral system used in the UK also means that governments can be voted into office on less than 50 per cent of the turnout, which indicates that government proposals are not necessarily backed by a majority of the public after all.

Answers should discuss the fact that the legitimacy of the Hunting Act 2004 and Parliament Act 1949 were challenged in the courts in *Jackson & Others v Attorney-General* (2005), culminating in a hearing before nine law lords in the Judicial Committee of the House of Lords (now the Supreme Court). The law lords unanimously upheld the legitimacy of both Acts (Lord Hope describing the procedure as a 'political reality' which had achieved 'general acceptance' by all of the main political parties), although some of their Lordships discussed the possibility that there might be some limits on its use (Lord Steyn gave an example of a bill to abolish judicial review).

Students could therefore conclude that the Parliament Act procedure remains justified. Nevertheless, it would be legitimate to take the position that the House of Lords in 1911 and that in the twenty-first century are sufficiently different (in terms of their composition and therefore democratic legitimacy) such that the Parliament Act procedure was no longer justified (in light of the reforms that have taken place). If so, it would be appropriate to consider that another means of resolving inter-House conflicts would be desirable to avoid deadlock. Possibilities include conciliation committees, where selected members of both houses meet to try to work out a compromise solution (found in the US Congress), or even dissolution of Parliament, which then gives the electorate the power to cast the deciding vote (an option of last resort available in Australia).

Further reading

- **Harlow, A., Cranmer, F.** and **Doe, N.** 'Bishops in the House of Lords: A Critical Analysis' [2008] PL 490

- **Muylle, K.** 'Improving the Effectiveness of Parliamentary Legislative Procedures' (2003) 24 Stat LR 169
  Identifies problems with the legislative process and discusses various options for reform.

- **Phillipson, G.** 'The Greatest Quango of them all, a Rival Chamber or a Hybrid Nonsense? Solving the Second Chamber Paradox' [2004] PL 352
  Discusses the various options for reforming the House of Lords.

- **Twomey, A.** 'The Refusal or Deferral of Royal Assent' [2006] PL 580
  Discusses whether or not the monarch has the power to refuse Royal Assent to bills that have been passed by Parliament (in Australia as well as the UK).

● **Weill, R.** 'Centennial to the Parliament Act 1911: the Manner and Form Fallacy' [2012] PL 105
  Examines the passage of the Parliament Acts of 1911 and 1949 and the House of Lords' ruling in *Jackson & Others* (2005).

 ## Online Resource Centre

You should now attempt the supporting multiple choice questions available at **www.oxfordtextbooks.co.uk/orc/wilson_els/**.

4 The interpretation of statutes

⊙ Learning objectives

By the end of this chapter you should:

- understand how problems of statutory interpretation may arise;
- be aware of the constitutional role of the courts in relation to statutory interpretation;
- be able to explain the nature and content of the 'rules' of statutory interpretation;
- appreciate the various approaches to the discovery of the intention of Parliament as expressed in the words of an Act of Parliament and the courts' use of a contextual and purposive approach to interpretation;
- be aware of the internal and external aids to interpretation of an Act of Parliament;
- understand the reasons for the rules and aids and their effectiveness in determining legislative intent; and
- appreciate the impact of the UK's membership of the European Union and the enactment of the Human Rights Act 1998 upon the process of statutory interpretation.

🅕 Talking point

....

The issue of abortion is controversial and gives rise to strong views. It is argued on one side that morally it is wrong to destroy life, while on the other that women should have the right to choose. By s.58 of the Offences against the Persons Act 1861 it is a crime to terminate a pregnancy. Up to 1967 there was a major social problem of back-street abortionists who unlawfully terminated pregnancies in unhygienic conditions and without proper skill. Such abortions often caused injury to or the death of pregnant women. With the passing of the Abortion Act 1967 a pregnancy could be lawfully terminated, in certain circumstances, by 'a registered medical practitioner', i.e. a doctor. When the Abortion Act 1967 was passed the method of abortion was surgical. By the early 1970s another method of abortion, medical induction, had replaced the need for surgery. With this advance in abortion techniques actions by a nurse became the effective cause of an abortion. Does the protection given by the Abortion Act 1967 also apply to nurses? The answer to the question is to be discovered from the words used by Parliament in the Abortion Act 1967 to express its intention. If the words do not cover the activities of a nurse in the termination of a pregnancy then a crime may be committed. How are the words of an Act of Parliament to be interpreted?

....

Introduction

At its most basic level, the interpretation of statutes is about the problem of communication. There are several viewpoints that need to be considered in the process of interpretation. The words used in a statute are drafted to convey a particular meaning, i.e. what is the intention behind the words used. Who are the words aimed at and what does the person reading the words take them to mean? What do the words used say; are the words capable of bearing only one meaning? The ideal is that the words used will express clearly the intention of the maker of the legislation and that intention will be clearly communicated to the person reading the words of the statute. Problems of communication arise when the words do not convey the intention clearly.

....

4.1 **Problems of language**

Problems that arise in relation to the interpretation of statutes are: first, the language used in a statute is vague or ambiguous; and second, new situations may arise that were unforeseen at the time the legislation was drafted and passed.

> ### Example
>
> *Vague or ambiguous language*
>
> Words may be vague, particularly when describing an abstract concept rather than a physical entity. The word 'obscenity' gives rise to problems of definition, as does an inherently vague word such as 'reasonable'. Definitions of physical entities are not without problems. For example, what is the definition of a 'building', what attributes must it have? Would a static caravan on a brick foundation constitute a 'building'?
>
> Ambiguity arises when words have more than one possible meaning. A word may be used in its ordinary sense or in a technical sense. For example, in *Fisher v Bell* [1961] 1 QB 394, it had to be decided whether a display of goods, in this case a flick knife, in a shop window was an 'offer'. A dictionary definition includes the meaning 'makes available for sale', which is probably seen as the ordinary meaning of offer. Alternatively, the technical legal meaning of offer from the law of contract is as follows: a party makes a proposal, containing terms which are certain together with an intention to be bound by the terms, which will become binding should the party to whom the proposal is addressed accept the proposal. The court in *Fisher v Bell* decided that Parliament had used the word in a technical sense so that a shopkeeper had not made an offer in displaying the flick knife in a shop window.
>
> *Unforeseen developments*
>
> In *Royal College of Nursing of the United Kingdom v Department of Health and Social Security* [1981] AC 800, the court had to consider the meaning of s.1(1) of the Abortion Act 1967. At the time that the Act was passed the main method of abortion was surgical; by 1980, the most common method was medical induction. This latter method involved the introduction of a chemical fluid into a mother's womb which caused the premature birth of the foetus. In the light of this latter procedure, the House of Lords was asked to consider whether s.1(1) of the Abortion Act 1967, which provides '...a person shall not be guilty of an offence under the law relating to abortion (ss.58 and 59 Offences Against the Person Act 1861) when a pregnancy is terminated by a registered medical practitioner', protected a non-registered medical practitioner, a nurse, who under the instructions of a registered medical practitioner, a doctor, effectively caused an abortion by introducing into a mother's womb an abortifacient fluid. The problem was whether Parliament in s.1(1) intended to cover this new method of abortion.
>
> Lord Wilberforce in a dissenting opinion said (at p.822):
>
>> when a new state of affairs, or a fresh set of facts bearing on policy, comes into existence, the courts have to consider whether they fall within the parliamentary intention. They may be held to do so, if they fall within the same genus of facts as those to which the expressed policy has been formulated. They may also be held to do so if there can be detected a clear purpose in the legislation which can only be fulfilled if the extension is made. How liberally

these principles may be applied must depend upon the nature of the enactment, and the strictness or otherwise of the words in which it has been expressed. The courts should be less willing to extend expressed meanings if it is clear that the Act in question was designed to be restrictive or circumscribed in its operation rather than liberal or permissive. They will be much less willing to do so where the subject matter is different in kind or dimension from that for which the legislation was passed. In any event there is one course which the courts cannot take, under the law of this country; they cannot fill gaps; they cannot by asking the question 'What would Parliament have done in this current case – not being one in contemplation – if the facts had been before it?' attempt themselves to supply the answer, if the answer is not to be found in the terms of the Act itself.

Whether a court will interpret a statute to cover a new situation unforeseen by Parliament at the time of the passage of an Act depends upon the nature of the legislation; whether it is designed to be restrictive or liberal. Note that Lord Wilberforce's statement as to how to approach this problem of the unforeseen development was approved by the House of Lords in *Fitzpatrick v Sterling Housing Association Ltd* [2001] 1 AC 27.

A similar problem was also seen in *R (Quintavalle) v Secretary of State for Health* [2003] 2 AC 687 (see later).

4.2 **Preliminary issues**

In understanding the process of interpreting a statute a number of preliminary questions need to be addressed.

First, in interpreting a statute what are the courts being asked to do? The primary task of the courts is to search for and give effect to the intention of Parliament (or the legislature) as found in the words of the statute. Lord Watson in *Salomon v Salomon* [1897] AC 22 said (at p.38):

> 'Intention of the Legislature' is a common but very slippery phrase, which, popularly understood, may signify anything from intention embodied in positive enactment to speculative opinion as to what the Legislature probably would have meant, although there has been an omission to enact it. In a Court of Law or Equity, what the Legislature intended to be done or not to be done can only be legitimately ascertained from that which it has chosen to enact, either in express words or by reasonable and necessary implication.

This quotation emphasises the relationship between parliamentary intention and the words used in the statute; whatever Parliament's intention might, or might not, have been the words used in the statute must be capable of bearing such a meaning.

The task for a court is to search for the true meaning of what Parliament has said. However, there are limits on how a court may interpret a statute. In *Jones v DPP* [1962] AC 635 Lord Reid said the words of a statutory provision were only to be given a meaning that they could reasonably bear; in the event of a word being ambiguous then a court could choose between the meanings. This principle of construction must be now read subject to s.3 of the Human Rights Act 1998 (see 7.3), but in general terms it still applies.

Second, is there a clear method for ascertaining the purpose of Parliament? You will find that there is no certain way of ascertaining the purpose of Parliament and in searching for such purpose the courts are asked to make choices between rival interpretations. The arguments as to the 'correct interpretation' to be given to a statutory provision are aided by use of the so-called 'rules' of statutory interpretation. As Lord Reid explained in *Maunsell v Olins* [1975] AC 373, 382 'they are not rules in the ordinary sense of having binding force. They are our servants not our masters.' The rules of statutory interpretation are used as aids to construction but may operate inconsistently as different rules may point to different answers (for an example, see later the case study on *Coltman v Bibby* [1988] 2 AC 276).

It is thus clear that the rules of statutory interpretation are not to be followed slavishly, they are helpful as tools in the search for the intention of Parliament, but their use is not certain to provide a 'right answer'. The rules may be used to support arguments as to the meaning of a statute but as the courts are not bound by the rules it is ultimately a choice for the courts as a matter of judgement which rule or rules are to apply. It is worth pointing out that the rules of statutory interpretation also may be employed in the interpretation of contracts, wills, and other legal documents; so do not compartmentalise what you are about to read as merely part of an English legal system module. The statements made by the courts concerning how to interpret statutes are not strictly binding in a doctrine of precedent sense, but they are *obiter dicta* (see chapter 5).

Third, if it is discovered that the words of a statute do not clearly communicate the intention or purpose of Parliament, from where may the intention be collected? This raises the issue of what can a court consult beyond the four corners of a statute. Rules have been developed as to what may, and may not, be considered in seeking the intention and purpose of Parliament.

Go to the Online Resource Centre where you will find an annotated statute which indicates the various features of an Act of Parliament.

> 🔑 **Key point**
>
> The rules of statutory interpretation are techniques for finding the true meaning of a statute, but do not comprise a system, application of which will ultimately produce the 'right' answer.

4.3 The traditional approach to statutory interpretation

Students have been traditionally taught the three rules of statutory interpretation: the literal rule; the golden rule; and the mischief rule.

4.3.1 The literal rule

The literal rule concentrates upon the words of the statute. Meaning is to be ascertained by application of the rules of grammar and the finding of dictionary definitions.

As Lord Diplock said in *Duport Steels Ltd v Sirs* [1980] 1 WLR 142, 157 'the role of the judiciary is confined to ascertaining from the words that Parliament has approved as expressing its intention what that intention was and to give effect to it'. At its most extreme an application of the literal rule only considers the words of the statute in the search for the intention of Parliament.

> ### Thinking point
>
> The literal rule operates on the assumption that the meaning of words and sentences are clear, which, of course, quite often is not the case. It is also apparent that sometimes the words of a statute and the perceived purpose of a statute may be at odds. The literal rule is artificial and now must be viewed in the light of a more contextual approach to interpretation (see later). Has a literal approach any role to play in the interpretation of statutes?

An example of the literal rule may be seen in the case of *Fisher v Bell* [1961] 1 QB 394. As outlined previously, this case concerned a shopkeeper who displayed in his shop window a flick knife with a ticket stating 'Ejector knife – 4s'. The Restriction of Offensive Weapons Act 1959 s.1 provided that '[a]ny person who manufactures, sells or hires or offers for sale or hire' a flick knife shall be guilty of an offence. It was argued by the prosecution that the knife was offered for sale in contravention of Restriction of Offensive Weapons Act 1959. The defendant said on the facts that no offer had been made.

It was held by the Divisional Court of the Queen's Bench Division that an offer had not been made and the Act was not contravened. Lord Parker CJ said under the ordinary law of contract the display of an article with a price on it in a shop window is merely an invitation to treat and not an offer for sale the acceptance of which would constitute a contract. There was no indication in the statute that Parliament had intended that the word 'offer' in the 1959 Act should have a meaning other than the one supplied by the general law of contract. In consequence, the defendant was not guilty of the offence charged.

See 4.6.2, 'Presumptions of legislative intent in cases of doubt or ambiguity'.

The court gave the word 'offer' a technical legal meaning by reading the statute against the general law of contract. The case may be viewed as an example of the literal rule. Alternatively, it may be seen, as Cross argues in *Statutory Interpretation* (p.73), 'as an example of the presumption that penal statutes should be strictly construed in favour of the accused'.

It is interesting to note that the 1959 Act was amended by the Restriction of Offensive Weapons Act 1961, the offence in s.1 being expanded to include where a person 'exposes . . . for the purpose of sale' a flick knife.

4.3.2 The golden rule

The classic statement of this rule is to be found in the words of Lord Wensleydale in the case of *Grey v Pearson* (1857) 6 HL Cas 61, 106 (note that this case concerned the interpretation of a will, but the rule also applies to statutes). The golden rule may be used where a literal interpretation of the words of a statute leads to an absurdity or to an inconsistency or repugnance with the rest of the statute. The inference to be drawn is that the meaning to be discovered by application of the literal rule cannot have been intended by Parliament. When faced with such absurdity or inconsistency or repugnance, Lord Wensleydale said, the grammatical and ordinary sense of the words of a statute may be modified to avoid the absurdity or inconsistency.

In deciding how to proceed to avoid the absurdity or inconsistency the court will look at Parliament's purpose in passing the legislation.

Adler v George [1964] 2 QB 7 illustrates how the golden rule may be used. By s.3 of the Official Secrets Act 1920 it is an offence for a person 'in the vicinity of any prohibited place' to obstruct any member of Her Majesty's forces. The defendant, Adler, had entered a Royal Air Force station, a prohibited place, and obstructed a member of Her Majesty's forces and was convicted by magistrates. On appeal, the defendant contended that no offence could be committed as the defendant was *in* the prohibited place and not, as s.3 provides, 'in the vicinity of any prohibited place'. Literally, 'in the vicinity of', it was argued, meant 'near' or 'close to,' but did not mean 'in' or 'on'. Lord Parker CJ rejected this interpretation and said that s.3 was designed to prevent interference with Her Majesty's forces when performing duties relating to security of prohibited places. Viewed against this purpose it would be absurd that an offence was created near a prohibited place and not within the place itself. His Lordship said that the words 'in or' may be inserted before 'in the vicinity of any prohibited place'. Clearly, it was strange that the more serious offence, obstructing in the prohibited place, was omitted while an offence of obstruction near the prohibited place was created. No doubt this anomaly convinced the court that the intention of Parliament must be to cover both situations.

It can be seen that Lord Parker CJ refers to absurdity to indicate that the words of the statute cannot wholly reflect the intention of Parliament and so words may be necessarily read into the statute. This is particularly so having regard to the context of the Act which is designed to prevent interference with members of Her Majesty's forces, in relation to a prohibited place. In this sense his Lordship is having regard to the purpose of s.3 of the Act.

Thinking point

Lord Wensleydale in *Grey v Pearson* does not indicate what is meant by absurdity or inconsistency and gives no clear indication as to what is to be done if such is found. His Lordship was somewhat cryptic when he said 'the grammatical and ordinary sense of the words may be modified'. Does this mean that the words of the statute must be capable of bearing an alternative meaning and the golden rule indicates that the meaning that does not lead to absurdity or inconsistency is to be chosen or does the rule allow for the reading in of words or the ignoring of words? *Adler v George* gives an illustration of words being read into a statute. Remember a judge must not legislate but only interpret statutes. Do you think Lord Parker crossed this line?

4.3.3 **The mischief rule**

The mischief rule is one of some antiquity. A classic formulation of the rule is to be found in *Heydon's* case (1584) 3 Co Rep 7a, 7b where it was said:

> And it was resolved by them that for the sure and true interpretation of all statutes in general (be they penal or beneficial, restrictive or enlarging of the common law), four things are to be discerned and considered:
>
> 1. What was the common law before the making of the Act,
> 2. What was the mischief and defect for which the common law did not provide,
> 3. What remedy the Parliament hath resolved and appointed to cure the disease of the Commonwealth, and
> 4. The true reason of the remedy;

and then the office of all the judges is always to make such construction as shall suppress the mischief and advance the remedy...

As can be seen, the courts were to interpret an Act so as to suppress the mischief and give effect to the remedy. However, the problem with this approach relates to the words of an Act and the extent to which it was permissible for a court to give a meaning to the words used that they were not capable of bearing. Additionally, the rule assumes that legislation is 'only designed to deal with evil and not to further a positive social purpose' (*The Interpretation of Statutes* Law Commission (Report No.21) 1969). While it is evident that the courts have embraced the notion of a purposive approach to interpretation, nonetheless references to 'mischief' are still to be found in the judgments of the courts. For examples of the use of the mischief rule in modern times, see *Smith v Hughes* [1960] 1 WLR 830 and *Royal College of Nursing of the United Kingdom v Department of Health and Social Security* [1981] AC 800.

In *Smith v Hughes* prostitutes in a house sought to attract the attention of men passing in the street by beckoning from balconies or tapping on windows. Under s.1(1) of the Street Offences Act 1959 it was 'an offence for a common prostitute to loiter or solicit in a street or public place for the purpose of prostitution'. It was argued on behalf of the defendant prostitutes that a balcony was not 'in a street', nor was tapping on a glass window from within a house. The defendants were convicted by magistrates and appealed to the Divisional Court of the Queen's Bench Division.

The problem was that the Act did not make clear where the prostitute had to be when the solicitation took place. Lord Parker referred to the mischief of the 1959 Act, which was well known, as a measure 'intended to clean up the streets' and to enable people to walk without being solicited by prostitutes. Against this background it mattered not that the prostitutes were indoors or on balconies; the solicitation was projected into the street and was aimed at a person walking in the street and fell within s.1(1) of the Street Offences Act 1959. The defendants' conviction was upheld.

Thinking point

Who decides upon the formulation of the 'mischief'? Which materials may a judge rely upon in seeking the 'mischief' of a statute? See the discussion later of aids to interpretation to be found inside and outside an Act of Parliament.

Identifying a mischief may be an exercise in interpretation too. Also an Act of Parliament may have more than one mischief.

Purposive approach – Heydon's case and the purposive approach contrasted

Strictly speaking, it is possible to differentiate between the rule in *Heydon's* case and a purposive approach although there are obvious similarities. The rule in *Heydon's* case was stated at a time when the role of Parliament was different – Parliament met infrequently and its supremacy had not been established, so the courts were more willing to go beyond the words of the statute to 'suppress the mischief and advance the remedy'. In ascertaining the mischief, the courts looked within the four corners of the statute itself not to external sources. The purposive approach seeks to ensure that the wording of an Act is interpreted in the light of the purpose underlying it. It is permissible to look within the Act and outside of the Act to discover the purpose. However, there are limits to the extent to which the courts may go beyond the words of the Act.

4.3.4 Application of the literal, golden, and mischief rules

The problem encountered with application of these three rules, i.e. the literal, golden, and mischief rules, was which rule was to be applied in any given situation? Professor John Willis in 'Statute Interpretation in a Nutshell' (1938) 16 Can Bar Rev 1 said, 'a court invokes whichever of the rules produces a result that satisfies its sense of justice in the case before it'. The literal rule was the one most frequently referred to by the courts expressly, but all three rules were valid and reference could be made to them as the situation demanded but no justification was given by the courts for their use or indeed any indication given of the circumstances of when each rule was to be employed.

The obvious shortcomings of this situation – excessive literalism and the lack of a systematic approach – led to calls for legislative reform in this area. In 1969, the Law Commissions produced a report, *The Interpretation of Statutes*, which proposed that 'a limited degree of statutory intervention is required in this field…to clarify, and in some respects to relax the strictness of, the rules which…exclude altogether or exclude when the meaning is unambiguous, certain material from consideration'. No legislation was ever passed in response to this report but since then academic writers have sought to make sense of the mass of conflicting dicta. Foremost in seeking to systematise have been Sir Rupert Cross in *Statutory Interpretation* and Francis Bennion in *Statutory Interpretation*. Their success may be measured by the frequent references made to their work by the courts. The approach identified by Cross is next considered.

4.3.5 **The unified contextual approach**

Sir Rupert Cross felt that the judges in practice used a combination of these rules in interpreting any one statutory provision. He called this a unified contextual approach to statutory interpretation and set out a purposive approach to interpretation. He described it as follows (at p.49):

1. The judge must give effect to the [grammatical and] ordinary, or, where appropriate, the technical meaning of words in the general context of the statute; he must also determine the extent of general words with reference to that context.

2. If the judge considers that the application of the words in their grammatical and ordinary sense would produce a result which is contrary to the purpose of that statute, he may apply them in any secondary meaning that they are capable of bearing.

3. The judge may read in words which he considers to be necessarily implied by words which are already in the statute and he has a limited power to add to, alter or ignore statutory words in order to prevent a provision from being unintelligible or absurd or totally unreasonable, unworkable, or totally irreconcilable with the rest of the statute.

4. In applying the above rules the judge may resort to certain aids to construction and presumptions…

5. The judge must interpret a statute so as to give effect to directly applicable European Community law, and, in so far as this is not possible, must refrain from applying the statutory provisions which conflict with that law.

See further 4.8 Interpretation of legislation and the Human Rights Act 1998.

To these points there must now be added a sixth point arising out of s.3 of the Human Rights Act 1998. In the 1998 Act, it is provided that a judge must interpret and give effect to primary legislation and subordinate legislation, in so far as it is possible to do so, in a way which is compatible with the Convention rights.

In considering the words of a statute the courts must consider the context in which they are being used. Lord Simon in *Maunsell v Olins* [1975] AC 373, at p.391 explained:

> [s]tatutory language, like all language, is capable of an almost infinite gradation of 'register' – i.e., it will be used at the semantic level appropriate to the subject matter and to the audience addressed (the man in the street, lawyers, merchants, etc.). It is the duty of a court of construction to tune in to such register and so to interpret the statutory

language as to give to it the primary meaning which is appropriate in that register (unless it is clear that some other meaning must be given in order to carry out the statutory purpose or to avoid injustice, anomaly, absurdity or contradiction). In other words, statutory language must always be given presumptively the most natural and ordinary meaning which is appropriate in the circumstances.

This makes the point that the intended meaning of words depends upon the circumstances in which they are used. Words may have an ordinary meaning or a technical meaning. See, for example, *Fisher v Bell* [1961] 1 QB 394. The aids to construction both internal and external to an Act, which are explained in what follows, help to establish the context of an Act. Lord Simon also explains that if the primary meaning to be given to the words do not fulfil the statutory purpose or would otherwise lead to injustice, anomaly, absurdity, or contradiction then a secondary meaning may be given if the words are capable of bearing such meaning.

In a contextual approach to interpretation an appreciation of the purpose of the Act is essential. Again, the internal and external aids to interpretation may be consulted to establish such purpose. In *R v Montila* [2004] 1 WLR 3141 the House of Lords, in a single opinion delivered by Lord Hope, said (at p.3151) 'it has become common practice for their Lordships to ask to be shown the Explanatory Notes when issues are raised about the meaning of words used in an enactment'.

See 4.4.2 on Explanatory Notes.

Statements by the House of Lords suggest that a contextual and purposive approach to the interpretation of statutes is to be adopted. Lord Steyn in *R (Quintavalle) v Secretary of State for Health* [2003] 2 AC 687 said (at p.700), 'nowadays the shift towards purposive interpretation is not in doubt. The qualification is that the degree of liberality permitted is influenced by the context, e.g. social welfare legislation and tax statutes may have to be approached somewhat differently.' See Bell, J. and Engle, G. *Cross Statutory Interpretation*, pp.180–3.

The following cases give examples of the application of the contextual and purposive approach.

In *R v Z (Attorney General for Northern Ireland's Reference)* [2005] UKHL 35, [2005] 2 AC 645 Z and others were charged under s.11(1) of the Terrorism Act 2000 with belonging to a proscribed organisation, the 'Real Irish Republican Army' (the Real IRA). By s.3(1) of the Act, 'an organisation is proscribed if (a) it is listed in Sch.2, or (b) it operates under the same name as an organisation listed in that schedule'. Schedule 2 includes the 'Irish Republican Army' (the IRA), but does not include 'the Real IRA'. The question for the House of Lords was simply whether 'the Real IRA' was a proscribed organisation.

It was argued on behalf of Z that the words used by Parliament had not made clear an intention to proscribe 'the Real IRA'; the organisation was not included in Sch.2 nor did 'the Real IRA' fall within s.3(1)(b) as it had a different name, separate membership, and different aims from those of 'the IRA'. Reliance was also placed on the principle of legal policy that any doubt in a penal statute should be resolved in favour of a defendant, as seen in *Tuck & Sons v Priester* (1887) 19 QBD 629. It can be seen that

Z's argument was based upon a literal interpretation of the Terrorism Act 2000, supported by a presumption of legislative intent.

However, Lord Bingham said (at p.655):

> the interpretation of a statute is a far from academic exercise. It is directed to a particular statute, enacted at a particular time, to address (almost invariably) a particular problem or mischief. As was said in *R (Quintavalle) v Secretary of State for Health* [2003] 2 AC 687,695 para 8: 'The court's task, within the permissible bounds of interpretation, is to give effect to Parliament's purpose. So the controversial provisions should be read in the context of the statute as a whole, and the statute as a whole should be read in the historical context of the situation which led to its enactment.'

His Lordship concluded that in approaching the issue in the present case the historical context was of fundamental importance. Looking at the legislation passed prior to and including the Terrorism Act 2000, the common object, with the exception of the Sentences Act 1998, was the suppression of Irish terrorism. Parliament had previously enacted statutes mindful of the IRA having split into two groups, the Official IRA and the Provisional IRA, and used the general label, the Irish Republican Army, for the purposes of proscription. This approach employed a blanket term 'to embrace all emanations, manifestations and representations of the IRA, whatever their relationship to each other'. The Terrorism Act 2000 was enacted against this background and of which Parliament must have been aware.

Lord Woolf agreed with Lord Bingham, and applying the approach of reading s.3 not only in the context of the Act as a whole but also in the light of the situation which led to its enactment, said (at p.660) 'there can be no doubt and any other view would be absurd, that the words of s.3 and Sch.2 were intended to include the Real IRA which was the most active of the different organisations at the time of enactment'. All of their Lordships agreed that 'the Real IRA' fell within the term 'the IRA', although they differed in their reasoning.

The case illustrates the purposive approach to interpretation with express reference made to the object of the Terrorism Act 2000; the identification of the intention of Parliament was reinforced by considering the absurdity that would result if 'the Real IRA', an active terrorist organisation at the time of enactment, was not included.

Another example of the purposive approach to interpretation is seen in *R (Quintavalle) v Secretary of State for Health* [2003] 2 AC 687. This case considered the difficult issue of the unforeseen development, as previously outlined. Could legislation be applied to a development that was unknown at the time of passage of an Act? The Human Fertilisation and Embryology Act 1990 was passed against a background of fast-moving scientific development. Under the Act a statutory licensing authority was established to regulate the creation of human embryos outside the human body. At the time of enactment it was thought that a human embryo could only be created by a process of fertilisation.

Later scientific developments allowed the creation of a human embryo by cell nuclear replacement (CNR), a process not involving fertilisation. By s.1(1) '...(a) embryo means a live human embryo where fertilisation is complete, and (b) references to an embryo include an egg in the process of fertilisation, and, for this purpose, fertilisation is not complete until the appearance of a two cell zygote' and by s.1(2) it was stated that the Act applies only to the 'bringing about the creation of an embryo outside the human body'. The House of Lords was asked whether an embryo created by CNR fell within the regulatory scheme established by the 1990 Act. It was argued that Parliament by defining 'embryo' by reference to fertilisation excluded embryos created by CNR. Lord Bingham having considered the background to the 1990 Act said that embryos created by CNR were subject to regulation.

His Lordship reasoned that the Act was directed to the creation of human embryos outside the human body and Parliament clearly could not have intended to distinguish between embryos on the basis of method of creation given the state of scientific knowledge in 1990. Lord Millett, relying in part upon the long title to the Act, 'an Act to make provision in connection with human embryos and any subsequent development of such embryos', said (at p.708):

> ...Parliament intended to make comprehensive provision for the protection of human embryos however created, and that the failure of particular provisions to capture embryos produced by a process not involving fertilisation is not because Parliament intended to leave them unregulated but because Parliament did not foresee the need to deal with them.

In the light of the purpose behind the Act s.1(1)(a) had to be read as directed to live human embryos created outside the body, irrespective of their manner of creation. Consequently, the words 'where fertilisation is complete' in s.1(1)(a) were interpreted as not being an essential part of the definition of an embryo but referring to the time at which an embryo became such.

Was this interpretation consistent with the guidance of Lord Wilberforce (see at 4.1)?

Lord Bingham posed and answered the following questions:

- Did live human embryos created by CNR fall within the same genus of facts as those to which the expressed policy of Parliament had been formulated? His Lordship answered yes as the embryos were similar and both forms were in need of regulation given the purpose of the Act.

- Was the operation of the 1990 Act to be regarded as liberal and permissive in its operation or restrictive and circumscribed? While considering this to be 'not an entirely simple question', his Lordship considered that the purpose of the Act required the regulation of 'activities not distinguishable in any significant respect from those regulated by the Act'.

- Was the embryo created by CNR different in kind or dimension from that for which the Act was passed? In his Lordship's view, given the reasons for the legislation, i.e. to address difficult moral, religious, and scientific issues relating to human embryos, the answer was no.

Lord Steyn said (at p.703): 'in order to give effect to a plain parliamentary purpose a statute may sometimes be held to cover a scientific development not known when the statute was passed. Given that Parliament legislates on the assumption that statutes may be in place for many years, and that Parliament wishes to pass effective legislation, this is a benign principle designed to achieve the wishes of Parliament.'

Thinking point

Can this statement of Lord Steyn be reconciled with the comments made by Lord Wilberforce (see at 4.1) in *Royal College of Nursing of the United Kingdom v Department of Health and Social Security* [1981] AC 800? Why did the majority of the House of Lords in the *Royal College of Nursing* case disagree with the decision reached by Lord Wilberforce?

To what extent does a purposive approach allow the courts to depart from the words of a statute?

The cases disclose that the courts, within very narrow limits, are willing to read words in and out as stated in Cross's third point. Remember, of course, that when the compatibility of legislation with the European Convention on Human Rights is in question the courts, by s.3 of the Human Rights Act 1998, are under a duty to interpret and give effect to legislation to ensure such compatibility, insofar as it is possible to do so.

Reading words in

Cross in point three said that judges may read words into a statute when the words are necessarily implied given the words which already are present in the statute. This was seen in *Adler v George* [1964] 2 QB 7, which is discussed earlier.

Reading words out

Cross said that a judge, using the yardstick of a statutory provision being absurd or unintelligible or totally irreconcilable with the rest of the statute, has a limited power to add to, alter, or ignore statutory words. In *McMonagle v Westminster City Council* [1990] 2 WLR 823, the House of Lords ignored words contained in the Local Government (Miscellaneous Provisions) Act 1982 as amended by the Greater London Council (General Powers) Act 1986. The appellant had been convicted of knowingly using premises as a 'sex encounter establishment' without a licence. 'Sex encounter establishment' was defined, inter alia, as '…(c) premises at which entertainments *which are not unlawful* are provided…' (emphasis added). It was argued on behalf of the appellant that the prosecution had to prove that the activities at the appellant's premises were not unlawful; that is the activities were not so indecent in character as to amount to an offence at common law. No licence was needed where the acts were unlawful.

Lord Bridge said that the purpose of the 1982 Act was to control sex establishments and that a literal interpretation of the words would have the effect of frustrating this purpose. To avoid this construction his Lordship treated the words 'which are not unlawful' as the product of poor draftsmanship and unnecessary. Usually effect must be given to every word of a statute, but if no sensible meaning can be given to a word or phrase and it frustrates the object of the legislation then such may be disregarded.

It is important to consider how far courts may depart from the wording of an Act of Parliament in the process of interpretation and are the courts consistent in this practice. As will be seen later when compatibility of English law with the European Convention on Human Rights is to be determined, s.3 Human Rights Act 1998 raises the same issue of how far the courts may go beyond the words used in legislation.

4.3.6 The rules of statutory interpretation in action

The case of *Coltman v Bibby* [1988] 2 AC 276 illustrates how the rules of statutory interpretation may be employed to determine the intention of Parliament.

The facts of the case were that Leo Coltman died when a ship, of some 90,000 tons, called the *Derbyshire*, in which he worked, sank. Damages were sought by the claimants, who were administering the estate of Coltman, from the defendant employers, Bibby Tankers Ltd. Under s.1(1) of the Employer's Liability (Defective Equipment) Act 1969, should an employee suffer personal injury in the course of his employment because of a defect in equipment provided by an employer for the purposes of the employer's business and the defect is due to the fault of a third party (for example, a manufacturer) then the injury is deemed to be also attributable to the negligence of an employer.

The case illustrates the difficulties that arise over the use of definitions in statutes; the House of Lords had to decide whether a ship was 'equipment' for the purposes of the Employer's Liability (Defective Equipment) Act 1969. If it was, the defendants would be liable to pay damages to the estate of Leo Coltman.

A starting point when considering the meaning of words in a statute is to see if Parliament has provided definitions of the terms used. These may be found sometimes in the section where the term is used or in the Interpretation section which is located at the end of a Part of an Act or at the end of an Act. The Employer's Liability (Defective Equipment) Act 1969 provided in s.1(3) that 'in the section "equipment" includes any plant and machinery, vehicle, aircraft and clothing;…"personal injury" includes loss of life…'.

The High Court held that the ship was 'equipment', whereas the Court of Appeal, by a majority, decided that it was not. The case was appealed to the House of Lords.

It is instructive to consider the arguments put forward by counsel before the House of Lords.

Arguments for the claimants

- There is no exhaustive definition of 'equipment' in the Act; note that s.1(3) uses the word 'includes' not 'means'. Parliament has used wide words and a ship falls within the meaning of 'equipment' or 'plant' or 'vehicle'.

- 'Equipment' is provided 'for the purposes of the employer's business' which is wider than providing equipment to a particular employee for use in the course of his work.

- The purpose of the Act is to protect employees who are injured due to defective equipment when that fault is attributable to the fault of a third party and not an employer.

- The 1969 Act applies to hovercrafts and for the purposes of taxation legislation a ship is treated as 'plant'.

- Given Parliament has used wide words and has not expressly excluded ships from the definition of 'equipment', ships are included; to arrive at any other interpretation would create absurd anomalies, e.g. a cross-Channel hovercraft is covered by the 1969 Act, but a cross-Channel ferry would not be so covered.

Arguments for the defendants

- The ordinary use of the word 'equipment' is something with which a person or thing is 'fitted out'. Support for this meaning is to be found for this meaning in the definition given by the *Oxford English Dictionary*.

- The claimants conceded that a factory or a hotel could not be 'equipment'. A large ship is like a factory, a place where an employee works. Liability attaches to 'equipment' within a factory or ship but not to the structure of the factory or ship.

- For the purposes of the Occupiers Liability Act 1957 and the Factories Act 1961, a ship is within the definition of 'premises'.

- 'Equipment' must be read in its context, particularly in the light of the word 'provided' which means 'supplied or furnished for use'. An interpretation which suggests that a ship is provided to the crew cannot be correct.

- Section 1(3) extends the ordinary meaning of 'equipment' to cover, for example, 'aircraft' and 'plant' that would not normally be covered. This would seem to preclude the inclusion, therefore, of a ship within the meaning of 'equipment'.

- The meaning of 'plant', defined by the *Oxford English Dictionary* as '[t]he fixtures, implements, machinery, and apparatus used in carrying out an industrial process', is not apt to include a ship. The same is true of 'vehicle', as a means of conveyance on land. If the word 'vehicle' was given a wider meaning, as encompassing any form of conveyance, so as to include a ship, then it would also cover an aircraft; however, Parliament has included an aircraft expressly, but made no mention of a ship. 'The Act is drafted in terms of inclusion, and anything not within the words of inclusion are excluded *sub silentio*.'
- The mischief behind the Act may be used if the words of the Act are in doubt.

The reasoning in the House of Lords

Lord Oliver delivered the leading opinion, with which the other Lords agreed, finding that the ship was indeed 'equipment'.

His Lordship first pointed to the mischief behind the 1969 Act that employees in the course of their employment may be injured by defective equipment provided by an employer. While the employer at common law might not have been negligent in supplying the defective equipment an employee might not be able to claim against the third person supplying the employer with such, as the third person may no longer be traceable or be insolvent or have ceased to trade. Parliament in consequence imposed a vicarious responsibility on an employer for defective equipment, making an employer liable to an employee; the employer then having a right of action against the third party. The purpose of the Act said Lord Oliver was to be found in the long title to the Act: 'to make further provision with respect to the liability of an employer for injury to his employee which is attributable to any defect in equipment provided by the employer for the purposes of the employer's business; and for purposes connected with the matter aforesaid'.

The word 'equipment' had to be read in its context of 'equipment provided by his employer for the purposes of the employer's business'. A ship owner to carry on business clearly needs ships; there is no misuse of language to say that these are the equipment of the business.

The analogy with a factory was rejected as a small boat would be 'equipment', for example a powerboat used for waterskiing training, so the size of the vessel and the fact that it also accommodates crew is not a justification to exclude it from the definition of 'equipment'.

A major argument that stood in the way of a ship being 'equipment', in his Lordship's view, was the need to read s.1(1) subject to s.1(3). 'Equipment' in s.1(1) may be given a wide meaning, but s.1(3) indicated how far the definition may extend, i.e. '"equipment" includes any plant and machinery, vehicle, aircraft and clothing'; the extended meaning does not include vessels and this must be deliberate given the enumeration of what 'equipment' includes. Lord Oliver rejected this argument, saying that s.1(3) was not restrictive as it used the word 'includes' and the items in the list are for the purpose of clarification. The use of the word 'any' in s.1(3) indicated, in the light of the purpose of the Act, that 'it should be widely construed so as to embrace every article of whatever kind furnished by the employer for the purposes of his business'.

Lord Oliver concluded (at p.300),

> [t]he omission is certainly curious but I find myself entirely unpersuaded that there can be deduced from it an intention to cut down the very wide meaning of 'equipment' in subsection (1) which is indicated both by the legislative purpose of the statute and by the width of the clarifying definition.

As the expression 'plant and machinery' includes machinery installed or affixed to a ship, it would be absurd if an employer was liable for injury caused by defects in such machinery, but not for injury caused by defects in the structure of the ship itself. If this approach were to be adopted, problems of demarcation would arise. Equally to exclude all vessels of whatever size would seem to run counter to the purpose of the Act. Undoubtedly, some vessels must be 'equipment' of a business, for example a dredger. If some vessels are 'equipment', then there is no justification for seeking to distinguish between vessels of different sizes.

As can be noted, his Lordship used various techniques to justify his decision that a ship was 'equipment' for the purposes of the Employer's Liability (Defective Equipment) Act 1969. An application of the literal rule was not possible as there was clearly an uncertainty caused by ss.1(1) and 1(3). Reference was made to the purpose of the Act and the various absurdities that would arise if vessels were not included in 'equipment'. The nature of definitions was considered and the use of the word 'includes' in s.1(3) meant that there was only a partial definition of 'equipment' which did not cut back the meaning of this word as used in s.1(1).

ⓘ Critical debate

In *Royal College of Nursing of the United Kingdom v Department of Health and Social Security* [1981] AC 800 the courts were faced with a problem caused by medical advances. Read the case and consider the following questions:

(a) How did the majority of the House of Lords arrive at a decision in favour of the interpretation placed on the 1967 Act by the DHSS? Identify the aids to statutory interpretation that were employed by the court.

(b) What would have been the consequences had the House of Lords affirmed the decision of the Court of Appeal and declared that it was not lawful for nurses to be involved in the termination of pregnancies by the medical induction procedure?

(c) Did the majority of the House of Lords in interpreting the 1967 Act go beyond the expressed intention of Parliament? Should the issue have been left to Parliament to resolve?

4.4 **Aids to construction**

The court in construing the words of a section of an Act may encounter ambiguity, uncertainty, or the provision may appear pointless. In such a situation a court may consult other parts of an Act as guides to the intention of Parliament or, within limits, go outside the Act in search of such intention.

4.4.1 **Aids to construction found within an Act of Parliament**

The features of an Act that may be used as aids to construction are: the long title; the preamble (if an Act has one); the short title; cross-headings; side or marginal notes; and punctuation. Lord Reid in *DPP v Schildkamp* [1971] AC 1 said that although punctuation, side or marginal notes, and cross-headings are not the product of anything done in Parliament (they are not capable of being amended by Parliament and are put in a statute by Parliamentary Counsel) (at p.10) 'it may be more realistic to accept the Act as printed as being the product of the whole legislative process, and to give due weight to everything found in the printed Act…'.

> ### Thinking point
>
> It is necessary to understand how legislation is made in order to follow the approach of the courts to the internal aids to construction. The long title, preamble, and short title, all may be amended by Parliament during the passage of a bill, but they do not create rules of law.
>
> The marginal or side notes are part of a bill not for the purposes of debate, but for ease of reference. They are included by Parliamentary Counsel, who is responsible for the drafting of a bill. While they cannot be amended by Parliament, they are a feature of a bill and ultimately part of the resulting Act of Parliament.
>
> What is important is that all the internal aids are part of the context of the Act and may be used to generally inform the reader of the purpose of an Act, but they are not the enacting words of the statute, i.e. the words of the sections, and must carry less weight as aids to interpretation. What do you think are the appropriate limits for the use of internal aids?

It is important to appreciate the limits within which these aids operate.

The long title

This gives an indication of the purpose of an Act. In *R v Bates* [1952] 2 All ER 842, Donovan J said that upon reading the words of a section, should doubt or ambiguity arise then the long title may be consulted as an aid to resolving the doubt or ambiguity. However, if the words of the section make a meaning clear, the long title cannot be used to restrict such meaning.

The preamble

Preambles are rarely seen in modern statutes but were more common in older statutes. Where a preamble exists it may set out the reasons for the passing of the statute. It may be consulted as part of reading the statute as a whole. Viscount Simonds said in *AG v Prince Ernest Augustus of Hanover* [1957] AC 436 (at p.461):

> [s]o it is that I conceive it to be my right and duty to examine every word of a statute in its context, and I use 'context' in its widest sense, which I have already indicated as including not only other enacting provisions of the same statute, but its preamble, the existing state of the law, other statutes *in pari materia*, [see later] and the mischief which I can, by those and other legitimate means, discern the statute was intended to remedy.

Once again the indication is that the courts are able to read beyond the words of a statute to establish the circumstances surrounding the making of the legislation. So a preamble may inform a court's reading of the words of an Act, but it cannot be used to cut down the plain meaning of the words.

The short title

The short title, while being part of an Act, is of limited interpretative value as it is merely a brief way of referring to an Act. Indeed, the short title may be positively misleading. For example, the Unfair Contract Terms Act 1977 does not cover all potentially unfair terms of a contract and its scope extends beyond contract terms to non-contractual notices also.

Cross-headings

These are to be found above a section or group of sections; they are there to help the reader find their way around an Act. A cross-heading may be consulted when the words of a section are ambiguous or unclear. However, in the light of a more contextual approach to the construction of statutes, it would appear (by analogy with Explanatory Notes and marginal and side notes) that ambiguity is not necessary to permit the use of cross-headings; see later *R (Westminster City Council) v National Asylum Support Service* [2002] 1 WLR 2956 and *R v Montila* [2004] 1 WLR 3141.

Side, or marginal, notes

These are so called as they originally appeared in the margin to an Act, sign-posting the content of a specific section. Since 2001, the note is placed in bold above the section to which it relates. As an aid to construction, a side note may be used in considering what the purpose of the section is and the mischief it is sought to address, but it cannot be used to restrict the clear meaning of a section ascertainable from its words. In *R v Montila* [2004] 1 WLR 3141, the House of Lords said that as side notes are included for ease of reference and not for debate before Parliament, they are to be accorded less weight; but, nonetheless, they provide a context for the examination of an Act.

An example of the use of side or marginal notes is seen in *Tudor Grange Holdings Ltd v Citibank NA* [1991] 3 WLR 750. In this case the claimants under a contract with the defendant bank alleged a breach of contract. This claim was contractually settled. The claimants later alleged that the settlement of the claim by reason of s.10 of the Unfair Contract Terms Act 1977 was subject to a test of reasonableness.

Section 10 provides:

> A person is not bound by any contract term prejudicing or taking away rights of his which arise under, or in connection with the performance of, another contract, so far as those rights extend to the enforcement of another's liability which this Part of this Act prevents that other from excluding or restricting.

It was argued by the claimants that the contractual settlement by its terms took away rights under the first contract with the defendant bank.

The High Court decided that Parliament never intended s.10 to apply to settlements of claims. In arriving at this conclusion, Browne-Wilkinson VC looked for the mischief behind the section and relied, in part, upon the marginal note which said 'Evasion by means of secondary contract'. This indicated that s.10 was aimed at the use of exemption clauses in secondary contracts to evade the control of Part 1 of the 1977 Act:

> …a contract to settle disputes which have arisen concerning the performance of an earlier contract cannot be described as an evasion of the provisions in the Act regulating exemption clauses in the earlier contract. Nor is the compromise contract 'secondary' to the earlier contract.

This case is further mentioned subsequently when considering Law Commission reports as an external aid to construction.

Punctuation

As has been seen in the words of Lord Reid in *DPP v Schildkamp*, punctuation may be considered as part of a statute and may be used as an aid to interpretation in the event of ambiguity.

4.4.2 Aids to construction found outside an Act of Parliament

Explanatory Notes

Since 1999, Explanatory Notes accompany a bill introduced by a government minister during its parliamentary passage. The Explanatory Notes are updated during this time and are published along with the new Act. They seek to explain the impact of the legislation in layman's terms and may be used as an aid to construction of the statute. In *R (on the application of S) v Chief Constable of South Yorkshire* [2004] 1 WLR 2196,

Lord Steyn said that, although Explanatory Notes are not approved by Parliament, they may cast light on the context of the statute and the mischief at which it is aimed.

The Explanatory Notes thus give the context of an Act and an indication of what the Act is intended to achieve and may be consulted. They may be used even in the absence of an ambiguity as it is permissible to read an Act of Parliament in its context. See the opinion of Lord Steyn in *R (Westminster City Council) v National Asylum Support Service* [2002] 1 WLR 2956 (at p.2959): '[i]n so far as the Explanatory Notes cast light on the objective setting or contextual scene of the statute, and the mischief at which it is aimed, such materials are therefore *always* admissible aids to construction' (emphasis added). Lord Steyn also indicated that Explanatory Notes may be accorded greater weight than Law Commission reports, government Green or White Papers, and the like as there is a closer connection between the Explanatory Notes and the proposed legislation, than with pre-parliamentary materials.

Interpretation Act 1978

This Act is important, but its title promises more than it actually delivers. It deals with details. Some examples serve to illustrate what it does.

1. Section 4 indicates that an Act comes into force either: (i) when provision is made for it to come into force on a particular day; or (ii) if there is no such provision then on the day the Act receives the royal assent. In each case, the Act is in force from the beginning of the day on which it comes into force.

2. Section 6 provides that unless a contrary intention appears in an Act:

   - where words used in an Act refer to the masculine gender they also include the feminine gender and vice versa; and

   - words appearing in the singular include the plural and words in the plural include the singular.

🔑 Key point

Be aware not only of the rules relating to the interpretation of statutes and the limits to their operation, but also consider the reasons for the rules.

Pre-parliamentary materials

Before a bill is presented to Parliament and then passes into law it may have been preceded by a royal commission, Law Commission, or other official committee report. Such reports may have explored problems in existing law or considered remedying perceived injustice. To what extent may such pre-parliamentary materials be used in the process of construction? It was said by the majority of the House of Lords in the *Black Clawson* case [1975] AC 591, that pre-parliamentary materials could be consulted to ascertain the state of the law before the Act and the mischief at which the Act was directed. However, the recommendations contained in a report, the draft bill, and any comments thereon, cannot be used in ascertaining the meaning of the words used in an Act.

Thinking point

Lord Reid in justifying this practice said that as the courts did not consult Hansard in ascertaining the intention of Parliament then with stronger reason the courts should 'disregard expressions of intention by committees or royal commissions which reported before the Bill was introduced'. Now it is permissible for the courts to use Hansard (see later) should the courts be able to consult the recommendations in a report as an indication of the intention of Parliament? See Lord Simon's opinion in the *Black Clawson* case that a draft bill and commentary annexed to a draft bill could be used to establish parliamentary intent. His Lordship said (at p.651):

> [t]o refuse to consider such a commentary, when Parliament has legislated on the basis and faith of it, is for the interpreter to fail to put himself in the real position of the promulgator of the instrument before essaying its interpretation. It is refusing to follow what is perhaps the most important clue to meaning. It is perversely neglecting the reality, while chasing shadows. As Aneurin Bevan said: 'Why read the crystal when you can read the book?' Here the book is already open: it is merely a matter of reading on. Certainly, a court of construction cannot be precluded from saying that what the committee thought as to the meaning of its draft was incorrect. But that is one thing: to dismiss, out of hand and for all purposes, an authoritative opinion in the light of which Parliament has legislated is quite another.

Obviously this must be read subject to the warning that Parliament might not have followed the recommendations of the committee in question and so the recommendations will be of little or, more likely, no interpretative value.

An illustration of the use of pre-parliamentary materials is seen in *Tudor Grange Holdings Ltd v Citibank NA* [1992] Ch 53. Browne-Wilkinson VC in seeking the mischief of the Unfair Contract Terms Act 1977 consulted the second report on exemption clauses of the Law Commission on Exemption Clauses (1975) (Law Com No.69). He commented (at p.66),

> [t]his report was the genesis of the Act of 1977. The report is wholly concerned with remedying injustices which are caused by exemption clauses in the strict sense. So far as I can see, the report makes no reference of any kind to any mischief relating to agreements to settle disputes.

This allowed him to conclude that the Act was not seeking to control contractual settlements of disputes, strengthening his interpretation of s.10, as already seen.

Parliamentary materials – Hansard

For many years the courts refused to allow the use of Hansard, the official record of parliamentary debates, as an aid to construction of an Act of Parliament. The practice was confirmed by the House of Lords in *Davis v Johnson* [1979] AC 264. This was criticised on the basis that an obvious source of elucidation of the intention of Parliament was being unnecessarily ignored.

In the case of *Pepper v Hart* [1993] AC 593, the House of Lords, consisting of seven law lords, by a majority of 6 to 1 decided that Hansard could be used as an aid to interpretation. However, the Lords in favour of permitting the reference to parliamentary materials clearly recognised the limits to the use of such materials. Hansard is only to be used within the following limits:

> first, the legislation must be ambiguous or obscure or a literal interpretation would lead to an absurdity; second, the statement or statements relied on were made by the minister or other promoter of a Bill, together if necessary with such other Parliamentary material as is necessary to understand such statements; and third, the statements relied upon are clear.

A literal interpretation of legislation is not possible where the words used are ambiguous or uncertain so another meaning may be sought by reference to clear statements made in Parliament by the promoter of the legislation. Reference may be made to Hansard where the material identifies the mischief behind the Act or the legislative intention behind the unclear language used. The House of Lords further seemed to indicate that reference to Hansard would only be permitted where Parliament addressed the very issue that a court was being asked to decide. In this sense it can be seen that the use of Hansard is very limited.

It is instructive to read the leading opinion of Lord Browne-Wilkinson and the dissenting opinion of Lord Mackay to discover the reasons for and against the use of Hansard in the interpretation of a statute. In essence the argument is, on one side, a matter of principle, that is, access to parliamentary words may throw light on the mischief behind a statute or the legislative intent; as opposed to, on the other side, considerations of cost, uncertainty in the parliamentary words themselves, and problems of access to Hansard.

Thinking point

Note that an argument as to the permitted use of parliamentary materials that did not find favour with the House of Lords in the late 1970s did find favour with a differently constituted House of Lords a mere thirteen years later; once again this illustrates the point that arguments may not have 'right' answers.

Be prepared to evaluate the reasons for and against the use of Hansard. In this respect what has happened subsequent to *Pepper v Hart* is significant. How useful has Hansard been in subsequent cases? Is Hansard readily available; note that Lord Mackay's comments were delivered before the power of the Internet was apparent. Nonetheless consider whether there are still difficulties in consulting Hansard and note that lawyers poring over Hansard will inevitably lead to increased costs.

The debate over the efficacy of *Pepper v Hart* has continued. Lord Steyn, writing extra-judicially ('*Pepper v Hart*: A Re-examination' (2001) 21 OJLS 59), has said that in his view, *Pepper v Hart* has substantially increased the costs of litigation to 'very little avail'. His Lordship also argued that the decision may have lead to a change in the behaviour of the executive, encouraging the making of statements in Parliament as to government understanding of the effect of legislation. The courts are aware of the implications of this practice. In *Evans v Amicus Healthcare* [2004] 3 WLR 681, Thorpe and Sedley LJJ said (at p.685),

> [i]n the absence of any intractable ambiguity of the sort contemplated in Pepper v Hart, it seemed at first sight an endeavour by the department of state responsible for drafting the legislation to introduce its own intentions as an aid to construction, something which is no more permissible in the construction of legislation than it is in the construction of contracts.

Given that Hansard may be consulted, it is important to evaluate how the rule has worked in practice, as seen in the subsequent case law.

The case of *Pepper v Hart* raised a problem that had been considered during parliamentary debates leading to the passing of the Finance Act 1976 and the minister had given a clear answer to the issue that had come before the courts. So the uncertainty in the meaning of the Finance Act 1976 was resolved by looking at the legislative history of the Act. It was fortunate that Hansard provided a clear answer. Another example of Hansard being used to successfully support a particular interpretation of a legislative phrase was seen in *Stevenson v Rogers* [1999] QB 1028. More recently in *R v JTB* [2009] UKHL 20 Hansard was used when the House of Lords decided that the defence of *doli incapax* for children between the ages of 10 and 14 had been abolished by s.34 of the Crime and Disorder Act 1998. Lord Philips accepted that that conclusion could not be reached from the words of s.34 but once extrinsic aids (the background of the mischief, the pre-legislative materials, i.e. consultation and White Papers, and the statements made in Parliament) were considered the intention of Parliament became clear. However, the rule in *Pepper v Hart* specifies that Hansard may only be used where the legislation is ambiguous or obscure, the statements to be relied upon are those of ministers or other promoters of a Bill and the statements are clear. It may be commented that in *R v JTB*, first, the legislation was not ambiguous and, second, the statements made in Parliament during the passage of the Crime and Disorder Act 1998 were not clear. See further Francis Bennion, 'Mens Rea and Defendants Below the Age of Discretion' [2009] Crim LR 757 where the use of Hansard is criticised.

The opinions of judiciary, particularly in the House of Lords, are divided on how Hansard is to be used. In *Jackson v Attorney General* [2006] 1 AC 262, the difference was apparent in the opposing views of Lords Nicholls and Steyn. Lord Nicholls, restating an opinion given in *R v Secretary of State for the Environment, Transport and the Regions, ex parte Spath Holme* [2001] 2 AC 349, said that it was permissible to consult clear ministerial statements in Hansard to discover the *purpose* that the words in a statute are seeking to achieve. In contrast, Lord Steyn sought to limit the operation of *Pepper v Hart* when he said (at p.301),

> [it] should be confined to the situation which was before the House in *Pepper v Hart*. That would leave unaffected the use of Hansard material to identify the mischief at which legislation was directed and its objective setting. But trying to discover the intentions of the Government from ministerial statements in Parliament is constitutionally unacceptable.

Reliance was placed upon the opinion of Lord Hope in *Spath Holme*, where he said (at p.408),

> the decision in *Pepper v Hart* should be confined to cases where the court is concerned with the meaning that is to be given to the words used in legislation by Parliament. It would be contrary to fundamental considerations of constitutional principle to allow it to be used to enable reliance to be placed on statements made in debate by ministers about matters of policy which have not been reproduced in the enactment. It is the words used by Parliament, not words used by ministers, that define the scope within which the powers conferred by the legislature may be exercised.

Thinking point

The use of Hansard may be contrasted with another method of discovering parliamentary intention, that of the golden rule. According to the golden rule, it may be argued that Parliament cannot have intended a meaning where it leads to absurdity. Such an approach is inferential not direct, whereas Hansard, in *Pepper v Hart* provided direct evidence of what was meant by s.63(2) of the Finance Act 1976. Consider other ways in which the intention of Parliament may be identified.

The case law seems to suggest that it is rare that Hansard will be determinative of a question of interpretation. In *R (Quintavalle) v Secretary of State for Health* [2003] 2 AC 687, Lord Hoffmann said '[a]s it is almost invariably the case when such statements are tendered under the rule in *Pepper v Hart*, I found neither of assistance'. Again in *R v Clinton* [2012] EWCA Crim 2 Lord Judge CJ said, '[e]ven on the most generous interpretation of *Pepper (Inspector of Taxes) v Hart*…, the debates did not reveal anything which assisted in the process of legislative construction'. However, his Lordship explained that the construction reached by the court was consistent with the views expressed in Parliament during the passage of the legislation.

Usually Hansard may not be used, where a criminal statute is ambiguous, to extend the scope of criminal liability created by the statute; a defendant is to receive the benefit of the ambiguity, see *Massey and Another v Boulden and Another* [2003] 1 WLR 1792. Lord Phillips LCJ in *Thet v DPP* [2006] EWHC 2701 said, '[i]f a criminal statute is ambiguous, I would question whether it is appropriate by the use of *Pepper v Hart* to extend the ambit of the statute so as to impose criminal liability upon a defendant where, in the absence of the parliamentary material, the court would not do so. It seems to me at least arguable that if a criminal statute is ambiguous, the defendant should have the benefit of the ambiguity.' However, in *R v JTB* [2009] UKHL 20 Hansard was used in a criminal case against a defendant. Should the use of *Pepper v Hart* aid a defendant in criminal proceedings then the position would seem to be that Hansard may be used. It may be further noted that Hansard was of no value in *Thet v DPP* as the statement by the minister indicated that the meaning of 'reasonable excuse' in the Asylum and Immigration (Treatment of Claimants) Act 2004 was best 'left to the circumstances of each individual case' and that ultimately it was for the courts to decide!

Statutes *in pari materia*

Sometimes there will be a number of statutes on the same subject area. These are known as statutes *in pari materia*.

Should the words of a statute be uncertain or ambiguous a court may consider as an aid to construction other statutes which are *in pari materia*. It is not clear when statutes are *in pari materia*, but those Acts on the same subject may fall within the phrase.

In *R v Wheatley* [1979] 1 WLR 144, the Court of Appeal was asked to decide whether the definition of 'explosive substance' in the Explosive Substances Act 1883 should be construed in the light of the definition of 'explosive' in the Explosives Act 1875. The court looked to the long titles to the Acts and noted that the 1875 Act dealt with 'explosive substances' and the 1883 Act was 'to amend the law relating to explosive substances'. It was determined that the 1883 Act was intended to amend the 1875 Act. Section 9(1) of the 1883 Act provides that 'explosive substance shall be deemed to include...'. This is not a complete definition and it was taken to be expanding the meaning of 'explosive substance'. Section 3 of the 1875 Act, however, gave a definition of 'explosive'. In the light of this, the court was convinced that both Acts were *in pari materia* and therefore it was permissible to use the 1875 definition in construing the 1883 Act.

An illustration of where statutes were considered not to be *in pari materia* was seen in *Stevenson v Rogers* [1999] QB 1028, where the phrase 'in the course of a business' in the Unfair Contract Terms Act 1977 and in the Sale of Goods Act 1979 was given different meanings.

Dictionaries

It is permissible to consult a dictionary if the meaning of a word used in a statute is unclear. Obviously, if a statute defines a word then that is the definition to be used. However, dictionaries are to be treated with caution. In *Customs and Excise Comrs v Top Ten Promotions Ltd* [1969] 1 WLR 1163 Lord Upjohn said (at p.1171):

[i]t is highly dangerous, if not impossible, to attempt to place an accurate definition on a word in common use; you can look up examples of its many uses if you want to in the Oxford Dictionary but that does not help on definition; in fact it probably only shows that the word normally defies definition. The task of the court in construing statutory language such as that which is before your Lordships is to look at the mischief at which the Act is directed and then, in that light, to consider whether as a matter of common sense and everyday usage the known, proved or admitted or properly inferred facts of the particular case bring the case within the ordinary meaning of the words used by Parliament.

4.5 Rules of language

These rules give an indication of the intention behind the use of words. They are really rules relating to grammar. It is important to note the limits to their operation. Next you will find illustrations of some of the rules of language.

4.5.1 *Expressio unius est exclusio alterius* rule

Under this rule the mention of one or more things of a particular class, excludes silently all other members of the class. A classic example of the use of the rule is seen in the interpretation of the following phrase: 'land, houses and coalmines'. The word 'land' potentially includes mines. However, the express inclusion of the word 'coalmines' in the phrase must be taken to mean that no mines are intended to be included by using the word 'land'.

The limits of the rule were explained in *Galinski v McHugh* (1989) P & CR 359. In this case, the claimant landlord wished to serve a notice under s.4 of the Landlord and Tenant Act 1954 on the defendant tenant. This was done by serving the notice on solicitors who were representing the defendant. The defendant claimed that this service was invalid. Section 4(1) of the 1954 Act requires notice 'to be given to the tenant' whereas s.66(4) of the Act, which deals with service of notices, incorporating s.23 of the Landlord and Tenant Act 1927 provides, inter alia, 'in the case of a notice to a landlord, the person on whom it is to be served shall include any agent of the landlord duly authorised in that behalf'. In consequence, it was argued by the defendant, using the *expressio unius est exclusio alterius* rule, that as s.66(4) indicated expressly that a notice to a landlord could be served on an agent but did not mention service on an agent of a tenant, such latter service was excluded.

The Court of Appeal held that the *expressio unius* rule was no more than an aid to construction, and it may not operate where it is possible to explain an express inclusion on grounds other than an intention to exclude other categories. Parliament may have made an express reference to service on a landlord's agent as landlords are more likely to have agents than are tenants and furthermore tenants may be accustomed to dealing with the agents of landlords. In the light of such, an express reference to agents of tenants was unnecessary, but that did not mean that Parliament intended notices to tenants to be only served upon them.

4.5.2 *Ejusdem generis* rule

Where general words follow specific words which form a class (or a genus) then the general words are to be read in the light of the specific words. For example, Lord Simon in a debate in the chamber of the House of Lords said if an animal transportation measure applied to 'calves, lambs and other animals' the general words, 'other animals' taken out of context could cover the whole of the animal kingdom. But this is not the intention of Parliament, as the specific words refer to the young of farm animals and are meant to cover say kids and foals and such like.

It is to be noted that the rule only applies where the specific words form a class.

In *Massey and Another v Boulden and Another* [2003] 1 WLR 1792, the Court of Appeal had to decide whether a village green fell within s.34(1)(a) of the Road Traffic Act 1988 which prohibited the driving of a motor vehicle, without lawful authority, on 'any common land, moorland or land of any other description, not forming part of a road'. It was decided that the specific words, 'common land' and 'moorland' did not create a class and therefore, 'land of any other description' was wide and encompassed a village green.

Also, the general words may be so general that on their natural meaning it is clear that they are not to be read in the light of the specific words, but given their natural meaning.

4.5.3 *Noscitur a sociis* rule

Simply put, words derive their meaning from, and so must be read subject to, the context in which they appear. As Viscount Simonds said in *AG v Prince Ernest Augustus of Hanover* [1957] AC 436, '…words, and particularly general words, cannot be read in isolation: their colour and content are derived from their context'. An example of the rule is seen in *Pengelley v Bell Punch Co. Ltd* [1964] 1 WLR 1055, where the Court of Appeal had to determine the meaning of s.28(1) of the Factories Act 1961. Section 28(1) provided:

> All floors, steps, stairs, passages and gangways shall be of sound construction and properly maintained and shall, so far as is reasonably practicable, be kept free from any obstruction and from any substance likely to cause persons to slip.

The court was asked if it was permissible to store boxes on a factory floor. The word 'floors' had to be read in context of the other words 'steps, stairs, passages and gangways', which indicated places used for the purposes of passage. In the light also of the word 'obstruction', which means to block or make impassable, s.28(1) was referring to floor used for the purpose of movement and did not apply to all 'floors'. So factory floors could be used to store materials.

4.6 **Presumptions of statutory intent**

Cross identifies two types of presumption, although noting that there is a tendency for these to merge into each other. First, there are presumptions of general application, such as when Parliament legislates against the background of constitutional and administrative principles; and second, presumptions of legislative intent in cases of doubt or ambiguity.

4.6.1 **Presumptions of general application**

These presumptions apply even if there is no ambiguity in the text of the legislation. They assume that a statute is drafted against the background of legal principles and thus allow for brevity on the part of the draftsman. Cross comments (at p.166) that the 'presumptions of general application not only supplement the text, they also operate at a higher level as expressions of fundamental principles governing both civil liberties and the relations between Parliament, the executive and the courts'. The presumptions have also been explained in terms of a principle of legality; this principle protects both procedural safeguards and substantive basic or fundamental rights. The principle only has prima facie force and can be displaced by clear words of a statute. See *R v Secretary of State for the Home Department, ex parte Pierson* [1998] AC 539 at pp.587–90, for Lord Steyn's explanation of the basis of presumptions of general application and a number of examples.

Examples of presumptions include:

- statutory decision-makers must follow the rules of natural justice;
- a mental element is required for crimes created by statute; and
- a sentence lawfully passed should not be increased, retrospectively.

See further *R v Secretary of State for the Home Department, ex parte Simms* [2000] 2 AC 115.

4.6.2 **Presumptions of legislative intent in cases of doubt or ambiguity**

Should a statute be unclear or so ambiguous that the intention of Parliament cannot be established then certain presumptions of intent may be employed. The following are examples of such presumptions.

Presumption in relation to penal statutes

If a penal statute is ambiguous, then the presumption of intent is that the statute should be strictly construed so as to avoid liability. Lord Esher MR in *Tuck & Sons v Priester* (1887) 19 QBD 629, 638 stated:

[i]f there is a reasonable interpretation which will avoid the penalty in any particular case we must adopt that construction. If there are two reasonable constructions we must give the more lenient one. That is the settled rule for the construction of penal sections.

A good illustration of how this presumption operates was seen in *Hobson v Gledhill* [1978] 1 WLR 215. Section 1(1) of the Guard Dogs Act 1975 provides that:

A person shall not use or permit the use of a guard dog at any premises unless a person ('the handler') who is capable of controlling the dog is present on the premises and the dog is under the control of the handler at all times while it is being so used *except* while it is secured so that it is not at liberty to go freely about the premises (emphasis added).

The section contains an ambiguity which relates to when the exception applies. Two possible meanings are apparent:

(a) there is no offence if there is always a handler, capable of controlling the dog, on the premises where a dog is being used *and* the dog is under the control of the handler unless the dog is secured; or

(b) there is no offence if there is a handler capable of controlling the dog where a dog is being used and the dog is under the control of the handler *or* there is no handler on the premises but the dog is secured.

In relation to meaning (a), the exception applies only to the words 'and the dog is under the control of the handler at all times while it is being so used'; whereas for meaning (b), the exception applies to all of the preceding words of the paragraph.

Having understood the ambiguity the question for a court is how to resolve the problem. Lord Widgery CJ in the Divisional Court of the Queen's Bench Division said, (at p.219) that he was unable to say 'which of the solutions canvassed was the intention of Parliament, and the right course in those circumstances is to favour the citizen'. Peter Pain J said (at p.218), in favouring meaning (b), that 'one comes to the rule that a penal statute, where there is an ambiguity, should always be construed in favour of the citizen who may find himself the subject of the penalty'. This restricted duty placed on the citizen was consistent with the mischief which Parliament was seeking to address, that is dogs should be secured so that persons entering premises, whether lawfully or not, would be able to remove themselves from the area of attack by a dog.

Presumption against the retrospective operation of a statute

It is a fundamental principle of any legal system that a citizen should be able to discover the law and be able therefore to avoid the consequences of breaking the law. If an Act of Parliament is retrospective this may mean that a citizen has broken laws at a time when the law did not exist. While Parliament is able to pass legislation that does have retrospective operation, in order to do so clear words must be used. Should Parliament not make this intention clear, the presumption is that no retrospective effect was intended.

Presumption against ousting the jurisdiction of the courts

Should a statute seek to exclude the jurisdiction of the courts then the words used must be clear; such provisions will be construed strictly so as to preserve the jurisdiction of the courts. In *Anisminic Ltd v Foreign Compensation Commission* s.4(4) of the Foreign Compensation Act 1950 provided that the 'determination by the commission of any application made... shall not be called in question in any court of law'. The House of Lords, by a majority, said while a valid determination of the commission could not be questioned, s.4(4) did not prevent the courts from inquiring whether an order of the commission was made on the basis of a misconstruction of their jurisdiction. The determination was not a 'determination' within s.4(4) and therefore the courts could declare it a nullity.

Presumption against Parliament being in breach of international law

The UK may enter into treaties with other sovereign states which have effect in international law, but do not become part of UK domestic law (remember to incorporate treaty obligations into UK law Parliament would have to pass an Act to that effect). Should an Act of Parliament be ambiguous it is presumed that Parliament does not intend to be in breach of its international obligations.

4.7 Interpretation of legislation and the European Union

The UK is bound to implement directives of the European Union fully. This means that domestic legislation (whether primary or secondary) must be passed in order to implement a directive. The courts must then adopt a purposive approach when interpreting this legislation, using the directive as an aid to interpretation. In *Litster and Others v Forth Dry Dock Co Ltd and Another* [1990] 1 AC 546, 559, Lord Oliver, when considering domestic regulations made to implement a directive, said:

> if the legislation can reasonably be construed so as to conform with those obligations, obligations which are to be ascertained not only from the wording of the relevant directive but from the interpretation placed on it by the Court of Justice of the European Communities, such a purposive construction will be applied even though, perhaps, it may involve some departure from the strict and literal application of the words which the legislature has elected to use.

As can be seen the courts may only give effect to the purpose of a directive where domestic legislation is reasonably capable of bearing the meaning to be given to it.

What happens, however, if the UK fails to implement the directive (in other words there is no domestic implementing legislation)? The answer is that the UK courts are, nevertheless, still obliged to adopt a purposive approach to any pre-existing domestic legislation that may exist in the same subject area, again using the directive as an aid to interpretation.

Such a situation occurred in *Webb v EMO Air Cargo (UK) Ltd* [1993] 1 WLR 49. The claimant was employed initially to replace a pregnant employee during the maternity leave of the latter, but was to continue to be employed after the return of that employee. Shortly after commencing her employment the claimant found that she too was pregnant and her employer dismissed her. Her claim under s.1 of the Sex Discrimination Act 1975 was rejected by an industrial tribunal, the Employment Appeal Tribunal, and the Court of Appeal. On appeal to the House of Lords, the claimant argued that the 1975 Act should be interpreted purposively using the Equal Treatment Directive (Directive 76/207). The problem for the claimant was that this directive was adopted in 1976, after the Sex Discrimination Act had been enacted in 1975.

Lord Keith stated that a UK court would have to interpret domestic legislation in any area subject to a directive in a way which accords with the purpose of the directive 'if that can be done without distorting the meaning of the domestic legislation'. His Lordship added, relying on *Marleasing SA v La Comercial Internacional de Alimentacion SA* (Case 106/89) [1990] ECR I-4135, that this approach applied whether the domestic legislation was passed before or after the relevant directive. The important point is that domestic law must be capable of bearing the meaning which accords with the purpose of a directive; if not, then it is for Parliament to legislate, not for the courts to arrive at a construction which the words will not bear. Before determining the claimant's appeal a ruling concerning the Equal Treatment Directive was sought from the European Court of Justice. The Court of Justice ruled that the directive precluded a dismissal in the claimant's circumstances on the grounds of pregnancy. In *Webb v EMO Air Cargo (UK) Ltd (No.2)*, the House of Lords [1995] 1 WLR 1454 decided that ss.1(1)(a) and 5(3) could be interpreted in a way which was consistent with the directive.

Example

The Unfair Terms in Consumer Contracts Regulations 1999 make reference to 'good faith', but do not indicate what the term means. (Note that a previous version of the Regulations, made in 1994, did expressly indicate the factors that were to be considered in assessing good faith.) It is permissible to consult the recitals to Directive 93/13 on Unfair Terms in Consumer Contracts [1993] OJ L95/29 in order to gain guidance on this term. The recitals provide:

> in making an assessment of good faith, particular regard shall be had to the strength of bargaining positions of the parties, whether the consumer had an inducement to agree to the term and whether the goods or services were sold or supplied to the special order of the consumer; whereas the requirement of good faith may be satisfied by the seller or supplier where he deals fairly and equitably with the other party whose legitimate interests he has to take into account.

See *Director General of Fair Trading v First National Bank plc* [2002] 1 AC 481.

4.8 Interpretation of legislation and the Human Rights Act 1998

The Human Rights Act 1998 places a duty upon the courts to interpret legislation to ensure compatibility with the European Convention on Human Rights. By s.3(1) of the Act it is provided:

> So far as it is possible to do so, primary legislation and subordinate legislation must be read and given effect to in a way which is compatible with the Convention rights.

The subsection applies to all legislation existing and future. The use of the word 'possible' gives rise to some uncertainty; how far may the courts depart from the wording of legislation in seeking to achieve compatibility? Parliament envisages that some legislation may not be compliant and by s.4 a court may make a declaration of incompatibility so there is a limit to the judicial task under s.3(1).

See chapter 7, 'Human rights and fundamental freedoms'.

Where a legislative provision is ambiguous then the court must choose the meaning which is compatible with Convention rights. However, it is not necessary for there to be ambiguity for s.3 to apply as was seen in *R v A* [2002] 1 AC 45, where words were read into s.41 of the Youth Justice and Criminal Evidence Act 1999 to ensure compliance with a defendant's right to a fair trial under Article 6 of the European Convention on Human Rights. This is a departure from the traditional approach to statutory interpretation where the task is to discover the meaning of legislation from the words used by Parliament.

The main question to be answered is to what extent are the courts constrained in their task under s.3 by the words used in legislation? This issue was considered in *Ghaidan v Godin-Mendoza* [2004] UKHL 30.

Section 3 of Human Rights Act 1998 is considered in further depth in Chapter 7, Human Rights and Fundamental Freedoms.

Summary

- The role of a judge in interpreting a statute is to discover and give effect to the intention of Parliament. The concept of intention of Parliament is not without problems.

- The principles of statutory interpretation are not rules binding on the courts but are tools that courts may use to find the intention of Parliament.

- The traditional approach to interpretation of three distinct 'rules' of statutory interpretation, it is arguable, has given way to a contextual and purposive approach.

- A court may read the whole of an Act of Parliament, but not every part of an Act carries equal weight.

- The words of the sections of an Act express the intention of Parliament and are paramount; the aids to construction cannot to be used to give the words of a section a meaning they cannot bear, except in limited circumstances. This is subject to the operation of s.3 of the Human Rights Act 1998.

- Internal aids – the long title, preamble, cross-heading, marginal or side notes, punctuation – may be used to establish the context for an Act but cannot be used to restrict the clear meaning of the words of a section.

- External aids may be consulted subject to the limits to their use. These aids are outside of an Act and include: Explanatory Notes; Interpretation Act 1978; pre-parliamentary materials; parliamentary materials – Hansard; statutes on the same subject area – statutes *in pari materia*; and dictionaries.

- The use of Hansard has given rise to some controversy. Hansard is only to be used within the following limits:

  (i)   the legislation must be ambiguous or obscure or a literal interpretation would lead to an absurdity;

  (ii)   the statement or statements relied on were made by the minister or other promoter of a bill; and

  (iii) the statements relied upon are clear.

- Presumptions are used as a last resort should an Act prove to be wholly unclear or ambiguous.

- The courts of the UK are to construe domestic legislation in any area subject to a directive in a way which accords with the purpose of the directive as stated by the Court of Justice, 'if that can be done without distorting the meaning of the domestic legislation'.

- The Human Rights Act 1998 has changed the role of the courts in interpreting legislation when issues of Convention rights are raised. The courts may go beyond the words of the legislation in seeking to make such legislation Convention-compliant.

Questions

1 Why is it misleading to refer to the 'rules' of statutory interpretation?

2 Explain the literal rule, golden rule, and mischief rule.

3 What is meant by the purposive approach to statutory interpretation?

4 From where may a judge find the purpose of an Act?

5 To what extent do you consider the use of Hansard as established in *Pepper v Hart* a useful development in the interpretation of statutes?

6 What is the impact on statutory interpretation of: (a) the UK's membership of the European Union; and (b) the Human Rights Act 1998?

 Sample question and outline answer

Question

The use of Hansard as an aid to statutory interpretation is fraught with difficulty. The courts have not found it a useful guide to the interpretation of statutes.
Discuss.

Outline answer

This question raises three main issues: first, when can Hansard be used as an aid to statutory interpretation; second, is using Hansard fraught with difficulties (this requires an evaluation of the basis for its use); and third, the experience of the courts in cases subsequent to *Pepper v Hart*.

In *Pepper v Hart* it was stated by Lord Browne-Wilkinson that the rule against the use of Hansard should be relaxed so as to permit reference to parliamentary materials in the following circumstances: first, the legislation must be ambiguous or obscure or a literal interpretation would lead to an absurdity; second, the statement or statements relied on were made by the minister or other promoter of a bill, together with such other parliamentary material as is necessary to understand such statements; and third, the statements relied upon are clear.

The House of Lords was setting out a limited relaxation of the rule against the use of Hansard in the interpretation of statutes. Indeed Lord Bridge suggested that Hansard should only be used where Parliament has considered the very issue of interpretation which the court faces and the minister has provided a clear answer to that issue. That was the very situation in *Pepper v Hart*. The reason for the limited approach was to ensure legal certainty.

An argument against the relaxation of the rule excluding the use of Hansard was that the costs of litigation would increase with the increased workload of consulting Hansard. One of the main difficulties is convincing a court that the conditions laid down in *Pepper v Hart* have been satisfied. It should be noted that even the judges are not in agreement as to how *Pepper v Hart* is to be interpreted, see for example *Jackson v Attorney General*. The criticisms made by Bennion of *R v JTB* can be usefully explored also.

The case law subsequent to *Pepper v Hart* does not present a clear picture as to the value of Hansard as an aid to interpretation. Some cases demonstrate the use of Hansard, for example, *Warwickshire County Council v Johnson* [1993] AC 583. In this case the House of Lords used Hansard to interpret s.20(1) of the Consumer Protection Act 1987. Under s.20(1) it was an offence to give a misleading price indication 'in the course of any business of his'. Here an employee of an electrical retailer was found by the Divisonal Court to have given a misleading statement 'in the course of [a] business of his'. It was argued on the employee's behalf that s.20(1) was ambiguous. The House of Lords agreed and resolved this issue by looking at the clear words of the minister in Parliament which indicated that it was not the intention of the statute to cover individual employees but to cover the 'business' of an employer. Equally, in *Stevenson v Rogers* Hansard was employed successfully.

However, there is a considerable case law which shows circumstances where Hansard has been of no assistance. In *R v Secretary of State for the Environment, Transport and the Regions, ex parte Spath Holme* the House of Lords refused to permit the use of Hansard as the statute, the Landlord and Tenant Act 1985, was not ambiguous, obscure, or giving rise to absurdity, nor were the statements made by ministers in Parliament clear. Indeed certain judicial comments suggest that Hansard is rarely of use, see Lord Hoffman's remarks in *R (Quintavalle) v Secretary of State for Health*. Usually Hansard may not be used, where a criminal statute is ambiguous, to extend the scope of criminal liability created by the statute, see *Massey and Another v Boulden and Another* and Lord Phillips in *Thet v DPP*.

While the use of Hansard does give rise to difficulties, including what are the precise limits of its operation, it has been used by the courts as an aid to the interpretation of statutes in some cases. The problems encountered by the courts revolve around whether the conditions for Hansard's use have been met. It would seem that in the case law subsequent to *Pepper v Hart* the courts have sought to limit the use of Hansard.

Further reading

To understand how the rules of statutory interpretation are employed it is necessary to read the leading cases. In reading such cases pay particular attention to the arguments raised by lawyers before the courts.

- **Beatson J.** 'Common Law, Statute Law, and Constitutional Law' (2006) Stat LR 1
  This article explores the relationship between common law and statute law and the impact of s.3 of the Human Rights Act 1998.

- **Bell, J.** and **Engle, G.** *Cross Statutory Interpretation*, 3rd edn, Oxford University Press (1995)
  Described in the Preface to the third edition as 'a short, systematic introduction to the general principles of statutory interpretation, intended primarily for law students'.

- **Bennion, F.** *Statutory Interpretation*, 5th edn, LexisNexis (2007)
  Bennion seeks to systematise the rules of statutory interpretation. It is excellent for reference purposes.

- **Bennion, F.** 'Mens Rea and Defendants Below the Age of Discretion' [2009] Crim LR 757
  The author criticises the decision in *JTB* in part because of the way in which the rules of statutory interpretation were used. Bennion argues that the rule in *Pepper v Hart* was misapplied.

- **Kavanagh, A.** '*Pepper v Hart* and Matters of Constitutional Principle' (2005) 121 LQR 98
  Examines the constitutional reasons against the use of Hansard in the process of interpretation and argues in favour of the courts giving effect to intention as enacted in the words of a statute.

- **Millett, Lord** 'Construing Statutes' (1999) Stat LR 107
  A short article considering the problems surrounding the discovery of the meaning of legislation and arguments against *Pepper v Hart*.

- **Steyn, Lord** '*Pepper v Hart*: A Re-examination' (2001) 21 OJLS 59
  Considers the arguments surrounding the use of Hansard in the interpretation of legislation and the legal and practical consequences of the decision in *Pepper v Hart*.

- **Twining, W.** and **Miers, D.** *How to Do Things with Rules*, 5th edn, Cambridge (2010)
  An insightful exploration of rules, problems of interpretation, and their solution.

 Online Resource Centre

You should now attempt the supporting multiple choice questions available at **www.oxfordtextbooks.co.uk/orc/wilson_els/**.

5

The doctrine of judicial precedent

◉ Learning objectives

By the end of this chapter you should:

- understand the basis of the doctrine of judicial precedent;
- be able to recognise the characteristics of *ratio decidendi* and *obiter dicta*;
- appreciate the factors involved in identifying both *ratio decidendi* and *obiter dicta*;
- know the hierarchy of the courts;
- be able to explain the rules of binding precedent in relation to each court; and
- understand the reasons why the courts are bound by precedents.

🅕 Talking point

. . . .

In 2012 the newspapers carried articles on the issue of the 'right to die'. These reports were prompted by a case in which the High Court was asked to declare that the common law should recognise that necessity is a defence to murder in a case of voluntary euthanasia. The declaration was sought by a claimant who wished to have the choice to end his life by voluntary euthanasia as he was incapable of ending his life himself due to catastrophic physical disabilities. For a doctor to terminate his life lawfully necessity would have to be a defence to murder.

Where is a court to find the answer to such a question? A court hearing a case will take account of individual circumstances and will want to achieve a just result, but this must be within the law as found in previous cases and legislation. If the law produces an unjust result can a court change the law if it considers it just to do so? This question raises issues of which body or bodies should be making law and should this power be limited. Within English law a court must always be mindful that its decision will create a precedent which has the capacity to affect many other cases in the future.

. . . .

Introduction

When a dispute arises a lawyer may be consulted. Having identified the legal area raised by the facts the lawyer will seek to discover what law is relevant to the problem. If the problem is one largely governed by case law, such as contract and tort, then recourse should be had to the decisions of judges to be found in law reports. The lawyer will need to extract from relevant cases the principles or rules which will assist in resolving the problem. What a lawyer is seeking is the principle or rule upon which the **decision** in a case is based; this is called the *ratio decidendi* of the case. Within a system of **binding** precedent this is the binding part of a case.

> **bound by a case or decision:** *Lawyers may refer to being bound by a case or a decision. The context should make clear that the words are being used as synonyms for the binding part of the case, the ratio decidendi. As will later become clear, the reasons for the ratio, the decision, or the case in its entirety are not binding in terms of the doctrine of precedent.*

The basis of the doctrine of judicial precedent is that like cases should be decided alike. So if the facts of a case are materially the same as the facts of a previous case then the principle or rule used to decide the previous case should be used to decide the instant case. In this way certainty is promoted and justice is served.

In English law, the doctrine is one of binding precedent, which means that within limits the lower courts must apply a *ratio decidendi* of the higher courts. R. Cross and J. Harris in *Precedent in English Law* pithily sum up the operation of the doctrine of binding precedent in the following words:

> [e]very court is bound to follow any case decided by a court above it in the hierarchy, and appellate courts (other than the House of Lords) are bound by their previous decisions.

The doctrine of binding precedent ensures that the courts decide cases in an orderly way and allow case law to be developed within the limits inherent in the doctrine.

....

🔑 Key point

The doctrine of binding precedent seeks to ensure the law is certain and that it may be allowed to develop in an orderly way. The operation of a system of binding precedent depends upon three things: the availability of reliable records of decisions; the identification of rules of law from the decisions in cases; and where there are several courts in a legal system, a settled hierarchy of courts.

5.1 Judicial precedent and law reporting

The prerequisite for the operation of a doctrine of judicial precedent is an effective system of law reporting. When judges make decisions there must be a mechanism to discover the rules that emerge from the cases. Accuracy is at a premium. In the English legal system, law reporting falls into two distinct phases, before 1865, and 1865 and after. Before 1865, law reporting was done privately and in individual series of reports named after the law reporter, e.g. Adolphus and Ellis, Espinasse and Campbell. In consequence of this latter point, the reports were known as the 'nominate' reports. The reports are now to be found collected together in the English Reports or the Revised Reports. A major problem of the 'nominate' reports is that they are of variable quality; quality depending very much upon who was the reporter.

In 1865, the Incorporated Council of Law Reporting commenced publishing the most authoritative set of reports, the *Law Reports*. While not published by the state they are the nearest that English law has to an official set of reports. They are systematic and accurate. The system follows the organisation of the courts: Appeal Cases (AC) comprising decisions of the Supreme Court/House of Lords and the Privy Council; and Chancery Division (Ch), Queen's Bench Division (QB), and Family Division (Fam) comprise cases both decided at first instance and on appeal from that court to the Court of Appeal. The organisation of the series of *Law Reports* has varied from time to time, mirroring the organisation and changes in the organisation of the courts. The criteria for inclusion in the *Law Reports* are that a case: introduces a new principle or rule; an existing principle or rule is materially modified; a doubt in the law is settled; or a case is peculiarly instructive.

The accuracy of the *Law Reports* is ensured by the editorial process which includes reporting by a barrister and checking by the judge(s) involved in the decision.

The Incorporated Council of Law Reporting also publishes the *Weekly Law Reports* which provide, as the name suggests, a regular source of recently decided cases. Many of the cases reported in the *Weekly Law Reports* will ultimately be included in the *Law Reports*. While the *Law Reports* may be considered the most authoritative set of reports, other series of reports are published. Foremost amongst these are the *All England Law Reports* published by LexisNexis in a weekly series. The *Weekly Law Reports* and the *All England Law Reports* are general in scope and include coverage of cases on many areas of English law. Additionally, there are many specialist sets of reports dealing with cases on particular areas of law. Examples of these include, the *Building Law Reports*, *Industrial Relations Law Reports*, and *Housing Law Reports*.

In recent years, law reports have become available electronically over the Internet. Lexislibrary and Westlaw each provide a searchable database of case law. Some reports of cases are provided without cost; for example see the British and Irish Legal Institute's website, **www.baili.org/** which contains certain case reports from 1996 onwards.

5.2 **Nature of judge-made law**

Case law is a major source of law for which the judges are responsible. Before discussing the mechanics of the doctrine of precedent it is important to understand some basic points about the nature of judicial law-making. The first point to appreciate about the law made by judges is that judges only get the opportunity to make pronouncements on an area of law should a case be brought before the courts on that area. It is not uncommon for a problem in the law to lie unresolved for many years due to no case being brought before the courts on this point. Second, the courts are constrained by precedents created by previous cases; they must work within the existing law and subject to the rules of the doctrine of judicial precedent. Third, the courts are wary of the retrospective effect of case law. Fourth, case law is unlike law made by Parliament: Parliament may legislate on any subject area it chooses, may sweep away any laws it wishes, in whole or in part, and usually legislation only affects the future, it is not retrospective.

It is now clear that within these limits, the courts do make law.

At one time, judges adhered to the declaratory theory of the common law. This stated that there was no such thing as judge-made law. When the judges made decisions, they were merely declaring what the law was and had always been, as if the law mysteriously existed in the ether. This concealed two important points. First, judge-made law is retrospective; a statement of law in a later case applies to situations that may have already occurred. So, for example, if at the time an act takes place there is no clear law governing it but a later case then makes clear that the law does apply to such an act, then the law as clarified will retrospectively apply. This is objectionable as citizens have no way of knowing what the law is at the time of the act. The declaratory theory said the law had always been there and that the later judge merely declared what it was.

Second, it may be argued that unelected judges should not be making laws in a democratic society. Again the declaratory theory masked this.

The declaratory theory is now seen for what it is, a fiction, and this has been recognised by the courts. Lord Lloyd in *Kleinwort Benson Ltd v Lincoln City Council* [1999] 2 AC 349 said (at p.393):

> [n]obody now suggests that the common law is static. It is capable of adapting itself to new circumstances. Is it then capable of being changed? Or is it only capable of being developed? The common-sense answer is that the common law is capable of being changed, not only by legislation, but also by judicial decision. This is nowhere clearer than when a long-standing decision of the Court of Appeal is overruled. Indeed in a system such as ours, where the Court of Appeal is bound by its own previous decisions, the main justification for the existence of a second tier appeal is that it enables the House to redirect the law when it has taken a wrong turning.

While judges do make law they do so within limits. C. K. Allen, in *Law in the Making*, explained the limits to judicial law-making in the following terms, 'the creative power of the courts is limited by the existing legal material at their command. They find the material and shape it. The legislature may manufacture entirely new material.' One writer likened judge-made law to a tapestry: all that the judges may do is insert stitches here and there when enabled by litigation to do so, that is when a dispute raising the area of law is brought before the courts. The insertions are limited by the surrounding fabric and judges must ensure that they are consistent with the existing body of law. In this sense judges make partial and piecemeal changes to the law; this is not, however, to say that judges do not make significant changes to the law. Parliament, on the other hand, can remove and replace sections of the tapestry or undertake sweeping reforms of the law by wholly replacing the fabric.

While there is no formal doctrine of the separation of powers in the British constitution the constitutional role of judges is to administer the law and that of Parliament is to make laws. This generalisation, of course, needs to be qualified by the judges' role in relation to the common law. Traditionally, judges, in developing the common law, have adopted a low-key role in relation to law-making, avoiding as far as possible controversial issues of policy so as to avoid accusations of undemocratic activity. The development of the law of contract, tort, and, to a lesser extent, property do not generate great public interest. Judicial law-making is thus more active in areas not attracting attention. However, the process of interpretation of statutes and the role expected of judges under the Human Rights Act 1998 clearly does raise potentially controversial issues.

The judicial role in relation to law-making was explained in *Knuller v DPP* [1973] AC 435 by Lord Simon when he said (at p.490):

it has been suggested that the speeches in *Shaw v. Director of Public Prosecutions* indicated that the courts retain a residual power to create new offences. I do not think they did so. Certainly, it is my view that the courts have no more power to create new offences than they have to abolish those already established in the law; both tasks are for Parliament. What the courts can and should do (as was truly laid down in *Shaw v. Director of Public Prosecutions*) is to recognise the applicability of established offences to new circumstances to which they are relevant.

Lord Lowry, in *C (A Minor) v DPP* [1996] AC 1, set out some general guidance in relation to judicial law-making when he said (at p.28):

[I]t is hard, when discussing the propriety of judicial law-making, to reason conclusively from one situation to another...I believe, however, that one can find in the authorities some aids to navigation across an uncertainly charted sea. (1) If the solution is doubtful, the judges should beware of imposing their own remedy. (2) Caution should prevail if Parliament has rejected opportunities of clearing up a known difficulty or has legislated, while leaving the difficulty untouched. (3) Disputed matters of social policy are less suitable areas for judicial intervention than purely legal problems. (4) Fundamental legal doctrines should not be lightly set aside. (5) Judges should not make a change unless they can achieve finality and certainty.

In relation to judicial law-making consider *R v R (Rape: Marital Exemption)* [1992] 1 AC 599 where the House of Lords overruled what was believed to be the law that a wife by marriage had given irrevocable consent to having sexual intercourse with her husband and therefore a husband could not be convicted of raping his wife. Do you think the House of Lords was making law? If so, is this objectionable? For further discussion of this case see Giles, M. 'Judicial Law-Making in the Criminal Courts: The Case of Marital Rape' (1992) Crim LR 407.

Thinking point

It is clear that the judges do make law. The questions to be addressed are: first, in what circumstances does such law-making occur; and, second, to what extent should the judges be making law? Is there a distinction to be drawn between the types of issues suitable for law-making through the process of (i) the courts, (ii) the Law Commissions, and (iii) political debate? On what information do judges base decisions in cases and consider and contrast the process that may be employed in preparing and passing legislation through Parliament.

It should be noted that sometimes judges will indicate that the law has been developed by the courts as far as it can be and it is now for Parliament to develop or amend it.

See *R (on the application of Nicklinson) v Ministry of Justice* and *R (on the application of AM) v DPP* [2012] HRLR 32 for an example of a judicial refusal to change the common law.

5.3 *Ratio decidendi*

A decision of a previous court will only be binding if the facts of the instant case are sufficiently similar to the previous case so that the *ratio decidendi* or rule of law from the previous case should be applied. Note that it is not the actual decision that is binding; under the doctrine of judicial precedent the only binding part of the case is the rule of law. Not all statements made by a court in a case will be part of the *ratio decidendi*. The *ratio* must be the basis or a basis for the determination of a case. The nature of case law is that usually a judge or judges will not state explicitly what the *ratio decidendi* is of the case being decided. In addition, a judge may also state other principles of law which do not relate directly to the basis for the decision in the case. These statements are termed *obiter dicta*. So the *ratio decidendi* must be 'constructed' by the lawyer from the judgment or judgments of the court. For a law student this is an essential skill to learn.

> ### 🔑 Key point
>
> The *ratio decidendi* of a case is not the decision reached in a case but the rule of law upon which the decision is based.

Ratio decidendi also has to be distinguished from the term *res judicata*. The decision in a case is binding on the parties to that case and is said to be *res judicata*; subject to any appeal, the same parties cannot re-litigate the same points already judicially determined. The *ratio decidendi* of a case, in accordance with the rules of binding precedent, is binding on other courts.

5.3.1 **Identification of the *ratio decidendi* of a case**

The first problem is to identify what is meant by *ratio decidendi*. The courts have not made many statements upon the nature of *ratio decidendi* and have not set out guidance as to how to discover the *ratio decidendi*. Most discussion of this has come from academic commentators. R. Cross and J. Harris, in *Precedent in English Law* (p.72), describe the *ratio decidendi* in the following terms:

> any rule of law expressly or impliedly treated by the judge as a necessary step in reaching his conclusion, having regard to the line of reasoning adopted by him, or a necessary part of his direction to the jury.

W. Twining and D. Miers, in *How to Do Things with Rules*, helpfully explain that the search for the *ratio* of a case is not like a hunt for buried treasure, meaning that if you continue to dig, ultimately the *ratio decidendi* will be found. A characteristic of the *ratio decidendi* of a case is that it is not in a 'fixed verbal form'. By this is meant that the words of a *ratio* must be chosen and the rule 'constructed'. Also, our appreciation of what is the *ratio decidendi* of a case may be changed by later cases. Identifying the *ratio* involves choices and counsel before a court may argue about how narrow or wide a *ratio decidendi* of a case is upon which reliance is placed.

In essence, in determining the *ratio decidendi*, the search is for the rule upon which the decision in a case is based. Crucial in this search is identification of the legal issues raised before the court, in other words what has the court been asked to decide? This point cannot be overstated and explains why consideration of how a case is argued is so important.

🗎 Example

Invitations to tender are requests for bids in relation to work or goods. The person inviting tenders gives details of the work or goods required and interested parties submit tenders, including an indication of price. Early in a law of contract module the question will be asked: does an invitation to tender amount to a promise to be bound by the lowest or highest bid submitted, in other words, an offer, or does it merely constitute an invitation to treat, inviting the bidders to make offers? Only an offer may be accepted and form the basis of a contract.

In *Spencer v Harding* (1870) LR 5 CP 561, the defendants issued a circular which identified goods which they were 'instructed to offer to the wholesale trade for sale by tender...'. The claimants submitted the highest tender, but the defendants refused to sell to them. The court was asked to decide if the circular amounted to an offer (in which there was a promise to sell to the highest bidder) or was the circular merely an invitation to treat? If the circular was an offer then the claimants had accepted and a contract was formed; if the circular was an invitation to treat then the claimants by submitting a tender had made an offer which the defendants had not accepted and hence there was no contract.

It was decided that the circular was an invitation to treat and judgment was given for the defendants. This statement does not indicate what the rule was underpinning the decision. The *ratio decidendi* of the case was:

> in the absence of words expressing a promise to sell to the highest bidder, the circular was merely an invitation to treat. No intention to be bound was expressed in the circular.

This rule was a necessary part in reaching the decision; or was necessary to answer the question asked of the court.

The most useful analysis of how to find the *ratio decidendi* of a case was undertaken by Dr A. Goodhart in 1931 in his *Essays in Jurisprudence and the Common Law*. In his view, the *ratio decidendi* is to be found in the facts treated by the judge as material and the decision based upon such facts. This has been seen as a test for finding the *ratio* of a case. While Goodhart's test is undoubtedly useful, it is flawed. Cross and Harris identify a number of criticisms that may be made of Goodhart's approach. One major problem is that highlighted by Professor J. Stone who said that the search for material facts often involves an element of choice. Facts that are considered to be material may be defined at various 'levels of abstraction'.

For example, in *Pharmaceutical Society of Great Britain v Boots Cash Chemists* it was asked whether a display of drugs and poisons, specified in the Pharmacy and Poisons Act 1933, in a self-service store amounted to an offer. It was decided that such a display was merely an invitation to treat and not an offer. It could be argued that the *ratio* of the case was that a display of drugs and poisons in a self-service store is an invitation to treat. The *ratio decidendi* of the case would therefore only apply when dealing with a display of drugs and poisons. However, is there any good reason to so restrict the *ratio*; drugs and medicines fall within a wider class, that of 'goods', and should the *ratio* of the case not govern displays of goods? The language of the judges in the *Pharmaceutical Society* case clearly indicated that the *ratio decidendi* concerned the display of goods. Thus, it can be seen that the more general the term, in this case 'goods', the wider the *ratio*. Conversely, the more restricted the term, 'drugs', the narrower will be the rule. For illustrations of some of these points, see the case study on *Blackpool & Fylde Aero Club Ltd v Blackpool Borough Council* [1990] 1 WLR 1195 later.

5.3.2 Cases on the interpretation of statutes

The rules of precedent apply to judge-made law, but also apply to cases interpreting statutes. When the courts interpret a statute then such determination becomes a precedent as to the meaning of the words or phrases used in the statute.

> ### ≣ Example
>
> In criminal law, theft is defined by s.1 of the Theft Act 1968 as the dishonest appropriation of property belonging to another with the intention of permanently depriving the other of it. A question that caused the courts some difficulty was the role of consent in relation to appropriation, namely, could property be appropriated in circumstances where the property owner consents. In *Lawrence v Metropolitan Police Commissioner* [1972] AC 626, a non-English speaking Italian, Mr Occhi, on arriving in England for the first time, got into a taxi and showed to the defendant driver a piece of paper identifying an address to which he wished to be taken. The defendant said that the journey was long and would be expensive. Mr Occhi gave the defendant £1, but from his open wallet the defendant removed a further £6. In fact, the journey was much shorter and the correct fare was approximately 10s 6d (53p). The defendant was convicted of theft, but appealed on the main ground that Mr Occhi had consented to the taking of £6 and, in consequence, there was no appropriation. The House of Lords held that the consent of an owner to a defendant taking property is irrelevant in establishing appropriation.
>
> In a later case, *R v Morris* [1984] AC 320, the House of Lords once again considered this issue of consent and appropriation. The appeal involved two related cases concerning the switching of price labels on goods in supermarkets i.e. removing a price label from goods and replacing it with a label with a lower price. In both cases the defendant was convicted and their subsequent appeals dismissed. In the House of Lords, there was apparent approval of *Lawrence*.

However, Lord Roskill said in the context of the meaning to be given to appropriation in s.1(1) of the Theft Act 1968, appropriation involves 'not an act expressly or impliedly authorised by the owner but an act by way of adverse interference with or usurpation of those rights'. This indicated that the absence of consent was crucial to a finding that there was an appropriation.

In *DPP v Gomez* [1993] AC 442, the defendant, an assistant manager of a shop, was asked by an acquaintance to supply goods from the shop in return for two stolen building society cheques. The defendant agreed and convinced the store manager to authorise the supply of the goods in return for one cheque, telling him that the cheque was 'as good as cash.' Further goods were supplied in return for the second cheque. The defendant was convicted of theft. The House of Lords was asked to decide as a point of law of general public importance:

> When theft is alleged and that which is alleged to be stolen passes to the defendant with the consent of the owner, but that has been obtained by a false representation, has (a) an appropriation within the meaning of s.1(1) of the Theft Act 1968 taken place…

Lord Keith said:

> [t]he actual decision in Morris was correct, but it was erroneous, in addition to being unnecessary for the decision, to indicate that an act expressly or impliedly authorised by the owner could never amount to an appropriation.… Lawrence makes it clear that consent to or authorisation by the owner of the taking by the rogue is irrelevant. The taking amounted to an appropriation within the meaning of s.1(1) of the Act of 1968.

It can be seen that the words of Lord Roskill in *Morris*, stated earlier, were an *obiter dictum* as on the facts there was no consent on the part of the owner of the goods. Lord Keith clearly deals with this point when saying that aspect of Lord Roskill's opinion was 'unnecessary for the decision'. Additionally, Lord Roskill was wrong, the case of *Lawrence* clearly raised the issue of consent which had been the subject of an authoritative statement by the House of Lords and was to be preferred.

In relation to the interpretation of statutes by the courts some caution must be exercised as the same words or phrases may be used in a different context or in different statutes. In these circumstances, a later court is not strictly bound by a previous court's interpretation of a statute if on a true construction of a statute Parliament intends the words to carry a different meaning. This was seen in *Stevenson v Rogers* [1999] QB 1028, in which the meaning to be attributed to 'in the course of a business' in s.14(2) of the Sale of Goods Act 1979 fell to be decided by the Court of Appeal. In an earlier decision of the Court of Appeal in *R & B Customs Brokers v UDT* [1988] 1 WLR 321, the meaning of this phrase, in s.12 of the Unfair Contract Terms Act 1977, had been decided. In *Stevenson v Rogers*, the Court of Appeal gave a different interpretation to 'in the course of a business' and restricted the application of the *R & B Customs Brokers* case to the meaning of the phrase in the Unfair Contract Terms Act 1977. See chapter 4, 'The interpretation of statutes' – subhead 'Statutes *in pari materia*'.

In *Partridge v Crittenden* [1968] 1 WLR 1204 the court had to consider the meaning of the words 'offer for sale' in the Protection of Birds Act 1954 and in so doing referred to *Fisher v Bell* (see at 4.1). While *Fisher v Bell* dealt with a different statute the approach adopted to the problem in that case was used to determine the issue in *Partridge v Crittenden*, i.e. Parliament, in using the words 'offer for sale', must have intended them to be read in the light of the general law of contract.

5.3.3 **Looking to later cases in determining the *ratio decidendi* of a case**

A later case may indicate what is perceived to be the *ratio decidendi* of an earlier case. Additionally, a later case may clarify the *ratio decidendi* of an earlier case by, for example, reclassifying what are, or are not, the material facts.

Example

Formation of contract depends upon there being an offer and acceptance of the offer. The general rule of communication of acceptance is that there must be actual communication of the acceptance of the offer to the person making the offer. There is a well-known exception to this rule: when the parties contemplate that the post will be used as the means of sending an acceptance, then acceptance is complete as soon as the letter of acceptance is posted. As new methods of communication were developed the courts were asked to decide in a series of cases when the postal rule applied.

In *Entores Ltd v Miles Far East Corporation* [1955] 2 QB 327 the Court of Appeal decided that when an acceptance to an offer is sent by telex, an instantaneous means of communication, the general rule of actual communication applied, not the postal rule.

The issue of which rule applies to an acceptance by telex was raised again before the House of Lords in the *Brinkibon* case [1983] 2 AC 34. The House of Lords agreed with the Court of Appeal that the rule of actual communication applied, but qualified the rule. Lord Wilberforce said (at p.42),

> [s]ince 1955 the use of telex communication has been greatly expanded, and there are many variants on it. The senders and recipients may not be the principals to the contemplated contract. They may be servants or agents with limited authority. The message may not reach, or be intended to reach, the designated recipient immediately: messages may be sent out of office hours, or at night, with the intention, or upon the assumption, that they will be read at a later time. There may be some error or default at the recipient's end which prevents receipt at the time contemplated and believed in by the sender. The message may have been sent and/or received through machines operated by third persons. And many other variations may occur. No universal rule can cover all such cases: they must be resolved by reference to the intentions of the parties, by sound business practice and in some cases by a judgement where the risks should lie...

This statement indicates that the general rule as to communication of acceptance only applies where telexes are sent and received by principals during office hours (indeed, in both *Entores* and *Brinkibon*, such were the facts). Lord Wilberforce said that the rule was not 'universal' and another approach may have to be adopted where the facts are different. *Brinkibon* thus confirmed the *ratio* of *Entores*, approved it, and explained its limitations.

> ### Thinking point
>
> Is Lord Wilberforce's statement part of the *ratio decidendi* of *Brinkibon*? Remember that the *ratio decidendi* must be necessary for the decision in the case; if the principle of law does not affect the outcome of the case it will not be the *ratio*. See the discussion of *obiter dicta* later in the chapter.

5.3.4 **Finding the *ratio decidendi* – an illustration**

In *Blackpool & Fylde Aero Club Ltd v Blackpool Borough Council* [1990] 1 WLR 1195, Blackpool Borough Council, the defendants, owned Blackpool Airport and granted a concession for the operation of pleasure flights. Blackpool & Fylde Aero Club Ltd, the claimants, had successfully tendered for the concession in the past, and in 1983 were invited along with six other parties to tender for the concession again. In the invitation to tender, it was provided 'The Council do not bind themselves to accept all or any part of any tender. No tender which is received after the last date and time specified shall be admitted for consideration.' The claimants submitted their tender in the correct form and before the deadline to the town hall. However, a failure by town-hall staff to empty the postbox meant that the claimants' tender was not considered to have been received in time and, in consequence, disregarded. The claimants had submitted the highest tender, but another operator's tender secured the concession.

The claimants sued the defendants.

At first instance in the High Court the judge found in favour of the claimants, holding that there was a breach of contract and a breach of a tortious duty of care. The defendants appealed to the Court of Appeal on both grounds of the decision of the High Court.

The issues

The first part of an analysis of a case is a careful identification of the issues raised by the parties. What is the court being asked to decide upon? In this case, the claimants sought damages for: (a) a breach of contract; and (b) common law negligence in tort.

So the legal issues relate to:

(a) the formation of contract, specifically had there been an offer and acceptance; and

(b) was a tortious duty of care owed by the defendants to the claimants?

More specifically in relation to issue (a), the claimants alleged that the council promised 'that if a tender was returned to the town hall, Blackpool before noon on Thursday 17 March 1983 the same would be considered along with other tenders duly returned when the decision to grant the concession was made'.

Material facts

In order to sift the facts and identify the material facts it is necessary to understand the law surrounding the legal issues that have been raised. In relation to issue (a), the law relating to offer, invitation to treat, and how to classify an invitation to tender needs to be explored.

The arguments

It was argued on behalf of the defendants that the invitation to tender was an invitation to treat, that is, an invitation to receive offers. There is, therefore, no obligation upon the defendants to accept the highest or any tender. On that basis, no contract could be formed unless and until the defendants accepted the offer of the claimants. Reliance was placed upon *Spencer v Harding* (1870) LR 5 CP 561 and *Harris v Nickerson* (1873) LR 8 QB 286.

Counsel for the claimants accepted that normally an invitation to tender was merely an invitation to treat, but in certain situations that contractual obligations could arise either from the express words of the invitation or from the circumstances surrounding the invitation or, as here, both. Counsel continued that if in the circumstances of the case it was asked 'How would an ordinary person reading the tender document construe it?' the answer, counsel for the claimants submitted, must include that a timely conforming tender would be considered along with all other tenders so submitted.

The decision

The Court of Appeal decided that the judge at first instance was correct in relation to issue (a) and that the invitation to tender was indeed an offer, but in the limited sense that the defendants would consider a timely and conforming tender, which had been accepted by the claimants submitting such a tender.

The ratio decidendi

The decision reached does not explain the basis upon which the case was decided. The basis for the decision, the *ratio decidendi*, may be stated as follows:

> where a local authority invites a selected number of parties to submit tenders and where the invitation prescribes a clear, orderly and familiar tendering procedure, including draft contract conditions available for inspection and plainly not open to negotiation, a prescribed common form of tender, the supply of envelopes designed to preserve the

absolute anonymity of tenderers and clearly to identify the tender in question, and an absolute deadline, that evinces an implied intention of the parties that a conforming tender will be considered and to that extent an invitation to tender is an offer capable of being accepted.

Note that this formulation of the *ratio* raises a number of questions: does the *ratio* only apply to local authorities; is it necessary that the tenderers be selected; and what form of procedure must be involved? Until later cases consider and decide these points uncertainty attaches to the application of the rule.

What has happened to *Blackpool & Fylde Aero Club Ltd v Blackpool Borough Council* in later cases?

In *Harmon CFEM Facades (UK) Ltd v The Corporate Officer of the House of Commons* (1999) 67 Con LR 1, the rule in the *Blackpool* case was considered to apply to tendering processes initiated by public sector bodies, suggesting that the rule in the *Blackpool* case does not apply to invitations to tender coming from private sector bodies. It was held in *Natural World Products Ltd v ARC 21* [2007] NIQB 19 that the impact of the *Blackpool* case was to create a rule 'in English law that in the public sector where competitive tenderers are sought and responded to, the contract comes into existence whereby the prospective employer impliedly agrees to consider all tenderers fairly' per Deeny J at para.5.

Endnote

Given that the Court of Appeal in the *Blackpool* case had decided the case on the basis of issue (a), it then declined, as unnecessary, to give a definitive answer in relation to issue (b).

Further note that although the defendants in breach of contract had failed to consider the claimants' tender, the court did not give any indication as to the damages that the defendants would have to pay. This issue was never raised before the Court of Appeal.

> ## 🔒 Key point
>
> Later cases may give an indication of what is the *ratio decidendi* of a previous case. As a *ratio decidendi* is a rule not in a fixed verbal form a *ratio* may change due to a later court deciding that a fact is not material or reformulating how facts are classified.

5.3.5 More than one *ratio*

It is possible that a case may have more than one *ratio decidendi*. This may occur where a court is asked to decide several issues, in which case each answer to the question posed must be based upon a rule. So there may be two or more *rationes decidendi*, depending upon the number of issues before the court. However, in *Blackpool & Fylde*

Aero Club Ltd v Blackpool Borough Council, the Court of Appeal had two issues before it but decided the case on the contractual issue and declined to decide the issue of whether a tortious duty of care arose as it was unnecessary to do so. In that case there is one *ratio*. If there is more than one *ratio decidendi* then they are both binding.

5.3.6 **The *ratio decidendi* of appellate courts**

In ascertaining the *ratio decidendi* of appellate courts, the difficulty faced is that there will often be multiple judgments, usually three in the Court of Appeal and five in the Supreme Court/House of Lords, and not always agreement amongst the judges. Care needs to be taken in reading judgments as sometimes judges will agree as to the outcome of a case but disagree as to the how the decision is reached; this will impact on what is the *ratio decidendi* of a case. Hence, it is necessary to determine the basis for each judge's decision and then count heads to see if there is a majority in favour of a particular ground for the decision. If a majority can be identified then this will found the basis for the *ratio* of the case, while a minority view may be considered to be persuasive.

It would seem that if a judge dissents as to the decision to be reached in a case then the judgment is to be ignored as far as the doctrine of precedent is concerned; the dissenting judgment will not be part of the *ratio decidendi* of the case. However, such dissent may point to an alternative view of the law which may be accepted by a later, but higher court. For example, see the dissenting judgment of Denning LJ in *Candler v Crane Christmas & Co* [1951] 2 KB 164 which was approved in *Hedley Byrne & Co Ltd v Heller & Partners Ltd* [1964] AC 465, while the case itself was overruled.

5.4 *Obiter dicta*

In a case, other statements as to the law under consideration may be made by judges which do not affect the outcome of a case. Such statements are referred to as *obiter dicta* (note that a single pronouncement by a judge is termed an *obiter dictum*). *Obiter dicta* are not binding on later courts, they are merely persuasive. The reason why *obiter dicta* do not carry the same weight as the *ratio decidendi* of a case is that, as the statements are not the basis for the decision in a case, they may not have been the subject of full argument or judicial consideration.

As with identifying the *ratio decidendi* of a case, the identification of *obiter dicta* is not without difficulty. The key is to consider whether the statement of law is the, or a, basis for the decision of the court. If the statement of law is not such, then it will be an *obiter dictum*. A case from the law of contract, *Partridge v Crittenden* [1968] 1 WLR 1204, provides an illustration of this point. In that case the appellant was convicted of an offence, under s.6 of Protection of Wild Birds Act 1954, of offering for sale a live wild bird, 'other than a close-ringed specimen bred in captivity'. The appeal raised two questions: first, were magistrates right to decide that an indication that birds were for sale in an advert, was an offer for sale; and second, were they right to hold that a bird was not a close-ringed specimen bred in captivity if the ring was removable from the bird's leg? The High Court held that no offence was committed as the advert did not constitute an offer. The rule relating to this issue was the basis for the decision and would clearly form the *ratio decidendi* of the case. However, the court considered in some detail what was meant by 'a close-ringed specimen bred in captivity' and concluded that the magistrates were correct in their decision, i.e. as the ring could be removed it was not a close-ringed specimen. This statement was not the basis of the decision, it supported a conviction rather than an acquittal, and therefore is to be classified as an *obiter dictum*.

Note that the *obiter dicta* of the Supreme Court/House of Lords, while still persuasive, carry more weight than *dicta* of the lower courts.

⬛ Example

Many instances of *obiter dicta* occur when judges speculate what would have been the outcome had the facts of the case been different. For example, in *Spencer v Harding*, discussed previously, Willes J said: '*If the circular had gone on, "and we undertake to sell to the highest bidder", the reward cases would have applied, and there would have been a good contract in respect of the persons'* (emphasis added), meaning that the circular would have been an offer which would have been accepted by the highest bid of the claimants. As can be seen, the judge indicated what would have been the outcome of the case if the facts had been different. Note also that this is clearly not the *ratio decidendi* as it does not support the decision that the circular was an invitation to treat.

Another example of *obiter dicta* is seen in *Hedley Byrne v Heller* [1964] AC 465, where the House of Lords said that a duty in the tort of negligence could be owed for statements causing economic loss but held that no such duty was owed on the facts of the case as the bank making the statement had expressly disclaimed responsibility for the statement. The *ratio decidendi* was clearly that no duty arose, but more importantly *dicta* of the House of Lords indicated that such duty could be owed under English law. These statements formed the basis for the development of the tort of negligent misstatement, being followed and developed by the courts in later cases.

5.5 **Nature of *stare decisis***

The doctrine of precedent is one of binding precedent (alternatively termed the doctrine of *stare decisis*); the courts are compelled to follow a *ratio decidendi* of superior courts or in certain instances of courts of equal standing. Underlying the doctrine is a desire to promote certainty and to allow the law to develop in an orderly way. To this end there is a hierarchical courts system, which is indicated in Diagram 5.1, starting with the highest courts and descending to the lowest courts.

In the House of Lords, Lord Hailsham in *Cassell v Broome* [1972] AC 1027, (at p.1054), explained the precedent relationship amongst the courts in the following terms:

> …in the hierarchical system of courts which exists in this country, it is necessary for each lower tier, including the Court of Appeal, to accept loyally the decisions of the higher tiers. Where decisions manifestly conflict, the decision in *Young v Bristol Aeroplane Co Ltd* [1944] KB 718 offers guidance to each tier in matters affecting its own decisions. It does not entitle it to question considered decisions in the upper tiers with the same freedom. Even this House, since it has taken freedom to review its own decisions, will do so cautiously.

Lord Hailsham outlines some of the issues raised by the doctrine of precedent: a higher court binds lower courts; certain courts bind themselves; and is it permissible in any circumstances for a lower court to question a decision of a higher court?

5.5.1 The Court of Justice of the European Union

The decisions of the Court of Justice of the European Union are binding on all English courts in relation to community law. The Court of Justice is free to depart from its previous decisions, but this is a rare occurrence.

5.5.2 The Supreme Court/House of Lords

Domestically, the Supreme Court/House of Lords is the highest court in the UK. Decisions of the Supreme Court/House of Lords bind all the courts beneath it in the

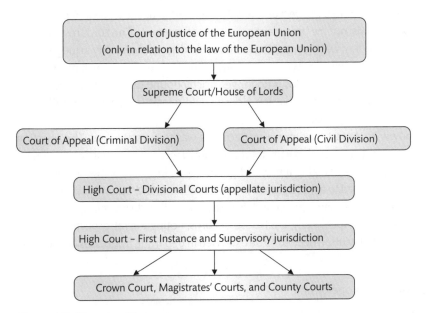

Diagram 5.1 Hierarchy of the courts

hierarchy of courts. References will, obviously, be made to the House of Lords in cases prior to 1 October 2009 and will be retained for the purposes of accuracy. In *Austin v Southwark London Borough Council* [2010] UKSC 28 it was made clear that the Practice Statement of 1966 was of application in the Supreme Court.

Until 1966, the House of Lords was bound by its own previous decisions, as established in *London Tramways Co. Ltd v London County Council* [1898] AC 375. In consequence, the development of areas of law was blocked, unless Parliament intervened to amend such law. This practice was altered by the Practice Statement (Judicial Precedent) [1966] 1 WLR 1234. A House of Lords of ten law lords agreed with the following statement delivered by Lord Gardiner LC:

> Their Lordships regard the use of precedent as an indispensable foundation upon which to decide what is the law and its application to individual cases. It provides at least some degree of certainty upon which individuals can rely in the conduct of their affairs, as well as a basis for orderly development of legal rules. Their Lordships nevertheless recognise that too rigid adherence to precedent may lead to injustice in a particular case and also unduly restrict the proper development of the law. They propose, therefore, to modify their present practice and, while treating former decisions of this House as normally binding, to depart from a previous decision when it appears right to do so.
>
> In this connection they will bear in mind the danger of disturbing retrospectively the basis on which contracts, settlements of property and fiscal arrangements have been entered into and also the especial need for certainty as to the criminal law.
>
> This announcement is not intended to affect the use of precedent elsewhere than in this House.

This statement is limited in effect as it is only intended to affect precedent practice in the House of Lords, not the precedent practice in other courts. The Lords restated that the role of precedent was essential to provide some degree of certainty in judge-made law and, in consequence, previous decisions of the House of Lords will normally be binding, but the House of Lords is no longer strictly bound by its own decisions. The Practice Statement indicated that the House could depart from a previous decision 'when it appears right to do so'.

See further on the retrospective nature of case law at 5.6.1.

The power to depart from previous decisions was thus established. The question arises, when is it right to depart from a previous decision? The Practice Statement gives some guidance as to this. It may be right to depart from a previous decision, first, where there is a need to avoid injustice in individual cases and, second, if the development of the common law is being unduly restricted. This is clearly guidance of a very general kind. More specifically, the House of Lords, noting the retrospective effect of case law, said that caution needed to be exercised in departing from cases concerning:

- contracts;
- settlement of property; and
- taxation.

> ### ⬛ Example
>
> If a solicitor advised a client on the creation of a contract relying on a precedent established by the Supreme Court/House of Lords and then in a subsequent decision of the Supreme Court the opinion was overruled the advice, although accurate when given, would need to redrawn. Any dispute relating to such a contract would be determined by reference to the later ruling. There was also seen to be an especial need to ensure certainty in the criminal law. Injustice could be caused if reliance had been placed upon a decision of the Supreme Court/ House of Lords and it was then decided by a later Supreme Court that the previous decision did not correctly state the law. The retrospective nature of the later decision may mean, for example, that an activity previously thought to be lawful has become criminal.

Since 1966, the House of Lords had rarely exercised its power to overrule one of its previous decisions. Examples of such exercise of the Practice Statement power are seen in: *R v Secretary of State for the Home Department, ex parte Khawaja* [1984] AC 74; *R v Shivpuri* [1987] AC 1; *Murphy v Brentwood District Council* [1991] 1 AC 398; and *R v G and Another* [2004] 1 AC 1034. In *Jones v Secretary of State for Social Services* [1972] AC 944, Lord Reid said that certainty in the law required that the Practice Statement power should be 'used sparingly'. He drew a distinction between cases where an old decision of the House of Lords raised a broad issue which might be ready for reconsideration and cases which concerned the construction of statutes or other documents. In relation to the latter category of cases, Lord Reid said that reconsideration should be rare, as answers to questions of construction may depend much upon approach, e.g. whether a literal or mischief approach to interpretation is adopted, and it is not possible to say which construction is right or wrong. In consequence, *Re Dowling* [1967] 1 AC 725 a previous decision of the House of Lords, which concerned the construction of a statute and did not involve a 'broad issue of justice or public policy...nor...any question of legal principle' was considered not to be a proper case from which to depart under the Practice Statement.

There is a need for finality and certainty in the law so the Supreme Court/House of Lords is reluctant to depart from its earlier decisions and merely because a previous decision is considered to be wrong will not be enough in itself to permit its overruling. If the approach were otherwise, future litigants might seek to argue that a decision is wrong in the hope that a differently constituted Supreme Court/House of Lords might find in their favour. In *Doherty v Birmingham City Council* [2009] AC 367 the House of Lords was invited to overrule its recent reasoning in *Kay and Others v Lambeth London Borough Council* [2006] 2 AC 465. This the House of Lords refused to do so. Lord Hope said that the power to overrule a recent decision should not be exercised unless there was a good reason for doing so.

The following cases indicate and illustrate the factors that the Supreme Court/ House of Lords takes into account in determining whether or not to depart from a previous decision. In *Horton v Sadler* [2007] 1 AC 307 the House of Lords departed from their previous decision in *Walkley v Precision Forgings Ltd* [1979] 1 WLR 606. The latter case had constrained the exercise of a discretion under s.33 of the Limitation Act 1980 to extend the time limit of three years in personal injuries claims. The House of Lords in departing from *Walkley* reasoned that it would not impact upon contracts, settlements of property, or fiscal arrangements as it was not a rule which had been relied upon in entering upon such dealings. The criminal law would be unaffected and there would be no detriment to public administration. Lord Bingham then gave three reasons for departing from *Walkley*: that it unfairly deprived claimants of a right Parliament intended them to have; that it had driven the Court of Appeal to draw distinctions which, while correct, were so fine as to reflect no credit on the law in this area; and that it subverted the clear intention of Parliament. Lord Brown added that *Walkley* was not a case where there were two tenable interpretations of a statute; there was only one interpretation which *Walkley* had failed to give to the statute. The decision was one that was plainly wrong. In the circumstances justice and certainty would be promoted by departing from it.

In *A v Hoare* [2008] UKHL 6, the House of Lords departed from *Stubbings v Webb* [1993] AC 498 as the decision was perceived to be unjust, in part due to other changes in the law, and gave rise to anomalies. The House of Lords argued that this could lead to uncertainty in the law as lower courts may be willing to distinguish on inadequate grounds and therefore in order to promote certainty it was right to depart from *Stubbings v Webb*.

Another case concerning the construction of a statute and departure from a previous precedent is *R v Shivpuri* [1987] AC 1. The appellant had carried a package from India which he believed to contain heroin or cannabis, but which actually contained harmless vegetable matter. He was convicted of attempting to be knowingly concerned in dealing with and harbouring a controlled drug, namely heroin, the importation of which was prohibited, contrary to s.1(1) of the Criminal Attempts Act 1981 and s.170(1)(b) of the Customs and Excise Management Act 1979. The House of Lords was asked:

> does a person commit an offence under s.1 of the Criminal Attempts Act 1981 where, if the facts were as that person believed them to be, the full offence would have been committed by him, but where on the true facts the offence which that person set out to commit was in law impossible?

On the facts the appellant had a guilty mind but was performing a lawful act; nonetheless their Lordships thought the answer to the question posed was yes and that an offence had been committed. However, this answer was inconsistent with that given in *Anderton v Ryan* [1985] AC 560, which had been decided by the House of Lords only in the previous year.

The House of Lords departed from its decision in *Anderton v Ryan* on the basis that the decision was wrong. Lord Bridge, although recognising the need for certainty in criminal law, felt that it was permissible to depart from the decision having regard to the following considerations:

- the fact that *Anderton v Ryan* was a recent decision was not influential. It was better to correct an error sooner rather than later;

- in the nature of the case no issue of reliance could arise which would mean that an innocent person would now be found to have committed a criminal offence;

- failure to depart from *Anderton v Ryan* would mean that the Criminal Attempts Act 1981 left the law unchanged following the decision in *R v Smith (Roger)* [1975] AC 476.

The case of *Austin v Southwark London Borough Council* [2010] UKSC 28 concerned the interpretation of s.82(2) of the Housing Act 1985. The Court of Appeal had stated the meaning of the section in *Thompson v Elmbridge Borough Council* [1987] 1 WLR 1425 which in turn had been followed by a number of later cases in the Court of Appeal. The House of Lords considered the interpretation in *Knowsley Housing Trust v White (Secretary of State for Communities and Local Government intervening)* [2009] AC 636 but refrained from overruling the decision in *Thompson*. In *Austin* it was argued that *Knowsley*, and therefore *Thompson*, should be departed from as the interpretation of s.82(2) was incorrect. The Supreme Court thought the interpretation was possibly wrong, but refused to depart from its previous decision in *Knowsley*. The reasoning for this was that as *Thompson* had been acted upon in 'tens of thousands of cases' the retrospective effect of such a departure would be incalculable. Also Parliament had passed legislation, the Housing and Regeneration Act 2008, dealing with the problem as to the future, so stating that *Thompson* was no longer good law would undermine the legislation and run counter to the intention of Parliament. The Supreme Court refused to depart from its previous decision.

Finally, in *Murphy v Brentwood District Council* [1991] 1 AC 398 the House of Lords had to consider the development of negligence in the law of tort. The previous decision in *Anns v Merton London Borough Council* [1978] AC 728 was considered not to have proceeded on any basis of principle at all and in the words of Lord Keith 'constituted a remarkable example of judicial legislation'. The effect of the decision in *Anns* was to cause great uncertainty in the law of negligence and was not one that citizens or local authorities would rely upon to a significant extent in conducting their affairs. Lord Keith in *Murphy* continued that the decision in *Anns* was not supported by 'any coherent and logically based doctrine behind it' and its effect was to put the law of negligence into a state of confusion. In consequence, the decision in *Anns* was considered to be wrong and was departed from.

It is important to discern from these cases the basis upon which the Supreme Court/House of Lords may, or may not, be willing to depart from one of its previous decisions. Cross and Harris, in *Precedent in English Law*, argue that the deliberations of their Lordships reveal factors that the House of Lords will consider in deciding whether to exercise its power. First, the Lords must be persuaded that the change will improve the law; *Miliangos v George Frank (Textiles) Ltd* [1976] AC 443. Second, something of significance must have been overlooked in arriving at the earlier decision or there has been a 'material change in circumstances'; see *R v Shivpuri*. Third, given the retrospective nature of overruling, consideration will be given to any reliance placed upon the House of Lords' precedent; *R v Shivpuri* and *Murphy v Brentwood DC*. Fourth, if Parliament has passed legislation which assumes the existence of a decision of the House of Lords, it is unlikely that such a decision will be overruled; see *British Railways Board v Herrington* [1972] AC 877. Fifth, and finally (at p.142):

> there is some support for the view that the House should not overrule an earlier decision, even if thought to be mistaken, where the issue is moot – that is where, on the facts of the instant case, it would make no difference to the outcome whether the impugned ruling were part of the law or not.

See *The Antclizo* [1988] 1 WLR 603.

It should be noted that the case of *R v Smith (Morgan)* [2001] 1 AC 146 was departed from in very unusual circumstances. See *Attorney General for Jersey v Holley* [2005] 2 AC 580, which is discussed later.

If a Supreme Court/House of Lords, decision is inconsistent with a later decision of the European Court of Human Rights should a lower court follow the decision of the Supreme Court/House of Lords or that of the European Court of Human Rights? See the House of Lords' decision in *Kay and Others v Lambeth London Borough Council* [2006] 2 AC 465 discussed later.

5.5.3 Court of Appeal

The Court of Appeal is split into two divisions: the Court of Appeal (Civil Division) and the Court of Appeal (Criminal Division). As the titles of the courts suggest, there is a division in workload between civil appeals and criminal appeals. The rules of precedent that operate in each division, while largely the same, differ in some important respects and need to be carefully noted.

Court of Appeal (Civil Division)

The Court of Appeal (Civil Division) is bound by the decisions of the Court of Justice of the European Union and the Supreme Court/House of Lords. It binds all the courts beneath it in the hierarchy of courts. Is the Court of Appeal (Civil Division) bound by its previous decisions? The answer is normally yes, subject to certain limited exceptions.

The precedent practice operating in the Court of Appeal (Civil Division) was established in *Young v Bristol Aeroplane Co Ltd* [1944] KB 718. Lord Greene MR said that the

Court of Appeal was bound by its own previous decisions and by decisions of courts of equal jurisdiction subject to the following exceptions:

(a) where the Court of Appeal is faced by two conflicting decisions of its own the present court must choose which decision to follow;

(b) the Court of Appeal must refuse to follow a decision of its own which conflicts with a Supreme Court/House of Lords decision, even though the decision of the Court of Appeal has not been expressly overruled; and

(c) if a previous decision of the Court of Appeal is considered to have been given *per incuriam* then the present Court of Appeal is not bound to follow it.

Each of these exceptions will now be considered in a little more detail.

(a) Conflicting decisions of the Court of Appeal

Such a difficulty should not arise as a later Court of Appeal is bound to follow previous binding decisions of the court. But, of course, an inconsistency in the case law might not be evident to a deciding court, it is only later that such conflict in the authorities becomes apparent.

A problem of this nature became evident in *Farley v Skinner* [2000] PNLR 441 which concerned a claim for damages for disappointment arising from a breach of contract. The rule which emerged from *Watts v Morrow* [1991] 1 WLR 1421 was that damages were payable for disappointment if the object of the entire contract was one to give pleasure, relaxation, or peace of mind and this had not been achieved. *Watts v Morrow* was followed in *Knott v Bolton* (1995) 11 Const LJ 375. However, two Court of Appeal decisions, *Jackson v Chrysler Acceptances Ltd* [1978] RTR 474 and *Branchett v Beaney* [1992] 3 All ER 910, suggested that disappointment damages were recoverable where an object or one of the objects of a contract (as opposed to being the object of the entire contract) was to provide enjoyment or peace of mind. Neither of these cases was cited in *Knott v Bolton*. In consequence, the Court of Appeal (Civil Division) in *Farley v Skinner* was faced with inconsistent authority. The court by a majority of 2 to 1 decided the case by following *Watts v Morrow*. The decision of the Court of Appeal in *Farley v Skinner* was reversed by the House of Lords. See 5.6.2 'Reversing'.

Another example of conflicting decisions was seen in *Tiverton Estates v Wearwell* [1975] Ch 146. The Court of Appeal in this case said that the court's decisions in *Griffiths v Young* [1970] Ch 675 and *Law v Jones* [1974] Ch 112 were in conflict with previous decisions of the Court of Appeal in *Buxton v Rust* (1872) LR 7 Exch 1 and *Thirkell v Cambi* [1919] 2 KB 590. The Court of Appeal decided that *Law v Jones* was wrongly decided and so declined to follow it and *Griffiths v Young*.

It was stated in *Patel v Secretary of State for the Home Department* [2012] EWCA Civ 741, relying on *Minister of Pensions v Higham* [1948] 2 KB 153 (the case related to first instance decisions), that where the Court of Appeal must choose between conflicting authorities, the general rule is that the later decision is to be preferred, if the later case has fully considered the earlier decision (Lord Neuberger MR at para.59).

(b) A Court of Appeal decision, though not expressly overruled, cannot stand with a decision of the Supreme Court/House of Lords

It would seem that Lord Greene had in mind the situation where a Court of Appeal decision is inconsistent with a *subsequent* decision of the Supreme Court/House of Lords. (See Cross and Harris, (p.147).) Obviously a Court of Appeal decision should not conflict with a *prior* decision of the Supreme Court/House of Lords. In *Iqbal v Whipps Cross University NHS Trust* [2007] EWCA Civ 1190, this exception was clarified. The Court of Appeal was faced with the problem of one of its own previous decisions being inconsistent with an *earlier* decision of the House of Lords. It was held that the exception does not apply where the inconsistency of a decision of the Court of Appeal is with a *previous* House of Lords decision, unless the Court of Appeal decision is given *per incuriam*. If an earlier Court of Appeal wrongly distinguishes or misinterprets a Supreme Court/House of Lords decision a later Court of Appeal is still bound by the decision of the previous Court of Appeal, as disagreement with the reasoning of the earlier court is an insufficient ground for not following the precedent. The correct approach is for the 'error' to be considered by the Supreme Court/House of Lords.

A situation may arise where the relationship of a Court of Appeal decision and that of the Supreme Court/House of Lords is not fully appreciated at the time of judgment. An example of this was seen in *Williams v Roffey Brothers & Nicholls (Contractors) Ltd* [1991] 1 QB 1. In this case the Court of Appeal decided that performance, by A, of an existing contractual duty owed to the other contracting party, B, could be consideration for a further promise from B, if B as a result of such performance obtained a practical benefit or the obviation of a disbenefit. Previously, the House of Lords in *Foakes v Beer* (1884) 9 App Cas 605 had approved the rule that part-payment of a debt does not release the debtor from the full debt, even if the creditor had agreed that such payment would, as no consideration is provided. It was argued before the Court of Appeal in *Re Selectmove Ltd* [1995] 1 WLR 474 that if a practical benefit was obtained by a creditor consequent upon part-payment of a debt this could be consideration for the discharge of the remaining debt.

This, of course, conflicts with the House of Lords decision in *Foakes v Beer*. In *Re Selectmove Ltd*, Peter Gibson LJ said that were the principle in *Williams v Roffey Bros & Nicholls (Contractors) Ltd* to be extended to cover situations of part-payment of a debt, then *Foakes v Beer* would be left without an application; indeed, *Foakes v Beer* was not even mentioned by the Court of Appeal in *Williams v Roffey Bros & Nicholls (Contractors) Ltd*. His Lordship continued that it was impossible consistently with the doctrine of precedent for the principle in *Williams v Roffey Bros & Nicholls (Contractors) Ltd* to be extended to situations governed by *Foakes v Beer*.

It can be seen that an extension of the *Williams v Roffey* principle would in effect 'overrule' *Foakes v Beer*, a power that the Court of Appeal does not possess under the doctrine of precedent. Thus, there is a conflict of principle in the law relating to consideration which will have to be resolved most likely by the Supreme Court, or, as Peter Gibson LJ suggested more appropriately, by Parliament after consideration by the Law Commission. The role of the doctrine of precedent is clearly seen as determining the issue before the court and the argument about principle and consistency in the law relating to consideration is curtailed. The Court of Appeal in *Re Selectmove Ltd* thus avoided an otherwise binding precedent of its own.

In *R v Wood* [2008] EWCA Crim 1305 the Court of Appeal effectively overruled the earlier Court of Appeal judgment in *R v Tandy* [1989] 1 WLR 350 on the issue whether alcoholism amounted to an 'abnormality of mind' for the purposes of the diminished responsibility defence. The court in *Wood* stated that *R v Dietschmann* [2003] UKHL 10, [2003] 1 AC 1209, a decision of the House of Lords, 'requires a re-assessment of the way in which *Tandy* is applied'.

(c) *Per incuriam*

In *Morelle v Wakeling* [1955] 2 QB 379, Sir Raymond Evershed MR explained *per incuriam* in the following terms:

> [a]s a general rule the only cases in which decisions should be held to have been given *per incuriam* are those of decisions given in ignorance or forgetfulness of some inconsistent statutory provision or of some authority binding on the court concerned: so that in such cases some part of the decision or some step in the reasoning on which it is based is found, on that account, to be demonstrably wrong. This definition is not necessarily exhaustive, but cases not strictly within it which can properly be held to have been decided *per incuriam* must, in our judgment, consistently with the stare decisis rule which is an essential feature of our law, be, in the language of Lord Greene MR, of the rarest occurrence.

Sir John Donaldson MR in *Duke v Reliance Systems Ltd* [1988] QB 108 added that had the court had the missing material before it 'it must have reached a contrary decision'. So the ignorance of an inconsistent statutory provision or a binding precedent must have an effect upon the decision in a case to make it one given *per incuriam*.

In *R (on the application of W) v Lambeth LBC* [2002] 2 ALL ER 901, the Court of Appeal (Civil Division) held that its previous decision in *R (on the application of A) v Lambeth LBC* [2001] EWCA Civ 1624 had been given *per incuriam*. Brooke LJ said that had the Court of Appeal in *A* been directed to s.122 of the Immigration and Asylum Act 1999 and s.17A of the Children Act 1989, and had appreciated that the housing allocation arrangements in 1989 were not as detailed and comprehensive as they became subsequently, it must have decided *R (on the application of A) v Lambeth LBC* differently.

In *Williams v Fawcett* [1986] QB 604, Sir John Donaldson MR emphasised that the concept of *per incuriam* did not merely apply in instances of ignorance or forgetfulness of an inconsistent statutory provision or binding precedent but also encompassed a 'manifest slip or error'. However, as already seen, such instances must be 'of the rarest occurrence'. Sir John Donaldson MR, in deciding that previous decisions of the Court of Appeal had been given *per incuriam*, said that the situation before him was 'exceptional'. The reasons for so deciding were: the growth of the error in the law could be clearly detected; the cases all concerned the liberty of the subject; and an appeal to the House of Lords, where the error could be corrected, was unlikely.

Further guidance as to what might be considered 'exceptional' was given by Lord Donaldson in *Rickards v Rickards* [1990] Fam 194. His Lordship said that a previous decision of the Court of Appeal could be treated as *per incuriam* where it concerned procedural rules (rather than substantive rules), in error it had been denied that the court had jurisdiction, and where an appeal to the House of Lords to correct the error was unlikely.

In *Boys v Chaplin* [1968] 2 QB 1, it was said that a decision by a two-judge court on an interlocutory matter was not binding on the Court of Appeal. The continuing validity of the basis for this exception has been doubted; see *Langley v North West Water* [1991] 1 WLR 697 and *Cave v Robinson, Jarvis and Rolf (a firm)* [2002] 1 WLR 581.

It was also said in *Young v Bristol Aeroplane Co Ltd* that a full court, consisting of six or nine judges has no greater power than a usual court consisting of three judges. Also, when the Court of Appeal sits with two judges, the decision has the same authority as a three-judge court, see *Langley v North West Water* and T. Prime and G. Scanlan, 'Stare decisis and the Court of Appeal; judicial confusion and judicial reform'? (2004) 23 CJQ 212.

Thinking point

Lord Denning during the 1970s waged a campaign to free the Court of Appeal (Civil Division) from the bonds of precedent, but was ultimately unsuccessful. See *Davis v Johnson* [1979] AC 264; compare Lord Denning's judgment in the Court of Appeal with the opinions of Lords Diplock and Salmon in the House of Lords. Why is the Court of Appeal bound by its previous decisions, whereas the House of Lords is not strictly bound by its own decisions?

The Court of Appeal is generally an intermediate court of appeal not a final court of appeal, unlike the Supreme Court. Lord Diplock in *Davis v Johnson* said (at p.326), 'In an appellate court of last resort a balance must be struck between the need on the one side for the legal certainty resulting from the binding effect of previous decisions, and, on the other side the avoidance of undue restriction on the proper development of the law'. The 'proper development of the law' may safely be left to the 'court of last resort', in other words, an appeal to the Supreme Court; while the need for legal certainty would be undermined if the Court of Appeal was not bound by its previous decisions. Indeed the danger to legal certainty would be multiplied by the Court of Appeal's practice of sitting in divisions of three judges.

Another exception to the operation of the doctrine of precedent in the Court of Appeal was considered by the House of Lords in *R (on the application of RJM) v Secretary of*

State for Work and Pensions [2009] AC 311. The issue arose of whether a previous decision of the Court of Appeal must be treated by a later Court of Appeal as binding, where the previous decision is inconsistent with a subsequent decision of the European Court of Human Rights. Lord Neuberger reaffirmed that the Court of Appeal should follow a decision of the House of Lords even if the decision of the House of Lords may be, or is, inconsistent with a subsequent decision of the European Court of Human Rights (save for wholly exceptional circumstances; see *Kay and others v Lambeth London Borough Council* [2006] 2 AC 465, para.45). However, his Lordship said that the situation is different when the Court of Appeal is considering the binding nature of its own previous decisions. While normally binding, Court of Appeal decisions may be departed from in certain situations, as stated in *Young v Bristol Aeroplane Co Ltd* [1944] KB 718, 729–30, but in the light of the Human Rights Act 1998 and s.2(1)(a) the exceptions in *Young* may be augmented. Lord Neuberger (at para.66) concluded that:

> the law in areas such as that of precedent should be free to develop, albeit in a principled and cautious fashion, to take into account…changes. Accordingly, I would hold that, where it concludes that one of its previous decisions is inconsistent with a subsequent decision of the ECtHR, the Court of Appeal should be free (but not obliged) to depart from that decision.

There are two points to note in this quotation. First, the 'changes' mentioned refer to the fact that when *Young* was decided the decisions of international courts, in this instance the European Court of Human Rights, did not have a direct impact within the English legal system, unlike the impact of the decisions now following the Human Rights Act 1998. Second, in order for the common law to develop in an orderly way it is important that the courts do not depart too freely from precedents. Lord Neuberger emphasised the need for caution when departing from otherwise binding precedent. It may be asked whether the precedent practice outlined by Lord Neuberger will also apply to Divisional Courts in the High Court as the precedent practice there is that the courts are bound by their own previous decisions subject to the exceptions in *Young*.

Court of Appeal (Criminal Division)

The Court of Appeal (Criminal Division) is bound by the decisions of the Supreme Court/House of Lords and binds all the courts beneath it. The rule in *Young v Bristol Aeroplane Co Ltd* also applies to the Criminal Division. A further exception was established by the Court of Criminal Appeal in *R v Taylor* [1950] 2 KB 368. In this case, Lord Goddard CJ said:

> [t]he Court of Appeal in civil matters usually considers itself bound by its own decisions or by decisions of a court of co-ordinate jurisdiction. For instance, it considers itself bound by its own decisions and by those of the Exchequer Chamber…In civil matters this is essential in order to preserve the rule of stare decisis. This court, however, has to deal with questions involving the liberty of the subject, and if it finds, on

reconsideration, that, in the opinion of a full court assembled for that purpose, the law has been either misapplied or misunderstood in a decision which it has previously given, and that, on the strength of that decision, an accused person has been sentenced and imprisoned it is the bounden duty of the court to reconsider the earlier decision with a view to seeing whether that person had been properly convicted. The exceptions which apply in civil cases ought not to be the only ones applied in such a case as the present, and in this particular instance the full court of seven judges is unanimously of opinion that the decision in *Rex v. Treanor*, 27 Cr.App.R. 35 was wrong...

The reference to the liberty of the subject justified a different approach to *stare decisis* in the Court of Criminal Appeal. It is argued that in criminal cases, justice is more important than certainty. Note also that the exception is exercisable by a full court (cf. the Court of Appeal (Civil Division)). In *R v Gould* [1968] 2 QB 65, this approach was approved as applying to the successor to the Court of Criminal Appeal, the Court of Appeal (Criminal Division).

An example of an application of this exception is to be found in *R v Simpson* [2004] QB 118, where the Court of Appeal (Criminal Division) concluded that the decision in *R v Palmer* [2002] EWCA Crim 2202 was wrong as the law had been misunderstood and misapplied.

This exception to *stare decisis* and the *per incuriam* doctrine were considered in *R v Rowe* [2007] QB 975. In this case, the Court of Appeal (Criminal Division) consisting of five judges, after considering *Simpson*, concluded that *R v M* [2007] EWCA Crim 298, a previous Court of Appeal (Criminal Division) decision, was wrongly decided as it was based upon 'wrong assumptions and false analysis'. However, the reason why the Court of Appeal (Criminal Division) refused to follow the decision in *R v M* was that it had been given, said Lord Phillips, 'in circumstances that were truly "per incuriam" '. *R v M* was not followed because the reasoning of the previous court:

- had not had regard to relevant authority and as a result arrived at false assumptions;
- had not followed the written submissions of the appellant with the consequence that the respondent's written submissions had not dealt with the points upon which the court based its reasoning; and
- the judgment was effectively extempore, being delivered the next day without time for research or reflection.

In *R v Varma (Aloke) and Others* [2011] QB 398 the Court of Appeal (Criminal Division) refused to overrule its previous decision in *R v Clarke* [2010] 1 WLR 223 after it had been argued by the Crown that the decision in *R v Clarke* was given *per incuriam*. While noting that *R v Simpson* allowed a five-judge court discretion, exercisable circumspectly, to escape a binding decision when it is wrong, the discretion in *Simpson* does have limits. Lord Judge CJ said (at p.411):

what Simpson does not establish, however, is that a five-judge constitution is entitled to disregard or deprive the only previous decision of the three-judge constitution of the court of its authority on a distinct and clearly identified point of law, reached after full argument and close analysis of the relevant legislative provisions. This principle applies with particular emphasis when the consequences of doing so would be to the disadvantage of the defendant.

The Court of Appeal held that the decision in *Clarke* was based on full relevant information; there was no possibility of conflict amongst relevant authorities; earlier decisions had not been misunderstood; the court had given a reserved judgment considered in meticulous detail; and, in consequence, it was not open to a five-judge court to hold that *Clarke* was wrongly decided. (Note that *R v Varma (Aloke)* was appealed to the Supreme Court [2012] UKSC 42 where *R v Clarke* was overruled.)

Should a Court of Appeal be faced with conflicting Supreme Court/House of Lords and Privy Council (see at 5.5.8) decisions the rules of precedent would seem to dictate that the Supreme Court/House of Lords decision, rather than that of the Privy Council, must be followed. However, in *R v James (Leslie)* [2006] QB 588, the Court of Appeal (Criminal Division) indicated that exceptionally the Court of Appeal may follow the decision of the Privy Council not that of the House of Lords.

In *Smith (Morgan)* [2001] 1 AC 146, the House of Lords by a majority held that the test of provocation as a partial defence to murder was that all the personal characteristics of a defendant were to be considered in determining whether a reasonable person in the defendant's position would have lost self-control. In *Attorney General for Jersey v Holley* [2005] 2 AC 580, the Privy Council (consisting of nine Lords of Appeal in Ordinary, 75 per cent of the judges in the House of Lords) by a majority of 6 to 3 held that under the test of provocation, loss of self-control was to be judged by reference to an objective standard of a person having and exercising ordinary powers of self-control. Lord Nicholls, delivering the judgment on behalf of the majority, said, '[t]his appeal, being heard by an enlarged board of nine members, is concerned to resolve this conflict and clarify definitively the present state of English law, and hence Jersey law, on this important subject.'

In *R v James (Leslie)* [2006] QB 588 the Court of Appeal (Criminal Division), sitting as a court of five judges, noted that the majority of the Privy Council had expressly stated that *Holley* was to 'clarify definitively' English law in relation to the defence of provocation, with which view the dissenting minority concurred, and that the deciding law lords in *Holley* largely still sat in the House of Lords and, in consequence, the Court of Appeal should follow *Holley* and not *Smith (Morgan)*. Strictly speaking, *Smith (Morgan)* has not been overruled, but given the highly unusual circumstances it would seem likely that the courts will follow *James* until the Supreme Court confirms that *Smith (Morgan)* no longer represents the law. It should be noted that the defendant in *James* sought leave to appeal to the House of Lords but this was refused by the Appeal Committee of the House of Lords. Given the circumstances outlined earlier, it may be readily seen that this is a very limited exception to the rules of the doctrine of precedent.

In *Sinclair Investments (UK) Ltd v Versailles Trade Finance Ltd (in administrative receivership) and others* [2011] 3 WLR 1153, the Court of Appeal had to consider whether to follow a Privy Council decision, *Attorney General of Hong Kong* [1994] 1 AC 324, in preference to previous decisions of its own, *Metropolitan Bank v Heiron* (1880) 5 Ex D 319 and *Lister & Co v Stubbs* 45 Ch D 1.

The Court of Appeal decided that it should follow its own previous decisions unless, in the words of Lord Neuberger, 'there are domestic authorities which show that the decisions of this court were per incuriam or at least of doubtful reliability'. The general position is that the Court of Appeal, where faced by a conflicting Privy Council decision, should follow its own precedents and leave it to the Supreme Court to overrrule the precedent if appropriate.

5.5.4 High Court - Divisional Courts at first instance

It is important to identify the jurisdiction being exercised by the Divisional Courts of the High Court. Divisional Courts may exercise appellate jurisdiction and supervisory jurisdiction.

Appellate jurisdiction

A Divisional Court in civil cases is bound by the Supreme Court/House of Lords and the Court of Appeal. It is bound by its previous decisions, subject to the exceptions in *Young v Bristol Aeroplane Co Ltd*. This was established in *Huddersfield Police Authority v Watson* [1947] KB 842.

A Divisional Court in criminal cases is bound by the Supreme Court/House of Lords and the Court of Appeal. It is bound by its previous decisions, subject to the exceptions in *Young v Bristol Aeroplane Co Ltd*. A further exception was established in *R v Manchester Coroner, ex parte Tal* [1985] QB 67. In the latter case, Robert Goff LJ said that in criminal cases, there was no material distinction between the exercise of appellate jurisdiction by a Divisional Court from decisions of magistrates by way of case stated and the exercise of appellate jurisdiction by the Court of Appeal (Criminal Division), with further appeals from each court lying to the House of Lords. In consequence (at p.79), '[i]t is difficult to imagine that nowadays, in such cases, a Divisional Court would adopt a different attitude from the Court of Appeal (Criminal Division) in *Reg v Gould* [1968] 2 QB 65'. So it appears that the precedent practice in the Court of Appeal (Criminal Division) also operates when a Divisional Court is exercising criminal jurisdiction.

In *Younghusband v Luftig* [1949] 2 KB 354, Lord Goddard CJ said that a Divisional Court of five judges had no more power than a court of three or two judges; a Divisional Court is bound by its own decisions, whatever the number of judges constituting it.

Supervisory jurisdiction

In *R v Manchester Coroner, ex parte Tal* [1985] QB 67, it was further decided that when a Divisional Court is exercising supervisory jurisdiction over inferior courts and tribunals by way of judicial review it is not bound by previous decisions of another

Divisional Court. It was expected that the power to depart from previous decisions would be exercised rarely.

Thinking point

Why did the Divisional Court in *R v Manchester Coroner, ex parte Tal* draw a distinction between the rules of precedent applying to appellate and supervisory jurisdiction? Robert Goff LJ explained that supervisory jurisdiction is in the nature of first instance jurisdiction, not appellate jurisdiction. The rules of precedent applying to first instance jurisdiction therefore should also apply to supervisory jurisdiction.

High Court at first instance

A judge sitting in the High Court at first instance is bound by the Supreme Court/House of Lords, the Court of Appeal, and Divisional Courts. Decisions of the High Court are binding on the county courts and magistrates' courts. At first instance, a judge will follow a decision of another judge of first instance, unless persuaded that that judgment is wrong; courts of equal jurisdiction do not bind each other (see *Huddersfield Police Authority v Watson* [1947] KB 842). A single judge exercising supervisory jurisdiction is not strictly bound, but the court in *ex parte Tal* said that it was difficult to imagine a single judge departing from a decision of a Divisional Court.

While judges at first instance are not strictly speaking bound by previous decisions of judges in the High Court, later judges will not lightly depart from such a decision. Judicial comity means that previous decisions are likely to be followed. Should a judge form the view that an earlier decision is wrong and depart from the earlier decision, this then leaves a problem in the law for a later judge. The approach to adopt was outlined in *Colchester Estates (Cardiff) v Carlton Industries* [1986] Ch 80. Nourse J, relying upon statements made by Denning J in *Minister of Pensions v Higham* [1948] 2 KB 153, said that where there are conflicting decisions of the High Court at first instance, the later decision is to be preferred if arrived at after a full consideration of the earlier case. The only exception to this would be where a third judge was convinced that the second judge was wrong in not following the first, due to, for example, a failure by the second judge to consider a binding or persuasive precedent.

Thinking point

The reason behind the approach of Nourse J is once again certainty and finality. There has to be an end to argument on a point of law for the sake of certainty. Given the non-binding nature of a High Court decision on later sittings of the High Court the point could be argued again and again. Obviously Nourse J's approach promotes certainty and invites a definitive ruling to be sought by way of an appeal to the Court of Appeal.

The following gives an example of where conflicting decisions have been made in the High Court. Section 2(2) of the Misrepresentation Act 1967 provides that damages may be awarded by a court in lieu of rescission of a contract. In *Thomas Witter Ltd v TBP Industries* [1996] 2 All ER 573, Jacob J held that damages could be awarded under s.2(2) where rescission was no longer available: 'the power to award damages under s.2(2) did not depend on an extant right to rescission – it only depended on a right having existed in the past'. This decision was not followed by Jack J in *Government of Zanzibar v British Aerospace (Lancaster House) Ltd* [2000] 1 WLR 2333. Jack J held that there is no power to award damages where rescission is no longer available. Consider what the High Court should do in a later case raising this point.

What is the position of a judge of a High Court when faced by conflicting decisions of the Supreme Court/House of Lords and Court of Appeal?

In *Miliangos v George Frank*, Bristow J faced conflicting authorities, *Re United Railways of Havana and Regla Warehouses Ltd* [1961] AC 1007 from the House of Lords and *Schorsch Meier v Hennin* [1975] QB 416 from the Court of Appeal. Bristow J chose to follow the decision of the House of Lords, deciding that the Court of Appeal's decision in *Schorsch Meier v Hennin* was given *per incuriam*. It was said in the House of Lords by Lord Simon that this was not an instance of *per incuriam*, as the Court of Appeal had considered *Re United Railways of Havana and Regla Warehouses Ltd* in reaching its decision. In any event, his Lordship continued that in such instances of conflict, the decision of the immediately superior court is to be followed. It was not for an inferior court to rule that a superior court's decision was *per incuriam*. Reliance was placed upon the words of Lord Diplock in *Baker v The Queen* [1975] AC 774, 788:

> the *per incuriam* rule…does not apply to decisions of courts of appellate jurisdiction superior to that of the court in which the rule is sought to be invoked: *Broome v. Cassell & Co. Ltd.* [1972] A.C. 1027. To permit this use of the *per incuriam* rule would open the door to disregard of precedent by the court of inferior jurisdiction by the simple device of holding that decisions of superior courts with which it disagreed must have been given *per incuriam*.

Thinking point

Lord Simon arrived at this conclusion on the basis that a failure to follow an immediately superior court was contrary to law and invited chaos in the law. Should the Court of Appeal have erred in its decision then the correct way forward would be by way of appeal to the House of Lords (now Supreme Court) which could be achieved from the High Court by the 'leapfrog' procedure under the Administration of Justice Act 1969. By s.12 of that Act an appeal may go directly from the High Court to the Supreme Court if a point of law of general public importance is involved and it is one 'in respect of which the judge is bound by a decision of the Court of Appeal or of the Supreme Court in previous proceedings, and was fully considered in the judgments given by the Court of Appeal or Supreme Court (as the case may be) in those previous proceedings'. In this way the costs of a needless appeal to the Court of Appeal could be avoided.

5.5.5 **The Crown Court**

The Crown Court is bound by all the courts above it in the hierarchy, including the Divisional Court of the Queen's Bench Division. Cross and Harris assert that:

> [i]t has been convincingly argued the precedential effect of Crown Court decisions does not vary with the status of the presiding judge and that, in view of the absence of any systematic reporting of such decisions, a Crown Court ruling does not bind another Crown Court or a magistrates' court.

Nevertheless, the decisions are persuasive.

5.5.6 **County courts and magistrates' courts**

These courts are bound by all the courts above them in the hierarchy, but do not bind themselves or other courts.

5.5.7 **Family court**

(Note at the time of writing the Crime and Courts Act 2013 which establishes the Family court had not been brought into force in this respect. This Act amends the Matrimonial and Family Proceedings Act 1984.)

As was seen in Chapter 2 the jurisdiction of the courts in relation to family law is to be exercised by the family court in place of the High Court (in part), county courts, and magistrates' courts. The jurisdiction of the court will be exercised by judiciary of all levels, e.g. High Court judges (puisne judges), Circuit judges, district judges, District Judges (Magistrates' Court), and justices of the peace (not being District Judges (Magistrates' Court). As the family court will comprise various levels of the judiciary an issue of judicial precedent arises, i.e. are the decisions within the family court of equal status? The Crime and Courts Act 2013 seeks to address this issue of precedent. Section 31C(2) Matrimonial and Family Proceedings Act 1984 (as amended by Sch.10, Crime and Courts Act 2013) deals with this by indicating decisions of which judges in the family court are to be followed by which other members of the judiciary sitting in the family court. For example, a decision of a High Court judge is to be followed by Circuit judges, district judges, District Judges (Magistrates' Court), and justices of the peace.

5.5.8 **Judicial Committee of the Privy Council**

While the judges sitting in the Privy Council will predominantly be Justices of the Supreme Court, decisions of this court are not binding on English courts. Such decisions are, however, persuasive. The reason for this is the Judicial Committee of the Privy Council hears appeals from, inter alia, the dominions outside the UK and some Commonwealth countries, where the law may differ from that of English law.

The Judicial Committee of the Privy Council does not strictly bind itself, but a decision may be departed from only with the greatest hesitation, *Gideon Nkambule v R* [1950] AC 379.

In *Worcester Works v Cooden* [1972] 1 QB 210, Lord Denning, while stating that the Court of Appeal (Civil Division) was not bound by decisions of the Privy Council, said that where the Privy Council disapproved of a previous decision of the Court of Appeal, or cast doubt on it, then the present Court of Appeal was at liberty to depart from their own previous decision.

It has been seen already that in exceptional and limited circumstances a decision of the Privy Council may be preferred to a decision of the Supreme Court/House of Lords.

5.5.9 Judicial precedent, the Human Rights Act 1998, and the European Court of Human Rights

By s.2(1) of the Human Rights Act 1998,

> A court or tribunal determining a question which has arisen in connection with a Convention right must take into account any
>
> (a) judgment, decision, declaration or advisory opinion of the European Court of Human Rights...
>
> whenever made or given, so far as, in the opinion of the court or tribunal, it is relevant to the proceedings in which that question has arisen.

See chapter 7, at 7.7.

While the English courts and tribunals are not strictly bound by the decisions of the European Court of Human Rights, they are under a duty to 'take into account' any relevant case law. This must be read alongside s.3 which provides that the courts so far as it is possible to do so must read and give effect to primary legislation and subordinate legislation in a way which is compatible with the Convention rights. By s.6(1) it is unlawful for a public authority, which includes a court or tribunal, to act in a way which is incompatible with a Convention right. Overall, the effect of this seems to suggest that a court may depart from a previous binding decision if to follow it would mean that the law of the UK is in contravention of the Convention. However, the House of Lords in *Kay and Others v Lambeth London Borough Council* [2006] 2 AC 465 decided that the ordinary rules of precedent applied, the lower courts should follow the decisions of the higher courts. Lord Bingham emphasised the need for certainty within the law. See further *Manchester City Council v Pinnock* [2010] UKSC 45 discussed in chapter 7. Should a lower court consider a binding precedent to be inconsistent with a later decision of the European Court of Human Rights it may say so and give leave to appeal. This approach is subject to one partial exception: where a Supreme Court/House of Lords decision preceded the passing of the Human

Rights Act 1998 and the Act had removed the policy considerations that dictated the Supreme Court/House of Lords decision, the decision may be departed from by the Court of Appeal.

The European Court of Human Rights is not strictly bound by its previous decisions, but the underlying reasons for a system of precedent are still apparent in the operation of the court. In *Coster v United Kingdom* (2001) 33 EHRR 20 it was said by the Court:

> [w]hile it is not formally bound to follow any of its previous judgments, it is in the interests of legal certainty, foreseeability and equality before the law that the European Court of Human Rights should not depart, without good reason, from precedents laid down in previous cases. Since the Convention is first and foremost a system for the protection of human rights, the court is to have regard to the changing conditions in contracting states and respond, for example, to any emerging consensus as to the standards to be achieved.

5.6 Methods of avoiding precedents

5.6.1 Overruling

Overruling occurs when a later court decides that the law as stated in an earlier and different case is wrong and no longer represents the law. Clearly, overruling can only be done within the bounds of the doctrine of *stare decisis*. For example, the Supreme Court can overrule its previous decisions and those of lower courts, such as the Court of Appeal, but the Court of Appeal cannot overrule a precedent of the Supreme Court/House of Lords. When a court overrules a previous case, as has been previously explained, the effect is retrospective; it is as if the previous case has never represented the law and the new case has always been the law. There is no such thing in English law as prospective overruling. This is a process whereby a court preserves the existing precedent but then declares that it will not apply as to the future; a new rule will apply in its place. An example of overruling involving the House of Lords is seen in *Murphy v Brentwood District Council*, where the House of Lords in effect overruled *Anns v Merton London Borough Council*.

As explained earlier, when overruling the courts are mindful of the uncertainty in the law that may be caused. This is because a principle of law in a case operates both retrospectively and prospectively, in the sense of applying to the future. If an established principle is overruled, e.g. where a higher court overrules a precedent set by a lower court, the new principle applies equally to the past and the future. This may operate unfairly should people have conducted their affairs in accordance with the law which has now been overruled. In some jurisdictions, such as the US, there is a practice of prospective overruling. With prospective overruling the newly established legal principle applies only to the future; the overruled principle of law remains in place for events and transactions occurring before the decision in the instant case and, depending upon the type of prospective overruling, to the facts of the instant case itself.

The House of Lords considered the temporal operation of judicial decisions in *Re Spectrum Plus Ltd (in liquidation)* [2005] 2 AC 680, exploring the arguments for and against prospective overruling. It was acknowledged that prospective overruling was not a practice in the English legal system. This, it was argued, was consistent with the judicial role as deciding what the law is and applying it to a set of facts, as opposed to Parliament's role of making law. However, Lord Nicholls said that exceptionally the House of Lords could alter judicial practice (the practice of judicial precedent derives from the common law and judges have the power to modify this practice) and prospectively overrule. Such overruling may be necessary, said Lord Nicholls (at p.699):

> to serve the underlying objective of the courts of this country: to administer justice fairly and in accordance with the law. There could be cases where a decision on an issue of law, whether common law or statute law, was unavoidable but the decision would have such gravely unfair and disruptive consequences for past transactions or happenings that this House would be compelled to depart from the normal principles relating to the retrospective and prospective effect of court decisions.

It is to be noted that Lord Nicholls suggested that this exceptional practice could potentially apply both to judge-made law and to the interpretation of statutes; however, in respect of the latter category Lords Steyn and Scott **dissented**. See also *Awoyami v Radford and Another* [2007] All ER (D) 183; and Lord Rodger 'A Time for Everything under the Law: Some Reflections on Retrospectivity' (2005) 121 LQR 57.

dissent
when a judge
disagrees with a
decision reached by
the other judges
in a case the judge
is said to dissent.

5.6.2 **Reversing**

Unlike overruling, which involves separate cases, reversing describes what a higher court does in relation to a decision given by a lower court in the same case. By reversing a decision, a higher court is saying that the lower court's decision is wrong. When a higher court states that a decision of a lower court is correct it is said to be affirmed.

This process occurred in *Farley v Skinner* [2002] 2 AC 732 where the House of Lords reversed the decision of the Court of Appeal in which it had been held that to claim damages for disappointment the object of the entire contract must be one to give pleasure, relaxation, or peace of mind. Lord Steyn in the House of Lords said there was no reason in law to limit recovery in this way. He said that it was 'sufficient if a major or important object of the contract is to give pleasure, relaxation or peace of mind'. Note further that the House of Lords also overruled a previous precedent set by the Court of Appeal in the separate case of *Knott v Bolton* (1995) 11 Const LJ 375.

5.6.3 Distinguishing

A technique which allows a court to escape a binding precedent is the process of distinguishing. A court may point to material differences in the facts of the case constituting a precedent and the instant case. In this way, it can be decided that the *ratio decidendi* of the previous case does not apply because of the differences.

An example of distinguishing is given by the case of *Holwell Securities v Hughes* [1974] 1 WLR 155. In this case, concerning the law of contract, the Court of Appeal (Civil Division) had to decide whether the postal rule applied to a letter of acceptance sent by post but never received. If the postal rule applied, a contract was formed. It was argued that the postal rule applied because of the rule in *Henthorn v Fraser* [1892] 2 Ch 27 and *obiter dicta* in *Bruner v Moore* [1904] 1 Ch 305. In the former case, the postal rule applied as it was in the contemplation of the parties that the post was to be used to communicate acceptance, while in the latter case the postal rule applied as the parties, by moving around Europe, clearly contemplated the use of the post for communicating acceptance. However, both were distinguished as in these cases there was nothing in the wording of the offers to exclude the operation of the postal rule, unlike in the *Holwell* case where the offer provided that it was to be 'exercisable by notice in writing'. These words, said the court, indicated that the letter of acceptance had to be received. In neither *Henthorn v Fraser* nor *Bruner v Moore* did the words of the offer deal with the manner in which acceptance was to be communicated.

5.7 Nature of the rules of judicial precedent

Note that the rules of precedent cannot be binding within themselves as they do not relate to the dispute before the court and therefore cannot be part of a *ratio decidendi*. Nonetheless, the House of Lords by the Practice Statement of 1966 changed the precedent practice of the court. This has been the subject of much academic comment as to the authority for the change, but the de facto situation is that the Practice Statement has been followed and no successful challenge has been mounted in the courts or Parliament.

Critical debate

The 'right to die' issue was highlighted in the cases of *R (on the application of Nicklinson) v Ministry of Justice* and *R (on the application of AM) v DPP* [2012] HRLR 32. The cases highlight the interplay of law and morality, the limits of judge-made law, and the relationship between the courts and Parliament. Read the cases and consider the following questions.

(a) The arguments concerning assisted dying raise issues of personal autonomy, of giving the individual control over the ending of his or her's life. In such circumstances the wishes of the individual should be paramount and should be reflected in the law. Do you agree?

(b) Why did the Court of Appeal refuse to develop the common law and introduce a defence of necessity?

(c) Were the judges right to refuse?

(d) In the context of these cases explain the relationship between the courts and Parliament.

5.8 Case analysis

On a practical level as a law student, it is important to develop good habits from an early point in your legal studies. In reading a case, it is important to record certain information. The following may be used as a template for the analysis of a case. As your skills of analysis develop, further sophistication may be introduced into the list of questions:

- **Legal issues:** the first task in reading a case is to identify what it is the court is being asked to decide. There may be more than one issue before a court. How the case is argued is important as this will indicate the question or questions asked of the court.

- **Material facts:** what are the material facts of the case (the facts the court considers relevant to the decision)?

- **The decision in the case:** although the outcome is of great importance to the parties involved, for a lawyer the decision is very much secondary to the *ratio decidendi* of the case.

- **Reasons for the *ratio decidendi*:** it is important to separate the reasons for the *ratio decidendi* from the *ratio decidendi* itself. Judges will seek to justify why a case is decided in a particular way; in other words, a justification will be given for the *ratio decidendi* of the case.

- **The *ratio decidendi*:** in relation to new cases, lawyers will have to attempt to formulate the rule of law upon which the decision in the case is based. As has been seen, this is a difficult process as judges will not usually neatly package a rule for the reader, instead the reader must 'construct' the *ratio*, looking for clues in the language used by the judge (or judges). If a case has been considered in later cases, then the later court may identify the *ratio decidendi* of the earlier case.

- **Other statements of law – *obiter dicta*:** statements of law which do not affect the outcome of a case are classified as *obiter dicta* and are not binding on later courts. *Obiter dicta* are, however, persuasive authorities.

- **The deciding court:** once the *ratio* of a case has been determined, the status of the deciding court must be noted so that the bindingness of the case may be assessed. Such information will influence how the case may be used.

- **Later cases:** consider what has happened to a decision in later cases. Has it been affirmed, reversed, followed, distinguished, or overruled?

➕ Summary

- Judicial precedent promotes certainty by ensuring that like cases are decided alike. Decision-making by the courts is governed by the doctrine of judicial precedent which allows for the law to develop in an orderly way. However, this aim is sometimes achieved at the expense of justice.

- Law is made by judges, but the law-making power is a circumscribed power. The courts must not usurp the role of Parliament as a law-maker. For example, the courts should not effect a major change to the common law if there are conflicting views, especially in relation to social policy, of how to resolve an issue or if Parliament has refused to introduce such changes.

- The *ratio decidendi* of a case is the basis upon which a case is decided. A case may have more than one *ratio*; this may depend upon the number of legal issues argued before a court and there being multiple grounds for a decision.

- A distinction must be drawn between the *ratio decidendi* of a case, which may bind later courts, and *res judicata* which indicates that the parties to case, subject to any appeal, are bound by the decision in the case.

- When determining the *ratio decidendi* of a case, later cases are important for two reasons. First, a judge in a later case may state what is the *ratio decidendi* of a previous case; and, second, a judge or judges in a later case may clarify the *ratio* of a previous case by restating what are the material facts, thus narrowing or widening a *ratio*.

- Unlike *ratio decidendi*, *obiter dicta* do not affect the decision in a case and are merely persuasive on other courts.

- In looking at the hierarchy of the courts, it is important to consider in relation to each court: (i) by which courts' decisions is the court under consideration bound; and (ii) does the court bind itself?

- The Supreme Court will normally follow its previous decisions but may depart from such decisions when it 'appears right to do so'. This discretion is to be exercised sparingly.

- The Court of Appeal is bound by the *rationes* of the courts above it and by its previous decisions, subject to exceptions.

- The High Court is bound by the courts above it in the hierarchy. Whether it is bound by its previous decisions depends upon the jurisdiction that the court is exercising, i.e. appellate, supervisory, or first instance. A divisional court exercising appellate jurisdiction is bound by its previous decisions, subject to the rule in *Young v Bristol*

Aeroplane Co Ltd. At first instance the High Court is not bound by previous first instance decisions, but will not lightly depart from such a decision. Supervisory jurisdiction is in the nature of first instance jurisdiction so the same rule of precedent relating to first instance decisions applies.

- The Crown Court, magistrates' courts, and county courts are bound by all the courts above in the hierarchy and do not bind themselves.

Questions

1 What is the doctrine of binding judicial precedent?

2 Under the doctrine of precedent, what is the binding part of a case?

3 Explain the characteristics of *obiter dicta*.

4 What factors does the Supreme Court/House of Lords take into account in exercising their power under the 1966 Practice Statement to depart from their previous decisions?

5 In what circumstances may the Court of Appeal (Civil Division) and (Criminal Division) refuse to follow previous decisions of the court?

6 How does the precedent practice in the High Court differ according to whether the court exercises appellate or first instance jurisdiction?

7 In relation to issues concerning human rights, what are the rules of precedent?

8 To what extent are the courts able to make law?

Sample question and outline answer

Question

The Practice Statement of 1966 indicated that the House of Lords (now the Supreme Court) would be more willing to depart from its own previous precedents.

Discuss the reasons and circumstances for the House of Lords/Supreme Court departing from its own precedents in decided cases.

Outline answer

An introduction must deconstruct the question and identify the issues to be discussed. The subject matter clearly relates to the House of Lords/Supreme Court practice in relation to its previous precedents. The answer will include an explanation of the following issues.

First, an explanation of judicial precedent with emphasis on the rules of precedent in relation to the House of Lords/Supreme Court must be given. Mention can be made of the need for certainty and the role of the doctrine of judicial precedent in seeking to achieve this aim.

Second, an exploration of the Practice Statement (noting that the statement applies equally to the Supreme Court as it did to the House of Lords, *Austin v Southwark London Borough Council* (2010)), concentrating on the reasons underpinning the approach to be adopted by the House of Lords/Supreme Court to its previous precedents.

One of the main issues arising out of the Practice Statement concerns the retrospective effect of precedents; precedents apply to the past as well as the future. The problems that this can cause need to be explored, especially the issue of reliance on a precedent by lawyers and citizens in ordering their affairs or as a guide to future action. The specific reference to contracts, settlements of property, and fiscal arrangements reflects the desire not to retrospectively disturb transactions or actions where reliance has been placed on existing precedent. Also note the need for certainty in the criminal law.

The main issue to then consider is in what circumstances the House of Lords/ Supreme Court will consider it 'right' to depart from a previous decision? Reference to a selection of decided cases is essential to highlight the basis for the House of Lords/ Supreme Court departing from its own previous precedents. The case law needs to be explained and analysed. It has been made clear in the case law that the Practice Statement power is to be used sparingly, *Jones v Secretary of State for Social Services* (1972). Clearly, the tension is between promoting certainty, but at the same time seeking to ensure that justice is done. If a change may be made without having an impact on the wider law and avoiding the problems of retrospectivity then a precedent may be departed from as in *Horton v Sadler* (2007). Merely because a previous decision is perceived to be wrong will not, of itself, necessarily be a reason to depart from it; the need for certainty may outweigh this consideration. An explanation of the House of Lords approach to the interpretation of statutes in previous precedents needs to be given, e.g. *Jones v Secretary of State for Social Services* (1972) and the refusal to depart from *Re Dowling* (1967). A comparison may be drawn with *R v Shivpuri* (1987).

If an old case of the House of Lords raises a broad issue of justice or public policy or legal principle then reconsideration of it may be appropriate. In *British Railways Board v Herrington* (1972), a previous House of Lords case, *Addie & Sons v Dumbreck* (1929), was reconsidered with the consequence that a duty of common humanity was owed by occupiers of premises to trespassers. Lord Pearson said at p.929 that 'the rule in Addie's case has been rendered obsolete by changes in physical and social conditions and has become an encumbrance to the proper development of the common law in this field'. Also if a precedent is causing great uncertainty and the case would not be relied upon by citizens or bodies to plan future actions then it may be right to depart from it, as in *Murphy v Brentwood DC* (1991). The views expressed in Cross and Harris will be of use and illustrations from the case law will need to be employed.

In conclusion you should state that the power to depart from previous precedents has been used sparingly by the Supreme Court/House of Lords. This is due to concerns over the retrospective nature of precedent and where reliance may have been placed on a previous precedent. However, as seen in *R v Shivpuri* (1987) and *Horton v Sadler* (2007) the House of Lords was willing to depart from its own previous decisions. The need to promote certainty may be consistent with a desire to do justice.

Further reading

At first year level your reading should be directed to two essential goals: a knowledge and understanding of the rules of judicial precedent and an appreciation of what underpins the rules. Reading what the judges have had to say in the case law is essential. Further case commentary may be available in journal articles.

- **Ashworth, A.** 'The Binding Effect of Crown Court Decisions' [1980] Crim LR 402
  Considers the reasons for decisions of the Crown Court not being binding precedents.

- **Cross, R.** and **Harris, J.** *Precedent in English Law*, 4th edn, Oxford University Press (1991)
  The leading text on the doctrine of judicial precedent.

- **Giles, M.** 'Judicial Law-Making in the Criminal Courts: The Case of Marital Rape' (1992) Crim LR 407
  Provides an illustration of how the common law may be adapted to reflect changing circumstances.

- **Gillespie, A.** 'Precedent and the limits of Simpson' (2010) 74 J Crim L 492
  Explores the precedent issue raised before the Court of Appeal (Criminal Division) in *R v Varma* (2010).

- **Holland, J.** and **Webb, J.** *Learning Legal Rules*, 8th edn, Oxford University Press (2013)
  Chapters 6 and 7 provide good practical illustrations of the doctrine of judicial precedent in action.

- **Prime, T.** and **Scanlan, G.** 'Stare Decisis and the Court of Appeal; Judicial confusion and judicial reform'? (2004) 23 CJQ 212
  Provides a review of the case law establishing precedent practice in the Court of Appeal from the *Young* case onwards.

Online Resource Centre

You should now attempt the supporting multiple choice questions available at **www.oxfordtextbooks.co.uk/orc/wilson_els/**.

6

The law and institutions of the European Union

Learning objectives

By the end of this chapter you should:

- know what are the main institutions of the EU and how they are comprised;
- understand the respective functions of the institutions;
- know the various sources of EU law;
- be able to distinguish between the various legislative acts adopted by the Union;
- understand the purpose and mechanics of the preliminary rulings procedure;
- explain why reform of the preliminary rulings procedure is regarded as important, and critically analyse the various reform proposals that have been made;
- understand the doctrine of supremacy;
- understand the principles of direct effect and indirect effect;
- understand the justification for the development of the principle of State liability.

🗨 Talking point

....

The UK has been a Member State of the EU since January 1973, when a Conservative government took the UK into what was then the European Economic Community (EEC). The Labour government that followed held a national referendum on whether the UK should retain its membership of the EEC in June 1975, which resulted in over 67 per cent of the electorate voting 'yes'.

Thirty-eight years later, in June 2013, James Wharton (Conservative MP for Stockton South), having earlier been placed first in the 2013/2014 ballot for private members' bills, introduced the European Union (Referendum) Bill into the House of Commons. Clause 1(1) states that '[a] referendum is to be held on the United Kingdom's membership of the European Union', and clause 1(2) adds that '[t]he referendum must be held before 31 December 2017'. Clause 1(4) states that the question to be put to the UK voters is 'Do you think that the United Kingdom should be a member of the European Union?'

The bill received unanimous support at its second reading (where the core principles of each bill are discussed) in the House of Commons in July 2013, with 304 votes in favour and none against. After the vote, the Prime Minister David Cameron tweeted: 'Referendum Bill passes first Commons stage, bringing us one step closer to giving the British people a say on Europe.' The bill has since completed its committee stage, in September 2013, although it may come up against opposition later. (Very few Labour MPs participated in the second reading vote and all of the Lib-Dem MPs boycotted that stage completely; Deputy PM Nick Clegg described the bill as a 'complete stunt'.)

Clearly the question of whether the UK should remain a Member State is a very complex, and controversial question involving issues of national identity, economics, and politics as well as law, much of which is outside the scope of this book. What this chapter will seek to explain are the history and core legal principles of the European Union, and the impact on the English legal system of the UK's membership of the EU. This will entail looking at key legal principles such as the 'primacy' or 'supremacy' of EU law over conflicting national law; the 'direct effect' of EU law which allows EU legislation to be enforced in UK courts and tribunals; the 'indirect effect' of EU law which requires judges in UK courts and tribunals to interpret UK legislation to bring it into line with EU legislation; and the 'preliminary rulings' procedure which enables judges in UK courts and tribunals to seek advice from the Court of Justice in Luxembourg on the true meaning of EU law. This knowledge might even help you to answer the question posed in Mr Wharton's bill . . .

....

Introduction

The UK joined what was then called the European Economic Community (EEC) in January 1973. However, at that date the EEC had already been in existence for fifteen years, formed when the Treaty of Rome came into effect in January 1958. The idea behind the EEC was to promote economic cooperation between different Member States for their mutual benefit. Over the years, the EEC expanded both geographically (as more countries joined) and legally, particularly when the decision was made to create the European Union (EU) in November 1993. No longer restricted to 'economic' matters, the EU is now a 'union' of twenty-eight Member States (with more waiting to join). It has its own institutions, including a Parliament and Courts, which ensure its (reasonably) smooth functioning. It has its own law-making powers, but the most important aspects of the 'law' of the EU are found in two international agreements, the Treaty on European Union of 1992 and the Treaty on the Functioning of the European Union of 2007. In addition, the Court of Justice of the European Union has established a number of key principles of EU law, including the doctrines of 'supremacy' (the principle that EU law overrides any conflicting provisions of national law); 'direct effect' (the principle that certain provisions of EU law are enforceable in the national courts); and 'State liability' (the principle that Member States are obliged to compensate individuals for any losses caused to them by a breach of their EU legal obligations).

....

6.1 The history of the European Union

6.1.1 The European Coal and Steel Community (ECSC)

The historical development of the EU dates back to the post-Second World War era. In 1951 the Treaty of Paris was signed by the governments of Belgium, the Netherlands, Luxembourg, France, West Germany, and Italy, establishing the European Coal and Steel Community (ECSC), creating a 'common market' in coal and steel. It was seen as a way of promoting cooperation between countries which had been at war with each other less than a decade previously. It was also seen as a means of accelerating post-war recovery and, by removing the raw materials for war from the control of the Member States, making another war less likely.

The ECSC was (for the time) an unusual organisation. There was a Council of Ministers, consisting of representatives of the Member States, with responsibility for the overall development and policies of the ECSC, and with supranational power (i.e. the power to make legally binding decisions without the intervention of national parliaments or governments). There was a permanent executive called the High Authority (subsequently re-named the European Commission), responsible for the day-to-day running of the ECSC, to which power could be delegated by the Council. The Treaty of Paris also established a Court of Justice, which was to resolve any disputes that arose between the Member States and to enforce the law in accordance with the Treaty.

For more detailed discussion of the institutions responsible for running the EU, see 6.2.

6.1.2 **The European Economic Community**

The Treaty of Rome was signed in 1957, establishing the EEC in January 1958. Its purpose was to promote the general economic integration of the six Member States who had formed the ECSC six years earlier. The EEC had a much wider remit than the ECSC and was designed to promote cooperation in a variety of 'economic' fields, such as agriculture, employment, fishing, trade, and transport. It is very important to note that these fields of operation are finite: the EEC only had power to act in those areas identified in the Treaty itself. In other areas, for example direct taxation, the individual Member States retained full control. The Treaty of Rome also created the 'Common Market', an area comprising all of the Member States in which goods, people, services, and capital would be free to move.

A second Treaty of Rome was also signed in 1957, establishing the European Atomic Energy Community (EURATOM), which was intended to promote cooperation in the generation and distribution of nuclear energy. Thus, from January 1958, there were three distinct European Communities, the ECSC, the EEC, and EURATOM. However, from 1969 they were run by a single set of institutions.

6.1.3 **Geographical enlargement and legal expansion**

Since 1958, the EEC/EU has grown from an initial membership of six to twenty-eight, following the accession of the UK, Denmark, and Ireland in 1973; Greece in 1981; Spain and Portugal in 1986; Austria, Finland, and Sweden in 1995; Cyprus, the Czech Republic, Estonia, Hungary, Latvia, Lithuania, Malta, Poland, Slovakia, and Slovenia in 2004; Bulgaria and Romania in 2007; and Croatia in 2013. Following the collapse of the Berlin Wall in 1989, Germany was reunited and the former East Germany was absorbed into the EU. At present, five other states are involved in formal negotiations to join: Iceland, Macedonia, Montenegro, Serbia, and Turkey.

Meanwhile, in 1986, the governments of the Member States signed the Single European Act (SEA), which came into effect in 1987. The SEA made a number of modifications to the (first) Treaty of Rome, the most important being:

● The list of fields in which the EEC was competent to act was expanded. For example, environmental protection was added.

- The Court of First Instance was created, to relieve some of the workload from the European Court of Justice.
- The 'Common Market' was re-named the 'Internal Market'.

6.1.4 The European Union and other developments

The legal expansion of the EEC, started in 1986, continued when the Treaty on European Union (TEU) was signed in 1992 and came into effect in November 1993. Amongst other things, the TEU:

- established the European Union (the EU);
- renamed the EEC as simply the EC;
- made various amendments to the (first) Treaty of Rome;
- renamed the Council of Ministers as the Council of the European Union;
- recognised the European Council as an institution of the EU;
- established the concept of 'citizenship' of the Union;
- paved the way for the adoption of the single European currency, the Euro, in 2002.

Two further treaties were signed: the Treaty of Amsterdam in 1997 and the Treaty of Nice in 2001. These made further amendments to both the (first) Treaty of Rome and the TEU but did not make any fundamental changes to the way in which either the EC or EU operated. In December 2000, the Charter of Fundamental Rights was approved by the governments of the EU's Member States. The Charter did not, initially, have binding legal force, but that changed in December 2009 (see later).

The Treaty of Paris, signed in 1951, was only ever intended to last for fifty years and it duly lapsed in 2002. As a result, the ECSC ceased to exist. The provisions of the Treaty of Rome were applied to the coal and steel industries instead. 2002 saw the introduction of the single European currency, the Euro, in twelve Member States: Austria, Belgium, Finland, France, Germany, Greece, Ireland, Italy, Luxembourg, the Netherlands, Portugal, and Spain. Slovenia adopted the Euro in 2007, followed by Cyprus and Malta in 2008, Slovakia in 2009, Estonia in 2011, and Latvia in 2014. There are now eighteen Member States in the 'Eurozone', overseen by the European Central Bank (ECB), based in Frankfurt in Germany.

6.1.5 The state of the Union

The latest EU treaty is the Lisbon Treaty, signed in 2007, which came into effect in December 2009. The main features are:

- the abolition of the EC;
- the (first) Treaty of Rome was amended and re-named as the Treaty on the Functioning of the European Union (TFEU);

- the TEU was amended;
- the Charter of Fundamental Rights was given legal force;
- the EU committed to becoming a signatory to the European Convention on Human Rights (ECHR);
- the establishment of a President and a Foreign Minister of the EU;
- combating climate change and global warming become official policies of the EU; and
- the Court of First Instance (CFI) was re-named as the General Court.

See 6.3 for discussion of the TEU, TFEU, and Charter.

6.2 The institutions of the EU

6.2.1 European Council

The European Council comprises all the Heads of State or Government of the Member States, its President, and the President of the European Commission. The European Council began with informal meetings in 1961 but adopted formal 'summits' in 1974. The Council meets in Brussels, four times a year. Although the European Council has no formal executive or legislative powers, it is required to 'provide the Union with the necessary impetus for its development' and to 'define the general political directions and priorities' of the EU (Article 15(1) TEU).

6.2.2 Council of the European Union

The Council of the European Union, formerly called the Council of Ministers, is usually referred to simply as 'the Council'. It is different to the European Council and should not be confused with it. According to Article 16(2) of the TEU, 'The Council shall consist of a representative of each Member State at ministerial level, who may commit the government of the Member State in question and cast its vote.' When the Council meets, its composition depends on the subject matter under discussion. For example, if the Council were to meet to discuss North Sea fishing stocks, agriculture ministers would attend. Article 16(1) of the TEU stipulates that the Council has the power to 'exercise legislative and budgetary functions'. However, the Council does not operate in isolation in this respect; rather, it interacts with the other institutions as part of the EU's legislative procedures.

6.2.3 European Commission

The Commission is headed by twenty-eight Commissioners, one per Member State, regardless of population size or economic strength (thus Germany has one Commissioner as does Malta), supported by some 25,000 employees. The twenty-eight

Commissioners are appointed together for a renewable five-year term. Commissioners are selected, by the Member States, rather than elected. Commissioners must be chosen on the 'ground of their general competence and European commitment from persons whose independence is beyond doubt' (Article 17(3) TEU). Once selected, they must act in the general interests of the EU, rather than in the interests of their Member State (Article 17(3) TEU). Each Commissioner is assigned a portfolio, but the Commission acts as a collegiate body. It is organised into 'directorates general' which correspond with the portfolios.

The Commission's specific functions and powers are found in Article 17(1) of the TEU. Amongst other things, the Commission:

- Is responsible for promoting the 'general interest' of the Union.

- Is authorised to take 'appropriate initiatives' to promote the Union. This essentially means the right to propose and draft secondary legislation, which it then passes on to the European Parliament and Council for approval and ultimate adoption. Most of the Commission's legislative proposals take the form of regulations and directives in areas such as consumer protection, health protection, and employment, but the Commission has recently moved into criminal law (e.g. criminalising the transportation of toxic waste).

- Is empowered to commence 'enforcement' proceedings against Member States if they are not complying with their obligations under EU law. The procedure for doing so is found in Article 258 of the TFEU. Initially, the Commission will issue a 'reasoned opinion' to the State in question giving it the opportunity to respond. If the Commission is dissatisfied with the response then the State can be brought before the European Court of Justice. In the event that it agrees with the Commission, the Court may require the State in question to take whatever 'measures' are deemed 'necessary' (Article 260(1) TFEU). If the State fails to comply with the Court's judgment then the Commission can bring the State back before the Court which can impose a punishment, either a 'lump sum or penalty payment' (Article 260(2) TFEU).

- Is responsible for enforcing EU competition policy. The Commission can prosecute corporations which form illegal cartels (prohibited by Article 101 of the TFEU), or abuse a 'dominant' position in the market (prohibited by Article 102 of the TFEU). The Commission can ultimately issue (very large) fines. In 2004, the Commission fined the Microsoft Corporation a then record €497m for breaching Article 102 of the TFEU. But this fine was dwarfed in May 2009, when the Commission imposed a fine of €1.06billion on the Intel Corporation for the same offence.

6.2.4 European Parliament

The Parliament was originally called the Common Assembly. In 1962 it began calling itself the Parliament, although this was only made official in 1986. The original

Members were delegates of Member States' own parliaments. The first direct elections were held across Europe in June 1979. Elections are held every five years, with the seventh election taking place in 2009 and the eighth in 2014. Prior to the 2014 election, there were 766 Members of the European Parliament (MEPs), with the proportions varying per Member State according to size and population. Thus, for example, Germany has ninety-six MEPs, France has seventy-four, the UK and Italy have seventy-three each, and so on. The four smallest countries have six MEPs each. After the 2014 election the number of MEPs will be capped at 751.

The functions of the European Parliament are:

- Participation in the legislative process. The Parliament's role here has been, and still is, controversial. Despite being the only directly elected (and hence most democratic) institution in the EU, the Parliament's role in the legislative process is purely reactive. It has the right to be consulted on all draft legislation and, in certain circumstances, can and does veto proposed legislation. But it has no powers to introduce legislation of its own (only the Commission can do this) and the Parliament cannot force through legislation if the Council opposes it.

- Supervisory functions (over the Commission).

- Budgetary powers.

6.2.5 **Court of Justice of the European Union**

The Court of Justice of the European Union (CJEU), usually referred to as the Court of Justice, consists of twenty-eight judges, one per Member State (Article 19(2) TEU). Each holds office for a renewable six-year term. Judges are selected from persons 'whose independence is beyond doubt' (Article 19(2) TEU). The judges elect one of themselves as 'President'. The CJEU may sit:

- as the 'full court' comprising all twenty-eight judges;

- in a 'Grand Chamber' comprising fifteen judges; or

- in chambers of three or five judges.

The Court sits as a 'full court' only in relatively rare cases, such as those considered of 'exceptional importance'. It sits in a Grand Chamber when a Member State or an EU institution which is a party to the proceedings so requests, and in particularly complex or important cases. Other cases are heard in chambers which allows for a degree of specialism and greater efficiency. Unlike English courts, the CJEU always gives a single, collegiate judgment; there are no minority judgments (dissenting or otherwise). The CJEU is assisted by eight Advocates-General (A-G), who are legal experts employed to give highly persuasive advisory 'opinions' to the Court before the judges retire to consider their judgment in some (but not all) cases. In most cases where an A-G is used, the CJEU follows the opinion when it gives judgment (often several months later).

Thus, once an A-G's opinion is available in a given case one can predict with some confidence how the CJEU will eventually rule.

6.2.6 General Court

The General Court began operations, as the 'Court of First Instance' (CFI), in 1989. Its name was changed in December 2009. There is 'at least' one judge per Member State (Article 19(2) TEU). At present there are twenty-eight judges. Unlike the CJEU, there are no Advocates-General. The General Court mainly handles cases involving EU competition law, and some judicial review cases. Appeals against General Court decisions – on points of law only – are heard by the CJEU.

6.2.7 European Central Bank

The European Central Bank, based in Frankfurt, Germany, is the central bank for Europe's single currency, the Euro. Its main task is to maintain the Euro's purchasing power and thus price stability in the eighteen European Union countries that presently make up the 'Eurozone'.

6.2.8 European Economic and Social Committee (EESC)

The EESC has 353 members, representing three groups: employers; workers; and various others which include agricultural and consumer interests. Its sole function is to advise the Council, the Commission, and the Parliament (Article 13(4) TEU)).

6.2.9 Committee of the Regions (CoR)

The CoR also has 353 members, representing regional and local bodies throughout the EU. Like the EESC, its sole function is also to advise the Council, the Commission, and the Parliament.

6.2.10 Civil Service Tribunal

The Civil Service Tribunal deals with cases involving disputes between the EU institutions and their employees. It is staffed by seven judges. Appeals against Tribunal decisions – on points of law only – are heard by the General Court.

6.3 Sources of EU law

6.3.1 The Treaties

All of the key provisions of EU law are contained in the TEU and the TFEU.

The Treaty on European Union

The TEU came into effect in November1993 and has been amended several times since, most recently when the Treaty of Lisbon came into force in December 2009. The TEU contains the fundamental principles relating to the EU and its institutions. It consists of a total of fifty-five Articles.

The Treaty on the Functioning of the European Union

The TFEU came into effect in December 2009, replacing the Treaty of Rome. The TFEU elaborates on the fundamental principles in the TEU, seeking (as its name suggests) to ensure that the EU functions smoothly. For example, Article 26 of the TFEU states that, 'The Union shall adopt measures with the aim of establishing or ensuring the functioning of the internal market', defined as 'an area without internal frontiers in which the free movement of goods, persons, services and capital is ensured'. The TFEU is much bigger than the TEU, containing a total of 358 Articles.

The Charter of Fundamental Rights

The Charter of Fundamental Rights was 'adopted' in December 2000 although initially it did not have binding legal force (it did have a persuasive influence, however, especially on the CJEU). That changed in December 2009, when the Charter acquired legal force. The Charter consists of fifty articles on a range of issues, such as human dignity (Article 1), the right to life (Article 2), respect for private and family life (Article 7), freedom of expression (Article 11), right to education (Article 14), right to asylum (Article 18), and equality between men and women (Article 23).

The Charter is not to be confused with the ECHR, which was signed in November 1950 and which came into effect in September 1953. The Charter and the Convention share a number of common features but are not identical. All twenty-eight Member States of the EU are signatories to the ECHR, along with nineteen non-EU countries including Norway, Russia, Switzerland, and Ukraine. Enforcement of the ECHR is the responsibility of the European Court of Human Rights in Strasbourg.

6.3.2 Secondary legislation: an introduction

See chapter 7, 'Human rights and fundamental freedoms'.

The TEU and TFEU are framework Treaties, which means that, although they contain the fundamental principles of law upon which the Union is founded and functions, detailed rules are necessary to 'flesh out' those general principles. To facilitate this, law-making powers are conferred upon the EU's institutions (Article 288 TFEU).

6.3.3 Regulations

The EU's institutions pass thousands of regulations each year. All regulations are cited by reference to a number followed by the year of enactment. Thus, for example, Regulation 1612/68 was number 1612 to be enacted in 1968. Regulations are described in Article 288 TFEU as having 'general application' and being 'directly applicable'. 'General application' means that regulations, like the Treaties, apply to both the Member States *and* individuals. The term 'directly applicable' means that regulations automatically become part of the domestic legal system of the Member States without the need for any national legislation. 'Direct applicability' is a powerful tool for ensuring legal uniformity throughout the EU. Regulations do *not* allow room for the exercise of any discretion to address national needs. For this reason, regulations tend to be used in highly regulated fields such as agriculture and competition.

6.3.4 **Directives**

Directives are very different to regulations. First, they are not necessarily of general application; instead, they are binding only upon those Member States to which they are addressed. (Having said that, directives usually are addressed to every State.) Second, directives are not binding in their entirely but only as to the 'result to be achieved'. As such, directives instruct Member States to do certain things, but do not specify how this should be done. Member States must 'implement' the provisions of directives into domestic law. All directives are cited by reference to the year of enactment followed by a number. Hence, for example, Directive 2004/38 was number 38 to be enacted in 2004. Here are some other examples:

- Directive 76/207 (the Equal Treatment Directive). This established a general principle of equal treatment for men and women in employment throughout the EU.
- Directive 92/85 (the Pregnant Workers Directive). This guarantees a minimum maternity leave period throughout the EU of fourteen weeks.
- Directive 93/104 (the Working Time Directive). This guarantees a maximum average working week throughout the EU of forty-eight hours.

Implementation of directives

Member States *must* introduce national legislation to 'implement' each directive. They must do this within a specified time period, stated in the directive itself. The time period varies from one directive to another, depending on the difficulty of achieving the required result, but the average time period is approximately two years. Member States must implement directives in a legally certain manner (for example, in the UK by an Act of Parliament or a statutory instrument). For example:

See chapter 3, 'Legislation and the law-making process'.

- Directive 92/85 was implemented into UK law by the Employment Rights Act 1996; and
- Directive 93/104 was implemented into UK law by the Working Time Regulations 1998.

Implications of failing to implement on time

If a Member State fails to implement a directive on time, certain implications may follow:

- The directive itself may be relied upon in litigation in national courts, subject to certain conditions (see 6.6).
- The State may find itself held liable to compensate any individual who has suffered loss as a consequence of this failure, again subject to certain conditions (see 6.7).
- The European Commission may bring an enforcement action under Article 258 of the TFEU, potentially leading to a fine imposed by the CJEU under Article 260 of the TFEU.

6.3.5 **Decisions**

Decisions are legally binding in their entirety upon those to whom they are addressed. Decisions may be addressed to Member States or to individuals.

6.3.6 **Recommendations and opinions**

Recommendations and opinions have, as their names suggest, no binding force. However, they cannot be ignored and have some persuasive authority.

6.3.7 **Case law**

The case law of the CJEU and the General Court form an essential source of EU law. Judgments of the two Courts are binding on national courts. The CJEU is not bound by a doctrine of precedent; however, it usually follows its previous decisions. Most of the Courts' workload consists of dealing with enforcement actions under Article 258 of the TFEU or giving 'preliminary rulings' under Article 267 of the TFEU (see 6.4). However, the CJEU has been very active in creating legal principles which underpin the whole of the EU's legal system, including 'supremacy' (see 6.5), 'direct effect' and 'indirect effect' (see 6.6), and 'State liability' (see 6.7).

Every case heard by the CJEU has a reference number. A C- prefix was introduced in 1989, in order to distinguish the CJEU's cases from the General Court's, which has a T- prefix. Thus, Case C-212/04 *Adeneler & Others* is case number 212 of the year 2004 and it was heard in the European Court of Justice.

6.4 **The preliminary rulings procedure**

6.4.1 **Introduction**

The preliminary rulings procedure is the mechanism by which national courts and tribunals may (or in some cases must) seek definitive 'rulings' from the CJEU on the interpretation of EU legislation.

> **Key point**
>
> The preliminary rulings procedure is *not* an appeal: the relationship between the CJEU and the national courts is not hierarchical, but based on mutual cooperation. Basically, the national courts are responsible for applying EU law and the CJEU is responsible for interpreting it.

6.4.2 **Purpose**

The procedure exists because of the need to secure the uniform application of EU legislation throughout the Union. After all, if EU law were to be applied differently in different Member States then it would cease to be 'EU law' (it would effectively become national law instead). To ensure uniform application, EU legislation must be interpreted consistently.

6.4.3 **Scope**

Article 267 TFEU stipulates that the CJEU has jurisdiction to give preliminary rulings on:

- The interpretation of 'the Treaties' – both the TEU and the TFEU.
- The interpretation of 'acts of the institutions, bodies, offices or agencies of the Union' – meaning legislative acts, primarily directives and regulations;
- The validity of those 'acts'. (The CJEU cannot rule on the validity of either of the Treaties.)

The CJEU's approach to its task of interpreting a provision of EU legislation was summarised in *Adidas* (Case C-223/98) [1999] ECR I-7081, where the Court stated that, 'it is necessary to consider not only its wording but also the context in which it occurs and the objects of the rules of which it is part…where a provision of [EU] law is open to several interpretations, only one of which can ensure that the provision retains its effectiveness, preference must be given to that interpretation.' This is a strong commitment to the 'purposive' approach to interpretation.

6.4.4 **Who can seek a preliminary ruling?**

Article 267 TFEU provides that 'any court or tribunal' may seek a preliminary ruling if a 'question' relating to the interpretation of EU legislation is raised in a case pending before it.

Whether a body qualifies as a 'court or tribunal' is a question of EU law. The CJEU has adopted a functional test, seeking to identify the characteristics of the body seeking a ruling, rather than its formal title, with the ultimate question being whether the body exercises a judicial function. In *Broeckmeulen* (Case 246/80) [1981] ECR 2311, various factors to be taken into account in deciding this test were identified:

See chapter 4, 'The interpretation of statutes'.

- whether the body is established by law;
- whether it is permanent;
- whether its jurisdiction is compulsory;
- whether its procedure is *inter partes*;
- whether it applies rules of law; and
- whether it is independent.

> ### 🔒 Key point
>
> A body does not necessarily have to have the name 'court' or 'tribunal' in order to be able to invoke the preliminary rulings procedure; the key is whether it carries out judicial functions.

For example, these bodies invoked the procedure: Immigration *Adjudicator* (UK); Alien Appeals *Board* (Sweden); Appeals *Committee* (Netherlands); Social Security *Commissioner* (UK); Competition *Council* (Finland).

Subsequent case law has confirmed that independence is critical. The CJEU in *Wilson* (Case C-506/04) [2006] ECR I-8613 identified two forms of independence: external (freedom from outside interference) and internal (lack of bias amongst the body's members). If either or both of these is missing then a body cannot invoke the procedure (*Schmid* (Case C-516/99) [2002] ECR I-4573). Other cases in which a body was not recognised as a 'court or tribunal' include *Nordsee* (Case 102/81) [1982] ECR 1095 (an arbitrator); *X* (Case C-74/95) [1996] ECR I-6609 (a prosecutor); *Victoria Film* (Case C-134/97) [1998] ECR I-7023 (a body acting in a purely administrative capacity).

The functional test for deciding whether or not a body is a 'court or tribunal' has attracted criticism. In *Alpe Adria Energia* (Case C-205/08) [2009] ECR I-11525, A-G Ruiz-Jarabo Colomer opined that the CJEU had become too generous with its interpretation of 'court or tribunal', opening up the procedure to what he described as 'quasi-judicial bodies'. He invited the Court to 'lay down a stricter and more consistent body of rules' on admissibility. However, when it gave judgment, the CJEU ignored the invitation.

Thinking point

1. Why could the bodies in *Nordsee*, *X*, and *Victoria Film* not seek preliminary rulings? Which factor(s) were missing?

2. Is the functional test for establishing whether or not a body is a 'court or tribunal' too generous, as A-G Ruiz-Jarabo Colomer contends? What are the advantages and disadvantages (if any) of the Court adopting a very wide interpretation?

6.4.5 **Discretionary and mandatory referral**

Article 267 of the TFEU distinguishes between two categories of courts and tribunals – those which 'may' refer a question to the CJEU and those which 'shall' do so. If courts or tribunals fall within the former category then they have complete discretion whether or not to refer. However, courts and tribunals from which there is no 'judicial remedy under national law' must request a ruling. These are often referred to as 'courts-of-last-resort'. Essentially, if there is no right even to seek leave to appeal against the decision of a particular body, then that body is a 'court-of-last-resort'.

The question of which UK courts and tribunals are subject to mandatory referral has attracted debate. The UK Supreme Court (and its predecessor, the Judicial Committee of the House of Lords) is certainly included but what about, for example, the Court of Appeal in the event that the Supreme Court refuses to give leave to appeal? The answer is that, generally speaking, the Court of Appeal is not a 'court-of-last-resort' because, according to the CJEU in *Lyckeskog* (Case C-99/00) [2002] ECR I-4839, the right to *seek* leave to appeal from the Supreme Court qualifies as a 'judicial remedy' (whether or not leave is given).

In *Bullmer v Bollinger* [1974] Ch 401, Lord Denning commented that mandatory referral applied only to the House of Lords. However, this is too restrictive. As Balcombe LJ noted in *Chiron v Murex* [1995] All ER (EC) 88, there are some situations when there is no right even to seek leave to appeal against a decision of the Court of Appeal, meaning that no 'judicial remedy' would be available, in which case the Court of Appeal should be regarded as a 'court-of-last-resort'.

6.4.6 **Avoiding mandatory referral**

Despite the wording of Article 267 of the TFEU, in *Da Costa* (Cases 28–30/62) [1963] ECR 61 and *CILFIT* (Case 283/81) [1982] ECR 3415 the CJEU has ruled that a 'court-of-last-resort' is under no obligation to refer if:

- The question is not relevant, in the sense that the answer to it cannot affect the outcome of the case.

- A previous decision(s) of the CJEU has already interpreted the provision of EU legislation in question.

- The correct application of the provision of EU legislation is so obvious as to leave no room for any reasonable doubt. This is known as *'acte clair'*. The CJEU has stressed that a national court should not easily reach the conclusion that a provision of EU law is *'acte clair'*. In *CILFIT*, the Court stated that 'the national court or tribunal must be convinced that the matter is equally obvious to the courts of the other Member States and to the Court of Justice'. The Court added that it had to be borne in mind that EU legislation was drafted in several languages, and that EU law uses terminology which was 'peculiar to it', emphasising that 'legal concepts do not necessarily have the same meaning' in EU law and in national law.

The *acte clair* doctrine is an important device for cutting out unnecessary, time-consuming requests. However, it can be abused, as happened in *R v Chief Constable of Sussex, ex parte ITF Ltd* [1999] 2 AC 418, where the House of Lords declined to seek rulings on the interpretation of the word 'measures' in Article 35 TFEU and the phrase 'public policy' in Article 36 TFEU, a decision which was criticised by commentators. Estella Baker, for example, said that 'At least three moot points lie buried in the case...there is a persuasive argument that a reference should have been made' ('Policing, Protest and Free Trade' [2000] Crim LR 95).

The UK Supreme Court also failed to invoke the preliminary rulings procedure – despite its obligation to do so as a 'court-of-last-resort' – in *Abbey National plc v OFT* [2009] UKSC 6, [2009] 3 WLR 1215, concerning the interpretation of a provision in Directive 93/13. Although all five judges decided that the case should not be referred to the CJEU, only Lord Mance paid any attention to the cautionary words in *CILFIT*. He decided that the possibility of the disputed provision having a different meaning in the other language versions of the directive was 'very limited' and that the likelihood of the CJEU or other Member States' courts reaching a different interpretation was 'remote'. In contrast, Lord Walker simply stated that 'we should treat the matter as *acte clair*'. Meanwhile, Lord Phillips said that the matter was not *acte clair*, but should not be referred anyway because 'it would not be appropriate'. This has attracted criticism. Paul Davies described the failure to refer in *Abbey National* as 'dubious', pointing out that the Supreme Court had actually reversed the rulings of the High Court and Court of Appeal ('Bank charges in the Supreme Court' (2010) 69 CLJ 21).

There are several other recent cases in which the UK Supreme Court decided a case involving a disputed point of EU law but without seeking a preliminary ruling. In *Jivraj v Hashwani* [2011] UKSC 40; [2011] 1 WLR 1872, the Supreme Court held (without requesting a preliminary ruling) that the word 'employment' in the Framework Directive 2000/78 (which prohibits discrimination on the grounds of religion or belief, disability, age, or sexual orientation) did not cover the situation where an arbitrator was appointed to resolve a contractual dispute. Rather, an arbitrator's role was that of an 'independent provider of services who is not in a relationship of subordination with the parties who receive his services' (per Lord Clarke). The *Jivraj* case echoed *Abbey National* (2009) insofar as the Supreme Court reached the opposite conclusion to that of the Court of Appeal (in which it had been held – unanimously – that an arbitrator was in 'employment') but did not feel the need to seek a ruling from the CJEU.

Similarly, in *X v Mid-Sussex Citizens Advice Bureau* [2012] UKSC 59, [2013] 1 All ER 1038, the Supreme Court held (again, without requesting a preliminary ruling) that the activities of a volunteer advisor with the Citizens' Advice Bureau fell outside of the scope of the same directive, not being an 'occupation'. *X* is particularly important as it establishes a precedent for the whole of the UK that those in the voluntary sector cannot rely on the directive and/or the UK implementing legislation to challenge alleged discrimination on the grounds listed in the directive. As the UK's 'court-of-last-resort' the Supreme Court was, in principle, obliged to refer to the CJEU a question on the meaning of the word 'occupation' but invoked the *acte clair* doctrine instead. The Supreme Court did at least give serious consideration to one of the *CILFIT* criteria – the possibility that other national courts in the EU might reach a different conclusion – but Lord Mance's judgment was emphatic: 'there is no scope for reasonable doubt about the conclusion that the Framework Directive does not cover voluntary activity'.

Thinking point

1. Baker commented that the House of Lords in *ITF* had displayed 'palpable reluctance' to seek a ruling. Why would the Lords be reluctant to invoke the procedure?

2. How could the Supreme Court in *Abbey National* and *Jivraj* conclude that the meaning of the disputed provision would be 'equally obvious to the courts of the other Member States and to the Court of Justice' when it was not even obvious to two other courts in England?

6.4.7 Docket control

There are exceptional circumstances in which the CJEU has declined to give a preliminary ruling. One such circumstance is when a ruling is elicited by means of a 'contrived dispute'. This occurred in *Foglia v Novello (No.1)* (Case 104/79) [1980] ECR 745 and *Foglia v Novello (No.2)* (Case 244/80) [1981] ECR 3045, where the Court refused to answer requests for preliminary rulings submitted to it by an Italian court on the basis that the dispute between the parties had been fabricated in order to have the Court resolve a disputed point of EU law. The Court stated that, 'The duty assigned to the Court by [Article 267 TFEU] is not that of delivering advisory opinions on general or hypothetical questions but of assisting in the administration of justice in the Member States'. Other situations in which a request for a ruling will be rejected include:

- Lack of factual and/or legal material. In *Telemarsicabruzzo & Others* (Cases C-320–322/90) [1993] ECR I-393 the Court declared that it was necessary for the national court or tribunal to 'define the factual and legislative context of the questions it is asking or, at the very least, explain the factual circumstances on which those questions are based'.

- Irrelevance. In *BP Supergas* (Case C-62/93) [1995] ECR I-1883 the Court stated that a request for a preliminary ruling may be rejected if it was 'quite obvious' that the ruling sought bore 'no relation to the actual nature of the case or the subject-matter of the main action'.

- No question of EU law is involved. In *Vajnai* (Case C-328/04) [2005] ECR I-8577 the CJEU rejected a request for a ruling because there was no question of EU legislation involved. A Hungarian man, Attila Vajnai, had been convicted of publicly displaying a five-point red star during a demonstration in Budapest, a criminal offence under Hungarian law. During his appeal hearing a preliminary ruling was requested but the CJEU declared that it had no jurisdiction to respond, because there was no provision of EU legislation which dealt with the criminal liability of those displaying political symbols.

6.4.8 Preliminary rulings on validity

Under Article 267 of the TFEU the CJEU can also deal with questions raised about the validity of EU secondary legislation (but not the Treaties). In *Firma Foto-Frost* (Case 314/85) [1987] ECR 4199 the CJEU stated that national courts do not have the power to declare EU secondary legislation invalid – only the CJEU has jurisdiction to do this. Where a question about the validity of secondary legislation is raised in legal proceedings, the national court must, therefore, either declare the legislation valid or make a reference to the CJEU.

6.4.9 The urgent procedure

In 2008, a new urgent procedure (known by its French acronym, PPU) was introduced. It is designed to allow preliminary rulings in exceptional cases to be prioritised. The national court must request that the PPU be applied and the CJEU must agree to the request (otherwise the ruling will be dealt with in the normal way). This allows for potentially enormous time savings. The normal preliminary rulings procedure takes, on average, nineteen months from request to judgment; under the PPU the waiting period can be measured in a matter of weeks. In the first case under the PPU, *Inga Rinau* (Case C-195/08 PPU) [2008] ECR I-5271, a ruling was requested in April 2008. Because the case involved a child custody dispute it was deemed to be urgent and judgment was delivered by the CJEU in July 2008, less than three months later. An ever faster turnaround was achieved in *Santesteban Goicoechea* (Case C-296/08 PPU) [2008] ECR I-6307, in the context of extradition proceedings. A preliminary ruling was requested in July 2008 and judgment was handed down by the CJEU in August, some five weeks later.

The PPU has been cautiously welcomed by commentators. Panis Koutrakos observed that 'there is a balance which must be struck: judges should be given time to reflect on the questions put before them, assess the arguments...and consider the wider ramifications of their conclusions...Whilst appropriate in certain exceptional circumstances, speed is not the only factor for the organisation of judicial proceedings' ('Speeding up the Preliminary Reference Procedure – Fast but not too Fast' (2008) 33 EL Rev 617).

6.4.10 Reform of the preliminary rulings procedure

The average waiting time for a preliminary ruling is approximately sixteen months, which has in fact come down from a previous record high of over two years. Even with this reduction in the waiting time, it is clearly unacceptable, for several reasons. First, the case at national level is suspended while the CJEU is preparing its ruling – meaning that the legal dispute which led to the case remains unresolved during that time. Second, national courts may be put off from asking questions because of the delay, meaning that (potentially) a number of very important questions which would otherwise be answered by the CJEU have to be answered by the national courts.

Thinking point

What do you think has caused, or contributed to, this problem? There are in fact several factors – see how many you can identify. A non-exhaustive list of these factors appears at the end of this section.

The solution adopted to deal with this problem is to allow the General Court to handle some of the preliminary rulings workload. Article 256(3) of the TFEU provides that the General Court has jurisdiction to respond to questions referred for a preliminary ruling under Article 267 of the TFEU, but only in 'specific areas', which have not, as yet, been identified. Article 256(3) of the TFEU goes on to state that where the General Court considers that the case requires a 'decision of principle likely to affect the unity or consistency of Union law', it may refer the case to the CJEU for a ruling, and that 'decisions given by the General Court 'may exceptionally be subject to review' by the CJEU 'where there is a serious risk of the unity or consistency of Union law being affected'.

This solution was agreed by the Member States in 2000, during the negotiations which led to the signing of the Treaty of Nice in 2001. Over ten years later, however, the reform is still not in use, because no agreement had been reached on what the 'specific areas' should be. Even assuming that some, or at least one, 'specific areas' are eventually identified, there are likely to be teething problems until the new procedure is fully developed. For example:

- The General Court may refer cases onto the CJEU when a 'decision of principle' is involved – but what does 'decision of principle' mean?
- Although the CJEU is only to review General Court rulings 'exceptionally', this arguably undermines the authority of those rulings. For one thing, national courts will be inhibited from applying a General Court ruling whilst a possible review is still pending.

As the CJEU's workload has increased over the years, many other reform proposals that have been made. Given that the Article 256(3) TFEU solution appears to have stalled, it is worth looking briefly at some of these alternatives.

- Appoint more judges. However, this could be counter-productive, as it increases the risk of inconsistent judgments. Anthony Arnull has observed that 'the larger the Court, the less effective it is at delivering prompt and intellectually compelling judgments' ('Refurbishing the Judicial Architecture of the European Community' (1994) 43 ICLQ 296).

- Abolish mandatory referrals. However, this would make little practical difference. First, 'courts-of-last-resort' only contribute about 10–15 per cent of the CJEU's workload. Second, national supreme courts already have considerable discretion thanks to the CJEU's *Da Costa/CILFIT* jurisprudence.

- Restrict to national 'courts-of-last-resort' only the right to seek references. A less drastic version of this reform involves abolishing the rights of first instance national courts (such as magistrates' courts, county courts, the First-tier Tribunal, and most other tribunals in the UK). This would almost certainly reduce the CJEU's workload, but could threaten the uniformity of EU law and the 'dialogue' that presently exists between CJEU and all national courts and tribunals. It could create workload problems for national systems, if litigants are encouraged to pursue appeals until they reached a point in the national judicial hierarchy where a ruling could be requested.

- 'Case filtering', whereby the CJEU would be allowed to select cases according to their novelty, complexity, and/or importance. The advantages are a reduced CJEU workload; national courts may become more selective; and it would allow the CJEU to concentrate on those cases which are fundamental to the uniformity and development of EU law. The disadvantages are that it threatens the uniformity of EU law and the open dialogue between the CJEU and national courts.

- 'Decentralisation'. This would involve renaming the CJEU as the European High Court of Justice (EHCJ), at the apex of a new hierarchy, with four new Regional Courts below it. Under this system, the EU would be divided into four regions, and all the national courts and tribunals in each region would submit ruling requests to the Regional Court for that region. The EHCJ would act as an appeal court, ensuring consistency between the Regional Courts. The idea was proposed by Jean Paul Jacque and Joseph Weiler, 'On the Road to European Union – A New Judicial Architecture' (1990) 27 CML Rev 185. This system is not dissimilar to that in the USA, where the Supreme Court oversees the Circuit Courts below it, each Circuit consisting of a number of states, so it is workable, but could be expensive, given the need to set up, equip, and operate four new courts.

- Abolition of the preliminary rulings procedure, to be replaced by a new system whereby national courts' interpretation of EU legislation would be subject to a review process undertaken by the European Commission. See further Allott, 'Preliminary Rulings – Another Infant Disease' (2000) 25 EL Rev 538.

Possible causes of the CJEU's workload problem

- The increasing number of Member States, meaning more requests for rulings.

- The increasing number of languages. Initially, the CJEU (and its translators) only had to deal with four language versions of EU legislation. Gradually that has increased as more States joined so that there are now twenty-three languages (twenty-four if Irish is included).

- The increasing scope and volume of EU secondary legislation. For example, Directive 2000/78, which prohibits discrimination on various grounds in employment, only came fully into effect in 2006 but has already generated at least thirty separate preliminary ruling requests.

6.5 **Supremacy of EU law**

Given that EU law and national law often deal with the same subjects, such as employment law, consumer protection, and protection of the environment, there is potential conflict between the two. In the event of a dispute, which law is to prevail? There is nothing explicitly in either of the Treaties, although a 'declaration' attached to the Treaty of Lisbon states that 'in accordance with well-settled case law [of the CJEU], the Treaties and the law adopted by the Union on the basis of the Treaties have primacy over the law of the Member States'. The Court touched on the issue of supremacy in *Van Gend en Loos* (Case 26/62) [1963] ECR 1 (see 6.6) but it was first considered in depth in *Costa v ENEL* (Case 6/64) [1964] ECR 585, concerning a conflict between the Treaty of Rome and Italian law. The Court stated that EU law had to prevail, because:

> By creating a [Union] of unlimited duration, having its own institutions, its own personality, its own legal capacity...and, more particularly, real powers stemming from a limitation of sovereignty or a transfer of powers from the States to the [Union], the Member States have limited their sovereign rights and have thus created a body of law which binds both their nationals and themselves. The integration into the laws of each Member State of provisions which derive from the [Union]...make it impossible for the States...to accord precedence to a unilateral and subsequent measure over a legal system accepted by them on a basis of reciprocity.

This decision was not particularly surprising, given that the Member States had signed the Treaty and could be considered to have agreed to bind themselves not to enact legislation contradicting it. In *Internationale Handelsgesellschaft* (Case 11/70) [1970] ECR 1125, however, the Court was asked to consider a much more contentious situation: a conflict between EU secondary legislation and German constitutional law. The CJEU was forthright, stating that '[t]he law stemming from the Treaty...cannot because of its very nature be overridden by rules of national law, however framed'. In other words, all forms of EU law, whether primary (the Treaties) or secondary (the 'law stemming from the Treaty'), had to prevail over any conflicting provisions of national law – even national constitutional law. This remains the CJEU's position today.

See chapter 2 on the
UK Parliament's view
of supremacy.

A practical problem remained: what was a judge in a national court to actually do if faced with a conflict between EU and national law? In *Simmenthal* (Case 106/77) [1978] ECR 629, the CJEU made it clear that:

> Every national court must, in a case within its jurisdiction, apply [EU] law in its entirety and protect rights which the latter confers on individuals and must accordingly set aside any provision of national law which may conflict with it, whether prior or subsequent to the [Union] rule... It is not necessary for the court to request or await the prior setting aside of such provision by legislative or other constitutional means.

The CJEU reiterated these points in *R v Secretary of State for Transport, ex parte Factortame Ltd* (Case C-213/89) [1990] ECR I-2433, adding that if a national court is prevented by a rule of national law 'from granting interim relief in order to ensure the full effectiveness of the judgment to be given on the existence of the rights claimed under [EU] law' then the court 'is obliged to set aside that rule'.

6.6 Direct effect

6.6.1 Introduction

The principle of 'direct effect' refers to those provisions of EU legislation which are capable of enforcement by individuals before national courts. The fact that individuals are capable of enforcing EU law in national courts clearly strengthens the impact of EU law. It also means that EU law is more likely to be observed, since the breach of 'directly effective' EU law (either by Member States or by other individuals) can potentially be challenged by individuals before national courts. Whether a particular provision of EU legislation is 'directly effective' depends on its language and purpose. Some provisions are only binding on, and enforceable by, Member States; others are too vague for enforcement by individuals; others are incomplete and require further implementation. To be directly effective, certain criteria must be satisfied. The key criteria are that the provision in question must be:

● sufficiently clear and precise; and

● unconditional.

The question whether or not a particular provision of EU legislation has direct effect is one that can only be answered by a court (not necessarily the CJEU; national courts can make rulings on this question).

6.6.2 Direct effect and Treaty articles

The principle of direct effect was first developed in relation to articles of the Treaty of Rome (now the TFEU) in *Van Gend en Loos* (Case 26/62) [1963] ECR 1, involving an alleged breach by the Dutch authorities of what is now Article 30 of the TFEU. The

CJEU confirmed that certain provisions of the Treaty were enforceable in national courts, at least in cases where the provision in question was being relied upon by an individual (in this case, a Dutch road haulage company) against one of the Member States. The Court stated:

> [EU] law...not only imposes obligations on individuals but is also intended to con-fer upon them rights which become part of their legal heritage. These rights arise not only where they are expressly granted by the Treaty, but also by reason of obligations which the Treaty imposes in a clearly defined way upon individuals as well as upon the Member States.

The CJEU has subsequently found several Treaty articles to be directly effective. The criteria (set out earlier) have been applied generously, with the result that many provisions which are not *particularly* clear or precise have been found to have direct effect.

Having established the principle of 'direct effect', the next question was whether EU legislation was capable of enforcement in actions brought against individuals, as opposed to the State. This arose in *Defrenne v SABENA* (Case 43/75) [1976] ECR 455, and the CJEU answered in the affirmative.

In *Defrenne v SABENA* (1976), an airline stewardess (Gabrielle Defrenne) brought a claim against her ex-employer (the Belgian airline company, SABENA) in the Belgian courts, alleging that she was being paid less than her male colleagues. At the relevant time, there was no Belgian legislation prohibiting pay discrimination. Defrenne there-fore relied upon what is now Article 157(1) of the TFEU (which guarantees equal pay for men and women doing the same work). The Labour Court in Brussels, Belgium requested a preliminary ruling from the CJEU under what is now Article 267 of the TFEU. The CJEU held that not only could Article 157(1) be relied upon in national courts, it could be relied upon against private employers. The Court stated that 'Since [Article 157 TFEU] is mandatory in nature, the prohibition on discrimination between men and women applies not only to the action of public authorities, but also extends to all agreements which are intended to regulate paid labour collectively, as well as to contracts between individuals'.

The idea that EU legislation may be enforced in the context of a dispute between an individual and the State is called 'vertical' direct effect, whereas the notion that EU legislation (or at least, Treaty articles) may impose obligations on individuals as well as the State is referred to as 'horizontal' direct effect. More recent examples of horizontal direct effect are:

- *Angonese* (Case C-281/98) [2000] ECR I-4139: an Italian national relied on Article 45(2) of the TFEU in a claim against an Italian bank.
- *Courage Ltd v Crehan* (Case C-453/99) [2001] ECR I-6297: Article 101 of the TFEU was invoked in a dispute between a British brewery/pub chain and a publican.
- *ITWF v Viking Line* (Case C-438/05) [2007] ECR I-10779: Article 49 of the TFEU was relied upon in litigation between the Viking Line ferry company and a trade union.

6.6.3 **Direct effect and regulations**

Provisions within regulations may also be directly effective, both vertically and horizontally, if they satisfy the key criteria. An example of provisions within regulations being relied upon horizontally occurred in *Muñoz v Frumar Ltd* (Case C-253/00) [2002] ECR I-7289.

6.6.4 **Direct effect and directives**

It was originally thought that directives, because they require implementation by Member States, were incapable of direct effect. However, in *Van Duyn v Home Office* (Case 41/74) [1974] ECR 1337, the CJEU ruled that provisions within directives are capable of direct effect, despite the need for implementation, so long as the result to be achieved is clear. However, there is an extra criterion to be met: a directive cannot have direct effect until its implementation date has expired (*Ratti* (Case 148/78) [1979] ECR 1629). Once a directive has been properly implemented into national legislation, an individual should rely on that legislation rather than on the directive. However, if a Member State fails to implement a directive on time (either at all or properly) then an individual may rely on the directive itself, if its provisions satisfy the criteria for direct effect.

However, this is subject to one final – but very significant – qualification. Having established that directives are capable of direct effect, the CJEU in *Marshall v Southampton Area Health Authority* (Case 152/84) [1986] ECR 723 drew a distinction between vertical and horizontal direct effect. In *Marshall*, the Court held that:

> It must be emphasised that…the binding nature of a directive…exists only in relation to 'each member state to which it is addressed'. It follows that a directive may not of itself impose obligations on an individual and that a provision of a directive may not be relied upon as such against such a person.

In *Marshall v Southampton AHA* (1986), Helen Marshall was employed by the defendant as a dietician. She was forced to retire at the age of 62 on the ground that she had exceeded the authority's compulsory retirement age, which was 60 for women, as opposed to 65 for men. This was permissible under the UK's Sex Discrimination Act 1975, which excluded 'provisions relating to death or retirement', but was allegedly in breach of Article 5 of Directive 76/207 (the Equal Treatment Directive), which prohibits discrimination between men and women in terms of 'dismissal' from employment. The Court of Appeal requested a preliminary ruling. The CJEU held that the word 'dismissal' could be interpreted to include compulsory retirement. It then held that provisions in directives were enforceable against the State, but not against private individuals, because directives were addressed to the Member States. However, Ms Marshall was still entitled to enforce Article 5, because the Authority could be regarded as part of the State. This was the case even though the Authority was acting in its capacity as an employer.

> ## 🔒 Key point
>
> Thus, according to *Marshall*, directives are only capable of 'vertical' direct effect (*Van Duyn* is an example). They are not capable of 'horizontal' direct effect.

The consequences of this are that provisions in an unimplemented directive dealing with some aspect of employment law (for instance) may be invoked by public sector employees against their employer (the State) but the same provisions cannot be invoked by a private sector employee against his/her employer. This particular anomaly led A-G Lenz in *Faccini Dori v Recreb* (Case C-91/92) [1994] ECR I-3325 to invite the Court to reconsider *Marshall*, but it declined to do so. Indeed, the Court has confirmed in several subsequent cases that directives are only enforceable 'vertically'.

However, although directives only have 'vertical' direct effect, in *Marshall* the CJEU held that Southampton AHA was part of the State, even in its capacity as employer. Indeed, in subsequent cases, the Court has emphasised that directives are potentially enforceable against the State in the sense of central government (as in *Van Duyn*), local government (*Constanzo v Municipality of Milan* (Case 103/88) [1989] ECR 1839), and its various 'emanations'. The CJEU has held the following are capable of being classed as 'emanations' of the State:

- health authorities (*Marshall*);
- the police (*Johnston* (Case 222/84) [1986] ECR 1651);
- the armed forces (*Sirdar* (Case C-273/97) [1999] ECR I-7403); and
- nationalised industries (*Foster v British Gas* (Case C-188/89) [1990] ECR I-3133).

The leading case here is *Foster*, where the CJEU stated that directives were enforceable 'against organisations or bodies which were subject to the authority or control of the State or had special powers beyond those which result from the normal rules applicable to relations between individuals'. This actually gives 'vertical' direct effect a much broader scope than might otherwise have been the case and ameliorates to some extent the decision in *Marshall* to deny 'horizontal' direct effect to directives.

> ## 🔒 Key point
>
> Although directives are only capable of 'vertical' direct effect, they are enforceable against the State in the sense of central and local government and 'emanations' of the State, such as the police.

Nevertheless, *Marshall* remains one of the CJEU's most controversial decisions and the distinction between vertical and horizontal direct effect of directives generates difficulties. For example, the claimants in *Marshall* and *Foster* were ultimately successful, as their cases were 'vertical', but in a third case, *Doughty v Rolls Royce plc* [1992] 1 CMLR 1045, the claimant was unsuccessful, her case being 'horizontal'. Yet the facts of all three cases were otherwise identical (the claimants were even seeking to enforce the same provision of the same directive).

Application of *Foster v British Gas* in UK courts and tribunals

Strictly speaking, the CJEU in *Foster* (1990) could only define in general terms the bodies against which directives were capable of being enforced. Since that judgment, several courts and tribunals in the UK have been called upon to apply *Foster* to various bodies in order to decide whether the provisions of an unimplemented directive could be enforced against them. Generally speaking, the courts have adopted a generous interpretation of *Foster*. The following is a summary of some of the cases:

- *Foster v British Gas (No. 2)* [1991] 2 AC 306. Here, the House of Lords held that British Gas (at least, when it was still a nationalised industry) was an 'emanation of the State'. Lord Templeman said that 'British Gas, which provided a public service, the supply of gas, to citizens of the State generally under the control of the State [and] was equipped with a special monopoly power which was created and could only have been created by the legislature [was] therefore a body against which the relevant provisions of the Equal Treatment Directive may be enforced'.

- *Doughty v Rolls-Royce PLC* [1992] 1 CMLR 1045. Here, the Court of Appeal held that the aerospace division of Rolls-Royce was not an 'emanation of the State' because it did not provide a public service and did not possess special powers.

- *Griffin v South-West Water Services Ltd* [1995] IRLR 15. In this case, the High Court found that the defendant company was an 'emanation of the State' despite being a private company, largely because it was regulated by OFWAT, the water regulator. Blackburne J held that the question was not 'whether the body in question is under the control of the State, but whether the public service in question is under the control of the State'. He added that it was also 'irrelevant that the body does not carry out any of the traditional functions of the State and is not an agent of the State... It is irrelevant too that the State does not possess any day-to-day control over the activities of the body.'

- *NUT v Governors of St Mary's Church of England Junior School* [1997] 3 CMLR 630. Here, the Court of Appeal held that school governors could be regarded as an 'emanation of the State'. Schiemann LJ said that although the governors did not have any 'special powers', they had been made responsible for providing a public service (education) and they were under the control of the State, which was sufficient.

- *Three Rivers District Council v Bank of England (No.3)* [2003] 2 AC 1; [2000] 2 WLR 1220, in which the House of Lords accepted without dispute that the Bank of England was an 'emanation of the state'.

- *Byrne v Motor Insurers' Bureau & Another* [2007] EWHC 1268 (QB), [2008] 2 WLR 234. Here, the High Court held that the MIB was not an 'emanation of the state', essentially because of the 'complete absence of special powers'.

- *Ministry of Defence v Wallis* [2011] EWCA Civ 231; [2011] 2 CMLR 42. Here, the Court of Appeal described the Ministry as an 'emanation of the state', although strictly speaking a central government department (like the Home Office in *Van Duyn*) *is* the State, as opposed to an 'emanation' of it.

- *NHS Leeds v Larner* [2012] EWCA Civ 1034, in which the Court of Appeal did not need to decide the issue after NHS Leeds accepted that it was an 'emanation of the state'.

The significance of all of this case law for the English legal system is that it demonstrates that directives are capable of enforcement against a wide variety of British bodies, such as British Gas (at least, when it was a nationalised industry), the Bank of England, and the NHS, even though directives are officially only 'addressed' to the Member States. The effect of this is to enable British claimants to enforce their rights under EU law in UK courts. Of course, not every claimant is able to do so: the ruling in *Marshall* continues to impose an obstacle to claimants wishing to enforce their legal rights in directives against other individuals. However, there is an alternative solution available for some of those claimants: indirect effect (see 6.6.6).

Several British cases have also involved the much less controversial enforcement of directives against local authorities. These include *Gibson v East Riding of Yorkshire Council* [2000] 3 CMLR 329 (Court of Appeal), *South Tyneside Metropolitan Borough Council v Toulson* [2003] 1 CMLR 28 (Employment Appeal Tribunal), and *Sayers v Cambridgeshire County Council* [2006] EWHC 2029 (High Court). These are less controversial because directives are 'addressed' to the Member States and this clearly includes local as well as central government.

No 'reverse' vertical direct effect of directives

Finally, it should be noted that while directives can be enforced vertically *against* the State, they cannot be enforced vertically *by* the State. In other words, there is no 'reverse' vertical direct effect of directives. This was established in *Kolpinghuis Nijmegen* (Case 80/86) [1987] ECR 3969, where the Court refused to sanction the prosecution by the Dutch authorities of a café for allegedly failing to comply with the provisions of Directive 80/777 relating to the marketing of natural mineral waters – because the directive had not been implemented into Dutch law.

6.6.5 **The incidental direct effect of directives**

Although it is clear from *Marshall* and *Faccini Dori* that directives cannot be enforced by one individual against another individual, in *CIA Security International* (Case

C-194/94) [1996] ECR I-2201 the Court held that a directive can be relied upon by an individual to prevent another individual from enforcing national law which is clearly contrary to it. In other words, directives cannot be used as a 'sword' but can be used as a 'shield'. This has been confirmed in several subsequent cases.

It is also possible to rely on a directive vertically even where this incidentally imposes obligations on another individual. This can be seen in *Wells* (Case C-201/02) [2004] ECR I-723, where Mrs Wells used Directive 85/337 to force the British government to carry out an environmental impact assessment of proposed mining operations at a neighbouring quarry even though that would impact adversely on the quarry's owners. The Court emphasised that the principle of vertical direct effect overrode the 'adverse repercussions' for the quarry's owners.

6.6.6 Indirect effect

The lack of 'horizontal' direct effect of directives clearly creates anomalies. However, there is an alternative remedy available to those wishing to enforce directives against other individuals: the 'obligation of interpretation', usually referred to as 'indirect effect'. This obligation was first identified in *Von Colson* (Case 14/83) [1984] ECR 1891, where the Court ruled that, where national legislation has been enacted to implement a directive, national courts are under a duty to interpret that legislation as far as possible in order to achieve the result required by the directive. This duty follows from the obligation placed upon Member States (including the courts) under Article 288 of the TFEU to achieve the results of a directive and their general duty under Article 4(3) of the TEU to take all appropriate measures to ensure fulfilment of their obligations.

An example of the *Von Colson* principle in the UK context is the case of *Litster* [1990] 1 AC 546, where the House of Lords interpreted UK legislation (the Transfer of Undertakings (Protection of Employment) Regulations 1981) in conformity with Directive 77/187, because the 1981 Regulations had been passed specifically in order to implement the 1977 directive.

The scope of the obligation of interpretation was significantly extended in *Marleasing* (Case C-106/89) [1990] ECR I-4135. The CJEU ruled that the obligation applied to all national legislation, including pre-existing legislation, not just legislation specifically implementing a directive. Prior to this ruling, the House of Lords had refused to apply *Von Colson* in a case involving pre-existing UK legislation (*Duke v GEC Reliance Ltd* [1988] AC 618). However, in subsequent cases, the *Marleasing* effect has been deployed between employees and their employers (or ex-employers) involving the interpretation of various sections of the Sex Discrimination Act 1975 (now repealed) in order to achieve results set out in the 1976 Equal Treatment Directive (Directive 76/207). For example, in *Webb v EMO (Air Cargo) Ltd* [1993] 1 WLR 49, Lord Keith said:

> It is for a UK court to construe domestic legislation in any field covered by a directive so as to accord with the interpretation of the directive as laid down by the [CJEU], if that

could be done without distorting the meaning of the domestic legislation...This is so whether the domestic legislation came after or, as in this case, preceded the directive.

In *Webb*, the House of Lords felt able to reinterpret a provision of the 1975 Act in a way which brought it into line with the Equal Treatment Directive, which resulted in the House giving judgment to Ms Webb. Other examples of cases in which courts and tribunals in the UK were able to reinterpret the 1975 Act in the light of the Equal Treatment Directive include *Coote v Granada Hospitality Ltd (No.2)* [1999] IRLR 452 (Employment Appeal Tribunal), *Hardman v Mallon* [2002] 2 CMLR 59 (Employment Appeal Tribunal), and *Relaxion Group v Rhys-Harper* [2003] UKHL 33; [2003] 4 All ER 1113 (House of Lords). You should note that all of these UK cases were 'horizontal', i.e. they were disputes between individual employees and their private (non-State) employers, such that direct effect would not have been available (because of the *Marshall* ruling), but indirect effect was available instead.

The obligation of interpretation was further expanded in *Pfeiffer* (Case C-397/01) [2004] ECR I-8835, where the Court indicated that the obligation extended to the 'whole body of rules of national law' – presumably including case law as well as national legislation. In *Impact* (Case C-268/06) [2008] ECR I-2483, the CJEU added that national courts were obliged to do 'whatever lies within their jurisdiction, taking the whole body of domestic law into consideration and applying the interpretative methods recognised by domestic law, with a view to ensuring that the directive in question is fully effective and achieving an outcome consistent with the objective pursued by it'.

In *Adeneler & Others* (Case C-212/04) [2006] ECR I-6057, the CJEU drew a parallel with its case law on direct effect (see *Ratti*) by deciding that the interpretative obligation arises only once the period for implementing the directive has expired. However, there is contradictory case law. *Mangold v Helm* (Case C-144/04) [2005] ECR I-9981 concerned the possible indirect effect of Directive 2000/78 (which required Member States to introduce legislation to tackle, inter alia, age discrimination) the implementation date of which was still in the future at the time of the dispute. Nevertheless, the Court decided that, because the principle of non-discrimination on grounds of age must 'be regarded as a general principle' of EU law, 'observance of the general principle of equal treatment, in particular in respect of age, cannot as such be conditional upon the expiry of the period allowed the Member States for the transposition' of Directive 2000/78.

The obligation of interpretation is subject to certain limitations. First, national courts are *not* expected to use directives to interpret national legislation in such a way as to create, or exacerbate, criminal liability (*Arcaro* (Case C-168/95) [1996] ECR I-4705). Second, the obligation on national courts is to interpret domestic legislation 'so far as possible, in the light of the wording and the purpose of the directive' (*Marleasing*). Thus, while indirect effect can be applied to most national legislation (although this may sometimes require a creative approach to interpretation), it will not apply to national legislation the wording of which clearly contradicts the directive (*Pupino* (Case C-105/03) [2005] ECR I-5285), or which is entirely unambiguous and therefore incapable of being interpreted (*QDQ Media v Omedas Lecha* (Case C-235/03) [2005] ECR I-1937).

> ### ! Critical debate
>
> Professor Michael Dougan has argued for the *Marshall* rule to be scrapped. In 'The "Disguised" Vertical Direct Effect of Directives?' (2000) 59 CLJ 586, he argued that '[t]he "incidental effect" case-law merely joins the unfortunate parade of bizarre nuances which already characterises this particular field…Ultimately, the case for toppling this house of cards simply by granting full horizontal direct effect to directives emerges still stronger.' Other academics, such as Professor Paul Craig ('The Legal Effect of Directives: Policy, Rules and Exceptions' (2009) 34 EL Rev 349) and Albertina Albors-Llorens ('Keeping up Appearances: the Court of Justice and the Effects of EU Directives' (2010) 69 CLJ 455), and a number of the CJEU's Advocates-General, have expressed similar views.
>
> On one hand, the Court of Justice has taken the view, based on the wording of the TFEU itself, that because directives are addressed to the Member States they are therefore binding only on the Member States. Hence, whilst the vertical direct effect of directives is possible (*Van Duyn*), the horizontal direct effect of directives is not (*Marshall*). It can also be argued that it would be unfair to allow an individual to enforce an unimplemented directive against another individual when it was not the fault of the (latter) individual that the directive had not been implemented into national law. Another argument can be made that, when a dispute involves individuals one of whom is seeking to enforce an unimplemented directive, indirect effect provides a more suitable remedy.
>
> On the other hand, academics point out the *Marshall* rule has been undermined by cases such as *Johnston* and *Foster v British Gas* (which have blurred the boundaries between vertical and horizontal direct effect), *CIA Security International* (which allows for directives to be enforced horizontally, provided the directive is being used as a 'shield' and not a 'sword'), and *Wells* (which allows a directive to be used by one individual to impose an obligation on another individual, provided that this is a side-effect of enforcing the directive vertically). They have also pointed out that reliance on indirect effect is not necessarily a perfect solution, as it relies on the national court being able and willing to interpret national law in conformity with EU law.
>
> In the light of this, should the Court of Justice change course and allow horizontal direct effect for directives? What would be the advantages and disadvantages (if any) for doing so? Bear in mind that Treaty articles and provisions in regulations already have horizontal direct effect.

6.7 **State liability**

6.7.1 Introduction

State liability for breaches of EU law was introduced in *Francovich & Others v Italy* (Cases C-6/90 and C-9/90) [1991] ECR I-5357, when the CJEU declared that the

Member States were 'obliged' to compensate individuals for loss and damage caused to them by breaches of EU law. There is nothing explicitly in either of the Treaties to support this, but the Court justified its decision by reference to what is now Article 4(3) of the TEU, according to which Member States have an obligation to ensure the fulfilment of their obligations arising under the Treaties.

6.7.2 The conditions for State liability

Francovich was concerned specifically with the failure of the Italian government to implement a directive. The obligation imposed on States to implement directives is clear (see Articles 4(3) of the TEU and 288 of the TFEU). However, two issues remained unclear:

- what the position might be in relation to other breaches; and
- the level of fault required to establish liability.

The CJEU addressed these issues in *Brasserie du Pêcheur SA v Germany; Factortame III* (Cases C-46 and 48/93) [1996] ECR I-1029. The Court made it clear that State liability was a general principle, not restricted to a failure to implement directives, and that three conditions had to be satisfied:

- the rule of EU law infringed must have been intended to confer rights on individuals;
- the breach must be sufficiently serious; and
- there must be a direct causal link between the breach of the obligation resting on the State and the damage sustained by the injured parties.

The burden of proof is on the claimant to establish all three conditions. State liability claims are brought in the national court of the defendant State.

An intention to confer rights on individuals

There is a strong link here to direct effect. As A-G Léger noted in *Köbler v Austria* (Case C-224/01) [2003] ECR I-10239, concerning an alleged breach of Article 45 TFEU (which confers the right of free movement on workers): 'The rule of law purportedly infringed... is directly effective and its purpose is therefore necessarily to confer rights on individuals.' This first condition has subsequently been held to be satisfied in the case of several directly effective Treaty articles, including Articles 34 and 35 TFEU (which facilitate the free movement of goods) and Article 49 TFEU (which confers the right of 'establishment' on companies and self-employed people). If the first condition is satisfied, the focus shifts to the second condition; but if not then the claim fails. This happened in *Paul & Others v Germany* (Case C-222/02), where the CJEU decided that Article 3(1) of Directive 94/19 was not intended to confer rights on individuals.

A sufficiently serious breach

The test for determining the second condition, a 'sufficiently serious' breach, is whether the Member State 'manifestly and gravely disregarded the limits on its discretion' (*Brasserie; Factortame III*). Although in principle it is national courts who decide this, the CJEU has identified various factors which may be used, as follows:

- the clarity and precision of the rule breached;
- the measure of discretion left by that rule;
- whether the infringement and the damage caused was intentional or involuntary;
- if there was an error of law, whether the error was excusable or not;
- any position taken by the Union's institutions; and
- the adoption or retention of national measures contrary to that rule.

The first two factors are intrinsically linked. As the CJEU pointed out in *Synthon* (Case C-452/06) [2008] ECR I-7681, the Member State's discretion is 'broadly dependent on the degree of clarity and precision of the rule infringed'.

Many State liability cases involve the failure to properly implement a directive. Such breaches may or may not be sufficiently serious. In *BT* (Case C-392/93) [1996] ECR I-1631 and *Denkavit International v Germany* (Case C-283/94) [1996] ECR I-5063, the failures by (respectively) the UK and Germany were held *not* to be serious, largely because the text of the directives were unclear, and both States had acted in good faith in trying to implement the directive correctly (suggesting the breach was excusable). Conversely, in *Rechberger & Others v Austria* (Case C-140/97) [1999] ECR I-3499 and *Stockholm Lindöpark v Sweden* (Case C-150/99) [2001] ECR I-493, incorrect implementation was deemed to be serious, because in both cases the relevant directives were clearly worded (suggesting the breach was inexcusable). Meanwhile, in *Dillenkofer v Germany* (Case C-178/94) [1996] ECR I-4845 the CJEU held that failing to implement a directive at all (as opposed to failing to do so properly) would always constitute a sufficiently serious breach, since the obligation to implement directives (under Article 288 of the TFEU) is absolute.

Where a Member State breaches another provision of EU law, typically in the TFEU, the question of liability depends upon the application of these factors to the factual circumstances. Thus the breach of Article 34 TFEU by the German government in *Brasserie du Pêcheur* was deemed to be insufficiently serious because it was an excusable error. However, the breach of Article 35 TFEU by the UK in *Hedley Lomas* (Case C-5/94) [1996] ECR I-2553 was deemed to be serious because of the lack of discretion available. Similarly, the breach of Article 49 TFEU by the UK in *Factortame III* was serious because the government had intentionally breached the provision in question.

Direct causal link

As to the third condition, the CJEU has held that it is, generally speaking, for the national courts to determine whether a direct causal link between breach and damage exists (*Rechberger & Others*).

6.7.3 **What is the 'State'?**

Most State liability cases involve actions against central government. However, in *Konle v Austria* (Case C-302/97) [1999] ECR I-3099 the CJEU decided that compensation need not necessarily be the responsibility of central government, and in *Haim* (Case C-424/97) [2000] ECR I-5123, the CJEU stated that state liability claims could be brought irrespective of the 'public authority...responsible for the breach'.

Even the judiciary may be held liable, according to the CJEU in *Köbler*. Although the claim in that case (against the Austrian Supreme Court) failed, the CJEU expressly ruled that national courts 'adjudicating at last instance' could face liability. This was confirmed in *Traghetti del Mediterraneo v Italy* (Case C-173/03) [2006] ECR I-5177, involving a claim against the Italian Supreme Court. However, the CJEU stressed that 'State liability can be incurred only in the exceptional case where the national court adjudicating at last instance has manifestly infringed the applicable law'.

Köbler creates the possibility that a State liability claim brought against a national court could end up being decided in the same court. This actually happened in *Cooper v Attorney General* [2010] EWCA Civ 464, [2010] 3 CMLR 28, when a State liability claim brought against the Court of Appeal had to be decided by the Court of Appeal. The claimant contended that two earlier Court of Appeal decisions (in 1999 and 2000) were in serious breach of EU law. The claim was brought in the High Court, and judgment was given to the defendants, but that decision was appealed to the Court of Appeal. The Court (in 2010) decided that the earlier Courts had committed a breach of EU law, but not a sufficiently serious breach to justify the imposition of State liability. (NB in the 1999 and 2000 cases, the Court of Appeal had been 'adjudicating at last instance' because no appeal was available to the House of Lords.)

Finally, in *AGM v Finland* (Case C-470/03) [2007] ECR I-2749 the CJEU introduced a form of vicarious liability when it stated that EU law 'does not preclude an individual other than a Member State from being held liable, in addition to the Member State itself, for damage caused to individuals by measures which that individual has taken' in breach of EU law'. Thus liability could, in principle, be imposed on a Member State for breaches of EU law made by individual government employees.

6.7.4 **Limitations**

Member States are allowed to impose conditions on the amount of damages that the claimant can recover in State liability claims. However, any such conditions must not be less favourable than those relating to similar domestic claims (the 'principle of equivalence') or framed in such a way as to make it in practice 'impossible or excessively difficult' to obtain reparation (the 'principle of effectiveness'). For example, reasonable limitation periods are permissible. In *Danske Slagterier v Germany* (Case C-445/06) [2009] ECR I-2119, the CJEU stated that reasonable time limits for bringing proceedings were justifiable 'in the interests of legal certainty which protects both the taxpayer and the authorities concerned'.

Summary

- The EU was formed in 1993, following the European Coal and Steel Community formed in 1952, and the European Economic Community formed in 1958.
- The EU has twenty-eight Member States with five applicant countries.
- The EU is run by several supranational institutions, including the Council, the European Commission, the European Parliament, and the CJEU.
- There are three main sources of EU law: primary legislation, secondary legislation, and case law of the CJEU.
- Primary legislation consists of the Treaty on European Union, the Treaty on the Functioning of the European Union, and the Charter of Fundamental Rights. These contain the fundamental principles of EU law.
- Secondary legislation includes regulations and directives, which add detail to the fundamental principles. Regulations seek to ensure uniformity throughout the Union. They do not require implementation. Directives are binding only as to the 'result to be achieved'. They require implementation into national law, within a specified time period.
- The CJEU deals with enforcement actions brought by the European Commission against Member States and preliminary rulings. The latter allows national 'courts and tribunals' to seek rulings on the interpretation of EU legislation, which ensures that EU law is interpreted consistently and applied uniformly. The CJEU has a heavy workload, which had led to long delays. Several reforms of the preliminary rulings procedure have been proposed.
- The CJEU has developed several key principles of EU law:
- 'Supremacy': any provision of EU law prevails over any conflicting provision of national law, even national constitutional law.
- 'Direct effect': sufficiently clear, precise, and unconditional provisions of EU legislation are enforceable by individuals in national courts. Treaty articles and regulations are enforceable 'vertically' (against the State) and 'horizontally' (against other individuals). Directives are enforceable once the implementation deadline has expired, but only 'vertically'. The State includes central and local government and 'emanations' of the State.
- 'Indirect effect': the obligation on national courts to interpret national legislation and case law, as far as possible, in conformity with any relevant directive, in order to achieve the result in the directive.

- State liability: Member States are obliged to compensate individuals for loss and damage caused by a failure to comply with EU law, subject to certain conditions.

? Questions

1 What are the main functions of the European Commission?

2 What the key differences between a regulation and a directive?

3 What is a 'court or tribunal' in the context of Article 267 TFEU?

4 What is a 'court-of-last-resort'?

5 Explain the circumstances in which the provisions of a directive could be given direct effect.

6 What is an 'emanation of the State'?

7 How was the principle of 'indirect effect' developed in (a) *Marleasing*; (b) *Pfeiffer*?

8 What are the conditions for State liability?

* Sample question and outline answer

Question

In the rare situations when direct effect of EU directives is not available, indirect effect ensures that individuals' rights under EU directives are adequately protected. Critically consider the extent to which you agree with this statement.

Outline answer

Answers to this question should begin by defining 'direct effect' – the concept that provisions of EU law are enforceable in national courts, subject to certain prerequisites being satisfied, i.e. that the provision in question is sufficiently clear, precise, and unconditional (*Becker*).

Answers should explain that provisions in directives are vertically enforceable, i.e. against the State (*Van Duyn*, *Becker*) but not horizontally, i.e. against other individuals (*Marshall*). This situation could usefully be contrasted with that involving provisions in the TFEU and/or provisions in regulations, both of which may be enforced horizontally as well as vertically (*Defrenne v SABENA*).

Explain the reasons for the *Marshall* rule – that directives are addressed to Member States and therefore only binding upon them (the so-called textual argument), who must not be allowed to benefit from their own failure to implement (the so-called estoppel argument); that it would be unfair to impose obligations via unimplemented directives on individuals.

Explain that, despite *Marshall*, directives are enforceable against local authorities and 'emanations of the State' such as the police (*Johnston*) as well as the 'State' in the sense of central government, which significantly ameliorates the strictness of the *Marshall* rule whilst simultaneously undermining it. After all, the possibility of enforcing directives against the police does not sit comfortably with the textual argument.

In particular, explain that CJEU in *Foster v British Gas* defined 'emanation of the State' very broadly, i.e. bodies subject to state authority/control or those with special powers, such as nationalised industries and hospitals, which only serves to blur the distinction between vertical and horizontal direct effect.

Explain the possibility of 'incidental' direct effect, i.e. where a directive may be used as a 'shield' in order to prevent contradictory national legislation from being enforced (*CIA Security v Signalson*) and 'triangular' direct effect, i.e. the situation where a directive is enforced (vertically) against the State even though there is a side-effect whereby obligations are imposed (horizontally) on a third party (*Wells*). Discuss the extent to which the presence of these concepts undermines the *Marshall* decision.

Note other limitations on the enforcement of directives, i.e. only available once implementation deadline has passed (*Ratti*); cannot be enforced by Member States against individuals, i.e. there is no reverse vertical direct effect (*Kolpinghuis*).

Answers should then explain 'indirect effect' – the obligation imposed on national courts to interpret implementing national legislation 'in the light of' EU directives (*Von Colson*). Note the subsequent expansion of indirect effect, in *Marleasing*, to all national legislation, whether implementing or not, and in *Pfeiffer* to all national law, i.e. case law as well as legislation. Explain the wide scope of indirect effect: in particular, observe that it is available in all cases, including 'horizontal' cases, as in *Marleasing* and *Webb*.

Discuss the limitations of indirect effect: the national legislation must be open to interpretation without 'distortion' (*Marleasing*) and therefore indirect effect will not apply to national legislation the wording of which clearly contradicts the directive (*Pupino*), or which is entirely unambiguous and therefore incapable of being interpreted (*QDQ Media v Omedas Lecha*); indirect effect is only available once the implementation deadline has passed (*Adeneler*); indirect effect cannot be used to create or exacerbate criminal liability (*Arcaro*).

Reach a conclusion. This will involve assessing whether direct effect of EU directives is not available only in 'rare' situations, and whether it is accurate to state that indirect effect ensures that individuals' rights under EU directives are adequately protected, given the various restrictions available on its enforcement. Academic commentary from the likes of Marson (2004) and Craig (2009), both of whom argue that the *Marshall* rule should be scrapped, could be usefully incorporated here.

🔾 Further reading

- **Craig, P.** 'The Legal Effect of Directives' (2009) 34 EL Rev 349
  Criticises the rule in *Marshall*, that directives cannot be enforced horizontally, in the light of the various exceptions to it that have been identified subsequently.

- **Davis, R.** 'Liability in Damages for a Breach of Community Law' (2006) 31 EL Rev 69
  Discusses the meaning and scope of the 'State' in the context of State liability.

- **Dougan, M.** 'When Worlds Collide: Competing Visions of the Relationship Between Direct Effect and Supremacy' (2007) 44 CML Rev 931

- **Drake, S.** 'Twenty Years after Von Colson' (2005) 30 EL Rev 329
  Provides an overview of the CJEU's indirect effect case law, and examines the relationship between indirect effect and incidental direct effect.

- **Lock, T.** *Is Private Enforcement of EU Law through State Liability a Myth? An Assessment 20 years after Francovich* (2012) 49 CML Rev 1675
  Examines the State liability case law in the two decades since the CJEU introduced the concept in 1991.

- **Marson, J.** 'Access to Justice: A Deconstructionist Approach to Horizontal Direct Effect' [2004] 4 Web JCLI (available at **webjcli.ncl.ac.uk**)
  Explores the arguments for and against horizontal direct effect of directives.

- **Rasmussen, H.** 'Remedying the Crumbling EC Judicial System' (2000) 37 CML Rev 1071
  Explores the various options for reform of the preliminary rulings procedure (including rewriting of the *CILFIT* criteria to encourage greater use of *acte clair*).

Online Resource Centre

You should now attempt the supporting multiple choice questions available at **www.oxfordtextbooks.co.uk/orc/wilson_els/**.

7

Human rights and fundamental freedoms

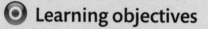

◎ Learning objectives

By the end of this chapter you should:

- understand the relationship between the law of the UK and the European Convention on Human Rights, particularly the impact of the Human Rights Act 1998 upon parliamentary sovereignty;

- appreciate the impact and consequences of UK law being incompatible with the European Convention on Human Rights;

- understand the significance of s.3 of the Human Rights Act 1998 for the process of statutory interpretation;

- be able to explain the operation of the doctrine of precedent in relation to decisions of the UK courts concerning human rights and the impact of decisions of the European Court of Human Rights;

- appreciate when Convention rights may be directly enforced, i.e. when the 1998 Act creates a direct cause of action;

- have knowledge of what constitutes a 'public authority'; and

- be able to explain the remedies available for contravention of a Convention right.

🌀 Talking point

. . . .

In certain sections of the British press the European Convention on Human Rights is viewed with suspicion and hostility. In some newspapers it is seen as a manifestation of EU interference (this is incorrect) and further evidence of the erosion of the United Kingdom's independence and the surrender of power to supranational bodies. For example, it is reported that because of the Convention suspected terrorists cannot be deported and also that the law depriving prisoners of the right to vote in parliamentary and local elections denies them their human rights and will have to be amended. In consequence, it has been suggested by a Conservative party minister that consideration be given to withdrawing from the European Convention on Human Rights.

As the European Convention on Human Rights appears to cause difficulty for the United Kingdom, and the perception is one of a government at loggerheads with the European Court of Human Rights, it might be asked why the United Kingdom was a signatory to the Convention in the first place and what does the Convention mean in the modern world?

. . . .

Introduction

By the end of the Second World War, it was clear how democracy and the law-making process could be manipulated to produce laws which were abhorrent to the prevailing morality of Western democracies. For example, in Nazi Germany, race laws were made which were morally repugnant but as they came from a recognised validating source could be viewed as laws.

It was against this backdrop that the Council of Europe, which consisted of ten states including the UK, created the European Convention on Human Rights. The aim of the Convention was to establish a common core of human rights and fundamental freedoms applicable to the signatory states. The Convention also sought to address a problem associated with most international treaties of how such a treaty was to be enforced, by establishing machinery for enforcement. To this end, the European Court of Human Rights was created by the Convention, to decide cases relating to the rights created by the Convention and provide remedies (see chapter 2 for further details on the court). Such a claim would be made against a state that was in breach of its Convention obligations. However, enforcement of decisions of the European Court of Human Rights ultimately depends upon states being willing to comply with

See 2.1.1, 'Recognised as being law'.

the obligations undertaken by them in the Convention. Such compliance is largely a political matter.

> ### 🔒 Key point
>
> The European Convention on Human Rights and the European Court of Human Rights are separate to the European Union and the Court of Justice of the European Union and should not be confused or interchanged. The European Court of Human Rights sits in Strasbourg whereas the Court of Justice of the European Communities sits in Luxembourg.

See 4.6, 'Presumptions of statutory intent'

As an international treaty, the European Convention on Human Rights was not part of the law of the UK and as such was not directly enforceable by the courts of the UK. Nevertheless, the UK courts construe domestic legislation if possible to ensure that it complies with international treaty obligations on the basis that it is a presumption of legislative intent that Parliament intends to comply with the treaty obligations of the UK.

While the Convention could not be relied upon before the UK courts, it was possible by 1966 for a claim to be made to the European Court of Human Rights once all forms of domestic legal redress had been exhausted, for example if a case had been tried before a court and all possible appeals made. During the latter years of the twentieth century, the UK was found to have contravened the Convention on numerous occasions, which the UK government then had to address by changing domestic law.

> ### 🗒 Example
>
> The reporting in *The Sunday Times* of its investigation into the thalidomide scandal was blocked by the UK contempt of court laws. A successful application to the European Court of Human Rights that the laws of contempt of court contravened the Convention right to freedom of expression was upheld (*Attorney General v Times Newspapers Ltd* [1979] 2 EHRR 245) and the law of the UK was subsequently changed by the Contempt of Court Act 1981.

By the 1990s, there were increasing calls for the incorporation of the Convention into UK law. These calls found a voice in the Labour Party's election manifesto pledge of 1997 to incorporate the Convention. Having been elected, the Labour government introduced the Human Rights Bill which was passed in 1998. Certain articles and Protocols of the Convention became part of the law of the UK when the Human Rights Act 1998 came into force on 2 October 2000. As the Act allowed the UK courts to consider domestic law in the light of Convention rights, this in turn enabled the courts to assess whether or not UK law was compliant with the rights laid down in the European Convention on Human Rights.

It is important to note that the European Convention on Human Rights was not incorporated into English law in its entirety. The only articles and Protocols incorporated are specified in s.1 of the Human Rights Act 1998 (see later).

....

7.1 The European Convention on Human Rights and the incorporation of Convention rights into UK law

In order to understand the relationship between the European Convention on Human Rights and UK law it is useful to look to the text of the Convention and Protocols. The full text of the European Convention on Human Rights and the Protocols may be found on the Council of Europe website at: **www.conventions.coe.int/**.

7.1.1 The European Convention on Human Rights

The main rights established under the European Convention of Human Rights are:

- Article 2 Right to life – everyone's right to life shall be protected by law.
- Article 3 Prohibition of torture – no-one shall be subjected to torture or to inhuman or degrading treatment or punishment.
- Article 4 Prohibition of slavery and forced labour.
- Article 5 Right to liberty and security.
- Article 6 Right to a fair trial.
- Article 7 No punishment without law – against the retrospective operation of law.
- Article 8 Right to respect for private or family life.
- Article 9 Freedom of thought, conscience, and religion.
- Article 10 Freedom of expression.
- Article 11 Freedom of association and assembly.
- Article 12 Right to marry.
- Article 13 Right to an effective remedy.
- Article 14 Prohibition of discrimination. Article 14 does not create rights within itself but must be linked to discrimination in respect of other Convention rights (see later, *A v Secretary of State for the Home Department* [2005] 2 AC 68 and *Ghaidan v Godin-Mendoza* [2004] UKHL 30).

See chapter 12, 'The criminal process: the suspect and the police', at 12.3.2 and 12.3.4.

The Convention rights have been augmented by a number of protocols. Under Protocol 1, three rights are created:

- Article 1 Right of natural and legal persons to peaceful enjoyment of their possessions.
- Article 2 Right to education.
- Article 3 The holding at reasonable intervals of free and fair elections in choosing the legislature.

Under Protocol 13, Article 1 abolishes the death penalty in any circumstances; no derogation is permissible.

Thinking point

The European Convention on Human Rights was drafted over sixty years ago. Do the rights need to be redrafted in the light of developments since 1949? What types of rights are protected by the Convention? Should economic rights also be included?

7.1.2 The Human Rights Act 1998 and incorporation of 'Convention rights' into UK law

Under s.1 of the Human Rights Act 1998, the 'Convention rights' to be incorporated into UK law are specified.

Section 1 provides that the 'Convention rights' are the rights and fundamental freedoms found in:

- Articles 2 to 12 and 14 of the Convention (note Articles 1 and 13 were not incorporated);
- Articles 1 to 3 of Protocol 1; and
- Article 1 of Protocol 13 as read with Articles 16 to 18 of the Convention.

It is to be noted that under the Convention, while some rights are absolute, many of the rights and freedoms are qualified, i.e. subject to exceptions. Examples of absolute rights are Article 3, Prohibition of torture, and Article 4, Prohibition on slavery and forced labour; whereas examples of qualified rights are that the right to liberty may be denied where a person is lawfully detained following conviction for a criminal offence before a court and see also restrictions on rights under Articles 8–11.

Article 13 (the right to an effective remedy) was not incorporated as the UK government stated that the Human Rights Act 1998 itself was an effective remedy. It has been argued, however, there are gaps in the remedial scheme in the UK.

'Margin of appreciation'

In qualifying rights, it is for states to decide how to balance the interests of society in general against the rights of individuals. An important principle of interpretation applied by the European Court of Human Rights is that of 'margin of appreciation'. So while human rights are universal in the abstract, such as the right to a fair trial, this does not mean that there has to be the same trial procedure in every national legal system. In an article, 'The Devaluation of Human Rights under the European Convention', T. Jones said that margin of appreciation 'refers to the degree of latitude which signatory States are permitted in their observance of the Convention'. The doctrine affords a measure of discretion to states and acts as a constraint on how far the European Court of Human Rights is able to interfere, for example with the balance struck between freedom of expression and religious sensibilities or between the rights of one individual and those of another. As there is no consensus amongst the European states on many moral issues, e.g. pornography, states are afforded a wide 'margin of appreciation'. A good example of this is seen in *Handyside v United Kingdom* (1976) 1 EHRR 737, where a sexually explicit book, directed at school children, was seized and destroyed under the Obscene Publications Act 1959. The book was freely available in many other states which were bound by the European Convention on Human Rights and it was argued by Handyside that UK law was in breach of Article 10. The European Court of Human Rights decided that there was no breach of Article 10 as it was for individual states to determine their approach in the light of the situation in their territories having regard 'to the different views prevailing there about the demands of the protection of morals in a democratic society'.

By Protocol 15 (at the time of writing this Protocol was yet to be ratified by all member states) express reference is made in the recitals to the Convention that in accordance with the principle of subsidiarity, member states have the primary responsibility to secure the rights and freedoms defined in the Convention and Protocols, and that they enjoy a margin of appreciation.

'Proportionality'

Another important principle applied by the European Court is that of 'proportionality'. Under this, any restriction of a Convention right must be proportionate to the legitimate aim to be achieved. In *de Freitas v Permanent Secretary of Agriculture, Fisheries, Lands and Housing* [1999] 1 AC 69, in assessing proportionality three questions had to be asked, namely whether:

- the legislative objective is sufficiently important to justify limiting a fundamental right;
- the measures designed to meet the legislative objective are rationally connected to it; and
- the means used to impair the right or freedom are no more than is necessary to accomplish the objective (per Lord Clyde).

In *Huang v Secretary of State for the Home Department* [2007] UKHL 11, the House of Lords accepted that in establishing proportionality that there was a fourth, overriding requirement, being the need to balance the interests of society with those of individuals and groups.

In *R (on the application of Daly) v Secretary of State for the Home Department* [2001] 2 AC 532, a policy whereby prisoners were excluded from their cells while the cells were searched by prison officers, including a search of privileged legal correspondence, was challenged on the ground of its lawfulness. It was argued on behalf of the applicant that the blanket policy of searching legally privileged correspondence without the presence of the prisoner infringed a basic right at common law and under the European Convention on Human Rights. The argument on behalf of the Home Department was that the search procedure was necessary for the maintenance of prison discipline and to prevent criminal activity and the exclusion of prisoners was intended to avoid the use of intimidatory or conditioning tactics by prisoners. The House of Lords said that the policy was unlawful. While the decision was based on the application of common law principles Lord Bingham said that the same result was also achieved by reliance on the European Convention on Human Rights. Under Article 8(1) of the Convention, the applicant had a right to respect in relation to his correspondence and the policy infringed this right to a greater extent than was necessary for the prevention of disorder and crime. The blanket policy of exclusion could not be justified as the evidence suggested that not all prisoners were likely to use intimidatory or conditioning tactics and other search practices respecting the privileged nature of the correspondence could be employed. The infringement of the right was greater than was justified by the objectives of the policy; the policy was not proportionate.

7.1.3 Derogation from Convention rights

It is possible for the UK government by Article 15 of the Convention to derogate from many of the Convention rights 'in time of war or other public emergency threatening the life of the nation'. Derogation means that Convention rights specified do not apply in the signatory state. Note that no derogation is permitted from Articles 2, 3, 4(1), and 7, and Protocol 13 Article 1.

By s.1(2) of the Human Rights Act 1998 the articles, establishing the 'Convention rights' specified in the 1998 Act, have effect subject to any designated derogation or reservation and s.14(1) of the Human Rights Act 1998 empowers the Secretary of State to make an order designating any derogation by the UK from an article of the Convention, or of any protocol to the Convention. (As to reservations, see s.15.)

🗖 Example

After the terrorist attacks of September 11, 2001, the UK government introduced legislation, the Anti-Terrorism, Crime and Security Act 2001, which by s.23 gave power to detain without trial suspected foreign terrorists resident in the UK. In order to achieve this detention the UK government made the Human Rights Act 1998 Order 2001 which derogated from Article 5, the right to liberty. This derogation was challenged in *A v Secretary of State for the Home Department* [2005] 2 AC 68 before nine law lords. The appellants were foreign nationals who were certified by the Secretary of State as suspected foreign terrorists and detained without trial under s.23. It was argued on their behalf that there was not a 'public emergency threatening the life of the nation' which permitted derogation within the meaning of Article 15(1).

The House of Lords refused to interfere with the derogation on this basis. The issue was largely political and the courts should give great weight to the judgement of the Home Secretary and Parliament on this question, as they were exercising 'a pre-eminently political judgement'.

However, s.23 was also challenged as discriminatory under Article 14 of the Convention in the appellants' enjoyment of liberty under Article 5; it was argued that s.23 was discriminatory in relation to rights under Article 5 as it only applied to foreign nationals suspected of being international terrorists and not to UK nationals suspected of being international terrorists.

The House of Lords decided that s.23 was indeed discriminatory; like cases were not decided alike. In consequence, it was declared under s.4 of the Human Rights Act 1998 (see later) that s.23 was incompatible with Articles 5 and 14, amongst other things, as a discriminatory provision.

7.2 Parliamentary sovereignty and the European Convention on Human Rights

While the UK played a major role in creating the European Convention on Human Rights and then ratified the Convention, the Convention was not incorporated into UK law. The argument for incorporation was resisted in part on the ground that incorporation risked upsetting the existing constitutional balance between Parliament and the courts. It has already been seen in chapter 2 that Parliament is supreme, able to make and unmake any laws, and that the courts cannot challenge the validity of an Act of Parliament. The incorporation of the Convention could have challenged the supremacy of Parliament and increased the power of the judiciary, by establishing a framework for challenges to the validity of legislation.

The Human Rights Act 1998 avoided this consequence by extending the role of the judiciary in the interpretation of legislation but not empowering the courts to strike down legislative provisions incompatible with Convention rights. In the case of *In Re S (Minors) (Care Order: Implementation of Care Plan)* [2002] 2 AC 291, Lord Nicholls said (at p.313):

> The Human Rights Act reserves the amendment of primary legislation to Parliament. By this means the Act seeks to preserve parliamentary sovereignty. The Act maintains the constitutional boundary. Interpretation of statutes is a matter for the courts; the enactment of statutes, and the amendment of statutes, are matters for Parliament.

The key to an understanding of the judiciary's role and its relationship with Parliament is the operation and interrelation of ss.3 and 4 of the Human Rights Act 1998, as illustrated in Diagram 7.1.

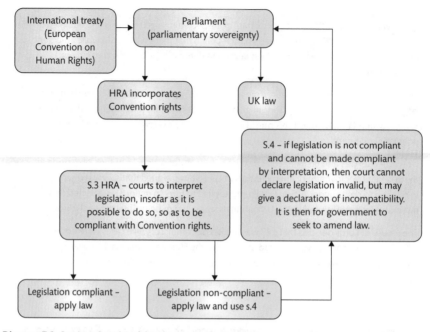

Diagram 7.1 Sections 3 and 4 of the Human Rights Act 1998

Thinking point

The Human Rights Act 1998 does not create a bill of rights for the UK. Does the approach adopted by the 1998 Act give rise to any difficulties?

7.3 Interpretation of legislation under section 3

By s.3(1), the courts are under a duty to read and give effect to primary legislation and subordinate legislation in a way which is compatible with the Convention rights in 'so far as it is possible to do so'. As will become apparent, the main issue concerns establishing the limits of the role of the courts in the interpretative process.

The duty under s.3(1) applies to primary legislation and subordinate legislation, whether enacted before or after the passing of the Human Rights Act 1998 (see s.3(2) (a)). Also, should the courts be unable to give effect to legislation in a way which is compatible with the Convention rights, this does not affect 'the validity, continuing operation or enforcement' of the legislation (both primary and subordinate, see s.3(2)(b) and (c)). In other words, the incompatible law is still valid and still applies, thus leaving a claimant in a position where it has been decided that UK law is not compatible with the Convention rights, but the UK law is still applicable to the claimant's case pending the intervention of the government and Parliament to change the law.

The question raised by the words 'so far as it is possible to do so' concerns the extent to which the courts may read words in or limit the meaning of words in the interpretation of domestic legislation. The concern is that by seeking to go beyond the language used in legislation, judges are not interpreting but are law-making and thereby usurping Parliament's legislative role.

How have the courts approached the task of interpretation under s.3(1)? Some guidance on this question was given by the House of Lords in *R v A (Complainant's sexual history)* [2002] 1 AC 45. In this case, the House of Lords had to decide whether s.41 of the Youth Justice and Criminal Evidence Act 1999, which restricted the admissibility of evidence relating to a complainant's sexual behaviour in relation to a defendant, contravened a defendant's right to a fair trial under Article 6 of the Convention. It was noted that while the words of an Act of Parliament are the primary source of interpretation, s.3(1) of the Human Rights Act 1998 placed a duty on the courts to interpret an Act, so as to ensure compatibility with Convention rights, if possible to do so. There was no need to find an ambiguity, in the sense of having two possible meanings, or absurdity in the wording of an Act for s.3 to apply. Indeed, in the view of Lord Steyn, the effect of s.3 may be that it is sometimes necessary to adopt an interpretation which appears linguistically strained. His Lordship concluded that it was permissible under s.3 to read s.41(3)(c), 'as subject to the implied provision that evidence or questioning which is required to ensure a fair trial under Article 6 of the Convention should not be treated as inadmissible'.

It may be seen that the interpretation of the House of Lords went beyond finding Parliament's meaning from the words used in the Youth Justice and Criminal Evidence Act 1999; instead, the House of Lords introduced a qualification to the operation of s.41 in order to give effect to the intention of Parliament in s.3 of the 1998 Act.

Example

The case of *Ghaidan v Godin-Mendoza* [2004] UKHL 30 concerned the interpretation of the Rent Act 1977. In this case, X, who was the tenant of a dwelling house, had lived with the defendant, in a stable homosexual relationship since 1972. On the death of X, the question arose of whether the defendant was entitled to succeed to the tenancy of the deceased. The Rent Act 1977 provided that:

Section 2(1) The surviving spouse (if any) of the original tenant, if residing in the dwelling-house immediately before the death of the original tenant, shall after the death be the statutory tenant if and so long as he or she occupies the dwelling-house as his or her residence.

(2) For the purposes of this paragraph, a person who was living with the original tenant as his or her wife or husband shall be treated as the spouse of the original tenant…

> A literal interpretation of the words of the statute meant that the survivor of a heterosexual relationship was entitled to a statutory tenancy but not the survivor of a homosexual relationship.
>
> The defendant argued that this difference in treatment was discriminatory in contravention of Article 14 read in conjunction with Article 8 and that this incompatibility could be resolved by s.3 of the Human Rights Act 1998. The House of Lords agreed and interpreted s.2(2) as applying to same-sex partnerships to ensure compatibility. In consequence, the defendant was entitled to succeed to the deceased's statutory tenancy.
>
> As to the process of reading in words, Lord Steyn endorsed the Court of Appeal's approach in interpreting the phrase 'as his or her wife or husband' to mean *as if they were* his wife or husband'. However, Lord Nicholls said that 'paragraph 2 should be read and given effect to as though the survivor of such a homosexual couple were the surviving spouse of the original tenant'. The precise words to be read into the Act were not significant, what was important was the substantive effect.

Are there limits to the duty under s.3(1)? Clearly, the use in the subsection of the phrase 'so far as it is possible to do so' envisages that there may be situations where the courts cannot achieve compatibility with the Convention. Lord Nicholls in *Ghaidan v Godin-Mendoza* explained the operation and limits of s.3(1). His Lordship said (at para.32):

> Section 3 enables language to be interpreted restrictively or expansively. But s.3 goes further than this. It is also apt to require a court to read in words which change the meaning of the enacted legislation, so as to make it Convention-compliant. In other words, the intention of Parliament in enacting s.3 was that, to an extent bounded only by what is 'possible', a court can modify the meaning, and hence the effect, of primary and secondary legislation.
>
> Parliament, however, cannot have intended that in the discharge of this extended interpretative function the courts should adopt a meaning inconsistent with a fundamental feature of legislation. That would be to cross the constitutional boundary s.3 seeks to demarcate and preserve. Parliament has retained the right to enact legislation in terms which are not Convention-compliant. The meaning imported by application of s.3 must be compatible with the underlying thrust of the legislation being construed. Words implied must, in the phrase of my noble and learned friend, Lord Rodger of Earlsferry, 'go with the grain of the legislation'. Nor can Parliament have intended that s.3 should require courts to make decisions for which they are not equipped. There may be several ways of making a provision Convention-compliant, and the choice may involve issues calling for legislative deliberation.

Clearly, the courts are permitted to go beyond the words used by Parliament in seeking to make domestic legislation compliant with the Convention. However, there are limits to the interpretative role of the courts under s.3. A court should not read in words to achieve compliance in the following situations:

- where Parliament has deliberately passed an Act which is intended not to be Convention-compliant then the courts must give effect to Parliament's intention to act in contravention of the Convention; and

- in the opinion of the court, Parliament, and not the courts, should decide the most appropriate way to make the legislation Convention-compliant.

In these two situations, the court may declare that the legislation is not Convention-compliant and this then is an issue for the government and Parliament to resolve.

Example

An example of a situation where the courts determined it was for Parliament to decide how to make legislation Convention-compliant was seen in *R (Anderson) v Secretary of State for the Home Department* [2003] 1 AC 837. The House of Lords decided that the Home Secretary's power under s.29 of the Crime (Sentences) Act 1997 to control when mandatory life sentence prisoners may be released was incompatible with Article 6 of the Convention (the right to have a sentence determined by an independent and impartial tribunal). It was not possible to interpret the section under s.3(1) as to do so would require removing the Home Secretary's powers which had clearly been intended by Parliament. This, said Lord Bingham, 'would not be judicial interpretation but judicial vandalism', giving an effect to s.29 quite different to that which was intended by Parliament. Indeed, in removing such powers, the House of Lords would then have been faced by the question of what should be put in place by way of substitution; this would have gone beyond any interpretative function. In consequence, the House of Lords made a declaration of incompatibility under s.4.

Another example is seen in *Bellinger v Bellinger* [2003] 2 AC 467. In this case the issue concerned the validity of a marriage between a male and a transsexual female; by s.11(c) of the Matrimonial Causes Act 1973, a marriage is void if the parties are not respectively male and female. It was argued that s.11(c) was incompatible with Articles 8 and 12 of the Convention. The House of Lords refused to use s.3(1) of the Human Rights Act 1998 to interpret the words 'male' and 'female' in the Matrimonial Causes Act 1973 as including a transsexual female. Lord Nicholls indicated that interpreting s.11(c) as including transsexuals would have far-reaching ramifications, raising issues which called for extensive enquiries and the widest public consultation and discussion. Such a change was to be left to Parliament, a body better suited to such wide-ranging reform and this was particularly so as the government had announced an intention to introduce primary legislation on this issue. In consequence, a declaration of incompatibility under s.4 of the Human Rights Act 1998 was made.

Kavanagh, in an article 'Statutory Interpretation and Human Rights after Anderson: A More Contextual Approach', argues that mere linguistic possibility is not the only factor that a court considers in determining whether an interpretation under s.3(1) is possible. Other factors such as: will Parliament reform the law; how imminent is such reform; and how radical a change to the legislation is needed to make it Convention-compliant, may be taken into account by the court.

Thinking point

Section 3 gives the courts much potential latitude in the interpretation of legislation. The courts are willing to read words into legislation, which may expand the scope of a provision, or read down, that is limit the scope of a provision. Does the case law demonstrate a consistent approach to interpretation under s.3?

When looking at this issue it is also important to consider when the courts are unable to interpret legislation consistently with Convention rights and instead issue a declaration of incompatibility.

7.4 **Declaration of incompatibility**

A declaration of incompatibility is seen as a measure of last resort should the courts be unable to interpret legislation under s.3 to ensure compatibility (see Lord Steyn's comments in *Ghaidan v Godin-Mendoza*). Section 4 of the Human Rights Act 1998 sets out the conditions for the making of a declaration of incompatibility. Where a court is satisfied that a provision of primary legislation, e.g. an Act of Parliament (for a full definition of primary legislation see s.21 of the Human Rights Act 1998), is incompatible with a Convention right, then it may make a declaration of incompatibility. In relation to a provision of subordinate legislation (for a full definition of subordinate legislation see s.21 of the Human Rights Act 1998), a court may make a declaration of incompatibility if it is satisfied that:

- the provision is incompatible with a Convention right; and
- the primary legislation under which the subordinate legislation is made prevents removal of the incompatibility (disregarding any possibility of revocation).

The only English courts that may make such a declaration are the Supreme Court, the Judicial Committee of the Privy Council, the Court Martial Appeal Court, the Court of Appeal, the High Court, and the Court of Protection in certain instances. It is made clear, by s.4(6), that a declaration of incompatibility 'does not affect the validity, continuing operation or enforcement of the provision' of the legislation in question. Rather, the declaration acts as a signal that the incompatibility needs to be addressed by the government and Parliament.

An example of a declaration of incompatibility was seen in *R (on the application of F (by his litigation friend F)) and Thompson (FC) v Secretary of State for the Home Department* [2010] UKSC 17. Here the Supreme Court had to consider whether s.82 of the Sexual Offences Act 2003 was incompatible with Article 8 of the European Convention of Human Rights, the right to respect for private and family life. Section 82 provides that anyone convicted of a sexual offence and sentenced to thirty months' imprisonment or more is under a lifelong duty to notify the police where they are living and of any travel abroad. Under the legislation there is no right of review.

The issue for the Supreme Court was 'does the absence of any right of review render lifetime notification requirements disproportionate to the legitimate aims that they seek to pursue?' It is to be noted that the notification provisions were not being challenged but rather the challenge related to the absence of a right to review the imposition of a duty to notify.

The Supreme Court upheld the decisions of the Divisional Court and the Court of Appeal that the indefinite notification requirements of the Sexual Offences Act 2003 were incompatible with Article 8 as there was no mechanism for review and, as such, the requirements constituted a disproportionate interference with such article. The declarations of incompatibility were repeated.

This case illustrates the operation of the concept of proportionality; the courts must seek to ensure that a balance is struck between the legitimate aims of legislation, i.e. the protection of the public from convicted sex offenders and the extent of the interference with an offender's Article 8 rights. In other words, were the unreviewable notification requirements of the 2003 Act proportionate to the legitimate aims? Given that it could be demonstrated that some offenders no longer presented a risk of re-offending, the absence of a system of review meant that the notification requirements were disproportionate in their interference with Article 8 rights.

Where a court is considering whether to make a declaration of incompatibility then by s.5, the Crown is entitled to be given notice of this and, in England, a minister of the Crown on giving notice is entitled to be joined as a party to the proceedings. See, for example, the Secretary of State for Trade and Industry's involvement in *Wilson v First County Trust Ltd (No.2)* [2004] 1 AC 816, where the Court of Appeal made a declaration of incompatibility. (Note that in this case, there was an appeal to the House of Lords where it was decided that s.127(3) was not incompatible with Article 6 of the Convention, a right to a fair trial, and with Article 1 of Protocol 1, a right to peaceful enjoyment of possessions.)

7.5 Statements of compatibility in Parliament

Section 19 of the Human Rights Act 1998 provides that a minister in charge of a bill in either the House of Commons or House of Lords must, before the second reading of the bill, make a statement in writing indicating whether or not the provisions of the bill are compatible in the minister's view with the Convention rights. While it is unlikely that the UK government would deliberately be in breach of its Convention obligations and usually a statement of compatibility will be issued, s.19 recognises the possibility of an Act being passed which is not compatible with Convention rights.

The making of a statement of compatibility indicates to the courts that the legislation is to be interpreted in accordance with s.3 of the 1998 Act. Should a minister state that he is unable to make a statement of compatibility, but nonetheless the government wishes the bill to proceed, it is more difficult to predict the approach of the

See 3.3, 'The passage of bills through Parliament'.

courts. In relation to the Communications Bill (which became the Communications Act 2003) which banned political advertising on television and radio, the minister did not make a statement of compatibility. While the government believed, and had been advised, that the ban on political advertising was compatible with Article 10, it could not be sure that the proposed legislation was Convention-compliant following the decision of the European Court of Human Rights in *VgT Verein gegen Tierfabriken v Switzerland* 10 BHRC 473. In *R (on the application of Animal Defenders International) v Secretary of State for Culture, Media and Sport* [2008] UKHL 15, the House of Lords decided that ss.319 and 321 of the Communications Act 2003, while restricting free-dom of expression, were necessary to protect the democratic process, given the potentially insidious effect of broadcast media. Parliament had clearly considered the issue in passing the Communications Act 2003 and in the opinion of the House of Lords, the legislation was not incompatible with Article 10. The decision of the European Court of Human Rights in *VgT* was considered but, on its facts, was found not to cover the situation that had arisen in the instant case.

7.6 **Remedying incompatibility**

7.6.1 **Primary legislation incompatible**

Section 10 of the Human Rights Act 1998 provides that a minister of the Crown has the power to take remedial action in relation to primary legislation in the following circumstances:

- either (a) a court has made a declaration of incompatibility and no appeal has been made or there is no appeal possible or (b) in the light of a finding of the European Court of Human Rights a legislative provision appears to be incompatible with the Convention; and

See 3.5.3 for an explanation of Henry VIII clauses.

- the minister of the Crown considers that there are compelling reasons for proceed-ing under s.10;

- then the minister 'may by order make such amendments to the legislation as he considers necessary to remove the incompatibility'.

The power given to the minister is an example of a Henry VIII clause; the minister may by delegated legislation repeal or amend the provisions of an Act of Parliament.

Thinking point

What are the dangers in permitting the amendment of primary legislation by delegated legislation? See 3.5.3.

7.6.2 **Subordinate legislation incompatible**

Under s.4 of the Human Rights Act 1998, a court may make a declaration of incompatibility if a provision of subordinate legislation is incompatible with a Convention right and the parent Act prevents removal of the incompatibility. Should such an incompatibility arise in relation to subordinate legislation, then by s.10(3) a minister of the Crown may by delegated legislation amend the primary legislation in the following circumstances:

- in order for the incompatibility to be removed, the primary legislation giving power to make the subordinate legislation must be amended; and
- the minister of the Crown considers there are compelling reasons for proceeding under s.10.

7.7 **The UK courts and the European Court of Human Rights**

The UK courts are not bound by the judgments of the European Court of Human Rights (see chapter 5, 'The doctrine of judicial precedent'). However by s.2(1) of the Human Rights Act 1998, a court or tribunal when determining an issue relating to a Convention right 'must take into account', inter alia, any judgment of the European Court of Human Rights whenever made or given (note that all judgments of the European Court of Human Rights whether given before or after the passing of the Human Rights Act 1998 fall within the ambit of s.2). The Act does not compel the courts to follow judgments of the European Court of Human Rights, but the courts must at least consider such judgments. However, in *R (Alconbury Developments Ltd and Others) v Secretary of State for the Environment, Transport and the Regions* [2003] 2 AC 295 Lord Slynn said (at para.26):

> [a]lthough the Human Rights Act 1998 does not provide that a national court is bound by [decisions of the European Court of Human Rights] it is obliged to take account of them so far as they are relevant. In the absence of some special circumstances it seems to me that the court should follow any clear and constant jurisprudence of the European Court of Human Rights. If it does not do so there is at least a possibility that the case will go to that court, which is likely in the ordinary case to follow its own constant jurisprudence.

It has been further stated in *R (Anderson) v Secretary of State for the Home Department* by Lord Bingham (at p.879) that:

> [w]hile the duty of the House under s.2(1)(a) of the Human Rights Act 1998 is to take into account any judgment of the European Court, whose judgments are not strictly binding, the House will not without good reason depart from the principles laid down in a carefully considered judgment of the court sitting as a Grand Chamber.

As has been seen, a Grand Chamber is a court consisting of seventeen judges. (See further 2.5.10.)

However, note Lord Hoffmann's comments in *Secretary of State for the Home Department v AF (No.3)* [2010] 2 AC 269. The case concerned control orders made under s.2(1) of the Prevention of Terrorism Act 2005 and whether the person subject to such an order, the controlee, had had a fair trial in compliance with Article 6 of the European Convention on Human Rights. The issue of a fair trial depended upon material which was undisclosed to the controlee on the grounds of national security. The European Court of Human Rights (ECtHR) in *A v United Kingdom* (2009) 49 EHRR 625 determined that a controlee must be given sufficient information about the allegations against him so as to enable him to give effective instructions with regard to those allegations. As the judgment of the ECtHR was clear and applicable in the *AF* case Lord Hoffmann said that although the House of Lords was not bound by *A v United Kingdom*, to reject the decision would put the UK in breach of the international law obligations under the Convention. In consequence, UK law should be read to ensure compatibility with the ECtHR's interpretation of the Convention. Here the House of Lords, given the clear judgment of the ECtHR, not only took the judgment into account but felt compelled to follow it.

In *Manchester City Council v Pinnock* [2010] UKSC 45 Lord Neuberger (delivering a single opinion on behalf of the Supreme Court consisting of nine Justices) said (at para.48):

> This court is not bound to follow every decision of the EurCtHR. Not only would it be impractical to do so: it would sometimes be inappropriate, as it would destroy the ability of the court to engage in the constructive dialogue with the EurCtHR which is of value to the development of Convention law (see e.g. *R v Horncastle* [2009] UKSC 14, [2010] 2 All ER 359, [2010] 2 WLR 47). Of course, we should usually follow a clear and constant line of decisions by the EurCtHR: *R (Ullah) v Special Adjudicator* [2004] UKHL 26, [2004] 2 AC 323, [2004] 3 All ER 785. But we are not actually bound to do so or (in theory, at least) to follow a decision of the Grand Chamber . . . Where, however, there is a clear and constant line of decisions whose effect is not inconsistent with some fundamental substantive or procedural aspect of our law, and whose reasoning does not appear to overlook or misunderstand some argument or point of principle, we consider that it would be wrong for this court not to follow that line.

So if the jurisprudence of the European Court is clear and constant then in effect the UK courts will be bound. (However, if the clear and constant line of decisions is inconsistent with some fundamental substantive or procedural aspect of our law or has omitted to consider or misunderstood an argument or point of principle then the decisions of the European Court need not be followed by the UK courts.) It has been argued that the impact of this approach is to make the jurisprudence of the European Court the engine for the development of human rights under the Convention and thus under UK law, rather than the UK courts taking an active approach to such development; as s.2 does not make the judgments of the European Court of Human Rights binding, it is argued that the UK courts may develop rights beyond the development of rights at the Strasbourg court. However, this argument has not found favour in the House of Lords. Lord Bingham in *R (Ullah) v Special Adjudicator* [2004] 2 AC 323, said (at p.350) that:

> [i]t is of course open to member states to provide for rights more generous than those guaranteed by the Convention, but such provision should not be the product of interpretation of the Convention by national courts, since the meaning of the Convention should be uniform throughout the states party to it. The duty of national courts is to keep pace with the Strasbourg jurisprudence as it evolves over time: no more, but certainly no less.

See also *R (Al-Skeini) v Secretary of State for Defence* [2007] UKHL 26, [2008] 1 AC 153, para.106. In *R (on the application of Animal Defenders International) v Secretary of State for Culture, Media and Sport* [2008] UKHL 15, Baroness Hale echoed this approach when she said, that certainly Parliament in passing ss.3 and 4 of the Human Rights Act 1998 was not intending to give the courts 'the power to leap ahead of Strasbourg in our interpretation of the Convention Rights'.

Lord Irvine, the former Lord Chancellor, has said that the courts have not correctly interpreted s.2(1) Human Rights Act 1998 (see 'A British Interpretation of Convention Rights' [2012] Public Law 237). He argues that Parliament intended by the choice of language in s.2(1), while having regard to judgments of the European Court of Human Rights, that a domestic court must ultimately decide a case for itself. The courts' current approach to judgments of the European Court of Human Rights is to make the decisions effectively binding. One argument that is raised to support the Supreme Court's approach to the judgments of the European Court of Human Rights is that if the UK courts do not follow the Strasbourg court's decisions then the UK as a state will be in breach of its international obligations. Lord Irvine contends that such a breach is a matter for the UK government not the courts. He says (at p.245),

> Parliament contemplated that the domestic courts would not follow Strasbourg in all cases. In doing so it implicitly approved the domestic courts reaching an outcome which might result in non-compliance with the UK's Treaty obligations. The judges should not abstain from deciding the case for themselves simply because it may cause difficulties for the United Kingdom on the international law plane.

ⓘ Critical debate

It may be argued that the UK courts should be more active in the development of human rights, but the interpretation by the Supreme Court of s.2 Human Rights Act 1998 is too restrictive. Read Lord Irvine 'A British Interpretation of Convention Rights' [2012] PL 237 and P. Sales 'Strasbourg Jurisprudence and the Human Rights Act: A response to Lord Irvine' [2012] PL 253 and then consider the following questions:

(a) Why does Lord Irvine believe that the UK courts have erred in their interpretation of s.2?

(b) What three reasons, in Lord Irvine's view, are given for the Supreme Court's following of the European Court of Human Rights' decisions?

(c) What counter-arguments to these three reasons does Lord Irvine express?

(d) Identify the major advantages should the UK domestic courts adopt a more critical approach to the 'Strasbourg jurisprudence'.

(e) Identify the reasons that Philip Sales argues support 'the mirror principle' adopted by the Supreme Court.

(f) Sales refers to 'rule of law values' underpinning 'the mirror principle' approach. What does this mean in principle and practice?

(g) What approach do you think should be adopted by the Supreme Court?

As to the approach that an English court should adopt in the face of a binding precedent under English law conflicting with the European Convention on Human Rights, see 5.5.8 'Judicial precedent, the Human Rights Act 1998, and the European Court of Human Rights'.

7.8 Unlawful for a public authority to act incompatibly with Convention rights

By s.6 of the 1998 Act, it is unlawful for a 'public authority' to act in a way which is incompatible with a Convention right. Any breach of a Convention right would be enforceable against the emanations of the state, such as government departments, and other public authorities by an individual or a company. Thus, the 1998 Act is creating a cause of action against a 'public authority' for contravention of Convention rights. Convention rights under s.6 are not directly enforceable as between individuals or companies; s.6 does not provide an independent cause of action in such circumstances.

However, as 'public authority' by s.6(3)(b) includes a court or a tribunal, (tribunal is defined by s.21 as meaning 'any tribunal in which legal proceedings may be brought'), for the purposes of the 1998 Act, in applying existing UK law the courts must not act in a way which is incompatible with a Convention right. This means that courts must seek to ensure that UK law is applied consistently with Convention rights. In consequence, the courts must develop the common law, as well as interpret legislation, consistently with Convention rights. So, an existing cause of action recognised by English law must be viewed by the courts against the backdrop of Convention rights. To this extent, an individual or company may enforce Convention rights indirectly against another individual or company by claiming under a cause of action established by UK law and then raising a supplementary argument that a Convention right has been breached.

Section 6(1) does not apply where an act by a public authority leading to incompat-ibility cannot be avoided because of (a) provisions of primary legislation, or (b) where the provisions of primary legislation cannot be read or given effect in a way compat-ible with the Convention rights and the authority was acting so as to give effect to or enforce those provisions. For example, if a court cannot read legislation in such a way as to ensure compatibility with Convention rights, s.6(1) does not apply to such a fail-ure to act. Table 7.1 shows the direct and indirect effect of the Human Rights Act 1998.

7.8.1 **Vertical and horizontal rights**

In your further reading, you will encounter references to vertical and horizontal rights: vertical rights refer to actions against public authorities, whereas horizontal rights relate to those rights, for example, as between individuals and companies. It appears that the Human Rights Act 1998 has a form of horizontal effect based upon the duty placed on the court as a public authority, by s.6, not to act inconsist-ently with Convention rights. So, the courts in developing the common law, must do so consistently with Convention rights. This was seen in *Venables v News Group Newspapers* [2001] 1 All ER 908. In this case, the High Court had to consider whether the Convention could be applied against newspapers, not being, of course, public bodies. Venables and Thompson, who as children had been convicted of murdering another child, were protected by injunctions preventing the publication of informa-tion concerning them. Upon reaching 18 years of age, they sought to have the injunc-tions extended, preventing publication of information concerning their new identities when released from their sentences. Newspapers argued that such injunctions would interfere with the freedom of the expression of the press.

Dame Butler-Sloss P, in the High Court, relying upon *Douglas v Hello! Ltd* [2001] QB 967 and s.12(4) of the Human Rights Act 1998, held that Article 10 had direct applica-bility between private parties to litigation. While not creating a free-standing cause of

Table 7.1 UK law and Convention rights

	Individual or Company v Public Authority	Individual or Company v Individual or Company
Direct effect under section 6	Claim using s.6 as cause of action	No claim under s.6 as no public authority involved (assuming the company is not a public authority)
Indirect effect using existing UK law		Bring a claim under UK law, e.g. for negligence, and then raise a supplementary argument that a Convention right has been breached

action, the courts had a duty to 'to act compatibly with Convention rights in adjudicating upon existing common law causes of action'. In consequence, the High Court under the domestic law of confidence, granted injunctions to prevent the newspapers revealing the whereabouts and identities of the claimants. In doing so, the court took into account that there was a real and strong possibility that the lives of Venables and Thompson would be at risk if such information was revealed, infringing their rights under Articles 2, 3, and 8. The right to freedom of expression under Article 10 was subject to the restrictions in Article 10(2). By Article 10(2) it is provided that:

> [t]he exercise of these freedoms, since it carries with it duties and responsibilities, may be subject to such formalities, conditions, restrictions or penalties as are prescribed by law and are necessary in a democratic society, in the interests of national security, territorial integrity or public safety, for the prevention of disorder or crime, for the protection of health or morals, for the protection of the reputation or rights of others, for preventing the disclosure of information received in confidence, or for maintaining the authority and impartiality of the judiciary.

Given the potential breaches of Venables and Thompson's rights under Articles 2, 3, and 8, the High Court decided that the right to freedom of expression of the press should be restricted. The granting of the injunctions to achieve the object sought was seen, by Dame Butler-Sloss P, as proportionate to the legitimate aim, i.e. the protection of Venables and Thompson from death or serious harm.

As can be seen, the court as a public authority ensured that UK law was compatible with the Convention and thus gave horizontal effect to Convention rights as between individuals and companies.

7.8.2 **Meaning of public authority**

Section 6 does not give a complete definition of 'public authority', but s.6(3) provides that the term *includes*: (a) a court or tribunal; and (b) any person certain of whose functions are of a public nature. By s.6(5), a person is not a public authority only by virtue of s.6(3)(b) in relation to a particular act 'if the nature of the act is private'.

The 1998 Act states that courts and tribunals are public authorities. It is equally clear that 'public authority' encompasses a minister, central government departments, local authorities, health authorities, armed forces, and the police. However, there is some doubt as to which other bodies fall within the term. The provisions of the 1998 Act are open-textured and it is for the courts to decide what constitutes a public authority, taking into account the jurisprudence of the European Court of Human Rights. In *Aston Cantlow and Wilmcote with Billesley Parochial Church Council v Wallbank* [2004] 1 AC 546, the House of Lords said that the phrase 'a public authority' is essentially a reference to a body whose nature is governmental in the broadest sense of that expression. It must encompass persons or bodies where all their functions are of a public nature – 'core' public authorities, such as the bodies already indicated.

Other bodies may not be governmental but, nonetheless, perform some functions of a public nature; such bodies will be a public authority for the purposes of s.6. The key is to concentrate on the nature of the function rather than on the nature of the body. This latter type of body is termed a 'hybrid' authority; it has some functions of a public nature. However, this may not be sufficient for it to be classed as a public authority if the nature of a particular act is private. In the *Aston Cantlow* case, a Parochial Church Council (PCC) was considered not to be a public authority as in seeking to enforce a liability to repair a chancel of a church the Council's act was private in nature; the obligation to repair arising from ownership of land. Lord Hope said (at p.570),

> The nature of the act is to be found in the nature of the obligation which the PCC is seeking to enforce. It is seeking to enforce a civil debt. The function which it is performing has nothing to do with the responsibilities which are owed to the public by the state.

Examples of a 'hybrid' authority include the Financial Services Authority and it has been suggested that Railtrack may be a public authority when exercising a regulatory function in relation to safety, but would not be a public authority when acting in a capacity as a commercial property developer. Problems have arisen over the status of housing authorities. In *YL v Birmingham City Council and Others (Secretary of State for Constitutional Affairs intervening)* [2008] 1 AC 95, the House of Lords by a majority of 3 to 2 held that the provision of care and accommodation by a private residential care home did not constitute a 'function of a public nature' within s.6(3)(b), even though Birmingham City Council arranged and paid for such care and accommodation, pursuant to ss.21 to 26 of the National Assistance Act 1948. See further on this case later. In *R (on the application of Weaver) v London and Quadrant Housing Trust* [2009] EWCA Civ 587, [2009] 4 All ER 865 the Court of Appeal held that a housing trust which was a registered social landlord, providing social housing, was a public authority for the purposes of s.6(3)(b) when terminating a tenancy.

Thinking point

What are the characteristics of a 'public authority'? Consider whether the following bodies are public authorities:

- the Law Society;

- the Solicitors Regulation Authority.

Do you think that 'public authority' should be further defined in the Human Rights Act 1998? If so, in what way?

Neither House of Parliament is a 'public authority'.

The classification of a person or body as a 'core' public authority is important for a further reason; a 'core' public authority cannot have Convention rights. See *Aston*

Cantlow and Wilmcote with Billesley Parochial Church Council v Wallbank [2004] 1 AC 546, per Lord Nicholls. In consequence, a public authority cannot make a claim for breach of Convention rights. Diagram 7.2 shows the stages to be considered in determining whether a public authority is in contravention of Convention rights and the effect of such contravention.

> ### 🔑 Key point
>
> A public authority cannot have Convention rights; it is possible for a hybrid public authority to claim for violation of Convention rights in relation to its private functions.

7.8.3 Determining what is a public authority

It is instructive to consider *YL v Birmingham City Council and Others (Secretary of State for Constitutional Affairs intervening)* [2008] 1 AC 95, as it demonstrates the difficulties in determining what is a public authority for the purposes of s.6 of the Human Rights Act 1998. In this case, there was a significant difference of opinion in the House of Lords with a 3 to 2 majority deciding that a care home did not possess functions of a public nature and therefore was not a public authority.

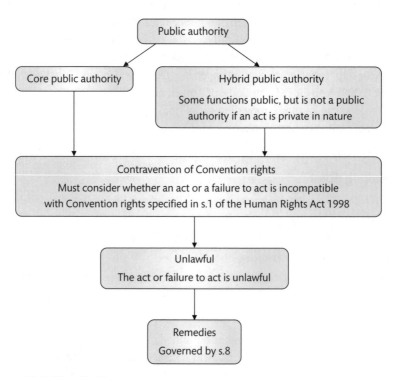

Diagram 7.2 Public authorities.

Facts

YL, the appellant, was 84 years old and suffered from Alzheimer's disease. She lived in the Southern Cross care home, a privately owned profit-making entity which provided accommodation and care facilities. The accommodation and care was largely paid for by Birmingham City Council and topped up by OL, the daughter of the appellant, under a tripartite agreement amongst Southern Cross, Birmingham CC, and OL. Birmingham CC entered into the agreement pursuant to its duty under s.21 of the National Assistance Act 1948.

The issue

Southern Cross wanted to terminate YL's residency in the care home and gave notice to this effect. It was argued on behalf of YL that the care home was performing functions of a public nature for the purposes of s.6(3)(b). Thus, Southern Cross was a 'public authority' and by giving notice had acted incompatibly with YL's rights under Article 8 (the right to respect for private or family life) of the Convention and, in consequence, such notice was unlawful under s.6(1) of the 1998 Act.

In *Aston Cantlow and Wilmcote with Billesley Parochial Church Council v Wallbank* [2004] 1 AC 546 Lord Nicholls said in determining whether a function is of a public nature, there is no single test of universal application; instead, a number of factors must be considered, none of which singly is likely to be determinative and weighting of the factors will differ from case to case. His Lordship identified a number of relevant factors, but stressed that such a list could not be exhaustive:

- the nature of the function, was it private or public;
- the role and responsibility of the state in relation to the matter in question;
- consideration of the nature and extent of any statutory duty or power with regard to the function;
- to what extent is the performance of the function regulated, supervised, and inspected by the state and are any criminal sanctions imposed for failure to meet set standards;
- the extent to which the state pays for the performance of the function;
- consideration of the risk that failure in performance of the function might impact on an individual's Convention rights.

Lord Bingham

Lord Bingham considered the following points in determining whether Southern Cross was performing a function of a public nature. The function was to provide accommodation and care for those unable to care for themselves; the state had accepted a social welfare responsibility in the last resort.

Sections 21 and 26 of the National Assistance Act 1948 conferred statutory powers and a statutory duty in this regard upon local authorities. A local authority may provide the care directly in a local authority-run care home or arrange for care to be provided by a voluntary organisation or by a private provider.

The provision of accommodation and care was subject to legal control and the application of criminal sanctions in the event of breach of prescribed standards.

Payment for the provision of accommodation and care fell on the state in respect of those, falling within ss.21 and 26 of the National Assistance Act 1948, who are unable to pay for such provision themselves. Lord Bingham said that 'it is indicative of a function being public that the public are, if need be, bound to pay for it to be performed'.

Finally, the risk of infringement of various human rights in care homes was understood by Parliament when passing the Human Rights Act 1998 and the intention must have been to extend the protection to residents of privately run care homes placed in such homes pursuant to the National Assistance Act 1998.

Lord Bingham thus concluded that a private care home was performing a function of a public nature.

Lord Scott

Lord Scott emphasised that Southern Cross was a private company carrying on a business for profit. In providing accommodation and care Southern Cross did so in pursuance of private law contracts with residents and local authorities. It had no public funding and enjoyed no special statutory powers; it was providing a service for a commercial rate of payment.

In his Lordship's view, the fact that residents were placed by local authorities with Southern Cross care homes pursuant to s.21 of the 1948 Act and paid for by local authorities carried little weight. Southern Cross was paid for a service and in no sense could be said to be subsidised out of public funds. It would be absurd to suggest that a private contractor performing cleaning or catering services at a local-authority-owned care home would be publicly funded and carrying on a function of a public nature, merely because payment was made out of public funds for that service.

It was argued in support of YL's contention that there was no difference in the nature of the function performed in the management of a local-authority-run care home and in that of a privately run care home. This was rejected on the basis that a local authority is under a statutory duty to arrange accommodation and care the costs of which are met out of public funds, whereas any duties owed by a private care home company are contractual or tortious and within the realms of private law. Merely because a local authority contracts out the performance of a function of a public nature to a private contractor does not mean that the contractor is a public authority under s.6(3)(b).

His Lordship thought it was not enough to consider the activity being performed and that it was necessary to look at the reason why the person in question is carrying on the activity that is being performed. The activity of a local authority running a care home is pursuant to public law obligations, whereas a privately owned care home acts in pursuance of private law contractual obligations.

Finally, Lord Scott said that the argument that vulnerable residents of care homes requiring the additional protection of s.6 of the 1998 Act added nothing. Other legal remedies already existed.

In consequence, Southern Cross was held not to be carrying on a function of a public nature.

Lord Scott also held that the service of the notice of termination was in any event an act, relating to the rights and obligations created by the contract between YL and Southern Cross, which was private in nature for the purposes of s.6(5).

Lords Bingham and Scott, as can be seen, identified a number of factors but disagreed on the weight and relevance to be attributed to the factors and in so doing arrived at different conclusions.

Note that it is important to read all of the opinions of the law lords (in this case, five opinions) in order to ascertain the basis upon which the case was decided. See chapter 5, 'The doctrine of judicial precedent'.

Note the effect of the actual decision in *YL v Birmingham City Council* was changed by s.145 of the Health and Social Care Act 2008 so that a care home for the purposes of s.6(3)(b) is to be taken to be exercising a function of a public nature. However, the reasoning of the majority is still good law.

Thinking point

Under s.6(3)(b) and s.6(5) it may not be sufficient for a body to be classed as a public authority in relation to a particular act if the nature of the act is private. How is the nature of an act, e.g. is it a private act, to be determined? See *R (on the application of Weaver) v London and Quadrant Housing Trust* [2009] EWCA Civ 587, [2009] 4 All ER 865, Elias LJ at paras 73–82.

7.8.4 Enforcement of Convention rights

As has been seen, s.6 creates a cause of action against a public authority where it is alleged that the public authority breached the Convention rights of a claimant. In order to enforce these rights s.7(1) provides that a claimant may:

(a) bring proceedings against the authority under this Act in the appropriate court or tribunal, or

(b) rely on the Convention right or rights concerned in any legal proceedings, but only if he is (or would be) a victim of the unlawful act.

Under s.7(1)(a), proceedings are brought against a public authority using s.6 as the cause of action, whereas under s.7(1)(b) legal proceedings may be brought against a public authority using an existing cause of action in English law along with an argument based upon Convention rights.

Under s.7(1), a claimant must satisfy the requirement of being a 'victim' of the unlawful act. In order to be a victim, a person must satisfy the test for being a victim under Article 34 of the Convention for the purposes of bringing proceedings in the European Court of Human Rights in respect of the act of which complaint is made, s.7(7). Article 34 indicates that a victim is '…any person, non-governmental organisation or group of individuals claiming to be the victim of a violation…of the rights set forth in the Convention or the protocols thereto'.

Thinking point

Does Article 34 indicate what is meant by 'victim'? Where can we look to find material which will give an indication of the meaning of 'victim'?

7.8.5 **Remedies**

By s.8, where a public authority is found to have acted unlawfully, then a court has a discretion to 'grant such relief or remedy, or make such order, within its powers as it considers just and appropriate'. A court may, for example, give the following relief or remedies, if the court has power to grant such relief or a remedy:

- damages;
- a declaration;
- an injunction;
- a **quashing order** (previously called *certiorari*);
- a mandatory order (previously called *mandamus*); and
- a prohibiting order (previously called *prohibition*).

> **quashing order:** *Note that quashing orders, mandatory orders, and prohibiting orders are public law remedies aimed at public bodies:*
>
> - *a quashing order quashes the decision of, for example, an inferior court, a tribunal, or a local authority where the decision-making process exhibits illegality, irrationality, or procedural impropriety;*
> - *a mandatory order compels, for example, an inferior court, a tribunal, or a public body to carry out its duty; and*
> - *a prohibiting order restrains, for example, an inferior court, a tribunal, a local authority, or a government minister from acting in excess of jurisdiction.*

Damages may only be awarded by a court which has power to award damages, or order a compensation payment, in civil proceedings; thus damages are not payable in criminal proceedings. Under s.8(3) of the Human Rights Act 1998, in considering whether an award of damages is appropriate (note that a court has the power to award damages but is not under a duty to do so), account must be taken of all the circumstances of a case, including 'any other relief or remedy granted, or order made' and the consequences of any decision of a court. Damages may be awarded where the court considers that an award is necessary to give just satisfaction. The case law suggests that in many instances, a declaration that Convention rights have been breached will suffice as a remedy.

In determining (a) whether to award damages, or (b) the amount of an award, a court must take into account the principles applied by the European Court of Human Rights in relation to awards under Article 41 of the Convention. The principles of the European Court of Human Rights are not easy to discern, but the basic principle is that the victim is to be placed in the position they would have occupied had the violation of their rights not occurred. Damages have been given in relation to both pecuniary losses, e.g. loss of earnings or medical costs and non-pecuniary losses, e.g. distress, inconvenience, and humiliation. While the basic principle is similar to the tortious measure of damages in English law, it is the Strasbourg Court's jurisprudence which is to be adopted in awarding damages. The award of damages, before the European Court of Human Rights, tends to be modest in amount. See generally on this issue *R (on the application of Greenfield) v Secretary of State for the Home Department* [2005] 1 WLR 673.

➕ Summary

- The European Convention on Human Rights is an international treaty. Unless a treaty is incorporated into the law of the UK it is not directly enforceable by the UK courts. Certain articles and Protocols of the Convention were incorporated into UK law when the Human Rights Act 1998 came into force on 2 October 2000.

- Primary legislation cannot be challenged using the Human Rights Act 1998 in the sense of the courts striking down legislation.

- The courts cannot decide that an Act of Parliament is invalid, they are limited to making a declaration of incompatibility should UK law contravene Convention rights; it then being for the minister or Parliament to amend UK law.

- By s.3 of the Human Rights Act 1998, both primary and subordinate legislation must be read and given effect in a way which is compatible with the Convention rights, in so far as it is possible to do so.

- By s.2, a court or tribunal determining a question which has arisen in connection with a Convention right must take into account any:

  (a) judgment, decision, declaration or advisory opinion of the European Court of Human Rights…

  whenever made or given, so far as, in the opinion of the court or tribunal, it is relevant to the proceedings in which that question has arisen.

But the courts of the UK are not bound to follow the decisions of the European Court of Human Rights.

- The Human Rights Act 1998 does not create a cause of action between individuals or companies for breach of Convention rights. However, an individual or company may sue under UK law and ask the courts to interpret the existing UK law to ensure compliance with the Convention rights in Human Rights Act 1998. This is achieved because as a court is a 'public authority' it is under a duty to ensure existing law is in compliance with Convention rights.

- However, it is unlawful for a public authority to act incompatibly with the Convention rights stated in the Human Rights Act 1998. Section 6 creates a direct cause of action against a public authority for contravention of Convention rights.

- Once all domestic avenues for redress of a grievance have been exhausted, a claimant may take a case to the European Court of Human Rights.

 Questions

1 How does the Human Rights Act 1998 ensure that the doctrine of parliamentary supremacy is not challenged?

2 Explain the impact of the Human Rights Act 1998 on law which contravenes a Convention right.

3 In ensuring that legislation is compatible with Convention rights what duty is placed upon the courts and how far have the courts been prepared to go in undertaking this task?

4 Are the UK courts bound by decisions of the European Court of Human Rights?

5 When does the Human Rights Act 1998 give a direct cause of action?

6 Explain what is meant by a 'public authority'.

Sample question and outline answer

Question

Under s.3 Human Rights Act 1998, in order to ensure that legislation is Convention-compliant, to what extent may the courts go beyond the words used by Parliament when interpreting a piece of legislation?

Outline answer

This question concerns the meaning and effect of s.3 Human Rights Act 1998. To understand the operation of s.3 it is first necessary to understand the context in which the section operates. After explaining the interpretative obligation that the courts must follow under s.3, the limits of its operation must be explored by reference to relevant case law.

The structure of the 1998 Act indicates that the courts cannot challenge the validity of legislation, even if it is not Convention-compliant. Indeed if the court decide that legislation is not Convention-compliant, under s.4 a declaration of incompatibility must be made and then it is for the government and Parliament to determine how the matter is to be resolved. The House of Lords has stated in *R v A* [2002] 1 AC 45 in the words of Lord Steyn 'that a declaration of incompatability is a measure of last resort. It must be avoided unless it is plainly impossible to do so.'

By s.3 Human Rights Act 1998 so far as it is possible to do so, primary legislation and subordinate legislation must be read and given effect in a way which is compatible with the Convention rights. This places on the courts an interpretative obligation by which Parliament instructs the courts to interpret legislation to ensure it is Convention-compliant, but subject to the important qualification that it is to be 'possible to do so'. However, this does not entitle the courts to make legislation, it is an interpretative process in accordance with the terms of s.3. (See Lord Woolf in *Poplar Housing and Regeneration Community Association Ltd v Donoghue* [2002] QB 48 at pp.72–3: 'When the court interprets legislation usually its primary task is to identify the intention of Parliament. Now, when section 3 applies, the courts have to adjust their traditional role in relation to interpretation so as to give effect to the direction contained in section 3 … Section 3 does not entitle the court to legislate (its task is still one of interpretation, but interpretation in accordance with the direction contained in section 3)'). Kavanagh's argument that even in relation to interpretation of legislation judges have a law-making role but within limits ('The Elusive Divide between Interpretation and Legislation under the Human Rights Act 1998' (2004) 24 OJLS 259) could be briefly explained here.

The question to be addressed is when is it possible by the process of interpretation to make legislation Convention-compliant? It is necessary to explore the case law and seek to draw some general conclusions. The courts go beyond the words of an Act by 'reading down' – limiting the extent of words in an Act, see *R v A* [2002] 1 AC 45 or 'reading in' – where the courts 'add' words to alter or expand the meaning of the Act, see *Ghaidan v Godin-Mendoza* [2004].

In *Ghaidan v Godin-Mendoza* Lord Nicholls said 'Parliament, however, cannot have intended that in the discharge of this extended interpretative function the courts should adopt a meaning inconsistent with a fundamental feature of legislation'. So if Parliament intends to pass an Act which is deliberately not Convention-compliant the courts must give effect to that Act. Also the intention of s.3 cannot have been to 'require the courts to make decisions for which they are not equipped'. The cases of *R (Anderson) v Secretary of State for the Home Department* [2003] 1 AC 837 and *Bellinger v Bellinger* [2003] 2 AC 467 illustrate these points. In *Anderson* the role of the Home Secretary in determining life sentences of prisoners contravened Article 6 but as this was a fundamental feature of the legislation s.3 could not be employed. Equally, in *Bellinger* the ramifications of interpreting legislation to include transsexuals represented a fundamental change to the law. A comprehensive review of the existing law was required rather than the courts merely dealing with one aspect of the law. Such a review required decisions on issues that Parliament ought to make.

In *Anderson* and *Bellinger* the House of Lords refused to use s.3 and instead made a declaration of incompatibility.

In conclusion, a number of points may be made. In following the interpretative obligation imposed by s.3 the courts must interpret, not legislate. It is arguable, however, that the courts will exercise a law-making role, but within limitations. For s.3 to engage, legislation must be incompatible with Convention rights. This may arise even though there is no ambiguity in the wording used by Parliament. The courts may go beyond the words used in legislation by limiting the operation of a provision by the process of 'reading down' or altering the meaning of a provision by 'reading in' words. However, there are limits and if an interpretation runs counter to a fundamental feature of legislation then a Convention–compliant interpretation under s.3 may not be possible. Also if a court is in effect asked to legislate, e.g. by making a wide-ranging change to the law or one which effects only a partial reform to a legal area, again this goes beyond the interpretative obligation in s.3.

Further reading

- **Irvine, Lord** 'A British Interpretation of Convention rights' [2012] PL 237
  Argues that UK courts are too deferential to judgments of the European Court of Human Rights in the domestic interpretation of Convention rights.

- **Jones, T.** 'The Devaluation of Human Rights under the European Convention' [1995] PL 430
  Considers the margin of appreciation doctrine as developed in the European Court of Human Rights.

- **Kavanagh, A.** 'Statutory Interpretation and Human Rights after Anderson: A More Contextual Approach' [2004] PL 537
  Considers the factors that the courts take into account when interpreting under s.3.

- **Kavanagh, A.** 'The Elusive Divide between Interpretation and Legislation under the Human Rights Act 1998' (2004) 24 OJLS 259
  Considers the judicial role under s.3 Human Rights Act 1998 and argues that the interpretative function under s.3 involves law-making but within limits.

- **Landau, J.** 'Functional Public Authorities after *YL*' [2007] PL 630
  Considers the nature of a 'public authority' in the light of the decision in *YL v Birmingham City Council*.

- Law Commission Report No.266, *Damages under the Human Rights Act 1998* (2000)

- **Masterman, R.** 'Section 2(1) of the Human Rights Act 1998: Binding Domestic Courts to Strasbourg?' [2004] PL 725
  Considers the operation of s.2(1) and the differing judicial approaches to its interpretation.

- **Sales, P.** 'Strasbourg Jurisprudence and the Human Rights Act: A response to Lord Irvine' [2012] PL 253
  It is argued that the Supreme Court has adopted the correct approach to s.2 in 'mirroring' the interpretation of European Court of Human Rights of the rights in the Convention.

- **Wright, J.** 'Interpreting Section 2 of the Human Rights Act 1998: Towards an Indigenous Jurisprudence of Human Rights' [2009] PL 595
  Examines s.2 and the approach of the UK courts to the case law of the European Court of Human Rights.

 Online Resource Centre

You should now attempt the supporting multiple choice questions available at **www.oxfordtextbooks.co.uk/orc/wilson_els/**.

8 The judiciary

 **Learning objectives**

By the end of this chapter you should:

- be aware of the different types of judicial appointment;
- be able to identify and understand the different types of judge and their roles and responsibilities;
- understand the way in which judicial appointments are made;
- be aware of the arguments concerning diversity of membership of the judiciary; and
- be familiar with the importance of the concept of independence of the judiciary, and the laws which safeguard it.

🛈 Talking point

....

In May 2013 the Times reported that the applicants for the post of Lord Chief Justice, the most senior judge in England and Wales, would have to go through an appointment process that included an eighteen-page application form, a reference from a senior civil servant, an interview and a 2,000-word essay (the subject of which had yet to be decided at the date of the opening of the application period). The intention was to ensure transparency and fairness in the appointment process and to ensure that the best candidate for the job was selected. As Chris Grayling the Lord Chancellor stated on the Judicial Appointments Commission website: 'the LCJ will be a vigorous, modernising, and imaginative individual who simultaneously will be a judge of exceptional quality, recognise the need for greater efficiency and effectiveness in the administration of justice and sustain the independence and standing of the judiciary.'

Commentators have expressed surprise that part of the process includes a reference from the most senior civil servant with whom the applicant has had most contact. Does this cast a shadow on the important principle of judicial independence? Do you think that it is appropriate, or reasonable, to expect an applicant for such a post to write an essay (especially since one of the other criteria is the ability to 'write high quality judgments'?) What would you suggest could be a suitable essay title?

....

Introduction

The role of judges is to decide disputes brought before the courts. In so doing, judges exercise a judicial function which involves deciding the facts of the case, based upon the evidence presented to the court, establishing relevant law, and then applying the law to the facts in order to reach a decision. It has been seen in chapter 4, in relation to legislation, that judges interpret and apply the law whereas Parliament makes the law. In the common law, the judiciary has a more active role but their law-making power is restricted and the judges generally exercise restraint in this regard.

When considering the judiciary it is important to understand how judges are appointed, what qualifications are required for the various judicial offices, and how judges may be removed. This information is needed when assessing the important and often controversial issues of diversity of the membership of the judiciary, its independence and accountability.

....

8.1 **The judicial hierarchy**

The structure of the courts is based upon a hierarchy and the same is true of the judges who sit in the courts.

Before the judicial hierarchy is explained, it is important to note that changes were made in the Tribunals, Courts and Enforcement Act 2007 to the qualifications required to become a judge and therefore any members of the judiciary appointed after the introduction of that Act will have been through a different process from those appointed before the Act came into force. The amendments to the eligibility criteria were made to promote diversity in judicial appointments. See further 8.2.1, 'Diversity in judicial appointments'. Prior to the introduction of this Act, qualification as a judge depended upon rights of audience (permission to appear and present cases) before the courts being held for a minimum period of time. In effect, only barristers and solicitors qualified for at least seven years (or in some cases ten years) were eligible for appointment. It was decided that the criteria for appointment were too narrow and in order to increase the numbers of people eligible for appointment, changes had to be made.

The role of the judiciary in making law is considered in chapters 3 and 4, as is the relationship between Parliament and the courts.

By s.50 of the Tribunals, Courts and Enforcement Act 2007, the 'judicial-appointment eligibility condition' must be satisfied for appointment as a judge. The condition is satisfied where:

- a person holds a 'relevant qualification', i.e. is a barrister or solicitor or, by s.51, holds a legal qualification specified in an order made by the Lord Chancellor (the Lord Chancellor, under the power given by s.51, has extended eligibility, for a number of judicial posts including district judges to Fellows of the Chartered Institute of Legal Executives and to registered patents agents and trade mark attorneys in relation to certain appointments); and

- the total length of the person's 'qualifying period' is N years (N years means the number of years specified in the statute under which the judicial appointment is to be made).

The 'qualifying period' is the period for which a person (a) has a 'relevant qualification'; and (b) gains experience in law. It is not sufficient to simply hold a legal qualification. A person must also accumulate experience in law during the qualifying period: this prevents qualified lawyers who have never practised as lawyers, or been academics in the law, applying for appointment. By s.52, experience in law means being engaged in a law-related activity. By s.52(4), a 'law-related activity' encompasses the following:

- the carrying-out of judicial functions of any court or tribunal;
- acting as an arbitrator;
- practice or employment as a lawyer;

- advising (whether or not in the course of practice or employment as a lawyer) on the application of the law;

- assisting (whether or not in the course of such practice) persons involved in proceedings for the resolution of issues arising under the law;

- acting (whether or not in the course of such practice) as mediator in connection with attempts to resolve issues that are, or if not resolved could be, the subject of proceedings;

- drafting (whether or not in the course of such practice) documents intended to affect persons' rights or obligations;

- teaching or researching law; and

- any activity of a broadly similar nature to an activity within any of the eight paragraphs in the bullet point sub-list.

Note that another change made by the Tribunals, Courts and Enforcement Act 2007 is to reduce the minimum length of time that a person must be suitably qualified before appointment to the judiciary. For example, prior to the Act, the qualification to be a Lord Justice of Appeal or to be a High Court judge had to be for a minimum of ten years: this has been reduced to seven years. The requirement that the qualification to be a district judge had to be held for a minimum of seven years was reduced to five years.

The changes made to the criteria for judicial appointment impacts upon the issue of diversity in judicial appointments, see 8.2.1.

8.1.1 **The Lord Chancellor**

Prior to the Constitutional Reform Act 2005, the office of Lord Chancellor carried with it a multiplicity of roles and duties. The Lord Chancellor occupied a unique position as a member of the government (sitting in the Cabinet), a member of the legislature (Speaker of the House of Lords), and, as well as being head of the judiciary, exercised a judicial role in the Appellate Committee of the House of Lords. This raised issues in relation to the separation of powers, essential to the constitution, and the independence of the judiciary. As a consequence of the disquiet over the overlapping roles of the Lord Chancellor, in 2003, the Labour administration under Tony Blair decided that the office of Lord Chancellor should be abolished. However, after concerns were expressed by the judiciary and others that abolition of the role could not be done without an Act of Parliament, and abolition would have major constitutional implications, the office was retained in a modified form.

As a result of the reforms, the Lord Chancellor no longer acts in a judicial capacity and is not the Speaker of the House of Lords. By s.3 of the Constitutional Reform Act 2005, the Lord Chancellor is under a duty, along with ministers and all others with responsibility for matters relating to the judiciary or otherwise to the administration of justice, to 'uphold the continued independence of the judiciary'. The section further states that 'the Lord Chancellor and other ministers of the Crown must not seek to influence particular judicial decisions through any special access to the judiciary' and that the Lord Chancellor must have regard to –

(a) the need to defend...[the independence of the judiciary];

(b) the need for the judiciary to have the support necessary to enable them to exercise their functions;

(c) the need for the public interest in regard to matters relating to the judiciary or otherwise to the administration of justice to be properly represented in decisions affecting those matters.

In relation to the appointment of judges, the Lord Chancellor's role has been curtailed with the establishment of a Judicial Appointments Commission (JAC). The holder of the office of Lord Chancellor is also Secretary of State for Justice.

Appointment of a Lord Chancellor is a political appointment made on the recommendation of the prime minister from those 'qualified by experience': s.2 Constitutional Reform Act 2005. The following may be taken into account by the prime minister: experience as a minister of the Crown; as a member of either House of Parliament; as a qualifying practitioner, for example, a person who has a Senior Courts qualification within the meaning of s.71 of the Courts and Legal Services Act 1990; as a university teacher of law; or other experience considered relevant by the prime minister. Because the appointment is political the Lord Chancellor has no security of tenure and the Queen, on the advice of the prime minister, may dismiss the Lord Chancellor at any time.

> ### 🔑 Key point
>
> The reforms have resulted in the appointment, in 2012, of Chris Grayling – the first holder of the office of Lord Chancellor since 1673 not to have a legal qualification.

8.1.2 Justices of the Supreme Court

In October 2009 the constitutional reforms led to the replacement of the Appellate Committee of the House of Lords, the highest court in the United Kingdom, by a Supreme Court. The most senior judges in the United Kingdom are the twelve Justices of the Supreme Court.

Appointment

A selection commission is convened by the Lord Chancellor and when the decision to appoint has been made, the Lord Chancellor, if content with the selection, forwards the name of the person chosen to the prime minister who then sends details to the Queen, who makes the final appointment. More details can be found here: **www.supremecourt.gov.uk/about/appointments-of-justices.html**.

Qualification

By s.25 of the Constitutional Reform Act 2005, to be appointed a justice of the Supreme Court a person must have: (a) held high judicial office for a period of at least two years; or (b) satisfied the judicial-appointment eligibility condition on a fifteen-year basis; or (c) been a qualifying practitioner for a period of at least fifteen years. (A qualifying practitioner means a person who is an advocate in Scotland or a solicitor entitled to appear in the Court of Session and the High Court of Justiciary, or is a member of the Bar of Northern Ireland or a solicitor of the Court of Judicature of Northern Ireland.)

House of Lords Reform – the creation of the Supreme Court

The Constitutional Reform Act 2005 contained provisions for establishing a Supreme Court for the whole of the United Kingdom. There had been criticisms of the law lords as the final judges of appeal, because they also had a legislative role as members of the House of Lords in scrutinising, debating, and at times amending government legislation. By convention the law lords did not engage in political debate to preserve the appearance of judicial impartiality. This dual role, both legislative and judicial, is however contrary to a concept of separation of powers and with the creation of the Supreme Court, the law lords are no longer entitled to sit in the legislative chamber of the House of Lords. Indeed, to emphasise the separation, the Supreme Court sits in a building separate from the Houses of Parliament.

The government announced its intention to create a Supreme Court in June 2003 and the court began operating in October 2009. The law lords already sitting in the House of Lords in October 2009 became the first Supreme Court judges. The senior law lord at that time, Lord Phillips of Worth Matravers, became the President of the court. In 2012 Lord Neuberger of Abbotsbury succeeded Lord Phillips. The Deputy President of the court is Lord Hope of Craighead. The other judges are referred to as Justices of the Supreme Court. Lady Hale is the only female Justice of the Supreme Court.

8.1.3 Lord Chief Justice of England and Wales

The Lord Chief Justice holds the office of President of the Courts of England and Wales and is head of the judiciary of England and Wales. As President of the Courts of England and Wales, the Lord Chief Justice is responsible for representing the views of the judiciary to government, maintaining appropriate arrangements for the deployment, training and guidance of the judiciary, and overseeing the allocation of work within the courts. The Lord Chief Justice is president of the Court of Appeal (Criminal Division), and is entitled to sit in any of the following courts: Court of Appeal; High Court; Crown Court; county courts; and magistrates' courts.

8.1.4 **Master of the Rolls**

The Master of the Rolls is President of the Court of Appeal (Civil Division) and is also the leading judge dealing with civil work in that court. The Master of the Rolls is also responsible for organising the work of the civil division.

8.1.5 **Heads of Division**

The Heads of Division act as judges in the Court of Appeal and, where appropriate, are also responsible for organising the work in their division and sitting as a judge in the relevant courts. (See chapter 2 for more information on divisions.)

To become the Lord Chief Justice, the Master of the Rolls, or a Head of Division, a person must be qualified for appointment as a Lord Justice of Appeal or be a judge in the Court of Appeal: s.10 Senior Courts Act 1981 (prior to 2009, known as the Supreme Courts Act 1981: the name was changed to prevent confusion that could have been caused by the naming of the new Supreme Court). In practice, they are selected from the Lords Justices of Appeal or Justices of the Supreme Court.

8.1.6 **Judges in the Court of Appeal**

Judges sitting in the Court of Appeal hear both civil and criminal appeals. The judges in the Court of Appeal are the Lords Justices of Appeal and the Heads of Division, that is the Master of the Rolls, the Presidents of the Queen's Bench Division and of the Family Division, the Chancellor of the High Court, and the Lord Chief Justice of England and Wales. Civil appeal cases are heard by a combination of Lords Justices of Appeal and Heads of Division and the court usually sits with three judges. Although criminal cases are also usually heard by three judges, the composition of the court may be a little different because one High Court Judge and one Senior Circuit Judge (or two High Court judges) may sit alongside either the Lord Chief Justice, the President of the Queen's Bench Division, or one of the Lords Justices of Appeal.

8.1.7 **Lords Justices of Appeal**

The Lords Justices of Appeal are selected from members of the High Court bench and sit in the Court of Appeal. To be appointed as a Lord Justice of Appeal, a person must satisfy the judicial-appointment eligibility condition on a seven-year basis, or be a judge of the High Court: s.10 Senior Courts Act 1981. In practice, only High Court judges are appointed as Lords Justices of Appeal.

8.1.8 **High Court judges**

High Court judges (sometimes known as puisne (literally 'inferior in rank') judges) hear important civil cases and criminal cases, including sitting in the Crown Court and sitting alongside Lord Justices of Appeal for appeals in the Court of Appeal (Criminal Division). These judges sit, primarily, in London but also travel to the major court centres outside London to hear cases. High Court judges are now selected through a process operated by the Judicial Appointments Commission. However, to be eligible for appointment they must satisfy the judicial-appointment eligibility condition on a seven-year basis or have held the office of circuit judge for at least two years, s.10 Senior Courts Act 1981.

8.1.9 High Court Masters and Registrars

Masters and Registrars sit in the Chancery and Queen's Bench Divisions to deal with the procedural aspects of civil cases, from commencement of proceedings until trial, if a matter proceeds that far. They are now appointed through the JAC selection process, the statutory qualification being to satisfy the judicial-appointment eligibility condition on a five-year basis. In the Supreme Court, there is a Senior Master, together with nine Queen's Bench Masters (one of whom is the Admiralty Registrar), five Chancery Masters and a Chief Master, and five Bankruptcy Registrars and a Chief Registrar.

8.1.10 Circuit judges

Circuit judges sit in one of seven regions throughout England and Wales and hear cases in the Crown Court and county courts of that region. They often specialise in either civil or criminal cases. Some judges also deal with specialist areas such as commercial or construction cases. They may sometimes be asked to sit in the Court of Appeal (Criminal Division). Circuit judges are appointed through the selection process operated by the JAC. By s.16 of the Courts Act 1971, to be appointed a circuit judge a person must:

- satisfy the judicial-appointment eligibility condition on a seven-year basis;
- be a recorder; or
- have held as a full-time appointment for at least three years one of the offices listed in Part IA of Sch.2 to the Courts Act 1971. These offices include:
- President of Social Security Appeal Tribunals and Medical Appeal Tribunals or chair of such a tribunal;
- President of the Employment Tribunals (England and Wales) or member of a panel of chairs for employment tribunals for England and Wales;
- President or member of the Immigration Appeal Tribunal;
- Master of the Queen's Bench Division;
- Master of the Chancery Division;
- District judge; and
- District Judge (Magistrates' Courts).

8.1.11 **Recorders**

Recorders are part-time judges in the Crown Court. By s.21 of the Courts Act 1971, to be appointed as a recorder a person must satisfy the judicial-appointment eligibility condition on a seven-year basis.

8.1.12 **District judges**

District judges deal with a whole range of civil matters, from divorce and other family proceedings to damages claims. They sit at county courts in a particular region (formerly known as a circuit). They may also sit at district registries of the High Court in a particular region, again dealing with civil business, although in these cases, their role will be that of case management rather than acting as trial judge. District judges are appointed through the JAC's application and selection process.

By s.9 of the County Courts Act 1984, for a person to be appointed a district judge or deputy district judge he or she must satisfy the judicial-appointment eligibility condition on a five-year basis.

> ### ⬚ Example
>
> **A day in the life of a district judge**
>
> There is no typical day for a district judge, the work is so varied. As a result of the Woolf reforms, matters that would have been dealt with at a court hearing where all the parties were present at court may now be dealt with by telephone conference call. For example, approximately thirty minutes will be allocated to a telephone case management hearing, with fifteen minutes added to this for reading the relevant papers beforehand. An attended appointment in front of a district judge would be the exception. On some days there may be a short appointments list, dealing with case management issues and interim applications, and perhaps short small claims trials. Another day may see a large and complex ancillary relief case (dealing with the allocation of assets in family proceedings) listed to last for three days. Family work would not be dealt with by telephone and a typical family list might see twenty-two hours of contested cases listed for hearing, although many of these would settle beforehand.
>
> This information is based on an interview with an experienced district judge.

8.1.13 **District Judges (Magistrates' Courts)**

District Judges (Magistrates' Courts) used to be known as stipendiary magistrates, and sit in the magistrates' courts to deal with a range of the more complex cases that come before these courts. These cases can be civil or criminal in nature and some District Judges (Magistrates' Courts) are able to hear cases in specialist areas such as family proceedings or extradition proceedings. District Judges (Magistrates' Courts) are appointed through the JAC application and selection process. By s.22 of the Courts Act 2003, the statutory qualification for appointment as a District Judge (Magistrates'

Courts) is satisfaction of the judicial-appointment eligibility condition on a five-year basis. The same requirements apply in relation to the appointment as a Deputy District Judge (Magistrates' Court).

8.1.14 **Magistrates – Justices of the Peace (JPs)**

There are around 300 magistrates' courts in England and Wales (although the number is decreasing as courts are closed as part of a costs saving exercise), hearing a range of criminal cases and some civil cases, such as family proceedings. However, the overwhelming majority of the work is criminal cases. All criminal cases commence in the magistrates' court and most are dealt with in their entirety in that court (see chapters 8 and 9). The magistrates' court deals with bail applications as well as trials and sentencing in relation to summary offences and either way offences, where appropriate. Magistrates may also be asked to issue a search warrant. Magistrates are lay people and generally have no legal qualifications, although having a legal qualification does not prevent a person becoming a magistrate. They are required to undertake practical training to prepare them for their role. Magistrates are unpaid, save for expenses. The system of training, development, and appraisal for magistrates is overseen by the Judicial College and delivered by Magistrates Area Training Committees. More details can be found on the Magistrates' Association website: **www.magistrates-association.org.uk/**. Under this system, all magistrates are appraised on a three- or four-year basis. Appraisal is undertaken by fellow magistrates trained for this purpose. Some magistrates, such as members of family court panels, receive specialist training to enable them to deal with their specific role.

Magistrates sit in panels (known as benches), usually made up of three magistrates, and are supported by a qualified legal adviser (the court clerk). One member of the panel, selected on a random basis, will chair the bench, and speak in court to ask questions and give judgments, and the other two magistrates are referred to as 'wingers'. All members of the bench have an equal role in making decisions upon the cases that come before them.

At present, magistrates are appointed by the Lord Chancellor following the recommendation of a local advisory committee for the area in question, which will advertise to encourage applications from members of the public. There was a recent advertising campaign on the back of buses to try to encourage wider participation by members of the public. Approval is then given by the Lord Chief Justice. The aim of the application process is to try to encourage applicants, whatever their gender or age, from a wide range of social and ethnic backgrounds, to ensure that the Bench (the term used for the magistrates as a group and not to be confused with the use of the term 'bench' to describe a panel of magistrates sitting in court!) is suitably diverse.

Magistrates are unpaid volunteers and they are usually asked to sit in court for twenty-six half-days per year. Magistrates may also be required to sit in the Crown Court to hear criminal appeals from the magistrates' court. In such appeals, two magistrates will sit together with a circuit judge. Magistrates are issued with structured decision-making guidelines, designed to ensure consistency between decisions made in different magistrates' courts and to assist the decision-making process. Magistrates are also given guidelines in relation to sentencing.

⬛ Example

A day in the life of a magistrate

If the court is due to begin sitting at 10 a.m. I usually arrive by 9.30 and sign into the diary. I am given a court list from the clerk and check through it, to get an idea of the nature of cases being dealt with and to ensure that none of the cases involve somebody known to me (in which case I cannot sit to hear that particular case). The list also indicates fellow panel-members and will identify the chair of the panel.

Ten minutes before going into court, I meet with the court clerk and discuss the list and any problem cases. The panel Chair is told the name of the prosecutor.

A typical day might involve dealing with bail applications, committals to the Crown Court, adjournments, pre-trial reviews, probation report cases (required to give guidance on sentencing), and road traffic cases. In some of these cases, the panel will retire from the court to consider their decision. Most of these matters are dealt with in the morning session, which usually ends at about 1 p.m. When the afternoon session commences, at 2 p.m., there may be some overspill cases from the morning to deal with and also a half-day trial, for example dealing with an offence of shoplifting. After all the cases have been heard, the panel and the clerk usually have a short discussion about how the day has gone.

This information is based on an interview with an experienced magistrate.

Table 8.1 shows the range of judicial offices, terms of appointment, and tenure.

8.2 **Appointment of the judiciary**

Historically, the selection and appointment of members of the judiciary has been solely in the hands of the Lord Chancellor, a government minister. This resulted in the judiciary being perceived as having a lack of independence from government. The selection requirements and process also led to criticism that members of the judiciary tend to come from a narrow social background and do not reflect diversity in the population, in terms of ethnicity, age, and gender.

8.2.1 **The Peach Report**

Sir Leonard Peach produced a report in 1999 entitled, *The Independent Scrutiny of the Appointment Processes of Judges and Queen's Counsel in England and Wales.* In the report he recommended the appointment of a Commissioner for Judicial Appointments and in March 2001, Sir Colin Campbell was appointed to this role. The

Table 8.1 Table of judicial offices and governing legislation

Title	Governing legislation-qualification	Tenure	Court to which assigned
Justice of the Supreme Court	Section 25 Constitutional Reform Act 2005	By section 33 Constitutional Reform Act 2005, office held during good behaviour but may be removed from such office on an address of both Houses of Parliament	Supreme Court
Lord Chief Justice	Section 10 Senior Courts Act 1981	By section 11 Senior Courts Act 1981, office held during good behaviour, subject to a power of removal by Her Majesty on an address presented to Her by both Houses of Parliament. Lord Chancellor to recommend exercise of the power of removal	President of Criminal Division of the Court of Appeal
Master of the Rolls	Section 10 Senior Courts Act 1981	As in section 11 Senior Courts Act 1981	President of the Civil Division of the Court of Appeal
Lord Justice of Appeal	Section 10 Senior Courts Act 1981	As in section 11 Senior Courts Act 1981	Court of Appeal
Chancellor of the High Court	Section 10 Senior Courts Act 1981	As in section 11 Senior Courts Act 1981	High Court (Chancery Division)
President of the Queen's Bench Division	Section 10 Senior Courts Act 1981	As in section 11 Senior Courts Act 1981	High Court (Queen's Bench Division)
President of the Family Division	Section 10 Senior Courts Act 1981	As in section 11 Senior Courts Act 1981	High Court (Family Division)
High Court judge (alternatively called a puisne)	Section 10 Senior Courts Act 1981	As in section 11 Senior Courts Act 1981	High Court – assigned to a Division by direction given by the Lord Chief Justice after consultation with the Lord Chancellor Crown Court
Circuit judge	Section 16 of the Courts Act 1971	By section 17 Courts Act 1971, a circuit judge may be removed from office on the ground of incapacity or misbehaviour if the Lord Chancellor thinks fit and if the Lord Chief Justice agrees	Crown Court, County courts

Commission was established to investigate individual complaints relating to judicial appointments and the Queen's Counsel procedures and to review the appointments process for judges (other than law lords and Heads of Division) and Queen's Counsel. Note that this Commission had no role in making or recommending individual appointments. In reports published in 2002, 2003, and 2004 by Sir Colin Campbell's Commission, the appointment of, and selection process for members of the judiciary was heavily criticised.

The Law Society also published two consultation papers in 2000 on judicial appointments, recommending the creation of an independent JAC with open and transparent selection procedures and a widening of the pool from which candidates for judicial appointment can be drawn, to include all qualified solicitors and barristers, whether or not in private practice.

In 2003, the government announced that it would establish a Judicial Appointments Commission for England and Wales and a consultation paper was published in 2003 entitled *A New Way of Appointing Judges*.

This consultation paper put forward a number of proposals concerning the manner in which the Commission would operate. For example, the Commission could have sole power to select and appoint all members of the judiciary; or could operate a selection procedure, but simply recommend appointments to the Queen or a government minister; or could select and appoint members of the judiciary, but only *recommend* appointments to higher office. The paper also dealt with the composition of the Commission, suggesting fifteen members, five of whom would be lawyers, five lay members, and five judges.

Sir Colin Campbell's Commission responded by suggesting that the majority of the JAC should be lay members and all members should be part-time, to try to attract high calibre applicants. The Commission also recommended that the JAC should be able to appoint certain members of the judiciary (up to Circuit Bench level) but only make recommendations for appointment to the High Court and above. It was felt that this approach would strike an appropriate balance between judicial independence and ultimate accountability to Parliament.

Following the consultation paper, and consideration of the responses to it, the Constitutional Reform Bill was introduced in 2004 and the Constitutional Reform Act was passed in 2005 which implemented the introduction of the JAC. From 3 April 2006, the JAC has been responsible for the recruitment and selection of judges. When selection of judges was a matter for the Lord Chancellor, it was increasingly perceived that this was inappropriate, because it might suggest that the judiciary were not independent from the government if they were selected by one of its members. The independence of the judiciary is important in all matters but particularly vital in situations where the courts are adjudicating on the lawfulness of acts of government.

The creation of the JAC is intended to make the appointment process clear and more accountable and also to review the way in which judges are appointed to try to broaden the diversity amongst members of the judiciary. As K. Malleson, in her article, 'Creating a Judicial Appointments Commission: Which Model Works Best', has commented:

> the rationale for the establishment of a commission must be that it will guarantee the independence of the system from inappropriate politicisation, strengthen the quality of the appointments made, enhance the fairness of the selection process, promote diversity in the composition of the judiciary and so rebuild public confidence in the system.

Thinking point

It is fundamental that the judiciary must be independent. Equally fundamental is that the judiciary must also appear to be independent so any process for appointment must be transparent. The decision to move the physical location of the Supreme Court from the Houses of Parliament to a separate location, Middlesex Guildhall, is to emphasise the independence of the judiciary from Parliament and the government. What else is important in safeguarding the independence, and the appearance of independence, of the judiciary?

The Lord Chancellor will continue to recommend individuals for appointment to the judiciary to the Queen, as the final step in the process, but will no longer be involved in the recruitment and selection process.

The JAC acts independently of government to select candidates for judicial office (those offices set out in Sch.14 to the Constitutional Reform Act 2005 as well as to the offices of Lord Chief Justice, High Court judges, Heads of Division, and Lords Justices of Appeal) on merit where a vacancy arises through fair and open competition and by encouraging a wide range of applicants. There are fifteen members of the JAC, drawn from a range of legal posts and professions but it also includes lay commissioners with no legal experience. However, the composition is a little different to that put forward in the consultation paper. There are five judges, three of whom are selected by the Judges' Council (see later), six lay members, two professional members (one barrister and one solicitor), one magistrate, and one tribunal chair or arbitrator. Other than those members selected by the Judges' Council, there is a competitive application process. The Chairman of the Commission must always be a lay member. The Commission is accountable to Parliament through the Lord Chancellor. The Judicial Appointments Commission undertook its first selection process in October 2006, advertising in the press for applicants for the post of High Court judge.

The JAC has the role of a recommending body, in that candidates for appointment are recommended to the Lord Chancellor. The process of appointment set out in the Act is broadly similar whatever the nature of the appointment, but, in the case of Supreme Court judges, does involve a symbolic recommendation to the Queen from the prime minister.

> **Thinking point**
>
> In assessing whether the aims of the reform of the judicial appointments have been met it is important to consider the composition and powers of the JAC and to review the nature of the appointments made by the commission. Do you agree with the composition of the JAC and the powers given to it?

The Constitutional Reform Act 2005 sets out various procedures for the selection of judges, as set out in Table 8.2.

For the selection and appointment of (i) the Lord Chief Justice, the Master of the Rolls, the President of the Queen's Bench Division, the President of the Family Division, and the Chancellor of the High Court, and (ii) Lords Justices of Appeal, initially the Lord Chancellor must make a recommendation to fill a vacancy in the offices mentioned. A request will be made to the JAC for a person to be selected for recommendation to fill the vacancy. On receipt of the request, the JAC appoints a selection panel, which must consist of four members, one of whom is the chair of the commission or nominee and one of whom is a lay member of the commission, to determine and apply the selection process and make a selection. (Note that senior judges are also to be members of the panel, depending upon the office to be filled; see s.71 in relation to the offices in (i), and s.80 in relation to (ii).)

The panel will submit a report to the Lord Chancellor with the name of the person recommended for appointment. Only one person must be selected for recommendation for each request. At this stage, the Lord Chancellor can either accept or reject the person selected (if in the Lord Chancellor's opinion the person is not suitable for the office), or ask the panel to reconsider their selection if, in the opinion of the Lord Chancellor, there is not enough evidence that the person selected is suitable for the office or there is evidence that the person selected is not the best candidate on merit.

If the Lord Chancellor rejects a selected person, the selection panel may not select that person again. Where the Lord Chancellor requires the panel to reconsider, the panel may select the same person again, or someone else. There are three stages in the Act

Table 8.2 Selection of judges

Selection of judges	Process
Judges of Supreme Court (section 26)	Sections 27–31
Lord Chief Justice, Master of the Rolls, and Heads of Division (section 67)	Sections 68–75
Lords Justices of Appeal (section 76)	Sections 77–84
Puisne judges and holders of offices under Schedule 14, e.g. circuit judges, recorders, district judges, tribunal members (section 85)	Sections 86–93

through which the selection process can progress if the Lord Chancellor rejects a selection or asks the panel to reconsider. At the third stage, the Lord Chancellor must accept the selection. The new process cannot therefore be thwarted by the Lord Chancellor continually asking a panel to reconsider or rejecting their selected candidate.

In March 2010, it was reported that a JAC selection panel had been asked by the then Lord Chancellor, Jack Straw, to reconsider their recommendation of Sir Nicholas Wall as preferred candidate for President of the Family Division. Sir Nicholas was subsequently appointed to the post.

Note that for appointment as a Justice of the Supreme Court, the Lord Chancellor must convene a selection commission for the selection of a person to be recommended by the prime minister. By Sch.8, the Selection Commission consists of: the President of the Supreme Court; the Deputy President of the Supreme Court; and one member of the JAC, the Judicial Appointments Board for Scotland, and the Northern Ireland Judicial Appointments Commission.

In October 2007, the government issued a further consultation document on judicial appointments, *The Governance of Britain, Judicial Appointments*. Examples of further options for change in the consultation document include:

- the JAC itself making all judicial appointments, without the need for the involvement of the Lord Chancellor;
- alternatively, the JAC appointing to more junior judicial posts, the Lord Chancellor retaining a role in relation to the appointment of senior judges;
- the further limiting or removal of the Lord Chancellor's ability to reject a candidate put forward by the JAC or to ask the JAC to reconsider; and
- a greater involvement for Parliament in judicial appointments.

On 25 March 2008, the prime minister and Secretary of State announced a White Paper and Draft Constitutional Renewal Bill to further the constitutional reform process. In the White Paper, the government proposed to reduce the role played by the Lord Chancellor in judicial appointments below the High Court, by removing the Lord Chancellor's power to reject a candidate or to ask the JAC to reconsider. The government also proposed to remove the prime minister from the process of appointing senior judges and to set out in legislation key principles representing best practice in making judicial appointments. These changes did not find their way into the final legislation which became the Constitutional Reform and Governance Act 2010.

8.2.2 Diversity in judicial appointments

The JAC has a statutory duty under the Constitutional Reform Act 2005 to encourage greater diversity amongst those available for selection as judges, see s.64. The JAC must, however, select solely on merit and ensure that those selected are of good character. The task facing the JAC in encouraging diversity within the judiciary is illustrated in Table 8.3 and Table 8.4.

Table 8.3 Gender and ethnicity, statistics as at 1 April 2012

Appointment name	Total in post	Gender			Ethnicity								Total in post
		Male	Female	% Female	White	Asian or Asian British	Black or Black British	Mixed	Any other back-ground	Total BME	Unknown	% BME	
Heads of Division	5	5	0	0.0%	3	0	0	0	0	0	2	0.0%	5
Lords Justices of Appeal	38	34	4	10.5%	26	0	0	0	0	0	12	0.0%	38
High Court Judges	110	93	17	15.5%	85	1	0	1	3	5	20	4.5%	110
Judge Advocates	8	7	1	12.5%	7	0	0	0	0	0	1	0.0%	8
Deputy Judge Advocates	5	4	1	20.0%	3	0	0	0	0	0	2	0.0%	5
Masters, Registrars, Costs Judges and District Judges (Principal Registry of the Family Division)	46	32	14	30.4%	32	1	0	0	0	1	13	2.2%	46
Deputy Masters, Deputy Registrars, Deputy Costs Judges and Deputy District Judges (PRFD)	67	41	26	38.8%	35	0	1	1	1	3	29	4.5%	67
Circuit Judges	665	551	114	17.1%	588	3	2	1	5	11	66	1.7%	665
Recorders	1155	967	188	16.3%	826	21	15	14	9	59	270	5.1%	1155
District Judges (County Courts)	447	330	117	26.2%	396	11	3	5	4	23	28	5.1%	447
Deputy District Judges (County Courts)	754	507	247	32.8%	571	20	6	6	6	38	145	5.0%	754
District Judges (Magistrates' Courts)	141	100	41	29.1%	104	4	0	0	0	4	33	2.8%	141
Deputy District Judges (Magistrates' Courts)	134	97	37	27.6%	81	4	0	2	0	6	47	4.5%	134
Total	**3575**	2,768	807	22.6%	2757	65	27	30	28	150	668	4.2%	3575

Source: Judicial Database 2012.

Table 8.4 Judiciary by gender and profession statistics as at 1 April 2012

Appointment name	Gender			Profession				% Non-Barrister	Total in post
	Total in post	Male	Female	Barrister	Solicitor	Legal Executive	Unknown		
Heads of Division	5	5	0	5	0	0	0	0.0%	5
Lords Justices of Appeal	38	34	4	38	0	0	0	0.0%	38
High Court Judges	110	93	17	108	1	0	1	1.8%	110
Judge Advocates	8	7	1	7	1	0	0	12.5%	8
Deputy Judge Advocates	5	4	1	5	0	0	0	0.0%	5
Masters, Registrars, Costs Judges and District Judges (Principal Registry of the Family Division)	46	32	14	28	18	0	0	39.1%	46
Deputy Masters, Deputy Registrars, Deputy Costs Judges and Deputy District Judges (PRFD)	67	41	26	37	30	0	0	44.8%	67
Circuit Judges	665	551	114	585	80	0	0	12.0%	665
Recorders	1155	967	188	1,096	59	0	0	5.1%	1155
District Judges (County Courts)	447	330	117	51	395	0	1	88.6%	447
Deputy District Judges (County Courts)	754	507	247	167	586	1	0	77.9%	754
District Judges (Magistrates' Courts)	141	100	41	53	88	0	0	62.4%	141
Deputy District Judges (Magistrates' Courts)	134	97	37	49	85	0	0	63.4%	134
Total	**3575**	2,768	807	2,229	1,343	1	2	37.7%	3,575

Source: Judicial Database 2012.

Traditionally, senior judicial appointments have been made from the ranks of barristers, because qualification was based upon being a barrister or, more recently, experience as an advocate. Clearly this limited the size and composition of the recruitment pool for the judiciary and therefore this impacted upon the people becoming judges. If the recruitment pool was small then the judiciary would simply reflect this limited group. Solicitors are now able to attain rights of audience in the higher courts and, as a consequence, are eligible for appointment as senior judges. The question to be answered, however, is how many solicitors have been appointed? Equally, the effectiveness of the recent changes made in the Tribunal, Courts and Enforcement Act 2007 to the eligibility criteria for appointment to the judiciary will have to be considered. The statistics on judicial diversity produced in 2012 are presented in a different format from previous years and do not break down the data by gender within the ethnicity and profession categories.

The JAC has been criticised in the press for failing to create a more diverse judiciary. *The Guardian* newspaper reported (28 January 2008) that the first ten High Court judges appointed under the new rules were all white, male, former barristers, six of whom had been privately educated at leading independent schools. The article also reported that, although at the time there were a further eleven candidates approved for appointment and waiting for a suitable vacancy, only three were women, none of the candidates were from a minority ethnic background, and none of them were solicitors. In a later piece in the same newspaper (19 May 2008), it was reported that, since the inception of the JAC, the percentage of judicial appointments at all levels given to women or members of an ethnic minority had actually decreased.

Thinking point

Is it necessary for the judiciary to reflect society as a whole? Is it not ability to do the job on merit, with no regard to race, gender, religion, or ethnicity that is important? Baroness Butler-Sloss during the debate on the Crime and Courts Bill in 2012 stated: 'I strongly support diversity when – and only when – it equals merit. It will be very important that women – particularly those from ethnic minorities – who may not be able to bear the strain of the judicial process are not placed in a position where they may find themselves failing because there has been too much enthusiasm for diversity and not enough for merit. This is very important. I have a vivid recollection of a woman judge many years ago who was a very fine pianist. She should have remained a pianist.' What do you think of this view?

The then Secretary of State for Justice, Jack Straw, acknowledged that the involvement of the JAC in the judicial appointment process had not fulfilled expectations of creating a more diverse judiciary. The situation since 2008 has improved marginally. The Equality and Human Rights Commission in its annual report of 2011, *Sex and Power*, see **www.equalityhumanrights.com/key-projects/sexandpower/**, noted that the percentage of women holding senior judicial posts (in the High Court and above) had risen slightly from 9.8 per cent in 2006 to 12.9 per cent in 2011, after a slight dip to 9.6 per cent in 2007–08. The Commission estimated at the present rate of progress, for women to achieve equality in terms of these judicial appointments it would take forty-five years, which is an improvement since the 2008 report which estimated a period of fifty-five years. Perhaps the appointment process is finally making progress in the right direction, although, as the report points out, the increase in percentages reflects, often, the appointment of only a small number of candidates in numerical terms.

In July 2010, the JAC reported that the first analysis of the appointment of women and black or minority ethnic candidates to judicial office over ten years (between 1998 and 2009) showed that more of these candidates are now applying for judicial roles than before the JAC was set up. It also found that more women candidates are being selected although the number of successful black or minority ethnic candidates remained constant.

In February 2010, the Advisory Panel on Judicial Diversity, chaired by Lady Neuberger, delivered its report into identifying the barriers to progress on judicial diversity and made recommendations to the Lord Chancellor on how to make progress to a more diverse judiciary at every level and in all courts in England and Wales.

> ## ! Critical debate
>
> *A comparative European study in 2012 reported that only Azerbaijan and Armenia have a lower ratio of women to men in the senior judiciary. The Ministry of Justice has praised its diversity task-force for implementing '20 of the 53 recommendations' made in Lady Neuberger's report on how to encourage more women to enter the profession. Is it fair to compare England and Wales with other jurisdictions in this respect?*

The Panel recommended a 'fundamental shift of approach from a focus on individual judicial appointments to the concept of a judicial career. A judicial career should be able to span roles in the courts and tribunals as one unified judiciary'. In order to deliver this change, the Panel recommended that a Judicial Diversity Taskforce, made up of the Lord Chancellor, the Lord Chief Justice, the Chairman of the JAC, leaders of the legal profession, and the Senior President of Tribunals, should oversee an agreed action plan for change.

You can access this report at: **www.gov.uk/government/publications/ improving-judicial-diversity**. The taskforce was set up and produced its first report in May 2011 and its second annual report in September 2012. The report can be accessed here: **https://www.gov.uk/government/publications/ improving-judicial-diversity-judicial-diversity-taskforce-annual-report**.

In relation to magistrates, until 2008 the proportion of male and female magistrates appointed was equal but between 2008 and 2012 more female magistrates than male magistrates were appointed. See the Ministry of Justice,

Judicial and Court Statistics 2011 **https://www.gov.uk/government/publications/judicial-and-court-statistics-annual**.

Thinking point

It is often stressed that the composition of the judiciary reflects a narrow social base. The criticism levelled at the judiciary is that it is unrepresentative of the general population because its members are predominantly male, white, public school and Oxbridge educated, and middle class. It is important to keep the judicial statistics under review in order to see who is being appointed to the judiciary, particularly noting the percentage of women, minority ethnic candidates, and solicitors. Of course, the composition of the judiciary may also reflect reluctance in certain groups to apply for judicial appointment. What steps need to be taken to widen the recruitment net and what steps are being taken by the JAC?

8.2.3 **Alternative methods of appointment**

Different countries around the world appoint their judges in different ways. Rather than have an appointments process the judges are appointed by standing for election, or by specifically training for the judiciary as a career.

In the United States of America, for example, some judges are elected, or their appointment is subject to confirmation, by the political electorate. Although this system is, arguably, a more democratic process than that used to appoint members of the judiciary in England and Wales, it does not necessarily mean that the best person for the job is the one who is appointed. In fact, it can result in the wealthiest candidates having the most success, due to well-financed promotional campaigns. The American Judicature Society (AJS), an independent body that works to maintain the independence and integrity of the courts and increase public understanding of the justice system, has commented that electing members of the judiciary is only effective if voters can make an informed choice – in some cases, due to the number of candidates this becomes impossible, and in other cases, where only one candidate runs for office, there is no choice at all. The AJS also suggests that in some circumstances, for a candidate to succeed, the support of a political party is essential. This may lead to charges that the independence and impartiality of the office holder can be in doubt, and may result in political credentials being more important than aptitude and suitability for the role.

Due to these concerns, some states use commissions to select candidates for judicial appointments. Although the membership of each commission varies, it would typically comprise both lay and legally qualified members and would be involved in advertising judicial posts, interviewing candidates, and making recommendations to the appropriate appointing authority.

You can find out more about how judges are appointed in the US and the role of the American Judicature Society at: **www.ajs.org/**.

In France, the École Nationale de la Magistrature (ENM) trains French law graduates to be judges. So, the judiciary includes judges appointed from the legal profession as well as career judges, straight from university, trained for two-and-a-half years by the ENM. This approach means that the average age of judges is lower than in many other countries and has also resulted in the appointment of more female than male judges in France. Of course this situation can lead to similar criticisms to those levelled in the United Kingdom, at an overwhelmingly male judiciary.

Thinking point

Academic lawyers can become judges of the Court of Justice of the European Communities in Luxembourg and of the European Court of Human Rights in Strasbourg. Do you think that academics, without legal professional qualifications, should be appointed to the judiciary in England and Wales?

8.3 **Removal and retirement**

The age for retirement of judges is usually 70. However, the Lord Chief Justice may allow certain judges to carry on above this age, up until age 75 (Judicial Pensions and Retirement Act 1993 s.26). It is possible to remove judges from office, but as has been seen in the Table of Judicial Offices and Governing Legislation (Table 8.1), removal may only take place under very specific circumstances. To summarise the position regarding the removal of judges, only the Queen, on the petition of both Houses of Parliament, can remove judges of the High Court or above. The last occasion on which this happened was in 1830, when Jonah Barrington, a judge of the High Court of Admiralty, was removed for fraudulently taking money that had been paid into court. The Lord Chancellor, with the agreement of the Lord Chief Justice, can dismiss other judges for incapacity, inability, or misbehaviour, depending upon the judicial office held. Bruce Campbell J (a circuit judge) was sacked in 1983 for smuggling spirits, cigarettes, and tobacco into England on his yacht. In April 2009, a district judge was removed from office by the Lord Chancellor and the Lord Chief Justice under s.11 (5) of the County Courts Act 1984. Also in 2009 a district judge, Margaret Short, was removed after a judicial investigation into complaints made about her behaviour towards solicitors appearing before her (this included, being 'petulant and rude') and 'a variety of other inappropriate behaviour'. In 2011 a deputy High Court judge was removed from office for 'bringing the judiciary into disrepute' after being convicted of assaulting his wife.

Thinking point

Why do you think it is so difficult to remove judges?

8.4 **Judicial independence**

Despite some perceived lack of independence in the judiciary arising as a result of the way in which they were appointed, prior to the Constitutional Reform Act 2005, the independence of judges is in fact protected in a number of ways. As has already been seen it is difficult to remove judges from office, which seeks to ensure that their decision-making is unaffected by external pressures political, or otherwise. The salaries of judges are substantial (but not as high as salaries for very successful lawyers) to maintain the quality of candidates seeking judicial appointment. Judges are paid from the Consolidated Fund, which was first set up in 1787 as 'one fund into which shall flow every stream of public revenue and from which shall come the supply for every service'. The significance of this is that the Consolidated Fund is not subject to an annual parliamentary vote, so judicial salaries are not the matter of political debate. By s.75 of the Courts and Legal Services Act 1990, certain judges, listed in Sch.11, are barred from private legal practice. The list includes, amongst others: Justice of the Supreme Court; Lord Justice of Appeal; Puisne judge of the High Court; circuit judge; district judge; and District Judge (Magistrates' Courts). Under the House of Commons Disqualification Act 1975, full-time judges are disqualified from membership of the House of Commons.

Another aspect of judicial independence is that judges are immune from being sued in connection with the exercise of their jurisdiction. The limits of this immunity were explored in the case of *Sirros v Moore* [1975] QB 118. Magistrates have statutory immunity, under ss.31 and 32 of the Courts Act 2003, for acts or omissions: (a) in the execution of duties as a Justice of the Peace; and (b) in relation to matters within their jurisdiction. The immunity extends to acts or omissions in the purported execution of duty beyond the jurisdiction of a Justice of the Peace so long as there is an absence of bad faith. In relation to defamation absolute privilege attaches to statements made by judges in the execution of their judicial office.

Thinking point

Can you suggest why judicial immunity from suit (being sued) is important?

Judges are, therefore, mostly independent of government and the legislature and do not become involved in political debate. However, judges may inevitably become involved in hearing, and deciding, cases with political implications. In the 1980s, cases such as *Duport Steel v Sirs* [1980] 1 WLR 142, concerning trade union activities in relation to a strike, *Bromley v Greater London Council* [1982] 1 All ER 129, dealing with pricing policy for the London Underground, and cases arising from the miners' strike

1984–85 thrust the courts into areas of political controversy. Indeed, it is said by some that the social and political background of judges predisposes them to favour certain sectional interests in the community and to be unsympathetic to other interests. (See J. A. G. Griffith *The Politics of the Judiciary*.) However, that is not to say that the judges are pro-government. The readiness of the courts to judicially review the decisions of the executive and find such decisions unlawful, particularly in the fields of immigration and sentencing, evidences judicial independence. Consider also the impact of the Human Rights Act 1998 and the courts' interpretation of United Kingdom law in the light of the European Convention on Human Rights (see chapter 7).

Consider also that judges may be requested to chair royal commissions and tribunals of inquiry. Inevitably such activity places judges in the political arena.

☰ Example

Examples include Lord Denning in relation to the Profumo affair in 1963, Lord Justice Scott's inquiry in the 1990s into the sales of arms to Iraq, and more recently Lord Hutton's report published in January 2004 into the death of the government arms expert, Dr David Kelly (HC 247). Judicial independence has been strengthened further, at least ostensibly, in the wake of the Constitutional Reform Act 2005. First, the Lord Chancellor no longer has a judicial role and, as has been seen, certain functions have been transferred to the Lord Chief Justice. Section 3 of the Constitutional Reform Act also imposes a duty on the Lord Chancellor to uphold judicial independence and not seek to influence judicial decisions through special access to the judiciary. Second, Justices of the Supreme Court are disqualified from sitting in the legislative chamber of the House of Lords and with the establishment of an independent Supreme Court there is a further apparent separation of the judicial and legislative functions. Third, the creation of the independent JAC has largely taken judicial appointments out of the hands of the executive.

On a personal level, to maintain their independence, judges must not engage in activities which might affect, or be thought to affect, their independence. A judge should disqualify him or herself from sitting in a particular case if an issue of bias arises, for example a financial interest in the outcome of a particular case (*Dimes v The Proprietors of the Grand Junction Canal* (1852) 3 HL Cas 759). The principle of natural justice, which includes the rule against bias, secures the impartiality of decisions made by judges. The other limb of the concept of natural justice is that that a hearing must be seen to be fair and judicial impartiality is an important safeguard for this. Successful appeals have been mounted against the decisions of judges who have interfered in a case by asking too many questions from the bench. These technical rules of natural justice do not however impact upon a perceived prejudice arising out of the social and political background of individual judges. See also the section on judicial conduct at 8.5.2.

Arguably, the leading case on judicial independence is *R v Bow Street Metropolitan Stipendiary Magistrate, ex parte Pinochet Ugarte (No.2)* [2000] 1 AC 119. The House of Lords had ruled, by a 3 to 2 majority, that the former president of Chile, Senator Pinochet, who was accused of various crimes against Spanish nationals resident in Chile in the 1970s, could be extradited to Spain to face trial. However, it subsequently emerged that one of the majority judges, Lord Hoffmann, had links with Amnesty International, a charity which campaigns for justice for political prisoners worldwide. The law lords decided that, because Lord Hoffmann had not declared this interest in advance, his presence in the case created an *impression* of bias sufficient to justify ordering a rehearing. Even the *theoretical possibility* of bias was enough. This was unprecedented, but shows the value placed on judicial independence in this country. At the rehearing, a new panel of judges confirmed that Pinochet could be extradited but the British government then intervened and decided that Pinochet was too ill to face trial in Spain and allowed him to leave the United Kingdom for Chile, where he managed to resist trial on grounds of ill health, until his eventual death in December 2006. Lord Browne-Wilkinson said:

> The fundamental principle is that a man may not be a judge in his own cause. This principle has two implications. First…if a judge is in fact a party to the litigation or has a financial or proprietary interest in its outcome then he is indeed sitting as a judge in his own cause [and this] is sufficient to cause his automatic disqualification…Second…where his conduct or behaviour may give rise to a suspicion that he is not impartial, for example because of his friendship with a party…In my judgment, this case falls within the first category of case. In such a case, once it is shown that the judge is himself a party to the cause, or has a relevant interest in its subject matter, he is disqualified without any investigation into whether there was a likelihood or suspicion of bias. The mere fact of his interest is sufficient to disqualify him unless he has made sufficient disclosure.

8.5 Governance of the judiciary

The way in which the judiciary is governed has changed following the Constitutional Reform Act 2005. The Lord Chief Justice, rather than the Lord Chancellor, is now responsible for deciding in which court judges sit and what sort of cases they hear. A new structure for the organisation of the judiciary has also been developed, which includes a new Judicial Executive Board and the existing Judges' Council.

Thinking point

An independent appointments process, the constraints on the removal of judges, as has been outlined in Table 8.1, and judicial immunity from suit, all ensure that judicial independence is safeguarded. Are further safeguards required?

The Judicial Executive Board is made up of the Lord Chief Justice, the Master of the Rolls, the Presidents of both the Queen's Bench and Family Divisions, the Chancellor of the High Court, the Vice-President of the Queen's Bench Division, and the Senior Presiding Judge. The Board is the vehicle through which the Lord Chief Justice exercises his executive responsibilities relating to issues such as providing leadership, direction, and support to the judiciary and determining roles and responsibilities of the judiciary; considering policies on complaints; developing policy and practice on judicial deployment and appointment to non-judicial roles and putting forward the requirements for new appointments of certain judges and discussing specific appointments with the JAC. Some aspects of the work of the Board will also be undertaken by subcommittees.

The original Judges' Council, dating from 1873, was in place until 1981. After much debate as to the pros and cons of having a Council representing the views of judges, the Judges' Council was resurrected in 1988 as a smaller body under the chairmanship of the Lord Chief Justice. The Council is primarily a representative body for the judiciary and advises the Lord Chief Justice on particular issues when requested to do so. The sort of issues upon which the Council presently advises includes judicial independence, the development of a judicial code of conduct, and terms and conditions of judges' employment. The Council includes representatives from all areas of the judicial hierarchy, meets a number of times each year, and publishes newsletters and an annual report.

The judiciary also has a number of other representative bodies, such as the Association of District Judges and the Magistrates' Association.

8.5.1 Training the judiciary

The responsibility for training the judiciary and magistrates lies with the Judicial College (JC). In April 2011, the College took over the training function that had been undertaken by the Judicial Studies Board since 1973. Membership of the College includes academics, practitioners, judges, and magistrates. The Lord Chief Justice has statutory responsibility for the College. You can find out more about the JC from the following website: **www.judiciary.gov.uk/training-support/judicial-college/index**.

The formal training of judges is now structured and the College has identified three aspects necessary for judicial training:

1. Substantive law, evidence, and procedure (and if appropriate, subject specific expertise);
2. Judicial skills;
3. Social context.

New appointees have to go through an induction programme and most are assigned a mentor to support them in the first few years of their appointment. The judges are then required to keep up to date by attending continuing education and training sessions. The College training strategy, 2011–14, sets out in detail what the body is trying to achieve: **www.judiciary.gov.uk/training-support/judicial-college/Strategy+2011+-+14**.

The College's predecessor, the Judicial Studies Board, published a competence framework for magistrates as part of the revised Magistrates' National Training Initiative. The College has put in place an induction and consolidation training programme to ensure that magistrates are fully trained to discharge their judicial function.

8.5.2 Judicial conduct

The Judges' Council, following consultation with the judiciary, drew up a Guide to Judicial Conduct in October 2004. A standing committee was instituted to keep the guide under review and the most recent version of the guide was published in March 2013. The guide is designed to assist judges in relation to issues of conduct that they might face and is designed to be read alongside their terms and conditions of appointment. The principles and aspirations set out in the guide include judicial independence, impartiality, integrity, propriety, competence, and diligence. These principles having been expressed, the guide goes on to consider a number of specific problems that may be faced by members of the judiciary, such as in respect of personal relationships and perceived bias and activities outside the court which includes areas such as commercial activities, participation in public debate and gifts, hospitality, and social activities. The guide can be found at **www.judiciary.gov.uk/Resources/JCO/ Documents/Guidance/judicial_conduct_2013.pdf**.

There is now an Office for Judicial Complaints (OJC). The purpose of this office is to try to ensure the fair and consistent treatment of disciplinary issues involving the judiciary.

You can find out more about the OJC at the following website: **www.judicialcom plaints.gov.uk/**.

The OJC deals with complaints about the personal conduct of members of the judiciary, rather than complaints about a judge's decision in a particular case.

Should anyone wish to complain about the OJC, then the complaint may be referred to the Judicial Appointments and Conduct Ombudsman. The role of the Judicial Appointments and Conduct Ombudsman encompasses the investigation of complaints concerning the judicial appointments process and issues arising out of judicial discipline or conduct.

You can find out more about the ombudsman at this website: **www.judicialom budsman.gov.uk/**.

Summary

- Judges are appointed to work in particular courts and may specialise in hearing particular types of cases, such as civil, criminal, and family. They are governed by the Lord Chief Justice through the Judicial Executive Board.

- The Justices of the Supreme Court are the most senior judges in the United Kingdom.

- The system under which members of the judiciary are selected and appointed has changed radically in recent years. This has been fuelled by criticisms of the make-up of the judiciary in terms of age, sex, gender, and ethnicity and in terms of their perceived lack of independence from government.

- From April 2006, the JAC has been responsible for operating a selection process for members of the judiciary and recommending appointments to the Lord Chancellor. The JAC is required, under the Constitutional Reform Act 2005, to encourage greater diversity amongst those selected for appointment and its creation is designed to make the selection process clearer, more accountable, and independent of government.

- The independence of the judiciary is protected in a number of ways, for example, by the process of appointment and by the constraints on the removal of judges.

- The Judges' Council is one of the representative bodies of the judiciary and publishes a Guide to Judicial Conduct. Judges receive training in their role through the Judicial College, which operates an induction process and continuing education.

Questions

1 Why do you think it was considered necessary to change the way in which members of the judiciary were appointed?

2 What is the role and function of the new Judicial Appointments Commission?

3 What are the obstacles to diversification of the composition of the judiciary?

4 Identify the safeguards in place to ensure judicial independence.

5 What sort of training do new members of the judiciary receive?

6 What key principles are contained in the Guide to Judicial Conduct?

Sample question and outline answer

Question

Lord Neuberger, President of the Supreme Court, commented in June 2013 that more had to be done to change the 'monolithic' senior judiciary. Should the judiciary be representative of the population as a whole?

Outline answer

Your introduction should set out what you understand the question to be asking and explain how you will set about answering it. This is a wide question that can be answered in a variety of ways. Provided you set out in your introduction how you intend to answer it, and then go on to do what you set out to do, you cannot go wrong! What follows are a few ideas about how the question could be approached.

The question requires you to discuss whether the make-up of the judiciary is similar to the population of the UK. This requires you to explain what is meant by representative, i.e. the contention that the members of the judiciary in age, social class, gender, ethnicity, and education should represent, in percentage terms, the population of the country.

You might wish to distinguish between the lay judiciary (magistrates) and the professional judiciary (judges). You could set out an overview of the composition of each and explain why that is the present situation.

You could explain the role of judges and why it could be important that they are drawn from a wide section of society and give an opposing view that the selection process should ensure that judges are able to do the job they are selected for whilst being drawn from a small pool of applicants. However you may also wish to investigate a contrary view, as expressed by Baroness Butler-Sloss. You could then go on to explain that the non-representative nature of the judiciary has generally been recognised as a problem and discuss the reforms brought about by the Constitutional Reform Act 2005, and the Tribunals, Courts and Enforcement Act 2007, together with the new procedures for appointment from the JAC.

In your conclusion you can sum up your arguments.

Further reading

Your reading should be directed to making sure you have an overview of the general structure of the judicial hierarchy in England and Wales and a general understanding of the jurisdiction and role played by judges. You should read in more depth about the debate relating to transparency and suitability of the appointment system and you should think about whether the process for removing judges from office is fit for purpose. Finally, the perennial debate about diversity in the ranks of the judiciary is a popular area for assessment. Make sure that you read the broadsheet newspapers: there are often articles and debate about the judiciary that will give you ideas to think about and explore further.

- **Bradley, A.** 'Judicial Independence under Attack' [2003] PL 397
  Considers the attack by David Blunkett against the judiciary arising from a case involving asylum seekers.

- **Derbyshire, P.** *Sitting in Judgment: the Working Lives of Judges*, Hart Publishing (2011)
  A discussion of the modern judiciary.

- Democratic Audit of the United Kingdom **www.democraticaudit.com/wp-content/uploads/2013/06/auditing-the-uk-democracy-the-framework-2.pdf**
  Discussion on the independence of the judiciary.

- Equality and Human Rights Commission *Sex and Power* (2011) **www.equalityhumanrights.com/key-projects/sexandpower/**
  The annual report dealing with the underrepresentation of women in positions of power.

- **Gerry, F.** 'Ensuring Gender Equality in the Judiciary' (2012) 176(48) CL & J 705
  Considers why there are so few women being appointed as judges.

- **Griffith, J. A. G.** *The Politics of the Judiciary*, 5th edn reissue, Fontana Press (2010)
  This is an important, and controversial, text. It considers whether the judiciary are able to be neutral or whether they must act politically.

- **Hale, B.** 'Equality and the Judiciary: Why Should We Want More Women Judges?' [2001] PL 489
  This article makes some interesting points about the judicial appointments system which was used to appoint many of the judges currently in post in England and Wales.

- Judicial appointments commission, their website is **http://jac.judiciary.gov.uk/**
  Includes lots of interesting information including the application forms and criteria for judicial posts.

- **Malleson, K.** 'Creating a Judicial Appointments Commission: Which Model Works Best?' [2004] PL 102
  An interesting discussion about the alternative ways that a JAC could be dealt with.

- Phillips of Worth-Matravers, Lord, Lecture on the Politics of Judicial Independence delivered at UCI in February 2011 **www.supremecourt.gov.uk/docs/speech_110208.pdf**
  This speech does exactly what its title suggests – it is an insider's view from the then President of the Supreme Court. You can see the speech being delivered here: **www.ucl.ac.uk/constitution-unit/events/judicial-independence-events/launch**

- **Small, J.** *'Quis Custodiet Ipsos Custodes?'* (2003) 153 NLJ 624
  In other words who oversees the judges? A discussion about the best way to appoint High Court judges.

Online Resource Centre

You should now attempt the supporting multiple choice questions available at **www.oxfordtextbooks.co.uk/orc/wilson_els/**.

9 The legal profession

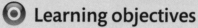 **Learning objectives**

By the end of this chapter you should:

- be able to describe the roles of solicitors and barristers in the English legal system;

- be able to identify the basic business models of legal practice and the constraints on such organisations;

- have an understanding of the rules affecting practice as a solicitor or a barrister;

- be able to identify the regulatory organisations overseeing solicitors and barristers and be able to discuss the issues concerning regulation; and

- be able to take part in the debate as to whether the two main branches of the legal profession should be fused into one.

🅛 Talking point

'Trucking giant Eddie Stobart enters legal market with barristers' business' was the eye-catching headline in The Lawyer in May 2012. The article explained that the trucking company planned to take advantage of the new opportunities afforded by alternative business structures (ABS) to launch a legal service to connect businesses directly to barristers without having to instruct a solicitor.

The article went on to state 'Stobart Barristers, the new service formed by the Stobart Group, has said it can cut the cost of barristers' services by charging clients a fixed fee and using paralegals instead of solicitors to help prepare a case.' In July 2013 the proposal became a reality when the Law Gazette reported that Stobarts had been granted an alternative business structure licence from the Solicitors Regulation Authority.

The idea of ABS is to open up the provision of legal services to management and input from non-lawyers. An ABS is a regulated organisation which provides legal services, but has some form of involvement from non-lawyers. The non-lawyer input can be either at management level or as an owner, such as an investor or shareholder.

Do you think that this is a good idea? Would you be happy to obtain legal advice via a company primarily known for its haulage business? Would the fact that the ABS is regulated by the Solicitors Regulation Authority influence your decision? Do you think that non-lawyers can add value to the provision of legal services?

Introduction

The past thirty years have seen major changes to legal practice and the legal professions. Some changes have been brought about directly by the professions, and some have been introduced by Acts of Parliament. Others have been necessitated by factors such as the increase in the volume and complexity of laws on the statute books and increased influence of the internet. A number of Acts of Parliament have sought to make legal services more readily available to members of the public and more responsive to the needs of consumers in order to break down barriers to competition to ensure that legal services are obtainable at the best price for the best service. The legislation includes the Administration of Justice Act 1985, which sanctioned licensed conveyancers and ended the conveyancing monopoly of solicitors and the Courts and Legal Services Act 1990, which stated in s.17(1), that the objective was:

the development of legal services in England and Wales (and in particular the develop-ment of advocacy, litigation, conveyancing, and probate services) by making provision for *new or better ways* of providing such services and *a wider choice of persons provid-ing them*, while maintaining the proper and efficient administration of justice (emphasis added).

Under this Act, the barristers' monopoly to appear as advocates before the higher courts was ended and solicitors were given the opportunity to gain higher rights of audience.

The Access to Justice Act 1999 continued reforms relating to legal services. In particular it established the Legal Services Commission to oversee legal aid via the Community Legal Service and the Criminal Defence Service. The Legal Services Commission was abolished in April 2013, as a result of provisions in the Legal Aid, Sentencing and Punishment of Offenders (LASPO) Act 2012, and replaced by The Legal Aid Agency which is now responsible for both civil and criminal legal aid and advice in England and Wales. (See chapter 11 on Access to Justice.)

In 2007 the Legal Services Act introduced alternative business structures for lawyers, with the aim of providing benefits for consumers by way of more choice, reduced costs, and greater convenience in accessing legal services. Sections of the Act have come into force on a number of different dates. The provisions in respect to ABS came into force in 2011. Under ABS, non-lawyers are permitted to part-own law firms and, it is hoped, the creation of multidisciplinary practices will lead to legal services and non-legal services being offered in combination. The Act has been referred to as 'Tesco law' because of an expectation, not yet realised, that supermarkets will provide legal services and compete with law firms.

The Legal Services Act also seeks to make the legal profession more accountable and transparent in relation to complaints. The self-regulation of the profession has been replaced by a scheme of independent safeguards. Regulation is undertaken by the Legal Services Board which has as its overriding mandate 'to ensure that regulation in the legal services sector is carried out in the public interest; and that the interests of consumers are placed at the heart of the system'.

The reforms have generated much comment, both positive and negative, and when studying the legal profession, the reforms should be considered and evaluated. In essence, the discussion revolves around what is 'in the public interest'. Lawyers view this as meaning that a strong independent profession is required with high ethical standards and a high level of expertise: the price being that there must be restrictions and the cost may be high. The opposing view is that public interest requires competi-tion, to improve efficiency, and that control by independent regulation is preferable to self-regulation. To assess the arguments it is necessary to understand the rules governing the work of the legal profession and how they operate.

9.1 **The legal profession**

In England and Wales, unlike in many other legal systems, the legal profession comprises two distinct branches: barristers and solicitors. In addition there are other personnel providing legal services, such as licensed conveyancers and legal executives. This chapter will look at these different branches of the legal profession.

9.2 **Solicitors**

The job description of a solicitor has altered over time but their role has always involved representing individuals and organisations in their dealings with the law. The title of solicitor in the present-day sense was first used in the late nineteenth century.

Traditionally solicitors worked in partnerships, based in local communities, and undertook a broad range of work associated with day-to-day legal concerns: divorce, conveyancing, drafting wills, dealing with criminal and civil litigation. This is still the case with small firms ('high street' firms) but, increasingly, solicitors work in large firms and as a result individual lawyers have to specialise in specific areas of the law. Large firms of solicitors ('commercial' firms) have a number of specialist departments, such as company/commercial, property, private client, and litigation. Many areas of the law are complex and the law can change on a daily basis. It is not possible for an individual solicitor to keep up to date with diverse areas of the law, as they may have done in the past, so solicitors have had to narrow their field of expertise and practice. In large law firms, within broad departments, smaller groups of solicitors will work in specialist units. For example, in the company department there may be sub-departments dealing with intellectual property, pensions, banking and finance, and insolvency. The biggest commercial firms have a huge array of specialist areas of expertise. It is instructive to look at the websites of some of the larger legal firms to find out how their business is organised on a departmental basis.

Example

A typical day for a commercial solicitor in a large specialist department

Work can be for a variety of clients or for one major client. A typical day may involve consideration of contractual documents, such as standard terms of business or contracts relating to intellectual property (e.g. computer software). The work often involves drafting, amending, or negotiating contracts on behalf of a client. The day might start with a client meeting to discuss a contract for software provision, followed by a business development lunch with a local accountancy firm. Business development is a very important part of a modern lawyer's work and involves promoting and marketing the firm to local, regional, and often national or international businesses. Part of the afternoon might be spent meeting colleagues, considering business development issues such as how the current work of the firm in a particular commercial area can be expanded. Throughout the day telephone calls and e-mails from clients will be dealt with as well as the post that has arrived in the morning. At the end of the day, post will be checked and signed to be sent out.

All time spent, both on client matters and on internal administrative tasks is recorded, whether through a computerised time-management clock that runs whilst working on a particular file (used if working in the office) or through time recording, entered manually on the system, for work undertaken away from the office, such as meeting a client at their premises or going to another firm of solicitors for a meeting. Time recording is an integral part of a modern solicitor's day. The data collected forms part of the billing system and is a vital tool to assess how individual lawyers within a firm are performing. Each solicitor will have a yearly target for billable hours, client development, and fees generated.

This account is based on an interview with an experienced commercial lawyer in private practice.

Solicitors may also work 'in-house', that is as employees of a business or other organisation or also may be employed by local or central government. Many large companies and local authorities have their own legal departments and solicitors, as well as acting for the company in legal matters, may also perform other roles, such as company secretary.

An important issue arises out of the growth in the volume and complexity of the law. This has led to the creation of larger law firms, often with branches in a number of cities or countries, and an increasing specialisation in legal practice and the development of expertise. Sole practitioners and smaller 'high street' firms undertake a wide range of work such as conveyancing, drafting wills, administering estates, and the provision of legal advice on a range of issues, such as boundary disputes, employment matters, claims arising from the purchase of faulty goods or services. The main income streams of smaller firms will usually be based on fees from conveyancing and litigation, particularly criminal work. If this income is reduced by competition from larger firms offering the savings generated by economies of scale, then smaller firms may be unable to survive. The work required to deal with small, low value disputes and claims, which may not be of interest to the larger firms, presently dealt with by sole practitioners and 'high street' firms, may therefore be left to pro bono organisations and individuals to deal with themselves.

Thinking point

The presence of law firms on high streets and in local communities is important with regard to access to justice. If large firms, which tend to be based in city centres, prosper at the expense of sole practitioners and smaller, local, firms then access to legal advice will be reduced.

9.2.1 The work of solicitors

Certain areas of work were once 'reserved' to the solicitors' profession. In other words, some types of legal work could only be undertaken on a commercial basis by qualified solicitors. Reserved areas of work included administering a deceased person's estate (probate), conveyancing, and the conduct of litigation. The solicitors' monopoly on conveyancing work was ended in 1985 by the Administration of Justice Act, which amended the Solicitors Act 1974 and created licensed conveyancers. Following the implementation of the Act, licensed conveyancers became entitled to conduct conveyancing transactions for a fee. Information about licensed conveyancers can be found at: **www.conveyancer.org.uk/**.

The Legal Services Act 2007 allows non-solicitors to carry out some types of legal work, subject to authorisation and regulation. By s.12, areas of legal work, 'reserved legal activity', can only be carried out by 'authorised persons' (see s.18) or otherwise 'exempt persons' (see s.19). 'Reserved legal activity' means:

- the exercise of a right of audience;
- the conduct of litigation (see Sch.2) which means:
  - (a) the issuing of proceedings before any court in England and Wales,
  - (b) the commencement, prosecution and defence of such proceedings, and
  - (c) the performance of any ancillary functions in relation to such proceedings (such as entering appearances to actions).' However, advocacy before a court is not part of the conduct of litigation;
- reserved instrument activity (for example, the preparation of any instrument of transfer or charge for the purposes of the Land Registration Act 2002);
- probate activities;
- notarial activities; and
- the administration of oaths.

(Note: an 'instrument' is a formal legal document in writing and 'notarial activity' is work carried out by a notary public.)

A person may be authorised to carry out a particular 'reserved legal activity' by a relevant approved regulator. As to the meaning of 'approved regulators' see s.20 and Sch.4. 'Approved regulators' include the Law Society, the General Council of the

Bar, the Institute of Legal Executives, the Council for Licensed Conveyancers, and the Chartered Institute of Patent Attorneys.

It will be an offence for a person to carry on a 'reserved legal activity' where a person is not entitled to carry out that activity.

The impact of Part 3 of the Legal Services Act 2007 is to allow individuals other than solicitors and barristers to undertake 'reserved legal activity' provided that they are authorised to do so under the Act.

See further chapter 11, 'Access to justice'.

Some legal services have always been able to be provided by non-lawyers. For example, advisors in law centres and Citizens' Advice Bureaux may give advice on employment, welfare, housing, or relationship issues. The roles played by these other individuals and bodies providing legal services are an important part of the discussion regarding access to justice. When considering the availability of advice to ordinary citizens it is important to consider the services provided not just by legal professionals but also by charitable organisations, pro bono schemes, and non-lawyers (see later).

9.2.2 Representation in court

Solicitors may appear on behalf of a client in certain courts, such as the Coroners' Court, magistrates' courts, and county courts. Solicitors may also represent clients at tribunals. Traditionally, a barrister had to be instructed where a client required representation in the higher courts. However, solicitors may now be awarded higher rights of audience, allowing them to represent clients in some or all of the following higher courts: the Crown Court, the High Court, the Court of Appeal, and the Supreme Court. Solicitors may be accredited for higher rights following the completion of an advocacy assessment based on the Solicitors Regulation Authority Higher Rights of Audience competence standards. There are separate awards for rights of audience for criminal and civil advocacy. Higher rights of audience were introduced by s.31 of the Courts and Legal Services Act 1990, as amended by the Access to Justice Act 1999. Further information on higher rights of audience can be found at: **www.sra.org.uk/ solicitors/accreditation/higher-rights-of-audience.page**.

Thinking point

At the end of 2012 approximately 4,000 solicitors (out of a total number of solicitors with practising certificates in excess of 120,000) had a higher rights qualification. Has this had an impact on competition in relation to the provision of advocacy services?

9.2.3 Sole practitioners and partnerships

The size of a legal firm can vary from one qualified solicitor (a sole practitioner) to firms with a global presence and over 3,000 solicitors. Some solicitors will be partners in their firm. Partners will be either equity partners, who own a share of the business and therefore are entitled to a share of the profits of the business, or salaried partners who do not own a share of the business and, as the name suggests, are paid a salary. The other solicitors in the firm are referred to as assistant solicitors or associate solicitors (often associate is a title given as a reward after a number of years of service). In a legal partnership formed under the Partnership Act 1890, the partners own the firm: each partner's share of the business depending upon the terms of the partnership agreement. Most firms designate one of the partners to act as managing partner and may also have a partnership committee to deal with the management of the firm.

Other partners may also be given specific roles within the firm, such as being in charge of recruiting trainee solicitors and managing them during their training contract. Assistant or associate solicitors can become partners through selection and promotion by the existing partners of the firm. Sometimes promotion to partnership can involve being asked to contribute capital (money) to the firm. This capital contribution will be reflected in the firms' partnership agreement.

Until 2001, solicitors were only able to practise as sole practitioners or in partnerships (under the Partnership Act 1890). Since the Limited Liability Partnerships Act 2000 was introduced in April 2001, solicitors have been able to form limited liability partnerships (LLPs). An LLP is a legal entity separate from its members. Therefore the LLP can own property, enter into contracts, bring legal proceedings, or have legal proceedings brought against it. In the same way as a partnership under the 1890 Act, the members (partners) of the LLP will usually have an agreement dealing with issues such as management of the business, admission of new members, and so on. Large commercial firms, and some smaller ones, have taken advantage of this opportunity.

Thinking point

Partnership under the 1890 Act or an LLP? One of the key attractions for adopting the new form of business structure is that the LLP is a separate legal entity from its members (the partners) and, as such, has liability for the debts of the business. If the LLP gets into financial difficulties, the partners are not personally liable for the debts. This position contrasts strongly with that of a partnership under the Partnership Act 1890, where each partner has unlimited liability for the debts of the partnership. However, this also means that it is the LLP, and not the individual partners, which owns the firm.

In his report reviewing legal services, published in December 2004, Sir David Clementi recommended that solicitors (and barristers) should be permitted to enter into 'legal disciplinary practices' (LDP). The recommendation was enacted under provisions in the Administration of Justice Act 1985 (AJA) and the Legal Services Act 2007 (LSA), and, as a consequence, amendments were made to the Solicitors Code of Conduct (the Code) to permit LDPs. An LDP is defined as 'a form of recognised body providing legal services where the owners and managers are not exclusively:

- solicitors of England and Wales
- registered European lawyers
- registered Foreign Lawyers.'

The change was introduced on 31 March 2009, allowing up to 25 per cent of the partners in firm to be non-lawyers. This has allowed barristers, legal executives and other professionals to become partners in law firms.

The Clementi Report is considered in more detail later.

9.2.4 **Qualification**

Qualification as a solicitor is generally achieved in three stages. The first academic stage is the completion of a qualifying law degree or the graduate diploma in law (GDL), for graduates with non-law degrees, or the Chartered Institute of Legal Executives (CILEX) Professional Qualification in Law. The Law Society and Bar Council prescribe the subjects that must be studied and passed in a qualifying law degree.

> **Thinking point**
>
> At present a qualifying law degree must include the following subjects: constitutional and administrative law, contract law, criminal law, equity and trusts, EU Law, land law, and tort. Why do you think that study of these particular areas of law is viewed as fundamental for all lawyers?

Further detail about the CILEX qualification is included subsequently under the heading, *Legal Executives*. Following successful completion of the academic stage, a student must then enrol on the vocational stage: the legal practice course ('LPC'). This is a one-year course that puts academic legal theory into practice and equips students for their training contract. Following satisfactory completion of the LPC, the practical stage of the training process must be commenced. This is a training contract with a firm of solicitors or local authority. The number of training contracts available is small compared to the number of students successfully completing the LPC and applying for a training contract. Competition is therefore fierce. The training contract is currently regulated by the Solicitors Regulation Authority and lasts two years, during which time the trainee must work in three different areas of practice. For example, a typical training contract at a medium sized firm could include four 'seats': family law, conveyancing, civil litigation, and crime. A minimum level of salary for trainees is also specified by the SRA. At the end of the successful completion of the two-year training period, a trainee is admitted as a fully qualified solicitor.

> ### ! Critical debate
>
> *The traditional training route to become a solicitor takes at least six years. The introduction of fees for undergraduate courses and the fees charged for GDL and LPC courses means that prospective trainee solicitors will have accumulated a great deal of debt before seeking a training contract. There is no guarantee of a training place after completion of the academic and vocational stages of training. Numerous studies and reports have suggested that the system discriminates against prospective lawyers from lower socio-economic groups and ensures that the profession remains the preserve of a narrow section of society. Do you agree?*
>
> *The Legal Services Board 2010 report 'Barriers to the Legal Profession' can be accessed at,* **https://research. legalservicesboard.org.uk/wp-content/media/2010-Diversity-literature-review.pdf**

Once qualified, the Solicitors Regulation Authority requires solicitors to undertake a minimum of sixteen hours per year of continuing education (CPD).

There has been much recent discussion as to whether the qualification route for solicitors is fit for purpose and there have been a number of reviews and proposals for change. The Solicitors Regulation Authority has undertaken a review of the way in which solicitors qualify – the Training Framework Review. The process focused primarily on the training contract period and the format and content of the legal practice course. A number of consultation papers were produced including the Training Framework Review, in July 2001, September 2003, and March 2005.

Despite a number of wide ranging proposals and suggestions for change, no concrete proposals were made and these plans for reform were shelved in 2005. However, the discussion and debate continued as to whether legal education was fit for the demands of the professions in the twenty-first century. On 19 November 2010, the Solicitors Regulation Authority, the Bar Standards Board, and the Institute of Legal Executives Professional Standards body announced a joint review of legal services education and training, the Legal Education and Training Review (LETR). As the introduction to its website states, this 'constitutes a fundamental, evidence-based review of education and training requirements across regulated and non-regulated legal services in England and Wales'.

The review body examined:

- the perceived strengths and weaknesses of the existing systems of legal education and training across the regulated and unregulated sectors in England and Wales;
- the skills, knowledge, and attributes required by a range of legal service providers;
- the potential to move to sector-wide outcomes for legal services education and training;
- the potential extension of regulation of legal services education and training for the currently unregulated sector;

- recommendations as to whether and, if so, how, the system of legal services education and training may be made more responsive to emerging needs;
- suggestions and alternative models to assure (sic) that the system will support the delivery of:
    i.   high quality, competitive, and ethical legal services;
    ii. flexible education and training options, responsive to the need for different career pathways, and capable of promoting diversity.

The LETR reported in June 2013. Many legal education providers, and the professions in general, had expected radical proposals for overhauling the provision of legal education; however the final report was generally regarded as a missed opportunity. It was hoped that the review would recommend that a requirement for regular reaccreditation of skills be introduced, as seen in the medical profession, but this was not included. The report did recommend greater emphasis on ethics and client care skills. It also recommended that lawyers should become more reflective practioners and that continued professional development (CPD) should provide 'intentional, meaningful learning' and not just be a box ticking exercise. The report can be accessed at: **http://ow.ly/moZtW**.

9.2.5 The composition of the solicitors' profession

Statistics are published annually by the Law Society. In 30 June 2013 there were 167,457 solicitors on the Roll, i.e. listed as being paid-up and qualified members of the profession. Inclusion on the Roll does not mean that the person can practise as a solicitor: a practising certificate is required in order to do this.; 127,068 of the enrolled solicitors had a practising certificate (76 per cent of those on the Roll). Of those solicitors holding practising certificates, approximately 47 per cent were women and 12 per cent were from minority ethnic groups.

The statistics show that the majority of law firms are relatively small, 86.2 per cent have four, or fewer, partners. Firms with twenty-six partners or more represent 2 per cent of law firms. However, this 2 per cent employ over 40 per cent of solicitors in private practice.

Statistics can be found at: **www.lawsociety.org.uk/aboutlawsociety/whatwedo/ researchandtrends.law**.

> ### 🔒 Key point
>
> In seeking to critically appraise any set of circumstances, it is important to have a sound empirical base for your argument. Part of this knowledge might be statistical information. It is worthwhile to look at the statistics to see if trends and patterns can be discerned.

9.2.6 The Law Society and the Solicitors Regulation Authority

The Law Society has traditionally both represented the interests of solicitors and regulated their activities in England and Wales. For example, it has dealt with allegations of
misconduct and complaints from the public and also represented solicitors' interests,
for example in any consultations with central government. Its powers and duties are
set out in the Solicitors Act 1974.

The dual roles, of enforcer and representative organisation, performed by the Law
Society were criticised on the basis that there was a potential conflict of interest. Sir
David Clementi, in the review of the regulatory framework for legal services (see later),
recommended that the roles should be split.

In the light of the recommendations, the Law Society established two regulatory
bodies, one dealing with consumer complaints, the Legal Complaints Service, and
one governing rule-making and legal education, the Solicitors Regulation Authority.

You can find out more about the Solicitors Regulation Authority at: **www.sra.
org.uk/**.

The representative function is still undertaken by the Law Society. Information
about the Law Society is found at: **www.lawsociety.org.uk/home.law**.

9.2.7 Complaints about solicitors

If a complaint is made about the standard of work carried out by a law firm or an individual within the firm, the complaint must first be directed to the firm.

All law firms are required to have a designated complaints handler who will try
to resolve any client complaints in the first instance. If the client is not satisfied
with the outcome of the internal investigation into the complaint they can contact
the Legal Ombudsman (LO). The LO was set up by the Office for Legal Complaints,
following the 2007 Legal Services Act. The service is free, independent, and impartial and the LO will investigate the complaint to try to assist the parties to resolve
the matter. If the matter cannot be resolved informally then a report will be produced which can then be accepted by the parties to the dispute or referred to an
Ombudsman for a final, binding decision. Details of the LO can be found at **www.
legalombudsman.org.uk/**.

9.2.8 Solicitors Regulation Authority Code of Conduct

All solicitors must act in accordance with the Code of Conduct that governs their
behaviour and sets out the manner in which their work must be conducted.

The Solicitors Regulation Authority publishes the conduct guide for solicitors (the
SRA Code of Conduct). The rules in this guide set out the duties and responsibilities of
solicitors towards their clients and deal with issues such as client confidentiality, conflicts of interest, information to be provided to the client, and complaints procedures.

The latest version of the Code is the SRA Code of Conduct 2011 and the most recent changes were published in April 2013. The new Code is part of a handbook which sets out the standards and requirements which are expected of any individual or body regulated by the SRA. The change in approach from the previous regime, which listed a set of rules, to the new outcomes-focused regulation (OFR) is designed to benefit clients as well as being in the general public interest. The SRA intend that the new Code of Conduct will 'support not only consumers of legal services, but will also support the independence of the legal profession and its unique role in safeguarding the legal rights of those it serves'. The Code comprises of a set of Principles requiring all solicitors to:

1. uphold the rule of law and the proper administration of justice;
2. act with integrity;
3. not allow...independence to be compromised;
4. act in the best interests of each client;
5. provide a proper standard of service to...clients;
6. behave in a way that maintains the trust the public places in...[solicitors] and in the provision of legal services;
7. comply with...legal and regulatory obligations and deal with...regulators and ombudsmen in an open, timely and co-operative manner;
8. run...business or carry out...role in the business effectively and in accordance with proper governance and sound financial and risk management principles;
9. run...business or carry out...role in the business in a way that encourages equality of opportunity and respect for diversity; and
10. protect client money and assets.

In order to achieve these Principles the Code goes on to list a number of Outcomes that firms and individuals are expected to achieve in order to comply with the Principles, and Indicative Behaviours that demonstrate the sort of conduct expected to establish compliance with the Principles. The handbook and Code of Conduct can be found at: **www.sra.org.uk/solicitors/handbook/welcome.page**. Failure to comply with the conduct rules may amount to evidence of inadequate professional services in the context of a complaint against a solicitor.

9.2.9 **Liability of solicitors**

When a solicitor is employed by a client, the relationship between them is contractual and each party may be sued should they fail to meet the obligations set out in the contract. Solicitors may also be sued for negligence if loss has been caused to someone to whom they owed a duty of care, such as a client or beneficiaries under a will (see later). The work undertaken must be carried out with the appropriate standard of care and skill.

> ### 📃 Example
>
> In *White v Jones* [1995] 2 AC 207, a law firm was sued in negligence by the beneficiaries of a will drawn up by a solicitor employed by the firm. The solicitor had failed to make amendments to the will, as instructed by the maker of it, which would have given a legacy to the beneficiaries. A delay on the part of the solicitor meant that the changes had not been made, and attested to, at the time of the maker's death. Despite the lack of a contractual relationship between the solicitor and the beneficiaries, the beneficiaries were able to bring a claim in negligence for the value of the legacies that they would have received, had the instructions been correctly carried out. In respect to liability in relation to litigation see at 9.3.12.

9.3 **Barristers**

Barristers are popularly portrayed wearing gowns and wigs, arguing their clients' case in a criminal court, perhaps the most famous depiction being Rumpole of the Bailey in the books by John Mortimer. However, barristers are not just criminal advocates.

They provide specialist legal advice and appear as advocates in both criminal and civil courts on behalf of their clients. Barristers' training focuses on, and reflects, the skills they are required to have to provide this support for clients. Most barristers operate as self-employed individuals, and they work in sets of chambers – essentially a group of barristers sharing premises and administrative facilities. The average set of chambers comprises of about thirty barristers, some of whom may be referred to as 'door tenants'. Door tenants are barristers who do not work full time in chambers, and who pay a reduced rent (sometimes a percentage on any cases coming to them through chambers).

Each set of chambers has a barrister's clerk who is responsible for administering the work that comes to the chambers by negotiating the brief fees and ensuring that the work is given to either the specific barrister instructed or, if no name is specified, to an appropriate advocate. The clerk acts as liaison between the barristers and the instructing solicitors. Part of their job is to organise the diaries of the barristers to ensure that the chambers work is dealt with efficiently. The chief clerk is usually supported by a number of junior clerks and fees clerks (responsible for billing) and, increasingly, by a manager who deals with marketing and human resources issues.

A barrister who is not a member of a chambers may be employed by a company, carrying out legal work for the company or, if employed by a law firm, to represent the solicitors' clients. Employed barristers may conduct litigation. Barristers may also be employed by central or local government or by the Crown Prosecution Service.

9.3.1 **'Cab rank' rule**

Barristers are subject to what is called the 'cab rank' rule, which means that a barrister must accept any case referred by a solicitor, provided that it is in their area of practice, they are available, and a reasonable fee is payable. The rationale for the 'cab rank' rule is ethical. It is designed to ensure that all defendants, however unpopular, can be represented in court and it also acts to protect barristers from the anger of the community if they are called to represent someone accused of a terrible crime. In *Arthur JS Hall & Co v Simon* [2002] 1 AC 615, Lord Steyn doubted the effectiveness of the rule. His Lordship said,

> [i]t is a valuable professional rule. But its impact on the administration of justice in England is not great. In real life a barrister has a clerk whose enthusiasm for the unwanted brief may not be great, and he is free to raise the fee within limits. It is not likely that the rule often obliges barristers to undertake work which they would not otherwise accept.

However the Bar Standards Board has suggested that any step to remove the cab rank rule would result in a major threat to justice. The BSB report can be accessed at: **www.barstandardsboard.org.uk/media/1460590/bsb_-_cab_rank_rule_paper_28_2_13_v6_final_.pdf**.

9.3.2 **Barristers' direct access to clients**

Traditionally, barristers could not accept instructions directly from members of the public and had to be instructed by a solicitor, on the client's behalf. This restriction was seen as anti-competitive and unnecessarily expensive because the cost of two lawyers was incurred when one would often be sufficient to do the work required.

A scheme was introduced by the Bar Council to allow some clients to instruct barristers directly. The scheme, known as Licensed Access, allows certain organisations, such as firms of accountants, or specific individuals, to apply to the Bar Council to be licensed to instruct barristers directly in an area of law in which those organisations or individuals are thought to have suitable expertise.

In 2004, the Bar Council's Public Access Rules came into force allowing barristers to accept instructions directly from members of the public in mainly civil work. Subject to certain exceptions barristers may not accept instructions from members of the public in the following areas of law: criminal, family, and immigration. The 'cab rank' rule does not apply when a barrister is 'instructed' by a member of the public.

See the Code of Conduct, Annex F2.

9.3.3 **Restrictions on partnerships**

Bar Council regulations used to prevent barristers from forming partnerships with one another. These rules were criticised by the Office of Fair Trading in a report published in March 2001, *Competition in Professions*.

Following the Legal Services Act 2007, and the introduction of Legal Disciplinary Practices, these rules have now changed. See 9.4.3 for further details.

9.3.4 **Qualification**

The qualification process for a barrister is similar to that of a solicitor. The academic stage is common to both barristers and solicitors. A qualifying law degree, or a non-law degree and the GDL, must first be successfully completed. Following the completion of the academic stage, the vocational stage must be passed. This is the Bar Professional Training Course (BPTC) which is a one-year course that aims to equip students with the skills and substantive knowledge they will need to practise as a barrister. The areas of study are:

Skills

- casework,
- legal research,
- general written skills,
- interpersonal skills,
- advocacy,
- conferencing,
- resolution of disputes out of court, and
- opinion writing.

Knowledge

- criminal and civil litigation,
- evidence,
- remedies,
- professional ethics, and
- sentencing.

Following completion of the BPTC, further work-based training with a set of chambers is undertaken. This is known as pupillage. A trainee barrister is called a pupil. During the one-year pupillage, the first six months are spent by the pupil observing and assisting his or her supervisor, undertaking legal research, becoming familiar with case papers, and attending court and case conferences. The pupil barrister may also shadow other members of chambers in order to see a wide variety of work. The pupillage supervisor will be an experienced member of chambers who has responsibility for supervising pupils and allocating work to them. A supervisor must be a barrister who has been called to the Bar (been qualified as a barrister) for at least seven years and is registered as a pupil supervisor with the Bar Council.

During the second six months of pupillage, the pupil will work as a barrister conducting his or her own cases, which may include making appearances in court on behalf of a client. Although still technically under the supervision of the supervisor, pupil barristers at this stage have a large degree of autonomy in the work that they do, although they are still covered by the professional indemnity insurance of their supervisor. When not practising, a pupil barrister will continue to gain experience through shadowing their supervisor. Some pupillages are split, with the six-month periods being spent in different sets of chambers. Although pupillages used to be unpaid, pupil barristers must now be paid a minimum salary of £12,000 by their set of chambers.

It is very difficult to be successful in finding a pupillage because there are many more students completing the BPTC than there are pupillages available. Competition is therefore intense. Following completion of pupillage, most newly qualified barristers will try to secure a tenancy either with the chambers where the pupillage was undertaken or at another set. Tenancy is also difficult to secure and is not guaranteed, particularly in London. The Law Careers Advice Network estimates that only half of the eligible number of pupils obtains a tenancy with a set of chambers in a given year. Following completion of pupillage, a barrister will be responsible for his or her own case load, although some may also continue to assist more senior members of chambers. All barristers in chambers are self-employed and therefore have no guarantee of regular work or a regular income. Average earnings vary according to location, area of law, and experience.

In the same way that solicitors have to carry out CPD, barristers are required to undertake continuing education. By the end of their first three years in practice they are required to have completed a minimum of forty-five hours continuing education in areas such as case preparation and advocacy. After this the requirement is for twelve hours of continuing education per year.

🗐 Example

The daily work of a criminal barrister

Perhaps the most exciting element of a criminal barrister's life is its unpredictability. The criminal law is in a state of perpetual flux, and every day is different. There is no such thing as a typical day. The job of a prosecuting barrister is very different from that of defence counsel, and one barrister may be required to act for defendants and for the prosecution, in different cases, on the same day.

Some trials, particularly the most serious ones, are scheduled in the barrister's diary months ahead. Such cases may last several weeks and sometimes several months. On other occasions a barrister will be instructed to prosecute or defend an accused person the night before the trial is to be heard. This might happen if the barrister who had been instructed in the case is delayed in another court in an ongoing case.

On any day a criminal barrister may deal with between one and half a dozen cases. Each set of instructions is known as a brief. Having prepared the papers overnight, or early in the morning, the barrister will have plenty to do at court before any trials or hearings commence. There may be sentencing hearings; concluding cases where the defendant pleaded guilty or was convicted some weeks before; and meetings with clients and instructing solicitors. If acting for the defence, a barrister will need to explain the likely sentence to the client and the client's family, and take instructions on potential points of mitigation.

Or there may be plea and case management hearings where a defendant will enter a plea of guilty or not guilty. If not guilty, a trial date will be set and the judge will make various orders to 'manage' the case and ensure it is ready for trial at the appropriate time.

On the day of a trial, prosecution counsel will need to check that witnesses are present, ensure all relevant evidence has been served, and then, in court, present the Crown's evidence. Defence counsel may, depending on the circumstances and the weight of the evidence, see if the client wishes to plead guilty to a lesser offence, and if so, try to negotiate this with the Crown prosecutor. If a trial is to take place, the client's instructions will need to be confirmed.

The official court day usually runs from 10 a.m. until 4.30 p.m. After court a barrister may have conferences to advise clients before collecting the next day's work from the clerks and the whole process begins again.

This information is based on an interview with an experienced criminal barrister.

Barristers undertaking civil work tend to make fewer court appearances than barristers working in criminal law; instead they will carry out more paper-based work to give specialist legal advice in writing (known as an opinion) or at a conference with instructing solicitors (with or without the client).

9.3.5 **The Inns of Court**

There are four Inns of Court: Gray's Inn, Lincoln's Inn, Middle Temple, and Inner Temple. The Inns date back to the fourteenth and fifteenth centuries and there used to be more than four of them. They were first established to provide accommodation and training for barristers and they therefore have a long and colourful history. But their chief function as the professional associations for barristers is to *call men and women to the Bar.*

> *called to the Bar:* To become a barrister a person must be 'called to the Bar' by one of the four Inns of Court. The prospective barrister attends a 'Call Night' at the Inn and is formally 'called to the Bar' in a ceremony watched by friends and family. The call to the Bar takes place after the successful completion of the BPTC.

Each Inn is governed by the Masters of the Bench (or Benchers). Benchers are elected from the senior members of the Inn (Queen's Counsel (QCs) or senior members of the judiciary). Students wishing to qualify as barristers must join an Inn before they begin the BPTC and they are required to attend a minimum number of twelve 'qualifying sessions' at their Inn before they can become barristers. Most of these will be completed by a student attending a dinner at the Inn. Each dinner counts as one qualifying session. Dinners are often accompanied by educational events, such as speeches or debates. Dining is also seen as an opportunity for students to meet practising barristers and senior members of the profession. Qualifying sessions can also be accumulated by attendance at other events, such as education days and advocacy training courses.

You can find out more about the Inns of Court at the websites listed:

- **www.graysinn.org.uk/**
- **www.innertemple.org.uk/**
- **www.lincolnsinn.org.uk/**
- **www.middletemple.org.uk/**

9.3.6 **Deferral of call**

A student can call him or herself a barrister once called to the Bar: that is having completed the BPTC and attended the requisite number of qualifying sessions at their Inn. This is the case even though the barrister cannot practise because he or she has not completed pupillage. The Bar Council considered that this system should change so that only those who had successfully completed pupillage would be entitled to call themselves barristers. This proposal is known as deferral of call and caused substantial debate amongst members of the Bar and providers of Bar Professional Training Courses. However, despite wide consultation in 2007, the proposals for reform were not implemented and the situation remains that a person who has passed the BPTC and been called to the Bar can call him or herself a barrister.

9.3.7 **Queen's Counsel (QCs)**

QCs are the most eminent and skilled members of the Bar. QC stands for Queen's Counsel. Appointments to Queen's Counsel are made by Her Majesty the Queen by Letters Patent following recommendation by the Secretary of State (if there is a king on the throne the title is KC or King's Counsel). A QC is often referred to, in colloquial terms, as a 'silk' because they wear silk gowns rather than the basic stuff gown worn by a junior barrister. All barristers, of whatever age or call, are known as juniors if they are not QCs. The purpose of the appointment to the rank of QC is to recognise outstanding ability as an advocate, although the overall legal abilities of an applicant and his or her professional qualities are also important.

The system of appointing Queen's Counsel has been the subject of consultation. In March 2001, the Office of Fair Trading published a report *Competition in Professions*, which questioned the relevance of the rank of QC as far as consumers were concerned, in part owing to the lack of direct access by members of the public to barristers at that time, the criteria used to award the rank of QC, and whether the award served to distort competition by the effective reservation of certain types of work to QCs and the increase in fees once QCs became involved in cases.

In July 2003, the Lord Chancellor, Lord Falconer, published a consultation paper, *Constitutional reform: the future of Queen's Counsel*. The paper sought views on the role of QCs, the advantages and disadvantages of the system, and possible changes to the way in which the rank is awarded. Responses to this consultation were published in January 2004.

Prior to 2005 the appointment system required application to the Lord Chancellor by barristers and, since 1994, solicitors with higher rights of audience. The Lord Chancellor would then recommend suitable applicants be invited to take silk after consultation with fellow members of the Bar, the judiciary, and solicitors. Published criteria were used against which the applicant's abilities were assessed and applicants were compared with existing QCs and other applicants in their area of practice. Those awarded the rank are regarded as leaders of their profession and all those who meet the necessary thresholds are appointed.

Since 2005, the appointment of QCs has no longer been a governmental recommendation but is by the independent Queen's Counsel Selection Panel, established by the Bar Council and the Law Society with the support of the Department for Constitutional Affairs, to administer the application process. A nine-person independent selection panel makes recommendations to the Secretary of State after consideration of individual applications. The Secretary of State cannot remove or add names to those selected by the panel and passes the recommendations to the Queen for approval. Applicants are assessed in relation to seven competences: integrity; understanding and using the law; oral and written advocacy; working with others, and diversity.

The independent nine-member panel includes a lay chair plus two solicitors, two barristers, a judge, and three further lay members.

You can find out more about the appointment of QCs at: **www.qcapplications.org/**.

9.3.8 **The composition of the barristers' profession**

Statistics are generally published annually by the Bar Council. As at December 2010 (the most recent date that published statistics seem to be available), there were 15,387 practising barristers (self-employed and employed), of which 65 per cent were male and 35 per cent were female.

The total number of chambers was 734, of which 347 were located in London and 387 outside of London. There were 419 sole practitioners and 2,967 employed barristers.

Statistics can be found at: **www.barcouncil.org.uk/about-the-bar/facts-and-figures/ statistics/**.

9.3.9 **The Bar Council**

The General Council of the Bar (Bar Council) is represents barristers and 'promote[s] [the role of barristers] at the heart of the justice system in England and Wales'. It was founded in 1894 and represents the interests of barristers on a range of matters. In the same way that the Law Society has been affected by the report of Sir David Clementi on the regulatory review of legal services, the Bar Council has also had to review its regulatory and representative roles. The Bar Standards Board was set up to oversee the regulatory side of the Bar and has a separate membership from that of the Bar Council. The Board deals with issues such as changes to the barrister's Code of Conduct as well as education and training and complaints against barristers. It has set up a number of regulatory committees to deal with these matters.

The Bar Council meets approximately seven times a year. Its members are barristers who represent chambers or court circuits in different parts of the country, or who are elected to the Council. Over 100 barristers are members of the Council. The Bar Council objectives include protecting the public interest and promoting and maintaining adherence to professional principles.

Details about the Bar Council can be found at: **www.barcouncil.org.uk/**.

9.3.10 **Complaints about barristers**

Prior to 2010 the Bar Standards Board investigated all complaints about barristers. From 6 October 2010, all complaints about barristers must be made to the Legal Ombudsman. As with complaints about solicitors, the Legal Ombudsman will deal with complaints about the service received from barristers. Any complaints about conduct, as opposed to professional service, will be referred by the Legal Ombudsman to the Bar Standards Board because complaints about conduct may amount to professional misconduct. This could include misleading the court or failing to act in a client's best interests, or acting contrary to instructions. Professional misconduct is a serious issue to be dealt with by the BSB and could result in the barrister concerned being disbarred (prevented from practising as a barrister).

9.3.11 **Barristers' professional Code of Conduct**

The Bar Council publishes a Code of Conduct of the Bar of England and Wales. The latest edition is the eighth, which came into effect in October 2004. It consists of a code of conduct covering issues such as a barrister's duty to the court, rules regarding the acceptance of instructions and confidentiality, and a set of written standards for the conduct of professional work. The latter are intended as a guide to the way in which a barrister should carry out his or her work. The 2004 Code is subject to amendment yearly, although it is still referred to as the 2004 Code. For example, it was amended following the Legal Services Act in 2007 to reflect changes in relation to Legal Disciplinary Practices.

9.3.12 **Liability of barristers**

The general common law position was that barristers could not be sued in negligence in relation to anything done by them in preparing a case for court, or for any of their actions in conducting the case in court. This was underlined in *Rondel v Worsley* [1969] 1 AC 191. However, this protection from being sued for negligence was removed in July 2000 following *Arthur JS Hall & Co v Simons* [2002] 1 AC 615. This case involved appeals to the House of Lords by three clients suing their solicitors in negligence. In each case, the solicitors claimed immunity from liability under the common law rule which prevented barristers being sued for negligence, and which had been extended to solicitors in *Rondel v Worsley*, albeit that the rule only related to acts concerned with the conduct of litigation. A majority of the House of Lords panel hearing the case concluded that the arguments relied upon in *Rondel v Worsley* no longer carried sufficient weight to sustain the claimed immunity for either barristers or solicitors, in relation to civil or criminal proceedings.

Example

It is interesting to note the reasons for upholding the immunity for advocates in *Rondel v Worsley* and then to compare this with the reasoning in *Arthur JS Hall & Co v Simons*. In the former case, the House of Lords supported the exemption on the following grounds: a barrister owed a duty not only to the client but to the court: a fear of being sued might impact upon the latter duty. The cab rank rule meant that a barrister could not refuse to represent a client and this principle might be under threat if a client appeared to be likely to sue his lawyer. Immunity existed in relation to judges, lawyers, and witnesses in relation to defamation, so immunity in relation to negligence is necessary to enable advocates to conduct litigation properly. Finally, it is against public policy to re-litigate a decided case and a claim for negligence would open up to review the decision in the original case.

In *Arthur JS Hall & Co v Simons* the House of Lords reviewed each reason supporting the advocates' protection from being sued in negligence. It was felt that there was no empirical basis for saying that immunity was needed so that duties owed to the court would be performed. Indeed, performing such duties could not be described as negligent. The cab rank principle, while recognised as valuable, could be circumvented in practice, and in any event had to be balanced against the potential injustice of a litigant suffering financial loss because of an advocate's negligence and being left without a remedy. The immunities in relation to defamation were founded on public policy grounds, seeking to encourage freedom of speech in court to allow the gathering of full information about the issues in the case, the reason for this immunity did not support the position in relation to negligence.

Tellingly, Lord Steyn commented:

…public confidence in the legal system is not enhanced by the existence of the immunity. The appearance is created that the law singles out its own for protection no matter how flagrant the breach of the barrister. The world has changed since 1967. The practice of law has become more commercialised: barristers may now advertise. They may now enter into contracts for legal services with their professional clients. They are now obliged to carry insurance. On the other hand, today we live in a consumerist society in which people have a much greater awareness of their rights. If they have suffered a

For the Supreme Court and departure from own previous decisions, chapter 5.

wrong as a result of the provision of negligent professional services, they expect to have the right to claim redress. It tends to erode confidence in the legal system if advocates, alone among professional men, are immune from liability for negligence.

In consequence, the immunity for barristers and solicitor advocates was removed and the House of Lords departed from *Rondel v Worsley*. Although that case was not wrongly decided, the House of Lords held that that due to developments since 1967 the decision no longer reflected public policy.

9.4 **Regulation of the professions and reform: The Clementi Review**

The basis for all the changes that have come about in the legal professions in the last ten years began following a report published in July 2003, *Competition and Regulation in the Legal Services Market* by the Department for Constitutional Affairs, the regulatory framework in place for barristers and solicitors was criticised as outdated and lacking in accountability. Sir David Clementi was asked to review the regulatory system for barristers and solicitors on behalf of the Department for Constitutional Affairs. The terms of reference for the review were to consider:

> what regulatory framework would best promote competition, innovation and the public and consumer interest in an efficient, effective and independent legal sector and to recommend a framework which will be independent in representing the public and consumer interest, comprehensive, accountable, consistent, flexible, transparent and no more restrictive or burdensome than is clearly justified.

Clementi published a consultation paper in March 2004, *Consultation Paper on the Review of the Regulatory Framework for Legal Services in England and Wales*, to which there were 265 written responses.

In the consultation paper, it was argued that the regulatory function and representative functions performed by the Law Society and the Bar Council were in conflict: what is in the best interests of the public might not be in the best interests of lawyers, for example, negotiating fee rates on behalf of their members. Five core functions of regulation were identified in the consultation paper:

(i)   **Entry standards and training:** setting minimum standards of entry qualifications usually linked to educational achievement for candidates wishing to become 'qualified'. It also encompasses matters such as continuing professional development.

(ii) **Rule-making:** formulation of rules by which members are expected to work and to adhere.

(iii) **Monitoring and enforcement:** checking the way in which members carry out their work, in the light of the prescribed rules, and enforcing compliance if rules are broken.

(iv) **Complaints:** systems for consumers to bring complaints about providers who have served them poorly, focused on redress to the consumer.

(v) **Discipline:** powers to discipline members where that person is, for example, professionally negligent, or in breach of the professional rules, focusing on action against that individual.

In December 2004, a final report was published, *Report of the Review of the Regulatory Framework for Legal Services in England and Wales.*

The report identified three key issues arising from the review. These were:

- concern about the complexity and inconsistency of the regulatory framework and its insufficient regard for consumers' interests;
- concern about the complaints system, both in terms of its efficiency and the principle of lawyers handling complaints against other lawyers; and
- concern about the restrictive nature of business structures within the legal profession.

The main recommendations in the report were:

- the creation of a new Legal Services Board as part of the establishment of a new regulatory framework;
- the creation of a new complaints system via the Office for Legal Complaints; and
- that alternative business structures for members of the legal professions should be established; it was also recommended that legal disciplinary practices should be permitted.

The recommendations have been brought into force and are discussed in what follows.

9.4.1 **The Legal Services Board**

The Board regulates the Law Society and Bar Council (and other professional organisations exercising regulatory functions in relation to legal professionals, such as the Institute of Legal Executives), and has the power to delegate regulatory functions to such bodies where appropriate. As already discussed these organisations have been required to alter their governance arrangements so that their regulatory and representative functions are separate. The Board also has statutory objectives including the promotion of the interests of the public and consumers.

9.4.2 **The Office for Legal Complaints**

The Office for Legal Complaints is an independent body, overseen by the Legal Services Board, dealing with consumer complaints against both barristers and solicitors through the Legal Ombudsman. The Legal Ombudsman website summarises the regime as follow: 'The new Legal Ombudsman replaces organisations like the Legal Complaints Service (LCS) and Bar Standards Board (BSB), who used to deal with legal service complaints. If an organisation such as one of these investigated a complaint and the client wasn't happy with the outcome or the service they received from these bodies, they could ask for their complaint to be independently reviewed by the Legal Services Ombudsman (LSO).'

The Legal Ombudsman is concerned primarily with the service offered by a lawyer. Clearly, there will be cases where poor service is linked with misconduct. In these types of cases, the Legal Ombudsman will still look at the service element of the complaint, but will refer the conduct part to the relevant regulatory body, such as the Solicitors Regulation Authority. Discipline remains the province of the Solicitors Regulation Authority and the Bar Standards Board.

Thinking point

The legal profession has consistently asserted that its independence should be protected. This is particularly important where a citizen wishes to challenge the decisions or actions of government. Any attack on the self-regulation of the professions must be seen in this light. The detail of how the Legal Services Board and the Legal Ombudsman are constituted and the nature of their functions must be evaluated to see if the independence of the legal profession is compromised. What balance has been struck by the Legal Services Act 2007?

9.4.3 Alternative business structures

One of Clementi's main recommendations was to suggest that legal disciplinary practices (LDPs) should be introduced to allow non-lawyers to own and manage law practices and different types of lawyers, such as solicitors and barristers, to work together in law firms for the purpose of providing legal services. An LDP is comprised of different types of lawyer (for example, barristers and solicitors) with a minority of non-lawyers in management posts.

Whilst being in favour of LDPs the Clementi Report identified and addressed a number of concerns. Of particular concern was the situation where the owners and managers of the firm were different. It was important that regulation ensured that inappropriate owners were not allowed to be part of firms and conflicts of interest and 'outside owners [bringing] unreasonable commercial pressures to bear on lawyers which might conflict with their professional duties' were avoided.

LDPs have to be regulated using a 'fit to own' test in respect of non-lawyers owning firms and an LDP would not be able to take instructions on a case where the owner had an interest in the matter. Furthermore, protection has had to be put in place, such as qualified lawyers holding key positions and managers adhering to a code of behaviour drawn up by the regulatory body. Qualified lawyers have to be a majority in the management group of the business.

In his report, Sir David Clementi explored the possibility of permitting multi-disciplinary practices (MDPs) to be established to bring together lawyers and other professionals to provide a variety of services, both legal and non-legal, for example, a partnership involving solicitors and accountants. MDPs became a reality in 2012, although many believe that LDPs are a more attractive business model.

> **Thinking point**
>
> What do you think are the advantages and disadvantages of allowing multidisciplinary partnerships (a form of alternative business structure)? One difficulty is that lawyers are subject to a code of conduct that would not apply to non-lawyers. For example, how can client confidentiality be protected in such an organisation?

The recommendations in the Clementi report were enacted in the Legal Services Act which received the royal assent on 30 October 2007. Provisions relating to the establishment of the Legal Services Board and the Office for Legal Complaints came into force on 7 March 2008.

Alternative business structures were allowed to exist after 6 October 2011. However, in the interim, the Act did allow limited forms of alternative business structures to be authorised. There are now approximately 300 LDPs, including a very small number with barristers as partners. The Bar Standards Board permits barristers to join LDPs.

Useful information on the Legal Services Act 2007 and its passage through Parliament may be found at: **www.publications.parliament.uk/pa/pabills/200607/legal_services.htm**.

The terms ABS, MDP, and LDP can be very confusing. In the Clementi report LDPs are classified as ABS; however the Solicitors Regulation Authority expressly states that their definition of an ABS *excludes* LDPs. The basic definitions are as follows: (more detail can be found on the SRA website: **www.sra.org.uk/home/home.page**):

- Alternative Business Structure (ABS): a firm with more than 25 per cent non-lawyer managers offering legal services and non-legal services;

- Legal Disciplinary Practices (LDP): a firm whose ownership is comprised of different types of lawyer and a minority of non-lawyers (up to 25 per cent) which carries out legal work. There cannot be any ownership or part ownership of the law firm by non-lawyers who are not managers of the firm;

- Multi Disciplinary Partnership (MDP): a firm, that is also an ABS, that includes ownership or part ownership of the law firm by non-lawyers who are not managers of the firm and which offers a combination of legal and non-legal services.

> ### 🔒 Key point
>
> When considering the legal profession much useful information and comment may be found in the weekly journals such as *New Law Journal*, the *Solicitors' Journal* and *Counsel*.

9.5 Should the professions of barrister and solicitor be amalgamated?

In many countries the legal profession is not divided as it is in England and Wales. The question as to whether the two professions should be fused is always topical. The traditional and distinct roles of solicitors and barristers are becoming blurred. For example the granting of higher rights of audience to solicitors and the direct access to barristers by some clients leads many to conclude that the two professions should in fact merge. Nevertheless, both the Bar Council and the Law Society have always argued against the idea of a single legal profession. In a March 2001 report, the Office of Fair Trading suggested that the dual structure of the legal profession added unnecessarily to costs but the Bar Council rejected this suggestion in its response to the report, arguing that there were benefits in a split profession.

Benefits of a split profession:

- Barristers do not conduct litigation (as already seen, this is the province of solicitors) so they are able to attain a much higher level of experience and skill in advocacy than would otherwise be possible.

- The detachment of barristers from clients means that a more objective approach may be adopted and this may lead, ultimately, to the time taken to conclude a case being shortened.

- Independent barristers can perform the advocacy and advisory work in which they specialise more efficiently and cheaply than solicitors because barristers' overheads are lower.

- Members of the public do not know what barristers do and have no idea of the specialisms and services offered therefore solicitors are needed to act as intermediaries to guide clients to the most suitable barrister. Solicitors will also be able to assess the quality of service provided by barristers and thus promote competition.

- The dual profession also promotes competition amongst solicitors because small firms of solicitors have access to the specialist legal services provided by barristers and are therefore able to compete with larger firms.

- The public interest lies not only in the promotion of competition but also in 'access to justice and the overriding moral duty of society to pursue the ideal of equality before the law'.

It may be that the reforms made to the professions, together with the organisational changes to the way lawyers work, will inevitably lead to the practical distinction between barristers and solicitors being no longer relevant.

9.6 Legal executives

Legal executives carry out a great deal of the day-to-day work in law firms. Members of the Chartered Institute of Legal Executives qualify as lawyers through a different route to the ones already discussed (see Solicitors and Barristers). To qualify, the Chartered Institute of Legal Executives (CILEX) Professional Qualification in Law must be attained. CILEX represents legal executives, admits legal executives to the profession, and administers the examination process. Legal executives specialise in a specific area of legal practice, such as conveyancing or criminal law and work alongside solicitors. The initial qualification process takes around four years and the academic study is usually undertaken as distance learning or day release whilst the trainee legal executive is working as a fee earner in a law firm. Legal executives are required to have at least five years' experience working in a legal environment under the supervision of a solicitor before they can become a Chartered Legal Executive (FCILEx).

Legal executives may decide to study further to qualify as solicitors by completing the Legal Practice Course. They do not usually have to complete a training contract.

You can find out more about legal executives at: **www.cilex.org.uk/**.

9.7 Licensed conveyancers

A licensed conveyancer is essentially a specialist in property law. Until the 1980s, conveyancing could only be undertaken on a professional basis by solicitors. Since then other people can qualify as licensed conveyancers and undertake conveyancing work. The Council for Licensed Conveyancers is the regulatory body for licensed conveyancers.

You can find out more about licensed conveyancers at: **www.conveyancer.org.uk/**.

9.8 Paralegals

In the increasingly competitive legal jobs market the role of paralegal has taken on an increasing importance. Paralegal used to refer to an unqualified legal clerk, or secretary, who undertook basic legal tasks to assist the qualified members of staff in a law firm. However, many paralegals now have legal qualifications, such as an LPC, and start their legal careers carrying out legal tasks that can range from assisting qualified lawyers, to handling large case loads. In this way it is hoped that they will eventually secure a training contract. The work is generally very poorly paid. A number of organisations offer paralegal training qualifications for school leavers and there are organisations that paralegals can join such as the Institute of Paralegals and the National Association of Licensed Paralegals.

Summary

- The legal profession in England and Wales comprises barristers, solicitors, and other legal professionals such as legal executives and licensed conveyancers.
- Solicitors can operate as sole practitioners, in partnership with other solicitors, either formed under the Partnership Act 1890 or through a Limited Liability Partnership, or in Legal Disciplinary Practices and Alternative Business Structures.
- Solicitors undertake a wide range of legal work, although those working in large firms tend to specialise in a particular area of law. Solicitors may now represent clients in every court, provided they have completed the necessary training or have sufficient experience to be granted higher rights of audience.
- The Law Society is the body that represents solicitors in England and Wales. The regulatory role that it used to have has been split off since the Clementi Report and the Solicitors Regulation Authority now regulates the profession.
- Barristers give clients specialist legal advice and appear in court on their behalf as advocates. They may be self-employed and operate from a set of chambers, be employed barristers in the public or private sector, or be part of a Legal Disciplinary Practice.
- All barristers must be a member of one of the Inns of Court.
- The General Council of the Bar (Bar Council) is the representative body for barristers. It, like the Law Society, has separated its regulatory and representative functions following the Clementi Report and the Bar Standards Board regulates the profession.
- The Legal Services Act 2007 has changed the way in which solicitors and barristers are regulated and the way in which they practise. The Act establishes the Legal Services Board to oversee both the Law Society and the Bar Council and to establish a new complaints system via the Office for Legal Complaints. The Act also allows solicitors and barristers to operate in alternative business structures which may be owned and managed by non-lawyers.

Questions

1 What do solicitors and barristers do?

2 How would you qualify as a solicitor?

3 Can barristers and solicitors be sued for negligence?

4 What reforms have been introduced to the way in which barristers and solicitors are regulated?

5 What sorts of business structures do barristers and solicitors currently operate under. Which model do you consider to be the most appropriate?

6 Do you consider that the Clementi reforms have gone far enough? What other reforms to the legal professions are necessary or desirable?

Sample question and outline answer

Question

A journalist in the *Economist* noted:

> The original reasons for dividing lawyers into two categories - barristers and solicitors - have long since disappeared, but the distinction remains. In theory the…barristers are supposed to be the specialists in advocacy or in particular areas of the law. The…solicitors are, often misleadingly, described as the general practitioners. In fact, some barristers are not specialists, some solicitors are. Some solicitors are better advocates than many barristers.

Is the division in the legal profession between solicitors and barristers still relevant in the twenty-first century, or should the professions be fused?

Outline answer

The introduction should set out what you understand the question to be asking and explain how you will answer it. The question expects you to discuss the differences between solicitors and barristers and the increasingly blurred distinctions between the two professions. You may then want to go on to discuss the advantages and disadvantages of having two branches of the profession before deciding whether you consider that the present division should remain or that the two professions be joined.

The professions of barrister and solicitor are separate and, traditionally, the work they carry out is different. You could outline the differences.

Fusion, in this context, can be defined as a union resulting from combining or merging different elements or parts. Is this the definition you wish to use?

When this was first investigated, by the Royal Commission on Legal Services in 1979 (the Benson Commission), the result was a strong recommendation to retain the two branches. What has happened since that committee reported? The Law Society view is that the legal profession should be similar to the medical profession. In other words all lawyers would have a standard training and then those who wished to specialise could apply to become consultants.

Discuss the fact that the granting of higher rights to solicitors and the opening of access to barristers has, perhaps, led to fewer calls for formal change Advantages/ disadvantages – you could discuss, amongst other issues, the following:

Lower costs – if only one lawyer is needed – however it may be argued that in practice two lawyers are often required: one to do the day-to-day work on the case and the other to represent a party at trial, for example.

Specialisation – using one lawyer prevents duplication of effort however, is it always necessary to have a specialist? Perhaps a lower paid lawyer could do the day-to-day work and call on a specialist for specific, difficult problems (as is the case in the medical profession.)

Advocacy – is it an advantage or a disadvantage that one profession specialises in advocacy?

Think about the roles, read widely, and develop your own views on advantages and disadvantages. Refer to the changes that have come about as a result of the Legal Services Act 2007.

Your conclusion will show that you have answered the question asked and will sum up your final view.

Further reading

The business structure of law firms, at the time of writing, has entered a new phase and the consequences of the advent of ABS, MDPs, and LDPs is not yet clear. It is important to read the legal press and quality newspapers to keep up to date with the changes that are taking place. The following list is a starting point for your reading.

- *Clementi Report of the Review of the Regulatory Framework for Legal Services in England and Wales*: **www.legal-services-review.org.uk/**
  This website includes both the final report and helpful questions and answers about the reporting process.

- Department for Constitutional Affairs 'The Future of Legal Services: Putting the Consumer First' (2005): **http://webarchive.nationalarchives.gov.uk/+/http://www.dca.gov.uk/legalsys/folwp.pdf**
  This is the white paper containing the proposals for changing the regulation of the legal profession. It is useful to look at this and consider the proposals in the light of the changes that have in fact taken place.

- **Greene, D.** 'Time for a New Model (2012) 162 NLJ 377
  This very readable article outlines the key provisions of the Legal Services Act 2007 and explains how they are being introduced gradually to allow the legal profession to adapt to the changes to regulation and to prepare for alternative business structures. The author considers how the licensing process may develop, the implications for traditional partnerships, and discusses legal disciplinary practices and alternative business structures.

- The Legal Education and Training Review **http://letr.org.uk/**
  This website includes the report, from June 2013, and a wealth of other information, including the literature review that was carried out in preparation for the report. It is a lengthy document, but the executive summary is clear and easy to read.

- **Mayson, S.** 'Something for Everyone' (2007) 157 NLJ 1073
  This article outlines the provisions of the Legal Services Bill 2006, which was enacted in 2007, allowing for lawyers to take part in alternative business structures, which permit the co-ownership of law firms by non-lawyers. It highlights the advantages to lawyers of being involved in 'multi-talented practices' and the ways in which the legal services market may change.

- Office of Fair Trading 'Competition in Professions' (2001): **www.oft.gov.uk/ advice_and_resources/publications/reports/professional_bodies/oft328/**
  This report is over ten years old but it provides an interesting starting point to consider the barriers to competition in the legal professions alongside other professions, such as accountancy.

- **Ward, R.** and **Akhtar, A.** *Walker and Walker's English Legal System*, 11th edn, Oxford University Press (2011), chapter 12
  A detailed and clearly written text book to supplement your reading of this chapter.

- Wilberforce Society Report: Reform of the Legal Profession **thewilberforcesociety. co.uk/wp-content/uploads/2012/05/Reform-of-the-Legal-Profession.pdf**
  The Wilberforce Society is a student society at Cambridge University. This is an excellent paper discussing the reform of the legal professions and all of the recent legislation in a very succinct and readable format.

Online Resource Centre

You should now attempt the supporting multiple choice questions available at **www.oxfordtextbooks.co.uk/orc/wilson_els/**.

10 The jury

⊙ **Learning objectives**

By the end of this chapter you should be able to:

- explain the criteria for eligibility for jury service;
- critically consider the merits of the changes to ineligibility, disqualification, and excusal for jury service in the Criminal Justice Act 2003;
- assess the case law and reform proposals in cases where defendants from an ethnic minority seek modification of the ethnic composition of the jury;
- critically consider the arguments for and against (a) the exclusion of jury trials in certain cases, and (b) jury waiver; and
- explain the policy of jury selection in England and compare it with that in the United States.

🛈 Talking point

....

In December 2012, Kasim Davey was serving as a juror at Wood Green Crown Court in London. The case involved an allegation that the defendant had committed the offence of sexual activity with a child, contrary to s.9 of the Sexual Offences Act 2003. After the first day in court, Davey posted a message on Facebook saying that he was in a jury deciding a paedophile's fate and that he was now able to ruin the paedophile's life (the language was much stronger than this). The next day, one of Davey's Facebook friends emailed the court about the post. The following day, Davey was asked to appear before the trial judge. He denied posting the message but the judge discharged him, and the case proceeded with the remaining eleven jurors. In a subsequent police interview, Davey admitted the Facebook post. The Attorney General applied for Davey to be committed for contempt of court. He denied liability, but the High Court in July 2013 held that he had done an act which was calculated to interfere with the proper administration of justice (Attorney General v Davey and Another [2013] EWHC 2317 (Admin); [2014] 1 Cr App R 1). He knew that, as a juror, he had a duty to act fairly towards the defendant but he posted a message making clear to his Facebook friends that he would use his prejudices in deciding the case. He was making clear not only his interference with the administration of justice by disregarding his duties to act as a juror, but his plain intention to do so.

This case raises a number of interlinked issues which will be addressed in this chapter: who should be eligible to serve on juries? Should the administration of justice in trials of serious criminal offences be entrusted to ordinary members of the public? Should there be some form of pre-trial vetting of jurors, to assess whether they might be biased? What should happen to a juror who uses social media to comment on an ongoing trial?

....

Introduction

The jury has been called the 'bulwark of the liberties' of the individual against the state and is seen by many as an essential part of the criminal justice system in England and Wales. One of the most distinctive features of the Crown Court trial is, undoubtedly, the input of the jury. However, its role may be more symbolic than most people realise. Crown Court trials represent no more than 2 per cent of all criminal trials, with the vast majority of criminal prosecutions taking place in the magistrates' courts. However, it should be noted that a jury does decide every criminal offence that is triable 'on indictment' (at least, where the accused pleads not guilty). This category includes the most serious offences such as murder, manslaughter, rape, and robbery. Furthermore, where a criminal offence is one 'triable either way', then the defendant can elect to have trial before a jury. The use of juries in civil proceedings, on the other hand, is very limited (see s.69 (1) of the Senior Courts Act 1981, discussed in 10.1.5).

The composition and operation of the jury has been subject of much debate in recent years and significant changes have been made to its composition. The starting point for an understanding of the jury is a thorough understanding of the basic law relating to it. To that must be added a critical awareness of the current issues relating to the workings of the jury.

10.1 The role of the jury

During a trial, the judge directs the jury as to the relevant principles of law and evidence. The jury's job in a trial is to determine issues of fact, i.e. what actually happened, and reach a verdict on that basis. In a civil trial, the jury's function is to determine whether the claimant has established his or her case on the balance of probabilities. As juries in civil trials are now very rare, in the remainder of this chapter all references to juries and jury trials will be to criminal prosecutions in the Crown Court, unless otherwise stated.

10.1.1 The jury's function in criminal trials

In a criminal trial, at the close of the case – that is, after the prosecution and defence have presented their version of events, examined and cross-examined the accused, the alleged victim, and any witnesses – the judge sums up the issues and legal principles, and then the jury retires to consider its verdict. This will either be 'guilty' if the prosecuting body, usually the Crown Prosecution Service (CPS), has established its case beyond reasonable doubt, or 'not guilty', if not.

> 🔑 **Key point**
>
> Although a judge may direct a jury to acquit, the judge may not direct the jury to convict. The decision whether or not the prosecution has proven its case is always a matter for the jury alone.

This principle was confirmed by the House of Lords in *R v Wang* [2005] UKHL 9, [2005] 1 WLR 661. The appellant, Cheong Wang, was indicted on two counts of having an 'article which has a blade or is sharply pointed' in a public place, contrary to s.139 (1) of the Criminal Justice Act 1988. He did not deny having the articles – a sword and a knife – with him but argued that he was a Buddhist and liked to stop at 'remote and uninhabited places' to practise a traditional martial art called Shaolin. However, the trial judge directed the jury that, as a matter of law, Wang had no defence and that they were therefore to return guilty verdicts. The jury duly convicted and the Court of Appeal dismissed Wang's appeal. However, on further appeal, the House of Lords quashed the convictions. Delivering a unanimous judgment, Lord Bingham said:

> No matter how inescapable a judge may consider a conclusion to be, in the sense that any other conclusion would be perverse, it remains his duty to leave the decision to the jury and not to dictate what that verdict should be.

Moreover, a judge cannot pressurise a jury into reaching a guilty verdict. Where this happens the Court of Appeal almost inevitably quashes the conviction. In *R v McKenna & Others* [1960] 1 QB 411, Cassells J said:

> It is a cardinal principle of our criminal law that in considering their verdict – concerning, as it does, the liberty of the subject – a jury shall deliberate in complete freedom, uninfluenced by any promise, unintimidated by any threat.

In *R v Watson & Others* [1988] QB 690, Lord Lane CJ said the jury:

> must not be made to feel that it is incumbent upon them to express agreement with a view they do not truly hold simply because it might be inconvenient or tiresome or expensive for the prosecution, the defendant, the victim or the public in general if they do not do so.

The principle that juries must not be pressurised into reaching a verdict was emphasised in *R v Buttle* [2006] EWCA Crim 246, the facts of which are given at 10.1.3 (the case also raised issues about the secrecy of jury deliberations). Gage LJ said that 'it is clear that a jury must not be put under undue pressure'. However, 'pressure' should be distinguished from 'exhortation'. In *Shoukatallie v R* [1962] AC 81, Lord Denning said that, 'the question…is whether the judge went beyond exhortation which is permissible, and exerted some measure of coercion which is not'.

10.1.2 Jury equity

One of the supposed strengths of jury trials is that a jury may acquit anyone, regardless of the law or the weight of the evidence. This is known as the principle of 'jury equity'. In *R v Ponting* [1985] Crim LR 318, a jury acquitted the accused of charges brought under the Official Secrets Act 1911. This was despite the fact that there was no argument that the accused had committed all the elements of the offence; and the judge had directed the jury that, as a matter of law, he had no defence.

> ### Example
>
> *R v Ponting* **[1985] Crim LR 318**
>
> In July 1984, Clive Ponting, a departmental head in the Ministry of Defence, sent two documents to Tam Dalyell, a Labour MP. The documents belonged to the ministry and related to parliamentary inquiries about the sinking of the Argentine warship, the *General Belgrano*, during the 1982 Falklands Conflict. Dalyell was a known critic of the government on the *Belgrano* sinking. The first document was unclassified but the second was marked 'Confidential'. Ponting was charged with an offence of disclosing confidential material under the Official Secrets Act 1911, although there was a defence if the disclosure was to 'a person to whom it is in the interest of the State to communicate it'. There was no argument that Ponting had committed all the elements of the offence; his only defence was that Dalyell was a person to whom it was his duty 'in the interest of the State' to communicate the documents. McCowan J directed the jury that, as a matter of law, the 'interest of the State' was synonymous with the 'interest of the government of the day'. However, despite this clear indication from the judge that the defence was unavailable, the jury returned a verdict of 'not guilty'.

According to D. Feldman's book, *Civil Liberties and Human Rights* (1993), at p.641, 'the jury acquitted Mr Ponting, probably reflecting public contempt for the government's attempt to conflate its own narrow political interest with the state's interest'. Birkinshaw, *Freedom of Information* (1989), at p.81, has suggested that the acquittal 'no doubt related to a jury refusing to be browbeaten by a judge'. Another example of 'jury equity' is the case of Bridget Gilderdale.

> ### Example
>
> *R v Gilderdale*, **The Times, 25 January 2010**
>
> In January 2010 Bridget Gilderdale was cleared by a jury at Lewes Crown Court of the attempted murder of her 31-year-old daughter, Lynn. Lynn had been suffering from myalgic encephalomyelitis (ME), otherwise known as chronic fatigue syndrome (CFS), which causes long-term tiredness which is not relieved by rest or sleep, since she was 14 years old. Her condition was particularly debilitating and she had previously attempted to take her own life to relieve her suffering. Bridget had cared for Lynn throughout the seventeen years and had tried to persuade her daughter not to take her own life. However, she eventually agreed to help Lynn to die by providing her with morphine and injecting air into her veins after Lynn told her mother that she wanted 'the pain to go'. After Lynn's death, Bridget pleaded guilty to aiding and abetting Lynn's suicide and was given a twelve-month conditional discharge. However, the prosecution proceeded with the attempted murder charge, which eventually led to a not guilty verdict. Given the strength of the prosecution evidence and the guilty plea to the assisted suicide charge, the jury's verdict is widely regarded as an example of jury equity. The trial judge, Bean J, was prompted to comment as follows: 'I do not normally comment on the verdicts of juries but in this case their decision, if I may say so, shows common sense, decency and humanity which makes jury trials so important in a case of this kind.'

Thinking point

In the magistrates' court the arbiters of fact are not a jury but the magistrates. Would a bench of magistrates have been more, or less likely, than a jury to acquit the defendants in these cases?

Penny Darbyshire, in 'The Lamp that Shows that Freedom Lives – Is it Worth the Candle?' [1991] Crim LR 740 (at p.748), is very critical of 'jury equity'. She writes that:

[j]urors will sometimes acquit, or convict, for a variety of extraneous reasons, which have nothing to do with replacing the law with their own sense of fairness or equity. They include the pressure of incarceration in the jury room and the replacement of the high standard of proof 'beyond reasonable doubt' with a lesser standard...Jurors also sometimes base their decisions on sympathy or hostility towards other trial participants, notably counsel and witnesses.

Thinking point

Is the jury's power to acquit someone in open defiance of the law and/or evidence a strength or a weakness of the jury system?

10.1.3 Appeals against decisions of the jury and the 'confidentiality' principle

Appeals by the prosecution

It is extremely rare for there to be an appeal by the prosecution against an acquittal by a jury. Until quite recently there was no possibility at all; however, s.76 of the Criminal Justice Act 2003 does allow the prosecution to apply to the Court of Appeal to quash an acquittal and order a retrial following a trial on indictment. The first occasion on which this happened was in *R v Dunlop* [2006] EWCA Crim 1354, [2007] 1 WLR 1657. William Dunlop had been charged with the murder of a young woman, Julie Hogg, but pleaded not guilty. At the trial in May 1991, the jury failed to reach a verdict and so a retrial was held in October 1991, with Dunlop again pleading not guilty. The second jury also failed to reach a verdict at which point the Crown withdrew the case and a verdict of not guilty was entered.

Several years later, whilst in prison for an unrelated offence, Dunlop admitted his guilt to a prison officer, and in April 2000 he was convicted of perjury for lying to the Crown Court during the 1991 trials. However, after the Criminal Justice Act 2003 came into force in April 2005, the Crown submitted an application to the Court of Appeal to have the 1991 acquittal quashed. The Court agreed and

Dunlop was duly tried for Julie's murder for a third time in September 2006. On this occasion he pleaded guilty.

Do not confuse this process whereby the Attorney General refers cases to the Court of Appeal following a defendant's acquittal by a Crown Court. Attorney General's References provide an opportunity for the Court of Appeal to state the law on a subject, but do not involve any change to the Crown Court's decision.

Appeals by the defence

Appeals against conviction are much more common. Usually this relates to an alleged misdirection by the judge on a point of law or evidence. However, the Court of Appeal is, in certain circumstances, prepared to hear evidence of events affecting the jury. If it finds an 'irregularity' serious enough to bring the conviction into doubt then it may quash a conviction. An issue that had to be carefully addressed here is s.8 of the Contempt of Court Act 1981, which forbids any investigation into things said during the jury's 'deliberations'. To what extent does this restrict the appeal courts' ability to hear appeals against alleged irregularities during a jury trial?

The classic example is *R v Young* [1995] 2 Cr App R 379, where allegations were made that the jury convicted the defendant of two counts of murder after consulting a makeshift Ouija board whilst they were sequestered in a hotel overnight. The Court of Appeal first had to decide whether the court itself was bound by s.8. Lord Taylor CJ held that s.8 did, in general terms, bind the court and so, unless s.8 could be avoided, it would be impossible to investigate what may or may not have happened prior to the jury returning their verdict. However, Lord Taylor then held that s.8 did not apply to the facts of the Young case, because when the jury was sequestered in the hotel, they were not 'deliberating'. Having decided that s.8 did not apply, the Court held that the use of the Ouija board was 'not merely objectionable but amounted to a material irregularity' and quashed Young's convictions (although it did order a retrial, at which Young was duly re-convicted).

In *R v Qureshi* [2001] EWCA Crim 1807, [2002] 1 WLR 518, the Court of Appeal decided, because of s.8, that it could not give leave to hear an appeal, despite one of the jurors, after conviction, alleging that a range of irregularities had occurred during the jury's deliberations. The allegations included making disparaging remarks about the defendant, bringing newspapers into the jury room, using mobile phones to contact outsiders during the trial, and adopting a bullying attitude. One juror was alleged to have fallen asleep during the evidence; another was alleged to have been deaf and unable to hear all the evidence. Despite all of this, the Court of Appeal felt it had no choice but to refuse leave to appeal because all the allegations related to matters protected by s.8.

In *R v Mirza* [2004] UKHL 2, [2004] 1 AC 1118, the House of Lords heard another case involving post-conviction allegations of irregularities having taken place during the jury's deliberations. One of the jurors alleged that at least some of the other jurors were racist and prejudiced against the defendant, who was from Pakistan but had been living in England since 1998. In a letter sent to the defendant's lawyers, it was alleged that ' [t]he bigots [on the jury] had decided that the case brought by the prosecution was not good enough for them, so they embellished it.' This prompted the defendant, who had been convicted of indecent assault, to appeal. The Court of Appeal dismissed his appeal as it considered itself bound by the decision in *Qureshi*. The defendant appealed again. The question for the Lords was whether the juror's letter could be used as a basis for allowing an appeal. The Lords held not, and dismissed the appeal.

However, the Lords actually disagreed with the Court of Appeal in *R v Qureshi* and held that s.8 of the Contempt of Court Act 1981 did *not* apply to the appeal courts (overruling *R v Young* on that point). However, the Lords decided that there was an even older common law rule to the same effect, preventing appeal judges from investigating appeals relating to alleged irregularities in the course of jury deliberations. The common law rule was designed to ensure the confidentiality of jury deliberations. There were several reasons given for this principle. Lord Hobhouse explained that 'nothing could be more destructive...than the juror coming out of court and communicating his or her views about the jury's deliberations to the media or to persons who are likely to disagree with the verdict'. Lord Hope said that 'the law recognises that confidentiality is essential to the proper functioning of the jury process, that there is merit in finality and that jurors must be protected from harassment'.

Thus, it is legally impossible to bring an appeal against conviction based on evidence of allegations of improprieties that may have occurred during the jury's deliberations (the confidentiality principle). However, the confidentiality principle does not apply when appeals are brought against conviction based on evidence of allegations of improprieties caused by or attributable to extraneous matters. The position in both Canadian and English law was neatly summarised by the Supreme Court of Canada in *R v Pan; R v Sawyer* [2001] 2 SCR 344, where Arbour J explained that the law:

> seeks to preserve the secrecy of the jury's deliberations, while ensuring that those deliberations remain untainted by contact with information or individuals from outside the jury. As a result, where the evidence establishes that the jury has been exposed to outside information or influences, it will generally be admissible.

A number of recent English cases have addressed the question of the difference between jury deliberations (which are subject to the confidentiality rule) and extraneous matters which might have influenced those deliberations (which are not):

- An example of the former situation is *R v Buttle* [2006] EWCA Crim 246. Buttle had been convicted of rape and assault by penetration. On appeal, it was contended that one of the jurors had been pressurised by three other jurors to return a guilty verdict. However, the appeal court dismissed Buttle's appeal. Gage LJ simply said that 'this Court cannot enquire into the privacy of what goes on in the jury room'.

- An example of the latter situation is *R v Karakaya* [2005] EWCA Crim 346, [2005] 2 Cr App R 5. Here, the accused had been convicted of rape. After the jury left court, it was discovered that a juror had taken into the jury's deliberating room extraneous documents (academic articles dealing with rape). Karakaya appealed, arguing that the presence of the documents in the jury room amounted to an irregularity. The Court of Appeal quashed the conviction (although a retrial was ordered) because the verdicts were not necessarily based purely on the evidence actually presented at trial. The Court of Appeal distinguished *R v Mirza* on the basis that this case involved consideration of extraneous documents.

- Another example of the latter situation is *R v Pintori* [2007] EWCA Crim 1700, [2007] Crim LR 997, where the defendant had been convicted of possession of heroin but appealed when it emerged, post-verdict, that one of the jurors had been employed by the police force (albeit in a civilian capacity) and knew some of the officers involved in bringing the prosecution. On appeal, it was submitted that this juror – and by extension, the whole jury – may have been biased against the defendant. The Court of Appeal allowed the appeal. *R v Mirza* was again distinguished as this case also involved the question of external influences on the jury's deliberation process.

- Another example of the latter situation is *R v Marshall & Crump* [2007] EWCA Crim 35, [2007] Crim LR 562, although in this case the Court of Appeal upheld the appellants' robbery convictions despite the fact that 'extraneous' material was found in the jury room after the trial had concluded consisting of printouts from three websites: the CPS, the Home Office, and a criminal solicitors' practice. Hughes LJ said that although the material was 'wholly extraneous', it was 'largely material which was in the public domain and to which an intelligent member of the public serving on the jury could perfectly legitimately have access'. As a result, the Court concluded that the guilty verdicts were 'safe'.

In *R v Thompson & Others* [2010] EWCA Crim 1623, [2010] 2 Cr App R 27, six appellants appealed against convictions for various offences. In each case the appellant had alleged, inter alia, jury irregularity. The irregularities alleged by each appellant were as follows:

(i) Benjamin Thompson had been convicted at Oxford Crown Court of causing grievous bodily harm with intent. After the trial, several jurors wrote a letter to the trial judge indicating that one of the jurors had used the Internet to bring extraneous material 'relating to the case and legal terminology' into the jury room;

(ii) Jason Crawford was convicted at Harrow Crown Court of two counts of cocaine possession with intent to supply. After the trial, one of the jurors made a phone call to Crawford's solicitor asserting that, although she had been inclined towards a not guilty verdict, she had been 'put under immense pressure by other jurors to change her decision';

(iii) Ahmed Gomulu was convicted at the Old Bailey of murder and wounding with intent. After his trial, members of Gomulu's family reported that the victim's brother had been seen talking to members of the jury during the trial;

(iv) Chris Allen was convicted of rape at Newport Crown Court. After his trial, it was claimed that the jury may have become aware that Allen was facing a second jury trial for an unrelated offence;

(v) David Blake was convicted at Newcastle Crown Court of having an article with a blade or point on school premises. After the trial, evidence emerged that one of the jurors had conducted 'experiments' involving nail clippers;

(vi) Kamulete Kasunga was convicted of assault occasioning actual bodily harm at Wood Green Crown Court. After the trial, it emerged that a juror had written to the judge expressing concerns over the verdict.

Only one appeal – Blake's – was successful. The appeals in the other five cases were dismissed. The alleged irregularities in Crawford's and Kasunga's cases were described as 'classic *Mirza* territory'; in other words, they related to allegations protected by the confidentiality principle which were therefore inadmissible. The allegation in Gomulu's case was rejected for lack of evidence. Allen's appeal failed for similar reasons. Thompson's appeal raised more difficulties. Lord Judge CJ said that the use of the internet would have constituted an irregularity. However, the verdict was nevertheless held to be safe on the basis that the jurors' letter to the trial judge 'does not suggest that the juror, or anything he or she said to the other members of the jury, led them, in dereliction of their duty, do other than follow the directions in law given by the judge, as supplemented by him in answer to the numerous notes in which the jury sought further directions'. On the specific issue of jurors using the Internet, Lord Judge CJ offered the following observations:

> The use of the internet has expanded rapidly in recent years and it is to be expected that many, perhaps most, jurors, will be experienced in its use and will make habitual reference to it in daily life… [The] use of the internet is so common that some specific guidance must now be given to jurors…Jurors need to understand that although the internet is part of their daily lives, the case must not be researched there, or discussed there (for example, on social networking sites), any more than it can be researched with, or discussed amongst friends or family, and for the same reason. The reason is easy for jurors to understand. Research of this kind may affect their decision, whether consciously or unconsciously, yet at the same time, neither side at trial will know what consideration might be entering into their deliberations and will therefore not be able to address arguments about it. This would represent a departure from the basic principle which requires that the defendant be tried on the evidence admitted and heard by them in court. [We] do not purport to lay down a standard form of words; the sense of the message is familiar to all judges. What matters is that it should be explicitly related to the use of the internet. We recommend a direction in which the principle is explained not in terms which imply that the judge is making a polite request, but that he is giving an order necessary for the fair conduct of the trial.

The principles laid down in the Contempt of Court Act 1981 and *R v Mirza*- that of the paramount importance of maintaining confidentiality of jury deliberations – can be starkly contrasted with the scenes immediately after the culmination of the Michael Jackson trial (*People of California v Jackson*) in Santa Maria, California, in June 2005. There, members of the jury held an impromptu, televised press conference to discuss the reasons for their not guilty verdicts, which was broadcast around the world. Had that conference taken place immediately after the end of an English criminal trial, the jurors would almost certainly have been prosecuted for contempt of court.

An example of this occurred in *Attorney General v Scotcher* [2004] UKHL 36, [2005] 1 WLR 1867. The defendant, S, who sat as a juror in a trial of two brothers accused of drug dealing in January 2000, was convicted of contempt of court after he wrote a letter to the mother of the accused after the trial telling her that he thought her sons' convictions were unsafe because some of the other jurors had been too keen to get the trial over with and go home. The House of Lords upheld S's conviction, holding that his motives in seeking to overturn a miscarriage of justice provided no defence to a charge of contempt.

Thinking point

Is it really an example of 'contempt' of court for the defendant in *Scotcher* to point out what appeared, to him, to be a glaring example of a miscarriage of justice?

Section 18 (1) of the Juries Act 1974 is designed to eliminate unnecessary appeals. It states that no judgment after verdict in any trial by jury in any court shall be stayed or reversed by reason –

(a) that the provisions of this Act about the summoning or impanelling of jurors, or the selection of jurors by ballot, have not been complied with; or

(b) that a juror was not qualified in accordance with s.1 of this Act; or

(c) that any juror was misnamed or misdescribed; or

(d) that any juror was unfit to serve.

Examples of this include:

- *R v Chapman & Lauday* (1976) 63 Cr App R 75 – evidence emerged after the trial that one of the jurors had such a severe problem with earwax that he could not hear the summing up. The defendants appealed, but the appeal was dismissed.

- *R v Bliss* (1987) 84 Cr App R 1 – after conviction, the defendant recognised one of the jurors as being a man with whom he had been involved in a fight in a pub some six months earlier. He appealed, arguing that the juror might have been 'hostile' to him, but this was rejected.

- *R v Richardson* [2004] EWCA Crim 2997 – evidence emerged after the defendant's conviction of rape and indecent assault that one of the jurors was actually disqualified because of his own conviction for indecent assault, but had served in any event. However, his appeal was dismissed.

10.1.4 Majority verdicts

The concept of majority verdicts was introduced by the Criminal Justice Act 1967 and is now regulated according to s.17 of the Juries Act 1974. This states that a jury's verdict 'need not be unanimous' where at least ten of them agree (s.17 (1) (a)) or, in the rare cases where there are ten jurors, at least nine of them agree (s.17 (1) (b)). The main advantage of majority verdicts is that it avoids the problem of one juror with extreme and/or intractable views from holding out against the rest, and should lessen the need for expensive and time-consuming retrials. Conversely, it has been argued that majority verdicts 'dilute' the concept of proof beyond reasonable doubt – on the ground that if one juror is not satisfied as to guilt, there must be a doubt – and hence gives less protection to the innocent. This, in turn, weakens public confidence in the system.

Thinking point

1. Are majority verdicts acceptable, given the requirement that the prosecution prove its case beyond reasonable doubt?
2. What might be the effect of a requirement to have unanimous verdicts?

10.1.5 The jury's function in civil trials

Section 69 of the Senior Courts Act 1981 lists the categories of civil cases that can be heard by a jury in the High Court. The list includes fraud, libel, and slander (collectively, this is known as defamation), malicious prosecution, and false imprisonment. For an example of the use of a civil jury in a malicious prosecution case, see *Morrison v Chief Constable of the West Midlands* [2003] EWCA Civ 271.

Even in one of these listed areas, s.69 (1) states that 'the action shall be tried with a jury unless the court is of the opinion that the trial requires any prolonged examination of documents or accounts or any scientific or local investigation which cannot conveniently be made with a jury'. For discussion of the application of s.69 (1), see the defamation cases of *Goldsmith v Pressdram Ltd* [1988] 1 WLR 64, *Viscount de L'Isle v Times Newspapers Ltd* [1988] 1 WLR 49, and *Beta Construction Ltd v C4 TV & Yorkshire TV* [1990] 1 WLR 1042. In March 1994, the Court of Appeal denied an application for trial by jury from two environmental campaigners of the libel action (the so-called 'McLibel' case) brought against them by the McDonald's restaurant chain. The court said that the scientific issues would make it impossible for the case to be heard satisfactorily by a jury. The case duly went to trial before a single judge and lasted over a year – the longest libel action in history.

10.2 **The selection of the jury**

10.2.1 **Liability to serve**

The rules as to eligibility to serve on a jury are contained in s.1 of the Juries Act 1974. The requirements can be summarised as follows. The individual must be:

- registered as an elector;

- aged between 18 and 70. The minimum age is 18. The maximum age, 70, was raised from 65 in 1988; and

- ordinarily resident in the UK, the Channel Islands, or the Isle of Man for five years from the age of 13.

In August 2013, the Ministry of Justice announced that the maximum age limit was to be raised to 75, which will increase the pool of eligible jurors by approximately 2 million. The change is expected to come into force in 2014. The government explained that the reform was to enable the criminal justice system to benefit from the 'knowledge and life experiences' of older people. It also reflected the fact that the life expectancy of the average British resident had increased significantly since the age limit was last raised, in 1988. Trial judges would be given the discretionary power to excuse those aged 70+ from jury service if they could show a good reason for not serving. Meanwhile, it is noteworthy that in many other countries which use jury trials, there is no upper age limit for jurors at all. For example, in Scotland, the upper age limit was abolished in 2011.

No other eligibility criteria are required. In particular, there is no requirement that jurors be British citizens. This may be contrasted with the position in Canada, for example, where citizenship is a requirement for eligibility for jury service.

Thinking point

1. What are the arguments for and against citizenship being a requirement for eligibility to serve on a jury?

2. Although the government intends to raise the upper age limit for jurors, what is the justification for having ANY upper age limit?

10.2.2 **Ineligibility**

Major changes have been made to this area of law in April 2004, when s.321 of the Criminal Justice Act 2003 came into effect. Previously, Sch.1 to the Juries Act 1974 listed various categories of people as being ineligible for jury service. There were four Groups:

- **The Judiciary** (Group A): this Group included judges and magistrates, both current and retired.

- **Other Persons Concerned with the Administration of Justice** (Group B): this was a very large Group. It included the police and barristers and solicitors 'whether or not in actual practice as such'.

- **The Clergy, etc.** (Group C): this Group included a 'man in holy orders; a regular minister of any religious denomination', and a 'vowed member of any religious order living in a monastery, convent or other religious community'.

- **Mentally Disordered Persons** (Group D): this Group includes a person 'liable to be detained' under the Mental Health Act 1983 (MHA) or 'resident in a hospital on account of mental disorder' as defined by the MHA (Schedule 1 of the Juries Act 1974 as amended by s.2 of the Mental Health (Discrimination) Act 2013).

Section 321 of the 2003 Act abolished Groups A, B, and C. This means that judges, lawyers, the police, and clergy all became eligible for jury service. Only those in Group D remain ineligible.

> ## 🔐 Key point
>
> The general rule in the English criminal justice system is that all people who are eligible to serve on a jury should do so if summonsed. Only the mentally disordered are ineligible for jury service.

The enactment of s.321 in the 2003 Act was the culmination of a reform proposal advanced by Lord Justice Auld in his Review of the Criminal Courts in England and Wales, commissioned by the government and published in September 2001. Auld LJ had recommended that English law should be brought into line with certain other jurisdictions, including a number of American states, where far fewer restrictions were placed on jury eligibility. The core objective of the reform was to broaden the pool of potential jurors, and to make the jury more representative of society.

> ## ❗ Critical debate
>
> *Composition of the jury has long been a vexed question. At one time it was said that the English jury was 'middle class, male, middle minded and middle aged'. This was mainly because at one time eligibility for jury service was linked to property ownership. Following the abolition of this requirement in the early 1970s, this criticism is no longer true, but the issue that the jury should be representative of society remains. What were the reasons for excluding from jury service: (a) judges and lawyers; (b) the police; and (c) the clergy? Do you agree with Parliament that these people should now be required to serve on a jury? What are the potential problems with having lawyers and police officers serving as jurors?*

The first case involving s.321 to reach the appeal courts was *R v Abdroikov & Others* [2007] UKHL 37, [2007] 1 WLR 2679. The case involved three separate cases, which were joined into a single appeal, where it was argued that the presence of certain jurors created a risk of 'apparent' bias, and hence the appellants' entitlement to a fair trial by an 'independent and impartial tribunal', guaranteed by Article 6 of the European Convention on Human Rights (ECHR), was not satisfied. The appellants in the three cases were:

(i) Nurlon Abdroikov, who had been convicted of attempted murder by an Old Bailey jury containing a serving police officer, although he had no connection to the case. The officer's presence on the jury was only revealed at a very late stage in the trial, when the jury had already retired to consider their verdict.

(ii) Richard Green, a heroin addict, who had been convicted at Woolwich Crown Court of ABH contrary to s.47 of the Offences Against the Person Act 1861, his jury also containing a police officer, PC Mason. In this case the victim, Sergeant Burgess, was also a police officer (he had pricked his finger on a used syringe in Green's pocket whilst conducting a search). PC Mason and Sergeant Burgess were both serving in the same London borough at the time of the incident and had once served in the same police station at the same time, although the two officers were not known to each other. PC Mason's presence on the jury was only discovered, by chance, after the trial.

(iii) Ken Williamson, who had been convicted at Warrington Crown Court on two counts of rape. His jury contained a solicitor, Martin McKay-Smith, who had been employed by the CPS since 1986. McKay-Smith had contacted the court in advance to inform them of his occupation and background, and defence counsel had sought to challenge his involvement, citing Article 6 of the ECHR. However, the trial judge had rejected this challenge, ruling that he was obliged by s.321 of the Criminal Justice Act 2003 to order McKay-Smith to serve.

The appellants invoked the principle established by Lord Hewart CJ in *R v Sussex Justices, ex parte McCarthy* [1924] 1 KB 256 that 'it is not merely of some importance but is of fundamental importance that justice should not only be done, but should manifestly and undoubtedly be seen to be done', a principle subsequently endorsed by the European Court of Human Rights. The appellants contended that this principle was not met in a case where one of the jurors was employed by a body (the police and the CPS) dedicated to promoting the success of one side in the adversarial trial process. However, the Court of Appeal rejected all of the appeals. Applying the test for 'apparent' bias laid down in earlier case law, namely 'whether the fair-minded and informed observer, having considered the facts, would conclude that there was a real possibility that the tribunal was biased' (*Porter v Magill* [2001] UKHL 67, [2002] 2 AC 357), Lord Woolf CJ held that a fair-minded and informed observer would *not* conclude that there was a real possibility that a juror was biased merely because his occupation was one which meant that he was involved in some capacity or other in the administration of justice.

The three appealed against that decision to the House of Lords which, albeit by a narrow majority of 3 to 2, allowed the appeals in two of the three cases. Giving the leading judgment, Lord Bingham said that:

> It must be accepted that most adult human beings, as a result of their background, education and experience, harbour certain prejudices and predilections of which they may be conscious or unconscious. I would also, for my part, accept that the safeguards established to protect the impartiality of the jury, when properly operated, do all that can reasonably be done to neutralise the ordinary prejudices and predilections to which we are all prone. But this does not meet the central thrust of the case made by [counsel] for the appellants: that these cases do not involve the ordinary prejudices and predilections to which we are all prone but the possibility of bias (possibly unconscious) which, as he submits, inevitably flows from the presence on a jury of persons professionally committed to one side only of an adversarial trial process.

Lord Bingham observed that, in the 2001 *Review of the Criminal Courts*, which eventually led to the enactment of s.321, Lord Justice Auld had indicated that police officers and holders of similar occupations should not sit in every case regardless of the circumstances, but that ultimately the trial judge should decide – on a case-by-case basis – whether their presence was compatible with the principle of justice being seen to be done. In Richard Green's case, the majority (Lord Bingham, Baroness Hale, and Lord Mance), pointed out that there was an evidential dispute between Green and Sergeant Burgess (the victim), and the jury had to choose to prefer the evidence of one or the other. As Sergeant Burgess and PC Mason (the juror) shared the same local service background, Lord Bingham held that the 'instinct' of a police officer juror to prefer the evidence of 'a brother officer' to that of the defendant 'would be judged by the fair-minded and informed observer to be a real and possible source of unfairness'. Lord Bingham stated that it 'is not a criticism of the police service, but a tribute to its greatest strength, that officers belong to a disciplined force, bound to each other by strong bonds of loyalty, mutual support, shared danger and responsibility, culture and tradition'. Green was, therefore, 'not tried by a tribunal which was and appeared to be impartial'. His appeal was allowed and the conviction was quashed.

In Ken Williamson's case, Lord Bingham held that it was 'clear that justice was not seen to be done where one of the jurors was a full-time, salaried, long-serving employee of the prosecutor'. His appeal was, therefore, also allowed and convictions quashed (although the door was left open for a retrial – presumably without CPS solicitors involved).

The majority did rule that there were situations where police officers and CPS solicitors would meet the tests of impartiality. Indeed, Nurlon Abdroikov's case was one of them and his attempted murder conviction was upheld. Lord Bingham stated that, although it was 'unfortunate' that the police officer's identity was only revealed to the trial judge at such a late stage, 'had the matter been ventilated at the outset of the trial, it is difficult to see what argument defence counsel could have urged other than the general undesirability of police officers serving on juries, a difficult argument to advance in face of the parliamentary enactment' (meaning s.321 of the 2003 Act).

Lords Rodger and Carswell dissented in the appeals of Green and Williamson. Lord Rodger, in a powerful dissent, said that many (if not most) jurors would harbour some prejudices of various kinds. He pointed out that there was a 'risk' in any Crown Court trial that some jurors may (for example) be homophobic, or sexist, or racist. However, he said that the law takes steps to minimise the risk by making jurors take an oath or affirm that they will 'faithfully try the defendant and give a true verdict according to the evidence', and by making the judge give them a direction that they must assess the evidence impartially. Lord Rodger said that it would 'be naïve to suppose that these safeguards will always work with every juror' – but he thought that the presence of the other eleven jurors would 'neutralise any bias on the part of one or more members and so reach an impartial verdict'. He later observed that allowing the appeals in Green's and Williamson's cases would 'drive a coach and horses through Parliament's legislation and will go far to reverse its reform of the law'. He thought that it was the 'rational policy of the legislature' to decide who was eligible to serve as jurors and then to treat them all alike. Applying these principles to the three appeals, Lord Rodger said:

> Like all other jurors, be they clergymen, defence lawyers, butchers, estate agents, prostitutes, petty crooks or judges, police officers and CPS lawyers sit as private individuals. Each brings his or her own particular experience to bear on the case they have to try…I can see no reason why the fair minded and informed observer should single out juries with police officers and CPS lawyers as being constitutionally incapable of following the judge's directions and reaching an impartial verdict…An observer who singled out juries with these two types of members would be applying a different standard from the one that is usually applied.

Referring more specifically to Green's case, Lord Rodger added that Parliament must have known, when passing s.321, that police officers had previously been ineligible for jury service. Nonetheless, Parliament had 'judged it proper in today's world to remove the bar and to rely on the officers' commitment to uphold the law…like any other juror'. Similarly, referring to Williamson's case, Lord Rodger said that 'one of the qualities required of any CPS lawyer is an ability to assess evidence and to take proper decisions based on his assessment of the evidence, regardless of any pressure from the investigating police officers or from the media'. His Lordship concluded that '[a] fair minded and rational observer might just think that such a person would be capable of bringing his realism, objectivity and skills to bear when acting as a juror. Why, at the very least, should the observer assume that they would desert him?'

The guidance provided by the House of Lords has been applied in subsequent cases. *R v I* [2007] EWCA Crim 2999 involved a trial at Carlisle Crown Court. Before the case even began, a potential juror told the judge that he was a police officer and he knew all the officers who were to give evidence. The defence objected to him sitting but the judge disagreed, ruling that the fact of knowledge of particular witnesses in itself was not a bar to an individual being on the panel. He described it as analogous to a barrister sitting on a jury and knowing particular witnesses and the judge. The trial went ahead with the police officer on the jury and the defendant was convicted of a number of offences. However, the Court of Appeal quashed the convictions, holding that 'there was here a real possibility of bias arising from the presence on the jury of a police officer who knew the police witnesses. The possibility that he might be likely to accept the words of his colleagues, irrespective of the dispute between the parties, is one which can only be described as real.'

In *R v Khan & Others* [2008] EWCA Crim 531, [2008] 3 All ER 502, there were five separate cases before the Court of Appeal; this time none of the convictions were quashed. The cases can be summarised as follows:

- Case 1: Bakish Khan and Ilyas Hanif had been convicted at Sheffield Crown Court of conspiracy to supply heroin. During the trial, a juror had informed the judge that he was a police dog-handler and knew one of the witnesses for the prosecution, who was another police officer. The trial judge, however, rejected an application to discharge the juror.

- Case 2: Martin Lewthwaite had been convicted at Bristol Crown Court of causing GBH with intent. At the beginning of the trial, a juror informed the judge that he was a police Detective Chief Inspector, but was involved with drugs crimes working outside the Nailsea area where the attack took place, and did not know any of the witnesses. The trial judge also rejected an application to discharge the juror. In both of these cases, the Court of Appeal held that the fact that a juror was a police officer and might seem likely to favour the evidence of a fellow police officer would not, of itself, lead to an appearance of bias and therefore did not automatically disqualify the juror.

- Case 3: Michael Khan had been convicted at Hull Crown Court of non-disclosure of property in his bankruptcy, contrary to s.351 of the Insolvency Act 1986. A juror at his trial was employed by the CPS as a media officer. The trial judge rejected an application to discharge the juror. The Court of Appeal upheld the conviction. Here, the Court pointed out that Khan had been prosecuted by the Department of Trade and Industry, not the CPS, and there could be 'no objection' to a member of the CPS being a juror in a case prosecuted by a different authority.

- Case 4: Roy Cross had been convicted of wounding with intent at Worcester Crown Court. After conviction he became aware that one of the jurors was a prison officer at a prison where he had been remanded before and during trial.

- Case 5: Stanley Hill had been convicted of the attempted murder of a woman called Wendy Crooks at Liverpool Crown Court and sentenced to life imprisonment. After conviction, he made essentially the same discovery as Cross. Cross and Hill both argued that there was a risk that the prison officers knew information detrimental to them. This was rejected by the Court of Appeal, which held that the mere suspicion that a juror might, by reason of having been employed as a prison officer, have acquired knowledge of that defendant's bad character could not, of itself, lead an objective observer to conclude that the juror had an appearance of bias.

Thinking point

Commenting on these case law developments, Nick Taylor ('Jury: Bias – Presence on Jury of Persons Concerned with Administration of Justice' [2008] Crim LR 641) observes that there is now a 'potentially very difficult burden upon the trial judge' to determine suitability. He suggests that Crown Court judges 'may be left wondering whether the clarity of the old exclusionary position was more desirable'. What do you think?

Two of the appellants in Case 1, Bakish Khan and Ilyas Hanif, successfully appealed to the European Court of Human Rights on the basis that the presence of the police officer on the jury in their case had infringed their right to a fair trial under Article 6 ECHR. In *Hanif and Khan v UK* (2012) 55 EHRR 16, the Strasbourg court held that, where there was a jury trial involving (1) an 'important conflict' relating to prosecution evidence and (2) one of the jurors was a police officer who was 'personally acquainted' with the police officer giving that evidence, then 'jury directions and judicial warnings are insufficient to guard against the risk that the juror may, albeit subconsciously, favour the evidence of the police'.

Hence, the *Hanif and Khan* ruling is a relatively narrow one, although there will almost inevitably be further case law exploring the concepts of 'important conflict' and 'personally acquainted', both of which are apparently required for a violation of Article 6. Intriguingly, however, the Strasbourg court stated that it was 'leaving aside the question of whether the presence of a police officer on a jury could *ever* be compatible with Article 6' (emphasis added). This may imply that, had it been required to confront the issue head on, the court would have ruled that the presence of any police officer on a jury (whether 'personally acquainted' with a prosecution witness or not) infringed the defendant's right to a fair trial. In 'Police Officers on Juries' (2012) 71 CLJ 254, John Spencer argues that:

> [i]n retrospect it surely was a bad idea to make police officers eligible to serve. In practical terms, the need for judges to question police jurors about their relationships (if any) with witnesses adds a new and needless complication to the trial, and where one does serve and the defendant is convicted, a new and needless ground for possible appeal. And in theoretical terms, however honest the individual officer, in public perception a policeman is a member of the opposing team.... The government should now make a

virtue out of necessity and, taking the initiative, reverse the change its predecessor made before another Strasbourg condemnation forces it to do so.

Meanwhile, the Court of Appeal continues to deal with domestic cases involving challenges to conviction on the basis of allegedly inappropriate jurors. In *R v L* [2011] EWCA Crim 65, [2011] 1 Cr App R 27, the appellant had been convicted of burglary and attempted burglary at the Central Criminal Court (the Old Bailey). He appealed on the basis that the jury had included an employee of the Crown Prosecution Service (CPS), a serving police officer, and a retired police officer – in other words, three out of the twelve jurors were individuals linked in some way with the prosecuting arm of the criminal justice system. The Court of Appeal emphasised that questions of eligibility or disqualification or excusal were directed to individual potential jurors, not to the jury as a whole, and so the mere fact that a quarter of the jury had connections to the police or the CPS did not of itself render the convictions unsafe. As far as the two police officers were concerned, the Court of Appeal decided that there was no reason why the position of either should cause any concern. Neither had any connection with the police force or the individual officers involved in the trial, nor with the Old Bailey.

However, the position of the CPS employee did cause concern. She had worked for the CPS for nine years, initially as a secretary to the Director of the Service's North East London Sector and subsequently providing administrative support to advocates at Snaresbrook Crown Court. Although stressing that each case had to be considered on its facts, Lord Judge CJ said that her service with the CPS was 'long enough and of sufficient importance' to fall within the ambit of the problem identified by Lord Bingham in *R v Abdroikov & Others* that 'justice is not seen to be done if one discharging the very important neutral role of juror is a full-time, salaried, long-serving employee of the prosecutor'. As a consequence, the court allowed L's appeal – but did order a retrial.

10.2.3 **Disqualifications**

Under Sch.1 to the Juries Act 1974, certain persons with a criminal record were disqualified either for life, ten years, or five years, depending on the sentence they received. This category has been preserved by the Criminal Justice Act 2003, although the rules have been simplified. The new position is that the following are disqualified:

- Persons sentenced to imprisonment:
  - those sentenced to five years or more: life disqualification; and
  - those sentenced to up to five years (including suspended sentences): disqualified for ten years;
- persons on bail.

Thinking point

Is it fair that someone who has committed a criminal offence could potentially (depending on the sentence imposed) face a life-time ban from jury service? After all, is imprisonment not meant to serve (at least in part) as a form of rehabilitation into society? What about those on bail – is the disqualification of those on bail not a contradiction of the fundamental legal principle 'innocent until proven guilty'?

10.2.4 Excusal

Under the Juries Act 1974, various categories of people were excused as of right from jury service if they did not wish to serve. This included:

- any person over 65 years of age;
- any person who had served on a jury within the last two years;
- MPs and MEPs;
- members of the Armed Forces;
- doctors, dentists, nurses, and vets; and
- members of Religious Societies or Orders.

Following enactment of the Criminal Justice Act 2003, however, the only people entitled to be excused as of right now are:

- any person who had served on a jury within the last two years; and
- members of the Armed Forces (and even here it will require a certificate from the individual's commanding officer that it would 'be prejudicial to the efficiency of the service if that member were to be required to be absent from duty').

Hence, those persons over 65 years of age, MPs, doctors, dentists, nurses, and vets all lost their entitlement to automatic excusal.

Do you agree with Parliament that MPs, doctors, dentists, nurses, and vets should now be required to serve on a jury, with no guarantee of excusal?

Persons may have their jury duty excused or deferred at the discretion of the Jury Central Summoning Bureau (JCSB) if they can show 'good reason'. A Home Office research study in 1999, based on a sample of 50,000 people summoned for jury service, found that 38 per cent of them were excused at the judge's discretion. The study found that the most common reasons were:

- medical (40 per cent);
- care of children and elderly relatives (20 per cent);
- work/financial reasons (20 per cent);
- non-residence (9 per cent);

- being a student (6 per cent);
- transport problems (1 per cent); and
- others (4 per cent).

10.2.5 **The process of selection**

Juries are selected from the electoral register. This is designed to ensure a random selection. In *R v Sheffield Crown Court, ex parte Brownlow* [1980] QB 530, Lord Denning MR said:

> Our philosophy is that the jury should be selected at random – from a panel of persons who are nominated at random. We believe that 12 persons selected at random are likely to be a cross-section of the people as a whole – and thus represent the view of the common man...The parties must take them as they come.

The case of *R v Salt* [1996] Crim LR 517 provides an interesting illustration of this. The defendant was convicted of burglary but appealed after it emerged that one of the jurors was the son of a court usher, who had been asked by his father to serve on D's jury owing to a shortfall in prospective jurors. D's conviction was quashed. The Court of Appeal actually denied that a random selection policy, as such, existed, but did state that every practicable effort should be made to make the selection random. This was not the case in D's trial.

However, the policy of random selection is not without problems, as certain groups in society (e.g. young people, students, and members of ethnic minority groups), tend to be under-represented on the electoral register – and hence on juries too. However, some of the problems have been alleviated (if not removed) by the introduction, in late 2000, of the JCSB computerised system, which now handles all jury summonses.

In his *Review of the Criminal Courts* (2001), Lord Justice Auld recommended that '[q]ualification for jury service should remain the same, save that entitlement to, rather than actual, entry on an electoral role should be a criterion. Potential jurors should be identified from a combination of a number of public registers and lists.' Something similar to this system operates in many American states, whereby driving licence records are used as a means of identifying potential jurors. After all, many people of voting age hold driving licences but are not registered to vote; these potential jurors will never be called for jury service under the present system.

Thinking point

1. Is there really 'random' selection of the jury in England?
2. How might the selection process be improved?

10.3 **Challenges to jury membership**

10.3.1 **Challenge 'for cause'**

Both prosecution and defence have the right to challenge all or any of the jurors 'for cause'. Challenges 'for cause' are very rare, mainly because the defence have very little information on which to base a challenge and challenges have to be based on a 'foundation of fact' (*R v Chandler* [1964] 2 QB 322). Since 1973, only jurors' names and addresses are known to the defence (prior to that date, jurors' occupations were also known). The only guidance provided by the 1974 Act is s.12 (4), which simply states that '[t]he fact that a person summoned to serve on a jury is not qualified to serve shall be a ground of challenge for cause; but subject to that… nothing in this Act affects the law relating to challenge of jurors.'

Useful guidance as to when challenge for cause may exist comes from the Supreme Court of Canada. In *R v Williams* [1998] 1 SCR 1128, McLachlin CJ stated that prejudice might occur in four situations:

- *Interest prejudice* – when jurors may have a direct stake in the trial due to their relationship to the defendant, the victim, witnesses, or outcome.

- *Specific prejudice* – when a juror had attitudes and beliefs about the particular case that may render them incapable of deciding guilt or innocence with an impartial mind. These attitudes and beliefs may arise from personal knowledge of the case, publicity through mass media, or public discussion and rumour in the community.

- *Generic prejudice* – when a juror holds stereotypical attitudes about the defendant, victims, witnesses, or the nature of the crime itself. Bias against a racial or ethnic group or against persons charged with sex abuse are examples of this.

- *Conformity prejudice* – when the case is of significant interest to the community causing a juror to perceive that there is strong community feeling about a case coupled with an expectation as to the outcome.

In the United States, by way of contrast, the jury are openly and routinely questioned about a whole range of issue – their occupations, political or religious beliefs, and so on, in order to eliminate bias. This process is known as 'voir dire' and can take hours, days, or even weeks. The examination of the jury for the trial of Jack Ruby for shooting Lee Harvey Oswald, the alleged assassin of President John F. Kennedy in Dallas in 1964, took fifteen days. That was nothing compared to the vetting of the jury for the trial of O. J. Simpson, for allegedly stabbing his wife to death, which took forty days (26 September to 4 November 1994). Both prosecution and defence (in criminal trials) and claimant and defendant (in civil trials) can then employ an unlimited number of challenges for cause to 'strike' unsuitable jurors. Both sides also have a limited number of peremptory challenges (see 12.3.3).

The voir dire is designed to produce juries that are unbiased. However, as well as being very time-consuming (and hence expensive) it has another obvious weakness: it is open to abuse by counsel seeking to secure a favourable jury. Alistair Bonnington ('The Jury: A Suitable Case for Treatment?' (1995) NLJ 847), commenting on the use of voir dire in civil trials in the US, pointed out:

> Now specialised firms have been set up to advise parties on jury selection techniques. They argue strongly that this work…will lead to the result desired by their client in virtually every case – in other words, the court process itself doesn't matter at all if you select the right jurors.

The Chief Justice of Canada was moved to speak out against the American voir dire system. In *R v Find* [2001] 1 SCR 863, McLachlin CJ said that voir dire 'treats all members of the jury pool as presumptively suspect'. She observed that 'prospective jurors are frequently subjected to extensive questioning, often of a highly personal nature' and that it was 'unclear that the American system produces better juries' than those systems, including the one in England and Wales.

However, two articles written by British lawyers who witnessed voir dire first-hand were much more positive about the US system. According to Mark George ('Jury Selection, Texas Style' (1988) NLJ 438) jury selection proceeded 'on a rational and logical basis' and that the jurors excluded – even those removed peremptorily – would have known that 'there was some reasoning behind their rejection'. Similarly, Richard May ('Jury Selection in the USA: Are there Lessons to be Learned?' [1998] Crim LR 270) commented that the 'care with which the proceedings were undertaken was impressive and leads one to ask whether enough is done in England to ensure that juries are unbiased'. However, in *R v Tracey Andrews* [1999] Crim LR 156, the Court of Appeal came out against introducing voir dire in England and Wales, on the basis that it contradicted the principle of random selection.

Thinking point

1 Compare and contrast the English system of jury challenges with the American system of voir dire.

2 Are there any arguments in favour of voir dire being introduced into England and Wales?

10.3.2 Challenge by the prosecution

The Crown may ask one or more potential jurors to 'stand by' before they take the juror's oath. Where this happens, the juror is moved to the back of the queue of potential jurors for that trial. No reason need be given, but the situations in which the Attorney General has authorised the use of 'stand-by' are restricted, especially since the defence lost its power of peremptory challenge in 1988 (see later). Guidelines issued by the Attorney General provide that 'it has been customary' for Crown prosecutors to invoke stand-by only 'sparingly and in exceptional circumstances…on the basis of clearly defined and restrictive criteria'. Furthermore, the 'prosecution should not use its right in order to influence the overall composition of a jury or with a view to tactical advantage'.

Two examples of circumstances in which it would be 'proper' for the Crown to exercise its stand-by power are given in the Guidelines. First, where a prospective juror is revealed to be 'manifestly unsuitable', for example if the case is complex and the juror is illiterate. Second, where a 'jury check' has revealed information justifying exercise of the right to stand by. One such case was *R v McCann & Others* (1991) 92 Cr App R 239, in which three Irish nationals were charged with conspiracy to murder the then Northern Ireland Secretary, Tom King. Because of the national security implications of the case, the Attorney General authorised a jury check and one juror was stood down as a result. The defendants were convicted and appealed, arguing that 'stand-by' was: (i) contrary to the principle of random selection; (ii) unconstitutional; and (iii) unfair, in that it gave the prosecution an advantage. However, the appeal was dismissed on this ground. Beldam LJ said that the Attorney General's guidelines were both a 'self-imposed restraint on the Attorney General's right of stand-by and in certain circumstances a safeguard for the interests of an accused'.

An example of what could happen if stand-by powers are not restricted occurred in Canada in the case of *R v Biddle* (1995) 96 CCC (3d) 321. The defendant (B) was charged with four counts of assault on women. He was convicted by an all-female jury, which itself is unobjectionable; however, prosecution counsel had set out to empanel an all-female jury and succeeded in doing so by virtue of the stand-by power given to them under Canadian criminal procedure rules. B successfully appealed to the Supreme Court, albeit on another ground. Interestingly, some of the judges who commented on the stand-by issue did not think that it was necessarily unfair on the defendant. L'Heureux-Dubé J stated that making findings of bias on the basis of 'assumed stereotypical reactions based on gender' was 'dangerous [and] contrary to our concepts of equality and individuality'. She held that there was nothing in the circumstances of the case that lifted the submission that an all-female jury could give rise to a reasonable apprehension of bias 'above the level of unwarranted stereotyping'.

10.3.3 Abolition of the defence 'peremptory challenge'

The right of the defence to challenge jurors 'without cause', otherwise known as the 'peremptory challenge', was abolished by s.118 of the Criminal Justice Act 1988. The Committee on Fraud Trials (the Roskill Committee) had recommended the abolition of the peremptory challenge in 1986 on the basis that it was being abused, for example by removing someone who looked like they might understand and/or sympathise with the prosecution and replacing them with someone who looked less likely to understand the case and/or more likely to sympathise with the defence; also, on the ground that it could upset and/or antagonise rejected jurors. There was also the danger that the peremptory challenge could be abused in cases where the race and/

or gender of the accused was a possible factor. As counsel for the defence had little information about prospective jurors when making peremptory challenges, this encouraged the application of stereotypes. The Committee's report concluded that: '[t]he public, the press and many legal practitioners now believe that this ancient right is abused cynically and systematically to manipulate cases towards a desired result. We conclude that…such manipulation is wholly unacceptable and must be stopped.' This recommendation was duly taken up by the government and then by Parliament when enacting the 1988 Act.

Thinking point

Up to 1988 it was possible for the defence in a criminal trial to challenge a juror without cause, a peremptory challenge. Was it right to abolish peremptory challenges? Should the Crown's right of 'stand-by' be removed as well?

10.3.4 **Challenge to the array**

Under s.12 (6) of the Juries Act 1974, the entire jury may be challenged (known as 'challenge to the array') if the official who summoned them was 'biased or acted improperly'. An unsuccessful 'challenge to the array' was brought in *R v Danvers* [1982] Crim LR 680, which is discussed at 10.5.

10.4 **Jury vetting**

In general terms, jury vetting refers to the covert investigation of potential jurors in order to assess their suitability for a particular trial. More specifically, jury vetting is a two-stage process. First, vetting involves the police checking potential jurors' records for previous criminal convictions (if any). Second, in limited circumstances, a further investigation by the security services may be required.

10.4.1 **Police vetting**

In *R v Sheffield Crown Court, ex parte Brownlow* [1980] QB 530, the Court of Appeal delivered a damning putdown of jury vetting. Both Lord Denning MR and Shaw LJ were adamant that it should not be introduced into English law, mainly on constitutional grounds. However, the Court of Appeal has subsequently endorsed the practice, in *R v Mason* [1981] QB 881. Lawton LJ stated that standard jury vetting by the police was necessary if only to ensure that disqualified persons – essentially those with criminal convictions – are excluded from juries.

He concluded that prosecutors may 'consider that a juror with a conviction for burglary would be unsuitable to sit on a jury trying a burglar; and if he does so he can exercise the Crown's rights [of stand by]. Many persons, but not burglars, would probably think that he should.'

10.4.2 Further vetting in 'exceptional cases'

In guidelines issued by the Attorney General in 1988, two 'exceptional types of case of public importance' are identified as justifying jury checks going beyond routine police investigation of criminal records. These are stated to be justified 'in the interests of both justice and the public'. They are:

- cases involving national security; and
- terrorism cases.

The particular aspects of these cases which may justify 'extra precautions' are: (a) in security cases a danger that a juror may make an 'improper use' of sensitive evidence; and (b) in both security and terrorism cases, the 'danger that a juror's political beliefs are so biased as to go beyond normally reflecting the broad spectrum of views and interests in the community, to reflect the extreme views of sectarian interest or pressure groups to a degree which might interfere with his fair assessment of the facts of the case or lead him to exert improper pressure on his fellow jurors'.

10.5 The ethnic composition of the jury

The Court of Appeal has turned down several claims to a 'right' to a multi-racial jury, stressing the overriding importance of random selection. The leading case is *R v Ford* [1989] QB 868, where Lord Lane CJ said that 'such a principle cannot be correct, for it would depend on an underlying premise that jurors of a particular racial origin or holding particular religious beliefs are incapable of giving an impartial verdict'. This is in line with the majority of earlier authorities on the point in which ethnic minority defendants were refused permission to have their all-white or predominantly white jury replaced or modified in order to ensure more ethnic minority jurors. In one such case, *R v Danvers* [1982] Crim LR 680, it was argued unsuccessfully that an all-white jury could not comprehend the mental and emotional atmosphere in which black families in England lived.

Two cases took a different view. *R v Binns & Others* [1982] Crim LR 522, 823 involved twelve young, male defendants, all but one of whom was of West Indian origin. The judge and the prosecution accepted the proposition that the jury should contain a reasonable proportion of black people. Eventually, a jury was sworn in containing one young man and two middle-aged women of West Indian origin and one young Asian man. All of the defendants were acquitted. *R v Thomas & Others* (1989) 88 Cr App R 370 involved four defendants of Afro-Caribbean origin charged with murder and wounding with intent. The alleged murder victim was white. The alleged wound-ing victim was African. When the Old Bailey jury appeared they were all-white. At the instigation of the defence, the trial judge ruled that he did have a power to stand by jurors in order to achieve a community balance, but that this power was to be 'used sparingly and in very exceptional circumstances'. He then ruled that the present case was not exceptional; the offences charged were not confined to the black community but could be and frequently were committed by all racial groups. He concluded by saying that he was not persuaded that 'an *à la carte* or specially selected jury' was required. However, both *R v Binns & Others* and *R v Thomas & Others* were disap-proved of in *R v Ford*, in the latter case for suggesting that judges had even an 'excep-tional' power to interfere with randomly selected juries to ensure a racial balance.

In 1993, the Runciman Commission recommended that in some cases race *should* be taken into account. It suggested that either counsel should be able to apply to the judge for a multi-racial (i.e. up to three people from ethnic minorities) jury. The judge would only grant this if the case had some special feature. More recently, in his *Review of the Criminal Courts of England and Wales*, Sir Robin Auld, a senior judge of the Criminal Division of the Court of Appeal, recommended that '[p]rovision should be made to enable ethnic minority representation on juries where race is likely to be relevant to an important issue in the case.' However, in its *Justice for All* White Paper (2002), the government rejected this proposal without explaining why it had done so other than to say that 'we have concluded that it would be wrong to interfere with the composition of the jury in these cases'. Objections can be advanced against the Runciman/Auld proposals on two grounds: (a) objections in principle; and (b) objec-tions in practice.

10.5.1 Objections in principle

On the first point it can be said that the Runciman/Auld proposals seem to presume that an all-white jury would be unable to return an unbiased verdict in a case involv-ing a defendant from a minority ethnic group (see the extract from the judgment in *Ford* earlier). Another objection is based on the 'floodgates' argument. Suppose that the law did allow black, Asian, or any ethnic minority defendant to request, or even demand, that an all-white jury be modified so as to include some ethnic minor-ity jurors. Would the law then be vulnerable to reform demands that other minority groups should have the same rights?

On this point, in *R v McCalla* [1986] Crim LR 335, the defendant, a young black man, was charged with conspiracy to rob. He applied for the jury to be 'racially balanced' or, alternatively, to have a minimum of two black members. The basis for the applica-tion was that only black jurors could fully appreciate the way in which the police treat young black people. Without such appreciation, he argued, he could not expect to receive a fair trial as the main thrust of his defence amounted to a challenge to the evidence of white police officers. This argument was rejected by the trial judge, who said that it would be wrong in principle to allow a defendant to stipulate the kind of jury to try him. If allowed in this case, the judge argued, it would be capable of 'infinite' extension to other minority groups, such as homosexuals, Freemasons, militant feminists, alcoholics, members of extreme political groups, and even criminals. The trial judge concluded that such a 'fundamental change' in the way juries are made up was not for judicial action but for Parliament.

10.5.2 Objections in practice

There are also practical objections to the proposals. Another reason given by the trial judge for rejecting the defendant's request in *R v McCalla* (1986) was that it would be impractical for the jury panel to be artificially enlarged in order to ensure that a 'proper' proportion of its members were black (or indeed from any minority ethnic group). Other practical objections relate to the details of the Auld proposal, which are set out in the questions on the Auld Review proposal next.

The Auld Review proposal

1   What does 'ethnic minority representation' actually mean?

2   Would an Afro-Caribbean defendant (for example) be entitled to Afro-Caribbean jurors, or would jurors of any ethnic minority group (i.e. not necessarily the same ethnic minority group as the defendant) suffice?

3   In which cases would it be that 'race is likely to be relevant'?

4   What test could be adopted to establish whether or not an issue is 'important'?

The Court of Appeal confirmed the correctness of the decision in *Ford* in *R v Smith (Lance Percival)* [2003] EWCA Crim 283, [2003] 1 WLR 2229. Smith, who was black, was charged with various offences including causing grievous bodily harm with intent. The alleged victim was white. The jury at Preston Crown Court was all-white. At trial, Smith did not raise any concerns about the jury but, after conviction, appealed that he had been denied a fair trial contrary to the guarantee of a fair trial in Article 6 of the European Convention on Human Rights. However, the Court of Appeal found that the trial was nevertheless fair. Giving judgment, Pill LJ said:

> We do not accept that it was unfair for the defendant to be tried by a randomly selected all-white jury or that the fair-minded and informed observer would regard it as unfair. We do not accept that, on the facts of this case, the trial could only be fair if members of the defendant's race were present on the jury. It was not a case where a consideration of the evidence required knowledge of the traditions or social circumstances of a particular racial group. The situation was an all too common one, violence late at night outside a club, and a randomly selected jury was entirely capable of trying the issues fairly and impartially. Public confidence is not impaired by the composition of this jury.

Pill LJ thought that the 'wider the experience of jurors and the deeper their wisdom the greater assistance it will give them in their deliberations', but this was not enough to make Smith's jury unfair.

> **Thinking point**
>
> At one point, Pill LJ states that '[i]t was not a case where a consideration of the evidence required knowledge of the traditions or social circumstances of a particular racial group.' Does this imply that, where a case did require such knowledge, that the outcome may be different? If so, in which cases might such knowledge be required?

10.6 Jury intimidation or 'tampering'

10.6.1 Juries in England and Wales

The problem of jury intimidation or tampering (or 'nobbling' as it is sometimes called) led to the suspension of jury trials for terrorist offences in Northern Ireland in 1973 (see 10.6.2). It has caused problems in England too. In 1982, several Old Bailey trials had to be stopped because of attempted 'tampering' – one after seven months. In 1984, jurors in the Brinks-Mat trial had to have police protection to and from the court and their telephone calls intercepted. In 1994, a four-month fraud trial at Southwark Crown Court was abandoned. Eventually, Parliament acted.

- Section 54 of the Criminal Procedure and Investigations Act 1996 allows for new prosecutions where 'tainted acquittals' are produced (that is, acquittals made by juries that had been intimidated). However, this provision has never been employed.

- Section 44 of the Criminal Justice Act 2003 allows the prosecution to apply to the court for a judge-only trial, which will be granted if two conditions are satisfied:

  - there is 'evidence of a real and present danger that jury tampering would take place' (s.44 (4)); and

  - the 'likelihood that [jury tampering] would take place would be so substantial as to make it necessary in the interests of justice for the trial to be conducted without a jury' (s.44 (5)).

Section 44 was invoked for the first time in England in *R v Twomey & Others* [2009] EWCA Crim 1035, [2010] 1 WLR 630. The case started with an armed robbery at Heathrow Airport in February 2004. In 2007, three men stood trial but after more than six months the number of jurors had dwindled to ten, and they were unable to reach a unanimous verdict. They were discharged and a retrial started in the summer of 2008, this time with four defendants. Some six months later, in December 2008, the prosecution informed the trial judge of evidence that approaches had been made to two of the jurors. The jury was again discharged and a second retrial ordered. At this point, the prosecution applied for that trial to be conducted without a jury. The trial judge accepted that a serious attempt at jury tampering had occurred. However, because of the importance of the issues raised, a senior circuit judge, Calvert-Smith J, was brought in to decide whether to invoke s.44. He found that there was a 'real and present danger' that jury tampering would happen again at the retrial. However, he also ruled a jury protection 'package' involving over thirty police officers and costing around £1.5million would reduce the risk of jury tampering to an acceptable level. He therefore rejected the application. The prosecution appealed and, in June 2009, the Court of Appeal held that both conditions in s.44 had been met and therefore allowed the appeal. The retrial was ordered to take place without a jury.

The standard of proof

The court said that, because s.44 applies to criminal proceedings, the criminal standard of proof had to be met for both conditions.

The Human Rights Act 1998 and the right to a fair trial

The Court of Appeal stated very clearly that ordering Crown Court trial by judge alone did not infringe the right to a fair trial by an independent and impartial tribunal, encapsulated by Article 6 of the European Convention. A judge-only trial ensured all of the necessary procedural safeguards would be met. Lord Judge CJ stated:

> [It] is important to emphasise that…the process of dispensing with a jury in a case where it is established that a jury trial is likely to be abused or subverted, the end result is not an unfair trial, but a trial by judge alone, where the necessary procedural safeguards available in a trial by jury are and remain available to the defendant. It therefore does not follow from the hallowed principle of trial by jury that trial by judge alone, when ordered, would be unfair or improperly prejudicial to the defendant. The trial would take place before an independent tribunal and, as it seems to us, for the purposes of article 6 of the European Convention for the Protection of Human Rights and Fundamental Freedoms, it is irrelevant whether the tribunal is judge and jury or judge alone.

The first condition: 'real and present danger'

Lord Judge CJ offered the following guidance on the operation of the first condition in s.44 (4), that there must be a 'real and present danger' that jury tampering may take place:

> The first condition addresses the risk that jury tampering may take place at any stage of the trial before the jury has returned their verdict. The real and present danger to be addressed therefore relates to the entire trial process. Where the court is sure that there is a real and present danger that the right to jury trial will be abused or misused by jury tampering, the first condition is established.

Applying these principles, Lord Judge CJ concluded that the first condition was 'emphatically established'.

The second condition: alternative measures to judge-only trial

The second condition in s.44 (5) requires that, after making due allowance for any reasonable steps which might minimise the danger of jury tampering, the judge should be sure that there would be a sufficiently high likelihood of jury tampering to make it necessary to have a trial by judge alone. On this issue, Lord Judge CJ referred to a case in the Northern Ireland Court of Appeal *R v Mackle & Others* [2008] NI 183, where s.44 had already been applied. That court had stated that 'the feasibility of measures, the cost of providing them, the logistical difficulties that they may give rise to, and the anticipated duration of any necessary precautions' were all relevant matters to be considered in deciding whether the second condition had been met. The court in *Mackle & Others* had further decided that it was relevant to consider whether the level of police protection required in order to counter the threat of jury tampering might 'affect unfavourably the way in which the jury approached its task. If a misguided perception was created in the minds of the jury by the provision of high level protection this would plainly sound on the reasonableness of such a step'. In *Twomey & Others*, Lord Judge CJ stated:

> We respectfully agree with this approach, and in the course of reaching our own conclusion, we examined some of the possible measures to ensure jury protection. We further examined their likely impact on the ordinary lives of the jurors, performing their public responsibilities, and considered whether, in some cases at any rate, even the most intensive protective measures for individual jurors would be sufficient to prevent the improper exercise of pressure on them through members of their families who would not fall within the ambit of the protective measures.

Lord Judge CJ concluded that the protection 'package' identified by Calvert-Smith J would not obviate the risk. A more extensive protection 'package' involving over eighty police officers and costing around £6million would be required, but even that did 'not sufficiently address the potential problem of interference with jurors through their families'. Lord Judge CJ stated that, even if it was accepted that the more extensive package dealt with 'the dangers posed to the integrity of trial by jury, it would be unreasonable to impose that package with its drain on financial resources and police manpower on the police, and, no less important, it would be totally unfair to impose the additional burdens consequent on the deployment of this package on individual jurors'. Therefore, the second condition was also established.

Defence rights to challenge the trial judge

The Criminal Justice Act 2003 allows the defence to make 'representations' to the trial judge when he or she is considering whether to discharge a jury and/or to proceed to judge-only trial in alleged jury tampering cases. Lord Judge CJ considered whether this right meant that the Crown had to disclose all of its evidence of jury tampering to the defence. The answer was no, because some of the evidence might be extremely sensitive. In Lord Judge's words, 'Experience suggests that the seriousness of jury tampering problems is usually proportionate to the seriousness of the alleged criminality' – meaning that jury tampering is more likely in cases involving organised crime and/or terrorism. Disclosing all of the Crown's evidence of jury tampering in such cases would be very dangerous for the wider community. Lord Judge CJ said:

> In short, the process [under s.44] could not apply where the actual or potential interference with the jury was of the most serious or sophisticated kind, and where, for example, disclosure of the evidence might imperil life or health or involve the disclosure of police operational evidence or methodology which, if disclosed, would be of considerable interest to the criminal world and damaging to the public interest. In such cases, faced with an order for disclosure, the Crown would be left with no alternative but to discontinue the prosecution. If so, the objective of the jury tampering would have succeeded. In short, therefore, we reject the submission that the evidence relied on by the Crown, or the bulk of it, must always be disclosed.

The implications for the trial judge

Lord Judge CJ also considered what a trial judge should do after having identified jury tampering, deciding that the provisions of s.44 are satisfied, and therefore discharging the jury. There were two options: (1) proceed directly to a judge-only trial with the same judge, or (2) terminate the trial (effectively forcing the CPS to bring a retrial, possibly in front of a different judge). Lord Judge CJ stated that the former option was preferable:

> [Given] that one of the purposes of [s.44] is to discourage jury tampering, and given also the huge inconvenience and expense for everyone involved in a re-trial, and simultaneously to reduce any possible advantage accruing to those who are responsible for jury tampering or for whose perceived benefit it has been arranged by others, and to ensure that trials should proceed to verdict rather than end abruptly in the discharge of the jury, save in unusual circumstances, the judge faced with this problem should order not only the discharge of the jury but that he should continue the trial.

This very issue arose subsequently, in *R v S* [2009] EWCA Crim 2377, [2010] 1 All ER 1084. The trial judge in that case had decided that, following evidence of jury tampering, the s.44 conditions were satisfied. He had discharged the jury but decided to continue as the judge in a judge-only trial. The appellant, S, had challenged that decision. The Court of Appeal in S allowed the appeal, but it did point out that the case was 'unusual' and 'indeed an extreme case'.

Twomey & Others: the aftermath

Following the Court of Appeal's ruling, the first Crown Court criminal trial in England and Wales without jurors for more than 350 years duly took place at the Old Bailey in

March 2010. At the end of the trial, Treacy J convicted all four defendants of robbery. Three of them were also convicted of possession of a firearm with intent to commit robbery. Appeals against conviction were subsequently dismissed by the Court of Appeal (*R v Twomey & Others* [2011] EWCA Crim 8, [2011] 1 WLR 1681) and the European Court of Human Rights (*Twomey & Others v UK* (2013) 57 EHRR SE15). The Strasbourg court noted that, although 'several' signatory states to the ECHR provided for jury trials, not all did so, and that 'there is no right under Article 6 of the Convention to be tried before a jury'. The Court stated that trial with a judge and jury, and trial with a judge alone, were 'two forms of trial which are in principle equally acceptable under Article 6'. For an excellent summary and discussion of the issues raised in *Twomey & Others* see Nick Taylor's case note in the *Criminal Law Review* ([2010] Crim LR 82).

In *R v J & Others* [2010] EWCA Crim 1755, [2011] 1 Cr App R 5, the Court of Appeal held that a trial judge's decision to order a judge-only trial was wrong, on the basis that the condition in s.44 (5) had not been met. The appeal court decided that, because the trial (for conspiracy to pervert the course of justice) was only estimated to last for two weeks, any protective measures needed to safeguard the jury against tampering would not 'impose an unacceptable burden on the jurors by intruding for a prolonged period on their ordinary lives'. Lord Judge CJ emphasised that judge-only trial must remain the 'decision of last resort' and hence that a trial judge had to be 'sure' that the conditions in the Act had been met.

In *R v Guthrie & Others* [2011] EWCA Crim 1338, [2011] 2 Cr App R 20, the four appellants were facing charges of six counts of conspiracy to defraud at Wood Green Crown Court in London. During deliberations, it emerged that jury tampering had taken place, albeit involving tampering carried out by a third party. Nevertheless the trial judge decided to discharge the jury and to continue the trial on her own. The appellants appealed, unsuccessfully, against that decision. In the Court of Appeal, Lord Judge CJ began by pointing out that the issues in a case like *R v Twomey* (2009) (where the trial judge has to decide whether a trial can *start* without a jury) and those in cases like *R v S* (2009) and the present case (where a jury has been discharged and the question was whether to *continue* without a jury) were 'not identical'. In the latter type of case, s.46 (3) of the Criminal Justice Act 2003 applied. This states that:

> Where the judge, after considering any such representations, discharges the jury, he may make an order that the trial is to continue without a jury if, but only if, he is satisfied (a) that jury tampering has taken place, and (b) that to continue the trial without a jury would be fair to the defendant or defendants.

Lord Judge CJ stated:

> Nothing in the legislation suggests that the trial judge who has made findings that the pre-conditions to the discharge of the jury and the continuation of the trial are satisfied must then recuse himself. Such a proposition would effectively extinguish the power created by s.46 (3). It would be strange if it were possible for a criminal or group of criminals to take extreme steps to undermine the process of trial by jury, and then to argue that judge who had made the necessary findings should not continue the trial.

Lord Judge CJ added that, although there were situations (for example where the trial judge had considered material on public interest immunity grounds which bore on the entire conduct of the prosecution) in which it might be right for the trial judge to disqualify him or herself, the 'normal approach' was that the case should continue with the same judge. The Court of Appeal also decided that the provisions in the 2003 Act were not limited to 'serious' criminal activity, nor were they confined to cases involving 'serious' intimidation. Finally, there was no need to ascribe responsibility for jury tampering to each, or indeed any, of the defendants in any given trial. The 2003 Act was concerned with the trial process, not the behaviour of the defendant (s). Applying these principles in *Guthrie & Others*, it was therefore irrelevant that:

- the charges faced by the appellants were not especially serious;
- the tampering did not involve 'serious' intimidation;
- the tampering had been carried out by a third party (in any case, a 'personal link' between the third party and one of the appellants was 'amply established').

10.6.2 **Criminal juries in Northern Ireland**

Between 1973 and 2007, all cases in Northern Ireland involving (or potentially involving) terrorism were heard by a single Crown Court judge without a jury. These were called 'Diplock courts' after Lord Diplock, who chaired the Commission that recommended this form of trial. The Northern Ireland (Emergency Provisions) Act 1973 (subsequently replaced by the Northern Ireland (Emergency Provisions) Act 1991 and most recently s.75 of the Terrorism Act 2000) created a presumption against jury trial in respect of various offences, including murder. Diplock courts were designed to deal primarily with the problems caused by sectarian 'troubles' involving Republican and Loyalist terrorism offences. Diplock courts were justified for two reasons:

- the threat of intimidation – not just of individual jurors but members of their family; and
- the danger of perverse verdicts by partisan jurors – for example, if a Catholic defendant was to be tried by a jury consisting predominantly of Protestant jurors (or vice versa).

Although designed as a means of allowing – as far as possible – unbiased trials involving, or potentially involving, crimes allegedly committed by organisations such as the IRA (Irish Republican Army) or the UDF (Ulster Defence Force), Diplock courts were used in other cases. In 2005, Abbas Boutrab, an Algerian national, was convicted by a single judge at Belfast Crown Court of possessing and collecting information 'for a purpose connected with the commission, preparation or instigation of an act of terrorism', contrary to s.57 of the Terrorism Act 2000. Boutrab had downloaded information from the internet on how to blow up a passenger jet. According to *The Times* newspaper, Boutrab's case was a landmark because he was the first 'Islamist terrorist' to be tried and convicted using the Diplock system.

In August 2006, however, the British government announced that Diplock courts were to be abolished for the majority of Crown Court trials in Northern Ireland, effective July 2007. According to the *Belfast Telegraph* in an article published in July 2007:

> [T]housands of cases have been tried using the [Diplock] system including the loyalist paramilitary gang, the Shankill Butchers, who were sentenced to life imprisonment in the 1970s for murdering Catholics in north and west Belfast. The number of trials being carried out at the courts has dropped dramatically over the last few years with just 61 cases last year and 49 in 2005.

However, according to a government consultation paper issued in August 2006 by the Northern Ireland Office (*Replacement Arrangements for the Diplock Court System*), judge-only trials are to be retained for 'exceptional' cases where juries could still be intimidated. The Director of Public Prosecutors will be authorised to decide which cases will be heard by a judge alone, with all other cases being heard by a jury, as in England and Wales. These reforms have now been implemented by the Justice and Security (Northern Ireland) Act 2007.

10.7 Juries in serious fraud trials

One area of jury trials that has attracted considerable attention in recent years is cases of serious fraud. By their very nature, allegations of fraud imply secrecy and deception. The issues involved in such cases tend to be very complex, with much accounting and financial information to be examined. There may also be several defendants. This all means that serious fraud trials are very time-consuming. The Roskill Committee (1986), the Home Office (1998), and Lord Justice Auld (2001) all examined the use of the jury in these cases, and all broadly concluded (the exact recommendations differed) that jury trials should be at least modified, if not entirely abolished, in serious fraud cases. The Home Office's 1998 consultation paper (*Juries in Serious Fraud Trials*) stated that a single judge offered a 'simple, viable alternative to jury trial' in 'long and complex fraud trials'. However, it also acknowledged that 'jurors could do a good job in complex fraud trials if they were selected in a special way'.

The Home Office proposed two such special selection processes: (a) 'some sort of screening procedure' for jurors; and (b) an 'entirely separate pool of jurors to be summoned exclusively to sit on serious fraud trials'. The latter proposal was acknowledged to be 'more radical and much more difficult'. The government observed that there was 'no lack of precedent for this'. It was observed that District Judges (Magistrates' Court) dealt with summary cases alone and that 'trial by judge alone is the general rule in civil cases in England'. Moreover, the government noted that 'the Northern Ireland experience' – meaning Diplock courts – 'provides an example of how such an arrangement can work...in relation to serious criminal offences'.

Lord Justice Auld's Review was more radical. It suggested that:

> in serious and complex frauds the nominated trial judge should have the power to direct trial by himself and two lay members drawn from a panel established by the Lord Chancellor for the purpose (or, if the defendant requests, by himself alone).

The panel would comprise of people identified as having expertise in financial matters – accountants, auditors, bankers, stockbrokers, and so on. Although this proposal retained some lay involvement in the trial process, it was a significant reduction from twelve randomly selected members of the public to only two people. Perhaps more significantly, this panel would not be deciding guilt or innocence on their own (as the present jury does) but would operate alongside the judge.

The Labour government's response, in the *Justice for All* White Paper (2002), accepted the principle of this idea but not the specific proposal. The government stated that 'identifying and recruiting suitable people raises considerable difficulties...we propose such cases are tried by a judge sitting alone'. Section 43 of the Criminal Justice Act 2003 implemented this latter proposal. It provided for judge-only trials where:

> [t]he complexity of the trial or the length of the trial (or both) is likely to make the trial so burdensome to the members of a jury hearing the trial that the interests of justice require that serious consideration should be given to the question of whether the trial should be conducted without a jury.

However, so controversial were the proposals that the Labour government only secured the approval of Parliament by agreeing not to implement s.43, unless Parliament was given a further opportunity to debate the issue. In the end, s.43 was never brought into effect and it has now been repealed, by s.113 of the Protection of Freedoms Act 2012. The Coalition government's explanatory notes accompanying the 2012 Act indicate that this repeal gave effect to their pledge to 'protect historic freedoms through the defence of trial by jury' ('Programme for Government': section 3: civil liberties).

Exclusion of juries from serious fraud trials: summary of the arguments

- Advantages: judge-alone trial saves time at trial because the judge does not have to explain so many matters to the jury. In theory, it should also lessen the risk of bias or outside influence. Judges are expected to explain and justify their decisions, unlike juries, who simply return a verdict of 'guilty' or 'not guilty'. Thus, where a judge reaches a guilty verdict, he or she must justify this decision with reasons; this provides greater transparency to the decision-making process and may give the defence an opportunity to consider an appeal which would not otherwise be possible.

- Disadvantages: judge-alone trial reduces the amount of lay participation in the legal system. There is the possibility that judges sitting alone would become 'case hardened' or 'prosecution-minded'. The extra burden on the judge may be too onerous. Although he or she would no longer have to direct the jury, the judge would now have to assimilate all the issues of fact *and* reach a verdict. The fact that judges are required to justify their decisions may open up new possibilities for expensive, time-consuming appeals.

10.8 **Jury waiver**

In his *Review of the Criminal Courts* (2001), Lord Justice Auld proposed that 'defendants in the Crown Court...should be entitled with the court's consent to opt for trial by judge alone'. This recommendation is known as 'jury waiver'. In many common law jurisdictions – Australia, Canada, New Zealand, and the US – where trial by jury exists, the defendant may nevertheless waive their 'right' to jury trial and instead opt for trial by a single judge. In *R v Turpin & Siddiqui* [1989] 1 SCR 1296, for example, Wilson J in the Supreme Court of Canada stated that a 'jury trial may not be a benefit and may even be a burden on the accused'. The obvious question to raise in response to this is, why would a defendant entitled to jury trial waive that right? According to the commentators S. Doran and J. Jackson ('The Case for Jury Waiver' [1997] Crim LR 155) there are three reasons:

- The notion of a jury as 'defence friendly' is outdated. Although juries may acquit against the evidence, there is a 'worrying phenomenon' of doubtful convictions.

- Judges may be better equipped to analyse certain kinds of evidence. In particular, juries are 'in awe' of scientific evidence and are 'neither willing nor qualified' to be critical of such evidence.

- Judges may be better equipped to handle certain types of issues than juries. A 'common view' among defence counsel was that sexual cases were 'difficult' to defend in front of a jury; they would prefer the case to be dealt with in a 'colder, unemotional fashion'.

Other possibilities involve cases where the defendant could appear unsympathetic or where the evidence was potentially inflammatory (for example, child abuse) or gruesome, where the jury might be shocked into a guilty verdict. Jury waiver may also be appropriate in cases that have attracted pre-trial publicity (especially publicity that was adverse to the accused). Recent examples in England and Wales of such cases include:

- Rose West, convicted of the 'Cromwell Street' murders of ten young women and girls, including her own 16-year-old daughter Heather;

- Tracey Andrews, convicted of her boyfriend's murder after publicly claiming he had been murdered in a 'road rage' incident by a stranger; and

- Dr Harold Shipman, Britain's most prolific serial killer (now deceased).

In many of these cases – including Rose West and Tracey Andrews – the defendants appealed against their convictions arguing that the adverse, pre-trial publicity prejudiced the jury against them and therefore denied them a fair trial. In all such cases the appeals were dismissed, the Court of Appeal taking the view that warnings given to the respective juries by the trial judges had ensured that justice had been done. In *R v West* [1996] 2 Cr App R 374, for example, Lord Taylor CJ stated that it would be 'absurd' if allegations of murder were 'sufficiently horrendous so as inevitably to shock the nation' that the accused could not be given a fair trial. Of course, no-one argues that the defendants should not be tried at all purely because the case has attracted publicity – but does it follow that jury trials will be fair?

A more recent Court of Appeal case dealing with pre-trial publicity is *R v Abu Hamza* [2006] EWCA Crim 2918, [2007] 2 WLR 226. The case involved Abu Hamza, the imam of Finsbury Park Mosque in north London, who was convicted in February 2006 of six counts of soliciting murder (in addition to a number of other offences). On appeal, it was argued that Abu Hamza had not received a fair trial, because of 'changes in attitude and public perception in relation to terrorism' following the attacks on New York on 11 September 2001 and London on 7 July 2005. It was contended that the adverse pre-trial media publicity meant that Abu Hamza's trial was unfair. It was argued that the media had led a 'sustained campaign' which was 'almost entirely hostile' and 'couched in particularly crude terms'. However, the appeal was dismissed. Lord Phillips CJ acknowledged that there had been a 'prolonged barrage' of adverse publicity, some of which treated the defendant as 'an ogre'. However, the Lord Chief Justice accepted the trial judge's conclusion that a properly directed jury would be able to return an impartial verdict. Abu Hamza had received a fair trial.

The government agreed with Lord Justice Auld's proposal to introduce jury waiver into English law. The government's *Justice for All* White Paper (2002) stated that 'defendants in the Crown Court should in future have the right to apply to the court for trial by a judge sitting alone. The judge will have discretion whether to grant the application and will have to give reasons for this decision.' The subsequent Criminal Justice Bill, when introduced into Parliament in 2002, stated that if defendants were to apply for waiver, the judge 'must' grant it, subject to a proviso. The judge would be entitled to refuse if 'satisfied that exceptional circumstances exist which make it necessary in the public interest for the trial to be conducted with a jury'. However, by the time the Criminal Justice Act 2003 was passed, the jury waiver reform had been dropped following opposition from Parliament, primarily in the House of Lords. At the time of writing, there seems little political incentive to try again to implement jury waiver.

Thinking point

1. Should the defendant faced with the prospect of trial by jury in the Crown Court be allowed to 'waive' that right? If so, should this be with the consent of the court, the prosecution, both, or neither (in which case it would effectively be 'waiver on demand')?

2. Can you think of any circumstances where the prosecution may object to a defendant seeking to 'waive' trial by jury?

3. When might the judge decide that 'exceptional circumstances...in the public interest' (to use the terminology from the Criminal Justice Bill 2002/03) would justify rejecting a plea for jury waiver and, effectively, forcing a reluctant defendant to face a jury?

10.9 **Jurors, social media, and the internet**

Section 8 (1) of the Contempt of Court Act 1981 states that 'it is a contempt of court to obtain, disclose or solicit any particulars of statements made, opinions expressed, arguments advanced or votes cast by members of a jury in the course of their deliberations in any legal proceedings'. This provision has already been discussed (in 10.1.3) in the context of its effect on the criminal appeal courts' ability to hear appeals based on alleged irregularities during the jury's deliberations (see in particular *R v Qureshi* and *R v Mirza*). However, a number of recent cases have examined s.8 in a very different context. These cases have highlighted the risks that jurors face of infringing s.8 if they either discuss a case on social media or conduct their own online research of the case.

In *Attorney General v Fraill & Sewart* [2011] EWHC 1629 (Admin), [2011] 2 Cr App R 21, Joanne Fraill had been a juror in a drugs trial at Minshull Street Crown Court, Manchester. At the start of the trial, the judge gave the jury an unequivocal direction that they must not use the internet 'to explore any issues which may arise'. He reminded the jurors of their obligation to decide the case 'solely on what you hear in the courtroom and upon nothing else'. One of the defendants, Jamie Sewart, was subsequently acquitted, although the trial continued in relation to the other defendants. That night, Fraill contacted Sewart on Facebook and, at Sewart's request, provided her with information about the jury's deliberations. The next day, Sewart informed her solicitor about the conversation on Facebook and the information was relayed to the trial judge, who decided that the jury had to be discharged, forcing a retrial to be arranged for the remaining defendants. Both Fraill and Sewart were subsequently convicted of being in contempt of court – Fraill for disclosing, and Sewart for soliciting, information about the jury's deliberations. Lord Judge CJ explained the applicable principles of law when he said:

> If jurors make their own inquiries into aspects of the trials with which they are concerned, the jury system as we know it, so precious to the administration of criminal justice in this country, will be seriously undermined, and what is more, the public confidence on which it depends will be shaken. The jury's deliberations, and ultimately their verdict,

must be based – and exclusively based – on the evidence given in court…The revolution in methods of communication cannot change these essential principles…Information provided by the internet (or any other modern method of communication) is not evidence. Even assuming the accuracy and completeness of this information (which, in reality, would be an unwise assumption) its use by a juror exposes him to the risk of being influenced, even unconsciously, by whatever emerges from the internet. This offends our long-held belief that justice requires that both sides in a criminal trial should know and be able to address or answer any material (particularly material which appears adverse to them) which may influence the verdict.

Commenting on the case in the *Criminal Law Review* ([2012] Crim LR 286), A.T.H. Smith stated that imposing contempt liability following a jurors' internet use had advanced the law by the 'crystallisation of underlying principles into a new rule. Jurors who flout a clear judicial instruction not to conduct their own research on the net are liable to sanctions that might include a period of imprisonment.'

In *Attorney General v Dallas* [2012] EWHC 156 (Admin), [2012] 1 WLR 991, Theodora Dallas, a Greek national but UK resident since 1996, had been a juror in the trial at Luton Crown Court of a man (Barry Medlock) for causing GBH with intent. The jurors had watched a video about their responsibilities and been told that they could not research the case or Medlock on the internet; there were notices in the jury rooms warning jurors that they could be in contempt of court if they did so. However, during the trial, Dallas conducted internet research about the case and disclosed the results of that research to her fellow jurors. Some of them objected to her doing so, and one of them raised the matter with court staff. Consequently the jury was discharged and Medlock was retried. Meanwhile, Dallas was charged with contempt of court. Dallas admitted that during the trial she had researched the meaning of grievous bodily harm on the internet, and then searched for the area in which the offence was alleged to have taken place, and then happened upon an online newspaper article regarding Medlock. In evidence, Dallas stated that she had not fully understood the warnings given to the jury, partly because English was not her first language, and had not realised that the trial judge was saying that she was not to do research on the internet *at all*. Despite her pleas, she was convicted. Lord Judge CJ stated that 'she did not merely risk prejudice to the due administration of justice, but she caused prejudice to it…The damage to the administration of justice is obvious.' This 'damage' manifested itself in at least five different ways, according to Lord Judge. First, the information which Dallas found online, although not adduced in evidence, might have played its part in her verdict. Second, when she disclosed some or all of that information to her fellow jurors. Third, the complainant had to give evidence of his ordeal again, at the retrial. Fourth, the time of the other members of the jury was wasted. Finally, the public was put to additional unnecessary expense in paying for the retrial.

In *Attorney General v Davey & Beard* [2013] EWHC 2317 (Admin); [2014] 1 Cr App R 1, the High Court examined two separate cases. The facts of *Davey* appear in the

Talking point at the start of this chapter. In *Beard*, one of the jurors in a fraud trial at Kingston Crown Court told one of the other jurors that he had conducted research on the internet about the case and related the information to him. That juror reported this to the court clerk, who told the judge, who discharged the whole jury. By this point the trial was into its sixth week, with total costs in excess of £300,000 already incurred. Both jurors were convicted of contempt of court. *Davey* therefore confirms *Fraill* whilst *Beard* confirms *Dallas*: if a juror uses the internet either to discuss or research an ongoing case then he or she faces their own criminal liability for contempt of court.

Thinking point

Do you agree that it is 'contempt' of court for jurors to discuss a case with their (Facebook) friends? Is is a 'contempt' of court for jurors to conduct their own research into a case or the issues involved in it? If you agree that it is 'contempt' in either or both situations, is criminal liability appropriate in such cases?

10.10 Advantages of jury trials

10.10.1 Public participation

Juries allow the ordinary citizen to take part in the administration of justice, so that verdicts are seen to be those of society rather than the judicial system. Lord Denning has described jury service as giving 'ordinary folk their finest lesson in citizenship'. According to W. R. Cornish, *The Jury* (1968 at p.255):

> The system has the intrinsic advantage that in drawing upon a steady stream of ordinary citizens it is not only educating them in the work of the courts, but also, since they are generally satisfied with their own performance, sending them back to their ordinary lives with a sense of the fairness and propriety of the judicial process in this country.

A Home Office consultation paper, *Juries in Serious Fraud Trials* (1998), postulated that the presence of members of the public on juries offered 'reassurance that the defendant's guilt or innocence is not being determined by the State…public involvement in the justice system is the sign of a healthy and democratic society'. Perhaps slightly optimistically – one might even say naively – it was asserted that ' [n]ot only is the quality of justice improved by the participation of the public but the community is enriched by it…jury trials keep the law in touch with the public and encourage the lawmakers to take account of their wishes.'

The alternative viewpoint has been put forward very forcefully by Darbyshire (1991 at p.746). She argued that this 'romanticism' about juries was 'quite devoid of constitutional or jurisprudential support'. She suggested that 'most of those who justify the jury as the quintessence of lay participation in a lawyer's paradise ignore the massive involvement of lay people' – meaning magistrates – in decision-making in the English legal system.

10.10.2 Juries are the best judges of facts

There is an argument that jurors (being, in the main, ordinary members of the public) are better equipped than judges or magistrates to assess issues such as the credibility of witnesses and whether the defendant in a theft trial was dishonest. Many defences in criminal law involve a 'reasonable man' test – diminished responsibility, duress, self-defence...who better to undertake this task than jurors? As most jurors only serve once, they should approach their cases relatively fresh and with an open mind; unlike judges and magistrates who are vulnerable to the argument that they can become 'case hardened' – meaning that they can become cynical, having heard similar arguments in similar cases perhaps over many years. Furthermore, there is a 'strength in numbers' argument or, put another way, twelve heads are better than three (magistrates) or one (judge). Weight of numbers arguably helps to minimise the possible risks of prejudicial views influencing the verdict.

10.10.3 Clear separation of responsibility

It has been argued that juries provide a better balance to proceedings in the trial courts, dividing the responsibilities of the trial into those who determine the law (the judge) and those who determine the facts (the jury).

10.10.4 Encourages openness and intelligibility

Because a jury is comprised of randomly-selected members of the public, the lawyers (especially those acting for the prosecution) have to present their evidence in a manner which the jury can understand. After all, the burden of proof in most matters of criminal law is on the prosecution (the main exceptions being the insanity and diminished responsibility defences), and to get a conviction the Crown needs to persuade the jury of the defendant's guilt 'beyond reasonable doubt'. In other words, if the jury are confused and do not understand the prosecution case, how can the jury be convinced of the defendant's guilt? Because of this, it should follow that the general public – who may be watching the trial from the public gallery or hearing about the trial on the TV or reading about it in the newspapers – are better able to understand what is going on. There is a risk that replacing the jury either with a single judge, a panel of judges, or some other alternative will encourage the lawyers to present their case in a more specialised, technical way with more legal jargon. This would in turn mean that trials may no longer be readily comprehensible to the public.

10.11 **Disadvantages**

10.11.1 **Cost and time**

Jury trials are much more expensive than trial by magistrates. It has been estimated that an uncontested case in the Crown Court costs five times as one in the magistrates' court, while a contested Crown Court case costs around eight times as much. Why is there such a dramatic cost disparity? The main reason is time: jury trials are much lengthier than trial by magistrates. The time factor leads to other disadvantages: defendants may spend months on remand awaiting a Crown Court trial, and it can also lead to witnesses' recollection of the events getting weaker. Not everyone agrees that the extra cost and time is a disadvantage, however. According to Heather Hallett QC (*Counsel*, October 1998, p.3): 'A jury trial is superior to a trial before magistrates and there is a greater chance of seeing justice done at the Crown Court than at the magistrates' court, if only because greater time, trouble and money are spent on jury trials.'

10.11.2 **Risk of perverse verdicts**

Excessive damages awards in civil actions

There are numerous examples of juries in civil trials in the High Court awarding large sums of money in compensation which are often contested and, sometimes, reversed on appeal. The leading cases all involve defamation, where the claimant seeks compensation for damage to their reputation caused by the publication of an untrue statement about them. The leading cases are:

- *Sutcliffe v Pressdram Ltd* [1990] 1 All ER 269 – in which Sonia Sutcliffe, the wife of Peter Sutcliffe, the Yorkshire Ripper, was awarded £600,000 against the publishers of *Private Eye* magazine which had published an article suggesting that she had been paid £250,000 by the *Daily Mail* for her story. She denied this claim and sought compensation. The jury's award was overturned on appeal; subsequently, Mrs Sutcliffe accepted £60,000 in out-of-court settlement.

- *Rantzen v Mirror Group Newspapers* [1993] 4 All ER 975 – in which Esther Rantzen, the erstwhile TV presenter and founder of the ChildLine charity, was awarded £250,000 against the publishers of *The People* newspaper for a series of articles which alleged that, despite her knowing that a boys' schoolteacher in Kent was guilty of sexually abusing children, she had nevertheless protected him because of his past services to her in assisting in the preparation of a TV programme about the sexual abuse of children. The award was overturned on appeal; the Court of Appeal substituting an award of £110,000. Neill LJ said that, ' [j]udged by any objective standards of reasonable compensation or necessity or proportionality the award of £250,000 was excessive.'

- *John v Mirror Group Newspapers* [1996] 2 All ER 35 – in which Elton John was awarded £350,000 against the publishers of *Sunday Mirror* newspaper. He had sued in respect of allegations made in the *Sunday Mirror* under the headline 'Elton's diet of death' that he was on a fad diet called 'Don't swallow and get thin', whereby he chewed food but spat it out instead of swallowing it. In particular, there were specific allegations that he had been spotted spitting food into a napkin at a dinner in Los Angeles. The jury's award was overturned on appeal, with the Court of Appeal awarding £75,000. The Court described the jury's awards as 'manifestly excessive'. Lord Bingham MR said that it was 'offensive to public opinion, and rightly so, that a defamation plaintiff should recover damages for injury to reputation greater, perhaps by a significant factor, than if that same plaintiff had been rendered a helpless cripple or an insensate vegetable'. He added that the time had come 'when judges, and counsel, should be free to draw the attention of juries to these comparisons'.

In *Grobbelaar v News Group Newspapers* [2002] UKHL 40, [2002] 1 WLR 3024, the Court of Appeal took the apparently unprecedented step of reversing a High Court jury's verdict in a defamation case as to liability – not just on the amount of damages. *The Sun* newspaper had published a series of articles in which it claimed that Bruce Grobbelaar, the former Liverpool FC goalkeeper, had fixed football matches for money. The allegations were based on covert video recordings in which Grobbelaar appeared to have confessed to having taken money to 'throw' matches. Grobbelaar was subsequently prosecuted on two counts of corruptly attempting to influence the outcomes of matches. He admitted the comments captured on video were true, but claimed that he had done so as a ruse to help bring those paying the bribes to justice. The Crown Court jury could not agree on a verdict. A retrial was ordered and this time the jury acquitted on one count, and failed to agree on the other, whereby a second not guilty verdict was entered.

Grobbelaar then began defamation proceedings against the publishers of *The Sun*. At the end of the trial, the High Court jury found for the claimant and awarded £85,000 damages. *The Sun's* publishers appealed, inter alia, on the ground that the verdict was perverse. Simon Brown LJ said that the Court of Appeal 'must inevitably be reluctant to find a jury's verdict perverse and anxious not to usurp their function' but that 'the experience of all of us that juries from time to time do arrive at perverse verdicts'. He went on to hold that the decision of the High Court jury was 'not merely surprising but unacceptable'; the result was 'an affront to justice'. Thorpe LJ agreed, saying that 'it would be an injustice' to allow the jury's verdict to stand.

On Grobbelaar's appeal to the House of Lords the Court of Appeal judgment was reversed, and that of the jury reinstated (mostly). The Lords ruled that the task of an appellate court was to seek to interpret the jury's decision and not to take upon itself the determination of factual issues. In the case, there was no justification for concluding that the jury must have acted 'perversely' in making its finding and so the jury's verdict that Grobbelaar had been defamed was reinstated. However, the Lords also ruled that the jury had fallen into serious error in its approach to the amount of damages. Grobbelaar had in fact acted in a way in which no decent or honest footballer would act and which could, if not exposed and stamped on, undermine the integrity of the game. It would be an affront to justice if a court of law were to award substantial damages to a man shown to have acted in such flagrant breach of his legal and moral obligations. Accordingly, the jury's award of damages was quashed and an award of £1 nominal damages substituted.

Criminal trials

Juries can, and do, return verdicts against the evidence (*R v Ponting* [1985] Crim LR 318, discussed earlier, is an example). A study by S. McCabe and R. Purves in 1972, *The Jury at Work* looked at 173 acquittals, and concluded that only fifteen (9 per cent) defied the evidence (the rest being down to a weak prosecution case, and/or a credible defence). In 1979, however, another study by J. Baldwin and M. McConville, *Jury Trials*, which examined 500 cases (both convictions and acquittals) found that 25 per cent of the acquittals were questionable. They described jury trial as 'an arbitrary and unpredictable business'. While there is evidence suggesting that jurors acquit at a higher rate than magistrates do, this *may* be down to magistrates convicting more innocent people that jurors acquitting more guilty ones.

P. Darbyshire ('The Lamp that Shows Freedom Lives' [1991] Crim LR 740), is very critical of this facet of the jury system, in particular the way that it is held up by defenders of the jury as an advantage. She asks (at p.750) 'What business have the jury to be rewriting the law?...The jury is an anti-democratic, irrational and haphazard legislator, whose erratic and secret decisions run counter to the rule of law.' She was particularly scathing about the reaction other commentators gave to a case when a hot-dog seller was acquitted by a 'sympathetic' jury on a charge of wounding on the ground of provocation – which is, as a matter of law, not a defence to that crime. One such commentator had suggested that the jury 'were saying...that provocation ought to be a defence' to wounding, 'and in saying this they would have the support of the bulk of the nation' (M. D. A. Freedman 'The Jury on Trial' (1981) 34 *Current Legal Problems* 65 at p.93). Darbyshire retorted by asking how could the jury, or anyone else for that matter, know what the 'bulk of the nation' wants? Instead, she supported the following assessment by P. Duff and M. Findlay ('The Jury in England: Practice and Ideology' (1982) 10 IJLS 253 at p.258): 'The jury, so irrationally selected, would appear to be a crude engine for the job of checking unpopular laws...The jury then may even be counterproductive in such situations, as the legislature may not feel constrained to intervene if they know that harsh or outdated laws are not being strictly applied.' If a jury can acquit despite the evidence, Darbyshire points out, then what is to stop them convicting despite the evidence? The answer is, of course, nothing.

Thinking point

In his *Review of the Criminal Courts* (2001), Sir Robin Auld recommended that '[t]he law should be declared, by statute if need be, that juries have no right to acquit defendants in defiance of the law or in disregard of the evidence.' The government in its response did not adopt this recommendation. Should juries be required, as Auld LJ suggested, to comply with the law? In other words, should 'jury equity' be abolished by Parliament?

10.11.3 Racist jurors in criminal trials

Article 6 of the ECHR confers the right to a fair trial by an impartial tribunal. This provision has been invoked in two cases before the European Court of Human Rights in Strasbourg where at least one juror has faced an accusation of racism: *Gregory v UK* (1998) 25 EHRR 577 and *Sander v UK* (2001) 31 EHRR 44. In *Gregory*, where one juror alleged – during the course of the trial – that other jurors had been making racist comments and jokes, which was collectively denied by the others, the trial judge allowed the trial to continue albeit after warning the jurors to remember their oath to try the case according to the evidence. The Strasbourg court held that the applicant's Article 6 rights had not been infringed. However, a very different result occurred in *Sander*. Here, after similar allegations, one juror admitted he may have made racist comments but denied actually *being* racist. The judge allowed the trial – albeit again after reminding the jurors of their oath – to continue and Sander was convicted. But his appeal to the Strasbourg court was successful (albeit by a majority verdict). The Court held that the trial judge should have discharged the jury and held a retrial. The difference in the two cases appears to be that in *Gregory* there was only an unsubstantiated allegation of racism whereas in *Sander* one juror did admit making racist comments.

It seems that the timing of allegations of racism is critical. In both *Gregory* and *Sander*, the juror involved raised the allegations during the trial and the appeals related to the judge's response to them. However, when allegations of racism are made after a verdict, it is much more difficult to investigate. You should refer back to the cases of *R v Qureshi* [2001] EWCA 1807, [2002] 1 WLR 518, and *R v Mirza* [2004] UKHL 2, [2004] 2 WLR 201, in which the Court of Appeal and House of Lords, respectively, declared themselves unable to investigate post-verdict allegations of jury impropriety, including allegations of racism. The guilty verdicts in both cases were upheld.

Thinking point

Is the decision in Sander compatible with the outcomes in the cases of Qureshi and Mirza, discussed earlier? If there is evidence of jury prejudice, should it matter whether the evidence was raised during the trial (as in Sander) or afterwards (as in Qureshi and Mirza)?

10.11.4 **Compulsory jury service**

While research has shown that many people find jury service a rewarding experience, others may have a negative attitude towards service. This may be because some people see jury service as an obligation rather than a privilege. It may be regarded by some jurors as time-consuming, inconvenient, and even financially disadvantageous. These attitudes may lead to people seeking excusal or deferral. Those who are unsuccessful in getting their jury service excused or deferred may then be resentful, and not take their responsibility seriously enough, or try to get the deliberations over with as quickly as possible. For an example of a case where this may have happened, refer back to *Attorney General v Scotcher* [2004] UKHL 36, [2005] 1 WLR 1867, discussed earlier.

10.11.5 **Distress caused to jury members**

Especially in murder, rape, and child abuse cases, the jury has to hear and, sometimes, see, very graphic and potentially distressing evidence. After Rosemary West's murder trial in 1995, some jury members were offered professional counselling. In *R v Wagner & Bunting*, the notorious Australian 'Snowtown' murders case in 2002, otherwise known as the 'Bodies in Barrels' murders, the evidence was so gruesome that three of the original jury dropped out, unable to cope with the evidence of sadistic torture and killing. Some of the jurors in South Australia's Supreme Court who did make it through to the end (and delivered guilty verdicts) had to receive counselling afterwards.

During his summing up at the end of the trial of the 'M25' rapist, Antoni Imiela, at Maidstone Crown Court in 2004, the trial judge told the jury to put aside feelings of 'revulsion, distress or dismay' and to decide their verdict in a 'calm and dispassionate manner'. He concluded that it was 'essential that you come to your decision based on the facts with your judgment unclouded and not distorted by emotions'. After deliberating, the jury returned seven guilty verdicts of rape.

More recently, at the start of the murder trial of Canadian pig-farmer Robert William Pickton in January 2007, accused of abducting and murdering six prostitutes and then feeding their remains to his pigs, the trial judge in British Columbia's Supreme Court had to warn the jury that their task would be grisly. He said that 'where evidence is particularly distressing, there is a concern that it may arise feelings of revulsion and hostility, and that can overwhelm the objective and impartial approach jurors are expected to bring to their task. You should be aware of that possibility and make sure it does not happen to you.' Pickton was eventually convicted of six counts of second-degree murder in December 2007.

10.11.6 **Lacking skill?**

Lord Denning MR once suggested that jurors should not be selected at random but should be selected in much the same way that magistrates are, with interviews and references required. This would, he thought, improve the decision-making skills of the jury as a whole. However, such a system would obviously be more time-consuming and expensive than the present system. There is also the danger that a jury capable of satisfying such a selection process would be self-selecting – more intelligent, better-educated people are likely to be drawn from a narrower socio-economic group than the population as a whole. Introducing a selection process would also appear to run counter to the government's policy in recent years to widen the pool of jurors as much as possible.

Summary

- The main use of the jury in the English legal system is for trial on indictment in the Crown Court. Civil juries are rare.

- The role of juries in criminal trials is to determine issues of fact and deliver a verdict. Juries cannot be directed to convict, nor must they be pressurised into returning a verdict. Juries are entitled to return a not guilty verdict, even if this appears to be in defiance of the law and/or evidence – this is 'jury equity'.

- The deliberations of the jury are secret and alleged irregularities which occur during them cannot form the basis of an appeal against conviction (*R v Mirza*). However, the situation is different if extraneous matters may have influenced the jury's verdict.

- The jury's verdict does not have to be unanimous – majority verdicts are allowed.

- The rules as to eligibility are contained in s.1 of the Juries Act 1974, but these rules were significantly amended by s.321 of the Criminal Justice Act 2003. Previously, the judiciary (including magistrates), lawyers, the police, and clergy (among others) were ineligible. Now, only the mentally disordered are ineligible. The fact that lawyers and police officers can serve on juries has been challenged in litigation which has reached the House of Lords (*R v Abdroikov & Others* (2007)) and the European Court of Human Rights (*Hanif & Khan v UK* (2012)).

- Various people are disqualified from jury service (e.g. people in prison) and others are entitled to be excused (e.g. members of the armed forces).

- Juries are selected from the electoral register. Both prosecution and defence have the right to challenge all or any of the jurors 'for cause', but the core principle in England and Wales is of random selection. This may be contrasted with the 'voir dire' system used in the United States.

- There is no 'right' to have the ethnic composition of a jury modified, although the introduction of such a 'right' has been proposed as a possible reform of jury trials.

- In cases of jury 'tampering' it is possible for a trial involving an indictable offence to be heard in a Crown Court by a judge acting alone, under s.44 of the Criminal Justice Act 2003, subject to stringent conditions being satisfied. 'Judge-only' trials do not infringe the right to a fair trial in Article 6 of the European Convention of Human Rights (*Twomey & Others v UK* (2013)).

- Section 43 of the Criminal Justice Act 2003 provided that serious fraud trials should be heard by a judge alone and not by a jury. However, this option was never brought into effect and has now been repealed by the Protection of Freedoms Act 2012.

- One option which exists in other countries is 'jury waiver', where the accused may opt out of jury trial. However, this is not an option in England and Wales.

- Jurors who discuss an ongoing case using social media and/or who conduct their own internet research into an ongoing case face criminal liability for contempt of court. The core principle here is that jurors must reach their verdict based only on the evidence heard in court.

? Questions

1 What are the eligibility criteria for jury membership under the Juries Act 1974?

2 Following the reforms introduced in the Criminal Justice Act 2003, which people are disqualified from jury service, and which people are entitled to be excused from jury service?

3 What rights do the prosecution and defence have at the outset of a Crown Court trial to challenge prospective jurors, either with or without cause?

4 In which circumstances may the prosecution apply for a Crown Court trial without a jury?

5 In which circumstances may a trial judge modify the ethnic composition of a Crown Court jury?

6 What is meant by 'jury vetting'?

✳ Sample question and outline answer

Question

In passing the Criminal Justice Act 2003, Parliament abolished most of the categories of persons either ineligible for, disqualified from or entitled to be excused from jury service. It was quite right to do this: after all, juries are supposed to reflect the public's involvement in the criminal justice system. Discuss.

Outline answer

Answers should briefly explain what 'jury service' means, especially in the context of the 'criminal justice system': i.e. twelve members of the public, randomly selected to decide guilt or innocence in a Crown Court trial.

Describe the basic eligibility rules (as set out in the Juries Act 1974): Minimum/maximum age limits; five-year residency in the UK (but not necessarily nationality); registration on the electoral roll.

Describe the ineligibility/disqualification/excusal rules prior to the CJA 2003: judges, magistrates, lawyers, police, clergy, mentally ill, etc. ineligible; certain criminals and people on bail disqualified; MPs, MEPs, peers, doctors, dentists, vets, armed forces, those with previous jury service, and those aged over 65 entitled to automatic excusal. Comment on the reasons for these rules: important jobs, possible bias, ability to influence other jurors, etc.

Explain the post-CJA 2003 legal landscape: only the mentally ill are ineligible; little change to disqualification; only those with previous jury service and armed forces entitled to be excused. Comment on the reasons for the changes: to produce a more representative jury by getting more middle-class professionals (judges, lawyers, police, doctors, etc.) involved; to reduce the likelihood of the same people being selected more than once because of a larger 'pool' of potential jurors, etc.

Discuss the post-CJA case law involving police officers, prison officers, and CPS employees on juries: *R v Abdroikov & Others* (2007), House of Lords; *R v I* (2007), Court of Appeal; *R v Khan & Others* (2008), Court of Appeal; *R v L* (2011), Court of Appeal; *Hanif & Khan v UK* (2012), European Court of Human Rights. Observe, for example, that in *Hanif & Khan* the ECHR stated that the defendant's right to a fair trial would be violated where a police officer on the jury was 'personally acquainted' with a police officer giving evidence on behalf of the prosecution, at least where there was an 'important conflict' about this evidence, which is ostensibly a narrow ruling. However, the Court seems to imply that the presence of any police officer on a jury might violate Article 6 ECHR.

Reach a conclusion as to whether or not the UK Parliament was 'quite right' to change the eligibility/disqualification rules.

Further reading

- **Corker, D.** 'Trying Fraud Cases without Juries' [2002] Crim LR 283

  This article explores a number of issues around the idea of 'judge-only' trials in fraud cases, such as the complex safeguards that would be required, and might help the reader to understand why s.43 of the Criminal Justice Act 2003 was never brought into force (and has now been repealed).

- **Crosby, K.** 'Controlling Devlin's Jury: What the Jury Thinks, and What the Jury Sees Online' [2012] Crim LR 15

  Analyses the ability of the criminal justice system to 'control' jurors (i.e. stop them from conducting their own research into a case) in a society where internet use is so prevalent.

- **Darbyshire, P.** 'The Lamp that Shows that Freedom Lives – Is it Worth the Candle?' [1991] Crim LR 740

  In which the author offers a powerful critique of 'jury equity'.

- **Doran, S.** and **Jackson, J.** 'The Case for Jury Waiver' [1997] Crim LR 155

  Presents arguments in favour of introducing into the English legal system an option for defendants to 'waive' their 'right' to jury trial in the Crown Court.

- **Hungerford-Welch, P.** 'Police Officers as Jurors' [2012] Crim LR 320

  Analyses the background to the Criminal Justice Act 2003 reforms on eligibility and the leading cases since, including *Abdroikov & Others* and *Hanif & Khan*.

- **Quinn, K.** 'Jury Bias and the European Convention on Human Rights: A well-kept secret?' [2004] Crim LR 998

  Assesses the principle of 'confidentiality' of jury deliberations and its compatibility with Article 6 ECHR, the right to a fair trial, as seen in cases such as *Mirza*, *Gregory*, and *Sander*.

- **Thornton, P.** 'Trial by Jury: 50 Years of Change' [2004] Crim LR 683

  Provides a valuable summary and analysis of the major changes to the system of jury trials from 1953–2003 (including the reforms introduced by the Juries Act 1974, the Contempt of Court Act 1981, and the Criminal Justice Act 2003).

 ### Online Resource Centre

You should now attempt the supporting multiple choice questions available at **www.oxfordtextbooks.co.uk/orc/wilson_els/**.

 **11** # Access to justice

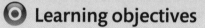 **Learning objectives**

By the end of this chapter you should:

- be aware of the arguments concerning access to justice;
- be able to discuss the impact of the proposed and actual changes to legal aid provision;
- be able to outline the basic principles relating to public funding in civil and criminal cases;
- be able to describe the differences between a conditional fee agreement and a contingency fee agreement; and
- appreciate the difficulties in evaluating whether there is 'access to justice' in the English legal system.

🅖 Talking point

....

When the proposals for legal aid reform were announced in June 2013 the Guardian produced a report by Saba Salman which included an interview with Breda Power, the daughter of Billy Power, one of the Birmingham Six whose wrongful conviction was quashed in 1991. The Birmingham Six had been convicted in 1975 of bombing two pubs in Birmingham, an act that was presumed to be the work of the Provisional IRA, killing 21 people and injuring 182. It was the most serious terrorist act that had taken place on the British mainland. The men were sentenced to life in prison. Their first appeal, in 1988, failed but following a lengthy campaign their second appeal was successful. Breda Powell suggests 'Under these reforms [the proposed reforms to criminal legal aid] the Birmingham Six wouldn't have been able to take out any kind of judicial review or instruct solicitors willing to do all that pro-bono work. What would have happened without that?'

The government has asserted that savings of £220 million have to be made in the legal aid budget. The initial proposals made by the Ministry of Justice, including preventing defendants choosing their own solicitors and price competitive tendering, have been rescinded following consultations during the summer of 2013. However, it seems that the proposal to end prisoners' access to legal aid as of right will be implemented. The government announced in September 2013 that they would publish a new consultation paper. How do you think the government should save money on legal aid and what impact do you think reforms will have on access to justice?

....

Introduction

This chapter is headed 'Access to justice' but what is meant by this phrase? Generally access to justice can be taken to refer to the fact that the advice necessary to obtain legal redress should be available to all and not be exclusive to any section of society. Justice should not be a commodity beyond the means of all but the wealthiest in society. Professor Richard Moorhead has emphasised that access to justice does not simply equate to legal aid. Access to justice means being 'treated fairly according to the law and if you are not treated fairly being able to get appropriate redress'. Over the course of the twentieth century, and into the twenty-first century, the English legal system has arguably become more difficult to navigate as a result of the growth in the volume and complexity of law on the statute books. It is instructive to visit a law library and compare the size of the yearly statute books from the beginning of the twentieth century with those of recent years. The labyrinthine legal system comprises a complex and detailed set of rights and responsibilities in areas such as welfare, housing, and employment law and accessing legal assistance when something goes wrong can be a difficult and costly process. Rights are only of use if an individual is aware of those rights and has the resources and ability to enforce them.

When discussing access to justice it is therefore important to consider whether those citizens who want to access legal remedies or assistance are able to do so, or whether they are prevented from doing so by a combination of lack of awareness of their rights and an inability to pay for legal assistance. It is also important, as in all aspects of the English legal system, to separate discussion of the availability of help and advice in criminal cases from consideration of the assistance available in civil matters. Access to justice can refer to the right to have representation if accused of a crime but it can also refer to the obtaining of legal help in a divorce case or employment matter or in relation to civil litigation.

The creation of the Legal Aid scheme in 1949 was intended to provide publically funded advice, assistance, and representation in criminal and civil cases. The scheme was regarded by many as the fourth pillar of the Welfare State. The costs of legal aid have increased beyond what had been envisaged by the designers of the scheme. Additionally, it is difficult to control costs due to the scheme being demand-led. Anyone requiring legal services, who is eligible under the rules, will receive financial assistance to obtain legal advice. From year to year, the costs have been impossible to predict as it cannot be known, for example, how many people might be arrested and require representation or how many individuals would require advice on marital breakdown.

The story of legal aid since the 1980s is one of governments trying to control legal aid expenditure in the face of escalating demand. Despite a number of initiatives, and the lowering of financial eligibility thresholds, legal aid costs rose from approximately £1.5billion in 1997 to over £2billion in 2012.

Within the legal aid budget, two areas of expenditure in particular have increased considerably: criminal defence expenditure in the Crown Court and the costs of child care proceedings. Governmental schemes and plans to control expenditure have given rise to the related problem of how to allocate the finite resources to meet potentially infinite needs. In recent years, the allocation of funds for civil legal aid has fallen while spending on criminal legal aid has increased. The government, in *Implementing Legal Aid Reform: Government response to the Constitutional Affairs*

Select Committee Report, Cmnd 7158 (June 2007), said of its proposals to reform the legal aid programme that:

> Controlling expenditure is not, in and of itself, the goal of the reform programme. The aim of improved efficiency and better control over spending is, ultimately, to ensure that more people can be helped by legal aid within the resources available, without any reduction in quality, and in a way that contributes to, and benefits from, improved efficiency in the wider justice systems. (para.33)

Major changes to the civil legal aid system in England and Wales were announced in November 2010. The proposals aimed to cut the legal aid bill by £350million a year by 2015. More detail on the changes will be given throughout the chapter. As well as the changes to civil legal aid, changes were also announced to the general funding of civil cases as a result of the report of Lord Justice Jackson who published his findings in January 2010.

When investigating and discussing access to justice it is important to consider the whole of the legal system and the wider picture. The issue is not simply that individuals cannot obtain funding for legal advice and representation but that even if money is available the funding arrangements may influence the legal profession's willingness to undertake certain types of legal work. For example, as a result of the withdrawal of legal aid for most divorce cases, some firms of solicitors no longer carry out matrimonial work, preferring to specialise in company and commercial work where fees are more lucrative. Many large firms have closed their matrimonial departments which has resulted in a lack of lawyers carrying out this work in some areas of the country or, more positively, niche practices being set up by the lawyers who have been made redundant. The issue of funding directly impacts upon the way in which the legal profession operates and the provision of legal services.

See chapter 9, 'The legal profession'.

Furthermore, a number of schemes to try to solve disputes without recourse to the courts have been established, such as mediation and arbitration services. The question may then arise as to whether the quality of justice being provided by the alternative forms of dispute resolution is equal to that of the courts.

The purpose of this chapter is to consider the ways in which access to legal advice and representation is funded in both civil and criminal cases, to consider alternative methods of paying legal costs, and the reform of the way in which the state funds legal advice and representation. Throughout this chapter consideration will be given to evaluating the effectiveness of the funding for legal services. Deciding how to fund legal advice and assistance is a major issue for governments. At the time of writing, proposals to reform criminal legal aid have not been finalised.

Thinking point

If a lack of funds means that many cannot pursue a remedy for a legitimate grievance, it may be argued that the rule of law, that all citizens are equal before the law, is more apparent than real.

11.1 Legal Aid Agency

The current system of funding legal advice and assistance is based on the Access to Justice Act 1999 and associated legislation, including the Legal Aid, Sentencing and Punishment of Offenders Act 2012, which came into force in April 2013. The 1999 Act introduced major changes to the way in which legal aid was delivered but many of the changes introduced by the Act were swept away by the 2012 Act. Legal aid is now administered by the Legal Aid Agency (LAA) which was established in April 2013. The priorities of the LAA are expressed to be to:

- improve casework to reduce cost, enhance control, and give better customer service;
- improve organisational capability to meet the challenges ahead, including developing and engaging our people;
- build and maintain strong partnerships to secure quality provision and contribute fully to wider justice and government aims.

The LAA includes the Public Defender Service which provides independent advice, assistance, and representation on criminal matters and the Civil Legal Advice Service.

Further details about the LAA can be found at **www.justice.gov.uk/about/laa**.

11.2 Civil Legal Advice Service

The Civil Legal Advice Service is the scheme under which advice and representation are provided in civil cases. The scheme is administered by the Legal Aid Agency, either through direct funding to firms of solicitors and other advice agencies or through coordination and partnership with other funders of legal services such as local authorities. Civil Legal Aid is provided for:

- benefit appeals;
- debt, if the applicant's home is at risk;
- special educational needs;
- housing;

- discrimination issues;

- help and advice for victims of domestic violence; and

- issues around a child being taken into care.

11.2.1 Availability of funding

Thinking point

The geographical location of firms of solicitors is important for access to justice. Not all solicitors have a contract to provide services under the Legal Aid scheme and therefore access will be difficult for many people. This is particularly true in small towns and in the countryside as the greatest concentration of firms of solicitors tends to be in the major urban areas.

There is a range of levels of service funded by the Legal Aid Agency in civil cases:

- **Legal help.** This is a service which offers advice on rights and options and help with negotiations and paperwork. This could include writing letters, negotiation, preparing a written case, and getting a barrister's opinion on the legally aided person's behalf. The eligibility for legal help is means-tested.

- **Help at court.** If legal aid is granted for help at court, a legal representative is appointed to help and speak for the assisted person in a civil court. This does not include formal representation. Again, eligibility depends upon a means test.

- **Family mediation.** Family mediation is used to help parties to a marriage to come to an agreement without going to court. Under family mediation, an independent mediator seeks to aid the parties in reaching an agreed settlement in relation to issues surrounding children, money, and the family home.

- **Legal representation.** This is available in very limited circumstances. Under the legal representation scheme, funding may be limited to investigative help, which will only cover investigating the strengths of the proceedings and is used in cases where the chances of the case being successful are not clear and the investigation is likely to be expensive. Alternatively, funding under this scheme can be for full representation. Representation is subject to a means and a merits test and if both tests are fulfilled a solicitor or barrister can be paid to prepare and handle the legal work required to prepare a case for court and representation at any court hearings.

Certain types of legal case are excluded from the Legal Aid scheme. These include personal injury cases, including, from April 2013, those involving clinical negligence (excepting children with brain injuries resulting in severe disability, which have arisen in the womb, during birth, or in the eight-week postnatal period), claims of negligence causing damage to property, boundary disputes, will writing, the creation of lasting powers of attorney under the Mental Capacity Act 2005, conveyancing, matters of trust law, company or partnership law, cases arising in the course of carrying on a business or concerning libel or slander, and private family law cases such as divorce, or disputes about children and finances unless the case involves domestic violence or abuse.

ⓘ Critical debate

A method of controlling the legal aid budget is to reduce eligibility. At first sight it appears strange that personal injury cases, which constitute a large proportion of civil claims, should not be eligible for legal aid. Personal injury cases were covered by legal aid until 2000, however the cost of supporting such claims was very high and therefore the government introduced legislation to remove legal aid from such cases and instead allow the claims to be funded by conditional fee agreements. The cost of bringing personal injury claims was therefore transferred from the public purse to the parties involved and to the claimants' lawyers. Lawyers undertaking work on a conditional fee basis take the risk of not receiving payment should a claim be lost. Is there a risk inherent to access to justice in adopting such an approach to the funding of litigation?

'Conditional fee agreements', 11.2.7.

The changes made to legal aid in 2000 did not affect clinical negligence claims due to the fact that such claims are likely to be difficult and costly and it was considered that lawyers might not be prepared to take the risk of medical negligence cases under a conditional fee agreement. However, as of April 2013 legal aid has been withdrawn from all but a small number of clinical negligence cases as a result of provisions in the Legal Aid, Sentencing and Punishment of Offenders Act 2012.

A very useful guide to legal aid reforms can be found at **www.justice.gov.uk/ downloads/legal-aid/legal-aid-reform/legal-aid-reform-faq.pdf**.

- The legal aid reforms have removed legal aid funding from a wide range of civil cases, including divorce, welfare benefits, school admissions and exclusions, employment, immigration (where the individual is not detained), consumer, and clinical negligence claims. When the proposals to remove legal aid in these areas were first put forward they were criticised by the Law Society chief executive, who expressed severe doubts that those who need help the most would still be protected, despite the fact that the government's stated aim was to ensure that the legal aid reforms ensured that the resources available were targeted at those in most need of help.

- The cuts to legal aid funding are likely to affect small legal aid providers the most. What potential impact may this have on access to justice?

Updates regarding the response to the final consultation will be posted on the Online Resource Centre which accompanies this book.

The April 2013 consultation paper for legal aid can be found at **consult.justice.gov. uk/digital-communications/transforming-legal-aid**.

There will be further consultation documents produced as the discussions and negotiations continue between the Ministry of Justice and interested parties such as the Law Society and the Bar Council.

Eligibility for funding for civil legal aid

Assessing eligibility for funding is complicated, with different thresholds of earnings, capital, and disposable income depending upon the level of service involved. The solicitor or adviser dealing with the case will give advice as to whether the person asking for help will be eligible for legal aid funding. There is also an online legal aid calculator which can be used to work out eligibility at: **www.gov.uk/check-legal-aid**.

As a general guide, in most cases, if disposable monthly income exceeds £733 or disposable capital exceeds £8,000 then the individual concerned will not be eligible. Contributions are required if disposable capital is over £3,000 or monthly disposable income is more than £315. The thresholds can alter depending, for example, on the number of dependant children in the family or for pensioners on low incomes but the levels are set at a very low sums. Where legal representation is provided, a contribution towards the cost of this service may be payable out of an applicant's capital or income. The level of contribution depends upon various financial thresholds. In some cases, a statutory charge is levied if money or property is recovered. For example, under the Legal Help scheme, if money or property is recovered, the solicitor or adviser concerned must use this towards paying the legal costs incurred.

11.2.2 Community Legal Service partnerships

In 1999 the Legal Services Commission, the forerunner of the Legal Aid Agency, set up community legal service partnerships to coordinate legal services on a regional level. These partnerships involved the Commission, the relevant local authority, and other funders of legal services in the area in question and were designed to allow the needs of the area to be monitored and provision of legal services planned and coordinated. However the partnerships are no longer facilitated and those local partnerships that still exist have been asked to evaluate the effectiveness of their work and to continue to meet only if they consider it is appropriate to do so.

11.2.3 Citizens' Advice Bureaux

Citizens' Advice is a national charity that sets and monitors standards, gives support and guidance, and provides services to Citizens' Advice Bureaux (CABs) throughout England, Wales, and Northern Ireland. All CABs are members of Citizens' Advice. The Citizens' Advice service helps people resolve a range of legal, financial, and welfare benefit related problems. The advice is free. Advisers in many bureaux have contracts with the Legal Services Board to provide legal help. Collectively, CABs help with over 5 million problems each year. The majority of advisers in the CAB are volunteers trained by the CAB although some volunteers have legal qualifications. In some CABs solicitors are employed directly or local solicitors provide services linked with the bureau. The CAB website is located at: **www.citizensadvice.org.uk/**.

11.2.4 **Law Centres**

Law centres were first established in the 1970s to address the legal needs of the poor and disadvantaged in their local communities. Today there are between fifty and sixty law centres in England and Wales, employing solicitors, barristers, and other legal advisers. They specialise in areas of social welfare law such as housing, employment, and welfare rights. Law centres do more than simply take on individual cases. They provide training and information about legal rights to local groups and may work with local authorities to address issues relevant to a particular section of the community, such as problems associated with inadequate social housing stock. Law centres are independent non-profit-making organisations and depend upon funding from central and local government, including funding from the Legal Aid Agency, trusts, and charities. The recent reforms have cut funding to law centres and a number have had to close. Local law centres may have their own websites but a great deal of information can be found at the Law Centres Network website: **www.lawcentres. org.uk/**.

11.2.5 **Student law clinics**

A number of Universities offer pro bono (free) legal services to members of the public through student law clinics. These schemes are set up to assist clients whilst giving students experience of legal work as part of their academic and professional development. The students may offer a full legal service to clients, like firms of solicitors, or may offer a basic advice-only service. Practising lawyers closely supervise the students' work and have overall responsibility for ensuring that clients receive a professional service. An example of a very successful law office at Northumbria University can be found at **www.northumbria.ac.uk/sd/academic/law/slo/**.

11.2.6 **Pro bono schemes**

Pro bono, shortened from the Latin phrase *pro bono publico* 'for the public good', services are sometimes offered by barristers or solicitors' firms to provide legal advice and assistance to clients without payment or for reduced fees. More details can be found on the website of the legal charity LawWorks: **www.lawworks.org.uk/**.

11.2.7 **Conditional fee agreements**

At common law, it had long been held that contracts for the conduct of litigation where payment is related to results are void as being contrary to public policy. Section 58 of the Courts and Legal Services Act 1990 changed this rule in relation to certain types of litigation. The Access to Justice Act 1999 allowed a number of different forms of agreement relating to the payment of fees. The most common, and the one which will be considered here, is the conditional fee agreement. These agreements are popularly known as 'no win-no fee' and the Access to Justice Act, and the general relaxation of the rules relating to the advertisement of legal services led to an explosion in no win-no fee litigation firms. Sections 44 and 46 of the LASPO Act 2012 changed the rules yet again regarding conditional fee agreements.

A conditional fee agreement is where a solicitor agrees with the client that the firm's legal fees will only be paid if the client wins the case. If the client wins the case then the solicitor will be paid an 'uplift' on the normal fees that would have been charged. This is known as a success fee and could include a percentage increase in the bill. However, until the law changed in April 2013 following LASPO, a solicitor carrying out contentious work was not allowed to be paid a fee which was a percentage of any damages that the successful client might be awarded. This type of arrangement, a contingency fee agreement, is not allowed at common law and was not permitted by legislation and therefore was not legal in England, although it is commonly used in the USA. LASPO introduced damages-based agreements (DBA), which are a form of contingency fee agreement. Since April 2013 DBAs are lawful for contentious work and a lawyer can agree to take a percentage of any damages awarded at the end of a successful case.

Thinking point

Conditional fee agreements allow a percentage increase in the fee payable should a claimant be successful. A DBA, on the other hand, allows a lawyer to claim a percentage of the damages recovered. Thus the additional fee payable in a conditional fee agreement is linked to costs, while in a DBA it is linked to the damages awarded. In the past it was suggested that contingency fee agreements might encourage lawyers who have a financial interest in the outcome of a case to employ dubious professional practices, e.g. inflating the claim for damages, coaching of witnesses, etc. and might encourage the pursuit of unmeritorious claims. What evidence is there to suggest that this will be the outcome of such agreements? Why did the government decide to allow DBAs? What regulation of such agreements is needed?

The reform of civil litigation funding and costs includes DBAs being permitted in civil litigation. The changes came about as a result of the recommendations in the Jackson report that both solicitors and barristers should be able to enter into contingency fee agreements with their clients in contentious civil cases, subject to controls on costs recovery and proper regulation and subject to a client receiving independent advice on the arrangement.

The rules governing conditional fee agreements (CFAs) are found in the Courts and Legal Services Act 1990 s.58 (as amended by the Access to Justice Act 1999). Clients must be given specific information to enable them to decide whether a CFA is appropriate. It is important that solicitors ensure that clients understand the risks and consequences of this type of agreement. CFAs are now permitted in all proceedings other than certain types of family proceedings and criminal proceedings.

> ### ≡ Example
>
> A solicitor enters into a CFA with a client injured as a result of tripping on a damaged paving stone. The case is straightforward and the client seems likely to be successful. The solicitor therefore includes a relatively small uplift of 10 per cent. The client wins the case and is awarded damages of £10,000. The legal fee for dealing with the case, if a CFA had not been entered into, is £4,000. However, as a result of the CFA, the final bill is increased by 10 per cent, bringing the total to £4,400.

A CFA covers liability for the costs of the claimant's solicitor but does not absolve liability for the costs of the other side if the claim is not successful (although there are special rules for personal injury cases that are outside the scope of this book). This may have a deterrent effect upon a claimant pursuing a claim. A claimant bears the risk of being ordered to pay the costs of the winning party if the claim is unsuccessful and therefore insurance to cover the risk is commonly taken out either at the start of the case or when it appears likely that the case is going to be decided by a court hearing. This type of insurance is known as after the event (ATE) insurance because insurance cover is bought after the cause of action has arisen. It may be contrasted with before the event (BTE) insurance which is explained at 11.2.8.

Ever since their introduction, CFAs have been subject to criticism. It has been argued that there is no incentive for lawyers to take on difficult cases because they will do so at their own risk; instead the tendency is to accept only clearly winnable or straightforward cases. There is also the issue of some lawyers having disproportionately increased fees under CFAs. As far back as September 2008, Jack Straw expressed concern that CFAs were not working as had been hoped. He said:

> It's claimed they have provided greater access to justice, but the behaviour of some lawyers in ramping up their fees in these cases is nothing short of scandalous. So I am going to address this and consider whether to cap more tightly the level of success fees that lawyers can charge.

Sir Rupert Jackson was commissioned in 2008 to review the rules governing the costs of civil litigation in England and Wales. Sir Rupert produced his final report in January 2010. The recommendations made in this report now form part of the reform of civil litigation funding and costs. The reform includes changing the system of conditional fees so that success fees and after the event insurance premiums are no longer recoverable from the losing party. This is because claimants under CFAs have no incentive in keeping their costs down because they do not have to pay them and these recoverable costs represent a significant burden for the losing party, who ends up paying more than the reasonable costs of litigating the case because the level of the success fee is often set too high. Since April 2013 any success fee has to be borne by the client. The reforms include a 10 per cent increase in general damages (for pain, suffering, and loss of amenity) in personal injury cases to make sure that claimants paying a success fee are still properly compensated and a cost-shifting mechanism (instead of ATE insurance) to protect the most vulnerable from adverse costs so that losing claimants only pay the costs of the winning defendant where, and to the extent that, it is reasonable to do so.

11.2.8 Before the event insurance (BTE)

Before the event insurance is an alternative way of funding legal fees, avoiding the need for a CFA or a DBA. This type of insurance is commonly available in motor insurance policies as 'legal expenses cover' and insures the policy holder against the costs of litigation arising out of a road traffic accident where the policy holder is the claimant. A solicitor advising a client on paying for legal advice must always check to find out whether BTE exists before advising the use of any other form of funding.

11.3 Criminal legal aid

The Legal Aid Agency provides advice and representation to the accused person in criminal cases. The service is available for people who have been arrested, questioned, or charged by the police.

The scheme is administered by the Legal Aid Agency either through direct funding to firms of solicitors and other advice agencies or through coordination and partnership with other funders of legal services such as local authorities.

11.3.1 Direct funding

The Legal Agency only funds advice or representation directly where the firm of solicitors concerned has a contract with the Agency.

There are a range of levels of service funded by legal aid in criminal cases:

- **Advice and assistance.** This covers general legal advice, letter writing, and negotiation, preparing a written case, and getting a barrister's opinion.
- **Police station advice and assistance.** This provides individuals being questioned by the police about an offence with free legal advice from a solicitor with a Legal Aid Agency contract. There will be a duty solicitor on call or one can be chosen from a list of local firms kept by the police.

Chapter 7, 'Human rights and fundamental freedoms'.

There is also a duty solicitor scheme operating in the magistrates' courts giving free advice and advocacy assistance on a first appearance in court, subject to some exceptions.

The right to advice and assistance can be seen in the light of the protection of basic human rights. By Article 6 a defendant has the right to a fair trial. Where a person is charged with having committed a criminal offence then as a minimum that person has a right:

> ...(b) to have adequate time and facilities for the preparation of his defence; (c) to defend himself in person or through legal assistance of his own choosing or, if he has not sufficient means to pay for legal assistance, to be given it free when the interests of justice so require.

- **Advocacy assistance.** Advocacy assistance covers the cost of case preparation and initial representation in certain proceedings in both magistrates' courts and the Crown Court but does not include full representation before a court.

- **Representation.** This covers the cost of preparation of a defence and representation in court, including, if the case is to be heard in the Crown Court, the cost of a barrister.

Representation under this scheme will only be granted if it is in the interests of justice to do so. Examples of instances where it is likely to be in the interests of justice for representation to be granted include the likelihood, if convicted, of a prison sentence or loss of employment, or where there are substantial questions of law in issue. The decision to grant legal representation is made by the magistrates' court where the case will be heard. If the court decides not to allow representation it must give reasons for doing so and a further application may be made to the court to review the case or, if the case is going to the Crown Court, an application may be made to that court.

Eligibility for funding

There is a means test for advice and assistance. The level of income/capital above which funding for advice and assistance is not available is generally above £99 disposable income per week and above £1,000 disposable capital. The methods of calculating disposable income/capital take account of a number of factors including the income of a partner and the number of children in the household. In most cases there is no financial eligibility test for advocacy assistance.

As already seen, advice at a police station under the duty solicitor scheme is free.

Under the provisions of the Criminal Defence Service Act 2006, from 2 October 2006, eligibility for free legal representation in the magistrates' court involves passing both a merits test (or interests of justice test) and a means test. Some applicants qualify automatically, such as those receiving income support. Others may qualify by meeting a simple means test, which involves applying a formula used to assess adjusted gross annual income and applying financial eligibility criteria. Applicants who fail to qualify automatically must pass a full means test. The full means test involves assessing an applicant's disposable income. To qualify under the full means test, an individual's annual disposable income must be less than £3,398. Means testing in the magistrates' courts, combined with the 'interests of justice' test results in around a third of all defendants being granted legal aid.

In January 2010 means-testing to assess eligibility for free representation in the Crown Court was introduced and this scheme has now been rolled out across the whole of England and Wales.

A calculator for eligibility for criminal legal aid can be found at **www.justice.gov.uk/legal-aid/assess-your-clients-eligibility/crime-eligibility/criminal-eligibility-calculator**.

11.3.2 **Public defenders**

The public defender has long been a feature of the courts system in the United States but it was not adopted in England and Wales until May 2001. The Legal Aid Agency directly employs solicitors, accredited representatives, and administrators to undertake criminal defence work. The aims of the public defender service are to provide independent, high-quality, and value-for-money criminal advice, assistance, and representation to defendants in criminal cases. The PDS lawyers are available 24 hours a day, seven days a week to give advice to people in custody and represent clients in magistrates' courts, the Crown Court, and higher courts if necessary.

The service is very unpopular with private firms contracted by the LAA. Public defenders effectively compete with private firms for work and are paid by the LAA and therefore it is considered by some that they constitute unfair competition. Research carried out to assess the cost of the PDS concluded that it was between 40 and 90 per cent more expensive than an equivilant service provided by contracted firms. There are currently four public defender service offices in England and Wales.

The PDS code of conduct can be found at: **www.justice.gov.uk/downloads/legal-aid/pds-code-of-conduct.pdf**.

Thinking point

Given the higher costs of the public defender service, what advantages of the service may be identified?

11.4 **Recent history of legal aid reform**

Legal aid has been an increasing burden on the public purse and the degree to which there should be state provision of legal advice and assistance has presented a difficult problem for politicians to solve. Proposals for reform lead to debate in relation to access to justice, the fees charged by lawyers, the merits of individual cases, and the income levels that should allow access to paid assistance in civil and criminal matters. The system has been subject to much tinkering and changes in the 65 years of its existence. Kenneth Clarke commented in the 2010 report *Proposals for the Reform of Legal Aid in England and Wales* that, '[s]ince 2006, there have been over thirty separate consultation exercises on legal aid.' Some of the history of past consultations and proposals are included in this section as well as a summary of the 2013 reforms and an outline of the proposals still under consideration.

In July 2005, the Department for Constitutional Affairs published a command paper, *A Fairer Deal for Legal Aid*. This paper set out the need to improve the way in which the legal aid system worked, especially in relation to criminal defence services.

In July 2006, Lord Carter published a review of legal aid procurement, *Legal Aid: A Market-Based Approach to Reform*. The review recommended moving to a market-based approach to legal aid, focusing on quality and value for money. Amongst the recommendations in the report were:

- best-value tendering for legal aid contracts based on quality, capacity, and price;

- fixed fees per case for legal aid work carried out in police stations, including travelling and waiting time;

- tighter controls on very high cost criminal cases; and new graduated fees for litigators in Crown Court matters.

Following Lord Carter's review, the Department for Constitutional Affairs and the Legal Services Commission published a joint consultation paper in July 2006 called *Legal Aid: A Sustainable Future*. The paper set out proposals as to the ways in which Lord Carter's recommendations would be implemented and included proposals to introduce a unified Legal Services Commission contract covering both civil and criminal work and both solicitors and not-for-profit providers of legal advice and assistance. Following this consultation, further proposals were made by the Department for Constitutional Affairs and the Legal Services Commission in November 2006, *Legal Aid Reform: The Way Ahead*, Cmnd 6993. The paper included some changes to the original implementation proposals and changes in the proposed start date for implementation of some schemes.

Many of the proposals were not favourably received by solicitors, particularly those relating to best-value tendering for legal aid contracts. For example, the Law Society lobbied the Ministry of Justice (previously the Department for Constitutional Affairs) regarding proposals to give judges powers to deal with delay in very high cost cases (including the power to order the withdrawal of representation). The plans were changed so that the Legal Services Commission would have the ultimate responsibility for terminating representation in a particular case. The Law Society also commenced judicial review proceedings against the Legal Services Commission in relation to aspects of the civil legal aid contract. These proceedings were discontinued in April 2008 following an agreement reached between the Law Society, the Legal Services Commission, and the Ministry of Justice.

The government proposals were also criticised by the Constitutional Affairs Select Committee, 'The Implementation of the Carter Review of Legal Aid' (May 2007), HC 223. Concerns expressed by the Committee included:

- the transitional arrangements based on fixed and graduated fees might drive providers of legal aid funded services out of the sector due to lack of profitability;
- fixed fees with little graduation may be a disincentive to the undertaking of difficult cases and may lead to the cherry-picking of cases to the detriment of needy clients;
- the inclusion of travel costs in fixed fees raises problems in relation to rural areas and small towns where specialist legal provision is uneven;
- again, the inclusion of waiting time, e.g. at police stations or at court, in fixed fees places the risk of such delay with the provider when waiting time is largely outside the control of providers; and
- the problem of maintaining quality of service in the face of reduced fees.

The transitional arrangements were seen as potentially damaging to the stability of the existing providers of legal services which would ultimately impact upon the operation of the proposed market-based best-value competitive tendering for legally aided work. The Constitutional Affairs Select Committee in its conclusions said:

239. The reform package is being implemented at too fast a speed. There has been no time for proper business planning by practitioners or even for them to understand the raft of proposals, counterproposals and consultations which have been emanating from the Legal Services Commission. Although it is clear that there is an urgent problem with Legal Aid expenditure, it is no solution to try to introduce changes in an atmosphere of panic.

240. A major part of the proposals involves the introduction of transitional arrangements which are over complex and too rigid. We think that the Government should reconsider whether they are necessary. We doubt whether the risk to the supplier base which they pose justifies their introduction. We would prefer to see competitive tendering – insofar as that is a solution to the problem – implemented directly, once there has been adequate piloting.

241. We are extremely concerned that the Department is trying to engage in such a far reaching change to the structure of Legal Aid on the basis of little or no evidence about which cost drivers have caused the problem or how its plans for a solution are likely to affect both suppliers and clients. We fear that if the reforms go ahead there is a serious risk to access to justice among the most vulnerable in society. It is clear that the Government has been unwise in attempting to reform the entire system rather than in concentrating on those areas which cause the problem: Crown Court and public law children cases.

In June 2007, the government responded to the report of the Constitutional Affairs Select Committee in a report entitled Implementing legal aid reform: Government response to Constitutional Affairs Select Committee report, Cmnd 7158. This report rejected the criticisms of the Committee.

> **Thinking point**
>
> The concern is that legally aided work will be so poorly funded that lawyers will decide to switch resources to other areas of legal work leaving a gap in provision or causing the quality of the service supplied by the remaining providers to diminish. Either way, access to justice suffers. What evidence would you have to collect to investigate these issues?

The reform agenda is now in the hands of the Coalition government who began with two consultations on reforming civil litigation funding and costs and reforming legal aid. The latter consultation included further changes to reform criminal legal aid fees.

The Legal Aid, Sentencing and Punishment of Offenders Act, which came into force in April 2013, reversed the position where legal aid has been available for all civil cases, except those specifically excluded by the Access to Justice Act 1999. The Act removes some types of case from the scope of legal aid funding, as discussed previously, and ensures that other cases will only qualify when they meet certain criteria. The legislation had a very difficult progression through Parliament and the bill was defeated fourteen times in the House of Lords before being passed by the narrowest of margins. Despite concerns from many quarters that the legislation would impact on the most vulnerable in society who would no longer be able to access legal assistance, the Ministry of Justice made clear that whilst it considered legal aid an 'essential part of the justice system' nevertheless, resources, provided by tax payers are limited.

One of the major concerns is that the lack of access to lawyers will result in individuals having to act in person which will make the court system slow and inefficient.

The changes brought into force in April 2013 are not the end of legal aid reform. At the same time as LASPO came into force, a consultation 'Transforming Legal Aid: Delivering a more credible and efficient system' was opened. The proposals for further changes included in the consultation document included:

1. The aim of improving public confidence in the Legal Aid scheme by ensuring that legal aid is not available for prisoners for matters that 'do not justify the use of public funds' and the introduction of a household disposable income threshold above which defendants would no longer receive criminal legal aid.

2. In relation to civil legal aid, the reduction of the use of legal aid to fund 'weak' judicial reviews.

3. The introduction of price competition in the criminal legal aid market, initially for the full range of litigation services and magistrates' court representation. In other

words, providers of legal aid services would have to tender for work, with the contracts going to the lowest bidder.

4. The reform of fees in criminal legal aid to reduce the cost of criminal legal aid fees for Crown Court advocacy and very high cost cases (both litigation and advocacy).

5. The reform of fees in civil legal aid to include reducing solicitor representation fees in family public law cases by 10 per cent, to align the fees for barristers and other advocates in non-family cases, and to remove the 35 per cent uplift in provider legal aid fees in immigration and asylum appeals.

6. The reduction of fees paid to experts in civil, family, and criminal cases by 20 per cent.

These proposals, full details of which can be read at **consult.justice.gov.uk/ digital-communications/transforming-legal-aid**, were open for comment until 4 June 2013. There was general agreement in the legal profession and the press that the proposals would narrow access to justice and could lead to miscarriages of justice and leave individuals without representation in critical cases. Sixteen thousand responses were received and the Ministry of Justice held fourteen 'stakeholder events' during the consultation period to listen to opinions on the proposals and to decide how to proceed.

As a result of the consultation exercise, in September 2013, Chris Grayling announced that the proposals to introduce competitive tendering and the proposed reforms to criminal advocacy fees were to be withdrawn and it was decided to undertake a second phase of consultation entitled 'Transforming Legal Aid: next steps'. At the time of writing, therefore, it remains to be seen, despite the clear need to save money and reform legal aid, exactly what the structure will be for the new system.

The consultation paper can be found at **consult.justice.gov.uk/digital- communications/transforming-legal-aid-next-steps/consult_view**.

🔑 Key point

Reform of the legal aid system, in order to try to balance the competing demands of the public purse and the needs of citizens who need legal advice, is a complex conundrum for both politicians and the organisations who represent lawyers. The fundamental reforms that have taken place in 2013 are not the end of the changes but the beginning. A general election in 2015 will ensure that the political parties set out their plans to secure an adequately funded legal aid system. The hope of the Law Society, and other bodies that represent lawyers, is that the result of the reviews, proposals, reforms, and discussions will be a system that offers quality representation and access to justice for all.

The Ministry of Justice website is at **www.gov.uk/government/organisations/ ministry-of-justice**.

Summary

- The Access to Justice Act 1999 introduced major changes to the way in which the state funded advice and representation in both civil and criminal cases.

- The Legal Aid Agency contracts directly with firms of solicitors and other advice agencies to provide advice and representation in both civil and criminal cases, where a range of levels of service are funded.

- Eligibility for funding depends on the level of service, whether civil or criminal work is involved, and whether a means test and/or merits test is satisfied. In some civil cases, a statutory charge is levied if money or property is recovered.

- Organisations involved in giving legal advice include Citizens' Advice Bureaux and law centres.

- Methods of funding legal advice and representation include CFAs, DBAs, and BTE insurance.

- Reform of the legal aid system is ongoing.

Questions

1 Does the entitlement of a suspect at the police station to free legal advice depend upon means-testing?

2 Can a person accused of a crime receive funding for legal representation: (a) in a magistrates' court; and (b) in the Crown Court?

3 In what circumstances is legal aid funding for legal representation available in civil proceedings?

4 Apart from funding via legal aid, in what other ways may civil litigation be funded?

5 Does the legal aid system cost too much?

6 Do you consider that the legal aid reforms have gone far enough?

7 Have the legal aid reforms gone too far and adversely affected access to justice for individuals?

8 What does access to justice mean?

Sample question and outline answer

Question

In 2011, when introducing proposals to reform legal aid, Kenneth Clark, the then Justice Secretary, declared 'I genuinely believe access to justice is the hallmark of a civilized society'. Do you agree? Have the recent changes to legal aid affected that access?

Outline answer

The introduction should set out what you understand the question to be asking and explain how you will answer it. It would be advisable to explain what you understand by 'access to justice'. Read widely and find some quotations and definitions that you can use to support your definition.

You may want to outline the purpose of legal aid, and perhaps distinguish between civil and criminal legal aid, and then explain why legal aid was introduced as the 'fourth pillar' of the Welfare State.

Try to put the question in context. Explain why changes to the system are necessary. For example, you could quote the Ministry of Justice which has stated: 'At around £2bn a year we have one of the most expensive legal aid systems in the world. At a time when everyone is having to tighten their belts we cannot close our eyes to the fact legal aid is costing too much and has mushroomed into something far bigger than it was intended to be.'

Set out your understanding of the changes proposed and suggest what effect you think they will have. You could refer to any of the case studies in the *Guardian* article at **www.theguardian.com/society/2013/jul/02/legal-aid-cuts-widespr ead-miscarriages-justice** or find your own examples. You can agree with the proposition made or disagree, so long as you support your view with evidence and sources.

Decide whether you think that access to justice, as you have defined it, have been affected by the changes and conclude accordingly.

Further reading

This is not a settled area of the law, due to the ongoing consultations on legal aid. Your reading should ensure that you can come to an informed decision about what access to justice means. Questions in this area will often ask you to decide whether you agree or disagree with the proposals for reform of legal aid or to discuss whether the various methods of paying for legal advice ensure justice for all. The newspapers are an excellent source of articles and examples to use in support of your arguments and, because this is such a topical issue, legal journals will have articles and discussion pieces dealing with the most recent proposals and changes. You will have to keep up to date with the reform proposals.

- **Bevan, C.** 'Self-represented Litigants: The overlooked and unintended consequence of legal aid reform' (2013) 35(1) J Soc Wel & Fam L 43–54
  This article is a thoughtful piece reviewing the research on the demographics, motivations, and case outcomes for litigants in person (people who represent themselves in front of courts and tribunals). In particular the author examines the concerns of family lawyers about the consequences of the expected increase in litigants in person participating in family proceedings due to legal aid reforms.

- **MacDonald, M.** 'Jackson Reforms: First impressions'. (2013) Post Mag 6 June, 22–5
  This is a report giving an overview of a roundtable discussion of specialists from the insurance and legal sectors on whether the Jackson reforms are producing the intended results. An interesting and readable discussion giving the views of those dealing with litigation under the reformed system.

- Ministry of Justice *Proposals for the Reform of Legal Aid in England and Wales,* CP12/10 (November 2010)
  This is the consultation document that formed the basis of Coalition government's proposals for the legal aid system. It is long but it is worth reading the executive summary, the introduction, and the background sections.

- Ministry of Justice *Transforming Legal Aid – Delivering a more credible and efficient system* CP14/2013 (April 2013)
  The website relating to this consultation paper contains a great deal of interesting material: **https://consult.justice.gov.uk/digital-communications/ transforming-legal-aid**. It is worth looking at the documents and reading the summaries and areas that interest you to get an overview of the consultation process. You will find the responses to the consultation document from the Bar Council and the Law Society online.

- Ministry of Justice *Transforming Legal Aid – Next Steps* (September 2013)
  The website **https://consult.justice.gov.uk/digital-communications/transforming- legal-aid-next-steps/consult_view** provides lots of information about the latest consultation. It will generate a great deal of discussion and responses from interested parties.

- **Moorhead, R.** 'An American Future? Contingency Fees, Claims Explosions and Evidence from Employment Tribunals' (2010) 73 MLR 752
  This article considers whether England and Wales will experience similar problems to America in relation to the use of contingency fees for litigation. The author discusses the link between contingency fees and a perceived increase in the number of civil claims commenced. The article also examines the inequalities in access to justice experienced by claimants and considers how far contingency fees address those concerns. Particular reference is made to the experience of lawyers in employment tribunals.

- **So, W.** 'A Brief History of the Law of Costs – lessons for the Jackson reforms and beyond' (2013) 32(3) CJQ 333–48
  If you are interested in the history and the development of the law of costs this is the article for you. The author comments on the Jackson reforms in the light of previous efforts to develop a system that is just, predictable, and efficient.

Online Resource Centre

You should now attempt the supporting multiple choice questions available at **www.oxfordtextbooks.co.uk/orc/wilson_els/**.

12

The criminal process: the suspect and the police

◉ Learning objectives

By the end of this chapter you should:

- have a basic knowledge of police powers of search, seizure, and arrest;

- have an understanding of police powers and duties when a suspect is at the police station;

- understand the law relating to confession evidence;

- understand the extent to which an accused person has a right to silence; and

- appreciate the factors that must be taken into account in deciding whether to prosecute someone for a criminal offence.

🔵 Talking point

In 2011 Lord Hanningfield, the former Conservative Party peer, was convicted of false accounting in connection with the MPs' expenses scandal and sentenced to nine months' imprisonment. While he was serving his sentence, the police commenced an investigation into allegations that Lord Hanningfield had committed fraud in relation to expenses claimed when he was the leader of Essex County Council.

Lord Hanningfield was released from prison on 9 September 2011. On 14 September, five police officers arrived at his home in two marked police cars at 6:45 a.m. They woke him up, arrested him, and searched his home without having first obtained a warrant from a magistrates' court. Lord Hanningfield claimed damages for unlawful arrest.

Section 24 of the Police and Criminal Evidence Act 1984 allows the police to arrest a person without a warrant if the arrest is necessary to allow the prompt and effective investigation of an offence. The police argued that Lord Hanningfield's arrest was necessary because, if they attempted to question him without first arresting him, he might become uncooperative. It was further suggested that he might hide or destroy evidence or alert others who were suspected of participating in the fraud.

The High Court ruled that Lord Hanningfield's arrest had not been necessary (Lord Hanningfield of Chelmsford v The Chief Constable of Essex Police [2013] EWHC 243 (QB)). There was no evidence to support the contention that he would not cooperate with the investigation; the idea that he might conceal or destroy evidence was pure speculation; and, although he had known of the investigation for some time, there was nothing to suggest that he had colluded with others or intended to do so.

The power of arrest is a power to deprive a person of their liberty and a decision to arrest someone is a serious matter. Lord Hanningfield's case confirms that police officers must give consideration to practicable alternatives to arrest, such as whether the suspect would attend a police station voluntarily to be interviewed. The law requires an officer to be able to justify a decision that it is necessary to arrest a suspect.

Introduction

A number of publicly funded local and national bodies have the power to investigate and prosecute offences. For example, the Department for Work and Pensions can investigate and prosecute those suspected of fraudulently obtaining benefits. Private individuals can also bring prosecutions. However, the vast majority of criminal offences are investigated by the police and prosecuted by the Crown Prosecution Service.

In order to investigate an offence, the police may need to exercise certain powers. They may wish, for example, to search a person or a building for evidence in connection with the offence, or to detain and question a suspect. The exercise of such powers will often involve infringing the rights and freedoms of individuals. The search of a house interferes with the occupier's right to respect for his home. The detention of a suspect interferes with his right to liberty. The law, therefore, aims to balance the public interest in ensuring that the police can investigate offences effectively, against the rights and liberties of individuals. This balance is achieved by giving the police powers but also by laying down rules that control and limit those powers and the circumstances in which they may be exercised.

This chapter is concerned in particular with police powers to search, arrest, detain, and question suspects. It will also look at the consequences that may follow where the police misuse their powers or break the rules. In relation to police interviews, it will consider both the rules that protect suspects and the extent to which the right to silence has been eroded.

Finally, not all investigations result in prosecution. We will examine who decides whether to bring a prosecution against a particular suspect and the criteria that are taken into account in making that decision.

12.1 **The structure and organisation of the police**

England and Wales has 43 local police forces, rather than a single national police force. The Police Reform and Social Responsibility Act 2011 provided that Police and Crime Commissioners were to be appointed for each force outside London. Police and Crime Commissioners are elected officials responsible for securing the maintenance of their police force and ensuring that it is efficient and effective. The first Police and Crime Commissioners were elected in November 2012 by an average of just 15 per cent of voters. They will remain in post until 2016 and have powers to decide local policing priorities, set policing budgets, and hire and fire chief constables.

As at 31 March 2013, there were 129,584 full-time equivalent police officers in the 43 police forces of England and Wales, which is the lowest recorded number since 2002. Police officers have a range of statutory and common law powers, the most significant of which are considered in this chapter. Some police powers are exercisable only on the authority of senior officers of specified ranks. Diagram 12.1 sets out the rank structure for forces outside London. (The Metropolitan Police and City of London Police have different titles for senior ranks and the head of these forces holds the rank of Commissioner.)

Police officers are supported by civilian staff, police community support officers (PSCOs), and special constables. PCSOs are uniformed civilians employed in a 'highly

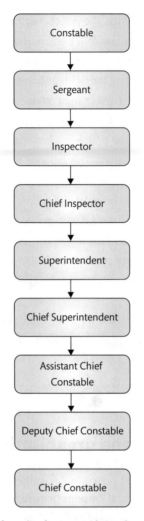

Diagram 12.1 The rank structure for police forces outside London

visible, patrolling role' (Home Office, *Police Service Strength*, SN00634, 25 July 2013). PCSOs have a number of standard powers, such as the power to issue a fixed penalty notice for littering and, in certain circumstances, the power to require the name and address of a person who has committed an offence. Chief Constables also have the authority to grant PCSOs a range of discretionary additional powers. Special constables are volunteers who are trained by their local police force to work with, and offer support to, police officers.

The Crime and Courts Act 2013 created the National Crime Agency (NCA), which will work with local and international police forces to address certain types of crime. The NCA will tackle organised crime; strengthen UK borders; fight fraud and cyber-crime; and protect children and young people. It will have the authority to coordinate a national response to organised crime. As with its predecessor, the Serious Organised

Crime Agency, NCA officers will have the combined powers of police constables, immigration officers, and customs officers.

12.2 **PACE and the Codes of Practice**

Prior to 1984, police powers were derived from a mixture of common law, statute, and bye-laws. In 1977, a Royal Commission on Criminal Procedure (RCCP) was established to examine the powers and duties of the police in respect of the investigation of criminal offences, and the rights and duties of suspects and accused persons. The RCCP, chaired by Sir Cyril Philips, was set up partly as a result of the miscarriage of justice that occurred in the *Maxwell Confait* case.

> ### Example
>
> In 1972 three youths, the eldest of whom was 18 but had a mental age of 8, were convicted of offences of murder, manslaughter, and arson, arising out of the killing of Maxwell Confait. Each of them had confessed during police questioning to some degree of involvement in the crimes. It was later discovered that none of the three could possibly have committed the offences and their convictions were overturned by the Court of Appeal (*R v Lattimore, Salih and Leighton* (1976) 62 Cr App R 53). The *Confait* case fuelled concerns about police interrogation procedures and techniques.

Following the report of the RCCP (Cmnd 8092), the Police and Criminal Evidence Act 1984 (PACE) was introduced. Police powers today are mostly to be found in PACE and in the Codes of Practice (Codes A to H) made under PACE. Among other things, PACE and the Codes of Practice govern the powers of the police to:

- stop and search persons and vehicles;
- enter and search premises;
- arrest, detain, and question people;
- take samples, photographs, and impressions; and
- conduct identification procedures.

PACE was designed to strike a balance between police powers and civil liberties. Since 1984, successive governments have sought to adjust that balance and PACE has been supplemented and amended by various Acts of Parliament. The Codes of Practice have also been amended on a number of occasions. The latest versions of PACE Codes A to H may be found at: **www.gov.uk/government/collections/police-and-criminal-evidence-act-1984-pace-current-versions**.

PACE is a statute and, as such, is binding upon the police. The Codes of Practice are made under PACE but are not part of the statute itself. PACE s.67 clarifies the legal status of the Codes of Practice by providing that they are admissible in evidence and that the court may take account of relevant provisions of the Codes when determining any issues that arise in criminal proceedings. However, although the police are required to comply with PACE and the Codes of Practice, failure to do so will not necessarily mean that any evidence obtained as a result is inadmissible.

> ### 🔑 Key point
>
> Where evidence is admissible in a criminal trial, this means that the jury may hear about it. Where a judge rules that a piece of evidence is inadmissable, the jury will not be made aware of it. In the context of a summary trial, the magistrates must decide whether a piece of evidence is admissible or not. If they decide that it is inadmissible, they must ignore it when deciding the case.

For examples of cases in which the courts have excluded evidence because of breaches of PACE or the Codes of Practice, see 12.4.4.

Thus, even where evidence is obtained by the police unlawfully or improperly, it can often still be used by the prosecution at trial (*Kuruma v R* [1955] AC 197). Breaches of PACE or the Codes of Practice could, however, lead to various other adverse consequences for the prosecution and/or the police, such as:

- the giving of an appropriate warning to the jury where evidence is admitted in the context of such a breach;

- a stay of criminal proceedings for abuse of process (i.e. bringing the criminal proceedings against the accused to an end);

- the instigation of police disciplinary proceedings; or

- the bringing of civil or criminal proceedings against the police (for example, if a police officer is alleged to have assaulted a suspect).

> ### Thinking point
>
> In some countries, whenever the police break the law (for example, by conducting an illegal search), any evidence obtained as a result is automatically inadmissible. Such evidence is sometimes referred to as 'the fruit of the poisoned tree'. Is this a good way of ensuring that the police always obey the laws or rules that govern the exercise of their powers? What if it means that a guilty person is acquitted because a police officer simply made a mistake?

12.3 Police powers to search, seize property, and make arrests

The principles that govern the powers of the police to search, seize property, and make arrests are mostly to be found in PACE and in the following Codes of Practice:

- Code A (the Revised Code of Practice for the Exercise by: Police Officers of Statutory Powers of Stop and Search; Police Officers and Police Staff of Requirements to Record Public Encounters, 2013);

- Code B (the Revised Code of Practice for Searches of Premises by Police Officers and the Seizure of Property Found by Police Officers on Persons or Premises, 2013); and
- Code G (the Revised Code of Practice for the Statutory Power of Arrest by Police Officers, 2012).

12.3.1 Powers to stop and search and seize articles

PACE s.1 gives police officers the power to search any person or vehicle for stolen or prohibited articles, bladed articles, or fireworks carried in contravention of fireworks regulations. 'Prohibited articles' are offensive weapons or articles made, adapted, or intended for use in connection with one of the offences listed in s.1(8) (which include burglary, theft, or criminal damage). In order to exercise this power, the officer must have reasonable grounds for suspecting that he will find a prohibited article, bladed article, or firework. This means that the police cannot normally carry out random, speculative searches.

The power to stop and search may only be exercised in a place to which the public have access and the person being searched may not be required to remove clothing other than a coat, jacket, or gloves in public (s.2(9)). If the officer does find a relevant article, s.1(6) gives them the power to seize it.

Section 1 is one of a number of police powers that can only be exercised if a police officer has reasonable grounds for suspicion. 'Reasonable suspicion' is not defined in PACE. The courts have held that the officer must personally suspect that he will find an article of a specified kind and there must be reasonable cause for that suspicion (*Castorina v Chief Constable of Surrey* (1988) 138 NLJ 180; *Howarth v Commissioner of Police of the Metropolis* [2011] EWHC 2818 (Admin)). Code A contains a reminder that the Equality Act 2010 makes it unlawful to discriminate against any person on the grounds of any of the 'protected characteristics' set out in the Act, which include age, sex and sexual orientation, race, and religion or belief. Code A also provides that there must be an objective basis for suspicion, based on facts, information, or intelligence. A person's appearance, including any of the protected characteristics, or the fact that a person is known to have a previous conviction, cannot form the basis of reasonable suspicion. Furthermore, reasonable suspicion cannot be based upon stereotypes that certain groups or categories of people are more likely to be involved in crime.

Example

PC O'Connell is on mobile patrol at 11:00 p.m. in a part of London in which a series of burglaries has been reported in the past week. All of the burglaries have taken place in the early hours of the morning and entry to each of the properties was gained using a screwdriver. One homeowner saw the burglar and described him as a black man.

At 11:30 p.m., PC O'Connell sees Omar, a young, black man, walking down a street. Upon seeing PC O'Connell's marked police car, Omar pulls his hood over his head and hunches his shoulders. He puts his right hand in his pocket, removes something, and places it under his jumper. PC O'Connell thinks that Omar must be concealing a screwdriver or similar implement and decides to stop and search him.

PC O'Connell clearly personally suspects that he will find a screwdriver when he searches Omar. A screwdriver would be a prohibited article if it was intended for use in connection with an offence of burglary. PC O'Connell's suspicion also appears to be objectively reasonable. The fact that Omar is black, or that he is young, cannot form the basis of reasonable suspicion but his furtive behaviour and the fact that he is seen to conceal something could give rise to reasonable suspicion.

Code A identifies certain information that must be given to a person prior to a search taking place, including a clear explanation by the officer of the purpose of the search. Code A indicates that it will generally be desirable for a brief conversation to take place prior to a search to avoid unsuccessful searches, to gain cooperation, and to reduce tension. This is necessary because the exercise of stop and search powers by the police has, at times, caused controversy; it has been alleged that the police use their powers to target particular categories or groups of people.

In order to ensure that stop and search powers are not used disproportionately against specific sections of the community, Code A also lays down procedures for the recording, monitoring, and supervision of stop and search powers. These require an electronic or paper record to be made of every search, which must include the object of the search, the grounds for reasonable suspicion, and the self-defined ethnicity of the person searched. Senior officers are expected to monitor these records and to address any trends or patterns that give cause for concern.

However, a recent report by Her Majesty's Inspectorate of Constabulary (HMIC) found 'disturbingly low levels' of supervision by senior officers of the conduct of stop and search encounters. Twenty-seven per cent of stop and search records did not contain reasonable grounds to search people. The Report concluded that there were low levels of understanding of the term 'reasonable suspicion', poor supervision, and lack of oversight by senior officers (Her Majesty's Inspectorate of Constabulary, *Stop and Search Powers: Are the police using them effectively and fairly?* (HMIC 2013)).

Further, it could be argued that records do not paint a complete picture because there is no requirement to make a record of a 'stop and account'. When an officer requests a person in a public place to account for themselves by asking what the person is doing, why they are in the area, where they are going, or what they are carrying, there is no national requirement for a record to be made. It is only if a stop and account results in a search that the encounter must be recorded.

The Home Office publishes statistics derived from records of stop and search encounters. The records show that in 2011/12, over 1.1 million stop and searches were carried out under s.1 PACE and less than 10 per cent led to an arrest. Table 12.1 sets out the ethnicity of persons searched under various search powers, including s.1 of PACE:

Table 12.1 Proportion of stops and searches by self-defined ethnicity, 2010/11 and 2011/12

		2010/11							2011/12						
		White	Black (or Black British)	Asian (or Asian British)	Chinese or Other	Mixed	Not stated	Total	White	Black (or Black British)	Asian (or Asian British)	Chinese or Other	Mixed	Not stated	Total
Section 1	E&W excl. MPS	83.4	4	6.2	0.5	2.1	3.7	100	83.6	4.1	6.3	0.5	2	3.6	100
	MPS*	43.3	30	15.7	2.5	3.7	4.7	100	43.7	28.6	15.8	2.5	4.1	5.2	100
	England & Wales	66.1	15.2	10.3	1.4	2.8	4.1	100	67.1	14.2	10.2	1.3	2.9	4.3	100
Section 60	E&W excl. MPS	62	17.7	7.3	0.9	4.8	7.3	100	62.9	15.1	10.4	0.8	4.3	6.5	100
	MPS	26.3	40.6	22	1.8	4.4	4.9	100	29.2	39.8	17.9	1.8	4.9	6.4	100
	England & Wales	31.4	37.3	19.9	1.7	4.4	5.2	100	34.6	35.8	16.7	1.6	4.8	6.4	100
Section 44/47A	E&W excl. MPS	59	5.9	14.1	4.7	1.8	14.6	100	-	-	-	-	-	-	-
	MPS	56.6	10.9	19.4	4.9	2.4	5.7	100	-	-	-	-	-	-	-
	England & Wales	57.1	9.9	18.4	4.9	2.3	7.4	100	-	-	-	-	-	-	-
All Searches	E&W excl. MPS	83.1	4.1	6.3	0.5	2.2	3.8	100	83.3	4.2	6.3	0.5	2.1	3.6	100
	MPS	42	30.7	16.3	2.5	3.8	4.8	100	42.6	29.5	16	2.4	4.2	5.3	100
	England & Wales	64.4	16.3	10.8	1.4	2.9	4.2	100	65.8	15.1	10.5	1.3	3	4.3	100

* MPS - Metropolitan Police Service.
Source: Home Office.

In July 2013, the Home Secretary, Theresa May, announced a public consultation on police powers of stop and search. She was critical of low search to arrest ratios and acknowledged concerns that people from ethnic minorities were being disproportionately targeted:

> The official statistics show that if you're from a black or minority ethnic background, you're up to seven times more likely to be stopped and searched by the police than if you're white. (**www.bbc.co.uk/news/uk-23140505** accessed 7 August 2013).

The consultation paper can be found here: **www.gov.uk/government/consultations/ stop-and-search**.

Although PACE s.1, is the main stop and search power that the police possess, there are a variety of other stop and search powers. For example, see s.23 of the Misuse of Drugs Act 1971 (which permits an officer to stop and search persons and vehicles if the officer has reasonable grounds to suspect that the person is in possession of controlled drugs); s.60 of the Criminal Justice and Public Order Act 1994 (which gives officers the power to stop and search in anticipation of violence); and s.47A of the Terrorism Act 2000 (which contains a power to search in specified locations to prevent acts of terrorism).

Section 47A of the Terrorism Act 2000 was inserted by the Protection of Freedoms Act 2012 to replace the power contained in s.44 of the Terrorism Act 2000. Under s.44 senior officers could authorise random searches of persons and/or vehicles. Such searches did not require the police to have any reasonable suspicion.

In *Gillan and Quinton v United Kingdom* [2009] ECHR 28, the European Court of Human Rights ruled that the use of s.44 constituted an interference with the right to respect for private life. Article 8 of the European Convention on Human Rights (ECHR) provides that there shall be no interference by a public authority with the right to private life except such as is in accordance with the law and is necessary to protect certain specified interests. The Court ruled that the interference created by s.44 was not in accordance with the law because it was not 'sufficiently circumscribed' and there were no 'adequate legal safeguards' to prevent misuse of the s.44 powers. The Court noted that the available statistics showed that the power was used disproportionately against black and Asian persons. As a result, the Court found that there had been a violation of Article 8 of the ECHR.

On 8 July 2010, Theresa May announced the government's intention to amend the law so that s.44 powers to stop and search were compliant with the ECHR. As a result, the Protection of Freedoms Act 2012 repealed s.44 and inserted a new s.47A in its place. Section 47A provides that a senior police officer may only give an authorisation to stop and search under the Terrorism Act if he reasonably suspects that an act of terrorism will take place. The senior officer must also consider both that the authorisation is necessary and that the geographical extent of the authorisation and its duration are necessary. Once a s.47A order is in place, an officer conducting a search in the specified area does not require reasonable suspicion. A new Code of Practice for the authorisation and use of stop and search powers under the Terrorism Act has been introduced. It contains a reminder that the Equality Act 2010 prohibits discrimination and states that officers must take care to avoid any form of racial or religious profiling when selecting people to search under a Terrorism Act authorisation.

12.3.2 **Powers to make arrests**

A person is under arrest when he is no longer at liberty to go where he pleases. An arrest is usually carried out by physically seizing or touching a person with a view to detaining him, although a person can be arrested by words alone (i.e. by being told that he is under arrest). Where PACE confers powers (such as the power of arrest), an officer may use reasonable force where necessary when exercising those powers (PACE s.117).

A magistrates' court may, in certain circumstances, issue a warrant for a person's arrest. A warrant is a written document which authorises the police to arrest a person in order to bring him before the court.

Where a warrant of arrest has been issued, the police may arrest the person who is the subject of the warrant at any time and take him into custody before bringing him before the court at the earliest opportunity. This is known as 'executing' the warrant. A warrant of arrest may be endorsed or 'backed' for bail. This means that, once arrested, the person is to be released on bail subject to a duty to appear before a magistrates' court on a specified date and at a specified time (s.117 Magistrates' Courts Act 1980).

Bail is defined later in the text.

However, a police officer will not always have time to go before the magistrates' court to apply for a warrant of arrest. An officer may need to arrest someone immediately in order to prevent an offence being committed. For this reason the police also possess a variety of powers to arrest *without* a warrant, the most notable of which is contained in PACE s.24.

Under PACE s.24, a police officer may arrest without a warrant:

- anyone who is in the act of committing, or about to commit, an offence; or
- anyone whom the officer has reasonable grounds to suspect is in the act of committing, or about to commit, an offence; or
- anyone who is guilty of an offence that has already been committed (or whom the officer has reasonable grounds to suspect is guilty of such an offence); or
- anyone whom the officer has reasonable grounds to suspect is guilty of an offence that the officer has reasonable grounds to suspect has been committed.

Thus, an officer does not have to wait until an offence has actually been committed before arresting someone. Nor do they have to be *sure* that the person they are arresting has committed (or was in the act of committing or was about to commit) an offence; they merely have to have *'reasonable grounds to suspect'*. In this context, the courts have held that 'reasonable suspicion' is partly subjective and partly objective. The officer must personally suspect that the person was, for example, about to commit an offence (the subjective element) but the grounds for that suspicion must be grounds that an ordinary person would regard as reasonable (the objective element) (*O'Hara v Chief Constable of the Royal Ulster Constabulary* [1997] AC 286).

⊜ Example

In *Alanov v Chief Constable of Sussex* [2012] EWCA Civ 234, the appellant (A) had been arrested when the police conducted house to house enquiries in an area where a particularly violent rape had occurred. The arresting officer suspected A of the offence because, when he knocked on A's door:

1. A's partner initially lied and said that A was not at home;

2. A's partner was nervous;

3. A remained in the bathroom and continued showering after his partner allowed the police into the house;

4. A became aggressive and was uncooperative; and

5. although the description of the rapist did not match A's appearance, that description might have been inaccurate.

The Court of Appeal held that these factors 'do not pass even the low threshold for establishing, objectively speaking…"reasonable suspicion"'.

In addition, the power of arrest under s.24 may only be exercised if the officer has reasonable grounds to believe that an arrest is *necessary* for one of the reasons specified in s.24(5), such as:

- to enable the person's name or address to be ascertained;

- to prevent the person causing injury to himself or another, or loss or damage to property;

- to protect a child or vulnerable person;

- to allow the prompt and effective investigation of the offence; or

- to prevent prosecution for the offence from being hindered by the person's disappearance.

Thinking point

Why do you think the law requires police officers to have 'reasonable grounds for suspicion' before they can make an arrest? And why must an arrest be 'necessary' if it is to be carried out without a warrant? Remember that an arrest is a serious infringement of personal liberty.

Code G emphasises that it is for the individual officer to decide whether to arrest, report for summons (for a definition of a summons see 13.2.4), grant 'street *bail*', issue a fixed penalty notice, or take any other action which is open to them. However, an officer who chooses to arrest is required to examine and justify the need to arrest the person and take them to a police station. This is because arrest and detention deprives a person of their liberty, which is a fundamental human right.

> *bail:* *Bail means the release from custody of an accused or convicted person. Bail may be granted either unconditionally or subject to conditions, such as a condition that the person resides at a particular address or reports to a police station at a particular time. 'Street bail' is the power that police officers now have to grant bail to persons who have been arrested without having to take them first to a police station. The only condition that an officer can impose on street bail is a condition that the person attends a named police station at a specified time.*

An officer must personally believe that arrest is necessary and that belief must be objectively reasonable (*Hayes v Chief Constable of Merseyside* [2011] EWCA Civ 911). In *Richardson v Chief Constable of Essex* [2011] EWHC 773 (QBD), the High Court held that the word 'necessary' is an ordinary English word and there is no need to paraphrase it. Before arresting a suspect, an officer must consider whether it is necessary to do so. If they conclude that it is necessary, they must be able to give reasons to support that conclusion. The officer should consider whether having the suspect attend the police station voluntarily is a practicable alternative to arrest.

Example

In *Richardson v Chief Constable of Essex* [2011] EWHC 773 (QBD), R was a schoolteacher with no previous criminal convictions or cautions. He was alleged to have assaulted a pupil and was asked to attend a police station for interview. When R arrived at the police station, the custody area was closed and he agreed to travel to an alternative police station. Upon arrival at the second police station, R was arrested.

The arresting officer maintained that she had arrested R because, as a voluntary attender, he would be entitled to leave at will, which could disrupt the interview. She claimed that R's arrest was, therefore, necessary to allow the prompt and effective investigation of the offence. R was interviewed whilst under arrest but was released without charge. He was later informed that no further action would be taken against him.

R successfully challenged the lawfulness of his arrest. The High Court held that R's status as a voluntary attender, meaning that he could leave during the interview, did not mean that his arrest was necessary. There was no basis for thinking that R would disrupt the interview by leaving, particularly given that he had voluntarily travelled to two different police stations for interview.

In *Lord Hanningfield of Chelmsford v Chief Constable of Essex* [2013] EWHC 243 (QB), the High Court reiterated the need for police officers to give consideration to alternatives to arrest. Mr Justice Eady stated that '[t]his process of addressing alternatives is not a matter of box-ticking. The record must show that genuine consideration was given to practicable options.' His Lordship added that s.24 of PACE should not be used to bypass the statutory safeguards that apply when an application is made for a warrant of arrest. In accordance with the jurisprudence on the necessity condition for arrest, Code G now provides that an officer 'must consider whether the suspect's voluntary attendance is a practicable alternative for carrying out the interview. If it is, then arrest would not be necessary.'

Article 5 of the European Convention on Human Rights guarantees the right to liberty and security of the person. Article 5 provides a definitive list of the circumstances in which a person may lawfully be deprived of his liberty. This includes the arrest or detention of a person on reasonable suspicion of having committed an offence, or where it is reasonably necessary to prevent him committing an offence, or to prevent him from escaping after having done so. Any such arrest must be carried out in accordance with procedures prescribed by national law and must be for the purpose of bringing the person before a competent legal authority. Thus, although arrest inevitably deprives a person of his liberty, it will not constitute a breach of the ECHR if it is necessary and is carried out in accordance with PACE and the Codes of Practice.

Under Article 5(2), an arrested person must be informed promptly, in a language that he understands, of the reasons for the arrest and of any charges. He must then be brought promptly before a court and is entitled to trial within a reasonable time or to release pending trial. He is entitled to have the lawfulness of his detention determined speedily by a court and his release must be ordered if the detention is unlawful.

In accordance with Article 5(2), PACE s.28 provides that at the time of arrest, or as soon as practicable thereafter, the arrested person must be informed both that he is under arrest and of the ground for the arrest. Failure to comply with these requirements renders the arrest unlawful. Code G provides that an arrested person must also be **cautioned**.

The wording of the caution is set out at 12.4.3. The alternative meaning of the term 'caution' is considered at 12.4.7.

caution: *The term caution can be used to mean two different things in criminal law. In this context a caution means the warning that must be given to a person about the implications of anything he might say (or not say) when asked questions about a criminal offence.*

Code C provides that once a decision to arrest a suspect has been made, the suspect must not be questioned concerning the offence except at a police station or other authorised place of detention. To question a suspect prior to his arrival at a police station would deprive him of various rights and entitlements under PACE and the Codes of Practice, such as the right to free legal advice. However, an exception may be made, and he may be questioned immediately upon arrest, if delay would be likely to lead to:

- interference with or harm to evidence or people;
- serious loss of, or damage to, property;
- the alerting of other suspects; or
- would be likely to hinder the recovery of property.

12.3.3 **Power to enter and search premises and seize articles**

Where the requirements of PACE s.8 are satisfied, a Justice of the Peace may issue a search warrant (i.e. a warrant authorising the police to enter and search premises). Section 8 applies where there are reasonable grounds to believe that an indictable offence has been committed and that there is material on the premises that is likely to be of substantial value to the investigation of that offence. Certain other criteria must also be met. For example, there must be one of a number of specified reasons for needing the warrant, such as that entry to the premises will not be granted without one. Further consideration of s.8 is outside the scope of this work.

The police also possess a variety of powers to search premises *without* a warrant. Under PACE s.17, a police officer may enter and search premises for one of the purposes specified in s.17(1), which include:

- to execute a warrant of arrest;
- to arrest a person for an **indictable offence**;
- to arrest a person for one of a number of specified summary offences, such as driving whilst under the influence of drink or drugs; or
- to save life and limb or prevent serious damage to property.

> **indictable offence:** *An indictable offence is an offence that either may or must be tried in the Crown Court. Conversely, a summary offence can only be tried in the magistrates' court. Thus, trial on indictment takes place in the Crown Court and summary trial takes place in a magistrates' court. For further details see 13.1.*

Other than in relation to saving life or limb, or preventing serious damage to property, s.17 powers may only be exercised if the officer has reasonable grounds for believing that the person he seeks is on the premises.

Alternatively, under PACE s.18, a police officer may enter and search premises occupied or controlled by a person who is under arrest for an indictable offence. However, this power may only be exercised if the officer has reasonable grounds for suspecting that there is evidence on the premises that relates to that offence or to a connected or similar indictable offence. Furthermore, the power to search under s.18 usually requires the authority of an officer of the rank of inspector or above.

All searches must be limited to the extent necessary to achieve the object of the search. Reasonable and proportionate force may be used to enter premises if necessary. Both s.17 and s.18 of PACE contain powers to seize relevant material discovered in the course of a search.

12.3.4 Power to search a person following arrest

Section 32 of PACE empowers a police officer to search an arrested person if there are reasonable grounds to believe that the person may present a danger to himself or others. An officer may also search an arrested person for anything which might be used in order to escape, or for evidence relating to an offence (if there are reasonable grounds for believing that such things may be concealed on the arrested person). Additionally, where the arrest was for an indictable offence, the officer may enter and search premises in which the arrested person was at the time of arrest or immediately before the time of arrest. This power may only be exercised if the officer has reasonable grounds to believe that there is evidence on the premises relating to the offence. This is different from the power in s.18 as it can be exercised even where the arrested person does not own or control the premises. Again, a search under s.32 is limited to the extent that is reasonably required to achieve the object of the search.

In accordance with Article 8 of the European Convention on Human Rights, Code B emphasises that the exercise of powers of entry, search and seizure must be fully and clearly justified because the exercise of such powers may significantly interfere with the privacy of the occupier.

12.3.5 Policing protestors

The police may exercise their usual powers under PACE in relation to demonstrators, such as the power to stop and search under s.1 of PACE. In addition, s.60 of the Criminal Justice and Public Order Act (CJPOA) 1994 may be used to stop and search protestors without reasonable suspicion in certain circumstances.

Section 60 of the CJPOA 1994 provides that an officer of the rank of inspector or above may authorise officers to stop and search persons and vehicles for offensive weapons or dangerous implements. The inspector must reasonably believe that:

- incidents involving serious violence may take place; or
- an incident involving serious violence has occurred and an offensive weapon or dangerous instrument used in the incident is being carried by someone in the area; or
- persons are carrying offensive weapons or dangerous instruments in the area without good reason.

An authorisation under s.60 must be limited to a specific area and must be for a specified period of no more than 24 hours. An officer of the rank of superintendent or above may extend the period for a further 24 hours. In 2012, a statutory stop and search authorisation under s.60 of the 1994 Act was issued in relation to the royal wedding of Prince William to Kate Middleton on the basis of police intelligence that demonstrators intended to disrupt the wedding. However, some officers continued to use their powers under s.1 of PACE when searching for items other than offensive weapons or dangerous implements (*R (on the application of Hicks) v Commissioner of Police for the Metropolis* [2012] EWHC 1947 (Admin)).

The death of Ian Tomlinson during the protests at the G20 summit in London in 2009 called attention to police tactics at demonstrations. Mr Tomlinson was a newspaper vendor who was on his way home when he found himself inside a cordon that the police had set up to contain protestors. When he tried to leave, a police officer (PC Harwood) hit him with a baton and pushed him to the ground. Mr Tomlinson got up and began to walk away but collapsed and died a short time later. The police at first denied that excessive force had been used and an initial police post mortem examination suggested that Mr Tomlinson had died of natural causes. However, video footage came to light showing Mr Tomlinson being pushed to the ground from behind by PC Harwood. A second post mortem examination established that Mr Tomlinson died as a result of internal bleeding caused by a blow.

PC Harwood was eventually charged with manslaughter but acquitted after trial. He was, nevertheless, sacked after a Metropolitan Police disciplinary panel found him guilty of gross misconduct. Despite the jury's verdict, the Metropolitan Police agreed to pay damages to Mr Tomlinson's family and, in July 2013, Deputy Assistant Commissioner Maxine de Brunner apologised for PC Harwood's use of 'excessive and unlawful force'.

The assault on Ian Tomlinson occurred as the police were setting up a cordon around demonstrators: a practice known as 'kettling'. Opponents of kettling argued that it amounted to a deprivation of the liberty of anyone caught inside the police cordon and was, therefore, unlawful under Article 5 of the European Convention on Human Rights (the right to liberty and security of the person).

In *Austin v UK* (2012) 55 EHRR 14, the European Court of Human Rights (ECtHR) considered a case in which the police cordoned off Oxford Circus on 1 May 2001 while protests against capitalism were taking place. For seven hours a crowd consisting of protestors and members of the public was contained inside the cordon, where conditions were uncomfortable. Although those inside the cordon were able to move about, it was cold and wet, there was no access to shelter or toilet facilities, and no food or water was provided. The ECtHR declined to rule that the kettling of protestors violated Article 5. The Court accepted that kettling might be the least intrusive and most effective means 'to isolate and contain a large crowd in volatile and dangerous conditions' so as to 'avert a real risk of serious injury or damage'. There is a distinction between a restriction on freedom of movement and the deprivation of liberty and the Court was unable to say that, in the instant case, a deprivation of liberty had occurred. However, if the police maintained a cordon after it was necessary for crowd control and in order to punish, or 'teach a lesson' to demonstrators, it is likely that Article 5 would be engaged and the detention of those inside the cordon would become unlawful.

12.4 The suspect at the police station

The principles that govern the treatment of a person who has been arrested and taken into custody by the police are to be found in PACE and in the following Codes of Practice:

- Code C (the Revised Code of Practice for the Detention, Treatment and Questioning of Persons by Police Officers, 2013);

- Code E (the Revised Code of Practice on Audio Recording Interviews with Suspects, 2013); and

- Code F (the Revised Code of Practice on Visual Recording with Sound of Interviews with Suspects, 2013).

12.4.1 Arrival at the police station

Where a person attends a police station voluntarily (i.e. without having been arrested), PACE s.29 provides that he may leave at will unless he is placed under arrest.

Where a person is under arrest, Code C requires him to be brought before the custody officer as soon as practicable. Section 36 of PACE provides that each designated police station must appoint one or more custody officers of at least the rank of sergeant. A custody officer must be independent and cannot be an officer who is involved in investigating the offence for which a person is in police detention.

The custody officer must open a custody record in which information relating to the person's detention is recorded. This information includes the offence for which the detainee has been arrested; the grounds for detaining him; whether legal advice was requested; details of periodic checks carried out; and all reviews of detention. The detainee's solicitor is entitled to consult the custody record.

Where an arrested person is brought before the custody officer, it is the custody officer's duty under PACE s.37 to make the decisions shown in Diagram 12.2.

If there is insufficient evidence to charge an arrested person then and there, he may be detained if there are reasonable grounds to believe that his detention is necessary to secure or preserve evidence relating to the offence or to obtain such evidence by questioning him. It is the latter that gives the police the power to detain a suspect in order to interview him.

A detainee has the right not to be held incommunicado. Under PACE s.56, he has the right to have someone informed of his whereabouts as soon as practicable. Under Code C, the detainee must also be given writing materials on request and allowed to

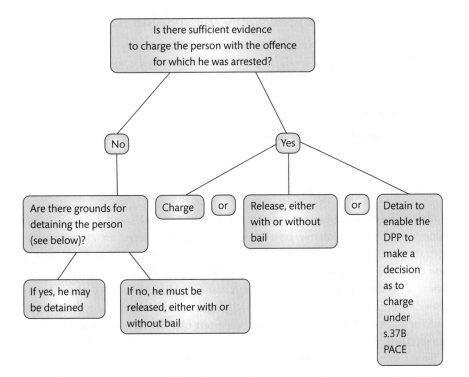

Diagram 12.2 A custody officer's decision-making process under PACE s.37

telephone one person. However, what he says or writes (other than in a communication to a solicitor) is not private as it may be read or listened to and used in evidence.

Thinking point

The Notes for Guidance to Code C state that a detainee's right to consult or communicate with his legal representative in private is 'fundamental'. Why should any communications between the detainee and his solicitor remain private? Is access to confidential legal advice an essential corollary of the right to a fair trial?

Under PACE s.58, a detainee has the right to consult a solicitor in private at any time, personally, in writing, or by telephone. Free independent legal advice is available from the duty solicitor. Code C provides that the custody officer must inform the detainee of his right to legal advice and that a detainee who requests legal advice should not be interviewed until that advice has been received. A detainee is entitled to have a solicitor present when he is interviewed, and the solicitor may properly intervene during the interview, for example:

• to seek clarification;

- to challenge an improper question or the manner in which a question is put;
- to advise the detainee not to answer a question; or
- where the solicitor wishes to give additional advice to the detainee.

> **Thinking point**
>
> Why is it important for a detainee to be allowed to see or speak to a solicitor? Why should he be allowed to have his solicitor with him during an interview? Consider whether his rights would necessarily be adequately protected without a solicitor.

Under PACE ss.56 and 58 and Annex B to Code C, the detainee's right to have someone informed of his detention may be delayed on the authorisation of an officer of at least the rank of inspector, and the right to legal advice may be delayed on the authorisation of an office of superintendant rank or above. These rights may only be delayed where a person is detained in connection with an indictable offence and there are reasonable grounds for believing that notifying someone would lead to interference with (or harm to) evidence or persons, the alerting of other suspects, or would hinder the recovery of property.

If a suspect is mentally disordered, or otherwise mentally vulnerable, or a juvenile (i.e. aged under 17), Code C requires the custody officer to ask an 'appropriate adult' to come to the police station to give the suspect advice and assistance. An appropriate adult is a responsible adult who is not a police officer or anyone employed by the police. The appropriate adult could be a parent, guardian, or social worker in the case of a juvenile. In the case of a person who is mentally disordered or vulnerable, the appropriate adult could be a relative, guardian, or someone experienced in dealing with those who have mental health difficulties. The right to an appropriate adult is in addition to the detainee's right to legal advice. Code C also imposes special requirements where the suspect cannot speak English or is deaf (in which case an interpreter must be provided) or where the suspect is blind or is visually impaired.

12.4.2 Detention conditions and care and treatment of detainees

Sections 8 and 9 of Code C set out minimum standards for the care and treatment of those detained in police custody. Where practicable, there should be one detainee to a cell, which should be adequately heated, cleaned, ventilated, and lit. There should be clean bedding and access to toilet and washing facilities. At least two light meals and a main meal must be offered every twenty-four hours, with drinks at mealtimes and on reasonable request. Normally, a detainee should be allowed a continuous eight-hour period every twenty-four hours, normally at night, which is free from interruption. Detainees should be checked at least every hour and the custody officer is responsible for ensuring that a detainee receives appropriate clinical attention if he is injured, ill, or appears to be suffering from a mental disorder.

Thinking point

The existence of minimum standards for the care and treatment of detainees ensures that a suspect's basic human rights are respected. Why is this important?

12.4.3 The police station interview

Code C 11.1A states that any questioning of a person regarding their involvement or suspected involvement in an offence constitutes an 'interview'. Following arrest, a suspect may usually only be interviewed at a police station or other authorised place of detention.

Before a detainee can be interviewed, Code C provides that the custody officer must assess whether he is fit to be interviewed or whether he is 'at risk'. This assessment may involve consulting a health care professional. A detainee may be at risk if interviewing him could cause significant harm to his physical or mental state or if anything he says *might* be considered unreliable in subsequent court proceedings as a result of his physical or mental state. In some circumstances, it may not be appropriate to interview a detainee at all. In other cases, safeguards, such as having an appropriate health care professional present, may enable the interview to take place.

The custody officer may have authorised detention on the basis that it was necessary in order to obtain evidence by questioning the detainee. However, the detainee cannot be compelled to answer questions and may choose to remain silent in interview. The police can interview him even if he will not answer questions. If he refuses to cooperate, for example by refusing to leave his cell, the interview may take place there.

Usually, however, interviews will take place in designated interview rooms. Code C provides that these should be adequately heated, lit, and ventilated and interviewees must not be required to stand. Breaks should take place at recognised mealtimes and there should also be short refreshment breaks roughly every two hours. Before questioning commences, Code C requires the interviewee to be cautioned.

The caution normally takes the following form:

> You do not have to say anything. But it may harm your defence if you do not mention when questioned something which you later rely on in court. Anything you do say may be given in evidence.

The first part of the caution is straightforward: it informs the person being interviewed that it is his right to refuse to answer questions. The second part of the caution is designed to alert the suspect to the fact that inferences (i.e. common sense conclusions) may be drawn against him if he relies at trial on any fact that he could reasonably

The right to silence and the circumstances in which inferences can be drawn from a suspect's failure to answer questions are dealt with at 12.4.5.

have been expected to mention in interview but did not so mention. The final part of the caution is to advise the suspect that anything that he does say may be introduced in evidence at his trial, usually by the provision to the jury or magistrates of a transcript or summary of the interview.

Code C 11.7 requires an accurate record to be made of all interviews. In relation to summary offences, this can be a written record, an audio recording, or a visual recording with sound. Where, however, a suspect has been cautioned in respect of an indictable offence, the police must make either an audio recording (to which Code E applies) or a visual recording with sound (to which Code F applies).

Requirements imposed by Code E concerning the conduct of audio recorded interviews include:

- the recording media must be unwrapped in the suspect's presence;
- once the recording has commenced, the police officers must identify themselves and must ask any others present to do so;
- the suspect must be cautioned and reminded of his right to free legal advice; and
- at the end of the interview, the master tape must be sealed in the suspect's presence.

These provisions are designed to instil confidence in the reliability of the recording as an impartial and accurate record of the interview. In addition to protecting suspects, the requirements imposed by PACE and the Codes of Practice may also protect interviewing officers from allegations of misconduct.

Code C provides that an interview must cease as soon as the officer in charge of the investigation is satisfied that all relevant questions have been put to the suspect and, taking into account any other available evidence, there is sufficient evidence to provide a realistic prospect of conviction.

12.4.4 Confessions made by the accused

Under PACE s.82(3), a confession is any statement that is either wholly or partly adverse to the person who made it. Thus the term 'confession' is not confined to statements in which the suspect admits the offence.

Example

Roger is shot and killed at his place of work. An eyewitness identifies Bryan, an employee, as the murderer. Bryan is arrested and interviewed by the police. Consider the following alternative scenarios:

(a) Bryan admits that he shot Roger;

(b) Bryan denies shooting Roger but admits being present at the time of the shooting;

(c) Bryan says that he was at home watching television at the time of the shooting.

Bryan's statement in scenario (a) is clearly a confession, as it is wholly adverse to Bryan. In scenario (b), Bryan's statement is a 'mixed statement' because his admission that he was present at the scene of the offence makes the statement partly adverse to him. Thus, the statement in scenario (b) is also a confession within the meaning of s.76, even though Bryan denied the shooting. Scenario (c) involves a wholly exculpatory statement. This statement is not adverse to Bryan in any way and is, therefore, not a confession.

The effect of PACE s.76(1) is that a confession made by the accused is admissible in evidence against him if it is relevant and is not excluded by the court under s.76(2).

Under PACE s.76(2) a confession will be inadmissible in either of two circumstances:

- if it was obtained by oppression (s.76(2)(a)); or
- if it was obtained in consequence of anything said or done which was likely, in the circumstances, to render any confession unreliable (s.76(2)(b)).

Section 76(2)(a)

Oppression is only partially defined in s.76(8) as including torture, inhuman or degrading treatment, and the use or threat of violence. The courts have held that oppression should be given its ordinary dictionary definition and that it includes the exercise of authority or power in a burdensome, harsh, or wrongful manner; unjust or cruel treatment; or the imposition of unreasonable or unjust burdens (*R v Fulling* [1987] QB 426). In *R v Miller* (1993) 97 Cr App R 99, the appellant was arrested on suspicion of murder. He was interviewed on a number of occasions for a total of thirteen hours. The police bullied and hectored him, shouting what they wanted him to say. After denying the offence 300 times, the appellant eventually confessed. The Court of Appeal held that the conduct of the interviewing officers constituted oppression and the conviction was quashed. *R v Fulling* [1987] QB 426 suggests that there must be impropriety on the part of the interrogator for conduct to amount to oppression.

Section 76(2)(b)

In contrast, it appears that the court may be required to exclude a confession for unreliability even if there is no suggestion of improper conduct on the part of the police. In *R v Barry* (1992) 95 Cr App R 384, police officers made statements that may have led the appellant to believe that he was more likely to be given bail if he confessed. The appellant had particularly strong reasons for wanting bail because he was the sole carer of his 9-year-old son. The statements made by the officers were 'something said' under s.76(2)(b). In the circumstances existing at the time (namely the appellant's concern for his son), the Court of Appeal found that his resulting confession was unreliable. The Court of Appeal held that this would be so whether or not the police officers' statements were *'flagrant or cynical or even deliberate'*.

If the defendant asserts that the confession may have been obtained in either of these ways, the prosecution must prove beyond reasonable doubt that the confession was not so obtained.

Thinking point

Why should the prosecution bear the legal burden of proving that the accused's confession was not obtained by oppression and was not unreliable in consequence of something said or done? Is this an example of what might be regarded as the 'weighting' of the criminal process in favour of the accused? When looking at the criminal process, note other rules that weight the system in favour of the accused. Consider whether this is an inevitable consequence of a system in which the accused is 'innocent until proven guilty' and in which prosecuting authorities have access to investigative and financial resources that are not available to the accused.

The question of the admissibility of a confession will be decided in a 'trial within a trial', known as a voir dire. In the Crown Court, the judge will hold the voir dire in the absence of the jury. If the prosecution is able to prove beyond reasonable doubt that the confession was not obtained by oppression or in consequence of something said or done which was likely to render it unreliable, the confession will be admissible. If the prosecution is not able to prove these things, then the judge must exclude evidence of the confession and the jury will never hear of it.

In a summary trial, the magistrates or district judge will make the decision as to the admissibility or otherwise of the confession. If they decide that it is inadmissible, they will be required to put it out of their minds for the remainder of the trial.

Thinking point

In the magistrates' court, questions of admissibility can be determined by the same magistrates who go on to hear the trial. If they determine that evidence is inadmissible, they will be required to put it out of their minds in deciding whether the defendant is guilty of the offence charged. Is it realistic to expect magistrates to 'forget' evidence in this way? Could this procedure unfairly prejudice the defendant?

Even where a confession upon which the prosecution seeks to rely is not excluded under PACE s.76(2), the court may still exercise its exclusionary discretion under PACE s.78. The s.78 discretion enables the court to exclude any evidence tendered by the prosecution. The test to be applied is whether, having regard to all the circumstances, including those in which the evidence was obtained, its admission would have such an adverse effect on the fairness of the proceedings that the court ought not to admit it. The court is likely to exercise the s.78 discretion so as to exclude a confession where there have been breaches by the police of requirements imposed either by PACE or by Code C which were significant or substantial.

In *R v Walsh* (1990) 91 Cr App R 161, the appellant confessed in interview to robbery with a firearm. He had been denied access to a solicitor. The police also breached Code C by failing to make a record of the interview. The Court of Appeal held that these were significant and substantial breaches of PACE and the Codes of Practice. The conviction was quashed on the grounds that the admission of the confession in those circumstances would have had such an adverse effect on the fairness of the proceedings that the judge ought to have excluded it under s.78.

> 🔒 **Key point**
>
> Unlike PACE s.76, the operation of PACE s.78 is not restricted to the exclusion of confessions. Section 78 may be used to exclude any prosecution evidence which it would be unfair to admit. Consequently, s.78 is a provision that is of fundamental importance in the context of criminal evidence.

12.4.5 The accused's silence at the police station

It is a fundamental principle of the criminal justice system that an accused person has a right to silence. However, where he exercises that right, the court may be entitled to draw an appropriate inference against him under s.34, s.35, or s.36 of the Criminal Justice and Public Order Act 1994. Section 34, which relates to the accused's silence in the police station, is the most important of these three sections and the only one that will be considered in detail in this chapter.

Section 35 of the 1994 Act, which concerns the silence of the accused in court, is considered at 13.16.7.

Under s.34 of the 1994 Act, the court may draw an adverse inference where the accused relies in his defence upon a fact that he failed to mention when questioned or charged, provided that the fact was one that he could reasonably have been expected to mention in the circumstances. An 'adverse inference' means that the jury or magistrates may conclude that the defendant remained silent either because he had no answer to give or because he had no answer that would stand up to questioning.

> **Thinking point**
>
> Is it always reasonable to infer that a defendant remained silent in interview because he had no answer to give, or no answer that would stand up to questioning? What other reasons could there be for a person in police custody not wanting to answer questions?

Adverse inferences can only be drawn where the accused relies at trial upon a fact that he *failed to mention* when questioned or charged. If he gives an account in interview and gives the same account at trial, no inference can be drawn.

> ### Example
>
> William witnesses a burglary and recognises the burglar as Daniel, someone he used to go to school with. Daniel is arrested and interviewed on suspicion of burglary. He says that at the time of the burglary he was at home watching television with his girlfriend and that William must be mistaken. He then refuses to answer any further questions. Consider the following two alternative scenarios:
>
> (a) At trial, Daniel gives evidence that he was at home with his girlfriend at the time of the burglary and that this is a case of mistaken identification.
>
> (b) At trial, Daniel gives evidence that he was at home with his girlfriend at the time of the burglary. He adds that William has held a grudge against him ever since Daniel had an affair with William's wife. He suggests that William is implicating him as an act of revenge.
>
> In scenario (a), Daniel has not relied at trial on any fact that he failed to mention in interview. Even though he failed to answer questions, the jury would not be able to draw an adverse inference from his silence.
>
> In scenario (b), Daniel relies on new facts that he could have been expected to mention in interview, namely that Daniel had an affair with William's wife and that William has held a grudge against him ever since. The jury could infer that he did not give that explanation in interview either because it is something that he has made up between interview and trial, or, although Daniel had thought of it prior to his interview, he knew it would not stand up to investigation.

Even where the accused relies at trial on a fact that he failed to mention in interview, an adverse inference cannot be drawn unless the fact is one that he could *reasonably have been expected to mention in the circumstances* existing at the time of interview. The courts have held that the expression 'in the circumstances' should be interpreted widely and might include matters such as the time of day, the accused's age, experience, mental capacity, state of health, sobriety, tiredness, and personality (*R v Argent* [1997] Cr App R 27).

The vast majority of cases on this issue, however, concern the relevance of legal advice. Can adverse inferences be drawn where the accused makes no reply in interview because his solicitor advised him to remain silent? Or can he argue that he could not reasonably have been expected to mention anything in those circumstances?

In *Condron v UK* (2001) 31 EHRR 1, the applicants were heroin addicts who were arrested and interviewed on suspicion of offences involving the supply of heroin. The Force Medical Examiner concluded that both were fit for interview but their solicitor disagreed. He formed the view that they were suffering from heroin withdrawal symptoms and advised them not to answer any questions at that time. The judge should have directed the jury that it could only draw an adverse inference if satisfied that the applicants remained silent because they had no answer to give, or none that would stand up to examination. However, the judge's direction left it open to the jury to draw an adverse inference even if the jury was satisfied that the applicants remained silent because of their solicitor's advice. The European Court of Human Rights ruled that the fact that a solicitor has advised his client to remain silent is a factor that should be given appropriate weight.

However, the Court of Appeal has subsequently emphasised that this does not mean that defendants can use their solicitor's advice as a convenient shield behind which to hide. In order for legal advice to be a valid reason for failing to mention a fact in interview, the defendant's reliance on that advice must be both genuine and reasonable (*R v Hoare* [2004] EWCA Crim 784).

> ### Thinking point
>
> Can the modifications to the right to silence introduced by the Criminal Justice and Public Order Act 1994 be regarded as part of a process of reducing the traditional weighting of the criminal process in favour of the accused?

Article 6 of the European Convention on Human Rights, which guarantees the accused the right to a fair trial, does not expressly guarantee the accused a right to silence. However, the European Court of Human Rights has indicated that the right to silence is an aspect of an Article 6 fair trial. Whilst the right to silence is not an absolute right, the denial of access to legal advice at the police station may give rise to a violation of Article 6. The court cannot draw an inference if the accused was not allowed an opportunity to consult a solicitor prior to being questioned. Even if the accused was allowed to consult a solicitor, the nature of the judge's directions to the jury concerning the drawing of inferences from silence may be crucial when determining whether there has been an Article 6 violation (*Murray v UK* (1996) 22 EHRR 29; *Condron v UK* (2001) 31 EHRR 1; and *Beckles v UK* (2003) 36 EHRR 13). Finally, the European Court of Human Rights has held that the jury must not convict wholly or mainly on the basis of an inference from silence.

12.4.6 Review and extension of detention

PACE sets out the maximum period for which a person can be detained without charge. PACE s.40 also provides that detention should be reviewed at regular intervals by the review officer to ensure that it is still necessary. If the detainee has been arrested and charged, the review officer is the custody officer. If the detainee has not been charged, the review officer must be an officer of the rank of inspector or above who has not been directly involved in the investigation.

The first review of detention should take place no later than six hours after deten-tion was first authorised. The second and subsequent reviews should take place at intervals of no more than nine hours. In some circumstances a review may be post-poned, for example, where the detainee is being questioned and the review officer is satisfied that interrupting the interview would prejudice the investigation.

Section 41 of PACE provides that a person should not normally be kept in police detention for more than twenty-four hours in total without being charged. This is either twenty-four hours from the person's arrival at the police station or twenty-four hours after arrest, whichever is earlier. Where the detainee is under arrest for an indict-able offence, PACE s.42 permits an officer of the rank of superintendent or above to authorise further detention for up to an additional twelve hours. To authorise such an extension, the superintendent must have reasonable grounds to believe that further detention is necessary to secure or preserve evidence relating to the offence or to obtain such evidence by questioning. They must also be satisfied that the investiga-tion is being conducted diligently and expeditiously.

Thus, the police have the power to authorise the detention of a suspect for up to thirty-six hours. Before this period expires, a magistrates' court may issue a warrant of further detention under PACE s.43, authorising the police to keep a person in detention for a further period not exceeding an additional thirty-six hours. The court may only issue a warrant of further detention if satisfied that there are reasonable grounds for believing that further detention is justified on the same grounds as those mentioned earlier in relation to s.42. Before that period expires, PACE s.44 provides that a magis-trates' court may extend the warrant of further detention by a maximum of an additional thirty-six hours (up to a maximum overall period of detention of ninety-six hours) if sat-isfied that there are reasonable grounds for believing that further detention is justified.

Parliament has deemed it appropriate to modify the safeguards provided by PACE and the Codes of Practice in the context of investigations into terrorist offences so as to permit additional periods of detention without charge. The Terrorism Act 2006 increased the maximum period for which a terror suspect can be held without charge from 14 days to 28 days. This controversial measure was originally intended to be only temporary; the Act provided that the maximum period of pre-charge detention would revert to 14 days after one year unless renewed by an affirmative order. However, the 28-day period was renewed annually until July 2010, when it was renewed for six months. On 24 January 2011, no renewal was sought and the maximum pre-charge detention period reverted to 14 days. The Protection of Freedoms Act 2012 perma-nently reduced the maximum period of pre-charge detention to 14 days in terrorism cases and removed the power to increase the period to 28 days by affirmative order. Whether the power to detain for 14 days prior to charge is an appropriate response to the threat of terrorism is an issue that has been hotly debated. Critics have pointed out that the maximum period of pre-charge detention in the USA is two days, and in Ireland is seven days (see **www.liberty-human-rights.org.uk/human-rights/terrorism/ extended-pre-charge-detention/index.php** accessed 30 September 2013).

12.4.7 **Photographs, fingerprints, and samples**

PACE s.64A empowers the police to take photographs of suspects in a variety of situations. For example, photographs may be taken of a detainee at a police station even if he does not consent. Code D provides that photographs obtained under s.64A may only be used or disclosed for purposes related to the prevention or detection of crime, the investigation of offences, the conduct of prosecutions, or the enforcement of sentences or other court orders. After being so used or disclosed, photographs may be retained but can only be used or disclosed again for the same purposes.

Under s.61 of PACE, the police can take fingerprints without consent in a variety of situations, most notably where a person detained at a police station has been arrested for, or charged with, a recordable offence. A recordable offence is one for which a conviction, *caution*, reprimand, or warning, may be recorded in national police records (basically, offences which carry a sentence of imprisonment, plus certain offences that do not).

> **caution:** *Where an offence has been committed, the police or the Crown Prosecution Service may be prepared to deal with the matter without instituting a criminal prosecution. Instead they may decide to caution the offender. A caution can only be given where the evidence is sufficient to have warranted prosecution. The offender must both admit his guilt and agree to accept the formal caution. A caution will usually be administered at a police station by an inspector. Although it does not have the same status as a conviction, a caution will be recorded on the Police National Computer.*

PACE s.61A empowers the police to take footwear impressions without consent from a person detained at a police station who has been arrested for, or charged with, a recordable offence.

Under PACE s.62, an intimate sample (which includes a sample of blood, semen, urine, or a dental impression) may be taken from a detainee, if authorised by an officer of the rank of inspector or above. The officer must have reasonable grounds both for suspecting the person's involvement in a recordable offence and for believing that the sample will tend to confirm or disprove the person's involvement in the offence. Where a person refuses consent to the taking of an intimate sample without good cause, the court or jury may draw an appropriate inference.

Under PACE s.63, a non-intimate sample (which includes a hair sample or a sample from, or under, a nail) may be taken from a person *without consent* in various circumstances. For example, a non-intimate sample may be taken without consent from a detainee who is under arrest for a recordable offence or from a person who has been charged with such an offence.

Code D governs the information that must be provided to a suspect before a photograph, fingerprint, footwear impression, or sample is taken, which includes the purpose for which it is being taken. Where a fingerprint, footwear impression, or sample is taken, the suspect must also be informed that it may be retained and may be the subject of a speculative search (i.e. the fingerprint, footwear mark, or DNA profile derived from the sample may be checked against records held by the police and other law enforcement authorities inside, and outside, the UK).

In 2001, PACE s.64 was amended to enable the police to retain DNA samples, finger-prints, and footwear impressions regardless of whether the person from whom they were taken was ultimately charged with, or convicted of, an offence. In *S and Marper v United Kingdom* [2008] ECHR 1581, the European Court of Human Rights held that this was a breach of the Article 8 right to respect for private life. As a result, the Crime and Security Act 2010 was enacted. The 2010 Act was passed under the previous Labour administration but the relevant sections were not in force by the time the current gov-ernment took office. Instead of bringing the provisions of the 2010 Act into force, the government introduced the Protection of Freedoms Act 2012, which sets out an alter-native scheme for the retention of biometric data. When the 2012 Act comes into force, it will repeal s.64 of PACE and insert ss.63D–63U in its place. Sections 63D–63U create an extremely complex statutory framework for the retention or destruction of fingerprints, footwear impressions, DNA samples, and DNA profiles obtained from such samples.

Under s.63C, footwear impressions may be retained as long as is necessary for pur-poses related to the prevention or detection of crime, the investigation of an offence, or the conduct of a prosecution, but must otherwise be destroyed within six months. The remainder of the new provisions focus on 's.63D material', which consists of fin-gerprints and DNA profiles derived from samples obtained under PACE. (Section 63R provides that the DNA sample itself must usually be destroyed as soon as a DNA pro-file has been obtained from it.)

Where s.63D material was taken unlawfully, or following an unlawful arrest, or where the arrest was a result of mistaken identity, it must be destroyed (s.63D(2)). Otherwise, where a person is convicted, warned, reprimanded, or cautioned, his fingerprints or DNA profile can be retained indefinitely. If he is not convicted, warned, reprimanded, or cautioned, the general rule is that s.63D material must be destroyed at the conclusion of the proceedings, or at the conclusion of the investigation if charges were never actually brought. However, this general rule is abrogated, and the police will be permitted to retain s.63D material in many cases, depending upon the offence with which the person was charged, his age, and the nature of any previous convictions. Thus, there remains a power to retain data that was obtained from unconvicted persons and, as Professor Ed Cape has suggested, '[i]t might be that the complexity of the new regime will make effective challenge on human rights grounds difficult' ('The Protection of Freedoms Act 2012: the retention and use of biometric data provisions' [2013] Crim LR 23).

12.5 Charging a detainee and the decision to prosecute

As we have seen, PACE s.37 provides that the custody officer is required to determine whether there is sufficient evidence to charge an arrested person with an offence.

In determining whether to charge him and what offence to charge him with, PACE s.37A requires the custody officer to have regard to guidance issued by the Director of Public Prosecutions (DPP). In most cases it is now Crown Prosecutors who determine whether a person is to be charged with an offence. Crown Prosecutors are lawyers employed by the **Crown Prosecution Service (CPS)**. For the purposes of providing charging advice, Crown Prosecutors are now deployed in police stations, and there is also a centrally managed out-of-hours duty prosecutor arrangement, known as CPS Direct. Crown Prosecutors also provide guidance and advice to investigators throughout the process of investigating and prosecuting an offence (for example, regarding evidential requirements).

See chapter 2, 2.6.2, 'The Attorney General' and 2.6.3, 'The Director of Public Prosecutions'.

For the Director's Guidance on charging go to: **www.cps.gov.uk/publications/ directors_guidance/dpp_guidance_5.html**.

> *Crown Prosecution Service (CPS):* The CPS is the main public prosecuting authority for England and Wales, its head being the Director of Public Prosecutions. The CPS is divided into areas, equating with police force areas, each area being under a Chief Crown Prosecutor. The CPS works with, but is independent of, the police. The Attorney General is accountable to Parliament for the Crown Prosecution Service.

Thus, in general, it is now Crown Prosecutors, rather than custody officers, who determine whether there is sufficient evidence to charge and whether, where there is sufficient evidence, a person should be charged or, for example, should be cautioned instead. There remain some circumstances, however, in which the police do still determine whether to charge, including in relation to certain road traffic offences. A custody officer may also release a person without charge and on bail for the purpose of enabling a Crown Prosecutor to subsequently make a charging decision under PACE s.37B.

Crown Prosecutors (and custody officers) should apply the Code for Crown Prosecutors (issued under s.10 of the Prosecution of Offences Act 1985) when determining whether to charge and, if so, what the charge(s) should be. The Code sets out the tests to be applied in deciding whether to prosecute a person for an offence.

The 'Full Code Test' has two stages: the 'evidential stage' and the 'public interest stage'. At the 'evidential stage', the Crown Prosecutor must decide whether there is enough admissible and reliable evidence to provide a realistic prospect of conviction. If the case passes the evidential stage, the next question is whether prosecution is in the public interest (the 'public interest stage'). Factors such as the age or state of health of the accused may persuade the Crown Prosecutor that prosecution is not in the public interest, unless the offence is serious or its repetition is likely. The Code also provides that the Crown Prosecutor must consider the circumstances of the victim and must take into account any views expressed by the victim as to the impact the offence(s) have had on them. 'However, the CPS does not act for victims or their families in the same way as solicitors act for their clients, and prosecutors must form an overall view of the public interest' (Code for Crown Prosecutors, para.4.12(c)).

Where all of the evidence in relation to an offence is not yet available and the Full Code Test cannot be applied at the time when the Crown Prosecutor is required to make the charging decision, the suspect should be released on police bail pending further enquiries. Alternatively, if it would not be appropriate to release the suspect on bail, for example because the offence is serious or there is a danger of the repetition of offences by the suspect if bailed, the Crown Prosecutor should decide whether to charge the suspect by applying the 'Threshold Test'. The Threshold Test is satisfied if there is a reasonable suspicion that the suspect committed an offence and it is in the public interest to charge the suspect. In such circumstances, the case must be reviewed under the Full Code Test as soon as is reasonably practicable.

For the Code for Crown Prosecutors go to: **www.cps.gov.uk/publications/docs/ code2013english_v2.pdf**.

A decision not to prosecute a suspect may be distressing for the victim. Historically, however, a victim had no right to challenge a decision not to institute proceedings, or to discontinue proceedings that had already commenced. Before the formation of the CPS in 1986, it was the policy of the Director of Public Prosecutions that, once a suspect had been informed of a decision that he would not be prosecuted, the decision should not be reappraised or reversed (HC Deb 25 April 1986, vol 96, col 640). The Director's policy was then revised so as to permit a decision not to prosecute to be revisited in exceptional circumstances. In 1993, the Attorney-General confirmed in Parliament:

> The fundamental consideration remains that individuals should be able to rely on decisions taken by the prosecuting authorities. The policy of the Director of Public Prosecutions is that a decision to terminate proceedings or not to prosecute should not, in the absence of special circumstances, be altered once it has been communicated to the defendant or prospective defendant unless it was taken and expressed to be taken because the evidence was insufficient. In such a case it would be appropriate to reconsider the decision if further significant evidence were to become available at a later date – especially if the alleged offence is a serious one. (HC Deb 31 March 1993, vol 222, col 200W)

More recently, the courts have become increasingly cognisant of the interests of victims in the prosecutorial process. The case of *R v Killick* [2011] EWCA Crim 1608 was a high point for victims' rights campaigners in this regard. In 2011, Christopher Killick was convicted of offences of sexual assault and non-consensual buggery against two disabled victims and was sentenced to three years' imprisonment. The CPS had originally decided not to prosecute Killick and a police officer wrote to the defendant informing him that the case against him would be discontinued. The victims challenged the decision not to prosecute, using the CPS procedure for general complaints about the level of service provided by the CPS. A new prosecutor looked at the case afresh and decided to bring charges. After Killick was convicted, he appealed against his convictions to the Court of Appeal, arguing that proceedings should not have been brought against him because he had been informed that he would not be prosecuted for the offences. Dismissing the defendant's appeal, the court held that victims have the right to a review of a decision not to prosecute. The court invited the DPP to consider introducing a clearer procedure and guidance to govern the review process.

Critical debate

Read *R v Killick* [2011] EWCA Crim 1608 and answer the following questions:

(a) Why did the Court of Appeal think it important that a decision not to prosecute should normally be a final decision?

(b) The court accepted that, where a defendant has been informed that he will not be prosecuted for an offence, any subsequent prosecution for that offence *may* constitute an abuse of process requiring the court to stay the indictment (i.e. stop the case). What criteria must be present before the court will find that there has been an abuse of process in these circumstances?

(c) In holding that victims have the right to a review of a decision not to prosecute, the court was influenced by the draft EU Directive on establishing minimum standards on the rights, support, and protection of victims of crime. What were the terms of the relevant provision of the draft directive?

(d) Why did the court suggest that it was inappropriate to require a victim to challenge a decision not to prosecute by way of the CPS complaints procedure?

The European Directive establishing minimum standards on the rights, support and protection of victims (2012/29/EU) was adopted on 25 October 2012. Subsequently, in June 2013, the Director of Public Prosecutions introduced the Victims' Right to Review (VRR) Scheme. The VRR Scheme provides that whenever a prosecutor decides not to bring charges against a suspect, or to stop a case that has already commenced, the victim of the offence must be notified of their right to request a review of that decision. The reviewing prosecutor will reconsider the evidence and the public interest before making a fresh decision as to whether a prosecution should take place. Details of the scheme can be found at: **www.cps.gov.uk/victims_witnesses/victims_right_to_review/index. html**. The VRR Scheme means that victims no longer have to rely on the CPS complaints procedure or apply to the courts for judicial review of a decision not to prosecute.

12.5.1 **After charge**

Except in terrorism cases, a detainee who has been charged may not be questioned further about the offence unless it is necessary: (i) to prevent or minimise harm or loss to a person or the public; (ii) to clear up ambiguity in a previous answer or a previous statement: or, (iii) in the interests of justice, to put information concerning the offence which has subsequently come to light to the accused for comment (Code C 16.5). Before such an interview takes place, the accused must be reminded of his right to legal advice and cautioned by being told '*you do not have to say anything, but anything you do say may be given in evidence*'. Thus, no inferences can be drawn from a person's failure to answer questions after he has been charged.

Section 22 of the Counter Terrorism Act 2008, which came into force on 10 July 2012, provides that a Crown Court judge may authorise post-charge questioning where the defendant has been charged with a terrorist offence, or the offence appears to the judge to have a 'terrorist connection'.

Thinking point

In a 2008 Home Office consultation entitled Modernising Police Powers, it was suggested that the police should be allowed to question a suspect after the decision to charge and before trial for all offences. Arguably, the additional evidence produced by such questioning could assist in determining whether additional charges are required or could lead to cases being discontinued. However, critics have argued that it could encourage the police to raise new issues via successive police station interviews rather than in the adversarial context of a criminal trial. Would this violate the basic principle that it is for the prosecution to prove the case against the accused and the accused is not required to help them to do so?

Once a person has been charged, PACE s.38 requires the custody officer to order the person's release unless certain specified circumstances apply. Examples of such circumstances are where:

- the person's name and address cannot be ascertained or there are reasonable grounds for believing that the person will fail to appear in court to answer bail;
- (if the person was arrested for an imprisonable offence) there are reasonable grounds for believing that detention is necessary to prevent the person from committing another offence;
- (if the offence is not an imprisonable offence) there are reasonable grounds for believing that detention is necessary to prevent the person from causing physical injury to another person or loss or damage to property;
- the charge is one of murder.

Where a person is kept in police detention following charge, PACE s.46 requires that the person be brought before a magistrates' court as soon as is practicable and no later than the first sitting after he was charged.

Summary

- Police powers are regulated by provisions of PACE and the Codes of Practice made under PACE.
- The police possess a variety of powers to search premises, to seize property, and to make arrests.
- The treatment of the suspect at the police station is subject to detailed requirements imposed by PACE and Code C.
- The admissibility of confessions is subject to the operation of PACE ss.76 and 78.

- Where the accused gives a no-comment interview at the police station, the jury may be entitled to draw inferences from the accused's silence.
- PACE imposes limits upon the maximum period for which a suspect may be detained at the police station.
- PACE permits the taking of fingerprints, footwear impressions, intimate samples, and non-intimate samples from a detainee. The regime governing the retention of fingerprints and DNA profiles obtained from such samples is extremely complex but, in general, material must be destroyed if the detainee is not charged or is ultimately acquitted of the offence.
- It is normally a Crown Prosecution Service lawyer, rather than the police, who decides whether a suspect should be prosecuted.

Questions

1 Do the police require a warrant: (a) in order to search a suspect's house; or (b) in order to search a suspect?

2 Identify three rights that an arrested person has upon arrival at a police station.

3 What are the potential consequences for a suspect who refuses to answer police questions?

4 What is a confession?

5 How long can a person be kept in police custody before being charged or released?

6 Can the police retain a person's fingerprints if he is subsequently acquitted of the offence with which he was charged?

Sample question and outline answer

Question

Seema is a 23-year-old classroom assistant. One morning, on her way to work, Seema passes the site of a demonstration about the refusal of planning permission to build a new mosque in the area. Some of the protestors have drawn slogans on the surrounding walls and pavements. As she is walking by, PC Odell approaches Seema and tells her that she is going to search her under s.1 of PACE. PC Odell tells Seema that she must take off her coat and hijab. PC Odell then searches the pockets of Seema's coat and finds two marker pens. She takes the pens and decides that she needs to interview Seema about them. She tells Seema that she is under arrest on suspicion of possessing items with intent to damage property.

Seema is taken to the police station where she is placed in a cold, damp cell and left unattended for seven hours. She is then taken to an interview room, where she is interviewed by PC Thomas. Seema tells PC Thomas that she was taking the marker pens to work. PC Thomas says that he does not believe her. He shouts at her over 100 times that she must admit that she was going to use the pens to write slogans. Seema eventually says that she intended to use the marker pens to damage property by writing on walls.

Advise Seema on whether the police officers acted lawfully and explain whether the evidence of the marker pens and her confession would be admissible at any subsequent trial.

Outline answer

There are two main types of question in law examinations: the discursive, essay-type question and the problem-based question, which requires students to apply the law to the facts of a given scenario. This is an example of the latter. When answering a problem question, you should work through the scenario in chronological order. At each stage, you should explain what the relevant law is and then apply the law to the facts set out in the question. You may find it helpful to use headings to structure your answer and to ensure that all of the problems in the scenario are covered.

Stop and search

Section 1 of PACE allows an officer to search a person if he has reasonable grounds to suspect that he will find a stolen or prohibited article, bladed article, or firework. Although prohibited articles include articles intended for use in connection with criminal damage (PACE s.1(8)), it does not appear that PC Odell had reasonable grounds for suspecting Seema. Seema was simply passing the site of a demonstration. Although the demonstration concerned the building of a mosque and may, therefore, have been attended by Muslim protestors, the fact that Seema is Muslim cannot form the basis of a reasonable suspicion (PACE Code A).

PC Odell ought to have had a conversation with Seema before searching her (PACE Code A). If she had asked Seema where she was going, she might have realised that there was no need to search her. Before searching Seema, PC Odell should have clearly explained the purpose of the search (PACE Code A). A person can only be required to remove an outer coat in public and not any other clothing (PACE Code A). Seema should not have been asked to remove the hijab.

Having discovered the marker pens, PC Odell was entitled to seize them (PACE s.1(6)). The fact that the search was not carried out in accordance with s.1 of PACE and Code A does not mean that evidence of the discovery of the marker pens will be inadmissible at Seema's trial (*Kuruma v R* (1955)).

Arrest

A police officer has a power to arrest a person without a warrant under s.24 of PACE if he has reasonable grounds to suspect that they are in the act of committing, or are about to commit, an offence. The officer must also have reasonable grounds to believe the arrest is necessary. Here the possession of the marker pens may well give PC Odell reasonable grounds to suspect that Seema intended to cause criminal damage. However, it is not clear why her immediate arrest was necessary. An officer who believes it is necessary to interview someone should consider whether the suspect's voluntary attendance at the police station would be a practicable alternative (Code G). PC Odell does not appear to have considered any alternatives to arrest (*Richardson v CC of West Midlands* (2011); *Hanningfield v CC of Essex* (2013)).

Detention

It is not clear whether Seema was brought before the custody officer immediately upon her arrival at the police station, as she ought to have been. She should have been informed that she had the right to have someone informed of her whereabouts (PACE s.56) and that she had the right to consult a solicitor (PACE s.58). The custody record will show whether she was informed of these rights.

Seema should not have been placed in a damp, cold cell. Cells should be adequately heated, cleaned, ventilated, and lit (PACE Code C). Seema should have been checked every hour (PACE Code C) and her detention should have been reviewed by the custody officer after six hours (PACE s.40). She should not have been left for seven hours unattended.

Interview

It is not clear whether the custody officer assessed whether Seema was fit for interview as required by Code C. Even if she was, the conduct of the interview was certainly unlawful. Seema should have been cautioned and informed of her right to have a solicitor present (PACE Code C). Shouting repeatedly at a suspect constitutes oppression within the meaning of s.76(2)(a) of PACE (*R v Miller* (1993)). Unless the prosecution can prove that Seema's confession was not obtained by oppression, it will not be admissible at her trial (PACE s.76(2)(a)). The interview should have been recorded (PACE Code C), so there should be no difficulty in establishing what took place.

Further reading

When reading articles and reports on the role of the police and the rights of suspects, your primary aim should be to grasp the nature and scope of the power or right that is being discussed. Consider also any criticisms of the way in which the power or right is exercised and note any problems that have arisen in practice.

- **Cape, E.** 'Case comment: *Hayes v Chief Constable of Merseyside*' [2012] Crim LR 35
  Discusses the increasing importance of the provision in s.24 of PACE which permits the power of arrest to be exercised only if it is necessary.

- **Cape, E.** 'The Protection of Freedoms Act 2012: The retention and use of biometric data provisions' [2013] Crim LR 23
  Explains the complex regime governing the retention of fingerprints, footwear impressions, and DNA profiles.

- **Cape, E.** 'The Counter-terrorism Provisions of the Protection of Freedoms Act 2012: Preventing misuse or a case of smoke and mirrors?' [2013] Crim LR 385
  Explains the changes that have been made to pre-charge detention periods in terrorism cases and discusses the circumstances in which post-charge questioning may take place.

- **Dennis, I.** 'Silence in the Police Station: The marginalization of section 34' [2002] Crim LR 25
  Analyses the circumstances in which inferences may be drawn from a suspect's silence in response to questioning in the police station.

- Her Majesty's Inspectorate of Constabulary, *Stop and Search Powers: Are the police using them effectively and fairly* (HMIC 2013)
  An official report based upon the inspection of stop and search records. Explores whether stop and search powers are used appropriately.

- **Leng, R.** 'Silence Pre-trial, Reasonable Expectations and the Normative Distortion of Fact-finding' (2001) 5(4) E & P 240
  Explores whether the power to draw adverse inferences from silence in response to police questioning is necessary and whether it promotes the interests of justice.

- **Malkani, B.** 'Article 8 of the European Convention on Human Rights and the Decision to Prosecute' [2011] Crim LR 943
  Discusses the relationship between Article 8 of the ECHR (right to respect for private life) and the decision to prosecute an individual for an offence.

- **Reid, K.** 'Race Issues and Stop and Search: Looking behind the statistics' (2012) J Crim L 165
  Explores whether official statistics indicate racism in the use of stop and search powers by the police.

- **Smith, J.C.** 'Exculpatory Statements and Confessions' [1995] Crim LR 280
  Explains the meaning of the term 'confession'.

- **Starmer, K.** 'Finality in Criminal Justice: When should the CPS reopen a case?' [2012] Crim LR 526
  Explains the circumstances in which it is permissible for the CPS to revisit a decision not to prosecute someone for an offence.

- **Zander, M.** 'Stop and Search is not Working Properly' (2013) 177 JPN 487
  Summarises the findings of the report of Her Majesty's Inspectorate of Constabulary on the use of stop and search powers.

 Online Resource Centre

You should now attempt the supporting multiple choice questions available at **www.oxfordtextbooks.co.uk/orc/wilson_els/**.

13 The criminal process: pre-trial and trial

Learning objectives

By the end of this chapter you should:

- be aware of the process by which a person may end up before a criminal court;

- appreciate the differences between the Crown Court and the magistrates' courts;

- be aware of the distinctions between summary trial and trial on indictment;

- be aware of the major pre-trial stages which occur in criminal proceedings;

- be familiar with the process of a criminal trial; and

- have a basic understanding of some of the key rules of criminal evidence.

🔵 Talking point

Operation Yewtree was set up to investigate hundreds of claims of sexual abuse that came to light following the death of Jimmy Savile in 2011. As part of Operation Yewtree, sixteen suspects have been arrested, the majority of whom have been named in the press. To date, charges have only been brought against five men. This has reignited the debate about whether those accused of sexual offences, particularly rape, should be granted anonymity prior to conviction.

Those who support pre-conviction anonymity for defendants accused of rape argue that a particular stigma attaches to rape allegations and suspicion remains, even if the defendant is ultimately acquitted. On the other side of the debate, it has been suggested that publishing the names of those accused of rape may give other victims the confidence to report sexual offences to the police.

*In the case of Stuart Hall, Lancashire Constabulary confirmed that the publicity surrounding the arrest of the former television presenter led to more of his victims coming forward. Stuart Hall eventually pleaded guilty to fourteen sexual offences against girls aged nine to 17. However, a ComRes survey for The Independent newspaper in May 2013 found that three out of four people still believe that those accused of sexual assaults should be given anonymity until they are proven guilty (***www.independent.co.uk/news/ uk/crime/exclusive-three-in-four-believe-those-accused-of-sexual-assaults -should-be-granted-anonymity-8599788.html*** accessed 30 September 2013).*

Introduction

This chapter will examine how cases progress through the criminal justice system. Not every person in respect of whom proceedings are instituted will necessarily appear in court. For example, a person who is convicted of speeding after being caught by a speed camera may be able to plead guilty by post and be sentenced in his absence. In the majority of cases, however, a defendant will have to appear in person and will appear first in the magistrates' court.

Most cases will remain in the magistrates' court, while more serious cases will be transferred to the Crown Court. The circumstances in which a case will be 'sent' to the Crown Court, and the procedures involved, depend upon the offence alleged. 'Summary only' offences, which are minor offences, will remain in the magistrates' court. Very serious offences are 'indictable only' offences and must be sent to the Crown Court to be tried on indictment. In between are a range of offences that are 'triable either way' and can be heard in either court.

The Crown Court and magistrates' courts each have their own rules and procedures. It is useful to have an understanding of the types of pre-trial hearing that take place in each venue and the steps that need to be taken prior to trial. You may be surprised to discover that, in the vast majority of cases, defendants plead guilty at one of these pre-trial hearings. Where a trial does take place, the major difference between Crown Court trial and summary trial is that the former takes place before a jury, whereas the latter takes place before either magistrates or a district judge. In both courts the format of a trial is very similar. The same evidential issues can also arise in the context of both summary trial and trial on indictment. This chapter will examine some of these evidential issues, such as the right to silence and the extent to which this has been eroded by statutory provisions that enable inferences to be drawn against a defendant who chooses not to testify.

13.1 The criminal courts of trial and the classification of offences

Criminal trials may take place in the Crown Court, the magistrates' court, or the Youth Court. Consideration of the constitution and operation of the Youth Court is outside the scope of this book. An adult defendant will be tried in either the magistrates' court or the Crown Court.

A magistrates' court comprises either a district judge or a bench of lay magistrates. Lay magistrates, who are not legally qualified, are advised on the law by a legally qualified clerk. District judges or magistrates are the sole arbiters of proceedings in the magistrates' courts. They decide both questions of law and questions of fact. As the tribunal of law, they are responsible for deciding all of the legal issues that arise in the proceedings, including issues as to the admissibility of evidence. For example, where a defendant suggests that a confession was made as a result of oppression, they will have to decide whether, as a matter of law, the confession is admissible or not. As the tribunal of fact, a district judge, or a bench of lay magistrates, is also responsible for judging the evidence, determining all of the relevant facts of the case, and deciding whether the defendant is guilty or not guilty.

In a jury trial, the judge decides questions of law and the jury decides the facts of the case. The dual role of the tribunal in the magistrates' court can lead to unfairness because, where the district judge or magistrates rule that evidence is inadmissible, they are nevertheless aware of its existence. If, for example, a defendant made a confession

For further information about the composition of magistrates' courts, see 1.5.1.

See 12.3.4 for further consideration of the difficulties that may arise where a district judge or magistrates are required to decide whether a confession is admissible.

to the police, which was ruled inadmissible by a bench of magistrates under s.76 of the Police and Criminal Evidence Act (PACE) 1984, the same bench of magistrates would go on to determine whether or not the defendant was guilty of the offence. Critics of this system argue that it is unrealistic to expect magistrates to put evidence, such as an inadmissible confession, from their minds when reaching a verdict.

The Crown Court comprises a judge, who is the tribunal of law, and a jury of twelve randomly selected members of the public, which is the tribunal of fact. In a Crown Court trial, the judge decides all questions of law, such as whether or not certain evidence is admissible. However, it is the jury that decides the facts of the case. On the basis of those facts, and applying any directions of law that the judge has given them, the jury decides whether the defendant is guilty or not guilty.

For further information in relation to juries see chapter 10.

Whether a defendant is tried in the magistrates' court or the Crown Court depends upon the classification of the offence(s) with which he is charged. For these purposes, all criminal offences fall into one of three categories:

- summary only offences;
- indictable only offences; or
- offences that are triable either way.

Summary only offences can usually only be tried in the magistrates' court. The sentencing powers of magistrates' courts are limited. For this reason, summary offences tend to be less serious offences, such as speeding, being drunk and disorderly, and common assault. In limited circumstances, summary offences may be tried in the Crown Court. For example, s.40 of the Criminal Justice Act 1988 provides that certain specified summary offences, including common assault or driving a motor vehicle whilst disqualified, may be included in an indictment if they are founded on the same facts or evidence as an indictable offence.

Example

John is charged with dangerous driving and is to be tried on indictment in the Crown Court. The evidence shows that he was disqualified from driving at the time of the offence. Section 40 of the Criminal Justice Act 1988 allows a charge of driving whilst disqualified to be added to the indictment even though driving whilst disqualified is a summary only offence.

Indictable only offences can only be tried 'on **indictment**' in the Crown Court. They include the most serious criminal offences, such as murder, robbery, and rape.

indictment: An indictment is a formal document that must be prepared for Crown Court proceedings. It sets out the charge or charges against the defendant and must include the name of the court, a statement of each offence, and brief particulars (i.e. details) of each offence.

Either way offences, as the name suggests, may be tried in either the magistrates' court or the Crown Court. Either way offences include theft, assault occasioning actual bodily harm, and affray. Where a defendant is charged with an either way offence, a formal allocation procedure must be held to determine the venue for trial. This procedure is considered at 13.7.2.

> ### 🔒 Key point
>
> It is important not to confuse the terms 'indictable' and 'indictable only'. An indictable offence is any offence that is capable of being tried on indictment in the Crown Court. There are, therefore, two types of indictable offence: those that are indictable only and *must* be tried in the Crown Court and those that are triable either way, which *may* be tried in the Crown Court.

All common law offences are indictable offences, whereas a statutory offence will be indictable if the statute specifies a penalty to be imposed if the offence is tried on indictment. Note that the classification of an offence is determined by the offence itself and not by the facts of the case. Thus, theft is always an either way offence, whether it is theft of diamond jewellery or theft of a bar of chocolate from a shop.

13.2 Instituting criminal proceedings

A variety of public bodies, as well as individuals, have the power to institute criminal proceedings. However, most prosecutions for both summary and indictable offences are brought by the Crown Prosecution Service (CPS).

13.2.1 The Crown Prosecution Service (CPS)

In 1981, the Royal Commission on Criminal Procedure (referred to at 12.2) recommended that an independent state agency should be set up to institute and oversee the prosecution of offences. As a result, the CPS was created by the Prosecution of Offences Act 1985. The CPS is a national prosecution service headed by the Director of Public Prosecutions (the DPP).

Section 3 of the 1985 Act gives the DPP the power to institute criminal proceedings. In practice, decisions as to whether to institute proceedings are taken by local Crown Prosecutors on behalf of the DPP. Where a prosecution is brought by another agency or by a private individual, s.6 of the 1985 Act gives the DPP the power to take over the conduct of the proceedings. The DPP even has the power to take over a case and then discontinue it in appropriate circumstances.

Thinking point

Prior to 1986, most prosecutions were brought by the police. What criticisms could be made of a system in which the police both investigated and prosecuted offences? Is the CPS, as an independent body, more likely to be able to assess evidence objectively and conduct cases fairly at court?

13.2.2 Commencing criminal proceedings

Although an indictable offence may eventually be tried in the Crown Court, criminal proceedings against adult defendants for both summary and indictable offences always begin in the magistrates' court. Perhaps the most obvious way in which criminal proceedings against a defendant commence is where the defendant is arrested and charged with a criminal offence. He will then either be detained and produced before a magistrates' court, or released by the police on bail with a condition of attendance before a magistrates' court on a specified day.

Alternatively, where a person has not been arrested, proceedings may be instituted by the issuing of a written charge and requisition, or the laying of an information and the issue of a summons.

13.2.3 Written charge and requisition

Where a defendant is not charged at the police station, a prosecutor may institute criminal proceedings by issuing a 'written charge' (which charges the defendant with an offence) and a 'requisition' (which requires him to appear before a magistrates' court to answer the written charge). The written charge and requisition must both be served on the defendant and copies must be served on the court. This is now the only procedure available to public prosecutors (such as the CPS), who can no longer lay an information to obtain a summons or warrant of arrest.

13.2.4 Information and summons

The procedure for laying an information to obtain a summons is still available to private prosecutors. An 'information' is a statement alleging that a person has committed an offence and providing brief details about that offence. An information may be laid (i.e. put before the magistrates' court) either orally or in writing. The prosecutor may then obtain a summons requiring the defendant to appear before a magistrates' court (Magistrates' Courts Act 1980 s.1). A summons is a formal document issued by the court calling upon a named person to present themselves before the court on a given date.

13.2.5 **Time limits**

Proceedings for a summary only offence must be brought within six months of the offence being committed (Magistrates' Courts Act 1980 s.127). There is no time limit for commencing proceedings for an either way or an indictable only offence.

Thinking point

Some countries have a 'statute of limitations' preventing criminal proceedings from being instituted after a given period of time. What reasons might there be for imposing time limits on prosecutions? Do they encourage the police to investigate offences promptly and efficiently?

Why do you think we only have time limits in relation to summary only offences in this country? Bear in mind that it may take time to investigate an offence and the absence of a time limit for indictable offences means that more serious offences can always be prosecuted.

A further time limit is applicable to some road traffic offences. Under ss.1 and 2 of the Road Traffic Offenders Act 1988, a conviction cannot be obtained in respect of certain offences, such as speeding, unless the driver was given notice of intended prosecution within 14 days of the commission of the offence.

13.2.6 **Fixed penalty notices for road traffic offences and penalty notices for disorder**

In relation to certain minor road traffic offences, such as speeding, the police may decide to issue a motorist with a fixed penalty notice. In this case, unless the motorist denies the offence, or requests a hearing for some other reason, he will pay the specified fine to the magistrates' court and, if appropriate, his licence will be automatically endorsed with a fixed number of penalty points. He does not need to appear in court.

Under s.2 of the Criminal Justice and Police Act 2001, the police can now issue a penalty notice for disorderly behaviour in relation to offences such as theft, littering, and possession of cannabis. A person who receives such a notice can request a hearing or can pay the specified penalty.

Table 13.1 shows the number of penalty notices for disorder in relation to various offences in the year ending September 2012.

Thinking point

What advantages do fixed penalty notices have for both the offender and the police? Note that a person who pays a fixed penalty for disorderly behaviour does not receive a conviction for the relevant offence. Consider the implications for police resources if every minor offender had to be charged, or requisitioned to attend court.

Table 13.1 Number of Penalty Notices for Disorder issued to offenders aged 16 and over, by gender and offence, 12 months ending September 2012

England and Wales

Offence	All offenders	Males						Females					
		All ages	%	Aged 16-17	%	Aged 18+	%	All ages	%	Aged 16-17	%	Aged 18+	%
Higher Tier Offences (£80)													
Wasting police time	2,536	1,564	62	68	3	1,496	59	972	38	40	2	932	37
Misuse of public telecommunications system	692	505	73	27	4	478	69	187	27	9	1	178	26
Giving false alarm to fire and rescue authority	39	36	92	-	-	36	92	3	8	-	-	3	8
Causing harassment, alarm or distress	18,896	16,158	86	815	4	15,343	81	2,738	14	146	1	2,592	14
Throwing fireworks	286	265	93	45	16	220	77	21	7	-	-	21	7
Drunk and disorderly	33,637	27,869	83	793	2	27,076	80	5,768	17	202	1	5,566	17
Criminal damage (under £500)	3,781	3,203	85	248	7	2,955	78	578	15	38	1	540	14
Theft (retail under £200)	29,187	15,472	53	821	3	14,651	50	13,715	47	596	2	13,119	45
Breach of fireworks curfew	12	7	58	2	17	5	42	5	42	-	-	5	42
Possession of category 4 firework	19	18	95	3	16	15	79	1	5	-	-	1	5
Possession by a person under 18 of adult firework	45	41	91	35	78	6	13	4	9	2	4	2	4
Sale of alcohol to drunken person	92	62	67	1	1	61	66	30	33	-	-	30	33
Supply of alcohol to a person under 18	48	36	75	1	2	35	73	12	25	-	-	12	25
Sale of alcohol to a person under 18	1,316	801	61	9	1	792	60	515	39	5	0	510	39
Purchasing alcohol for a person under 18	173	134	77	8	5	126	73	39	23	2	1	37	21
Purchasing alcohol for a person under 18 for consumption on the premises	23	21	91	4	17	17	74	2	9	1	4	1	4

Delivery of alcohol to a person under 18 or allowing such delivery	66	52	79	1	2	51	77	14	21	–	–	14	21
Possession of cannabis	15,750	14,852	94	341	2	14,511	92	898	6	14	0	884	6
Lower Tier Offences (£50)													
Trespassing on a railway	1,071	959	90	75	7	884	83	112	10	17	2	95	9
Throwing stones at a train/ railway	9	8	89	1	11	7	78	1	11	–	–	1	11
Drunk in a highway	516	422	82	16	3	406	79	94	18	2	0	92	18
Consumption of alcohol in a designated public place	664	585	88	3	0	582	88	79	12	–	–	79	12
Depositing and leaving litter	625	558	89	41	7	517	83	67	11	13	2	54	9
Consumption of alcohol by a person under 18 on relevant premises	17	9	53	8	47	1	6	8	47	6	35	2	12
Allowing consumption of alcohol by a person under 18 on relevant premises	–	–	–	–	–	–	–	–	–	–	–	–	–
Buying or attempting to buy alcohol by a person under 18	21	17	81	13	62	4	19	4	19	2	10	2	10
Depositing and leaving litter in a Royal Park	1	1	100	–	–	1	100	–	–	–	–	–	–
Use of pedal cycle in a Royal Park	114	91	80	–	–	91	80	23	20	–	–	23	20
Failing to remove animal faeces from a Royal Park	–	–	–	–	–	–	–	–	–	–	–	–	–
Totals													
Total Higher Tier Offences	106,598	81,096	76	3,222	3	77,874	73	25,502	24	1,055	1	24,447	23
Total Lower Tier Offences	3,038	2,650	87	157	5	2,493	82	388	13	40	1	348	11
Total all offences	109,636	83,746	76	3,379	3	80,367	73	25,890	24	1,095	1	24,795	23

Source: Ministry of Justice.

13.3 **The Auld Review**

In 1999, the Lord Chancellor, the Home Secretary and the Attorney General appointed Lord Justice Auld to conduct a review into the working of the criminal courts. In announcing the appointment, the Lord Chancellor stated:

> The Government's aim is to provide criminal courts which are, and are seen to be:
>
> - modern and in touch with the communities they serve;
> - efficient;
> - fair and responsive to the needs of all their users;
> - co-operative in their relations with other criminal justice agencies; and
> - with modern and effective case management to remove unnecessary delays from the system. (Auld LJ, *Review of the Criminal Courts of England and Wales*, 2001, Foreword, para.2)

A study carried out by the Law Commission for the Auld Review in 2000 found that there were 207 Acts of Parliament containing provisions relating to criminal procedure and/or evidence, one of which dated back to 1795. There were also 64 pieces of secondary legislation containing rules that differed in application according to whether they governed summary trials or trial on indictment. These statutory provisions were supplemented by Guidance issued by both the Lord Chief Justice and the Attorney General (*Auld Review*, Chapter 10, para.272). Lord Justice Auld stated:

> Fairness, efficiency and effectiveness of the criminal justice system demand that its procedures should be simple, accessible and, so far as practicable, the same for every level and type of criminal jurisdiction. There are many features of criminal procedure that are common to summary proceedings and those on indictment, yet at present they are separately provided for in each jurisdiction and in a multiplicity of instruments and, often, in quite different language. Such a mix of different provisions providing for common procedural needs is an impediment to understanding by courts, legal practitioners, parties and others of the workings of the courts, and thus to the accessibility of the law…(*Auld Review*, Chapter 10, para.271)

The Auld Review recommended that there should be a unified criminal court with a single procedural code. A unified court came into being in 2005 when Her Majesty's Courts Service was created. HM Courts Service amalgamated with the Tribunals Service in 2010. HM Courts and Tribunals Service is now a single, integrated agency of the Ministry of Justice, which is responsible for the administration of the criminal, civil, and family courts and tribunals in England and Wales (see **www.justice.gov.uk/about/hmcts**). A single procedural code was created by the Criminal Procedure Rules 2005. The approach for the Criminal Procedure Rules was based on the Civil Procedure Rules, which had been introduced seven years earlier (see chapter 15).

13.4 **The Criminal Procedure Rules 2013**

Procedure in the criminal courts is now governed by the Criminal Procedure Rules 2013 (CrimPR) (see **www.justice.gov.uk/criminal/procrules_fin/rulesmenu.htm**). CrimPR Part 1 states that the 'overriding objective' of the criminal justice system is to ensure that cases are dealt with justly, which includes:

- acquitting innocent defendants and convicting the guilty;
- dealing with the parties fairly;
- recognising the defendant's rights (and, in particular, the right to a fair trial under Article 6 of the European Convention on Human Rights);
- respecting the interests of witnesses, victims, and jurors;
- dealing with cases efficiently and expeditiously; and
- dealing with cases in ways that take into account the gravity of offences, the complexity of issues, the severity of the consequences, and the needs of other cases.

The court is required to further the overriding objective and the parties are also required to prepare and conduct the case in accordance with it.

> **Key point**
>
> The overriding objective seeks to balance the interests of the prosecution and the defence. Throughout the remainder of this chapter, consider the extent to which the criminal justice system as a whole achieves this aim.

The CrimPR are divided into eleven sections that correspond with the different stages of a criminal case, from 'preliminary hearings' to 'appeals'. The CrimPR are supplemented by the Criminal Practice Directions (CPD) ([2013] EWCA Crim 1631), which came into force on 7 October 2013. The CPD replaced the Consolidated Criminal Practice Direction, which has been revoked. The text of all of the CPD can be found in a single document at **www.judiciary.gov.uk/publications-and-reports/ practice-directions/criminal-practice-directions**.

13.5 **First hearings**

As previously discussed, a person who is offered, and pays, a fixed penalty will not need to appear before the court. In all other cases involving adult defendants, whether proceedings are instituted by arrest or by the issuing of a written charge and requisition, the defendant's first hearing will take place in the magistrates' court.

Where an adult appears before a magistrates' court charged with an offence triable only on indictment, s.51(2)(a) of the Crime and Disorder Act 1998 requires the magistrates' court to send him to the Crown Court forthwith. In other cases the nature of the further hearings that will take place after the first appearance and prior to trial varies according to the type of offence with which the defendant is charged.

13.6 Pre-trial hearings: summary only offences

A defendant charged with a summary only offence may wish to plead guilty. This can usually be done at his first appearance before the magistrates' court and the court will either proceed straight to sentence or adjourn for pre-sentence reports (see chapter 14). In some cases, however, the prosecution and/or the defence will have good reason for requesting more time for preparation and the proceedings will be adjourned at the first hearing. Where there is to be a not guilty plea, steps will be taken to prepare for trial. These steps include setting the trial date and dealing with pre-trial issues, such as disclosure.

For further information about disclosure, see 13.13.

13.7 Pre-trial hearings: either way offences

Where the defendant is charged with an either way offence, formal 'allocation' proceedings must take place to determine the trial venue. The allocation provisions have replaced the old 'mode of trial' provisions, although the procedure involved is very similar. If the case is allocated to the Crown Court for trial, the defendant is sent forthwith to the Crown Court under s.51(1) of the Crime and Disorder Act 1998. Committal proceedings, which used to take place following a decision that a case should be tried in the Crown Court, have been abolished.

One of the main considerations for both the court and the defendant in deciding allocation is that the sentencing powers of the magistrates' court are limited to six months' imprisonment (or 12 months where the defendant is charged with two or more offences that are triable either way), whereas the Crown Court will usually have the power to impose a longer sentence up to the statutory or common law maximum for the offence in question.

13.7.1 Plea before venue

Before the allocation procedure commences, the defendant must be given an opportunity to indicate whether, if the offence were to proceed to trial, he would plead guilty or not guilty (Magistrates' Courts Act 1980 s.17A). This is known as the 'plea before venue' procedure. If the defendant indicates that he would plead guilty to the offence, the magistrates' court should record a conviction against him

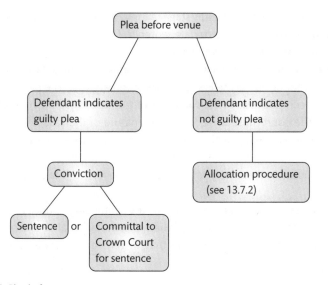

Diagram 13.1 Plea before venue

without hearing any evidence. The magistrates (or district judge) must then decide whether they can sentence him or whether he should be committed (i.e. trans-ferred) to the Crown Court for sentence. If the defendant indicates that he would plead not guilty, or declines to indicate what his plea would be, the court must fol-low the allocation procedure laid down by ss.19 to 23 of the 1980 Act (as amended by s.41 and Sch.3 of the Criminal Justice Act 2003). Diagram 13.1 illustrates the plea before venue procedure.

The defendant obviously cannot be expected to indicate his likely plea unless he knows the substance of the charges he faces. CrimPR Part 10 provides that the prose-cution must serve initial details of the prosecution case prior to the allocation hearing.

13.7.2 **Allocation procedure**

If the defendant either indicates a not guilty plea, or declines to indicate a plea at all, allocation proceedings will take place. At the allocation hearing, the magistrates' court must first decide whether the case is suitable for summary trial or whether it is not suitable for summary trial, for example, because it is too serious. If the court decides that the case is *not* suitable for summary trial, the case will be sent to the Crown Court and the defendant will have no choice in the matter. However, if the court decides that the case *is* suitable for summary trial, the defendant can either accept summary trial or elect trial by jury in the Crown Court. Before making a decision, the defend-ant may ask the court for an indication as to whether he would receive a custodial or a non-custodial sentence if he were to plead guilty. The court does not have to give an indication but may do so if asked. In practice only scant information about a case tends to be available at such an early stage in the proceedings, which makes it difficult for a court to determine the appropriate sentence. Diagram 13.2 shows the procedure that will be followed at an allocation hearing.

There are a number of factors that the magistrates' court must take into account in deciding whether or not a case is suitable for summary trial. The parties are entitled to make representations as to the suitability of the case for summary trial or trial on indictment. The court must also consider the nature of the case, the seriousness of the offence, the adequacy of the magistrates' court's sentencing powers, and any other relevant circumstances. The court should be informed of the defendant's previous convictions, as these may affect the likely sentence (Magistrates' Courts Act 1980 s.19).

An Allocation Guideline has been issued by the Sentencing Council to provide guidance to magistrates when determining whether summary trial or trial on indictment is more suitable. The Guideline provides that, in general, either way offences should

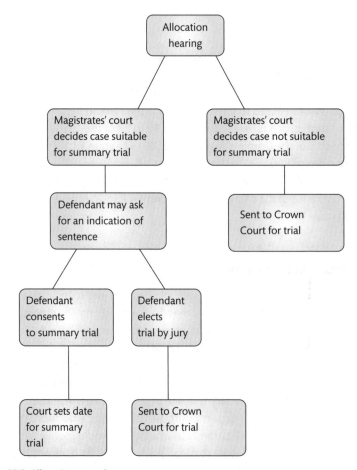

Diagram 13.2 Allocation procedure

be tried summarily unless it is likely that the magistrates' court's sentencing powers will be insufficient (**http://sentencingcouncil.judiciary.gov.uk/docs/Allocation_guideline2.pdf**).

If the magistrates' court decides that summary trial would be more suitable, the defendant must be told that he may either consent to summary trial or may choose to be tried on indictment in the Crown Court. The following factors may influence his decision:

- Statistically, there is a greater chance of acquittal before a jury.

- A jury, unlike magistrates, will not hear potentially prejudicial evidence that has been excluded by the judge in their absence (e.g. if a judge rules that a confession is inadmissible, the jury will never get to hear of it, see 12.4.4).

- A Crown Court judge may be better equipped to deal with issues of law than lay magistrates.

Conversely:

- The Crown Court has greater sentencing powers than a magistrates' court.

- A Crown Court trial is more expensive and a defendant who is convicted may be ordered to pay the costs of the case.

- A defendant may have to wait longer for a Crown Court trial, although the new allocation provisions and the abolition of committal proceedings are designed to shorten the period between a defendant's first appearance and trial on indictment.

Before deciding whether to accept the jurisdiction of the magistrates' court, the defendant may ask for an indication of sentence. Any indication that is given should be limited to an indication as to whether a custodial or a non-custodial sentence would be passed if the defendant were to plead guilty at that point. The court does not have to give an indication but, if an indication is given, it is binding on the court if the defendant pleads guilty immediately.

If the magistrates' court does not consider the case suitable for summary trial, or if the defendant chooses trial by jury, the case must be sent forthwith to the Crown Court under s.51(1) of the Crime and Disorder Act 1998. A preliminary hearing in the Crown Court will usually be held 14–21 days after the case is sent, followed by a Plea and Case Management Hearing (see 13.9).

13.7.3 **Abolition of committal proceedings**

Before s.41 and sch.3 of the Criminal Justice Act 2003 came into force on 28 May 2013, either way offences had to be 'committed' to the Crown Court if the magistrates' court declined jurisdiction or the defendant elected trial on indictment. The purpose of committal proceedings was to ensure that a defendant was only committed to the Crown Court if there was sufficient evidence against him. When asked to commit a case to the Crown Court for trial, the role of the magistrates was to inquire into the case as 'examining justices'. This meant that the court had to decide whether the case against the defendant was strong enough to put him on trial before a jury.

Prior to the committal taking place, the prosecution had to serve a 'committal bundle' on the defence, consisting of the evidence relied upon by the prosecution. Where the defence accepted that there was sufficient evidence to put the defendant on trial, the proceedings took the form of a committal without consideration of the evidence under s.6(2) of the Magistrates' Courts Act 1980 and the magistrates' court simply agreed to commit the defendant to the Crown Court for trial.

However, if the defendant's legal representative submitted that there was insufficient evidence to put the defendant on trial in the Crown Court for the offence (or if he was unrepresented), s.6(1) of the 1980 Act required the magistrates' court to consider the evidence. The prosecutor had to read out the evidence contained in the committal bundle and the court could only commit the defendant for trial if of the opinion that there was sufficient evidence to put the defendant on trial for an indictable offence.

Committal proceedings were abolished by s.41 and Sch.3 of the Criminal Justice Act 2003, which came fully into force on 28 May 2013. The aim of the new allocation provisions is to ensure that, where Crown Court trial is more appropriate, the case arrives at the Crown Court as soon as possible. Although the magistrates' court no longer considers the evidence in a case, the defendant is entitled to make an application to the Crown Court for the charges in the case to be dismissed. A Crown Court judge must then consider the evidence and shall dismiss a charge if it appears that the evidence would not be sufficient for the defendant to be properly convicted (Sch.3 para.2 of the Crime and Disorder Act 1998).

13.8 Pre-trial hearings: indictable only offences

As was seen at 13.5, where a defendant appears before a magistrates' court charged with an offence triable only on indictment, s.51(2)(a) of the Crime and Disorder Act 1998 provides that he must be sent to the Crown Court forthwith. (Under s.51B and s.51C of the 1998 Act, complex or serious fraud cases and certain cases involving child witnesses or child complainants may also be transferred to the Crown Court without an allocation hearing. Further consideration of these types of case falls outside the scope of this work.)

Between 14 and 21 days after the sending of a case by the magistrates' court, the Crown Court will usually hold a preliminary hearing (sometimes referred to as a 'Narey hearing'), at which a timetable will be set for the future progress of the case. This will include a date by which the prosecution must serve its evidence on the defence and a date for the Plea and Case Management Hearing (PCMH). The PCMH should normally take place within 13 weeks after the defendant is sent for trial if the defendant is in custody or within 16 weeks after sending for trial if the defendant is on bail (Criminal Practice Directions 3A.10).

13.9 **Plea and Case Management Hearings in the Crown Court**

In order to promote the overriding objective of the CrimPR, courts are required to actively manage cases, for example by setting time limits for the various steps that need to be taken in preparation for a trial. This is the purpose of the Plea and Case Management Hearing (PCMH). A PCMH will always take place in the context of trial on indictment, regardless of whether any other form of pre-trial hearings take place.

At the PCMH the defendant will be arraigned. This means that the indictment will be read out and the defendant will be asked whether he pleads guilty or not guilty to the charges contained therein.

For further consideration of indictments, see 13.10.

Where the defendant is arraigned and pleads guilty to the indictment, there will obviously be no need for a trial. The judge may sentence the defendant then and there. Usually, however, sentence will be adjourned for the preparation of reports about the defendant. The purpose of such reports is to assist the judge in determining the appropriate sentence (see chapter 14).

If the defendant pleads not guilty, the judge will require information from the parties in order to set a timetable for trial. The advocates in the case are, therefore, required to complete a questionnaire, concerning matters such as:

- the time estimate for the trial;
- which prosecution witnesses the defence requires to attend;
- whether the prosecution has complied with statutory disclosure requirements;
- whether the parties intend to rely on expert evidence (see 13.16.4);
- whether issues arise in relation to the admissibility of any evidence; and
- whether there are to be any bad character or other applications (see 13.16.5).

Under s.40 of the Criminal Procedure and Investigations Act 1996, the judge at a pre-trial hearing (such as the PCMH) may make rulings concerning the admissibility of evidence or other questions of law. Such rulings are binding until the case is disposed of, although a judge may subsequently discharge or vary a ruling made under s.40 in the interests of justice. In practice, however, issues concerning the admissibility of evidence are often deferred in order to be determined by the trial judge either prior to, or on the day of, the trial.

Additional hearings may take place after the PCMH if it is necessary to deal with any further issues that arise prior to trial. Such issues may include, for example, disclosure (see 13.13). However, para.3A.13 of the Criminal Practice Directions indicates that a further hearing should only be held if it is needed for some compelling reason. The aim is to streamline the criminal process and save court costs by reducing to a minimum the number of hearings that take place prior to trial.

13.10 **Indictments**

Crown Court trial is known as 'trial on indictment' because the document that contains the charges against the defendant is called an indictment. An indictment may contain one or more **counts**.

> **count:** A count charges the defendant with an offence. A count must contain both a statement of the offence with which the defendant is charged and particulars (i.e. brief details) of the offence (CrimPR Part 14.2). The statement of the offence should describe the offence in ordinary language and identify any legislation that creates the offence. The particulars of the offence should make clear what the prosecutor alleges against the defendant.

The following is an example of an indictment.

> **Example**
>
> INDICTMENT
>
> IN THE CROWN COURT AT NEWCASTLE UPON TYNE
> THE QUEEN – v – JOHN ROBERT PARKER
> JOHN ROBERT PARKER is charged as follows:
>
> Count 1
>
> STATEMENT OF OFFENCE
> BURGLARY, contrary to section 9(1)(b) of the Theft Act 1968
>
> PARTICULARS OF OFFENCE
> JOHN ROBERT PARKER, on the 9th day of August 2013, having entered as a trespasser a building, being a dwelling known as 31 Seaview Road, Newcastle upon Tyne, stole therein a television set, DVD player and twelve DVDs.
>
> Count 2
>
> STATEMENT OF OFFENCE
> BURGLARY, contrary to section 9(1)(b) of the Theft Act 1968
>
> PARTICULARS OF OFFENCE
> JOHN ROBERT PARKER on the 12th day of August 2013, having entered as a trespasser a building, being a dwelling known as 82 Regent Road, Newcastle Upon Tyne, stole therein a laptop computer and £120 in money.

Normally, a single count should charge the defendant with a single offence. A count that charges the defendant with more than one offence is said to be 'duplicitous'. Thus, where the defendant is alleged to have committed more than one offence, there should normally be one count on the indictment for each offence. In order for a number of counts to be contained (or 'joined') in the same indictment, they must either be founded on the same facts, or must form or be part of a series of offences of the same or a similar character.

More than one defendant may appear on the same indictment and more than one defendant may be charged in a single count. This would be the usual course where two or more defendants have committed an offence together.

Where a number of counts have been properly joined in an indictment, the Crown Court may still order that a count or counts be tried separately (under s.5 of the Indictments Act 1915). This is known as 'severing' the indictment. The court may order severance if, for example, the defendant would be prejudiced if the offences were tried together. This might be the case where trying several counts together would result in a very complicated case or might make the jury hostile to the defendant (*Ludlow v Metropolitan Police Commissioner* [1971] AC 29). Equally, the court has the power to order separate trials of co-defendants charged in the same indictment (*R v Grondkowski* [1946] KB 369).

13.11 **Plea bargaining**

As discussed earlier, not all cases result in trials being held because many defendants plead guilty at some stage of the court process. Indeed, if all cases were to result in trials, there would be too much work for the courts and the criminal justice system would inevitably grind to a halt. The courts, therefore, offer certain incentives to defendants to plead guilty and have begun to move towards establishing a plea bargaining system.

A 'plea bargain' is an agreement under which the defendant enters a guilty plea to an offence in return for an undertaking that he will receive a specified sentence. Plea bargaining is common practice in some countries but, until relatively recently, was not an acceptable practice in England and Wales.

One of the difficulties with plea bargaining is that a defendant could feel pressurised into pleading guilty to something that he has not done in order to benefit from a concession in relation to his sentence. For example, if a defendant were told that he would receive a custodial sentence if convicted after trial but would not be sent to prison following a guilty plea, he might feel that, realistically, he was left with little choice but to plead guilty.

Prior to 2005, the only form of 'bargaining' that was acceptable in this country was what is sometimes known as 'charge bargaining'. Charge bargaining occurs where the defendant is charged with an offence, but offers to plead guilty to a lesser offence. In some cases, this may be acceptable to the prosecution and, if so, the defendant will then not be prosecuted for the more serious charge.

Example

A defendant charged with wounding with intent to cause grievous bodily harm contrary to s.18 of the Offences Against the Person Act 1861 may be prepared to admit that he wounded the victim intending to cause some harm but may deny that he intended to cause grievous bodily harm. He may therefore offer a guilty plea to the lesser offence of wounding contrary to s.20 of the 1861 Act. The prosecution may accept the lesser plea if, for example, the evidence as to the defendant's intent is not strong. Even if there is some evidence of intent, the prosecution might be persuaded to accept the lesser plea because a judge would still have significant sentencing powers (the maximum sentence for s.20 wounding being five years' imprisonment). The acceptance of the plea also avoids potential further trauma to the victim by having to give evidence in court.

Similarly, the courts have long followed the practice of awarding a discount in sentence to a person who pleaded guilty. In most cases, a defendant who pleaded guilty could be expected to receive a discount of up to one third (see 14.4.2).

However, prior to 2005, a judge was not permitted to indicate the type or length of sentence he would pass in advance of a guilty plea. In particular, a judge was not allowed to indicate that on a plea of guilty he would impose one sentence but on conviction following a trial he would impose another, more severe sentence (*R v Turner* [1970] 2 WLR 1093). Thus, although charge bargaining was relatively commonplace, plea bargaining in the strict sense was not allowed.

Thinking point

A defendant would always know that he was entitled to a discount in sentence if he pleaded guilty and judges were permitted to remind defendants of this. Why do you think judges were nevertheless restricted from indicating the exact sentence they were prepared to impose in order to encourage defendants to plead guilty? Was there a danger that defendants would feel that they were being unfairly pressurised into admitting offences whether or not they were actually guilty?

In *R v Goodyear* [2005] 3 All ER 117, the Court of Appeal relaxed the rules and a defendant is now permitted to formally seek an 'indication' as to the sentence they will receive. An indication is essentially a promise that the defendant will receive a particular sentence, or type of sentence, if he pleads guilty at the point at which the indication is given. The nature of the *Goodyear* indication procedure is summarised in the Criminal Practice Directions, Division VII, at paras C.1–8.

The Court of Appeal anticipated that a *'Goodyear* indication' would normally be sought at the PCMH, although agreed that a defendant could seek an indication at any time after that. In practice, indications are often sought on the day of trial before the jury is sworn.

The judge is entitled to refuse to give an indication. However, if an indication is given and the defendant pleads guilty immediately, the court is bound by the indication and must pass the promised sentence. If the defendant declines to plead guilty following an indication, the indication ceases to have effect. Thus, if the defendant pleads guilty at a later stage the judge will not be bound by the indication given on the earlier occasion and may pass a more severe sentence.

13.12 **Bail**

At most court appearances, the issue of bail will be considered and the court will decide whether the defendant should be in custody, or 'on bail' in the community, until the next court hearing.

13.12.1 **Remand in custody**

The decision to *remand* a defendant in custody prior to trial is a serious matter. Article 5 of the European Convention on Human Rights recognises that the right to liberty is a fundamental human right. Thus, there is normally a presumption in favour of granting bail to a defendant who has not yet been convicted of an offence. Where bail is refused, there are strict time limits that apply to the period for which a defendant can be remanded in custody pending trial, although these may be extended if there is good cause and the prosecution can show that they have acted with diligence and expedition.

remand
A remand is an order that the defendant be kept in custody or granted bail between court appearances.

Under s.128 of the Magistrates' Courts Act 1980, the court may remand a defendant in custody for a maximum of eight clear days. In practice, defendants do not always have to be brought back before the court after this time as s.128 also provides that a defendant who is legally represented may consent to being remanded in his absence on up to three consecutive occasions before he has to be brought back before the court. Furthermore, s.128A provides that where a court fixes a date for the next stage in the proceedings to take place, a defendant who has already been remanded once, may be remanded for a maximum period of 28 clear days for the next stage of the proceedings to take place (s.128A).

To ensure that defendants awaiting trial are not imprisoned indefinitely, regulations made under s.22 of the Prosecution of Offences Act 1985 set down maximum periods for which a defendant may be kept in custody pending trial. For example, the maximum period between first appearance and summary trial is usually 56 days. Where a defendant appears before the magistrates' court for an indictable only offence, or elects Crown Court trial for an either way offence, the maximum period for which he may be remanded in custody by the Crown Court before the start of his trial is usually 182 days, less any period during which he has been in the custody of the magistrates' court.

Thinking point

The regulations allow the courts to remand a defendant in custody for a longer period if he is to be tried in the Crown Court. Why do you think this is? Bear in mind that the Crown Court has the power to try more serious cases, which may take longer to prepare.

13.12.2 Remand on bail

Bail is the release of a defendant subject to a duty to surrender to custody (Bail Act 1976 s.3). This simply means that the defendant has a duty to return to court on the date set.

Under s.4 of the 1976 Act, a defendant appearing before either the magistrates' court or the Crown Court has a general right to bail. However, Sch.1 to the Act provides that this right does not apply in certain circumstances, such as: where the instant offence has been committed while the defendant was on bail in respect of another offence; where the defendant has previously been released on bail and failed to surrender to custody; or if the court is satisfied that the defendant should be kept in custody for their own protection. A defendant may also be refused bail if he has tested positive for a Class A drug and the conditions in Sch.1, para.6B of the 1976 Act are established.

Section 25 of the Criminal Justice and Public Order Act 1994 provides that where the defendant is charged with a specified offence, such as murder or rape, and has a previous conviction for such an offence, he will only be granted bail in exceptional circumstances. Section 114(2) of the Coroners and Justice Act 2009 adds that, where a defendant is charged with murder, he may not be granted bail unless there is no significant risk of his committing an offence that would be likely to cause physical or mental injury to another person.

More generally, Sch.1 to the 1976 Act allows a court to refuse bail in relation to any offence where there are substantial grounds to believe that, if released on bail, the defendant would fail to surrender to custody, commit further offences, or interfere with prosecution witnesses or otherwise obstruct the course of justice. In taking its decision, the court should take into account:

- the nature and seriousness of the offence;

- the strength of the evidence;

- the defendant's character, antecedents, associates, and community ties;

- the defendant's record in relation to fulfilling his obligations under previous grants of bail; and

- any other factors that appear to be relevant.

Thinking point

Community ties may be relevant because, for example, a person with family ties and a job has strong connections to the area and is therefore less likely to abscond if granted bail. Consider how the other factors set out in Sch. 1 may be relevant to the decision to grant bail.

The Legal Aid, Sentencing and Punishment of Offenders Act 2012 inserted a new para.2ZA into Sch.1 of the 1976 Act. Paragraph 2ZA provides that a defendant need not be granted bail if the court is satisfied that there are substantial grounds to believe he will commit further offences by engaging in conduct that would be likely to cause physical or mental injury to an 'associated person'. An associated person is defined to include: a current or former spouse, civil partner, or cohabitee; anyone who has had an intimate personal relationship with the defendant which was of a significant duration; a relative; or, a person who lives or has lived with the defendant (other than as an employee, tenant, lodger, or boarder). Similarly, s.114 of the Coroners and Justice Act 2009 provides that, where the court is satisfied that there are substantial grounds to believe that the defendant would commit further offences if granted bail, the court should have regard to the risk that such offending would be likely to cause physical or mental injury to another person (Bail Act 1976 Sch.1 para.9(e)). It is difficult to see what these provisions add to Sch.1, which has always provided that a court may refuse bail if there are substantial grounds to believe the defendant will commit further offences.

Under s.3 of the 1976 Act, the court may require the defendant to provide a **surety or a security** before releasing him on bail.

Section 3 also allows the court to set such other conditions of bail as appear to be necessary, for example, to ensure that the defendant surrenders to custody, does not commit further offences, or does not interfere with witnesses. Such bail conditions might require the defendant to live at a specified address, to report regularly to a police station, to stay out of a particular area, or not to contact specified persons. A defendant who is released on bail and fails to surrender without reasonable cause commits an offence under s.6 of the 1976 Act, which is punishable by imprisonment.

surety/security
A surety is a person who agrees to forfeit a sum of money if the defendant fails to surrender. A security is a sum of money or assets that the defendant may forfeit himself if he fails to surrender.

13.13 Pre-trial issues: disclosure

Before a trial can take place, the parties need to be in possession of the relevant material to enable them to properly prepare and present their case. A defendant is entitled to copies of the evidence upon which the prosecution proposes to rely. This may include, for example, witness statements, transcripts of interviews, and documentary exhibits. The defendant is also entitled to copies of certain types of material that the prosecution do not intend to use. The provision of this other material is known as 'disclosure'.

13.13.1 Section 9 of the Criminal Justice Act 1967

If the prosecution wishes to rely upon the evidence of a witness at trial, a copy of the witness's statement must be supplied to the defence. A witness statement must comply with the requirements of s.9 of the Criminal Justice Act 1967. A defendant who receives a section 9 statement has seven days to object to it being used in evidence. If no objection is received, the statement will simply be read out at trial as agreed evidence, thus removing the necessity of calling the witness. This can be an important device to save court time and costs.

A defendant is not obliged to serve copies of the statements of defence witnesses, although they may do so if they wish.

13.13.2 Unused material

disclosure
Disclosure means that the prosecutor must either provide the defendant with a copy of any such material or allow the defendant to inspect it.

Material that the prosecution has which is relevant but which it does not intend to rely upon is known as 'unused material'. In addition to giving the defendant the evidence upon which it proposes to rely, the prosecution is also required to review all of the unused material in a case to assess whether there is anything that ought to be *disclosed* to the defence. The prosecution is not required to disclose material that is neutral or damages the defence case. However, s.3 of the Criminal Procedure and Investigations Act 1996 imposes a duty on a prosecutor to disclose any material in their possession, or which they have inspected, that 'might reasonably be considered capable of undermining the case for the prosecution against the defendant or of assisting the case for the defendant'. The Attorney General has issued Guidelines on Disclosure, which can be found at **www.cps.gov.uk/legal/a_to_c/ attorney_generals_guidelines_on_disclosure/**.

Following this 'initial disclosure' by the prosecution, s.5 of the 1996 Act requires the defendant to provide a 'defence statement'. Section 6A sets out the matters that a defence statement must address and provides that it must include the nature and particulars of the defendant's defence, particulars of any alibi, and details of any issues of law which the defendant wishes to raise. Under s.6C, the defendant must also provide the name, address, and date of birth of any witnesses he proposes to call to give evidence. In the past, there was no obligation upon defendants to disclose their defence. It was suggested that some defendants took advantage of this by raising new issues at trial and thereby 'ambushing' the prosecution. The courts have emphasised that a criminal trial is a search for the truth and not a 'game' (*R v Gleeson* [2003] EWCA Crim 3357; *R (on the application of Firth) v Epping Magistrates' Court* [2011] EWHC 388 (Admin)). It is, therefore, important that a defence statement now highlights the real issues in the case. (In the context of summary trial, s.6 of the 1996 Act continues to provide that the giving of a defence statement by the defendant is voluntary.)

Following initial disclosure, the prosecution is under a continuing duty to keep the question of disclosure under review (s.7A of the 1996 Act). The prosecutor is also required to specifically review the position in light of the defence statement and provide any material that might reasonably be expected to undermine the prosecution case or assist the defence.

A defendant who has given a defence statement can apply for disclosure under s.8 of the Act if he has reasonable cause to believe that there is prosecution material that is required to be disclosed but has not been so disclosed. This may include material that is in the hands of third parties to which the prosecutor has access. This is one reason for giving a defence statement in the magistrates' court, where it would otherwise be optional.

In summary, the prosecution is obliged to supply the defence with copies of all of the evidence it intends to present at trial. There are also strict duties to disclose material the prosecution does not intend to use where such disclosure is necessary to ensure a fair trial. There is no corresponding duty on the defence to disclose material in the defendant's possession which might undermine the defence case or assist the prosecution. In fact, defendants are not even required to serve the statements of defence witnesses on the prosecution. However, under s.6C of the Criminal Procedure and Investigations Act 1996, which came into force on 1 May 2010, defendants are now required to notify the prosecution and the court of the names and addresses of all defence witnesses. This enables the prosecution to investigate these witnesses in advance of trial.

Thinking point

Why do you think the defence is not under a duty to disclose material that is adverse to the defendant's case? Is this another example of the weighting of the criminal justice system in favour of the defendant? Or is it simply a facet of the principle that the defendant is innocent until proven guilty?

13.14 **Trial on indictment**

Where the defendant has pleaded not guilty to a count, or counts, with which he is charged, it will be necessary for a jury to be sworn. The defendant will then be 'given in charge' to the jury. This is the point at which the jurors will be informed of the charges and told that it is for them, having heard the evidence, to determine whether the defendant is guilty or not. Under s.44 of the CJA 2003, the prosecution may apply to have a trial conducted by a judge without a jury where there is a real and present danger of jury tampering. This is an exceptional course, which happens very rarely in practice.

Normally, the defendant will be present at his trial, but the court does possess discretion to try the defendant in his absence, for example, where the defendant deliberately absconds from the trial or disrupts the trial (*R v Jones* [2003] 1 AC 1).

Criminal trials normally take place in public, but there are exceptions to this general rule. For example, where a person is charged with an offence under the Official Secrets Acts of 1911 or 1920, the public may be excluded if it would be prejudicial to national safety. Similarly, there are restrictions on the information that the press may publish. For example, under s.1 of the Sexual Offences (Amendment) Act 1992, information identifying a sexual offence complainant may not be published.

Legislation preventing the publication of the identity of rape complainants was first introduced in 1976 (Sexual Offences (Amendment) Act 1976 s.4). The 1992 Act extended this protection to victims of all types of sexual offence. In 2010, the government announced its intention to extend anonymity in rape cases to defendants (HM Government, *The Coalition: Our programme for government*, 2010, para.20). Proponents of the view that those who are accused of rape ought to remain anonymous unless and until they are convicted argue that a special stigma attaches to a rape allegation, which does not go away, even if the defendant is ultimately acquitted. Those in favour of maintaining the status quo suggest that publishing the name of a man accused of rape may encourage other of his victims to come forward. It may be that further research is needed in this area. The government's proposal to grant anonymity was ultimately abandoned on the ground that there was insufficient empirical evidence on which to base a decision to afford anonymity to those accused of rape.

13.14.1 The case for the prosecution

Once the jury has been sworn, the prosecution advocate makes an 'opening speech'. In this speech, the advocate will outline the case against the defendant so as to enable the jurors to more easily understand the evidence they will hear. Following the opening speech, the prosecution advocate 'calls' the prosecution evidence. This will involve bringing witnesses into court to give evidence that will prove the elements of the offence. Where the prosecution calls a witness, the witness is first examined in chief by the prosecution advocate. He may then be cross-examined by the defence advocate. If there are several co-defendants, the witness will be cross-examined by the advocate for each of them in the order in which the defendants' names appear on the indictment. Following all cross-examination, the witness may be re-examined by the prosecution advocate.

In general, where the prosecution serves a witness statement on the defence, the prosecution should call the witness to give live evidence. However, if the defence agrees, the prosecution may read the witness's statement instead (Criminal Justice Act 1967 s.9).

A party is only likely to serve the statement of a witness whose evidence will support his own case. The advocate will have a witness statement, or 'proof of evidence', which will contain the evidence that the witness is expected to give. The advocate will hope that the witness will 'come up to proof', i.e. give evidence in accordance with his statement. Even if the witness fails to come up to proof when giving evidence, the advocate who called the witness is not normally permitted to cross-examine the witness by asking leading questions.

As a general rule, advocates may not ask their own witness 'leading questions' in order to elicit evidence, unless the evidence to which the question is directed is not in dispute. A leading question is one that either suggests the answer to the witness or assumes the existence of facts about which the witness has not yet given evidence. For example, if one of the issues in the case is whether a car was blue, a witness may not be asked 'Was the car blue?' in examination in chief. Instead the advocate should ask 'What colour was the car?'

Unlike examination in chief, leading questions may be asked during cross-examination (*Ex parte Bottomley* [1909] 2 KB 14). The key rule in cross-examination is that the advocate must put his case to the witness to give the witness the opportunity to respond to it. However, cross-examination of a sexual offence complainant relating to that complainant's sexual behaviour on other occasions will require leave of the trial judge under s.41 of the Youth Justice and Criminal Evidence Act 1999.

Leave is not normally required before asking particular questions of a witness. Section 41 of the 1999 Act was passed to address concerns that sexual offence complainants were being questioned inappropriately about their previous sexual behaviour. These types of question could be designed to unsettle the witness, to scandalise, and to attack the victim's character, rather than to elicit the truth about what happened. The law now prevents such questioning unless it is relevant to the case.

Where the defendant has not appointed a defence advocate and is conducting his case personally, the provisions of Chapter 2 of Part 2 of the Youth Justice and Criminal Evidence Act 1999 prohibit him from personally cross-examining sexual offence complainants and certain child witnesses. The court also possesses discretion to prevent the defendant from personally cross-examining witnesses in other types of case. If the defendant declines to appoint an advocate to cross-examine the relevant witness, the court can appoint a qualified legal representative to cross-examine the witness on the defendant's behalf.

The provisions of the 1999 Act concerning cross-examination by the defendant in person provide another example of recent legislation intended to make the process of giving evidence as a witness in a criminal trial less unpleasant. The provisions were enacted in response to two widely publicised cases, in which defendants acting in person cross-examined complainants who had made allegations of rape against them.

Following cross-examination, the advocate for the party who called a witness is entitled to re-examine the witness. Essentially, the rules that govern examination in chief also govern re-examination, but re-examination should normally only relate to matters that were raised in cross-examination (*Prince v Samo* (1838) 7 Ad & El 627).

13.14.2 Defence submissions of no case to answer

At the close of the prosecution case, the defence may make a submission of 'no case to answer'. This is a submission that no jury, properly directed, could convict on the prosecution evidence. The judge will hear submissions from both defence and prosecution advocates in the absence of the jury and will direct an acquittal if either:

- there is no evidence that the defendant committed the offence with which he is charged; or

- the evidence is so inherently weak or tenuous that, even taken at its highest, a properly directed jury could not properly convict (*R v Galbraith* [1981] 1 WLR 1039).

> ### Example
>
> Bob is charged with theft of a watch. One of the elements of theft which the prosecution must prove is that the property in question belonged to another person. In Bob's case, the prosecution calls no evidence to prove that the watch that was found in Bob's possession belonged to someone else. The jury should be directed to acquit Bob following a defence submission of no case to answer because there is no evidence in relation to an element of the offence with which he is charged.

13.14.3 The case for the defence

If the defendant intends to give evidence himself and call other witnesses of fact, the defence advocate may make an opening speech outlining the defence case and the evidence that will be called on his behalf (under s.2 of the Criminal Evidence Act 1898). In practice, defence opening speeches are rare. Indeed, if the defendant is to be the only defence witness, or if he does not intend to give evidence, the defence advocate is not entitled to make an opening speech.

Where the defendant does testify, s.79 of the Police and Criminal Evidence Act 1984 provides that he must be called before any other defence witnesses unless the court orders otherwise. Defence witnesses (including the defendant) are examined in chief by the defendant's advocate. They may be cross-examined by the advocate for the prosecution, and may then be cross-examined by advocates for any co-defendants, before being re-examined by the defence advocate. Where written statements are admissible on behalf of the defendant because their contents are agreed, the defence advocate will read them to the jury.

If there are several co-defendants, their defence cases will be presented in the order in which the defendants' names appear on the indictment.

The prosecution should not normally be permitted to call further evidence following the close of the prosecution case. In an appropriate case, however, the prosecution may be entitled to call rebuttal evidence (i.e. evidence to contradict or nullify defence evidence). For example, if the defendant gives evidence that wrongly suggests that he is of good character, the prosecution may be entitled to call bad character evidence in rebuttal.

13.14.4 **Closing speeches by prosecution and defence advocates**

Following the close of the case for the defence, the prosecution advocate is usually entitled to make a closing speech. (The prosecution advocate is not entitled to make a closing speech where the defendant is not legally represented and has called no witnesses other than himself.) Finally, the defence advocate is entitled to make a closing speech. Section 1 of the Criminal Procedure (Right of Reply) Act 1964 provides that the making of a closing speech by the prosecution must take place prior to the making of a speech by or on behalf of the defendant. This means the defence is entitled to the last word before the judge sums up the case.

For the admissibility of bad character evidence see 13.16.5.

13.14.5 **The trial judge's summing up**

Before the jury retires to consider its verdict, the judge sums up the case for the jury. In the course of summing up, the judge will remind the jury of the evidence and give the jury directions on the relevant law, including explaining the elements of the offence and the burden and standard of proof. The judge may also be required to direct the jury concerning a variety of other matters, such as:

- the drawing of inferences from silence (see 12.4.5 and 13.16.7);
- the fact that the jury is not bound to accept the opinion of an expert witness (see 13.16.4); and
- the significance of evidence of the defendant's good or bad character (see 13.16.5).

To assist judges in formulating their directions to the jury, the Judicial Studies Board provides guidance and examples of appropriate directions. These can be found at: **www.judiciary.gov.uk/Resources/JCO/Documents/Training/benchbook_ criminal_2010.pdf**. Finally, the judge should direct the jury to retire to the jury room to reach a unanimous verdict.

13.15 **Summary trial**

Where the defendant pleads not guilty in the magistrates' court, he will be tried by either lay magistrates or by a district judge, who will act as both the tribunal of law and the tribunal of fact. Thus, the magistrates, or district judge, decide both whether evidence is admissible and whether the defendant is guilty. The procedure at a summary trial is otherwise similar to trial on indictment.

Where the tribunal in the magistrates' court consists of lay magistrates assisted by a legally qualified clerk, the clerk will advise the magistrates on any issues of law that have arisen during the case before they retire to consider their verdict. This advice should be given in the presence of both the prosecution and the defence advocate so that the advocates may make submissions if the clerk says anything with which they disagree.

13.16 **Evidential issues**

The law of evidence is a complex subject. A course on the English legal system cannot hope to cover all relevant areas. This section outlines a few of the key evidential issues that are likely to arise in the context of both summary trial and trial on indictment.

13.16.1 **Burden and standard of proof**

Where the defendant pleads not guilty to an offence, the prosecution will bear the legal burden of proving the defendant's guilt to the criminal standard of proof. In general, the prosecution bears the legal burden both of proving the elements of the offence with which the defendant is charged and of disproving any defences raised by the defendant (*Woolmington v DPP* [1935] AC 462). Consequently, where the defendant relies upon a defence such as self-defence, provided that there is some evidence before the court to raise the defence, the prosecution bears the legal burden of disproving the defence to the criminal standard of proof (*Mancini v DPP* [1942] AC 1).

Thinking point

The '*Woolmington* principle' imposes the legal burden of proof in criminal proceedings upon the prosecution, subject to limited exceptions. Is this an example of the weighting of the criminal justice system in favour of the defendant?

At common law there is only one exception to the general rule that the prosecution bears the burden of proof in a criminal case. Where the defendant relies upon the common law defence of insanity, the defendant bears the legal burden of proving this defence (*M'Naghten's case* (1843) 10 Cl & Fin 200). Some statutes also impose the legal burden of proving a defence upon the defendant, either expressly or by implication. Thus, for example, s.2 of the Homicide Act 1957 states that the defendant bears the legal burden of proving the defence of diminished responsibility.

The criminal standard of proof is proof beyond reasonable doubt. This means that the jury must not find the defendant guilty unless they are 'satisfied so they feel sure' of the defendant's guilt (*R v Summers* [1952] 1 All ER 1059). Where, exceptionally, the defendant bears the legal burden of proving a defence, the requisite standard of proof is merely proof on the balance of probabilities (*R v Carr-Briant* [1943] KB 607).

Article 6(2) of the European Convention on Human Rights guarantees the defendant the right to be 'presumed innocent until proved guilty according to law'. Consequently, the courts have held that the statutory imposition of a legal burden of proof upon the defendant may violate Article 6, although it will not necessarily do so (*Salabiaku v France* (1988) 13 EHRR 379). Whether or not imposing a legal burden of proof on the defendant violates Article 6 will depend upon factors such as the reason for imposing a legal burden of proof upon the defendant, how difficult it would be for the defendant to discharge that burden, and the potential consequences for the defendant if he fails to discharge the burden (*Attorney General's Reference (No.4 of 2002)* [2004] 3 WLR 976).

In circumstances in which imposing a legal burden of proof upon the defendant would violate Article 6, the court may be able to 'read down' the relevant statutory provision (under s.3(1) of the Human Rights Act 1998) as merely imposing an 'evidential burden' upon the defendant (*Attorney General's Reference (No.4 of 2002)* [2004] 3 WLR 976). The effect of reading down a provision in this way is that, provided that there is evidence before the court to raise the relevant defence, the legal burden of disproving the defence to the criminal standard of proof is borne by the prosecution.

In relation to limiting the meaning of statutory provisions, see chapter 4.

13.16.2 Competence and compellability of witnesses

Sometimes there may be doubt as to the capacity of a witness to give evidence. The judge, in the absence of the jury, will then have to decide whether the witness in question is 'competent' to give evidence. Similarly, a witness may be reluctant to testify and an issue may arise as to whether he can be 'compelled' to give evidence.

Section 53 of the Youth Justice and Criminal Evidence Act 1999 provides that persons who cannot understand questions and give understandable answers are not competent to give evidence in criminal proceedings. The issue of competence might arise, for example, where the witness is a young child or a person who is mentally impaired.

As regards compellability, the basic rule is that all persons can be required to give evidence in criminal proceedings. Where a witness is competent and compellable but does not wish to attend court to give evidence in the proceedings, a party may apply to the court under s.2 of the Criminal Procedure (Attendance of Witnesses) Act 1965 for a witness summons in order to secure the witness's attendance. A witness summons is a document issued by the court requiring a witness to attend court and give evidence. A witness who fails to attend after receiving a witness summons may be arrested and brought to court.

The major exception to the rule that all persons are compellable in criminal proceedings concerns defendants. Under s.1 of the Criminal Evidence Act 1898, the defendant is competent but not compellable on behalf of the defence. Thus, a defendant is entitled to give evidence in his own defence, or on behalf of a co-defendant, but he cannot be forced to do so.

There are also particular rules relating to the compellability of spouses and civil partners. Under s.80 of PACE, a defendant's spouse or civil partner is compellable on behalf of the defendant but is not normally compellable on behalf of the prosecution or a co-defendant. Thus, the prosecution usually cannot force a defendant's wife to give evidence against him. However, a defendant's spouse or civil partner can be compelled to give evidence if the defendant is charged with an offence specified in s.80(3) of PACE. Specified offences include those involving assault, injury, or threat of injury to the spouse or to a child. It is the legal nature of the offence with which the defendant is charged, rather than the underlying facts, that determines whether it is a specified offence (*R v A(B)* [2012] EWCA Crim 1529).

Thinking point

The effect of s.80 of PACE is that where, for example, a defendant is charged with an offence involving violence upon his wife, she can be forced to give evidence about what happened even if the parties are reconciled and she no longer wishes to testify against him. Is this in the interests of justice? Is it an example of the state intruding into people's private lives, or does the state have a responsibility to protect its citizens from themselves?

13.16.3 **Special measures directions**

Before a trial takes place, either the prosecution or the defence may apply to the court for a 'special measures direction' to be made in relation to a witness under the Youth Justice and Criminal Evidence Act 1999 (YJCEA 1999). The Coroners and Justice Act 2009 amended the YJCEA 1999 so as to reduce the discretion available to the court in deciding whether to grant an application for special measures. The regime contained in Chapter 1, Part 2 of the YJCEA 1999 (as amended) is designed to make it less unpleasant for victims and other witnesses to give evidence in criminal proceedings.

A witness may be eligible for special measures because of the witness's age (i.e. if the witness is under the age of 18), or if the quality of the witness's evidence is likely to be diminished due to physical or mental incapacity (YJCEA 1999 s.16). A witness may also be eligible if the quality of his evidence is likely to be diminished by reason of fear or distress about testifying, of if the witness is a complainant in a case involving a sexual offence (YJCEA 1999 s.17). Although the special measures regime applies to both prosecution and defence witnesses, it does not apply to the defendant.

The following special measures are available to a witness who is eligible under s.17 YJCEA 1999 (i.e. fear or distress in connection with testifying):

- screening the witness from the defendant (s.23);
- the giving of evidence by live link (s.24);
- the giving of evidence in private (e.g. excluding members of the public from the courtroom) (s.25);
- removal of wigs and gowns (s.26); and
- the playing of a pre-recorded interview with the witness to replace examination in chief (s.27).

Section 28 also allows cross-examination and re-examination of a witness to be pre-recorded but this provision has not yet been brought into force.

Where the witness is eligible for special measures by virtue of s.16 (i.e. due to age or incapacity), the court may additionally direct that examination of the witness be conducted through an intermediary (s.29) or that the witness be provided with an appropriate device to aid communication (s.30).

Upon receiving an application for special measures in relation to an eligible witness, the court must consider whether any of the special measures available would be likely to improve the quality of the witness's evidence. The court will apply those measures which would tend to maximise the quality of the witness's evidence. In relation to child witnesses, the primary rule is that a video recorded interview will be admitted as the witness's evidence in chief, and cross-examination and re-examination will take place via TV live link (s.21). If the witness is a complainant in proceedings relating to a sexual offence, the court must similarly direct that a pre-recorded interview be admitted as evidence in chief (s.22A) unless this would not be likely to maximise the quality of the complainant's evidence.

The procedure governing the making of an application for special measures, including the content of an application, is laid down by CrimPR Part 29. For example, an application must explain why the witness is eligible for assistance and must propose the measure or measures that the applicant thinks would be likely to maximise the quality of the witness's evidence.

Sections 16 and 17 of the YJCEA 1999 specifically state that the accused is not eligible for special measures even though Article 6 of the European Convention on Human Rights requires there to be 'equality of arms' between the prosecution and the defence. However, human rights jurisprudence confirms that the court has inherent powers to vary the way in which defendants give evidence to ensure that they are not disadvantaged (*R (on the application of D) v Camberwell Green Youth Court* [2005] 1 WLR 393). In *R (on the application of C) v Sevenoaks Youth Court* [2009] EWHC 3088 (Admin), the Divisional Court held that the youth court had a duty at common law to appoint an intermediary to assist a defendant who had learning difficulties.

13.16.4 **Expert evidence**

In some cases, parties to criminal proceedings may wish to rely upon the evidence of an expert. An expert is a person who is suitably qualified to give an opinion in his field of expertise. In order to ensure that all of the parties have a proper opportunity to consider and respond to such evidence, CrimPR Part 24 imposes pre-trial disclosure requirements relating to expert evidence, which apply to both prosecution and defence.

CrimPR Part 33, which applies to persons who are required to give or prepare expert evidence for criminal proceedings, makes it clear that expert witnesses must give objective, unbiased, evidence that relates to matters within their expertise. Their duty to do so overrides their duty to the party instructing them. Moreover, guidance for experts issued by the CPS indicates that prosecution experts are required to 'retain, record and reveal' (*Guidance Booklet for Experts' Disclosure: Experts' Evidence, Case Management and Unused Material*, May 2010). This means that they must retain all material relevant to the case, make a record of any work that they carry out, and reveal everything they have recorded to the prosecution team so that consideration can be given to whether there is any material that ought to be disclosed to the defence.

> ### 🔑 Key point
>
> Miscarriages of justice may occur (as in *R v Clark* [2003] EWCA Crim 1020) when prosecution experts fail to disclose to the CPS information which could assist the defence or damage the prosecution case, as a prosecutor obviously cannot disclose such information to the defence if the prosecutor is not aware of it.

Expert evidence is admissible in criminal proceedings in order to provide the court with information that is outside the court's experience and knowledge. However, such evidence is not admissible if the court is capable of forming its own conclusions without expert assistance. For example, in *R v Turner* [1975] QB 834, a psychiatrist was not permitted to give evidence as to how an ordinary person, who was not mentally ill, would react to provocation, as this was something that would be within the experience and knowledge of the jury.

Expert evidence will only be admissible if the witness is 'qualified' in the relevant field (*R v Barnes* [2005] EWCA Crim 1158). This does not necessarily require the witness to have had formal training or to possess formal qualifications. The crucial question is whether the witness possesses a skill that the court lacks (*R v Silverlock* [1894] 2 QB 766).

Crucially, experts may only give expert evidence concerning matters that are within their area(s) of expertise. In the trial of Sally Clark for the murder of her two sons, the prosecution relied on the evidence of an eminent paediatrician to refute the defence suggestion that the deaths were due to sudden infant death syndrome. In addition to giving evidence as to the cause of death, the paediatrician's evidence touched upon the statistical improbability of two children in the same family both dying of natural causes. Sally Clark's conviction was subsequently overturned (*R v Clark* [2003] EWCA Crim 1020) and the paediatrician was criticised for putting forward what was in fact a thoroughly misleading theory of probability when he had no expertise in the field of statistics (*GMC v Meadow* [2007] 1 All ER 1).

Where expert evidence is admissible, the court is not bound by the opinion of the expert. It is the opinion of the jury or the magistrates, and not that of an expert witness, which determines the issues before the court (*R v Stockwell* (1993) 97 Cr App R 260). However, as the Law Commission acknowledged in its 2011 Report, *Expert Evidence in Criminal Proceedings* (Law Com No 325), a jury comprised of lay persons may not be properly equipped to evaluate technical or complex expert opinion evidence. There is, therefore, a risk that jurors will simply defer to an expert's opinion.

The Law Commission's Report was prepared following calls for reform from various personnel concerned with the criminal justice system, including scientists, legal practitioners, legal academics, and the House of Commons Science and Technology Select Committee. A number of high-profile miscarriage of justice cases had led to fears that 'expert opinion evidence was being admitted in criminal proceedings too readily, with insufficient scrutiny' (Law Com No 325, para.1.2). The Report proposes a new statutory test under which expert opinion evidence will only be admissible if it is 'sufficiently reliable'.

! Critical debate

Read G. Edmond, 'The Law Commission's report on expert evidence in criminal proceedings' [2011] Crim LR 844, and answer the following questions:

(a) The Law Commission's proposals envisage a 'gatekeeping' role for the trial judge in relation to expert evidence. What is meant by this term?

(b) What are the traditional trial safeguards that have been thought to be sufficient to protect defendants from unreliable expert opinion evidence?

(c) If the Law Commission's proposals were brought into force, on what grounds could a court conclude that an expert's opinion is not sufficiently reliable to be admitted?

(d) Under the Law Commission's proposals, a court would have to have regard to certain generic factors when deciding whether evidence is sufficiently reliable. Do you think the proposed list of generic factors would be helpful to a court deciding on the reliability of such evidence?

13.16.5 **Bad character**

Section 98 of the CJA 2003 defines bad character as evidence of misconduct, namely criminal offences or other reprehensible behaviour. Evidence which has to do with the facts of the offence with which the defendant is charged, or which concerns the investigation or prosecution of that offence, does not constitute evidence of bad character. The most common form of evidence of bad character will be a person's previous convictions.

Prior to 2003, a defendant's bad character could not be used against him save in very limited circumstances. The circumstances in which such evidence can be used was expanded significantly by the CJA 2003. Critics have argued that this is another example of the rebalancing of the criminal process to favour the prosecution. However, it is important to note that a defendant remains entitled to adduce bad character evidence under the 2003 Act. For example, the defendant may wish to introduce the previous convictions of a prosecution witness or a co-defendant to undermine that person's evidence.

The bad character of the defendant

Evidence of the defendant's bad character will only be admissible under the CJA 2003 if one of what the Court of Appeal in *R v Hanson* [2005] 1 WLR 3169 described as the 'gateways' created by s.101(1)(a) to (g) of the CJA 2003 is applicable.

- Under gateway (a), evidence of the defendant's bad character is admissible by agreement between the parties.

- Gateway (b) permits the defendant to adduce evidence of his or her own bad character.

- Gateway (c) renders evidence of the defendant's bad character admissible if it relates to the background history of the offence with which the defendant is charged.

- Under gateway (d), which is the most important gateway, evidence of the defendant's bad character is admissible if it is relevant to an important matter in issue between the defendant and the prosecution. This can include evidence that the defendant has the propensity to commit offences of the kind with which he is charged, or evidence that he has a propensity to be untruthful.

- Under gateway (e) one co-defendant may adduce evidence of another co-defendant's bad character if it has substantial probative value in relation to an important matter in issue between them.

- Under gateway (f), evidence of the defendant's bad character may be adduced to correct a false impression that the defendant has given, either at the police station or in court. This gateway may be used, for example, where the defendant wrongly suggests when giving evidence that he has no previous convictions.

● Under gateway (g), evidence of the defendant's bad character is admissible where the defendant has attacked another person's character, either at the police station or in court.

Where evidence is tendered under gateway (d) or (g), the defence may object under s.101(3), in which case the court must not admit the evidence if to do so would have such an adverse effect on the fairness of the proceedings that the court ought not to admit it.

Where evidence of the defendant's bad character is admitted in criminal proceedings, it will be necessary for the judge to give the jury careful directions concerning matters such as the relevance of the previous convictions and the fact that the jury should not assume that the defendant is guilty merely because he has previous convictions (*R v Hanson* [2005] 1 WLR 3169; *R v Highton* [2005] 1 WLR 3472).

Traditionally, English courts were reluctant to admit evidence of the defendant's previous convictions due to the danger that the jury might find him guilty because of his previous convictions rather than on the basis of the evidence. Although evidence of the defendant's bad character was admissible in exceptional circumstances, the provisions of the CJA 2003 now make it much easier for the prosecution to introduce such evidence.

Thinking point

The CJA 2003 makes evidence of bad character potentially admissible as evidence of the defendant's propensity to commit offences of the type with which he is charged. Do you think that this is a valid reason for making the jury aware of a defendant's prior offences? What arguments might there be for suggesting that evidence of a person's propensity to commit offences is prejudicial? Consider the danger that the jury will place too much emphasis on a defendant's previous behaviour, rather than focusing on the evidence specific to the offence.

The bad character of non-defendants

Evidence of the bad character of persons other than the defendant (such as witnesses) will only be admissible under the CJA 2003 if a s.100 gateway is applicable. The main example is s.100(1)(b), under which evidence of the bad character of a person other than the defendant is admissible if it has substantial probative value in relation to an issue of substantial importance in the case. Traditionally, evidence of a witness's bad character was admissible in order to discredit the witness. Section 100 of the CJA 2003 now restricts the ability of parties to criminal proceedings to adduce evidence of the bad character of a witness other than the defendant.

Key point

Along with the special measures regime considered at 13.16.3, s.100 forms one of a number of provisions in recent years that, potentially, make it less unpleasant for witnesses to give evidence in criminal proceedings.

13.16.6 Good character

At common law the defence was entitled to adduce evidence of the defendant's good character in the form of evidence as to his general good reputation (*R v Rowton* 1865 Le & Ca 520). This common law rule was preserved by s.118 of the CJA 2003. Where the defence adduces evidence of the defendant's good character, the jury should be directed that a man of good character is both less likely to be guilty and more likely to be truthful (*R v Vye* [1993] 1 WLR 471).

13.16.7 Silence: failure of the defendant to testify

The options available to a defendant in a criminal trial have changed significantly since the late nineteenth century. Prior to the Criminal Evidence Act 1898, the law did not permit a defendant to give evidence on oath on his own behalf, although it had become common practice for defendants to make unsworn statements from the dock. Section 1 of the 1898 Act amended the position to make defendants competent to give sworn evidence.

The 1898 Act faced opposition from those who felt that it would effectively require a defendant to prove his innocence. Supporters of the Act argued that defendants were entitled to decline to give evidence and therefore retained the right to silence. The prosecution was not permitted to make any adverse comment concerning a defendant's failure to give evidence and the trial judge's ability to comment was limited.

By the latter part of the twentieth century, criticisms of the law in this area were mounting. It was felt by many that the ability to choose whether or not to give evidence gave defendants an unfair advantage. It was suggested that defendants should not be allowed to remain silent with impunity. Eventually, Parliament enacted the Criminal Justice and Public Order Act 1994. Section 35 of this Act provides that a jury is entitled to draw an inference in respect of a defendant's silence at trial, unless the physical or mental condition of the defendant makes it undesirable for him to testify (Criminal Justice and Public Order Act 1994 s.35). This means that the jury is now entitled to conclude that the defendant did not give evidence because he had no answer to the prosecution's case, or none that would stand up to cross-examination.

For inferences from the defendant's silence at the police station under s.34 of the 1994 Act, see 12.4.5.

The judge must direct the jury that they may only draw an inference against the defendant if satisfied that the prosecution's case is so strong that it calls for an answer. As in the case of s.34, the jury must also be directed that a conviction cannot be based wholly or mainly on a s.35 inference.

Thinking point

Section 35 of the 1994 Act makes it dangerous for the defendant to offer no defence and require the prosecution to prove his guilt. Is this unfair to the defendant or is it an example of the rebalancing of the criminal process?

13.17 **Verdicts**

If the defendant is tried on indictment, the jury decides whether he is guilty or not guilty. If the defendant is tried summarily, it is the magistrates (or the district judge) who determine whether he is guilty or not guilty.

13.17.1 **Trial on indictment**

If a jury decides that the defendant is not guilty of the offence with which he is charged, the jury may be entitled to find the defendant guilty of a lesser offence, which he is not specifically charged with. Thus, for example, where the jury finds the defendant not guilty of murder, it may find him guilty of the lesser offence of manslaughter (Criminal Law Act 1967 s.6(2)). Generally, the jury may find a defendant guilty of a lesser offence if the allegation in the indictment amounts to or includes an allegation of the lesser offence (Criminal Law Act 1967 s.6(3)).

Example

Joe is charged with burglary contrary to s.9(1)(b) of the Theft Act 1968. It is alleged that Joe entered 12 Elmfield Park as a trespasser and stole therein a television set and DVD player. If the jury is not satisfied that Joe was a trespasser, he cannot be guilty of burglary. However, if the jury is satisfied that Joe stole the items, he may be convicted of theft instead, because burglary of this type includes an allegation of theft (R v Lillis [1972] 2 QB 236).

Initially, the judge must require the jury to reach a unanimous verdict. Sometimes, however, a jury may be unable to reach a unanimous verdict. After at least two hours and ten minutes have elapsed from the time the jurors retired to consider their verdict, the judge is entitled to accept a majority verdict (Juries Act 1974 s.17; Practice Direction (Criminal Proceedings: Consolidation), para.IV.46). A majority verdict is a verdict on which at least ten of twelve jurors agree. If the jury has been reduced to eleven jurors (for example, due to a juror falling ill during the trial), a majority verdict still requires at least ten jurors to agree. In exceptional cases where there are ten jurors, a majority verdict requires nine jurors to agree. Where a guilty verdict is returned by a majority, the foreman must state in open court the number of jurors who agreed with the verdict and the number who dissented from it. The ability to accept a majority verdict is necessary because of the risk that, otherwise, it might be impossible for a jury to reach a verdict as a result of a single juror having particularly extreme and intransigent views.

If the jury cannot reach a majority verdict, the judge will discharge the jury, in which case a retrial may follow.

13.17.2 **Summary trial**

Where a case is tried by lay magistrates, a unanimous verdict is not required. Magistrates may reach a verdict upon which two of them agree. Subject to limited statutory exceptions, if a magistrates' court finds the defendant not guilty of the offence with which he is charged, he may not be convicted of a lesser offence (*Lawrence v Same* [1968] 2 QB 93).

13.17.3 **Re-trials**

A guilty verdict is final, subject to any right of appeal (see chapter 16). A not guilty verdict is also usually final as the prosecution generally has no power to appeal against a not guilty verdict. The rule against 'double jeopardy' means that a defendant who has been acquitted of an offence may not subsequently be charged with the same offence again, even if new evidence is discovered against him.

The double jeopardy principle was called into question by the Macpherson Inquiry into the case of Stephen Lawrence, a black teenager who was stabbed to death in a racist attack by a gang of white youths in 1993. After failings in the police investigation into the murder, Stephen Lawrence's parents brought a private prosecution in 1996 against three of the youths alleged to have killed their son. The private prosecution failed and the youths were aquitted. The investigation continued and it was hoped that new evidence might be discovered against the killers. The Macpherson Report recommended that consideration be given to permitting a person to be prosecuted after an acquittal where fresh and viable evidence against him was discovered.

In 2001, the Law Commission also recommended a limited exception to the double jeopardy principle. The Commission proposed that, in cases of murder only, the Court of Appeal should have the power to quash an acquittal where there was reliable and compelling new evidence of the defendant's guilt. In response, Parliament introduced Part 10 of the Criminal Justice Act 2003, which is wider than the Law Commission's proposals. Under s.76 of the 2003 Act, where a person has been acquitted of a 'qualifying offence', a prosector may apply to the Court of Appeal for an order quashing the acquittal and ordering a re-trial. Qualifying offences include murder, manslaughter, rape, arson endangering life, and certain serious drugs offences. The Court of Appeal must order a re-trial if there is new and compelling evidence against the acquitted person (s.78). Compelling evidence means evidence that is reliable, substantial, and highly probative in the context of the case. An order under s.76 may only be sought with the consent of the DPP, who must be satisfied that it is in the public interest to seek a re-trial.

In 2010, new scientific evidence was discovered in relation to the Stephen Lawrence case. Two men were charged with murder, including Gary Dobson, who had been acquitted in 1996. The Court of Appeal quashed his acquittal and ordered a re-trial. Both defendants were subsequently convicted of the murder of Stephen Lawrence.

Summary

- The criminal courts of trial are the Crown Court and magistrates' courts. Trial on indictment (i.e. trial by jury) takes place in the Crown Court whereas summary trial takes place in magistrates' courts.

- Criminal proceedings are usually instituted by arresting and charging the defendant or by issuing a written charge and requisition. Some cases will then remain in the magistrates' court, whilst others will be 'sent' to the Crown Court.

- At a criminal trial on indictment, the basic procedure is that the prosecution case is heard first. The defence may then (where appropriate) submit that there is no case to answer. If this submission is unsuccessful, the defence case follows. Closing speeches are then made, followed by the judge's summing up. At the end of the trial the jurors retire to reach their verdict. The summary trial procedure is very similar.

- The prosecution bears the burden of proving the case against the defendant beyond reasonable doubt.

- A variety of other evidential issues may arise at trial, such as: the competence and compellability of witnesses; the availability of special measures for vulnerable witnesses; the admissibility of expert evidence; the admissibility of character evidence; and, the implications of a defendant's failure to testify.

Questions

1 (a) How are criminal offences categorised?

  (b) What sort of offences are summary only?

  (c) What is meant by trial on indictment?

2 What factors are taken into account when deciding whether an either way offence should be tried in the magistrates' court or in the Crown Court?

3 Is plea bargaining allowed in the courts of England and Wales?

4 Who bears the burden of proof in criminal proceedings and what is the standard of proof?

5 Which party to criminal proceedings is entitled to cross-examine a witness?

6 What special measures are available to assist vulnerable witnesses when giving evidence?

 Sample question and outline answer

Question

Suraya, who is 22 years old and works as a care assistant, has been charged with theft of a bicycle. She has a previous conviction for handling stolen goods. Suraya admitted to the police that she stole the bicycle but now says that she only confessed because the police bullied her. Suraya intends to plead not guilty. She is frightened about attending court. Advise Suraya about the following matters:

(i)   What procedure will be used to determine whether her case is tried in the magistrates' court or in the Crown Court?

(ii) If Suraya is given the choice, should she opt for a magistrates' court trial or elect Crown Court trial?

(iii) Will Suraya have to testify in her own defence?

Outline answer

Theft is triable either way. The first part of the question requires you to demonstrate your knowledge of the procedure that applies to all either way offences. Part (ii) requires you to discuss the relative advantages and disadvantages of summary trial and trial on indictment and to give your opinion as to which venue would be preferable. Part (iii) tests your knowledge of one of the fundamental rules of evidence applicable to criminal trials, namely the right to silence.

(i)   Theft is an either way offence, so is subject to the plea before venue (PBV) and allocation procedures. Suraya must attend the magistrates' court for the PBV hearing, which may take place before a magistrate sitting alone. Under s.17A of the Magistrates' Courts Act 1980, Suraya should be informed of the PBV procedure and warned that she could be committed for sentence if the magistrates' sentencing powers are insufficient. Suraya will then be asked whether she intends to plead guilty. If she indicates a not guilty plea, the court must determine whether the offence appears more suitable for summary trial or trial on indictment (Magistrates' Courts Act 1980 s.19). The prosecution and defence advocates will make representations and the court will be informed about Suraya's previous conviction. The court must also consider the Sentencing Council's Allocation Guideline, which states that either way offences should generally be tried summarily unless it is likely that the court's sentencing powers will be insufficient. If the court decides that the case is not suitable for summary trial, Suraya will be sent to the Crown Court (Crime and Disorder Act 1998 s.51(1)). If the court decides that summary trial would be more suitable, Suraya may consent to be tried summarily or may elect Crown Court trial. Before making this decision, Suraya is entitled to ask for an indication as to whether, if she pleaded guilty, she would receive a community sentence or a custodial sentence.

(ii) A Crown Court trial is more expensive and the Crown Court has greater sentencing powers than a magistrates' court. However, acquittal rates are higher in the Crown Court. A Crown Court judge decides questions of law, including questions about the admissibility of evidence. This means that, if the judge decides that Suraya's confession is inadmissible, the jury will never hear it. Conversely, in the magistrates' court, the magistrates or district judge decide questions of law and fact, and will therefore have heard a confession even if they subsequently rule it inadmissible. Given that Suraya's case involves an argument about the admissibility of a confession, a Crown Court trial would probably be in her best interests.

(iii) A defendant is entitled to testify but cannot be compelled to do so (Criminal Evidence Act 1898 s.1). If Suraya does not give evidence, an inference can be drawn from her silence unless her physical or mental condition makes it undesirable for her to testify (Criminal Justice and Public Order Act 1994 s.35). The fact that Suraya is frightened about attending court would not be enough to preclude the drawing of an adverse inference. Thus, if Suraya chose not to testify, the magistrates or jury would be entitled to conclude that her silence was due to her having no answer to the charge against her, or none that would stand up to cross-examination.

Further reading

Your reading should be directed to understanding the process by which a criminal case comes before the courts. Because the criminal justice system is about balancing the rights of the accused against the rights of victims and the public at large, you should consider whether the particular procedure or rule you are reading about favours the prosecution or the defence and whether, if it does favour either party, this is justifiable.

- **Buxton, R.** 'The Private Prosecutor as a Minister of Justice' [2009] Crim LR 427
  Explores some of the practical and ethical difficulties with private prosecutions.

- **Edmond, G.** 'The Law Commission's Report on expert evidence in criminal proceedings' [2011] Crim LR 844
  Discusses whether the Law Commission's proposals on expert evidence would be an improvement on the current tests for admitting expert evidence.

- **Garland, F.** and **McEwan, J.** 'Embracing the Overriding Objective: Difficulties and dilemmas in the new criminal climate' (2012) 16(3) E&P 233
  Describes a study into the practical effect of the case management provisions of the Criminal Procedure Rules.

- **Hamer, D.** 'The Presumption of Innocence and Reverse Burdens: A balancing act' (2007) 66(1) CLJ 142
  Explains the circumstances in which placing the burden of proof on the defendant has been deemed to be compatible with the presumption of innocence enshrined in Article 6 of the European Convention on Human Rights.

- **Kirk, D.** 'How do you Solve a Problem like Disclosure' (2013) 77(4) J Crim L 275
  Explains the reasons why disclosure is of fundamental importance to the criminal process and explores some of the problems with the disclosure regime.

- Part VI of the Law Commission's Report, *Double Jeopardy and Prosecution Appeals* (Law Com No 267)
  Explains why reform was needed to the rule that a person who had been acquitted could not subsequently be charged with the same offence.

- **Ragavan, S.K.** 'The Compellability Rule in England and Wales: Support for the spouse of the defendant' (2013) 77(4) J Crim L 310
  Outlines the circumstances in which a spouse is compellable to give evidence and discusses whether sufficient support is available to victims and witnesses who are compelled to testify.

- **Vamos, N.** 'Please don't Call it "Plea Bargaining"' (2009) 9 J Crim L 617
  Examines the advantages and disadvantages of plea bargaining in the United States and contrasts the US approach with the approach taken in England and Wales.

- **Waine, L.** 'The New Mode of Trial and Committal for Sentence Regimes' (2013) 6 Arch Rev 7
  Outlines the new plea before venue and allocation procedures.

- **Wolchover, D.** 'Rape Defendant Anonymity' (2012) 176 JPN 5 and 'Rape Defendant Anonymity Part 2' (2012) 176 JPN 24
  Highlights the arguments for and against protecting the identities of those accused of rape.

Online Resource Centre

You should now attempt the supporting multiple choice questions available at **www.oxfordtextbooks.co.uk/orc/wilson_els/**.

14 Sentencing

⊙ Learning objectives

By the end of this chapter you should:

- be familiar with the aims of sentencing;
- be aware that the maximum sentence available varies from one offence to another;
- appreciate the factors that the court must take into account in determining the appropriate sentence to impose on an offender;
- understand the role of sentencing guidelines and be familiar with how guidelines are structured;
- have a basic knowledge of the types of sentence that may be imposed upon an adult; and
- have a basic knowledge of the types of sentence that may be imposed upon a young offender.

🅕 Talking point

. . . .

Between 6 and 10 August 2011, riots occurred in towns and cities across England. At 10:30 p.m. on 8 August, 21-year-old Jordan Blackshaw created a public event on facebook entitled 'Smash down in Northwich Town', inviting people to meet in a restaurant in Northwich the following lunchtime. He referred to the ongoing riots, adding 'we'll need to get on this, kicking off all over'. The police were notified of the event and closed the webpage down.

Blackshaw was subsequently arrested and charged with doing an act capable of encouraging riot, burglary and criminal damage, believing that one or more of those offences would be committed. He described his actions as a 'sick joke' that had gone too far. On 16 August he pleaded guilty and was sentenced to four years' imprisonment, even though the event that he had encouraged never actually took place.

Some commentators opined that the sentences imposed upon Blackshaw and others who committed offences during the riots were too harsh. Civil liberties organisations argued that many of the sentences were disproportionate; the courts had placed too much weight upon the context in which the offences took place, rather than focusing on the offences themselves. Others argued that harsh sentences were appropriate. The Prime Minister, David Cameron, praised the courts for sending a 'tough message'.

Blackshaw's sentence was upheld by the Court of Appeal. The Lord Chief Justice stated that, having regard to the courts' duty to protect the public, '...the imposition of severe sentences, intended to provide both punishment and deterrence, must follow' (R v Blackshaw and Others [2011] EWCA Crim 2312).

. . . .

Introduction

The final stage of the criminal process is the sentencing of a convicted defendant. There are a variety of sentencing options available to the courts, ranging from an absolute discharge to custodial sentences.

The Powers of Criminal Courts (Sentencing) Act 2000 (PCC(S)A 2000) and the Criminal Justice Act 2003 (CJA 2003) currently govern the making of custodial sentences, including life imprisonment and extended sentences for dangerous offenders. The CJA 2003 also empowers the courts to make community orders, enabling offenders to serve their sentences in the community. Requirements that are commonly attached to such orders include supervision by a probation officer, unpaid work in the community, and curfews.

Successive governments have struggled to strike the appropriate balance between the different aims of sentencing, which include punishment, rehabilitation, and reparation. The primary purpose of a prison sentence is to punish an offender, whereas a community sentence is more likely to be directed towards rehabilitation. This chapter will explore the purposes of sentencing before considering different types of sentence in more detail. The separate regime governing the sentencing of youths is dealt with at the end of the chapter.

14.1 **Statutory provisions governing the sentencing of offenders**

The sentencing regime in England and Wales is largely governed by the PCC(S)A 2000 and the CJA 2003. There has been a recent flurry of legislation, however, amending and supplementing these statutes, including the Criminal Justice and Immigration Act 2008, the Coroners and Justice Act 2009, the Legal Aid, Sentencing and Punishment of Offenders Act 2012 (LASPO Act 2012), and the Crime and Courts Act 2013. Sentencing practice is complicated by the fact that not all of the provisions of all of these statutes are in force. Sentencing legislation is, therefore, extremely difficult to navigate.

Sentencing is also a complicated exercise because, when Parliament changes the law, the new provisions are rarely retrospective. A person will usually fall to be sentenced in accordance with the law that was in force at the time the relevant offence was committed (*R v H* [2011] EWCA Crim 2753). As the number of historic offences that are being prosecuted increases, practitioners must be au fait not only with the current law, but also with sentencing provisions that have been in force at various points in the past.

Example

In May 2013, veteran television presenter Stuart Hall pleaded guilty to fourteen offences of indecent assault, which were committed between 1967 and 1986 upon victims aged 9 to 17. At that time, the maximum sentence for indecent assault was two years' imprisonment, or five years' imprisonment if the victim was under the age of 13. In Hall's case, the maximum sentence for most of the offences was, therefore, two years' imprisonment.

Hall was sentenced to fifteen months' imprisonment in total for the offences. The Attorney-General considered the sentence to be unduly lenient and referred it to the Court of Appeal. (For consideration of Attorney-General's References, see Chapter 16). In July 2013, the Court of Appeal increased the total sentence to thirty months' imprisonment by ordering that two of the fifteen-month sentences be served consecutively. (For discussion of consecutive and concurrent sentences, see 14.7.4.)

The imposition of the original sentence of fifteen months' imprisonment generated a degree of public outrage. However, the sentencing judge was constrained by the maximum sentence that was in force at the time the offences were committed. Attitudes towards sexual offending have changed dramatically in recent decades. The sentences that are now handed down for sexual offending are significantly higher than they would have been in the 1960s, '70s and '80s. Indeed, the offence of indecent assault was repealed by the Sexual Offences Act 2003 and replaced by two new offences: sexual assault and assault by penetration, which carry maximum sentences of ten years' imprisonment and imprisonment for life respectively.

It is simply not possible, or necessary, to cover all of the sentencing provisions that have ever been in force in an English legal system course. This chapter will, therefore, outline the sentencing principles and provisions that would be applicable in the case of an offender who committed an offence at the time of writing.

14.2 **The purposes of sentencing**

The purposes of youth sentencing are discussed at 14.8.1.

When passing sentence, a court must bear in mind the purposes of sentencing, which are set out in s.142 of the CJA 2003, namely:

- punishing offenders;
- reducing crime (including by deterring others from committing similar offences);
- reforming and rehabilitating offenders;
- protecting the public; and
- reparation by defendants to those affected by their offences.

> 🔑 **Key point**
>
> The aims listed in s.142 are not necessarily compatible with one another. For example, a community sentence involving supervision by a probation officer has rehabilitation as its primary aim and is not generally regarded as a punitive sentence.
>
> One advantage of having a 'menu' of purposes is that it promotes flexibility, enabling courts to promote a particular purpose when the interests of justice so dictate. However, the failure to give any guidance to judges as to how they should choose between competing aims creates the risk that sentencing decisions will be inconsistent.

> **Thinking point**
>
> How else might the aims of sentencing set out in s.142 of the CJA 2003 conflict with one another?

Governments have, at various times, elevated certain sentencing aims above others. A government wanting to be seen to be 'tough on crime' will tend to promote the aims of punishment and deterrence above reform and rehabilitation. When the current Coalition government first came to power, statements were made suggesting a move away from the 'prison works' orthodoxy. Former Justice Secretary, Kenneth Clarke, publicly acknowledged that credible community sentences were often preferable to short custodial sentences. In a bid to reduce the burgeoning prison population, Mr Clarke indicated a preference for expanding the use of community penalties.

However, the policies of Mr Clarke's successor, Chris Grayling, are focused on punishment rather than rehabilitation. In early 2013, the government introduced legislation to ensure that all community sentences have a punitive element, such as a curfew, or unpaid work. Meanwhile, prison overcrowding remains a pressing problem. A parliamentary briefing paper published in July 2013 confirmed that 69 prison establishments in England and Wales (representing 56 per cent of the prison estate) are currently overcrowded, with nine establishments having a population of at least 150 per cent of the Certified Normal Accommodation figure (Source: SN/SG/4334).

Thinking point

Do you think that the number and length of custodial sentences that are imposed should be curbed in order to reduce the prison population?

14.3 **Maximum sentences**

Before sentencing an offender, the first thing the court needs to know is what its sentencing powers are in relation to the relevant offence(s). Where a defendant has been convicted of a common law offence, such as kidnapping, sentencing is said to be 'at large'.

Where a defendant has been convicted of a statutory offence, the maximum penalty that the court may impose for the offence will be set out in the Act of Parliament that creates the offence. If the offence is triable either way, the Act will specify the maximum sentence that can be imposed if a defendant is either convicted on indictment or committed to the Crown Court for sentence.

If a defendant is convicted following summary trial, or pleads guilty before the magistrates' court and is not committed for sentence, the maximum penalty the magistrates' court can impose is never more than six months' imprisonment for a single offence (s.78 Powers of Criminal Courts (Sentencing) Act 2000). However, if a defendant falls to be sentenced for two or more either way matters, the magistrates'

sentencing at large
Where sentencing is at large, the Crown Court can impose any sentence up to and including life imprisonment.

court may impose up to 12 months' imprisonment (s.133(2) Magistrates' Courts Act 1980).

> ### 🔑 Key point
>
> A statute may specify a maximum penalty of less than six months' imprisonment following summary conviction. For example, s.5 of the Public Order Act 1986 provides that the maximum sentence for the offence of causing harassment, alarm or distress is a fine. However, a statute cannot currently permit a magistrates' court to impose more than six months' imprisonment for a single offence.

> ### 🗐 Example
>
> Theft is an either way offence. Section 7 of the Theft Act 1968 provides: 'A person guilty of theft shall on conviction on indictment be liable to imprisonment for a term not exceeding seven years.' If a defendant is convicted of theft in the Crown Court, or if he is committed to the Crown Court for sentence, he may receive a sentence of up to seven years in prison. If a defendant is convicted of theft in the magistrates' court and is not committed for sentence, the maximum penalty the magistrates' court can impose is six months' imprisonment. (See 13.7.1 for further information about committal for sentence.)

Section 154 of the CJA 2003, which has not been brought into force, would increase magistrates' courts' sentencing powers to 12 months' imprisonment for any one offence. The Magistrates' Association, which represents lay magistrates, has lobbied for greater sentencing powers, arguing that it would be cheaper to process more cases in the magistrates' courts. The extension of magistrates' courts' sentencing powers from six to 12 months' custody formed part of the Conservative Party's manifesto for the 2010 general election but was not subsequently included in the Coalition Agreement. In August 2013, Justice Minister Damian Green confirmed that the government did not intend to bring s.154 of the CJA 2003 into force, which would give magistrates higher sentencing powers, because of the risk that this would lead to a rise in the prison population.

> ### Thinking point
>
> What other arguments could be made for and against increasing magistrates' courts' sentencing powers? Remember that lay magistrates are not legally qualified and that anyone who is sentenced by a magistrates' court has an automatic right of appeal to the Crown Court.

The Court of Appeal has consistently held that the maximum sentence for an offence should normally be reserved for the most serious examples of that offence. The following section will explore how the courts decide precisely what sentence to impose within the available sentencing range.

14.4 Determining the appropriate sentence

In addition to the factors set out in s.142 of the CJA 2003 (see 14.1), the seriousness of the offence is a key consideration in passing sentence.

☰ Example

Lewis burgles a house while the occupier is asleep in bed. He smashes a window to gain entry, then ransacks the downstairs rooms and takes a computer, a stereo, a DVD player, television, and a stack of DVDs. He also steals a piece of jewellery of sentimental value to the homeowner.

Donna burgles a house during the daytime while the homeowner is out. She gains entry via an open window and does not cause any damage. She takes a purse that had been left on the table but does not steal anything else.

The burglary committed by Lewis is more serious than the burglary committed by Donna and will attract a higher sentence.

In determining the appropriate sentence, the court must also have regard to any aggravating or mitigating factors apparent from the facts of the case, and to any sentencing guidelines (CJA 2003 s.172). The court will often be assisted by a pre-sentence report.

14.4.1 Pre-sentence reports

When a defendant is convicted, either following a trial or by pleading guilty, the court may either sentence him immediately or adjourn so that a **pre-sentence report** can be obtained.

An example of a pre-sentence report can be found on the Online Resource Centre that accompanies this book.

> *pre-sentence report: A pre-sentence report will be written by a probation officer after meeting the defendant. The report will explore the reasons for the defendant's offending behaviour, assess the risk of future offending, and make recommendations as to the defendant's suitability for various types of sentence.*

Section 156 of the CJA 2003 provides that the court must normally obtain a pre-sentence report when considering a custodial sentence or certain community sentences.

14.4.2 Offence seriousness, aggravating and mitigating factors

In determining the seriousness of an offence, the court must have regard to both the culpability of the offender and the harm the offence caused (or was intended to cause, or might foreseeably have caused) (s.143, CJA 2003). For detailed guidance on offence seriousness, including important *aggravating and mitigating factors*, see the sentencing guideline 'Overarching Principles: Seriousness' (available at **sentencingcouncil. judiciary.gov.uk/docs/web_seriousness_guideline.pdf**).

> *aggravating factors:* Aggravating factors are features which indicate a higher than usual level of culpability on the part of the defendant, or a higher than usual degree of harm, or both.

> *mitigating factors:* Mitigating factors are features that indicate that the defendant's culpability is unusually low, or that the harm caused by the offence is less serious than would be usual for an offence of that type.

Examples of aggravating factors identified in the guideline include professional offending, use of a weapon, abuse of a position of trust, an especially serious physical or psychological effect on the victim, or where the victim is particularly vulnerable. Mitigating factors include provocation, the fact that a defendant has a mental illness or a disability, the youth or age of the defendant, and personal mitigation, such as remorse or admissions to the police.

Under s.143 of the CJA 2003, the court must treat a previous conviction as an aggravating feature if it is reasonable to do so, having regard to the nature, relevance, and age of the earlier offence. Similarly, where a defendant commits an offence on bail, this will be an aggravating factor (s.143(3)). A sentence should also be increased where an offence was racially or religiously aggravated, or aggravated in relation to the victim's disability, sexual orientation, or transgender identity (ss.145 and 146).

The sentencing court is entitled to take into account any matters that appear to the court to be relevant in mitigation of a defendant's sentence (s.166). For example, a guilty plea is normally regarded as a mitigating feature. Section 144 of the CJA 2003 requires the court to take into account the stage in the proceedings at which the offender indicated his intention to plead guilty. The sentencing guideline entitled 'Reduction in Sentence for a Guilty Plea' provides that courts should discount sentences by up to one-third where a defendant pleads guilty (**sentencingcouncil.judiciary. gov.uk/docs/web_seriousness_guideline.pdf**). There is a sliding scale for discounting the sentence, ranging from a one-third discount where a guilty plea is entered at the earliest opportunity, to a discount of one-tenth or less where a plea is entered at the last minute, for example, on the day of trial. In certain circumstances, the court does not have to give any discount at all for a guilty plea, such as where the prosecution case against the defendant is overwhelming.

Thinking point

What are the advantages and disadvantages of allowing the courts to impose lesser sentences on those who plead guilty? If there were no discount at all, and therefore no incentive for a defendant to plead guilty, would this result in more trials?

14.4.3 Sentencing guidelines

Section 118 of the Coroners and Justice Act 2009 created a Sentencing Council for England and Wales. Section 120 of the 2009 Act empowers the Sentencing Council to issue *sentencing guidelines* relating to the sentencing of offenders.

> 🔑 **Key point**
>
> The Sentencing Council is an independent body, whose role is to issue guidelines to be used by all courts with a view to achieving transparency and consistency in sentencing (see **www. sentencingcouncil.org.uk/index.htm**). The Sentencing Council replaced the Sentencing Guidelines Council, which no longer exists.

Section 125 of the Coroners and Justice Act 2009 provides that a court 'must follow' any applicable sentencing guidelines, unless it would be contrary to the interests of justice to do so. This is an important change from the previous legislation, which provided only that the court had to 'have regard to' any sentencing guidelines (s.172 CJA 2003).

> *sentencing guidelines: In s.125 of the Coroners and Justice Act 2009, the term 'sentencing guidelines' encompasses definitive guidelines that have been issued by either the Sentencing Council, or its predecessor, the Sentencing Guidelines Council. Also included are guidelines laid down in any judgment of the Court of Appeal before 27 February 2004, unless they have been superseded by definitive guidelines.*

It has often been said that guidelines are not 'tramlines' and that 'slavish adherence' to guidelines is not required (see, for example, *R v Blackshaw and Others* [2011] EWCA Crim 2312). Nevertheless, where a judge does not follow an applicable sentencing guideline, he must explain why he is of the opinion that it would be contrary to the interests of justice to do so.

> ❗ **Critical debate**
>
> Read s.121 of the Coroners and Justice Act 2009, then read the Sentencing Council's definitive guideline for burglary offences (available at **http://sentencingcouncil.judiciary.gov.uk/ guidelines/guidelines-to-download.htm**). Answer the following questions:
>
> (a) What is an offence 'category' and what is a 'category range'? (See page 2 of the guideline)
>
> (b) Look at pages 7–10 of the guideline. In relation to domestic burglary, what factors would bring an offence within Category 3?
>
> (c) What is the starting point for a Category 3 domestic burglary, and what is the category range?
>
> (d) What factors should result in a court imposing a sentence *below* the starting point for a Category 3 domestic burglary?

(e) Do you think it is a good idea to require judges to follow sentencing guidelines in most cases, or should judges always be able to use their discretion to pass any sentence up to the maximum for the offence?

14.5 Newton hearings

Sometimes, a defendant pleads guilty to an offence but does not accept all the facts alleged against him by the prosecution. If the differing versions would attract different sentences, the court must either accept the defence version of the facts and sentence on that basis, or hold a 'Newton hearing' (see R v Newton (1983) 77 Cr App R 13). At a Newton hearing, the judge (or magistrates, or district judge) will hear evidence and must decide whether the prosecution has proved beyond reasonable doubt that its version of the facts is correct.

Example

Steve is charged with robbery. Robbery involves the use or threat of force in order to steal. The prosecution case is that Steve held a knife to John's throat, then punched him in the face and stole his wallet. Steve admits punching John and stealing his wallet but denies having a knife. Steve thus admits the offence of robbery. However, the presence of a knife is an aggravating feature, since if it were proved that Steve had a knife, he would receive a longer prison sentence. A judge would, therefore, be likely to require a Newton hearing to determine whether Steve did have a knife before proceeding to sentence.

During the Newton hearing John, and any other witnesses on this point, would be called by the prosecution to give evidence to establish the presence of the knife at the time of the robbery. Steve would then be entitled to give evidence in his own defence, to say that he did not have a knife, and also to call any other witnesses to support his version of events. Unless the judge is sure that Steve had a knife, he must sentence on the basis that Steve did not have a knife.

14.6 Offences taken into consideration

A defendant who is being sentenced in respect of an offence may wish to have other offences 'taken into consideration', even though he has not been charged with those offences. Such offences are referred to as 'TICs'. If the court is prepared to take offences into consideration, the defendant is not convicted of the TICs but the court will take them into account. This may or may not add to the sentence that the defendant receives, depending upon the number and seriousness of the offences in question. The advantage to the defendant is that TICs may not add greatly to his sentence, and he cannot later be separately prosecuted and punished for them (R v Miles [2006] EWCA Crim 256).

14.7 **Types of sentence**

The criminal courts have a range of sentences open to them. The types of sentences available will now be considered in ascending order of seriousness.

14.7.1 **Absolute and conditional discharges**

At the bottom of the scale, under s.12 of the Powers of Criminal Courts (Sentencing) Act 2000, come the 'absolute discharge' and the 'conditional discharge'. The court must be of the opinion that it would be inexpedient to inflict punishment for the offence. In the case of an absolute discharge, the defendant remains convicted but is not punished at all. In the case of a conditional discharge, the defendant will not be punished unless he commits another offence within a specified period. If he does commit a further offence, he may be sentenced both for the new offence and the offence for which he received the conditional discharge. The maximum period of a conditional discharge is three years; there is no minimum period.

14.7.2 **Fines**

Fines are the most common penalty imposed by the criminal courts. In the year ending March 2013, 68 per cent of offenders were issued fines. There is no limit to the amount of fine that the Crown Court may impose (s.163 Criminal Justice Act 2003). The maximum fine that a magistrates' court can impose for an offence is £5,000, but this limit will be removed when s.85 of the Legal Aid, Sentencing and Punishment of Offenders Act 2012 comes into force. However, the maximum that can be imposed for a particular offence may be limited by the statute that creates the offence (and may be considerably less than £5,000).

> ### Example
>
> Using threatening, abusive, or insulting words or behaviour likely to cause harassment, alarm, or distress is an offence contrary to s.5 of the Public Order Act 1986. Section 5(6) states that a person who is guilty of this offence is liable to 'a fine not exceeding level 3 on the standard scale' (s.5(6)). The standard scale of fines is set out in s.37 of the CJA 2003. Under s.37(3), there are five levels of fine and a level 3 fine is £1,000. Thus, the maximum sentence that can be imposed on a person who is convicted of an offence contrary to s.5 Public Order Act 1986 is a fine of £1,000.

Section 164 of the CJA 2003 provides that a fine must reflect the seriousness of the offence but that the court must also take into account the circumstances of the case, including the financial circumstances of the defendant.

14.7.3 **Community orders**

The sentencing court may impose a community order (CJA 2003 s.177), which is an order that the defendant abide by one or more specified requirements. In the year ending March 2013, the courts imposed community orders on 26 per cent of offenders who were sentenced for indictable offences. The requirements that may currently be imposed upon a defendant under a community order are:

- unpaid work for between 40 and 300 hours (formerly known as 'community service');
- supervision (colloquially known as 'probation');
- a curfew, for up to 16 hours a day for a maximum of 12 months;
- a prohibited activity requirement (preventing the offender from participating in specified activities);
- an exclusion requirement (preventing the offender from entering a specified area for up to two years);
- a programme requirement (requiring the offender to attend a specified course, such as an anger management course);
- an activity requirement (requiring the offender to participate in specified activities, such as basic skills training);
- mental health treatment, alcohol treatment, or drug rehabilitation;
- a foreign travel prohibition (preventing the offender from travelling outside Britain for up to 12 months);
- residence (requiring the offender to live at a specified address).

Section 150A of the CJA 2003 provides that a community order can only be imposed if the offence in question is punishable by imprisonment, or if the defendant is a persistent offender who has previously been fined. Furthermore, under s.148, the court may only impose a community order if it is of the opinion that the particular offence is sufficiently serious to warrant it. Indeed, even where this s.148 'threshold' for making a community order has been passed, the court may decide that a financial penalty or a conditional discharge is appropriate (see 'Overarching Principles: Seriousness' at the Sentencing Council's website).

Under s.148, the requirement(s) imposed under a community order must be those which, in the opinion of the court, are the most suitable for the offender, and any restrictions on liberty must be commensurate with the seriousness of the offence. However, when s.44 and Sch. 16 of the Crime and Courts Act 2013 come into force, courts will be required to impose a punitive element (such as unpaid work, an exclusion requirement, a curfew, or a fine) as part of every community order.

A defendant who fails to comply with the requirements of a community order may be returned to court. Where a court finds the defendant to be in breach of the order, it must issue a fine, impose more onerous conditions, or revoke the order and re-sentence the offender for the original offence.

14.7.4 Custodial sentences

In the year ending March 2013, 27 per cent of all those sentenced for indictable offences received custodial sentences. Unsurprisingly, the proportion of offenders who received custodial sentences was higher in the Crown Court, which deals with more serious offences, where 58 per cent of offenders received an immediate custodial sentence.

Determinate custodial sentences

> ### 🔒 Key point
>
> Where a custodial sentence is an available option, s.152 of the CJA 2003 provides that the court must not pass such a sentence unless of the opinion that the offence (or the combination of the offence and associated offence(s)) is so serious that neither a fine nor a community order can be justified.

The factors that will influence the court's decision as to the length of sentence to impose are considered at 14.4. Where the court does pass a custodial sentence, it must normally be for the shortest term that is commensurate with the seriousness of the offending (CJA 2003 s.153). Moreover, the fact that the s.152 'custody threshold' has been passed does not automatically mean that the court should impose a custodial sentence. Circumstances such as mitigation relating to the offender's personal circumstances may enable the court to impose a community sentence instead (see CJA 2003 s.166 and see 'Overarching Principles: Seriousness' at the Sentencing Council's website).

> ### Thinking point
>
> The sentences imposed upon defendants for offences committed during the riots of 2011 were criticised by many as being too harsh. For example, in addition to the case of Jordan Blackshaw (discussed in the Talking point at the start of this chapter), the media reported that a 23-year-old man had been imprisoned for six months for stealing bottled water worth £3.50. To what extent were these sentences commensurate with the seriousness of the offences committed?

As we have already seen, the maximum custodial sentence that the magistrates' court can impose on a defendant is six months for a single offence. Where the defendant is charged with two or more 'either way' offences, the magistrates' court may aggregate the terms of imprisonment imposed in respect of each offence up to a maximum of 12 months. In the case of either way offences, if the magistrates' court considers that this is insufficient, it can, of course, commit the defendant to the Crown Court for sentence.

Offenders do not commonly serve the full period of imprisonment to which they are sentenced. Instead, they are released on licence well before the end of that period. For example, under s.244 of the CJA 2003, offenders sentenced to imprisonment for 12 months or more will normally be released on licence after serving half of their sentence and will remain on licence until the expiry of the sentence. Some prisoners who are serving a sentence of at least 12 weeks will be eligible to be released before the half-way period under the home detention curfew scheme. A prisoner on home detention curfew will be confined to their home for a specified period and will have to wear an electronic tag, usually around their ankle.

Extended sentences

The controversial indeterminate sentence of imprisonment for public protection ('IPP') was abolished by the Legal Aid, Sentencing and Punishment of Offenders Act 2012. IPPs were imposed on offenders who were deemed to be 'dangerous'. When sentencing an offender to an IPP, the judge had to specify the minimum term of imprisonment to be served. However, the offender did not have the right to be released after serving the minimum term and could only be released if the parole board was satisfied that he was no longer dangerous. Thus, an offender sentenced to an IPP did not know when, or if, he would be released. Furthermore, in order to demonstrate that he was no longer dangerous, an offender had to complete certain courses or training programmes in prison, yet funding difficulties meant that places on such courses were very often unavailable. The IPP provisions were ultimately abolished in response to heavy criticism from the judiciary, the legal profession, and academics.

Under the current law, where an offender is deemed to be 'dangerous', in accordance with the provisions of s.225 of the CJA 2003, the court may impose an extended licence period (known as an 'extended sentence'). An offender will be regarded as 'dangerous' if they have been convicted of an offence specified in Sch.15 of the CJA 2003, and the court considers that there is a significant risk that the offender will cause serious harm to the public by committing further specified offences. The court must also be satisfied that either the offence would normally attract a custodial sentence of at least four years, or the offender has a previous conviction for one of the serious offences listed in Sch.15B to the CJA 2003. If so satisfied, the court may impose an additional licence period of up to five years for a specified violent offence, or up to eight years for a specified sexual offence.

Minimum terms of imprisonment

In certain circumstances, statutes lay down the *minimum* custodial sentence that the court must impose. For example, s.111 of the Powers of Criminal Courts (Sentencing) Act 2000 provides that, subject to certain conditions, where a person is convicted of a domestic burglary and has already been convicted of two other domestic burglaries, the court must impose a sentence of imprisonment for a term of at least three years. This is sometimes known as the 'three strikes' rule.

Consecutive or concurrent prison sentences

Where an offender is convicted of more than one offence and custodial sentences are imposed, the sentences may be consecutive or concurrent. For example, where the court intends to impose a period of imprisonment of three months for one offence and nine months for another offence, these may either be ordered to be served consecutively, making a total sentence of 12 months, or they may be served at the same time, making a total sentence of nine months. The judge or magistrates should state in the presence of the defendant whether the terms of imprisonment are consecutive or concurrent (see the Criminal Practice Directions, VII E). Concurrent sentences will normally be appropriate where the offences of which the defendant was convicted arose out of the same incident (*R v Noble* [2003] 1 Cr App R (S) 65). Where consecutive sentences are imposed, the court may mitigate the sentence by considering the totality of it (CJA 2003 s.166). In other words, the appropriate overall sentence may be less than the aggregate of the sentences that would otherwise be imposed for each of the individual offences.

Suspended sentence orders

Perhaps in recognition of the fact that there may be a limit to what can be achieved during a short prison sentence, the courts have long had the power to suspend sentences in certain circumstances. Under s.189 of the CJA 2003, where the court imposes a sentence of imprisonment of between 14 days and two years, the court may suspend the sentence for between six months and two years (known as the 'operational period'). If the offender commits another offence within the operational period specified, a future court may, and usually will, order that the custodial sentence be served. This is intended to ensure a defendant's good behaviour for the period of the suspension.

A court imposing a suspended sentence may also order the offender to comply with one or more of the requirements of a community order (see 14.7.3). A failure to comply with these requirements would also place the offender in jeopardy of being ordered to serve the custodial sentence.

Thinking point

Consider why the courts have the power to suspend prison sentences. Do you think the imposition of a suspended sentence, coupled with a community order, is likely to act as a greater incentive to good behaviour than the imposition of a community order alone?

Deferred sentences

Either a magistrates' court or the Crown Court may defer sentencing an offender for up to six months. The court may impose requirements on the offender during the deferral period, such as a residence requirement or a supervision requirement. Deferring sentence enables the court to have regard to the offender's conduct between the date of the offence and the date on which he is finally sentenced. For example, where an offender is already subject to other court orders, deferring sentence enables the court to give the offender an opportunity to comply with those orders before sentence is passed. If the offender does comply with existing orders during the deferral period, the court may impose a community sentence where it would otherwise have imposed a period of imprisonment.

When s.44 and Sch.16 of the Crime and Courts Act 2013 come into force, courts will have the power to defer sentence where the offender and victim agree to take part in restorative justice (RJ). The court may then have regard to the offender's engagement, or lack of engagement, in the RJ process when passing sentence. RJ is considered further at 14.8.4.

In relation to community sentences, deferred sentences, custodial sentences, and suspended sentences see the sentencing guideline 'New Sentences: Criminal Justice Act 2003', which can be found at the Sentencing Council's website.

Life sentences

At the top end of the scale of prison sentences comes the life sentence for murder, which is 'fixed by law' (Murder (Abolition of Death Penalty) Act 1965 s.1). Although called a 'life sentence', the court is required to order that the 'early release provisions' will apply unless the offence is so serious that, in the court's opinion, such an order should not be made (CJA 2003 s.269). This means that the trial judge will order a 'minimum term' that the offender must serve before being considered for release. On rare occasions where the seriousness of the offence(s) is exceptionally high, the court may make a 'whole life order' and life will actually mean life. On 31 March 2013, there were 7,576 prisoners serving life sentences in England and Wales, of whom only 42 were subject to whole life orders.

> ### Example
>
> On 13 June 2013, Dale Cregan was sentenced to life imprisonment for the murders of father and son David and Mark Short, and PCs Fiona Bone and Nicola Hughes. In passing sentence, Mr Justice Holroyde observed that the seriousness of the offences was exceptionally high because Cregan had murdered more than one person and each of the murders involved a substantial degree of premeditation and planning. In particular, Cregan had lured the two police officers to a house by falsely reporting that he had been the victim of an offence. When the unarmed officers arrived, Cregan opened fire upon them in an act of 'pre-meditated savagery'. His Lordship imposed a whole life order, adding: 'That means, in plain terms, that you will never be released from prison.'

In *Vinter and Others v UK* [2013] ECHR 645, however, the European Court of Human Rights (ECtHR) held that the imposition of a whole life order violates Article 3 of the European Convention on Human Rights, which prohibits inhuman or degrading treatment or punishment. The ECtHR ruled that a life sentence must include both a possibility of release and a possibility of review. Parliament has yet to introduce legislation to give effect to the judgment in this case.

Under Sch.21 to the CJA 2003, the 'minimum term' for an offence of murder will usually be at least 15 years, although it can be significantly more (see also Division VII M of the Criminal Practice Directions, which can be found at **http://www.judiciary.gov.uk/JCO%2fDocuments%2fPractice+Directions%2fConsolidated-criminal%2fnew-cpds-consolidated-with-amendment-no-1.pdf**). If and when an offender is released from such a sentence, he remains on licence for life. This means that he will be released subject to certain conditions, such as residence requirements, a curfew, or maintaining contact with a probation officer. If he breaches the conditions of the licence, for example by committing an offence or by failing to comply with other conditions, his licence may be revoked and he will be recalled to prison.

Certain other serious offences have a maximum sentence of life imprisonment, and these include manslaughter, wounding with intent to cause grievous bodily harm, robbery, and rape. The court retains the discretion to impose a life sentence in such cases (*R v Saunders and others* [2013] EWCA Crim 1027). However, the court will usually only impose a life sentence if the conditions in s.224A or s.225 of the CJA 2003 are satisfied. Section 224A deals with those who are convicted of a second serious offence, and s.225 deals with offenders who are deemed to be dangerous.

Under s.224A, the court may be required to impose a life sentence if the offender falls to be sentenced for an offence listed in Sch.15B to the CJA 2003 and has a previous conviction for such an offence. Offences listed in Sch.15B include manslaughter, wounding with intent to cause grievous bodily harm, robbery with a firearm, and certain serious sexual offences.

serious harm
Death or serious
physical or
psychological injury
(CJA 2003 s.224(3)).

Under s.225, the court must impose a life sentence if the offender has been convicted of a 'serious offence' and there is a significant risk that he would cause '**serious harm**' to members of the public by committing further specified offences. The court must also be satisfied that the seriousness of the offence justifies the imposition of a life sentence. 'Specified offences' are those offences that are listed in Sch.15 to the CJA 2003. In addition to the serious offences listed in Sch.15B, Sch.15 includes a number of less serious offences, such as malicious wounding, assault occasioning actual bodily harm, and sexual assault.

14.7.5 **Other sentences and orders upon sentence**

Examples of other orders that a criminal court might make or sentences that it might impose include:

- An offender may be bound over to keep the peace and be of good behaviour (Justices of the Peace Act 1967 s.1(7)), whereby a person agrees to forfeit a sum of money if he fails to comply with the terms of the bind over.

- An offender may be disqualified from driving (Powers of Criminal Courts (Sentencing) Act 2000 s.146). In addition to the courts' powers to disqualify those convicted of certain road traffic offences, s.146 of the 2000 Act gives any court the power to disqualify an offender from driving on conviction for any offence, even if the offence is not connected with the use of a motor vehicle.

- Banning orders under the Football Spectators Act 1989 can be used to prohibit a person from attending football matches.

- Anti-social behaviour orders can be imposed upon conviction if it is necessary to protect the public from further anti-social acts by the offender (Crime and Disorder Act 1998 s.1C). The effect of an 'ASBO' is to prohibit the offender from doing certain things described in the order. An ASBO is not a sentence in itself but may be imposed in addition to the sentence that is passed for an offence.

- Notification requirements may be imposed under the Sexual Offences Act 2003, under which a person convicted of a sexual offence must notify the police of a variety of matters including their home address.

- Compensation orders can be made, which require an offender to pay compensation for personal injury, loss, or damage resulting from an offence (Powers of Criminal Courts (Sentencing) Act 2000 s.130). The imposition of a compensation order must be considered in any case where the court has the power to do so. A compensation order may be the only sentence imposed for an offence or it may be imposed in addition to most other types of sentence.

- Confiscation orders may be made, under which the amount by which an offender has benefited from criminal conduct may be confiscated (Proceeds of Crime Act 2002).

Thinking point

Imposing a sentence upon an offender may potentially have a variety of consequences. For example, it may prevent the offender from committing other offences by keeping him out of circulation; it may assist in reforming the defendant; it may deter others from committing similar offences; it may punish the defendant; or it may satisfy the needs of the victim, the victim's family, or the public at large for retribution. Which types of sentence do you think may have any or all of these consequences?

14.8 Sentencing youths

For the purposes of sentencing, a youth is an offender under the age of 18. (Note that children under the age of 10 are deemed to be incapable of committing criminal offences and cannot appear before a criminal court.) In certain circumstances, such as where the youth is charged alongside an adult, an offender aged 10–17 may appear before a magistrates' court. In exceptional circumstances, where the offence is particularly serious, a young offender may be sent to the Crown Court. However, the vast majority of offenders under the age of 18 are dealt with before youth courts. A youth court tribunal consists of three specially trained magistrates or a district judge. Its procedures and atmosphere are less formal than those of an adult magistrates' court.

14.8.1 Aims of youth sentencing

The Criminal Justice and Immigration Act 2008 inserted s.142A into the CJA 2003. Section 142A, which is not yet in force, emphasises that the principal aim of the youth justice system is to prevent re-offending by those under the age of 18. Under s.142A(3), the purposes of sentencing youths are:

- the punishment of offenders;
- the reform and rehabilitation of offenders;
- the protection of the public; and
- reparation by offenders to those affected by their offences.

Thinking point

Consider the purposes of sentencing set out in s.142 of the CJA 2003, outlined at 14.1. How will the purposes of youth sentencing differ from the purposes of adult sentencing if s.142A becomes operational?

The types of sentence available for youths are considered next in ascending order of severity.

14.8.2 Absolute and conditional discharges

For absolute and conditional discharges in relation to adult offenders, see 14.7.1.

Absolute and conditional discharges under s.12 of the Powers of Criminal Courts (Sentencing) Act 2000 are available for youths as they are for adults.

14.8.3 Fine

A young offender may be fined. As with an adult offender, any fine that is imposed should reflect both the seriousness of the offence and the offender's ability to pay. In the case of a youth under the age of 16, it is the young offender's parent or guardian who is legally responsible for paying the fine and it is their ability to pay that must be taken into account.

14.8.4 Referral orders

Where a youth court or magistrates' court does not intend to impose an absolute or a conditional discharge, an offender under the age of 18 who has no previous convictions and pleads guilty to an offence that is punishable with imprisonment, must normally be sentenced to a referral order. The court also has the power to make a referral order where the offender has previous convictions, but is not required to do so.

A referral order requires a young offender to attend a youth offender panel and to agree a contract with the panel. Such a contract may require the young offender to make restitution or reparation to the victim of the offence, for example, by repairing any damage caused by the offence. The offender may also be required to undertake a programme of interventions and activities aimed at addressing their offending behaviour.

Referral orders commonly utilise 'restorative justice' (RJ) approaches. RJ enables a victim to tell an offender what impact the crime has had on them. Victims are able to ask the offender questions and obtain an apology. The majority of victims who agree to RJ choose to attend a face-to-face meeting with the offender. A study commissioned by the Ministry of Justice, which began in 2001, has suggested that RJ is likely to result in a 27 per cent reduction in the frequency of re-offending (Shapland, J. et al, 'Restorative Justice: Does Restorative Justice affect reconviction. The fourth report from the evaluation of three schemes.' Ministry of Justice, 2008).

14.8.5 Youth rehabilitation orders

Where the circumstances do not make a referral order mandatory, a youth rehabilitation order may be made under s.1 of the Criminal Justice and Immigration Act 2008 if the offence is sufficiently serious to warrant it. The requirement(s) imposed under a youth rehabilitation order must be those which, in the opinion of the court, are the most suitable for the young offender, and the restrictions on liberty must be commensurate with the seriousness of the offence.

The court must specify a period no more than three years from the date of sentence within which the requirements imposed under the order must be completed. The following requirements may be imposed under a youth rehabilitation order:

- an activity requirement for no more than 90 days in total;
- supervision;
- unpaid work for between 40 and 240 hours (which can only be imposed on an offender aged 16 or 17);
- a programme requirement;
- an attendance centre requirement;
- a prohibited activity requirement;
- a curfew for between 2 and 16 hours a day for up to 12 months;
- an exclusion requirement;
- residence with a specified person or at a specified address;
- mental health treatment, intoxicating substance treatment, drug treatment, or drug testing;
- an education requirement; and/or
- intensive supervision and surveillance.

An electronic monitoring requirement may also be imposed to monitor the young offender's compliance with other requirements of the order.

For adult community orders see 14.7.3.

14.8.6 **Custodial sentences**

Detention and training orders

A detention and training order (DTO) may only be made in respect of an offence which is punishable by imprisonment. Additionally, where the young offender is under the age of 15, a DTO may only be made if the offender is a 'persistent offender'. At the date of writing, a DTO cannot be imposed upon an offender under the age of 12.

A DTO may be imposed for a period of 4, 6, 8, 10, 12, 18, or 24 months. If the court imposes consecutive sentences on an offender who has committed more than one offence, the aggregate term of the DTO must also be one of these periods. Thus, two DTOs of 4 and 8 months may be made consecutive, giving a total sentence of 12 months. However DTOs of 4 and 10 months could not be made consecutive, as the aggregate would be 14 months, which is not a permissible term.

An offender who is sentenced to a DTO will be detained in a secure children's home, a secure training centre, or a young offender institution for half of the term of the order, after which they will be released into the community, where they will be supervised and will undergo appropriate training and education until the expiry of the DTO.

Detention under s.91 of the Powers of Criminal Courts (Sentencing) Act 2000

Where an offender aged 10–17 is charged with an offence punishable by at least 14 years' imprisonment, the case may be sent to the Crown Court under s.91 of the Powers of Criminal Courts (Sentencing) Act 2000. Section 91 also applies to youths charged with certain sexual offences and to youths aged 16–18 who are charged with certain firearms offences. If the young offender is subsequently convicted before the Crown Court and the judge is of the opinion that neither a youth rehabilitation order nor a DTO is suitable, the young offender may be sentenced to detention for any period up to the maximum for the offence in question. In an appropriate case, the court may pass a sentence of detention for life. The term 'detention' is used instead of the term 'imprisonment' because a youth will be detained in secure accommodation or, more commonly, a young offender institution, rather than an adult prison.

Life imprisonment

A person who is convicted of murder and was under the age of 18 at the date on which the offence was committed must be sentenced to be detained 'during Her Majesty's pleasure'. This is effectively a life sentence and the judge will set a minimum term that the young offender must serve before being considered for parole. The starting point when a court is sentencing a youth for murder is usually 12 years, as opposed to 15 years for an adult (see 14.7.4).

Summary

- There are a number of different aims of sentencing, which may conflict with one another.
- Sentencing is governed by a complex statutory regime and the courts have a variety of sentencing options available to them, ranging from absolute discharges to custodial sentences.
- There is a maximum sentence that may be imposed in relation to each offence. For some serious offences, the maximum sentence will be life imprisonment. For some minor offences, the maximum sentence is merely a fine.
- In deciding what sentence to impose, the court will take into account the seriousness of the offence and any aggravating and mitigating factors. The court must also follow any sentencing guidelines unless it would be contrary to the interests of justice to do so.

- The court may find it necessary to adjourn in order to obtain pre-sentence reports before sentencing.
- If the defendant disputes the prosecution's account of the facts of the case, the magistrates or judge may be required to hold a *Newton* hearing to determine the appropriate basis upon which to sentence.
- Youth sentencing is subject to different considerations and different types of sentence are available.

Questions

1 What are the aims of sentencing adult offenders?

2 Can the court take a defendant's previous convictions into account when sentencing him or her?

3 What is the 'custody threshold'?

4 What sort of requirements may be attached to a community order?

5 What types of order may be available in addition to a sentence?

6 How do the sentencing options for a court dealing with a young offender differ from the sentencing options for a court dealing with an adult offender?

Sample question and outline answer

Question

Monique, who is 21 years old and has no previous convictions, has been charged with a single offence of theft. Monique works in a photography shop and the prosecution allege that she stole a sum of money from the shop's safe. Monique's first appearance before the magistrates' court will take place next week. She intends to plead guilty.

Discuss the factors the court will consider in deciding whether to sentence Monique to a period of imprisonment.

(Note that theft is an either way offence carrying a maximum sentence of seven years' imprisonment. The Sentencing Guidelines Council issued definitive guidelines on sentencing for theft in 2008, which have not been superseded.)

Outline answer

The question is deliberately vague about the facts of the offence and so requires you to discuss general sentencing principles. Because theft is an either way offence, you will need to discuss the position in both the magistrates' court and the Crown Court.

Introduction

Monique could be sentenced in the magistrates' court or her case could be committed to the Crown Court for sentence if the magistrates/district judge considers their powers to be insufficient.

Maximum sentences

If Monique is sentenced in the magistrates' court, the maximum sentence would be six months' imprisonment. If she is committed to the Crown Court, the judge could pass a sentence up to the seven-year maximum for the offence.

Determining the appropriate sentence

Either court must have regard to the purposes of sentencing, which include punishment and deterrence but also the rehabilitation of offenders (s.142 CJA 2003). Before imposing a custodial sentence, a pre-sentence report should normally be obtained (s.156 CJA 2003). The court must consider the seriousness of the offence and any aggravating and mitigating factors (s.143 CJA 2003). The sum of money stolen will be important in determining offence seriousness. The fact that Monique is an employee is an aggravating feature as an employee is in a position of trust. Her exact position in the company and the degree of trust invested in her will, therefore, be relevant. However, Monique is young, which is a mitigating feature. Monique's guilty plea is also a mitigating factor. In accordance with sentencing guidelines, Monique will probably be entitled to a discount of up to one-third for her early guilty plea.

The court may only pass a custodial sentence if the offence is so serious that neither a fine nor a community order can be justified (s.152 CJA 2003). It must pass the shortest term that is commensurate with the seriousness of the offence (s.153 CJA 2003).

The court must follow any applicable sentencing guidelines unless it would be contrary to the interests of justice to do so (s.125 Coroners and Justice Act 2009). 'Sentencing guidelines' include guidelines issued by the now defunct Sentencing Guidelines Council. If the court chooses to depart from the guidelines it must explain the reasons why.

If the proposed sentence is between 14 days' and two years' imprisonment, the court may suspend the sentence. The court may order Monique to comply with requirements, such as supervision, unpaid work, or a curfew, during the period of suspension.

Further reading

- **Epstein, R.** 'What is the Role of Community Sentences in the Criminal Justice System?' (2011) 175 JPN 671
  Discusses a report concerning the effectiveness of community sentences compared with prison sentences.

- Ministry of Justice, *Criminal Justice Statistics Quarterly Update to March 2013* (2013)
  Pages 8–11 set out sentencing statistics for the year ending March 2013.

- **Roberts, J.V.** 'Points of Departure: Reflections on sentencing outside the definitive guidelines ranges' [2012] Crim LR 439
  Explores the circumstances in which courts may depart from definitive sentencing guidelines.

- **Roberts, J.V.** 'Sentencing Riot-related Offending' (2013) 53(2) Br J Criminol 234
  Examines public attitudes to the sentencing of those involved in the 2011 riots and discusses the divergence of perspectives between the community and the courts.

- Sentencing Council, *Overarching Principles: Seriousness* (2004)
  Sets out the factors that a court must take into account in determining what sentence to pass on an offender.

- **Shapland, J.**, Robinson, G., and Sorsby, A. *Restorative Justice in Practice*, Routledge (2011)
  Evaluates the work of three restorative justice (RJ) projects and considers the effect of RJ on the frequency of re-offending.

- **Von Hirsch, A.** and **Roberts, J.V.** 'Legislating Sentencing Principles: The provisions of the Criminal Justice Act 2003 relating to sentencing purposes and the role of previous convictions' [2003] Crim LR 639
  Discusses the aims of sentencing and reviews the principal sentencing provisions in the CJA 2003.

Online Resource Centre

You should now attempt the supporting multiple choice questions available at **www.oxfordtextbooks.co.uk/orc/wilson_els/**.

15 The civil process

⊙ Learning objectives

By the end of this chapter you should:

- be able to describe the process by which a civil claim will be dealt with in a county court or in the High Court;

- be aware of the major case management powers possessed by the civil courts and appreciate that these powers must be exercised so as to further the overriding objective of the Civil Procedure Rules 1998 (as amended);

- be able to list the major differences between civil and criminal trials;

- have a basic understanding of some of the major principles of civil evidence;

- be familiar with the procedures and principles which govern the award of costs in civil proceedings; and

- be able to describe how civil judgments can be enforced.

🛈 Talking point

. . . .

Lord Justice Jackson was asked, in 2009, to consider the civil courts' procedures and rules and to continue the reform process begun by Lord Woolf in the 1990s. Jackson's concern was that in some areas of the civil litigation process there was no correlation between the value and complexity of the claims and the costs of pursuing litigation. He considered that costs were 'disproportionate and impede access to justice'. As a result of his investigations and report, in April 2013 the Civil Procedure rules were substantially amended. Perhaps the most far reaching change was to the overriding objective of the rules. Lord Woolf's reforms had led to the overriding objective, expressed in CPR 1, being that courts should deal with cases justly. As of 1 April 2013 the overriding objective is to deal with cases justly AND AT PROPORTIONATE COST. When you are reading this chapter, and considering the civil courts' process think about whether you believe the rules will achieve this stated aim. What will the courts, and lawyers, have to do to ensure the new overriding objective is met? Do you think that justice and proportionality can sit along side each other on an equal basis? Can you think of a case where justice would only be achieved with disproportionate expenditure? What does disproportionate mean?

. . . .

Introduction

The civil court process is the means by which the state enables individuals to settle disputes. It is clearly in the public interest to ensure that those disputes that are incapable of informal resolution and must go to court are dealt with as quickly and efficiently as possible. The civil justice system was criticised for being too slow, expensive, complicated, and inaccessible. In 1994, Lord Woolf, the then Master of the Rolls, was commissioned to investigate the civil justice system and produce a report to recommend reforms to the system to improve access to justice. Lord Woolf's final report 'Access to Justice', published in July 1996, recommended a complete overhaul of the system, including a new set of rules and procedures and a change in the courts' attitude towards case management. As a result, the Civil Procedure Rules (CPR) came into force in 1999.

This chapter will consider the major changes introduced by the CPR and by the practice directions, protocols, and guides that accompany them. Although the CPR have largely been welcomed by practitioners, the judiciary, and academics, the extent to which they have actually improved access to justice has been a matter of some debate. Indeed, the problem of spiralling civil litigation costs led to a second major review of the system by Lord Justice Jackson, whose final report was published in January 2010.

In addition to considering the nature and impact of the Woolf reforms, this chapter will also look at five stages of the civil process:

- the civil process prior to the commencement of proceedings;
- the civil process between the commencement of proceedings and trial;
- the civil trial itself;
- the awarding of costs in civil proceedings; and
- the enforcement of civil judgments.

In the context of the civil trial, some of the basic principles of civil evidence will be discussed.

15.1 The nature of civil proceedings

A criminal case is usually brought by the state (in the name of the Queen) against an individual. Conversely, a civil case is commenced by an individual or organisation against another individual or organisation. Sometimes a particular event may give rise to both criminal and civil liability. Criminal law governs an individual's obligations to people in general and civil law oversees specific relationships.

> ### Example
>
> After having a few pints of beer, Joe decides to see how fast his new Porsche Turbo sports car can go. He drives it at high speed around a blind bend and crashes into an oncoming car driven by Anne. Anne is injured in the collision and her car is written off.
>
> Joe could be prosecuted in the criminal courts for offences such as driving after consuming alcohol above the prescribed limit and driving dangerously. The criminal charges would be determined in either the magistrates' court or the Crown Court.
>
> Anne could also bring a claim against Joe in the civil courts for negligence (a tort). Anne's aim would be to recover damages to compensate her for her personal injuries and the damage to her car. Her civil claim would be heard in either the county court or the High Court.

15.2 The Woolf reforms

In 1994, Lord Woolf was appointed by the Lord Chancellor to conduct a comprehensive review of the civil justice system. This was a result of widespread concern that the existing system was outdated and cumbersome, leading inevitably to tortuous and expensive litigation and inadequate access to justice.

Following an extensive programme of consultation with individuals and interest groups, Lord Woolf concluded that the system was too slow, too expensive, and too complicated. In particular:

- the cost of litigation often exceeded the value of the claim;
- the system favoured wealthy litigants over those who lacked resources;
- there were difficulties in predicting how long litigation might last and how much it would cost, which created uncertainty;
- the system lacked a coherent structure;
- there was a general lack of openness and cooperation between opposing parties; and
- rules and court orders were too often ignored.

One of the major aims of the Woolf review was to improve access to justice for individuals and small businesses. Those who want to bring cases in the civil courts will often have to fund the litigation themselves and may be unable to afford legal advice or representation. Lord Woolf felt that the system should therefore be clear and accessible to ordinary people. In practice, however, the High Court and the county courts had separate procedural rules, which were unnecessarily convoluted. Even the basic terminology was confusing: for example, a person bringing a claim was referred to as 'the plaintiff' and proceedings were commenced in the county court by a 'summons' and in the High Court by a 'writ'. Time limits were different in each court.

Lord Woolf made extensive recommendations for reform of the system in his report, *Access to Justice*, (see **http://webarchive.nationalarchives.gov.uk/+/http://www. dca.gov.uk/civil/final/contents.htm**). The majority of his recommendations were implemented through the CPR, which came into force on 26 April 1999.

15.2.1 **The Civil Procedure Rules**

Other than in relation to certain specialised forms of proceedings (e.g. family proceedings and insolvency proceedings), the CPR now govern all proceedings in county courts, the High Court, and the Civil Division of the Court of Appeal.

The CPR are divided into 'parts', with each part containing the basic rules to be followed in relation to a particular aspect of procedure, with more detailed guidance in accompanying *practice directions*. The procedures to be followed before proceedings commence are contained in the pre-action protocols. At present there are thirteen pre-action protocols.

> *practice directions: Practice directions are sets of rules and procedures which supplement and support parts of the CPR. They tell parties what the courts expect of them and also what may happen if they do not comply with rules or court orders.*

Throughout the remainder of this chapter, CPR means the Civil Procedure Rules 1998. Thus, for example, CPR 26 means Part 26 of the Civil Procedure Rules 1998 and CPR 7 PD refers to the practice direction that supplements CPR Part 7. The CPR can be found at: **www.justice.gov.uk/civil/procrules_fin/menus/rules.htm**.

The CPR are designed to be easily accessible and are supposed to be more user-friendly and intelligible than the rules they replaced. When they were introduced they were designed to be a completely new start. For example, a party bringing a claim is now referred to as a 'claimant' and claims in both the county court and the High Court are commenced by a 'claim form' (see Thinking point in 15.5).

Thinking point

Critics have suggested that the CPR have not simplified the civil process as intended. As well as being supplemented by numerous practice directions, pre-action protocols, and court 'guides', the CPR themselves have been updated sixty-six times since 1999. Is this consistent with a system that is supposed to be intelligible to non-lawyers?

The overriding objective of the CPR, expressed in CPR 1.1 is to deal with cases justly and, following the changes to the rules in 2013, at proportionate cost. This is the governing purpose of the CPR and is to be borne in mind by the parties and the court when conducting the litigation. In order to achieve the overriding objective, major changes were introduced to streamline the processes and allocate resources appropriately.

New processes and procedures introduced by the Woolf reforms include:

- claims are now allocated to one of three 'tracks' according to the value of the claim;
- the courts are responsible for setting timetables and ensuring that rules and procedures are complied with. Sanctions may be imposed upon a party who does not comply;
- costs in many cases are now fixed;
- in cases where costs are not fixed, the courts have wide powers to control costs;
- any party to the proceedings can make offers to settle the whole or part of a dispute, with sanctions for those who turn down appropriate and reasonable offers;

issued
a claim form is issued
when it is dated by the
court and stamped
with the court seal.

- there is an expectation of cooperation and openness between parties both prior to commencement of proceedings, in the hope that litigation will be avoided, and once the case has been *issued* at court;
- encouragement to use alternative dispute resolution.

The CPR made a variety of changes which increased the powers of the civil courts. Judges and court staff are given power to manage cases so as to reduce the extent to which the conduct of the parties might determine the progress of a case. The CPR also seek to restrict the adversarial nature of civil proceedings by encouraging cooperation and openness.

A good example of the reforms introduced by the CPR is provided by the ability of the civil courts to limit the admissibility and nature of expert evidence. Under the pre-CPR regime, the duration and cost of civil trials was often increased by disproportionate reliance upon expensive expert evidence. Under the CPR, the courts now possess the power to restrict expert evidence to that which is reasonably required, to direct that expert evidence be given by a single joint expert (i.e. one expert instructed by the parties jointly), and to limit such evidence to written reports rather than oral testimony, thereby ensuring speedier, less expensive, and less complex trials.

Expert evidence in civil proceedings is considered further at 15.14.4.

! Critical debate

Is the emphasis on the need for cooperation and openness in civil proceedings consistent with the maintenance of an adversarial system?

The Civil Procedure Rules emphasise the importance of using court as a last resort and encourage parties in dispute to try alternative dispute resolution methods, such as mediation before issuing court proceedings. Indeed, a party who fails to try ADR may be penalised in costs see the cases of Dunnett v Railtrack [2002] EWCA Civ 302, Halsey v Milton Keynes General NHS Trust [2004] EWCA 3006 Civ 576 and Burchell v Bullard [2005] EWCA Civ 358.

However, this encouragement to cooperate before litigation commences, and during the preparation for trial is very different from what happens in a court room if the parties finally end up there. Perhaps it is time to get rid of the adversarial process in civil cases completely? Are there any circumstances, do you think, that an adversarial process is more appropriate to settle a dispute than a more conciliatory approach?

15.2.2 The overriding objective and the court's duty to manage cases

The CPR has an 'overriding objective' of dealing with cases justly at proportionate cost. The court must have regard to the overriding objective when exercising its powers under the CPR and when interpreting the CPR. CPR Part 1 provides that dealing with a case justly and at proportionate cost includes:

- ensuring that the parties are on an equal footing;
- saving expense;
- dealing with the case in ways which are proportionate –
  - (i)   to the amount of money involved;
  - (ii) to the importance of the case;
  - (iii) to the complexity of the issues; and

(iv) to the financial position of each party;

- ensuring that it is dealt with expeditiously and fairly;
- allotting to it an appropriate share of the court's resources, while taking into account the need to allot resources to other cases; and
- enforcing compliance with rules, practice directions and orders.

The parties must help the court to further the overriding objective and the court itself must further the overriding objective by active case management. CPR Part 1 explains that active case management includes:

- encouraging cooperation between the parties;
- identifying the issues at an early stage;
- deciding promptly which issues need full investigation and trial and accordingly disposing summarily of the others;
- deciding the order in which issues are to be resolved;
- encouraging the parties to use an alternative dispute resolution procedure if the court considers that appropriate and facilitating the use of such procedure;
- helping the parties to settle the whole or part of the case;
- fixing timetables or otherwise controlling the progress of the case;
- considering whether the likely benefits of taking a particular step justify the cost of taking it;
- dealing with as many aspects of the case as it can on the same occasion;
- dealing with the case without the parties needing to attend at court;
- making use of technology; and
- giving directions to ensure that the trial of a case proceeds quickly and efficiently.

Thinking point

Professor Michael Zander has argued that the multiple considerations of the overriding objective are potentially conflicting. This leads to a risk of inconsistent decisions, as different judges can come to different decisions in similar cases. Can you foresee a situation in which the different aspects of the overriding objective conflict? Are some of the terms used by the overriding objective, such as 'fairness', easy to define or are they open to interpretation?

15.2.3 The Jackson Review

Supporters of the Woolf reforms claim that the CPR have introduced greater efficiency and reduced delays. Unfortunately, however, the costs of civil litigation have increased. The lack of proportionality between the value of claims and the cost of litigating them remains a major concern. For example, in 2009 it was reported that a defendant in a boundary dispute between neighbours had been ordered to pay £70,000 in costs to the claimant. The area of land involved in the dispute was approximately six square metres. Although this may be an extreme example, excessive and disproportionate costs are a problem.

In 2008, Lord Justice Jackson was appointed by the Master of the Rolls to undertake a review of the rules and principles governing costs in civil litigation. His final report, published in January 2010, made a number of recommendations that are designed to control costs. Key recommendations included:

- legal expenses must reflect the nature and complexity of the case and must be proportionate;
- qualified one way costs-shifting (i.e. a claimant who is unsuccessful should not be ordered to pay the defendant's costs);
- fixed costs in fast track cases.

There are also a number of major recommendations concerning the funding of civil litigation, which are considered in chapter 11. These recommendations and the subsequent implementation of the recommendations will be considered later.

15.3 **The civil courts**

The main civil courts are the county courts and the High Court, although magistrates' courts have a limited civil jurisdiction in relation to family law cases. A magistrates' court in its civil jurisdiction is known as the family proceedings court. Magistrates have the power to decide family matters such as adoption, residence, contact, and maintenance. Further consideration of the civil jurisdiction of magistrates is outside the scope of this chapter.

15.3.1 **The county courts**

At present there are approximately 160 county courts in England and Wales. The government has recently implemented a programme of court closures to save money backed up by the introduction of more online and electronic handling of cases.

The Crime and Courts Act 2013, s 17, sets out a provision to establish one County Court, on similar lines to the High Court. This too is designed to be a costs saving measure, and follows a recommendation made by Sir Henry Brooke in his 2008 report 'Should the Civil Courts be Unified?' Section 17 will come into force on a date decided by the Lord Chancellor. Clearly, although the provision is made in s.17 for a unified court to be established, a great deal of work will be needed to actually carry out the unification process.

Most of the judicial work of a county court is carried out by district judges. Circuit judges and recorders deal with the more complex matters. This includes pre-trial case management decisions, the trial of cases that are allocated to the small claims *track* and, in some court centres, the trial of cases that are allocated to the fast track. A district judge may also try a multi-track case with the consent of the Designated Civil Judge (i.e. the senior civil judge at the relevant trial centre). However, the county court trial of most cases that are allocated to the multi-track or the fast track takes place before a circuit judge or a recorder.

> **tracks:** *Each civil case is allocated to one of three tracks, namely the 'small claims track', the 'fast track', or the 'multi-track'. The appropriate track depends upon the value and complexity of the case. In essence, the lowest value cases are allocated to the small claims track (up to £10,000 in cases except personal injury and housing disrepair claims where the limit is £1,000), the medium value cases (up to £25,000) to the fast track, and the high value cases to the multi-track. Value of a case is the starting point for allocation but issues of complexity, importance, and numbers of witnesses are also taken into account. See CPR 26. Each track has its own rules that govern the conduct of a case.*

In some civil cases, liability will not be in issue and the court only needs to determine the amount of damages to be paid. For example, a defendant may admit breaching a contract but dispute the amount that he should have to pay to the claimant. Depending upon the value involved, and the complexity of the issues, a district judge may conduct the hearing to determine the amount of damages regardless of the track to which the case has been allocated. Part 7 of the CPR and Practice Direction 7A provide that certain proceedings must be commenced in the county court. These include proceedings where the value of the claim does not exceed £25,000 or, if the case involves personal injuries, where the value of the personal injuries claim is less than £50,000.

Thus, the vast majority of civil claims commence in the county court. In 2011, 1,553,983 cases started in the county court, compared to 49,166 in the High Court (see **www.gov.uk/government/uploads/system/uploads/attachment_data/file/162459/judicial-court-stats-2011.pdf.pdf**). These figures demonstrate a downward trend, commencing in 2006, in the number of court proceedings issued. There are, however, some limitations upon county court jurisdiction. For example, in accordance with s.15(2) of the County Courts Act 1984, a county court does not normally possess jurisdiction to hear defamation proceedings. There are special procedures for starting 'designated money' claims, which must now be issued out of the Northampton County Court, County Court money claims centre. Before issuing a claim it is important to check CPR7 and the associated practice directions to ensure that the issuing procedure is correctly followed.

Note: The Crime and Courts Act 2013 establishes a dedicated Family Court, s.17(3). However this provision is not yet in force, and, like the change to a unified County Court, will require change to the present system before the provision is enacted.

15.3.2 **The High Court**

The High Court is made up of three divisions, namely the Queen's Bench Division, the Chancery Division, and the Family Division.

The Queen's Bench Division (QBD) deals predominantly with claims in contract and *tort* although it can deal with a variety of other matters.

The QBD has specialist subdivisions which include the Commercial Court and the Admiralty Court, where judges with specific expertise determine matters of commercial law and shipping, respectively. There is also the Divisional Court of the QBD (as distinct from the QBD itself). The Divisional Court of the QBD has appellate jurisdiction and can determine appeals by way of case stated (an appeal decided on an agreed set of facts) and applications for judicial review.

The Chancery Division deals with matters such as the sale of land, mortgages, trusts, bankruptcy, and patents and encompasses the Bankruptcy Court and the Companies Court. Cases dealt with by the Family Division include matrimonial matters and proceedings under the Children Act 1989.

Many types of claim may be brought before more than one division (e.g. professional negligence claims may be brought in either the Queen's Bench Division or the Chancery Division). However, certain types of claim must be brought before a particular division (e.g. cases concerning the execution of trusts must be brought in the Chancery Division).

The High Court is based at the Royal Courts of Justice in London. There are also approximately 50 district registries around England and Wales at which a claimant may commence High Court proceedings.

At the Royal Courts of Justice, pre-trial case management is mainly undertaken by masters (they have a similar jurisdiction to that of a judge sitting in chambers; in other words, not in open court). At district registries, such work is mainly undertaken by district judges (who will be appointed both as county court district judges and as High Court district judges). Trials are conducted by a High Court judge or a deputy High Court judge. Certain other functions must also be performed by a High Court judge or a deputy High Court judge, such as making a 'freezing order' (which prevents a person from disposing of assets) or a search order (CPR 25A PD).

For some types of case, the rules do not specify where the case should commence. Where proceedings may be commenced either in the High Court or in a county court, it will be for the claimant to decide where to commence the proceedings. The claimant should commence proceedings in the High Court, rather than in a county court, if he believes that a High Court judge should deal with the case in view of:

- the financial value of the claim;
- its complexity; or
- the importance of its outcome to the public (CPR 7A PD).

Where a party chooses to commence proceedings in the High Court, the High Court may order the proceedings to be transferred to a county court if appropriate (s.40 County Courts Act 1984). Similarly, where a party chooses to commence proceedings in a county court, either the county court or the High Court may order the proceedings to be transferred to the High Court (ss.41–42 County Courts Act 1984).

tort
a tort is a civil wrong for which the victim is entitled to some form of redress. Examples of torts include negligence, nuisance, and defamation.

More information about High Court judges, district judges, and masters can be found in chapter 8.

15.4 **Case management powers**

Prior to the Woolf reforms, there were rules that set out the procedural steps to be taken by litigants and the time limits within which those steps were to be taken. However, these were often ignored. One of Lord Woolf's main objectives was to ensure that the courts began to control proceedings effectively. CPR Part 3 therefore confers a variety of general case management powers upon the civil courts. One of the main ways in which the court controls proceedings is by making orders, such as orders to:

- extend or shorten time limits laid down by the CPR;
- adjourn a hearing or bring it forward;
- require a party or his lawyer to attend court;
- hold a hearing by telephone;
- stay (i.e. suspend) the proceedings;
- determine the order in which issues are to be tried; or
- exclude an issue from consideration.

statement of case
a statement of case is a document in which a party sets out the basis of his case. Examples of statements of case are: particulars of claim; defences; counterclaims and replies (see 15.5.3 and 15.6.1).

A party to litigation may apply to the court for an order but the court may also make an order without application, in order to manage the proceedings. Thus, the conduct of litigation is not simply left to the parties. A court order may contain conditions and may specify the consequences of a party's failure to comply. For example, an 'unless order' may specify that 'unless' a party complies with the order, his *statement of case* will be struck out. Even where no 'unless order' has been made, the court may strike out a statement of case if there has been a failure to comply with a rule, a practice direction, or some other court order. As a result of the Jackson reforms, judges have been told, and trained accordingly, to be much tougher on default than they have been. Parties to litigation are advised to have their case in first class order at all times. There is no guarantee that a court will grant an extension of time to carry out a step in the process, or to make amendments to the case or replace an expert. See for example *Guntrip v Cheney Coaches Ltd* (2012) EWCA (a case decided under the old CPR rules but reflecting the new approach introduced in 2013) when a late request to appoint an alternative expert, after the initial expert changed his mind, was refused.

Thinking point

Striking out means that the court will order a document, or part of a document, to be deleted so that it may no longer be relied upon. Striking out a party's statement of case will often effectively mean that proceedings are decided in favour of the opposing party. Should the court be allowed to impose such a severe sanction for the breach of a procedural rule?

Instead of exercising the power to strike out a party's statement of case, the court may impose other sanctions where a party fails to comply with a rule, a practice direction, or a court order. Alternative sanctions include ordering the party at fault to pay costs, or refusing to give that party permission to rely on evidence to which the rule or order related.

However, a party may apply to the court for relief (i.e. that the sanction be removed or not enforced) from any of the aforementioned sanctions. It used to be the case that CPR Part 3 required the court, when considering an application for relief from sanctions, to consider all of the circumstances including:

- the interests of the administration of justice;
- whether the application was made promptly;
- the explanation for the failure to comply with rules;
- the extent to which the party has complied with other rules, practice directions, or court orders;
- whether the failure was caused by the party or his legal adviser;
- whether the trial date can still be met if the relief is granted; and
- the effect of granting the relief on the parties.

However, the Jackson reforms have simplified part 3.9 to introduce a much stricter approach to default. As well as considering 'all the circumstances of the case so as to enable it to deal justly' with an application for relief, the court must also now take into account the need:

(a) for litigation to be conducted efficiently and at proportionate cost; and

(b) to enforce compliance with rules, practice directions, and orders.

The system of sanctions introduced by the CPR was said to be an integral part of case management (*Access to Justice*, ch.6, para.16). Lord Woolf stated that the threat of punishment was necessary to ensure compliance with court orders and procedural rules. However, he acknowledged that the judiciary would need to take a much more robust approach if sanctions were to have any real effect. Critics of the Woolf reforms have suggested that, in practice, judges have been too willing to exercise mercy and grant relief from sanctions (see e.g. Zuckerman, A. 'Litigation management under the CPR' in Dwyer (ed.), *The Civil Procedure Rules Ten Years On*, Oxford University Press (2009)). Lord Justice Jackson clearly took this view on board and as a result failure to comply with orders, and the resultant increases in costs, will no longer be tolerated. The new approach of the courts can be seen in *Fred Perry (Holdings) Limited v Brands Plaza Trading Ltd* (2012) EWCA Civ 224 – a judgment of Lord Justice Jackson. The Master of the Rolls, Lord Dyson, has indicated that the appeal judges will support robust case management decisions at first instance.

15.5 Commencing civil proceedings

issued
a claim form is issued when it is dated by the court and stamped with the court seal.

In most straightforward cases, a person wanting to begin civil proceedings must complete a claim form and deliver it to the court. Proceedings commence when the claim form is *issued*. The person issuing the claim form is referred to as the claimant, while the person against whom the claim is made is the defendant. A single case may involve more than one claimant and/or more than one defendant.

15.5.1 Preliminary matters

Prior to commencing proceedings (i.e. prior to issuing the claim form) there is a variety of matters that a party and/or his solicitor must consider. In the first instance, the solicitor and client will need to discuss the various methods by which civil litigation may be funded. (This is discussed in more detail in chapter 11, 'Access to Justice'.)The primary considerations, in relation to the claim itself, are the nature of the claim and the remedy being sought. For example, it may be that a person seeks damages (compensation) for personal injuries or for breach of contract. Alternatively, he may be seeking a remedy such as an injunction to prevent a nuisance from continuing.

The nature of the claim is particularly important because there are statutory time limits within which claim forms must be issued. If proceedings are not commenced within the applicable limitation period, this will provide the defendant with a defence.

> ### Example
>
> Under the Limitation Act 1980, in relation to a claim for breach of contract, the claimant must issue the claim form within six years from the date of the breach. In relation to a personal injury claim, the claimant must usually issue the claim form within three years of the personal injury being suffered. In disease cases, the general rule is that proceedings must be issued within three years of the claimant's date of knowledge (see s.14 Limitation Act 1980).

Alternative dispute resolution is considered in chapter 17.

Prior to commencing proceedings, the solicitor will begin to collect evidence. The solicitor will take statements from his client and from other witnesses of fact (i.e. not expert witnesses). Decisions will also be made about what other evidence should be obtained. Evidence to support the case might include: copies of written records, such as accident reports from the police or from an employer; photographs of the scene of an accident; medical notes and records and evidence from an expert in a particular field, such as a consultant surgeon or an engineer. The solicitor and client must also consider whether some form of alternative dispute resolution may be more appropriate than litigation.

15.5.2 **Pre-action protocols**

The funding of civil cases is considered in chapter 11.

One of the aims of the CPR is to encourage the early resolution of cases. For this reason, the CPR are supplemented by 'pre-action protocols'. There are several pre-action protocols and each is applicable to a particular type of action, such as personal injury claims, defamation claims, housing disrepair cases, and judicial review. There is also now a practice direction on pre-action conduct (PDPAC), which contains a protocol that is applicable to *all* claims even if a specific protocol does not exist for the type of claim. The number of protocols is under scrutiny and it is likely that there will be a complete overhaul and simplification of their contents before the end of 2015.

The pre-action protocols and the PDPAC protocol lay down rules and procedures to be followed before a claim form can be issued. The main aim of the protocols is to encourage the exchange of early and full information, which is known as the 'cards on the table' approach. It is hoped that this will enable the parties to avoid litigation by settling the claim without recourse to court proceedings. Where litigation is unavoidable, early disclosure should support the efficient management of the proceedings. To encourage the parties to abide by the protocols, the court may take account of any failure to comply when determining costs. The pre-action protocols can be found at: **www.justice.gov.uk/civil/procrules_fin/menus/protocol.htm/**.

Most of the protocols require the claimant to notify the defendant of an intention to make a claim by sending a letter of claim. The defendant then has a period of time to investigate the claim before the claimant can commence court proceedings. For example, under the pre-action protocol for personal injury claims, the claimant should send two copies of a letter of claim to the defendant before proceedings are issued (one copy being for the defendant's insurer, if he has one). The letter of claim should summarise the facts and indicate the nature of any injuries and any financial loss. If neither the defendant nor his insurer replies within twenty-one days, the claimant is entitled to issue proceedings. If the defendant and/or insurer replies, they have up to three months to investigate the claim. By the end of that period, the defendant or insurer should indicate in a letter of reply whether liability is denied and, if so, why it is denied. This system is designed to allow cases to be settled at an early stage and to allow defendants to fully investigate claims and make offers to settle if appropriate, ensuring that very few cases will remain to be decided by the courts. If the defendant does not comply with the deadlines the claimant could issue a pre-action disclosure application.

The exception to the letter of claim approach applies to low value personal injury claims in road traffic cases, where the accident occurred on or after 30 April 2010, and low value personal injury claims (public liability and employer's liability claims) after July 2013, where the protocols prescribe the use of an electronic portal to notify claims, file documents, and deal with the cases. The draft protocols can be found at: **www.justice.gov.uk/civil-justice-reforms/personal-injury-claims/ extending-the-road-traffic-accident-personal-injury-scheme** and the portal can be found at: **www.claimsportal.org.uk/en/**. The aim of this electronic handling of claims is to reduce costs and streamline the process. Cases that are handled through the portal are subject to fixed costs.

In addition to requiring the early notification of a potential claim, the pre-action protocols contain rules relating to expert evidence. This is because the expense of expert witnesses was a major reason for the high cost of civil litigation. For example, in a personal injury case, a medical expert will usually need to provide evidence as to the nature and extent of the claimant's injuries and their likely prognosis. Before the CPR, both parties would instruct expert witnesses and the fees of both experts would usually, ultimately, be borne by the losing party. Most CPR pre-action protocols now provide that before instructing an expert witness, a party should give the other party a list of suitable experts. The expectation is that opposing parties will then share the same expert, who is referred to in the CPR as a single joint expert.

> ### Thinking point
>
> Is the introduction of single joint experts consistent with the adversarial nature of the English legal system? If there is more than one valid point of view that an expert could hold on an issue, might the requirement for a single expert effectively pre-judge the case?

CPR Part 36 offers, which may be made before or after proceedings commence, are considered at 15.9.

Finally, the pre-action protocols encourage the parties to settle claims rather than commence court proceedings. For example, under the pre-action protocol for personal injury claims, the parties are required to consider whether it is appropriate to make a pre-proceedings offer to settle the claim under CPR Part 36. If such an offer is made, the party making the offer must provide sufficient evidence or information to enable it to be properly considered. The protocol also provides that the parties should consider whether some other form of alternative dispute resolution, such as mediation, is appropriate.

In 2010, the Pre-Action Protocol for Low Value Injuries in Road Traffic Claims came into force. This protocol applies to claims where the value of personal injuries is between £1,000 and £10,000. It was introduced because these cases form a high proportion of all civil claims but were, it was suggested, often subject to delays and disproportionate costs. The aim of the protocol is to ensure that claimants receive fair compensation in a timely manner and at a proportionate cost. It introduces strict timetables and fixed costs, which vary in amount depending upon the stage at which a case is settled.

15.5.3 **Claim forms**

Civil proceedings commence when a claim form is issued by the court at the claimant's request (CPR Part 7).

In accordance with CPR Part 16, the claim form must state the nature of the claim, specify the remedy sought and, where money is sought, contain a statement of value. The claim form should confirm whether the claimant expects to recover:

- no more than £10,000;
- more than £10,000 but no more than £25,000; or
- more than £25,000.

If the value of the claim is unknown, the claim form should state that the claimant cannot say how much he expects to recover.

Where a claimant has suffered personal injuries, he may be entitled to claim a sum of money for general damages. General damages are intended to compensate a claimant for his pain, suffering, and loss of amenity (the way in which life has been changed by the injury). If these are to be claimed, the form must state whether the claimant expects to recover not more than £1,000 or more than £1,000 in respect of general damages.

These figures are designed to enable the court to allocate the case to the appropriate track.

The claimant must complete the necessary steps to serve the claim form on the defendant within four months of the claim form being issued by the court, although the court may extend this period. CPR Part 6 sets out the ways in which documents may be served (i.e. given to the defendant). These include: personal service (by leaving the document with the relevant person); posting the document by first class post or via a document exchange service; or sending the document by fax or by other means of electronic communication. Where the parties to civil litigation have appointed solicitors, the solicitors should be asked if they are authorised to accept service. If the solicitors confirm that they are authorised to accept service then the documents will be served on the solicitors rather than on the parties themselves. It is important not to serve the solicitor direct unless express consent has been given.

If the *particulars of claim* are not written on the claim form itself, these must either be served with the claim form in a separate document or served as a separate document within 14 days thereafter. See **www.justice.gov.uk/courts/procedure-rules/ civil/forms** for the claim form templates.

> *particulars of claim:* The particulars of claim is the document in which the claimant sets out the basis of the case against the defendant. It will set out the allegations being made and the facts relied upon in support of those allegations. It must contain the matters specified in CPR Part 16 and the associated practice direction.

In the context of a personal injury claim, the particulars of claim must include the claimant's date of birth and details of his injuries (CPR 16 PD). Where the claimant relies on medical evidence, a report from a medical practitioner concerning the alleged injuries must be attached.

All statements of case have to be verified by a 'statement of truth'. The significance of this requirement is considered at 15.14.2.

15.5.4 **Part 8 claims**

Rather than commencing proceedings under CPR Part 7, a claimant may be entitled (or may be required) to commence proceedings under CPR Part 8. A claimant may follow the CPR Part 8 procedure, for example, where he seeks a decision on a question which is unlikely to involve a substantial dispute of fact, or where he seeks to recover costs in the context of a claim that was settled before proceedings commenced.

Where a claim is commenced under CPR Part 8, the claim form will contain less information. The main information required by the Part 8 procedure is the question which the claimant wants the court to decide, or the remedy which the claimant seeks and the legal basis for claiming it.

15.6 **Responding to particulars of claim, acknowledgement of service, admissions, and default judgments**

Once particulars of claim are served on a defendant under CPR Part 7, the defendant may, in accordance with CPR Part 9, respond by:

- filing or serving an admission (under CPR Part 14);
- filing a defence (under CPR Part 15);
- doing both of these things if he only admits part of the claim; or
- filing an acknowledgement of service (under CPR Part 10).

15.6.1 **Filing a defence or a reply**

file
Where a party is required to file a document this means that the party is required to deliver the document to the court.

Where a defendant wishes to defend all or part of the claim, he should *file* a defence. CPR Part 16 provides that, amongst other matters, the defence must state which of the allegations in the particulars of claim the defendant denies, which of the allegations are admitted and which allegations the defendant is unable to admit or deny but requires the claimant to prove. In relation to an allegation that is denied, it is not sufficient to simply deny the allegation being made; the defendant must set out the reasons why it is denied and set out his own version of events. Under CPR Part 15, the general rule is that a defence should be filed within fourteen days of service of particulars of claim.

When a defence is filed, copies are served on all other parties to the proceedings. The claimant may then file a reply to the defence, although this is not compulsory. The claimant may file a reply if, for example, he wishes to allege further facts in response to the defence. Sometimes a defendant may make a counterclaim under CPR Part 20. A counterclaim means that the defendant makes his own claim against the claimant.

Example

Assume that a road traffic accident took place between Clare and Dave. Both Clare's car and Dave's car were damaged. Clare brings civil proceedings against Dave. Clare alleges in the claim form, and particulars of claim, that the accident was caused by Dave's negligence. She seeks damages to compensate her for the cost of repairs to her vehicle. In response, Dave files a defence denying liability for the accident and putting forward his version of the accident circumstances. His defence includes a counterclaim, in which he claims that the accident was caused by Clare's negligence and in which *he* seeks damages from *Clare*.

Where a defendant makes a counterclaim under CPR Part 20, the claimant should file a defence to it, just as a defendant must file a defence if he wishes to defend a claim.

15.6.2 Filing an acknowledgement of service

Where a defendant needs to have more time to file a defence, he may file an acknowledgement of service within 14 days of service of the particulars of claim (CPR Part 10). He then has a further 14 days in which to file his fully pleaded defence. The effect of these provisions is to give the defendant 28 days in total in which to file a defence instead of the basic 14 days. The claimant and defendant can also agree in writing to allow the defendant a further 28 days to file and serve the defence, giving the defendant a possible 56 days in total (CPR Part 15).

15.6.3 Default judgments

Where a defendant neither files a defence, nor an acknowledgement of service, within the time periods laid down by the CPR, the claimant may be able to obtain judgment against the defendant. This is known as a 'default judgment' (CPR Part 12). (Note that the defendant is not required to file a defence at all in the context of a Part 8 claim, so a *default judgment* may not be obtained in the context of a Part 8 claim.)

Equally, the defendant may be able to obtain a default judgment against the claimant in the context of a counterclaim under CPR Part 20 where the claimant fails to file a defence within the time limit.

The claimant may obtain a default judgment by simply filing a *request* if the claim is either for a sum of money, or for delivery of goods where the claim form gives the defendant the alternative of paying the value of the goods. Otherwise, the claimant must *apply* for a default judgment.

CPR Part 12 therefore provides an incentive to defendants to respond promptly when particulars of claim are served upon them. A defendant who fails to respond within the time limits prescribed by the CPR, may find that the case is decided against him by way of judgment in default. However, where the claimant obtains a default judgment, that is not necessarily the end of the matter. CPR Part 13 gives the court

default judgment
a default judgment is a judgment without trial against the party who has 'defaulted' by failing to file an acknowledgement of service or a defence as required.

CPR Part 23, which governs the making of applications for court orders, is considered at 15.11.

discretion to set aside or vary a default judgment upon application by the defendant. The court may set aside or vary a default judgment if the defendant has a real prospect of successfully defending the claim, if there is some other good reason why it should be set aside or varied, or if there is some other good reason why the defendant should be allowed to defend the claim. The matters which the court should consider in exercising this discretion include whether the defendant applied to have the judgment set aside promptly.

15.6.4 **Formal admissions**

Of course a party to civil proceedings does not have to contest the whole or part of the claim made against him. A formal admission may be made, whereby the truth of all or part of the other party's case is admitted. CPR Part 14 provides that an admission must be made in writing, such as in a statement of case or in a letter. The basic rule is that an admission should be made within 14 days following service of the claim form, or within 14 days of service of the particulars of claim. Where a party makes a formal admission, the other party may apply to the court for judgment on the admission.

The court's permission is usually required for a party to amend or withdraw a formal admission. Special rules concerning the making of formal admissions apply when the claimant only seeks the payment of money.

15.6.5 **Stay of proceedings**

What happens if the defendant has not served or filed an admission, a defence, or a counterclaim and the claimant has not entered or applied for a default judgment or summary judgment? CPR Part 15 provides that, in these circumstances, once six months have expired from the deadline for filing a defence, the claim will be stayed. This means that the proceedings are suspended unless and until the stay is lifted. Either party may apply to have the stay lifted.

CPR Part 20 applies to counterclaims made by a defendant. It also applies to other forms of additional claim, such as a claim for contribution or indemnity made by a defendant against another person.

> ### ⊜ Example
>
> A claim for contribution may be made, for example, where a defendant alleges that the negligent conduct of a third party was partly responsible for the accident to which a negligence claim relates.

Under Part 20, a defendant who wishes to make a counterclaim against the claimant must file particulars of the counterclaim. If the defendant wishes to counterclaim against a party other than the claimant, he must apply to the court for permission to have the other person added to the counterclaim as an additional party.

Similarly, a defendant who wishes to claim a contribution, or indemnity, against an existing party must file a notice stating the nature and grounds of his additional claim and serve it on the relevant party. Where the defendant wishes to make an additional claim against a person who is not already a party, the additional claim will be made when the court issues the additional claim form. The defendant does not require the court's permission to make such an additional claim if it is issued at the time the defence is filed, or within 28 days of filing the defence. Where an additional claim is served on a person who was not already a party, the effect is that the person becomes a party to the proceedings. The purpose of CPR Part 20 is to enable counterclaims and additional claims to be managed in the most convenient and effective way. If practicable, the court will ensure that the original and additional claims are managed together.

15.7 **Allocation and case management tracks**

Civil proceedings are allocated to one of three case management tracks, namely the small claims track, the fast track, or the multi-track. Subject to exceptions, Part 26 provides that:

- the small claims track is the track where the financial value of the claim does not exceed £10,000 (the limit was raised from £5,000 in April 2013) and where the financial value of a claim for damages for personal injuries does not exceed £1,000;

- the fast track is the normal track where the financial value of the claim exceeds £10,000 but does not exceed £25,000, provided both that the trial is not likely to last for more than one day and that oral expert evidence will be limited to two expert fields and to one expert per party in each expert field; and

- the multi-track is the normal track for all other claims (Part 8 claims being automatically allocated to the multi-track).

The financial boundaries of the fast track have not been changed, even though the ceiling for the small claims track has been increased. It is probable that further changes will be made to the boundaries by the end of 2015.

Some claims (e.g. rent possession and mortgage possession) are not allocated to any track, but the court may allocate them if they become defended. Otherwise, they will simply be given a date for a short hearing.

When a defence is filed by the defendant, a court officer will provisionally decide which track the claim should be allocated to and then notify the parties of this, along with some preliminary directions (CPR Part 26). The aim is to streamline the allocation process and ensure that, if possible, the administrative tasks required are centralised and many steps, such as initial allocation and taking steps when parties do not return

Alternative dispute resolution is considered in chapter 17.

documents, are carried out by court staff rather than judges. The parties are required to complete a directions questionnaire (formerly called an allocation questionnaire) and file it by a specified date. The directions questionnaire asks the parties questions about a variety of matters, such as:

- Whether the solicitor has explained to the client the importance of trying to settle the claim without court proceedings and the costs consequences of failing to do so;
- whether the parties would like a stay (i.e. a suspension of proceedings) for one month to attempt to settle the claim by informal discussion or alternative dispute resolution;
- whether there has been compliance with the applicable pre-action protocol;
- what witnesses of fact they intend to call;
- whether they consider a single joint expert to be suitable;
- the names of any experts/single joint experts they wish to rely upon;
- whether they want their experts to give oral evidence;
- which track they consider to be most suitable for their claim;
- how long they estimate the trial will take;
- what case management directions they regard as appropriate; and
- what they estimate their costs are likely to be.

The purpose of directions questionnaires is to assist the court in exercising its case management powers.

Thinking point

The directions questionnaire specifically invites the parties to consider whether proceedings should be suspended to enable them to take part in alternative dispute resolution. The court also provides a free mediation service in small claims track cases. Should alternative dispute resolution, such as mediation, be a compulsory prerequisite to bringing a claim before the civil courts?

Usually the court will allocate the claim to a track when every defendant has filed a directions questionnaire or upon the expiry of the period for filing the questionnaires. The court may order a party to provide further information and/or may decide that it is necessary to hold an allocation hearing to determine the appropriate track in the presence of the parties.

The court does not have to allocate a case to the track to which it appears to belong by virtue of the monetary value of the claim. When deciding whether to allocate a claim to its normal track, CPR Part 26 requires the court to consider:

- the financial value of the claim;

- the nature of the remedy sought by the claimant;
- the complexity of the case;
- the number of parties;
- the value and complexity of any Part 20 claim;
- the number of witnesses required to give oral evidence that may be required;
- the importance of the claim to anyone who is not a party; and
- the views of the parties and their circumstances.

Where a claim has no financial value, the court will allocate it to the track which it considers most suitable, taking into account the remainder of the matters referred to earlier.

15.7.1 The small claims track

Where a claim is allocated to the small claims track, simplified procedures apply. Consequently, various parts of the CPR do not apply. CPR Part 27 provides that where a claim is allocated to the small claims track:

- hearings will be informal;
- the strict rules of evidence will not apply;
- evidence need not be given under oath;
- the court may limit cross-examination; and
- expert evidence, written or oral, may only be given at a hearing with the court's permission.

When a case is allocated to the small claims track, the court will generally fix a date for the trial and give standard directions (CPR Part 27). These include requiring the parties to file and serve copies of all documents on which they intend to rely at least fourteen days prior to trial. The parties will be given at least 21 days' notice of the trial date, unless they agree to accept less, and will be informed of the length of time allowed for the trial.

In appropriate circumstances, the court may find it necessary to give special directions as well as, or instead of, standard directions (CPR Part 27). An example of a non-standard direction would be a direction that expert evidence is required in relation to a specific issue and that such evidence should be given by a single joint expert.

Where a case is allocated to the small claims track, there will usually be no pre-trial hearings. The first time the parties or their representatives appear before the court will therefore be on the day of trial. However, the court may hold a preliminary hearing before the trial if necessary. A preliminary hearing may be held, for example, to give special directions to the parties; to enable the court to dispose with the claim on the basis that a party has no real prospect of success at trial; or to enable the court to strike out a statement of case on the basis that it discloses no reasonable grounds for bringing or defending the claim.

The expectation is that the parties will attend trial in person. However, under CPR Part 27, where a party gives the court and the other parties at least seven days' written notice that he will *not* attend the trial and requests the court to decide the claim in his absence, the court will do so, taking into account both the party's statement of case and any documents that the party has filed and served, such as witness statements. If a claimant fails to attend the trial without giving such written notice the court may strike out the claim. If a defendant fails to attend the trial without giving written notice, the court may decide the claim solely on the basis of the claimant's evidence. If neither party attends the trial and both parties fail to give written notice, the court may strike out both the claim and any defence or counterclaim.

Finally, it should be noted that CPR Part 27 imposes limits upon the costs that a party may recover where a claim is allocated to the small claims track. The basic position (under CPR Part 27 and CPR 27 PD) is that unless the party who is ordered to pay costs has acted unreasonably, the costs that may be recoverable from him essentially comprise:

- fixed costs in respect of issuing the claim;
- costs for legal advice and assistance (not exceeding £260) if the proceedings involve a claim for an injunction or an order for specific performance;
- court fees and expenses incurred by the other party or a witness in travelling or staying away from home (limited to £90 per day per person);
- a sum for loss of earnings by the other party or a witness; and
- a sum not exceeding £750 in respect of an expert's report.

15.7.2 **The fast track**

Upon allocating a case to the fast track, the court will give case management directions and will set a timetable for the steps that are to be taken prior to the trial (CPR Part 28). The parties will be required to file a directions questionnaire; the questionnaire is in the same format for fast track and multi-track cases. The proposed directions should be agreed between the parties if possible. In fast track cases the directions should follow those set out in CPR 28.

When the case is allocated, the court will either fix the trial date or fix a period of up to three weeks within which the trial will take place. There will usually be a period of no more than thirty weeks between the giving of directions and the trial. Case management directions given at this time will relate to matters such as disclosure of documents (see 15.8), service of witness statements (see 15.14.2) and expert evidence (see 15.14.4). A typical timetable for preparing a fast track case, running from the date of the notice of allocation, would be:

- disclosure – four weeks after allocation;
- witness statements exchanged – ten weeks;
- experts' reports exchanged – 14 weeks;
- pre-trial checklists sent by the court – 20 weeks;
- completed pre-trial checklists filed – 22 weeks; and
- the trial itself – 30 weeks (CPR 28 PD).

A pre-trial checklist (listing questionnaire) deals with matters such as confirming that the party has complied with directions; how many witnesses the party intends to call; questions relating to expert evidence; and whether the estimate of the time needed for the trial has changed.

Following the date for filing pre-trial checklists, the court will confirm the trial date, give any directions for the trial which it considers appropriate (including a trial time-table), and specify any further steps that must be taken before the trial.

The expectation is that directions at both allocation and listing stages will be given without a hearing (CPR 28 PD). Thus, as in small claims cases, the first time that the parties or their representatives appear before the court will usually be at trial. However, the court does have the power to hold pre-trial hearings in fast track cases if necessary. A hearing may be necessary, for example, to discuss any non-standard directions that may be required to ensure proper preparation of the case, or where a party has failed to comply with directions that have already been given.

Fast track costs will normally be assessed summarily by the judge at the end of the trial. Under CPR Part 45.38, the fast track *trial costs* which the court may award are as follows:

- £485 where the value of the claim does not exceed £3,000;
- £690 where the value of the claim is more than £3,000 but does not exceed £10,000;
- £1,035 where the value of the claim is more than £10,000 but does not exceed £15,000; and
- £1,650 where the value of the claim exceeds £15,000.

CPR part 45 also sets out what fixed costs can be awarded in a variety of other claims such as road traffic accidents and low value personal injury claims.

> ### 🔑 Key point
>
> Trial costs are, essentially, the advocate's fee. All other reasonable costs are also recoverable. In his report on the costs of civil litigation, Jackson LJ proposed that all costs on the fast track should be fixed for certain types of case, including personal injury cases. In other types of fast track case, he suggested that costs should be limited. The report argued that this would promote certainty and ensure that costs are always proportionate. Fixed costs have been introduced in personal injuries cases.

15.7.3 **The multi-track**

Upon allocating a case to the multi-track, the court will either give case management directions and set a timetable for the steps to be taken prior to the trial, or will arrange a case management conference or a pre-trial review (CPR Part 29). It will also deal with costs management, or budgeting, as required from April 2013 in CPR 3. Budgeting will apply to all multi-track cases, except Chancery, Commercial Court, Technology/Construction Court, and Admiralty cases, issued on or after 1 April 2013. The parties will have to submit a budget for the projected costs of the continued conduct of the case for the court's approval. For an interesting discussion and over-view of the budgeting provisions, see the article by HHJ Simon Brown 'Teaching Old Dogs New Tricks' in the *New Law Journal* 28 March 2013, and part two published on 12 April 2013.

As soon as is practicable the court will fix the trial date or the trial period. When the court does so, the parties will be notified and a date will be specified for filing a pre-trial checklist. If the parties agree case management proposals and the court considers that they are suitable, the court may approve the proposals without holding a case management hearing and may give appropriate directions. If a party wishes to vary the trial date, the trial period, or the date fixed by the court for a case management conference, a pre-trial review, or the return of a pre-trial checklist, the permission of the court will be required. Other directions may be varied by agreement between the parties, provided that the trial date is not moved.

The matters considered at a case management hearing might include the disclosure of documents and what expert evidence is required (CPR 29 PD). The *Queen's Bench Guide* (at 7.6) and the *Chancery Guide* (at 3.22) indicate that at a pre-trial review, the court will review the state of preparation of the respective parties, will deal with outstanding matters, and will give any necessary directions (such as directions concerning the order in which witnesses will be called). The *Guides* may be seen on the CPR website at: **www.justice.gov.uk/courts/procedure-rules/civil/court_guides**. In multi-track cases, the parties will be required to complete pre-trial checklists within time limits specified by the court. These checklists deal with matters such as whether trial bundles have been completed, which witnesses of fact and expert witnesses are to be called, as well as asking the parties to provide estimates of the minimum and maximum length of the trial.

After the parties have filed completed pre-trial checklists, or after the court has held a listing hearing or a pre-trial review, the court will set a trial timetable. In accordance with CPR Part 39, the court should consult with the parties when setting a trial timetable.

If the successful party has completed the case within the stated budget, it is likely that the trial judge will simply allow the costs without further process. If the party has overstepped the budget then it is likely that costs will subsequently be assessed by a costs judge via a detailed assessment of costs under CPR Part 47. New rules on costs apply to cases issued after April 2013, and for work carried out after April 2013.

15.8 **The disclosure and inspection of documents**

One of the main aims of the Woolf reforms was to improve openness and cooperation between parties. Part of this means ensuring that all parties to civil proceedings have access to relevant documents, some of which may be in the hands of an opponent. However, the requirement to disclose documents had been a long-standing feature of the civil justice system in England and Wales. Arguably, the Woolf reforms refined this requirement rather than extending it.

CPR Part 31 concerns the disclosure and inspection of **documents** and applies to claims that are allocated either to the fast track or to the multi-track.

Previously, where the court ordered disclosure under CPR Part 31 this meant standard disclosure. Standard disclosure required a party to disclose:

- the documents upon which he relies;

- any documents which adversely affect his case;

- any documents which adversely affect the case of another party; and

- any documents which support the case of another party.

A party was under a *duty* to make a reasonable search for documents of the latter three types. However under the Jackson reformed rules standard disclosure no longer applies in multi-track cases, except in personal injury cases. The idea is to prevent pointless lists of copious documents being disclosed and to make sure that the parties concentrate on the issues in the case that are disputed. A list of options will be considered by the court to ensure that relevant documents only need to be disclosed, dealing with the substantial issues in dispute.

Disclosure of a document means stating that the document either exists or has existed. A party gives disclosure by serving a list on the other parties which identifies the relevant documents. In most cases, CPR Part 31 also provides that the other party then has the right to inspect the document or to have a copy of it.

A party may claim that it is his right to withhold inspection of a document, for example, as a result of legal professional privilege. Legal professional privilege applies to confidential communications between a party and his legal representatives, which were made for the purpose of giving or obtaining legal advice. It also extends to confidential communications with third parties, which were made in connection with actual litigation or in contemplation of litigation. A party does not have to allow inspection of privileged documents.

Where a party believes that the documents disclosed by another party do not fulfil the party's duty to give the appropriate disclosure, he may apply to the court for an order for specific disclosure, requiring the other party to disclose specified documents, to carry out a search, and to disclose any documents located in consequence of the search. The duty to give the appropriate agreed disclosure continues throughout the proceedings and, consequently, where documents to which the duty applies

documents
under CPR Part 31, documents does not refer only to paper hard-copy documents but also anything in which information is recorded; including, for example, information stored on a computer.

come to a party's attention following service of the list of documents, the other parties must be notified of this.

> ## Thinking point
> Why do you think a party does not have to disclose documents containing communications with his solicitor for the purpose of seeking advice about his case? Is it in the public interest for clients to be able to speak freely to their lawyers?

15.8.1 **Without prejudice communications**

Negotiations with a view to settlement in the context of civil proceedings may be subject to the 'without prejudice privilege'. The without prejudice privilege arises where the purpose of the negotiations is to resolve a dispute between the parties. Where it applies, the content of the negotiations is not admissible in evidence unless both parties agree to waive the privilege. Thus, where there are negotiations on a without prejudice basis aimed at settling a dispute but no settlement is reached, the trial judge cannot be told of any admissions or concessions that were made by any party during the course of the negotiations. The reason for this rule is to encourage the parties to enter into correspondence with a view to settling their dispute without fear that anything that is said could later be used against them.

The privilege may arise whether or not correspondence is headed 'without prejudice', although it is good practice to use this heading when parties intend to negotiate on a without prejudice basis (*Rush and Tompkins v Greater London Council* [1988] 3 WLR 939). Conversely, the privilege will not arise where a party makes clear that negotiations are taking place on an 'open' basis (*Dixon's Stores Group Ltd v Thames Television plc* [1993] 1 All ER 349). There are also a number of exceptions to the privilege. For example, where a negotiating party makes an offer which is expressed to be without prejudice except as to costs, the privilege does not prevent the judge from considering the content of the negotiations in relation to the issue of costs (*Cutts v Head* [1984] Ch 290).

15.9 **Part 36 offers**

Either the claimant or the defendant may make an offer to settle the claim under CPR Part 36. Such an offer is referred to as a 'Part 36 offer'. If the offer is accepted, the defendant must pay the agreed sum to the claimant within 14 days. In order to encourage parties to settle disputes, CPR Part 36 provides that there may be costs consequences where either party unreasonably refuses to accept an offer. In cases to which the Pre-Action Protocol for Low Value Personal Injury Claims in Road Traffic

Accidents applies, offers to settle are referred to as 'RTA Protocol offers'. The rules are similar to those that apply to Part 36 offers, although the costs consequences differ as such cases are normally subject to fixed costs.

A Part 36 offer must comply with the strict requirements laid down by CPR Part 36. For example, it must be made in writing, must state that it is intended to have the consequences set out in Part 36, and must specify a period of at least 21 days within which the other party may accept the offer. Failure to comply exactly with the requirements will result in the defective Part 36 offer having no Part 36 effect.

If the defendant makes a Part 36 offer which is not accepted by the claimant, the case will proceed to trial in the usual way. If after trial the claimant fails to obtain a judgment that is more advantageous than the Part 36 offer, the general rule is that the defendant is entitled to costs and interest upon those costs, from the date when the **relevant period** expired. CPR Part 36.14 introduces amendments to the rules for offers made after 1 April 2013 to specify an additional amount to be paid by defendants who do not accept claimant's Part 36 offers and then fail to beat that offer at trial. The uplift can be substantial. For awards up to half a million pounds, an extra 10 per cent is added and for sums between £500, 000 and one million pounds an extra 5 per cent is added, up to a limit of £75,000. Clearly this provision is designed to ensure that defendants consider claimants' offers very carefully and that claimants pitch their offers at an appropriate level.

relevant period
the relevant period is the period of at least 21 days, specified in the Part 36 offer, within which the offer may be accepted.

Example

Carrie claims damages for breach of contract. Daniel denies that there has been a breach of contract but is nevertheless prepared to settle the case to avoid the time and expense of going to court. He makes a Part 36 offer in the sum of £3,000. Carrie does not accept this offer and the case proceeds to trial. At trial, the judge finds that there has been a breach of contract and awards Carrie damages in the sum of £2,500.

The general rule is that the successful party is entitled to his costs (see 15.15). However, although Carrie has succeeded in proving her claim for breach of contract, the outcome is less advantageous for her than it would have been if she had accepted the Part 36 offer. This means that she must pay Daniel's costs from the date that his offer expired.

The claimant may also make a Part 36 offer. If this is not accepted by the defendant and the judgment after trial is equal to, or less than, the sum specified in the claimant's offer, the general rule is that the claimant is entitled to interest on the whole or part of the money awarded for some or all of the period following expiry of the relevant period. The claimant will also be entitled to costs on an **indemnity basis** (and interest on those costs) from the date on which the relevant period expired.

indemnity basis: Where costs are assessed on a standard basis, the court will only allow costs that have been reasonably incurred, are reasonable in amount, and are proportionate to the matters in issue. Where costs are assessed on an indemnity basis, the court will still only allow costs that are reasonably incurred but will give the benefit of the doubt to the receiving party if any items are in dispute. Furthermore, the proportionality test does not apply.

CPR Part 36 provides that a Part 36 offer is made without prejudice except as to costs. Thus, subject to exceptions, e.g. where the proceedings have been stayed following acceptance of the offer, the fact that the offer has been made should not be communicated to the trial judge until the case has been decided.

The Part 36 procedures are designed to provide a strong incentive to parties to settle their disputes. However, Lord Justice Jackson was of the view that Part 36 does not go far enough. In order to provide an even greater incentive to defendants to settle cases, his report recommended that where a defendant fails to beat a claimant's Part 36 offer, the amount that the claimant recovers should be enhanced by 10 per cent. This measure was implemented in CPR Part 36.14 (see earlier discussion). In many cases this will have a significant impact and concentrate the minds of the lawyers during the conduct of the case. Opponents of this measure argue that it places defendants under too much pressure to settle cases even though their defence may have merit. It is another indication of the intention of the courts to control and limit litigation to the most contentious matters.

15.10 **Qualified One Way Costs Shifting**

Under CPR 44.13 to CPR 44.17, for personal injury cases, Qualified One Way Costs Shifting (QOCS) has been introduced by the April 2013 amendments. The rule is that the claimant will not be required to pay the defendant's costs if the claim fails, but if the claim succeeds the defendant must pay the claimant's costs in the usual way.

The aim of this is to avoid the need for the claimant to take out after-the-event insurance. The Legal Aid, Sentencing and Punishment of Offenders Act 2012, which came in to force in relation to insurance policies taken out after 31 March 2013, made the premiums non-recoverable from the defendant. The disadvantage to defendant insurers of not recovering costs in cases that they win is outweighed by not having to pay after-the-event insurance premiums when they lose.

The aim of the reform is to ensure that claimants in personal injury cases can proceed in the knowledge that they will not be liable for defendants' costs and therefore it is no longer necessary to take out after-the-event insurance.

However, QOCS does not sit comfortably alongside Part 36. A claimant who is successful at trial but fails to beat a defendant's Part 36 offer will be ordered to pay all of the defendant's costs from the date of expiry of the time for accepting the offer, although the order is only enforceable, without leave of the court, up to the level of damages awarded by the court. Thus the claimant may actually receive no payment of damages because the awarded sum has to be used to pay the defendant's costs. It remains to be seen how QOCS will affect the litigation process, but it is likely to ensure that claimants and defendants will have to be extra careful to consider all aspects and consequences of Part 36 offers.

15.11 Applying for court orders

CPR Part 23 deals with applying for court orders. The CPR and the directions and timetables imposed by the court are designed to cover most eventualities that arise in the course of proceedings. However, any party to the proceedings has the option of applying to the court for a specific order should it become necessary. In other words, if a party wants something, and agreement cannot be reached with the opponent, an application can be made to ask the court to make an order.

For example, where a party has failed to comply with a standard rule or direction, his opponent may apply under CPR Part 23 for an order that unless the respondent complies with the relevant rule or order, his claim will be struck out or judgment will be entered against him. This is known as an 'unless order' (see 15.4). The CPR Part 23 procedures must also be used to make an application for default judgment or summary judgment. Application may also be made for an extension of time to take a step in the proceedings, to ask for permission to instruct an expert, or to instruct an alternative expert. Under the new tough court regime, an application for the latter may well be refused.

Default judgment was considered at 15.6.3. Summary judgment will be considered at 15.12.

A party may also apply for an order for an interim remedy. The court may grant a variety of interim remedies, such as:

- *interim injunctions*;
- *freezing injunctions*; and
- *search orders*.

interim injunctions: An injunction is an order that a person does something or refrains from doing something. An example would be an injunction restraining a party from causing a nuisance. An interim injunction, as the name suggests, is a temporary injunction which takes effect pending the final decision in a case.

freezing injunctions: Sometimes a party may fear that his opponent will dispose of assets prior to the final decision in a case and thereby evade justice. In such a case the concerned party may apply to the court for a freezing injunction to prevent his opponent from removing his assets from the jurisdiction or from dealing with assets either within or outside the jurisdiction. Freezing injunctions were formerly known as Mareva injunctions after the case Mareva Compania Naviera SA v International Bulkcarriers SA [1975] 2 Lloyd's Rep 509.

search orders: A party may also apply for a search order which allows him to enter premises for the purposes of preserving evidence. Search orders were formerly known as Anton Piller orders.

A party seeking any of these types of interim remedy must abide by the rules in both CPR Part 23 and Part 25.

CPR Part 23 provides that, whatever the nature of the court order that is applied for, an application notice must be served by the party seeking the order (the applicant) on the person against whom the order is sought (the respondent). Service should take place as soon as possible after the application notice is filed and, unless the CPR or a practice direction or court order provide otherwise, must take place at least three days before the court deals with the application. Thus, the opposing party will usually be aware of the application at least three days before it is heard. An application notice must state both the order that the applicant seeks and why the order is sought. When served, it should be accompanied by a copy of any supporting witness statement(s).

In limited circumstances an application may be made without notice being given to the other party. Applications without notice were formerly known as *'ex parte'* applications.

Thinking point

Consider the reasons why a party might apply for a search order or a freezing order. Why might it be desirable to make such an application on a without notice basis? If the opposing party was aware in advance that a certain order might be made, could he frustrate the purpose of the order, for example by disposing of evidence that might be found if a search order was executed?

The court may also make an order on its own initiative without an application. In such circumstances, any party affected by the order may apply for it to be varied or set aside.

An application for an order may be dealt with without a hearing if the parties agree the terms of the order, if the parties agree that there should not be a hearing, or if the court does not consider that a hearing would be appropriate. Moreover, where a party fails to attend the hearing of an application, the court may proceed in the absence of that party. Often hearings for interim orders will be dealt with by telephone conference call which saves the costs of the parties attending court in person.

15.12 **Summary judgment**

Under CPR Part 24, the court may be able to dispose of a claim or an issue without holding a trial by entering judgment on a claim or dismissing the claim. This is known as summary judgment. The court may grant summary judgment against a claimant or a defendant where the claim or defence has no real prospect of success, provided that there is no other compelling reason for holding a trial.

As was seen at 15.4 the court may strike out a statement of case which discloses no reasonable grounds for bringing or defending a claim (CPR Part 3).

There is no precise dividing line between the scope of the court's powers under Parts 3 and 24, although examples of cases in which an application to strike out would be more appropriate are set out in CPR 3A PD. These include cases where the particulars of claim fail to set out the facts of the claim, fail to show a legal basis for a claim, or where the particulars of claim make no sense.

15.13 Civil trial

Under CPR Part 39, the court is entitled to conduct a trial in the absence of a party. Alternatively, if neither party attends, the court may strike out the proceedings. If the claimant does not attend, the court may strike out both the claim and the claimant's defence to any counterclaim; and, if the defendant does not attend, the court may strike out the defence and/or any counterclaim. Where the court gives judgment or makes an order against a party who failed to attend the trial, the party may make an application to the court to have the judgment or court order set aside. The application must be supported by evidence. The court may only grant such an application if the party made the application promptly, had a good reason for failing to attend and had a reasonable prospect of succeeding at the trial.

Under CPR Part 39, the general rule is that civil trials and other hearings (e.g. applications for interim remedies) will be held in public. There are exceptions where, for example, the hearing involves confidential information. The court also possesses a general discretion to hold a hearing in private in the interests of justice.

Thinking point

Why do you think that court hearings are held in public? Is it important that justice is not just done but seen to be done? It would assist your understanding of the court process if you could find time to attend your local court to see justice in action. Tou do not have to make an appointment, just turn up and go in. You can find your local court at: **http:// hmctscourtfinder.justice.gov.uk/hmcts/**.

A civil trial which is allocated to the fast track or the multi-track will usually start with an opening speech on behalf of the claimant, although where the judge has read the papers he may decide to dispense with an opening speech (CPR 28 PD and 29 PD).

The claimant's witnesses will give evidence first. The rules provide that a witness' statement will usually stand as the witness's evidence in chief, in other words the witness will not be required to repeat the contents of his statement but will be cross examined on it. However, a witness may be permitted to amplify the witness statement or to give evidence in chief about matters that have arisen since the witness statement was served (CPR Part 32). He may be cross-examined on behalf of the defendant and may then be re-examined on behalf of the claimant. The same procedure is then followed in relation to any defence witnesses.

The trial will conclude with closing speeches, first on behalf of the defendant and then on behalf of the claimant. Finally, judgment will be given by the judge who has been hearing the trial. In the context of a fast track trial, judgment will often be followed immediately by the summary assessment of costs by the trial judge. Where the trial is long or complex, however, the judge may decide to reserve judgment (i.e. to give it at a later date). Under CPR Part 40, a judgment takes effect either on the day it is given or on a later date specified by the court. A party is usually required to comply with a judgment or order for the payment of money within 14 days.

In general, civil trials take place without a jury, but an application for jury trial may be made within 28 days of the defence being served in the context of claims of fraud, libel, slander, malicious prosecution, and false imprisonment (Senior Courts Act 1981 s.69; County Courts Act 1984 s.66; CPR Part 28). Where trial by jury takes place in a county court, the jury consists of only eight jurors, rather than the usual 12 (County Courts Act 1984 s.67).

15.13.1 **Burden and standard of proof in civil proceedings**

In civil proceedings, a party who raises a fact in issue bears the legal burden of proving it (*Wakelin v London and South Western Railway* [1886] 12 AC 41). Thus, for example, in the context of a civil claim for battery, the claimant bears the burden of proving the elements of battery. If the defendant merely asserts in his defence that the battery did not take place, the defendant does not bear the legal burden of proving this defence, as it merely amounts to a denial of the claimant's assertion. If, however, the defendant raises new facts in issue, such as alleging that he acted in self-defence, the defendant bears the burden of proving the defence (*Ashley v Chief Constable of Sussex Police* [2007] 1 WLR 398).

The standard of proof in civil proceedings is proof on the balance of probabilities. This means that a party discharges the legal burden of proof if he persuades the court that the facts that he asserts are more probably true than not (*Miller v Minister of Pensions* [1947] 2 All ER 372).

This does not necessarily mean that the court must decide in favour of one party and against the other as it may be that neither party's version of events is credible. In *Rhesa Shipping v Edmunds* [1985] 1 WLR 948, a ship sank in the Mediterranean. The cause of its sinking was unknown. Its owner was insured against 'the perils of the sea', but the insurance did not cover loss due to wear and tear. The insurers refused to pay the insurance claim and the owner issued proceedings in the civil courts against the insurers. At trial, the owner put forward the theory that the ship had struck a submerged submarine (a peril of the sea). The insurers suggested that prolonged wear and tear caused the hull of the ship to open up.

The trial judge found that the claimant's and the defendant's versions of events were both improbable. However, he preferred the claimant's evidence, so gave judgment for the claimant. On appeal the House of Lords held that the judge did not have to decide between the two explanations. The burden of proving that the loss was caused by a peril of the sea was on the claimant. If the trial judge, having heard all of the evidence, was not satisfied that the claimant's version of events was more probably true than not, then the claim should have been dismissed.

Some criminal offences are also capable of being tried as civil wrongs. For example, a battery is both a criminal offence and a tort. (See also the example given at 15.1.) Where a *serious* allegation of a criminal nature, such as fraud or rape, is alleged in the context of civil proceedings, questions have arisen as to what the standard of proof should be. The courts have held that, in a civil case, the standard of proof remains proof on the balance of probabilities. It has been suggested that, given the rarity of such conduct compared to that of an ordinary civil wrong, it would take strong evidence to persuade the court that the facts alleged were more probably true than not (*Re H and Others (Minors) (Sexual Abuse: Standard of Proof)* [1996] 2 WLR 8). However, in *Re B (Children)* [2008] UKHL 35, the House of Lords again emphasised that the standard of proof remains proof on the balance of probabilities.

Finally, it should be noted that in certain exceptional circumstances, the criminal standard of proof (i.e. proof beyond reasonable doubt) is applicable in civil proceedings. The best known example of this is provided by proceedings for civil **contempt of court**.

In *Re Bramblevale* [1970] Ch 128, a civil case, the appellant's company went into liquidation. The liquidator asked the appellant for copies of the company books and papers. The appellant at first admitted that he had these but later claimed that they had been destroyed in a road traffic accident. He was ordered on several occasions to produce the papers but only produced some of them. He was eventually committed to prison by a judge for contempt of court. In this case the contempt proceedings were in the context of a civil case and were determined by a civil court. However, it was held that proceedings for contempt were always criminal in nature because the liberty of the individual is at stake.

contempt of court
contempt of court means conduct which interferes with the administration of justice. Contempt may arise in the context of civil or criminal proceedings.

15.14 Evidence in civil proceedings

CPR Parts 32 to 35 contain rules concerning a variety of other aspects of civil evidence, the major examples of which are considered next.

15.14.1 Exclusionary discretion

CPR 32.1 empowers the civil court to control the evidence that it receives by giving directions as to the issues on which it requires evidence, the nature of the evidence required, and the way in which the evidence should be given. Rule 32.1 also allows a judge to exclude evidence and to limit cross-examination. This rule is therefore an important example of the court's power to manage its cases. The court should, of course, exercise this discretion so as to further the overriding objective.

15.14.2 The evidence of witnesses in civil proceedings

Under CPR Part 32, the general rule is that the evidence of witnesses will be proved at trial by their oral testimony. At a hearing other than a trial, the general rule is that evidence will be given by written statements. A party may also rely upon matters set out in a statement of case or an application notice if verified by a statement of truth. At a hearing other than a trial, a party may apply to the court for permission to cross-examine the person whose written evidence is relied upon.

> ### 🔑 Key point
>
> CPR Part 22 requires that various documents (including statements of case, witness statements, and experts' reports) be verified by a statement of truth. A statement of truth is essentially a sentence stating that the party believes the facts stated to be true. The statement of truth must be signed by the person making it. Where a *statement of case* is not verified by a statement of truth, CPR Part 22 provides that the court may strike it out and, until struck out, it may not be relied upon as evidence of the matters in it. Where a *witness statement* is not verified by a statement of truth, CPR Part 22 provides that the court may direct that it is not admissible in evidence. The wording of the statement of truth will be different when a solicitor is signing on behalf of a client, instead of the client himself.

Where a witness is called to give evidence in civil proceedings, the general position, under CPR Part 32, is that the witness' written statement will stand as his evidence in chief. He can then be cross-examined and re-examined on the witness statement. The court may, however, permit a witness to give oral evidence in chief, for example to supplement his witness statement.

Although a witness statement will often be drafted by a solicitor, it should be in the witness' own words. The court will give the parties directions concerning the service of witness statements on the other parties. Where a party fails to comply with such directions as to service, the witness may only be called to give evidence with the court's permission.

Where a party who wishes to call a witness is unable to obtain a statement from the witness, the court may permit him to serve a witness summary. This is a summary of the evidence that would be in the witness statement or a summary of the matters about which the witness is to be questioned.

The provisions concerning the service of witness statements and witness summaries are necessary to ensure openness in civil proceedings. The parties should know what evidence will be called and will not be permitted to ambush their opponent by failing to disclose the nature and detail of a witness' evidence in advance. Part 32 of the CPR, amended in 2013, allows the court to define and limit the scope and extent of the factual evidence that may be called, taking into account the overriding objective. This is another area in which the court's case management powers will be demonstrated.

15.14.3 Witness summonses and the competence and compellability of witnesses

As was seen at 13.16.2 in relation to criminal proceedings, there may sometimes be doubt as to the capacity of a witness to give evidence. A decision must then be made as to whether the witness in question is 'competent' to give evidence. Similarly, a witness may be reluctant to testify and an issue may arise as to whether he can be compelled to give evidence.

In civil proceedings, the test of competence is the common law test of whether the witness can understand the nature and significance of the oath (*R v Hayes* [1977] 1 WLR 234). Consequently, an adult witness who is unable to satisfy this test, such as a witness of very low IQ, will not be competent to testify.

Conversely, a child witness in civil proceedings (i.e. someone aged under 18) may still be competent to give unsworn evidence, even if he is incapable of understanding the nature and significance of the oath (s.96 of the Children Act 1989). A child may give unsworn evidence provided that he understands that he has a duty to speak the truth and has sufficient understanding to justify his evidence being heard.

The court may issue a witness summons to secure the attendance of a witness at court (CPR Part 34). A witness summons may require the witness to attend to give evidence or to produce documents. Thus, a reluctant witness may be compelled to attend court.

Where a witness fails to attend a High Court hearing in compliance with a witness summons, he may be liable to be punished for contempt of court for which he may be sentenced to imprisonment (CPR Sch 1 RSC Order 52). Where a witness fails to attend a county court hearing in compliance with a witness summons, the witness may be liable to a fine (s.55 County Courts Act 1984 and CPR Sch 2 CCR Order 34).

15.14.4 Expert evidence in civil proceedings

The admissibility of expert evidence in civil proceedings is governed by s.3 of the Civil Evidence Act 1972. Section 3 equates with the common law principles that relate to criminal proceedings, which are considered at 13.16.4. Expert evidence will be admissible to provide the court with information that falls outside the court's experience and knowledge, provided that the witness possesses the requisite skill that the court lacks. For example, in a personal injury case an orthopaedic surgeon may be called to give evidence about the nature and extent of a claimant's leg injury.

However, both CPR Part 35 and CPR 32.1 (which was considered at 15.15.1) confer broad case management powers upon the civil courts, enabling the judge to exclude or limit expert evidence and to determine the means by which such evidence will be given.

CPR Part 35 provides that expert evidence should be restricted to that which is reasonably required. The parties must also provide the court with an estimate of the cost of the proposed expert evidence. In line with the overriding objective of proportionality, the court will then consider whether the costs are reasonable and proportionate to the matters in issue. The general rule is that expert evidence will be given by written report and the court's permission is required if an expert is to be called to give oral evidence. The court may also set out precisely what issues the expert evidence should address: this may be limited to one narrow point. The court is also empowered to limit the amount of the expert's fees and expenses that the instructing party can recover from other parties.

Further, the court may direct that expert evidence in relation to an issue must be given by a single joint expert (i.e. an expert who is instructed by all of the parties). Where the parties cannot agree upon a single joint expert, the court may select one from a list prepared or identified by the parties or may direct some other manner of selecting the single joint expert. The Jackson reforms of 2013 extended and emphasised the judges' powers to oversee and control litigation. As well as identifying the name and speciality of an expert that a party wants to instruct, the cost of the expert must also be disclosed before permission is given to rely upon that expert.

Thinking point

The power of the courts to direct that the parties instruct a single joint expert was a major change introduced by the CPR. Critics argued that to force opposing parties to use the same witness was to usurp the adversarial process. However, there are many who regard the single joint expert as one of the successes of the CPR. There has even been support for the suggestion that court-appointed experts should be introduced. Court-appointed experts are common in civil law jurisdictions.

Under CPR Part 35, a party is entitled to put written questions either to expert witnesses instructed by other parties, or to a single joint expert, within twenty-eight days of receiving the expert's report. The expert's answers form part of the report. Where each party is permitted to instruct his own expert, the court may direct that a discussion between experts take place in order to identify and discuss the issues and, where possible, to reach an agreed opinion.

> **Thinking point**
>
> In Australia, a practice known as 'hot tubbing', or concurrent evidence, takes place between experts. Under this procedure, instead of giving evidence sequentially, experts sit in the witness box together at trial and the judge chairs a discussion between them. In this way experts help the court to reach a conclusion together, rather than being pitted against one another. As a result of Lord Justice Jackson's recommendations concurrent expert evidence may be directed under Practice Direction 35.11. Is this another way in which the civil justice system is becoming less adversarial?

CPR Part 35 makes provision concerning the contents of experts' reports and also makes it clear that the overriding duty of an expert witness is to the court and not to the party who instructed him. Thus, for example, CPR 35 PD makes clear that an expert should consider all material facts, including those which detract from his opinion.

The court will give directions concerning the disclosure of experts' reports and simultaneous disclosure will normally be required. Under CPR Part 35, where a party fails to disclose an expert's report, the expert evidence will only be admissible with the court's permission.

15.15 **Costs**

All parties to civil litigation inevitably face costs in relation to the conduct of the proceedings, such as court fees and legal expenses. CPR Part 44 gives the court discretion as to whether costs are payable by one party to another, the amount of those costs and when they are to be paid.

As was indicated at 15.8.1 and 15.5.2, the CPR limits costs to fixed costs in certain types of case, unless the court orders otherwise. In other cases, the general rule is that 'costs follow the event'. This means that the unsuccessful party pays both his own costs and the costs of the successful party. However, in deciding what order to make in relation to costs, the court should consider matters such as the conduct of the parties, whether a party whose case was not wholly successful was partially successful, and any payment into court or offer to settle (including a CPR Part 36 offer). CPR Part 44 provides that costs which have been unreasonably incurred or which are unreasonable in amount will not be allowed.

> **Thinking point**
>
> Would it be better if costs did not 'follow the event' and, as in the United States of America, each party was responsible for their own costs? One obvious advantage of this approach would be to encourage the parties to keep costs to a minimum. What might be the disadvantages of this approach? Might a person be dissuaded from seeking justice by the thought that he would have to pay his own legal expenses?

Under the reforms following the Jackson report, a defendant will be required to pay the claimant's costs if the claimant is successful, but the claimant will not be required to pay the defendant's costs if the claim is unsuccessful. This is known as 'qualified one way costs shifting' (see 15.10). There will be an exception to this general rule if the claimant has behaved unreasonably. The aim of this proposal is to obviate the need for claimants to take out 'after the event' (ATE) insurance, thereby reducing the cost of civil litigation.

15.15.1 **Costs-only proceedings**

Sometimes a dispute may be settled before proceedings are commenced but the parties, having agreed which party is to pay the costs, may fail to agree the amount of the costs to be paid. CPR Part 44 provides that either party may start 'costs-only proceedings' under CPR Part 8. The effect of this is that the court will either order costs in an amount to be determined by detailed assessment or dismiss the claim.

15.16 **Enforcement of judgments and orders**

Parties do not always comply with judgments or orders made at the conclusion of civil proceedings. It is therefore essential that mechanisms are in place to enable remedies awarded by the courts to be properly enforced.

judgment creditor/ judgment debtor
a judgment creditor is a person who has obtained a judgment or order. A judgment debtor is a person against whom a judgment was given or an order was made.

CPR Parts 70–74 provide a number of methods by which a **judgment creditor** may enforce a judgment or order against a **judgment debtor**.

CPR 70 PD indicates that a judgment or order for the payment of money (including a judgment or order for the payment of costs) may be enforced by a **writ of fieri facias**, a **warrant of execution**, a **third party debt order**, a **charging order**, or an **attachment of earnings order**.

writ of fieri facias: *A writ of fieri facias (or 'fi fa') may be obtained in the High Court to enforce a judgment for the payment of money (see CPR Sch 1 RSC Orders 45 and 46). Under a writ of fi fa, goods belonging to the person against whom the judgment was given or the order was made are seized and sold by a High Court enforcement officer in order to satisfy the judgment debt, interest, and costs.*

warrant of execution: *The county court equivalent to a writ of fi fa is a warrant of execution. A warrant of execution will be executed by a bailiff rather than by a High Court enforcement officer (see CPR Sch 2 CCR Order 26).*

third party debt order: *Sometimes a third party may owe money to a judgment debtor. For example, the judgment debtor may have an account with a bank or building society which is in credit. In such cases CPR Part 72 provides that a third party debt order may be made, requiring the third party, such as the bank or building society, to pay the judgment creditor directly.*

charging order: *CPR Part 73 and the Charging Orders Act 1979 enable a judgment creditor to obtain a charge on specified property belonging to the judgment debtor in order to secure* the payment of money due under a judgment or court order. A charge on a property means that if the property is sold, the charge usually has to be paid first before any of the proceeds of the sale can be given to the judgment debtor. The charging order itself does not compel the judgment debtor to sell the property. However, once a charging order has been made, the judgment creditor can apply for an order for sale of the property to satisfy the debt.

attachment of earnings order: A county court may make an attachment of earnings order to satisfy a judgment debt under CPR Sch 2 CCR Order 27 and the Attachment of Earnings Act 1971. This is an order requiring a judgment debtor's employer to deduct sums from the judgment debtor's earnings and pay them to the court.

Where a judgment creditor requires information in order to enforce a judgment, application may be made for an order requiring the judgment debtor to attend court to provide information concerning his means and any other matters in relation to which information is required, such as details concerning the judgment debtor's bank accounts (CPR Part 71). When the judgment debtor attends the hearing, he will be questioned by a court officer under oath, but not normally in the presence of a judge.

Summary

- The main civil courts are county courts and the High Court.
- Procedure in relation to most civil proceedings is governed by the Civil Procedure Rules 1998 (as amended).
- The civil courts must seek to give effect to the 'overriding objective' of the CPR.
- The CPR confers extensive case management powers upon the civil courts.
- Civil claims are allocated to the small claims track, the fast track, or the multi-track.
- The civil courts possess discretion to restrict or exclude evidence in civil proceedings.
- The court possesses discretion concerning the payment of costs, but in general costs 'follow the event' and in certain types of case costs are limited to fixed costs.
- Civil judgments may be enforced by a variety of methods.

Questions

1 What is meant by 'the overriding objective'?

2 What are directions?

3 What is meant by a Part 36 offer?

4 How does the standard of proof in civil proceedings differ from that in criminal proceedings?

5 Where a civil court awards a claimant damages, how can the claimant enforce the judgment against the defendant?

✳ Sample question and outline answer

Question

In his article 'The Civil Justice System and the Legal Profession – the Challenges Ahead' (2003) 22(Jul.) CJQ 235, Mr Justice Lightman stated:

> …on the whole the defects inherent in the adversary system have been aggravated rather than remedied by recent developments. The inflated expectations and returns of members of the legal profession and the parasitic costs of our case law system have made access to civil justice increasingly a luxury few can afford. The legal landscape has changed, but in my view we are today even further from our goal of a system delivering justice to all than we were 40 years ago.

Have the reforms to the civil litigation process, brought about by Lord Woolf's reforms, resulted in increased access to justice and an improved civil justice system?

Outline answer

This question requires you to have understood and thought about the Woolf reforms, and the later Jackson reforms, and the reasons for the changes to the process and procedures of civil justice.

The answer should include reference to the problems that led to the need for reform and a critical discussion of the changes made (this may be broad or focused depending upon how you interpret the question. In order to achieve a good mark you should set out in your introduction the parameters of their answer).

There should be a definition of, and consideration of, what 'adversary system' means. What problems were identified by Lord Woolf in the previous system?

What did the CPR set out to do? Make justice quicker, fairer, and more open – the overriding objective.

In what ways has it been successful? What is justice for all?

Why was it necessary for the Jackson report to be commissioned? Have the latest changes broadened access (or is it too early to tell)? Is the civil system, based on precedent, too complex? Remember, that the CPR was designed as a code for civil justice but is now, arguably, just as unwieldy as the rules that it replaced. The White Book is full of precedent and complex argument after each 'straightforward' rule.

Is the system cheaper? Make reference to no win-no fee and the contraction of civil legal aid.

If this question was set as course work you would be advised to read the article from which the quotation was taken. You must quote from your own reading and develop an argument to either agree or disagree with the proposition.

Further reading

Your reading should be directed to making sure you appreciate the changes that have been made to the civil justice system not only as a result of the Woolf reforms but also more recently following the Jackson review. Lord Justice Jackson's proposals have not yet been fully implemented and there are still changes to come. This is a fast moving area and you should keep an eye on the legal press to find out what other changes are proposed. For example, it is likely that the limit for personal injury cases in the small claims track will be increased, and perhaps the upper limit for fast track cases. The post-April 2013 changes are bedding in and practitioners are holding back on issuing proceedings to get to grips with the rule changes. The promised tougher attitude expected of judges will be shown as cases make their way through the system. Watch for Court of Appeal decisions dealing with the new rules. You should read in more depth about the debate about costs savings and dealing with cases justly and proportionately. Think about whether you consider that the CPR has had the effect of encouraging early settlement and more efficient and cheaper access to justice.

- **Blackie, K.** and **Bates, J.** *Civil Litigation in Practice: An integrated guide to the law and practice of civil litigation*, Northumbria Law Press (2013)
  This is a straightforward practical guide to the Civil Procedure Rules and how they work on a day-to-day basis. The book includes case studies and illustrated examples and is a very readable introduction to civil procedure.

- **Brooks, A.** 'Expert Meetings and Joint Reports' (2002) 2 JPI Law 180
  A general practical guide to the process of meetings between experts and how joint reports are compiled.

- **Dwyer, D.** (ed.) *The Civil Procedure Rules Ten Years On*, Oxford University Press (2009)
  This is a book resulting from a conference discussing ten years of the CPR. It is useful to gain a historical perspective and to consider some of the chapters in the light of the 2010 Jackson report. In particular the first part (the book comprises 24 chapters divided into seven sections) comprising reflections on the historical basis of, and comparative background to, the CPR is a thought provoking read.

- **Sime, S.** *A Practical Approach to Civil Procedure*, 15th edn, Oxford University Press (2012)
  This is a standard text book on civil procedure. It is comprehensive and includes access to an online updating service.

- **Sorabji, J.** 'Late Amendment and Jackson's Commitment to Woolf: Another attempt to implement a new approach to civil justice' (2012) 31(4) CJQ 393–412
  This article, written by Professor Sorabji, Barrister and Legal Secretary to the Master of the Rolls, considers the approach of the civil courts towards the late amendment of claims and

the effect of the civil justice reforms advocated by Lord Woolf in the 1990s that developed into the CPR. It looks at the likely impact of the proposals of Lord Justice Jackson's report and is a good starting point to think about the CPR changes introduced in 2013.

- **Sorabji, J.** 'Prospects for Proportionality: Jackson implementation' (2013) 32(2) CJQ 213–30
  This article considers whether the implementation of the civil procedure reforms put forward in the Jackson report is likely to achieve the aim of ensuring that litigation is conducted at no more than proportionate cost. The author discusses the causes of the costs crisis that the Jackson reforms seek to address and considers whether proportionality is an appropriate aim for the civil litigation process.

- **Zander, M.** 'The Government's Plans on Civil Justice' (1998) 3 MLR 61
  Although this article is now of historical interest, it is a helpful criticism of the Woolf reforms and discusses the expectation that the reforms will not do what they set out to do. It is a useful article to read as a starting point to consider the effect of the changes to the civil justice system.

 ## Online Resource Centre

You should now attempt the supporting multiple choice questions available at **www.oxfordtextbooks.co.uk/orc/wilson_els/**.

16 Criminal and civil appeals

◉ Learning objectives

By the end of this chapter you should:

- understand how decisions of magistrates' courts may be appealed or reviewed;

- understand the ways in which decisions of the Crown Court may be appealed or reviewed;

- be aware of the test applied by the Court of Appeal (Criminal Division) to determine an appeal against conviction;

- understand the role of the Criminal Cases Review Commission (CCRC);

- be aware of the mechanisms for appealing or reviewing decisions in civil proceedings;

- know the composition and powers of the various appellate courts; and

- appreciate the nature of the various civil and criminal appellate processes.

🅕 Talking point

In 2008, Colin Norris, a former nurse, was convicted of the murder of four elderly hospital patients and the attempted murder of a fifth. Newspapers at the time labelled Mr Norris 'the angel of death'. The first four women suffered hypoglycaemic episodes in hospital while Mr Norris was on duty and died as a result. The fifth woman also suffered a hypoglycaemic episode but died of unrelated causes. The prosecution alleged that Mr Norris had induced the hypoglycaemic states by injecting the women with insulin or a similar drug. Experts for the prosecution testified that naturally occurring hypoglycaemia in non-diabetics was very rare and it was 'outside the bounds of possibility' that five such cases could occur within a short space of time in the same hospital.

Mr Norris appealed against his convictions to the Court of Appeal (Criminal Division). The Court of Appeal will allow an appeal against conviction if they think the conviction is 'unsafe' but will dismiss such an appeal in any other case. Mr Norris's appeal was dismissed ([2009] EWCA Crim 2697).

Recent articles in the press have reported that there is now fresh scientific evidence suggesting hypoglycaemia in non-diabetics is more common than was first thought (see, for example, Duncan Campbell, 'Fresh Evidence Challenges 'Angel of Death' Nurse Colin Norris's Conviction' (The Guardian, 20 May 2013) **www.guardian.co.uk/law/2013/may/20/ fresh-evidence-angel-of-death-colin-norris** accessed 2 March 2013). This evidence has been given to the Criminal Cases Review Commission (CCRC), which has the power to refer Mr Norris's case back to the Court of Appeal. The CCRC will refer the conviction if it considers there is a 'real possibility' that the conviction would be quashed were the reference to be made.

The CCRC has referred a number of high-profile convictions to the Court of Appeal, including the cases of Sally Clark, who was convicted of murdering two of her infant sons; and Barry George, who was convicted of murdering the television presenter Jill Dando. Both of these appellants had their convictions quashed. Despite successes in cases such as these, the CCRC has been criticised for being too cautious and failing to refer a sufficient number of cases back to the appeal courts.

Introduction

A party to criminal or civil proceedings who is unsuccessful may wish to challenge the court's decision. This chapter is concerned with the various mechanisms by which the decisions of courts may be appealed or reviewed. It will also consider the nature, composition, and powers of the appellate courts and the procedures involved in bringing appeals before those courts.

As was seen in chapter 2, the appeal court system in England and Wales is hierarchical. Where a decision of a court of first instance has been challenged on appeal or by way of judicial review, a party who is dissatisfied with the outcome of the appeal or review may sometimes be able to appeal against the decision of the appellate court itself to the next court in the hierarchy.

16.1 **Criminal appeals**

As was seen in chapter 13, there are two criminal ***courts of first instance***, namely the magistrates' court and the Crown Court. The avenues of appeal from each will be considered separately.

court of first instance
a court of first instance is a court in which a case is first tried.

A number of factors need to be considered in studying the appeals process. In relation to criminal appeals, you should consider the following points as you read this section:

- the decision that is the subject of the appeal or review may be a decision of fact or a decision of law;
- not all avenues of appeal are available to both the prosecution and the defence;
- the decision that the appellant wishes to challenge may relate to a conviction, or sentence, or both; and
- some avenues of appeal or review require the appellant to obtain leave (i.e. permission) to appeal.

16.1.1 **Appeals from magistrates' courts**

The decisions of magistrates' courts can be appealed to the Crown Court (see 16.1.2) or to the High Court by way of case stated (see 16.1.3). Alternatively, application may be made to the High Court for judicial review of a decision of a magistrates' court (see 16.1.4). The most appropriate avenue of appeal for a party to criminal proceedings will depend upon whether they wish to appeal against a decision of fact or a decision of law.

16.1.2 **Appeals to the Crown Court from magistrates' courts**

Under s.108 of the Magistrates' Courts Act 1980, a defendant who pleaded *guilty* may appeal to the Crown Court against sentence. A defendant who pleaded *not guilty* and was convicted after trial, may appeal against either conviction, or sentence, or both.

Thinking point

A person who pleaded guilty may only appeal against conviction in limited circumstances, for example if his plea was equivocal (i.e. ambiguous), or if it was made under duress. Why do you think this is? If there was a general right of appeal against conviction following a guilty plea, is there a risk that there would be too many appeals for the courts to cope with? It was said in *R v Durham Quarter Sessions, ex parte Virgo* [1952] 2 QB 1 that '[i]f everybody who pleaded guilty and found that the sentence was one which he did not like could appeal…against his conviction there would be no end to it.'

A defendant must give notice of appeal to the Crown Court no more than 21 days after sentence, although the court may extend this period (Crim PR 63.2).

The Crown Court in its appellate capacity consists of a judge plus at least two lay magistrates. An appeal against conviction takes the form of a complete rehearing of the case. Any witnesses who testified at trial will need to do so again and the Crown Court will consider the evidence afresh. This is, therefore, the most appropriate avenue of appeal for a defendant who is dissatisfied with a magistrates' court's decisions of fact.

Under s.48 of the Senior Courts Act 1981, the powers of the Crown Court on appeal include the power to confirm, reverse, or vary all or part of the magistrates' decision, or to remit the matter to the magistrates' court with the Crown Court's opinion (i.e. send the case back to the magistrates' court). In relation to an appeal against conviction, the Crown Court will usually either allow the appeal and quash the conviction or dismiss the appeal and affirm the conviction of the lower court.

When considering an appeal against sentence, the Crown Court's role is to decide what is the appropriate sentence for the relevant offence. In making this decision, the Crown Court should disregard the sentence that was passed by the magistrates' court. In relation to an appeal against sentence (and also following an unsuccessful appeal against conviction), the Crown Court has the power to impose any punishment that would have been available to the magistrates' court, whether more or less severe than that imposed by the magistrates' court.

Thinking point

The power to impose a more severe sentence means that a defendant who appeals to the Crown Court risks having his sentence increased. Is this unfair to defendants? Or is it necessary for the Crown Court to have the power to impose harsher punishment on appeal in order to deter frivolous appeals?

The prosecution does not have the right to appeal to the Crown Court against either conviction or sentence. This prevents a person who has been acquitted from having to face a second hearing in another court.

16.1.3 Appeals by way of case stated from magistrates' courts to the High Court

Under s.111 of the Magistrates' Courts Act 1980, a party to proceedings before a magistrates' court who asserts that the magistrates (or district judge) made an error of law or exceeded their jurisdiction may appeal to the High Court 'by way of *case stated*'. The aggrieved party must apply to the relevant magistrates' court within 21 days after the decision appealed against, asking the magistrates to state a case for the opinion of the High Court. Where a defendant applies to the magistrates to state a case, his right to appeal to the Crown Court comes to an end.

> **case stated:** *A case stated is a document in which the court states its findings of fact, summarises any submissions made by the parties, sets out its decision, and sets out the question on which the opinion of the High Court is sought (CrimPR Part 64).*

If the magistrates consider that an application to state a case is frivolous, they may refuse to state a case. 'Frivolous' means that the application is futile, misconceived, hopeless, or academic. The applicant may then apply to the High Court for a mandatory order requiring the magistrates to state a case. If the magistrates refuse to comply with such an order, they may personally be required to pay the costs of further applications to the High Court (*R v Huntingdon Magistrates' Court, ex parte Percy, The Times*, 4 March 1994).

> 🔑 **Key point**
>
> An appeal by way of case stated may be brought by either the prosecution or the defence. This means that the prosecution is entitled to appeal decisions of law made by magistrates' courts, but not decisions of fact.

An appeal by way of case stated will be heard in the Queen's Bench Division of the High Court, by a tribunal consisting of at least two High Court judges of the Division. An appeal by way of case stated is not a rehearing and no evidence will be called. Rather, the appeal will be decided following legal argument by the parties. The High Court has the power to reverse, affirm, or amend the magistrates' decision or may remit the matter to the magistrates' court with the opinion of the High Court (s.28A Senior Courts Act 1981).

16.1.4 Applications for judicial review of decisions made by magistrates' courts

Alternatively, a party who wishes to challenge a decision made by a magistrates' court may apply to the High Court for judicial review of the decision. As with appeals by way of case stated, this avenue is available to both prosecution and defence. An application for judicial review requires the leave of the High Court (see s.31 of the Senior Courts Act 1981 and CPR 54.4).

Judicial review is a review of the way in which the court made its decision. It will be appropriate where, for example, a party asserts that there has been procedural impropriety, unfairness, or bias (*Council of Civil Service Unions v Minister for the Civil Service* [1985] AC 374). Where, however, the case stated procedure is available (for example, where the challenge is based upon an error of law or excess of jurisdiction), an appeal by way of case stated, rather than an application for judicial review, will be the appropriate route by which to challenge a decision made by a magistrates' court (see *R v Morpeth Ward Justices, ex parte Ward* [1992] 95 Cr App R 215).

16.1.5 **Bail: appeals from magistrates' courts**

Where a defendant is in custody following his conviction for an offence, a magistrates' court may grant him bail if he has given notice of appeal to the Crown Court or has applied to the magistrates to state a case (Magistrates' Courts Act 1980 s.113). The High Court may grant bail in the context of appeals by way of case stated or applications for judicial review (Criminal Justice Act 1948 s.37 and Criminal Justice Act 1967 s.22). The Crown Court may also grant the defendant bail (under s.81(1)(b) of the Senior Courts Act 1981) where the defendant is appealing to the Crown Court from a magistrates' court.

16.1.6 **Appeals from the Crown Court**

For further information about trial on indictment see 13.1.

An appeal from the Crown Court relating to trial on indictment lies to the Criminal Division of the Court of Appeal (Senior Courts Act 1981 s.53).

Under s.55 of the Senior Courts Act 1981, the Court of Appeal will normally consist of three judges when hearing an appeal against conviction (although, exceptionally, it may consist of an odd number exceeding three). When hearing an appeal against sentence, the Court of Appeal may consist of two judges but will normally consist of three. In either case, the judges in question will usually be Lords Justices of Appeal or more senior judges (such as the Lord Chief Justice). High Court judges and circuit judges may also sit in the Court of Appeal, although a court may not include more than one circuit judge.

Appeal against conviction

Following trial on indictment, a defendant may appeal against conviction to the Court of Appeal either if the Court of Appeal gives leave to appeal or if the trial judge certifies that the case is fit for appeal (s.1 Criminal Appeal Act 1968). In accordance with s.18 of the 1968 Act and CrimPR Part 68, notice of appeal, or notice of application for leave to appeal, must be given within 28 days from conviction, although the Court of Appeal may extend this time limit.

Applications for leave to appeal against conviction are made in writing and go before a single judge of the Court of Appeal, who makes a decision based on the papers. If the single judge does not grant leave to appeal, the appellant is entitled to renew his application for leave to appeal before a fully constituted court (Criminal Appeal Act 1968 s.31).

Unlike a defendant who is convicted in the magistrates' court, a defendant who is convicted following a trial on indictment does not have an automatic right of appeal against conviction. In particular, a defendant who is convicted on indictment cannot appeal simply because he disagrees with the verdict of the jury.

> ### 🔑 Key point
>
> An appellant will only be granted leave to appeal against conviction if there are arguable grounds upon which the Court of Appeal may conclude that the conviction is unsafe.

Prior to its amendment by the Criminal Appeal Act 1995, s.2(1) of the 1968 Act provided that the Court of Appeal should allow an appeal if it thought:

(a) that the conviction was unsafe or unsatisfactory; or

(b) that the judgment of the court of trial should be set aside on the ground of a wrong decision of any question of law; or

(c) that there was a material irregularity in the course of the trial.

However, even if any of these conditions was made out, s.2 provided that the Court could dismiss the appeal if satisfied that no miscarriage of justice had occurred. This was known as 'the proviso'.

In its 1993 Report, the Royal Commission on Criminal Justice (the Runciman Commission) criticised the wording of s.2, stating that it was confusing. In relation to the first condition upon which an appeal could be allowed, the Commission observed that the Court of Appeal rarely distinguished between cases that were 'unsafe' and those that were 'unsatisfactory'. The Commission queried whether the latter term was necessary. The Commission also pointed out that if either s.2(1)(b) or s.2(1)(c) was satisfied, this would mean that the conviction was unsafe or unsatisfactory. Thus, even where paragraphs (b) or (c) were applicable, the Court of Appeal tended to rely upon paragraph (a). The Commission recommended replacing the complex wording of s.2 with a simple test, namely 'whether the conviction is or may be unsafe'. The Commission added that the proviso was redundant: 'if no miscarriage of justice has occurred, the proviso is unnecessary, since the conviction need not then be regarded as unsafe'.

The Criminal Appeal Act 1995 amended s.2 of the 1968 Act so that the Court of Appeal must now allow an appeal against conviction if it thinks that the conviction is unsafe. There is, therefore, now a single test for quashing a conviction.

A conviction may be unsafe because of an error or procedural irregularity at trial, for example, where the trial judge:

- misdirected the jury;
- failed to give the jury an important direction, such as a direction concerning the relevance of a defendant's previous convictions (see 13.16.5);
- admitted inadmissible evidence; or
- excluded admissible evidence.

There has been considerable debate as to whether the Court of Appeal ought to have the power to quash a conviction in the absence of any error or procedural flaw in the court below. The issue is whether the Court of Appeal should be permitted to allow an appeal simply on the ground that it has a 'lurking doubt' about the safety of the conviction.

> ### ☰ Example
>
> In *R v Cooper* [1969] 1 QB 267, the Appellant had been convicted of assault occasioning actual bodily harm. He contended that his identity had been mistaken for that of another man, to whom he bore a striking resemblance. On appeal, no criticism was made of the trial judge and the Appellant accepted that his trial had been fair. The Court of Appeal underlined that it would be 'very reluctant indeed to intervene' in a case where all of the relevant issues were put before the jury and the jury was properly instructed by the trial judge. The court nevertheless allowed the appeal, acknowledging that
>
> > '[i]n cases of this kind the court must in the end ask itself a subjective question, whether we are content to let the matter stand as it is, or whether there is not some **lurking doubt** in our minds which makes us wonder whether an injustice has been done. This is a reaction which may not be based strictly on the evidence as such; it is a reaction which can be produced by the general feel of the case as the court experiences it' (emphasis added).

Subsequent cases revealed a lack of enthusiasm on the part of the Court of Appeal for the subjective, instinctual approach suggested in *Cooper*. Indeed, in 1993 the Runciman Commission criticised the Court of Appeal's general reluctance to consider whether juries had reached the wrong decisions. The Commission observed that most appeals that were allowed involved errors at trial, such as a mistake by the trial judge when summing up the case. In its Report, the Commission concluded: 'We are all of the opinion that the Court of Appeal should be readier to overturn jury verdicts than it has shown itself to be in the past' (p.162). Although the phrase 'lurking doubt' continued to be used, it was only in the rarest of cases that appeals were allowed on this ground alone. Recently, in *R v Pope* [2012] EWCA Crim 2241, the Court of Appeal held,

[i]t can…only be in the most exceptional circumstances that a conviction will be quashed on this ground [of lurking doubt] alone, and even more exceptional if the attention of the court is confined to a re-examination of the material before the jury.

> ### ! Critical debate
>
> Read *R v Cooper* [1969] 1 QB 267 and then read L.H. Leigh's article, 'Lurking Doubt and the Safety of Convictions' [2006] Crim LR 809. Now answer the following questions:
>
> 1. Is it appropriate for the Court of Appeal to take an instinctual approach and allow an appeal on the ground that their Lordships have a general feeling of unease, or lurking doubt, about the safety of the conviction? Does such an approach usurp the function of the jury?
>
> 2. In how many cases has the Court of Appeal's approach been purely instinctual? Can any of the 'lurking doubt' cases also be justified on the basis that there was an error or procedural irregularity in the original proceedings?
>
> 3. Read *R v Pope* (earlier). On what grounds did the Appellant's counsel argue that there was a lurking doubt about the safety of his conviction for murder?
>
> 4. What did the Court of Appeal say about the concept of lurking doubt in *Pope* (earlier)? To what extent will this judgment restrict the use of the lurking doubt ground of appeal?

In addition to the grounds already discussed, an appeal may also be based on new evidence. Under s.23 of the 1968 Act, the Court of Appeal may receive 'fresh evidence' (i.e. evidence that was not available at the original trial) where this is in the interests of justice. In deciding whether to admit fresh evidence, s.23(2) of the 1968 Act provides that the Court must take the following factors into account:

(a) whether the evidence appears to the Court to be capable of belief;

(b) whether it appears to the Court that the evidence may afford any ground for allowing the appeal;

(c) whether the evidence would have been admissible in the proceedings from which the appeal lies on an issue which is the subject of the appeal; and

(d) whether there is a reasonable explanation for the failure to adduce the evidence in those proceedings.

Again, the appeal must be allowed if the conviction is unsafe in light of the new evidence. In *R v Pendleton* [2001] UKHL 66, the House of Lords ruled that, in a case of any difficulty, 'it will usually be wise for the Court of Appeal…to test their own provisional view by asking whether the evidence, if given at the trial, might reasonably have affected the decision of the trial jury to convict'. This is sometimes referred to as the 'jury impact test'.

Where the Court of Appeal allows an appeal against conviction, thus quashing the appellant's conviction, it may order a retrial if it appears that this would be in the interests of justice (see s.7 of the 1968 Act).

In 2011, the Court of Appeal received 1,535 applications for leave to appeal against conviction. Of those cases in which leave to appeal was granted, just 196 appeals against conviction were allowed.

Appeal against sentence

Under ss.9 and 10 of the 1968 Act, the defendant may appeal against sentence to the Court of Appeal both where sentenced by the Crown Court following trial on indictment and where sentenced following committal for sentence. In accordance with s.11 of the 1968 Act, the defendant may only appeal against sentence to the Court of Appeal either if the Court of Appeal gives leave or if the sentencing judge certifies that the case is fit for appeal. Notice of appeal, or notice of application for leave to appeal, must be given within 28 days from sentence being passed. As in the case of appeals against conviction, written applications for leave to appeal are determined by a single judge of the Court of Appeal. Again, if the single judge refuses leave to appeal, the appellant may renew his application before the full court.

Section 11 of the 1968 Act empowers the Court of Appeal to quash the sentence and to pass any sentence that the Crown Court could have imposed. However, the Court of Appeal cannot increase the appellant's sentence.

Thinking point

The Crown Court in its appellate capacity has the power to increase an appellant's sentence if appropriate. Should the Court of Appeal have similar powers? Note that the Court of Appeal has the power to direct that any time served in custody by the appellant between the date of sentence and the date of appeal should not count towards his sentence (see s.29 of the 1968 Act). This means that the appellant can effectively be ordered to start serving his sentence afresh from the date of his appeal, regardless of how long he has spent in prison since originally being sentenced. It is this power that helps to deter frivolous appeals.

In 2011, the Court of Appeal received 5,623 applications for leave to appeal against sentence. Of these, 1,386 appeals were ultimately allowed.

16.1.7 Miscarriages of justice and the Criminal Cases Review Commission

There is no single agreed definition of the term 'miscarriage of justice'.

Example

Under s. 133 of the Criminal Justice Act 1988, compensation is available to a defendant whose conviction is reversed on the ground that a newly discovered fact shows beyond reasonable doubt that there has been a miscarriage of justice. In *R (Adams) v Secretary of State for Justice; In re MacDermott; In re McCartney* [2011] UKSC 18, the three Appellants challenged decisions that they were not entitled to compensation following the quashing of their convictions for murder. Lord Phillips observed that the phrase 'miscarriage of justice' is capable of having a number of different meanings but the following four categories of case 'provided a useful framework for discussion':

(1) Where...fresh evidence shows clearly that the defendant is innocent of the crime of which he has been convicted. (2) Where...fresh evidence is such that, had it been available at the time of the trial, no reasonable jury could properly have convicted the defendant. (3) Where...fresh evidence renders the conviction unsafe in that, had it been available at the time of the trial, a reasonable jury might or might not have convicted the defendant. (4) Where something has gone seriously wrong in the investigation of the offence or the conduct of the trial, resulting in the conviction of someone who should not have been convicted.

There can be no doubt that miscarriages of justice do occur, for all of the reasons identified in *R (Adams) v Secretary of State for Justice; In re MacDermott; In re McCartney* [2011] UKSC 18. High-profile miscarriage of justice cases include the 'Guildford Four' and the 'Birmingham Six'. The eventual release of the appellants in these two cases fuelled concerns about the potential for defendants to be wrongly convicted. As a result, a Royal Commission on Criminal Justice (the Runciman Commission) was established in 1991. The Commission recommended that an independent body should be set up to examine potential miscarriages of justice and to refer matters to the Court of Appeal where appropriate. Consequently, the Criminal Cases Review Commission (CCRC) was set up in 1997.

The CCRC is an independent public body. Its principal role is to review or investigate cases in which an appeal to the Court of Appeal against conviction or sentence has been unsuccessful, or where leave to appeal was refused. Under the Criminal Appeal Act 1995, the CCRC may refer a conviction or sentence of a defendant back to the Court of Appeal if there is a real possibility that the conviction or sentence would not be upheld if the reference were made (Criminal Appeal Act 1995 s.13). Thus, for example, where fresh evidence is discovered, the CCRC may cause a case to return to the Court of Appeal several years after the defendant's original appeal to the Court of Appeal was unsuccessful. Similarly, where a defendant was originally convicted and sentenced by a magistrates' court, the CCRC may refer the conviction or sentence back to the Crown Court.

Between 1 March 1997 (when the CCRC was set up) and 31 December 2012, the CCRC received a total of 15,710 applications. (This figure includes 279 cases that were transferred from the Home Office C3 department, which had responsibility for advising the Home Secretary on miscarriages of justice prior to the formation of the CCRC.) By 31 December 2012, the CCRC had referred just 512 cases to the Court of Appeal; 466 had been heard by the Court, of which 328 were 'quashed'.

It appears that a relatively high proportion of cases referred by the CCRC has resulted in successful appeals. However, investigative journalist Bob Woffinden, who has written extensively about miscarriage of justice cases, contends that the statistics create a misleading impression. For example, some of the cases referred were appeals against sentence. Any reduction in sentence, even a minor one, is counted by the CCRC as a 'quashed' case and a success. In relation to appeals against conviction, a quashed conviction may not absolve the appellant of liability altogether as sometimes the Court of Appeal substitutes a conviction for an alternative offence, such as manslaughter for murder. Woffinden also points out that a number of the CCRC's successes involve relatively minor convictions, including dishonestly obtaining a telecommunication service; allowing a dog to be dangerously out of control in a public place; failing to comply with a notice requiring proper maintainance of land under the Town and Country Planning Act; and, keeping a disorderly house. Although the CCRC was set up in response to miscarriages of justice in major cases, it has referred very few serious cases to the Court of Appeal.

In addition to criticisms that the CCRC is overly cautious and refers too few cases to the Court of Appeal, its limited resources mean that it can take many months, or even years, for it to evaluate cases and make a decision about referral. For example, solicitors for Colin Norris, who is currently serving life imprisonment for the murder of four elderly women and the attempted murder of a fifth woman, state that they lodged an application to the CCRC on 20 October 2011 on the basis that fresh scientific evidence cast doubt on the safety of Mr Norris's conviction. To date, the CCRC has not made a decision as to whether to refer the case back to the Court of Appeal.

Thinking point

The CCRC will only refer a case to the Court of Appeal if it thinks there is a 'real possibility' that the appeal will be allowed. This means that the CCRC must focus on what the Court of Appeal will think. Should the focus instead be on the CCRC's own view of the safety of the conviction? The Innocence Network UK (INUK) suggests that the 'real possibility' test 'subordinates the CCRC entirely to the appeal courts' (**www.innocencenetwork.org.uk/ criminal-justice-system-still-failing-the-innocent** accessed 4 June 2013). INUK proposes that there should be an alternative test for referral, namely whether the CCRC thinks that the applicant 'is or might be innocent'. Do you agree that this would be a better test?

16.1.8 Bail: appeals from the Crown Court

The Court of Appeal possesses the power to grant bail pending appeal (under s.19 of the 1968 Act). Alternatively, the Crown Court may grant bail where the Crown Court has certified that a case is fit for appeal (Senior Courts Act 1981 s.81(1)(f)).

16.1.9 Attorney General's references

So far, we have only considered the rights of the defence to appeal from the Crown Court against sentence or conviction. In certain circumstances, the prosecution may have a right of appeal from decisions of the Crown Court in criminal cases. For example, where a defendant is tried on indictment and is acquitted, the Attorney General may refer a point of law that arose in the case to the Court of Appeal in order to obtain the opinion of the Court (see s.36 of the Criminal Justice Act 1972 and CrimPR Part 70). However, no matter what the Court of Appeal's ruling is, the defendant's acquittal will not be affected.

Thinking point

This means that even if the Court of Appeal agrees that a point of law was wrongly decided in the defendant's favour (and against the prosecution), the defendant cannot be retried for the offence. Why do you think this is? How important is it to have certainty and finality in criminal proceedings?

Additionally, where the Attorney General considers that a sentence passed by the Crown Court was unduly lenient, he may refer the case to the Court of Appeal under s.36 of the Criminal Justice Act 1988. The Court of Appeal may quash the sentence and pass any appropriate sentence that the Crown Court had the power to pass. An Attorney General's reference may only be made in relation to an indictable only offence or to certain specified either way offences.

Moreover, under Part 9 of the Criminal Justice Act 2003, the prosecution is now entitled to appeal against 'terminating rulings' made by the trial judge in the context of trial on indictment. A terminating ruling is a ruling that has the effect of bringing the prosecution to an end, such as a ruling that the defendant has no case to answer. The Court of Appeal may confirm, reverse, or vary the judge's decision. The result may be that the proceedings resume, or that a retrial takes place, or that the defendant is acquitted.

If further provisions of Part 9 of the Criminal Justice Act 2003 are brought into force, the prosecution will also be entitled to appeal to the Court of Appeal against certain 'evidentiary rulings', i.e. rulings relating to the admissibility or exclusion of prosecution evidence.

16.1.10 Appeals by way of case stated from Crown Court decisions

In accordance with s.28 of the Senior Courts Act 1981, a party wishing to challenge a decision of the Crown Court that does not relate to trial on indictment may appeal by way of case stated. Thus, the case stated procedure described at 16.1.3 may be used to challenge a decision made by the Crown Court upon an appeal from a magistrates' court. This route of appeal will be available if the Crown Court has made an error of law or exceeded its jurisdiction.

16.1.11 Applications for judicial review of decisions of the Crown Court

Alternatively, decisions of the Crown Court that do not relate to trial on indictment may be challenged by way of application for judicial review (s.29 Senior Courts Act 1981). For examples of the grounds upon which such a challenge may be based see 16.1.4.

16.1.12 Appeals to the Supreme Court

Appeal from the Court of Appeal (Criminal Division)

Under s.33 of the Criminal Appeal Act 1968, the defence or the prosecution may appeal from the Court of Appeal to the Supreme Court, but the leave of the Court of Appeal or the Supreme Court is required. Leave will not be granted unless the Court of Appeal certifies that a point of law of general public importance is involved, and then only if it appears to the Court of Appeal or the Supreme Court that the point of law is one that should be considered by the Supreme Court.

An application for leave to appeal to the Supreme Court should usually be made within 28 days of the Court of Appeal's decision (see s.34 of the 1968 Act and CrimPR Part 74), although the Court may extend this time limit.

For further information about the Supreme Court see 2.5.9.

When hearing an appeal, the Supreme Court must consist of an uneven number of at least three Justices of the Supreme Court (Constitutional Reform Act 2005 s.42). In disposing of an appeal, the Supreme Court may exercise any of the powers of the Court of Appeal or may remit the case to the Court of Appeal (Criminal Appeal Act 1968 s.35). The Court of Appeal may grant bail where a person appeals, or applies for leave to appeal, to the Supreme Court (Criminal Appeal Act 1968 s.36).

Appeal from the High Court

Under s.1 of the Administration of Justice Act 1960, there is also a right of appeal from decisions of the High Court in 'any criminal cause or matter' to the Supreme Court. This right of appeal is available to the prosecution or the defence. It is subject to leave and certification requirements which equate to those considered immediately above in relation to appeals from the Court of Appeal to the Supreme Court.

16.2 Civil appeals

Subject to certain limited exceptions (such as committal orders, by which a person in contempt of court may be committed to prison), a party who wishes to appeal from a decision of a county court or High Court judge will require permission to do so (CPR

52.3). Permission will only be given where the court considers either that the appeal would have a real prospect of success or that there is some other compelling reason for hearing the appeal (CPR 52.3(b)).

An appeal in a civil case may relate to the final decision of the court, such as a judgment given at the conclusion of a trial. Alternatively, the appeal may be against a decision taken before trial, such as a decision about case management (for example, decisions relating to disclosure, directions about the trial timetable, or security for costs). When the court is deciding whether to grant permission to appeal against a case management decision, CPR 52A PD provides that the court is entitled to consider:

- whether the issue is sufficiently significant to justify the costs of appealing;
- whether the procedural consequences of appealing, such as losing the trial date, outweigh the significance of the decision which the party wishes to appeal; and
- whether it would be more convenient to determine the issue at the trial or after the trial.

These criteria are designed to restrict the number of appeals against case management decisions in order to save time and expense.

16.2.1 Permission to appeal

CPR 52.3(2)(a) provides that a party may apply for permission to appeal to the court that made the decision to be appealed. Such an application should be made at the hearing at which the decision to be appealed was made. If the court refuses permission to appeal, application may be made to the appeal court. Alternatively, an application may be made directly to the appeal court by way of an appeal notice (CPR 52.3(2)(b)).

> **Thinking point**
>
> Is it fair that a party to civil proceedings should require permission to appeal? What purpose does the requirement of permission serve? Is it necessary to have this process to filter out hopeless appeals?

Where a party applies to the appeal court for permission to appeal, CPR 52.4 requires the party to file an appellant's notice, either within 21 days after the date of the decision which is to be appealed, or within such period as the lower court directs.

The appeal court may vary the time limits for filing appeal notices and may permit appeal notices to be amended. Where there is a compelling reason to do so, it may even strike out all or part of an appeal notice and may fully or partially set aside permission to appeal. If the appeal court refuses permission to appeal without holding a hearing, the party seeking permission to appeal may ask the court to reconsider the decision at a hearing (CPR 52.3(4)). However, if the application is totally without merit and the judge who refused permission to appeal was a judge of the Court of Appeal or the High Court, or was a Designated Civil Judge or a Specialist Circuit Judge, the judge may make an order preventing the decision from being reconsidered at a hearing (CPR 52.3(4A)).

16.2.2 **The nature and consequences of a civil appeal**

Normally, in accordance with CPR 52.11, an appeal will take the form of a review of the decision made by the court below, although the appeal court possesses discretion to order a rehearing if it is in the interests of justice to do so. Indeed, in certain, limited circumstances, the appeal court may be required to hold a rehearing. The appeal court will not normally receive fresh evidence or evidence that was not before the court below, but does possess discretion to receive such evidence.

An appeal will be allowed where the decision of the court below was wrong, or was unjust in consequence of serious procedural or other irregularity. The appeal court may: affirm, set aside, or vary the order or judgment of the court below; refer a claim or issue back to the lower court for determination there; order a new trial or hearing; order the payment of interest; and, make a costs order.

16.2.3 **Avenues of appeal**

Ignoring the possibility of a leapfrog appeal (see 16.2.5 'Leapfrog appeals in civil courts'), the main avenues of appeal are as follows (see CPR 52A PD and Destination of Appeals Order 2000 (SI 2000/1071)):

- From a decision of district judge in the county court to a circuit judge in the county court (unless the decision is a *final decision* in a case which has been allocated to the multi-track or in specialist proceedings, such as probate claims etc., in which case appeal is to the Court of Appeal).

  final decision: A final decision is a decision that would finally determine the proceedings, regardless of the way in which the court decided the issue. A decision to strike out a statement of case or to grant summary judgment will not be a final decision (Destination of Appeals Order 2000 (SI 2000/1071) CPR PD 52).

- From a decision of circuit judge in the county court to a single judge of the High Court (unless the decision is a final decision in a case that has been allocated to the multi-track or in specialist proceedings, in which case appeal is to the Court of Appeal).

- From a decision of a Master or a district judge sitting in a district registry to a single judge of the High Court (unless the decision is a final decision in a case that has been allocated to the multi-track or in specialist proceedings, in which case appeal is to the Court of Appeal).

- From a decision of a High Court judge to the Court of Appeal.

It should be noted that appeal routes are different in the context of insolvency proceedings and family proceedings. In relation to routes of appeal in civil proceedings in general and to the position in family proceedings, see HM Courts and Tribunal Service, *Form 201: Routes of Appeal* (available at **http://hmctsformfinder.justice. gov.uk/courtfinder/forms/form-201-eng.pdf**). In relation to insolvency proceedings, see Practice Direction – Insolvency Proceedings.

16.2.4 Composition of the Court of Appeal (Civil Division)

In accordance with s.2 of the Senior Courts Act 1981, the judges who sit in the Civil Division of the Court of Appeal are Lords Justices of Appeal (or Lady Justices of Appeal) plus certain other senior judges (such as the Master of the Rolls, who is the president of the Court of Appeal's Civil Division). Section 54 of the Senior Courts Act 1981 provides that the Civil Division of the Court of Appeal is duly constituted if it consists of one or more judges. However, whilst applications for permission to appeal are normally dealt with by a single Lord Justice, a court which hears a full appeal usually consists of three Lords Justices. Where a two-judge court sits and is equally divided, a party may apply to have the appeal reheard by an uneven number of three or more judges (s.54(5) of the 1981 Act).

16.2.5 Leapfrog appeals in civil courts

Under CPR 52.14, an appeal that would normally be heard in the county court or in the High Court may be transferred to the Court of Appeal where it raises an important point of principle or practice, or where there is some other compelling reason for the Court of Appeal to hear the case. Such a transfer may be ordered by the court which made the decision to which the appeal relates, or by the court from which permission to appeal is sought, or by the Master of the Rolls (Access to Justice Act 1999 s.57 and CPR 52.14(1)). This is known as a 'leapfrog' appeal. However, the Court of Appeal or the Master of the Rolls may subsequently remit the appeal back to the original appeal court.

Another form of leapfrog appeal is an appeal from the High Court to the Supreme Court. In accordance with ss.12 and 13 of the Administration of Justice Act 1969, a High Court judge may, with the consent of the parties, certify that a case involves a point of law of general public importance which either:

- wholly or mainly relates to statutory construction; or
- is one in relation to which the judge is bound by a previous decision of the Court of Appeal or the Supreme Court.

The Supreme Court may then grant leave to appeal directly to the Supreme Court.

16.2.6 'Second appeals' to the Court of Appeal and appeals to the Supreme Court

In addition to the appellate routes outlined previously, 'second appeals' are possible in civil cases. A 'second appeal' is an appeal to the Court of Appeal following an initial appeal to a county court or to the High Court. A 'second appeal' is possible only with the permission of the Court of Appeal. In accordance with s.55 of the Access to Justice Act 1999 and CPR 52.13, such permission should only be given either where the appeal raises an important point of principle or practice or where there is some other compelling reason why the appeal should be heard by the Court of Appeal. A second appeal may only be made to the Court of Appeal, thus neither the county court nor the High Court may hear a second appeal (Destination of Appeals Order 2000 (SI 2000/1071)).

A party may appeal against a decision of the Court of Appeal to the Supreme Court. In accordance with s.40 of the Constitutional Reform Act 2005, the leave of the Court of Appeal or that of the Supreme Court is required.

✛ Summary

- From magistrates' courts, a defendant may appeal to the Crown Court or the High Court or may apply to the High Court for judicial review.

- From the Crown Court, appeal normally lies to the Court of Appeal. However, certain Crown Court decisions may be appealed to the High Court or may be subject to judicial review by the High Court.

- Where a defendant appeals against conviction following a Crown Court trial, the Court of Appeal will only allow the appeal if it deems the conviction to be 'unsafe'.

- The Criminal Cases Review Commission may refer cases to appellate courts.

- The Attorney General may refer a point of law to the Court of Appeal on behalf of the prosecution.

- The route of appeal in civil proceedings depends upon the nature of the decision to be appealed, the type of judge who made it, and the court in which it was made.

- Following an initial appeal to a county court or the High Court, a 'second appeal' to the Court of Appeal is possible in a civil case.

❓ Questions

1 To which court would the defendant appeal if convicted following trial on indictment and to which court would he appeal if convicted following summary trial?

2 (a) What is the role of the Criminal Cases Review Commission?

   (b) What is meant by an Attorney General's reference?

3 What are differences between an appeal by way of case stated and judicial review?

4 To which court may a party appeal against a final judgment made by a district judge in the county court?

5 In what circumstances may a party to civil proceedings appeal to the Court of Appeal?

6 What powers do the different appellate courts possess in both criminal and civil proceedings?

Sample question and outline answer

Question

'The time has now come to acknowledge that [the Criminal Cases Review Commission] was an experiment that failed.' Bob Woffinden, guardian.co.uk, 30 November 2010.

Discuss the role of the CCRC and its effectiveness in rectifying miscarriages of justice.

Outline answer

Your introduction should identify any key terms and set out the issues to be addressed. In the context of this question, you should recognise the importance of the term 'miscarriages of justice' and explain that you will discuss whether the Criminal Cases Review Commission (CCRC) has been an effective mechanism for addressing such cases. Your answer should address the following issues.

First outline what the term 'miscarriage of justice' means. There is no agreed definition of the term but Lord Phillips suggested four categories of case in which a miscarriage of justice could be said to have occurred. The first three of these relate to cases in which fresh evidence is discovered. The fourth category refers to cases in which there was a serious flaw in the conduct of the investigation or trial.

You should provide some background information by discussing why the CCRC was set up. Refer to the high profile wrongful convictions that finally persuaded the establishment that an independent body was needed to examine such cases and refer them back to the Court of Appeal where appropriate.

Before you can analyse the CCRC's performance, you need to outline the legal test that the CCRC must apply. The CCRC will refer a case if there is a 'real possibility' that the conviction would not be upheld by the Court of Appeal (Criminal Appeal Act 1995 s.13).

You can now discuss whether the CCRC is 'effective' or whether it is an 'experiment that failed'. Refer to the CCRC's own statistics, which indicate that a high proportion of cases that are referred result in successful appeals. Discuss whether these statistics are misleading. Given the number of applications that the CCRC has received, very few cases have been referred to the Court of Appeal. Reasons for this may include scarce resources resulting in significant delays.

The 'real possibility' test has also been criticised as it prevents the CCRC from forming a view itself as to whether a conviction ought to be overturned. Rather, the CCRC must consider what the Court of Appeal will do. This may be a particular problem given that appeals are only likely to be successful where there was an identifiable error or procedural irregularity, or where there is fresh evidence. One reason that applications to the CCRC rarely result in referral back to the Court of Appeal is that any mistakes of fact or law, or procedural flaws, will usually have been identified and dealt with at the applicant's original appeal. There is no real possibility of success before the Court of Appeal where an issue has already been considered. As the Runciman Commission observed, the Court of Appeal is reluctant to simply consider whether a jury made the wrong decision. The recent case of *R v Pope* (2013) places further restrictions on the Court of Appeal's ability to allow an appeal solely on the ground of a lurking doubt about the safety of the conviction.

In conclusion, you should state whether you agree that the CCRC is 'an experiment that failed'. Summarise the main issues that you have identified, including the lack of resources to enable the CCRC to investigate cases more expeditiously and the difficulties with the legal framework within which the CCRC must operate.

Further reading

Your wider reading should develop your understanding of the court hierarchy and grounds of appeal in both the civil and criminal justice systems. Focus on some of the controversial concepts found in the appeal system, such as 'lurking doubt', 'fresh evidence', and 'miscarriages of justice'.

- **Elks, L.** *Righting Miscarriages of Justice? Ten Years of the Criminal Cases Review Commission* (JUSTICE 2008)
  One of the first CCRC Commissioners analyses cases referred to the Court of Appeal by the CCRC and explains how miscarriages of justice are dealt with.

- **Leigh, L.H.** 'Lurking Doubt and the Safety of Convictions' [2006] Crim LR 809
  Discusses the extent to which the Court of Appeal has allowed appeals against conviction solely on the ground of lurking doubt.

- **Foster, R.** 'Trials and Error' (2012) 109(17) LS Gazette 9
  A reply by the Chair of the CCRC to criticisms made by speakers at a symposium organised by the Innocence Network UK.

- **Grist, R.** 'The Jury Impact Test – an Optional Extra?' (2013) 177 JPN 71
  Explores whether the Court of Appeal is obliged to allow an appeal against conviction where a jury might reasonably have acquitted in light of fresh evidence.

- Report of the Royal Commission on Criminal Justice (Cm 2263), Ch 10 (available at **www.official-documents.gov.uk/document/cm22/2263/2263.pdf**)
  Explains the law prior to the Criminal Appeal Act 1995 and recommends that an independent body should be set up to rectify miscarriages of justice.

- **Robins, J.** 'Wrongly Accused' (2011) 175 JPN 675
  Explains the role and functions of the CCRC.

- **Taylor, P.** 'R v Pope – case comment' [2013] Crim LR 421
  Discusses whether the judgment in *R v Pope* unnecessarily restricts the concept of 'lurking doubt'.

- **Woffinden, B.** 'The Criminal Cases Review Commission has failed', *The Guardian*, 30 November 2010 (available at **www.guardian.co.uk/commentisfree/ libertycentral/2010/nov/30/criminal-cases-review-commission-failed**)
  Sets out criticisms of the CCRC and explains why the CCRC's published statistics are misleading.

Online Resource Centre

You should now attempt the supporting multiple choice questions available at **www.oxfordtextbooks.co.uk/orc/wilson_els/**.

17 Tribunals and alternative dispute resolution

Learning objectives

By the end of this chapter you should be able to:

- understand the reasons for the existence of tribunals and alternative methods of dispute resolution, such as arbitration and mediation;

- explain the nature and types of tribunal and understand the problems associated with tribunals;

- describe the different forms of alternative dispute resolution;

- compare and contrast the different forms of alternative dispute resolution; and

- assess the relative advantages and disadvantages of different forms of alternative dispute resolution, compared to civil litigation.

🗨 Talking point

In October 2013, horse-racing pundit John McCririck brought an action against Channel 4 in the Central London Employment Tribunal. McCririck, 73, was removed from his position as one of the team presenting Channel 4 Racing in October 2012. He immediately accused his ex-employers of 'ageism' and, 12 months later, began proceedings in the tribunal alleging a breach of the Equality Act 2010 and seeking compensation.

McCririck told BBC News: 'The Equality Act in 2010 said you cannot sack somebody because of their age, and there are hundreds of thousands of people in this country, in their 30s to their 70s, who dread, who fear the threat of the sack just because someone younger is chosen by one of the suits and skirts... That is wrong, that is illegal, and that is who I'm fighting on behalf of.'

The Employment Tribunal (ET) is often in the news. Other tribunal cases to have hit the headlines recently include those of David Drew and Wendy Williams. Dr Drew was a consultant paediatrician in the West Midlands, who was sacked after quoting bible passages in emails to colleagues. He sued Walsall Healthcare NHS Trust alleging unfair dismissal and religious discrimination but he lost at the Birmingham ET (a decision which was confirmed by the Employment Appeal Tribunal in September 2013). Group Captain Wendy Williams, meanwhile, won her sex discrimination case against the Royal Air Force in June 2013. She successfully argued that the RAF had wrongly selected a less experienced male colleague as the RAF's candidate to become commodore of the Defence Medical Group. The ET in Birmingham concluded that Gp Capt Williams 'was not selected because of her sex', in clear breach of the Equality Act 2010.

This chapter will examine the role of tribunals, including the ET, and various other forms of dispute resolution other than the courts, such as arbitration and mediation. It will seek to establish why these alternative forms of dispute resolution exist, and what are their advantages and disadvantages.

Introduction

There is no accepted definition of a 'tribunal'. Essentially, they are like courts in that they are dedicated places where people can go to try to resolve legal disputes. However, there are key differences. Whereas courts – especially civil courts – often have a very broad jurisdiction, tribunals specialise in specific subject areas such as employment or social security. Another notable difference is the presence in many tribunals of lay members – non-legally qualified people who sit alongside a legally qualified chair and contribute fully to the decision-making process.

'Alternative Dispute Resolution' (ADR), meanwhile, is an umbrella term which describes a range of methods of resolving legal disputes without recourse to litigation in the courts. ADR covers arbitration, conciliation, mediation, and 'med-arb', amongst others. There are certain similarities between all of these methods – there is no judge and there need not be any lawyers present either. They tend to be less formal than going to court, and with more flexibility in terms of where and when the parties to the dispute meet. Arbitration is the most formal of the various forms of ADR, and is typically used for resolving contractual disputes. An arbitrator will listen to the arguments presented by both sides and then give a binding decision. With mediation, a mediator will try to help the parties to the dispute to negotiate a compromise agreement – but, unlike arbitration, the mediator has no power to impose a solution on the parties. Conciliation is similar, but a conciliator has more scope to suggest possible solutions to the parties. Again, however, the conciliator has no power to impose a solution on the parties. 'Med-arb', as the name might suggest, is a combination of mediation and arbitration. The remainder of this chapter will look at tribunals and the different forms of ADR in more detail, and will seek to explain why tribunals and ADR exist in the first place.

....

17.1 **Tribunals**

17.1.1 **Background**

The earliest tribunals date back some 200 years. For example, the General and Special Commissioners of Income Tax were established in 1799 and 1805, respectively. The Railway and Canal Commission, established in 1873, subsequently evolved into the Transport Tribunal (and is now part of the General Regulatory Chamber of the First-tier Tribunal – see 17.1.3). However, the present system has grown up since the 1940s. The main reason has been the expansion of legislation in many areas previously regarded as outside of the control of the state – such as education, employment, housing, social security, and town and country planning. This legislation gave people rights – to a school place, to benefits, to protection from eviction, to keeping a job – and imposed obligations on government departments, local authorities, and employers. Naturally this led to disputes. Given the vast number of disputes, it was recognised that the ordinary courts could not cope with the workload: the Royal Commission on Legal Services discovered (in 1979) that the number of cases being dealt with by tribunals was six times that of the number of contested cases in the county and High Courts *combined*. More recently, the Administrative Justice and Tribunal Council (AJTC) reported that, in 2010, tribunals dealt with 650,000 cases compared to 223,000 criminal cases and 63,000 civil cases that were heard in the courts. As Elliott and Thomas, 'Tribunal Justice and Proportionate Dispute Resolution' (2012) 71 CLJ 297 put it, 'tribunals are big business'.

Nor would the ordinary courts have been the best forums for resolution of many of these disputes: given the detailed nature of the legislation, and the complexity of some of the issues raised in the disputes, it was perhaps inevitable that specialised tribunals would be needed. Indeed, new tribunals are still created, usually by statute, to deal with increased demand for a means of resolving legal disputes in a specialised area. For example, the Charity Tribunal and the Consumer Credit Appeals Tribunal were both created by statute in 2006 and began work in 2008. (Note: both of these tribunals have already been abolished and their functions transferred to the General Regulatory Chamber of the First-tier Tribunal (see 17.1.3).)

17.1.2 **What is a tribunal?**

What distinguishes a tribunal from a court? As already indicated, they are specialist, and (compared to courts) relatively informal bodies, designed for resolving legal disputes within their area of expertise quickly and relatively cheaply. A particular feature of most (but not necessarily all) tribunals is the presence of non-legally qual-ified (lay) members alongside a legally qualified judge, to provide an extra level of specialist expertise. According to the Franks Committee Report on Tribunals (1957, p.9), the defining qualities of tribunals are 'cheapness, accessibility, freedom from technicality, expedition and expert knowledge of their particular subject'. However, there has been an increasing trend for some tribunals, at least, to become more like courts – with greater use of legal representation, greater reporting of decisions and reliance on them as precedents, and more procedural rules – such that it is getting harder to distinguish them from courts. There are, however, two distinct types of tribunal:

- those established by the state, generally described as 'administrative tribunals' to perform judicial functions, typically reviewing decisions made by some govern-ment department; and
- those established by non-state institutions such as professional and sporting associations and trade unions as part of their disciplinary procedures.

Thinking point

Do the advantages of tribunals over courts justify having this extra tier of dispute resolution? Would the English legal system be better served by having more specialised courts?

17.1.3 The organisation of tribunals: the Tribunals Service

Until quite recently, there was very little coherence or structure to the administrative tribunal system. Individual tribunals had been set up by different Acts of Parliament with little or no consistency when it came to procedures, and related matters such as the availability of appeals. In May 2000, Lord Irvine, the then Lord Chancellor, appointed Sir Andrew Leggatt, a former Court of Appeal judge, to undertake a review of the administrative tribunal system. Sir Andrew published his report, entitled *Tribunals for Users – One System, One Service*, in 2001 (available at: **www.tribunals-review.org. uk/**). Sir Andrew identified a number of serious problems with the system.

Lack of independence

Many tribunals dealt with disputes between citizens and government departments. When looking at these tribunals, Sir Andrew found that there was an 'uneasy relationship' between most tribunals and the government departments whose decisions were being challenged. He found that many tribunal members did not feel that they had sufficient independence from those departments. Sir Andrew concluded that 'plainly they are not independent'. This was especially the case with tribunals funded by government departments but, even where that was not the case, Sir Andrew thought that 'there can be an unhealthy closeness'.

Lack of coherence

Sir Andrew found that most tribunals are 'entirely self-contained', and operated separately from other tribunals, which meant that they were all using different practices and standards. This meant confusion: not just for ordinary members of the public who are the users of tribunals but also solicitors and other advisers.

Inconsistency of appeals

Lord Justice Woolf, 'A Hotch-Potch of Appeals – the Need for a Blender' [1988] CJQ 44, wrote that the various appeal routes available from different tribunals' decisions were a 'hotch-potch'. Sir Andrew agreed that the structure of appeal routes was 'haphazard, having developed alongside the unstructured growth of the tribunals themselves'. He noted that, while some tribunals had a two-tier structure (for example, appeals from the employment tribunal were (and indeed still are) heard by the Employment Appeal Tribunal), most did not. Sir Andrew was particularly concerned that people wishing to challenge decisions in 'important areas', such as decisions of the Mental Health Review Tribunal, were 'effectively left with no recourse apart from judicial review'. His conclusion was that the inconsistent appeal system was 'not satisfactory'. The solution was obvious: 'to simplify, to ensure that appeal routes are rational and clearly defined. There should be a single route for all appeals from tribunals.'

Sir Andrew's 2001 report's key recommendation was the creation of a Tribunals Service, designed to provide a common administrative service for all tribunals, and streamline the appeal structure. The new Service would provide:

- **independence**: a Tribunals Service would break the relationship (described as 'indefensible') that currently exists whereby certain tribunals receive administrative support from the government department whose decisions are being challenged;
- **coherence**: all of the existing tribunals would be brought together under the umbrella of the Tribunals Service; and
- **consistency of appeals**: there would also be a single appellate tribunal, with a subsequent appeal to the Court of Appeal.

Sir Andrew's report received widespread support. A. W. Bradley 'The Tribunals Maze' [2002] PL 200, for example, commented that:

> one of the great advantages of the new comprehensive structure…is that it would prevent a new maze of tribunals growing up in future. Inevitably, as new legislation affecting the powers of government over individuals is needed in the future, there will be a need for rights of appeal to be created against official decisions made under the new powers.

The government accepted Sir Andrew's recommendations and in April 2006 a Tribunals Service was established as an 'executive agency' of (what is now) the Ministry of Justice (MoJ) to provide administrative support for several (but not yet all) of the country's biggest tribunals. At a stroke, a large number of tribunals became independent of the government departments whose decisions they reviewed. Five years later, in April 2011, the Tribunals Service was amalgamated with HM Courts Service, creating the HM Courts & Tribunals Service, which provides administrative support for the country's courts and (most, but still not all of its) tribunals.

The First-tier and Upper Tribunals

The establishment of the Tribunals Service was by no means the end of the reform of the tribunal system. The problem of the 'hotch-potch' appeals procedures had still to be addressed. The Tribunals, Courts and Enforcement Act 2007 was passed in order to achieve this. The Act creates two new 'generic' tribunals, the First-tier Tribunal (FTT) and the Upper Tribunal (UT), which came into existence in November 2008. The functions and personnel of dozens of pre-existing tribunals have now been transferred to the new 'generic' tribunals, with the consequent abolition of those pre-existing tribunals. The First-tier Tribunal is presently subdivided into seven 'chambers', as follows:

- The General Regulatory Chamber. This carries out the functions of a variety of now abolished separate tribunals, such as the Charity Tribunal, the Consumer Credit Appeals Tribunal, the Gambling Appeals Tribunal, the Immigration Services Tribunal, and the Information Tribunal, among others.

- The Social Entitlement Chamber. This has taken over the functions of the Asylum Support Tribunal, the Criminal Injuries Compensation Appeals Panel, and the Social Security & Child Support Appeals Tribunal.

- The Health, Education & Social Care Chamber. This has replaced the Care Standards Tribunal, the Mental Health Review Tribunal, and the Special Educational Needs & Disability Tribunal, among others.

- The Property Chamber. This has taken over the functions of the Adjudicator to the Land Registry, the Agricultural Land Tribunal, and the Residential Property Tribunal.

- The War Pensions & Armed Forces Compensation Chamber.

- The Tax Chamber. This carries out the functions of what used to be the VAT & Duties Tribunal and the General and Special Commissioners of Income Tax. Since the Parliamentary Standards Act 2009, it also deals with appeals against decisions of the Compliance Officer involving MPs' expenses.

- The Immigration & Asylum Chamber. This replaces the Asylum & Immigration Tribunal.

Section 11 of the 2007 Act provides that appeals (on points of law) from the First-tier Tribunal will be heard by the Upper Tribunal. This Tribunal is subdivided into four chambers, as follows:

- Administrative Appeals Chamber. This body deals with all appeals from the General Regulatory Chamber, the Social Entitlement Chamber, the Health, Education & Social Care Chamber, and the War Pensions & Armed Forces Compensation Chamber of the First-tier Tribunal.

- Tax and Chancery Chamber. This body hears appeals from the Tax Chamber of the First-tier Tribunal.

- Lands Chamber. This body replaces the Lands Tribunal. It hears appeals from the Property Chamber of the First-tier Tribunal.

- Immigration & Asylum Chamber. This hears appeals from its namesake in the First-tier Tribunal.

Section 13 of the 2007 Act provides that appeals (on points of law) from the Upper Tribunal will go to the Court of Appeal. There is also the possibility of taking a case to the High Court in order to seek judicial review of a tribunal decision. This is not provided for in the 2007 Act but, in *Cart & Another v Upper Tribunal* [2011] UKSC 28,

[2012] 1 AC 663, the Supreme Court held that judicial review was available. However, this possibility will only be available in cases where there was an 'important point of principle or practice' or some other 'compelling reason' for the case to be reviewed (per Lord Phillips in *Cart*). These conditions are designed to be restrictive and, if anything, subsequent case law has narrowed them. In *PR v Home Secretary* [2011] EWCA Civ 988, [2012] 1 WLR 73, Carnwath LJ in the Court of Appeal explained that 'compelling' meant '*legally* compelling, rather than compelling, perhaps, from a political or emotional point of view, although such considerations may exceptionally add weight to the legal arguments' (emphasis in the original).

It was deemed necessary to provide the High Court with the power to judicially review tribunal decisions because 'there is a real risk that the exclusion of judicial review will lead to the fossilisation of bad law' (per Lord Dyson in *Cart*). However, it was simultaneously deemed necessary to restrict the availability of judicial review, for several reasons, including:

- Legal certainty: the desirability of ensuring that, in most cases at least, tribunal decisions were final, without the possibility of disputes being prolonged by contesting those decisions in the courts.

- Cost: the need to ensure that resources were not needlessly expended in litigating cases through the courts which had already been decided at tribunal level.

- Specialisation and mutual respect: the recognition that the Upper Tribunal, in particular, is staffed by subject specialists who are experts in what are often complex areas of law such as social security and immigration, whereas the High Court is a court of general jurisdiction.

- High Court workload: the need to avoid overburdening the High Court with judicial review cases.

As already noted, not all of the pre-existing tribunals have been transferred to the 'generic' First-tier and Upper Tribunals. For example, employment tribunals and the Employment Appeal Tribunal have not (yet) been transferred because of the nature of the cases that come before them, which involve one party against another, unlike most of the other tribunals which involve citizens challenging decisions made by government departments. Other tribunals which (for the time being at least) remain outside of the First-tier/Upper Tribunals structure include the Competition Appeal Tribunal (**www.catribunal.org.uk/**), the Copyright Tribunal (**www.ipo.gov.uk/ctribunal. htm**), the Gender Recognition Panel, the Investigatory Powers Tribunal (**www.ipt-uk. com/**), and the Special Immigration Appeals Commission.

17.1.4 **Membership of tribunals**

Membership of tribunals varies. Some, such as the First-tier Tribunal (Gambling) and the Lands Chamber of the Upper Tribunal, usually sit with a judge sitting alone.

However, many tribunals sit with a panel of three people: a judge who acts as the chairperson, and two non-legally qualified (lay) members, sometimes known as 'wing members'. The reason why some tribunals have wing members differs according to the tribunals concerned.

Some tribunals' wing members are chosen for their expertise in a particular subject matter. For example, medically qualified people sit in cases before the Gender Recognition Panel. People experienced in data protection matters sit as wing members on the First-tier Tribunal (Information Rights). Wing members of other tribunals are chosen for their representative qualities. For example, the lay members of the Employment Tribunal have experience representing employees' or employers' interests. The First-tier Tribunal (Mental Health) has both types of wing member: a medically qualified member (usually an experienced consultant psychiatrist) who provides expertise and a lay member who represents the wider community.

Thinking point

It is important to note the composition of tribunals. Many include both legally qualified people and lay people. When looking at specific tribunals, note the composition of the tribunal and how the members are appointed. A legally qualified chairperson for a tribunal is considered to be essential for resolving any points of law that may arise. Many tribunals deal with specialist fields of activity, such as immigration, mental health, or tax, whereas other tribunals deal with the problems of ordinary people in their capacities as employees or benefit claimants. Lay membership of a tribunal reflects the work of the tribunal. Choose three tribunals with lay membership and identify the role of its lay members.

17.1.5 Appointment of tribunal judges and lay members

Tribunal members (both judicial and lay) are usually appointed by the Lord Chancellor. It has been acknowledged that this raises questions regarding the members' independence and impartiality (similar to those questions involving the judiciary that have led to Parliament changing the appointment system of judges; see chapter 8). Section 1 of the Tribunals, Courts and Enforcement Act 2007 provides that the guarantee of judicial independence in s.3 of the Constitutional Reform Act 2005 also applies to most tribunal members. The Judicial Appointments Commission is now involved in the appointment of some tribunal members, such as the First-tier Tribunal (Gambling).

17.1.6 Supervising the tribunal system

Until quite recently, a body called the Council on Tribunals had the task of supervising the constitution and working of tribunals in the UK. However, the Council was described as conspicuously lacking in powers and suffered from a lack of resources. Consequently, ss.44 and 45 of the Tribunals, Courts and Enforcement Act 2007 replaced the Council with a new body called the Administrative Justice and Tribunals Council (AJTC), which had a broader remit over the whole of the administrative justice system. Under the 2007 Act, the functions of the Council were to keep the administrative justice system under review; to consider ways to make the system accessible, fair, and efficient; and to make proposals for research into the system. In August 2013, however, the AJTC was abolished under the Public Bodies Act 2011 (the Coalition government's legislation designed to reduce the number of public bodies in the UK). At the time of writing this chapter, it is not clear whether the government intends to replace the AJTC.

Thinking point

In July 2013, the AJTC itself submitted a report on its own (imminent) demise entitled 'Future Oversight of Administrative Justice'. In the report, the AJTC posed the following (rhetorical) questions:

How will the Administrative Justice system be overseen without the AJTC to perform that role as an independent statutory body? How will users' needs be identified and represented? How will the accessibility, fairness, and efficiency of the system be assessed? Where will proposals for its improvement come from?

17.2 **Arbitration**

17.2.1 **Commercial arbitration – general principles**

Arbitrators typically aim to resolve disputes as to a contract, having been nominated in advance by the parties themselves for that very reason. Commercial arbitration is governed by the Arbitration Act 1996. Section 1(a) states that: 'the object of arbitration is to obtain the fair resolution of disputes by an impartial tribunal without unnecessary delay or expense'. Section 33(1) provides that the tribunal shall (a) 'act fairly and impartially as between the parties, giving each party a reasonable opportunity of putting his case and dealing with that of his opponent', and (b) 'adopt procedures suitable to the circumstances of the particular case, avoiding unnecessary delay or expense, so as to provide a fair means for the resolution of the matters falling to be determined'.

17.2.2 **Arbitrators**

An arbitrator will typically be an expert in the particular field of commerce to which the contract relates. There is no rule preventing legally qualified persons from being arbitrators and judges can and do sit as arbitrators. Once appointed, the arbitrator is obliged to act in an impartial manner (like a judge) but will have been appointed because of his specialist knowledge, thus avoiding the need to have technical points explained to him by expert witnesses (unlike a judge). Section 15 of the 1996 Act provides that, in any arbitration, the parties are free to agree on the number of arbitrators; if there is no agreement as to the number of arbitrators, then the tribunal shall consist of a sole arbitrator.

17.2.3 Appeals and judicial review

Section 68(1) of the Arbitration Act 1996 states that '[a] party to arbitral proceedings may...apply to the court challenging an award in the proceedings on the ground of serious irregularity affecting the tribunal, the proceedings or the award.' Section 69(1) states that, 'unless otherwise agreed by the parties, a party to arbitral proceedings may...appeal to the court on a question of law'. Appeals require either the agreement of all the other parties to the proceedings, or leave of the court. Appeals on findings of fact were abolished by the Arbitration Act 1979, primarily for the reason that the possibility of lengthy and expensive appeals to the High Court subverted the whole point of having the case heard by an arbitrator in the first place. There is also the possibility of judicial review. If the proceedings were allegedly not conducted in a 'judicial manner', the case may be reviewed in the High Court.

Thinking point

Arbitration for many years was the main alternative to litigating a case before the courts. In recent times, arbitration has been seen as beset by similar problems to those associated with litigation before the courts. What do you think are the problems?

17.3 Mediation

Mediation can be defined as the process whereby a neutral third party, the mediator, helps both sides to a dispute to come to a mutually acceptable agreement. If an agreement is reached it can be written down and form a binding contract which, if necessary, is enforceable in court. If not, traditional civil litigation is still open to the parties.

🔑 Key point

Mediation is a process which depends on the voluntary participation of both parties to the dispute. The aim is to establish a mutually acceptable compromise through negotiation and, eventually, agreement. The outcome can therefore be very flexible: it is whatever the parties agree upon. However, there is no guarantee that any agreement will be forthcoming, which is one of the drawbacks of mediation.

17.3.1 **The scope of mediation**

Mediation is a form of ADR which had, until relatively recently, been associated primarily with the resolution of matrimonial disputes. Indeed, this is still an area where mediation has a key role, as its informality and privacy is ideally suited to such disputes. Until recently, mediation was regarded as a novelty and of little importance (see Lind, 'ADR and Mediation – Boom or Bust?' (2001) NLJ 1238). However, the situation has changed dramatically since then. The landmark cases of *Dunnett v Railtrack* and *Cowl v Plymouth City Council* led to a massive increase in the profile of ADR in general and mediation in particular. The following section explores the areas of dispute resolution where mediation is now firmly established.

Divorce and subsequent disputes

A court may be a particularly inappropriate place for divorce and subsequent disputes over property and custody, since the adversarial nature of the system can aggravate the differences between the parties. This is likely to be especially harmful where children are involved, since the couple will normally have to maintain some kind of contact after divorce. Hence, mediation has been available to divorcing couples for some time – not necessarily to try to get them back together, but to try to ensure that any arrangements between them are made as amicably as possible. Part II of the Family Law Act 1996 aimed to make mediation for divorcing couples compulsory, as opposed to voluntary. However, there were various objections to this reform, and in February 2001 the then Lord Chancellor, Lord Irvine, announced that Part II was to be repealed. The Court of Appeal has subsequently decided (in *Halsey v Milton Keynes NHS Trust* [2004] EWCA Civ 576, [2004] 1 WLR 3002, a medical negligence case) that mediation in all circumstances must be voluntary and that, although courts can strongly encourage mediation, it is going too far for any outside party – whether government, Parliament, or the courts – to insist that parties with a dispute try mediation.

Negligence and judicial review action

Mediation is now well established in the context of negligence claims, covering personal injury (*McCook v Lobo* [2002] EWCA Civ 1760), claims for property loss (*Dunnett v Railtrack* [2002] 1 WLR 2434), and professional negligence (*Hurst v Leeming* [2002] EWHC 1051). In *Cowl v Plymouth City Council* [2001] EWCA Civ 1935; [2002] 1 WLR 803, a judicial review action, Lord Woolf CJ was adamant that mediation had a role to play in such cases:

> Even in disputes between public authorities and the members of the public for whom they are responsible, insufficient attention is paid to the paramount importance of avoiding litigation whenever this is possible... both sides must now be acutely aware of

the contribution [ADR] can make to resolving disputes in a manner which both meets the needs of the parties and the public and saves expense and stress.

Trust and probate disputes

Mediation has a potentially invaluable role to play in the context of trust and probate disputes. The privacy and confidentiality, flexibility and informality of the process may well help to avoid, or at least minimise, conflicts between family members over the distribution of assets.

Property disputes

The same arguments can be made in support of the use of mediation in property disputes between neighbours. In *Valentine v Allen* [2003] EWCA Civ 915, involving a complicated dispute between neighbours over rights of way, the trial judge encouraged the parties to consider mediation. Although it was unsuccessful in that case, it nevertheless illustrates that the judge considered the dispute could potentially have been resolved outside of court.

Landlord and tenant disputes

The case of *Shirayama Shokusan v Danovo Ltd* [2003] EWHC 3306 (Ch) involved a dispute between a landlord and tenant in a commercial tenancy. Blackburne J in the Chancery Division ordered the parties to attempt mediation. (Note: the notion that judges had a power to compel parties into mediation was disapproved of in *Halsey*; see further later.)

Commercial disputes

Cable & Wireless PLC v IBM (UK) Ltd [2002] EWHC 2059 and *Leicester Circuits v Coates Brothers* [2003] EWCA Civ 333 are examples of cases where mediation has been used (albeit not necessarily successfully) in the context of commercial disputes.

Defamation, employment, and housing disputes

Other areas where mediation should, in principle, be able to provide a solution include defamation (see R. Shillito 'Mediation in Libel Actions' (2000) NLJ 122), employment, and housing disputes (see R. Mahendra 'Popular but no Panacea' (2004) NLJ 1398).

17.3.2 The 'cost consequences' of a failure to mediate

In *Dunnett v Railtrack plc* [2002] 1 WLR 2434, the Court of Appeal controversially ordered that the successful party in negligence litigation should pay the losing side's costs – because of the former's failure to respond positively to the court's suggestion that they should enter into mediation. This was despite the fact that mediation was first proposed after the defendant had already won in the county court. Brooke LJ said:

> Skilled mediators are now able to achieve results satisfactory to both parties in many cases which are quite beyond the power of lawyers and courts to achieve. This court has knowledge of cases where intense feelings have arisen, for instance in relation to clinical negligence claims. But when the parties are brought together on neutral soil with a skilled mediator to help them resolve their differences, it may very well be that the mediator is able to achieve a result by which the parties shake hands at the end and feel that they have gone away having settled the dispute on terms with which they are happy to live. A mediator may be able to provide solutions which are beyond the powers of the court to provide…It is to be hoped that any publicity given to this part of the judgment of the court will draw the attention of lawyers to their duties to further the overriding objective…and to the possibility that, if they turn down out of hand the chance of ADR when suggested by the court…they may have to face uncomfortable costs consequences.

Example

Dunnett v Railtrack plc [2002] 1 WLR 2434

Facts: Susan Dunnett brought a claim against Railtrack plc seeking damages for negligence arising out of the deaths, in July 1996, of three of her horses which had been struck by an express train on the Swansea-to-London mainline. The judge in the county court dismissed her claim, but she was given leave to appeal to the Court of Appeal. Pending the appeal, Dunnett suggested ADR to Railtrack, but they flatly rejected it. Accordingly, the appeal proceeded. At the Court of Appeal in London, the appeal was dismissed, and Railtrack sought its costs from Dunnett. However, the Court ordered Railtrack to pay its own costs. This decision was highly controversial, as it created an exception to the 'normal' rule which is that the losing party in any litigation pays the winning party's costs. The Court of Appeal took the view that the advantages of mediation over litigation were so obvious that Railtrack had to be 'punished' for not responding more positively to the suggestion of mediation.

The Court of Appeal followed and applied *Dunnett* in *Leicester Circuits v Coates Brothers* [2003] EWCA Civ 333. Here, after both sides had agreed to mediate in an attempt to resolve their dispute, Coates withdrew, forcing the case to proceed to litigation. Judge LJ regarded this as unreasonable. He said that the:

> unexplained withdrawal from an agreed mediation process was of significance to the continuation of this litigation…We take the view that having agreed to mediation it hardly lies in the mouths of those who agree to it to assert that there was no realistic prospect of success.

However, *Dunnett* has been distinguished in several subsequent cases, on the basis that a party to litigation will be entitled to reject a mediation proposal when it is

'justified' in doing so. This is when mediation would have no 'realistic prospect of resolution of dispute'. In *Hurst v Leeming* [2002] EWHC 1051 (Ch), Lightman J held that:

> Mediation is not in law compulsory…but [ADR] is at the heart of today's civil justice
> system, and any unjustified failure to give proper attention to the opportunities afforded
> by mediation, and in particular in any case where mediation affords a realistic prospect
> of resolution of dispute, there must be anticipated as a real possibility that adverse con-
> sequences may be attracted…If mediation can have no real prospect of success a party
> may, with impunity, refuse to proceed to mediation. But refusal is a high-risk course to
> take…Further, the hurdle in the way of a party refusing to proceed to mediation on this
> ground is high…the starting point must surely be the fact that the mediation process
> itself can and does often bring about a more sensible and more conciliatory attitude on
> the part of the parties than might otherwise be expected to prevail before the media-
> tion, and may produce a recognition of the strengths and weaknesses by each party of
> his own case and of that of his opponent, and a willingness to accept the give & take
> essential to a successful mediation.

In *Société Internationale de Télécommunications Aeronautiques SC (SITA) v Wyatt
Co (UK) Ltd* [2002] EWHC 2401 (Ch), Park J also refused to penalise a litigant as to
costs despite refusing to mediate. He explained that this was because of the attitude of the other party in trying to instigate mediation, which he variously described
as 'self-serving', 'disagreeable', 'off-putting', and 'bullying'. In *McCook v Lobo* [2002]
EWCA Civ 1760, Pill LJ said that 'this was not a case where there was scope for mediation' and hence there was no order to deprive the winning litigant of his costs.
Similarly in *Valentine v Allen* [2003] EWCA Civ 915, Arden LJ decided not to penalise
either of the parties for their failure to respond to the judge's entreaties to mediate: 'it
is not clear that [they] could by mediation have come to any agreement. The failure
to go to mediation is of no cause or effect'. In *Halsey v Milton Keynes General NHS
Trust* [2004] EWCA Civ 576, [2004] 1 WLR 3002, the Court of Appeal confirmed these
developments. Dyson LJ said:

> In deciding whether to deprive a successful party of some or all of his costs on the grounds
> that he has refused to agree to ADR, it must be borne in mind that such an order is an
> exception to the general rule that costs should follow the event. In our view, the burden is
> on the unsuccessful party to show why there should be a departure from the general rule.
> The fundamental principle is that such departure is not justified unless it is shown (the
> burden being on the unsuccessful party) that the successful party acted unreasonably in
> refusing to agree to ADR…We accept that mediation and other ADR processes do not
> offer a panacea, and can have disadvantages as well as advantages: they are not appro-
> priate for every case. We do not, therefore accept that there should be a presumption
> in favour of mediation. The question whether a party has acted unreasonably in refusing
> ADR must be determined having regard to all the circumstances of the particular case.

The Court of Appeal significantly reduced the scope of the *Dunnett* rule by emphasising that, when a court was deciding whether to impose cost sanctions for a failure to
mediate, the burden of proof fell on the losing party to prove that there was a realistic

prospect of mediation being a success. Dyson LJ stated that the losing party had to prove that a refusal to mediate was unreasonable; there was no burden on the winning party to prove that their refusal to mediate was reasonable. He stated that, 'it would not be right to stigmatise as unreasonable a refusal by the successful party to agree to a mediation unless he showed that a mediation had no realistic prospect of success'. According to Dyson LJ, there were at least six factors which may be relevant to the question of whether a party has unreasonably refused mediation:

(a) the nature of the dispute;

(b) the merits of the case;

(c) the extent to which other settlement methods had been attempted;

(d) whether the costs of ADR would be disproportionately high;

(e) whether any delay in setting up and attending the ADR would have been prejudicial; and

(f) whether the ADR had a reasonable prospect of success.

He did emphasise that 'in many cases no single factor will be decisive, and that these factors should not be regarded as an exhaustive checklist'. Reaction to the decision in *Halsey* has generally been positive (see, e.g., M. Supperstone, D. Stilitz, and C. Sheldon, 'ADR and Public Law' [2006] PL 299).

Example

Halsey v Milton Keynes General NHS Trust [2004] EWCA Civ 576, [2004] 1 WLR 3002

Lillian Halsey brought an action against the Milton Keynes NHS Trust alleging negligent treatment of her late husband, Bert. He had been admitted to hospital in June 1999 with serious health problems. A 'nasogastric' feeding tube was fitted – allegedly negligently, so that, instead of directing liquid food into Bert's stomach, it went instead into his left lung, resulting in his death. This was denied. Mrs Halsey (via her solicitors) contacted the trust in January 2000, indicating that she would accept £7,500 damages. The trust (through its solicitors) replied in February indicating that they would 'take all necessary steps to resist a claim'. A few days later, Mrs Halsey contacted the trust again proposing mediation. In March, the trust again insisted there was no claim to mediate about. In April 2001, Mrs Halsey indicated that she would settle for £12,500.

The trust refused to settle or mediate. In May 2002, Mrs Halsey issued her claim; although she again proposed mediation. This was rejected in September 2002. In April 2003, Mrs Halsey again proposed both settlement and/or mediation. After this was rejected, she wrote another letter to the trust pointing out the decisions in *Dunnett* and *Hurst v Leeming*. In May 2003, the trust replied that mediation would have 'little chance' of success and that the mediation (being doomed to failure) would be a waste of money. Trial took place in June 2003, and judgment was given to the trust. The trial judge also held that the trust should not be deprived of any of its costs. Mrs Halsey appealed. The Court of Appeal dismissed the appeal.

The *Halsey* factors were considered in detail by the Court of Appeal in *Burchell v Bullard* [2005] EWCA Civ 358.

> ### Example
>
> *Burchell v Bullard* [2005] EWCA Civ 358
>
> Nick Burchell, a builder, had agreed to build two large extensions to the Bullards' home in Bournemouth, payment in stages. The Bullards refused to make the third payment as they were unhappy with the work. Burchell's solicitor wrote to the Bullards, suggesting the case be referred to 'a qualified construction mediator'. The Bullards (on advice from their surveyor) rejected this on the basis that the issues were technically too complex. Burchell duly made a claim for over £18,000; the Bullards counterclaimed for over £100,000. In court, the judge awarded Burchell his £18,000 but also awarded the Burrells £14,000 of their counterclaim. Thus, the Bullards had to pay him the difference of some £5,000 once VAT and interest had been added on. On costs, the parties were ordered to pay each other's costs. Burchell appealed against the costs order. The Court of Appeal was scathing of the Bullards, in particular their gross exaggeration of their counterclaim, and their dismissive attitude towards Burchell's offer to mediate. The court said that 'the defendants cannot rely on their own obstinacy to assert that the mediation had no reasonable prospect of success'. The court thought that the nature of the dispute was suitable for ADR, the merits of the case also favoured mediation, the costs of ADR would have been relatively small. However, because the offer to mediate was made before the decision in *Dunnett*, the Court thought that the defendants' decision not to mediate had to be judged against the prevailing legal circumstances at the time, and hence ordered that no costs sanction be imposed against the Bullards. However, the Court of Appeal did modify the trial judge's costs order by ordering the Bullard's to pay 60 per cent of all of the costs (on both sides) and hence leaving Burchell with only 40 per cent to pay.

For other, more recent, cases applying the *Halsey* factors see *Nigel Witham Ltd v Smith* [2008] EWHC 12 (TCC), *Carleton (Earl of Malmesbury) v Strutt & Parker (A Partnership)* [2008] EWHC 424 (QBD), and *S v Chapman* [2008] EWCA Civ 800.

17.3.3 The importance of the voluntary nature of mediation

It is important to emphasise that mediation, at least in England, is a voluntary process. There are two main reasons for this: first, if mediation was compulsory or participants were forced to participate, it could create barriers between the parties and the mediator and inhibit the negotiation process. Second, the typical outcome in a successful mediation process is a compromise solution to which both parties have agreed. As both can be satisfied with the outcome (sometimes referred to as a 'win/win' outcome), there is therefore a greater chance that the agreement will continue. Conversely, forcing one, or even both, unwilling parties into mediation would probably achieve nothing in terms of a settlement, and would just prolong the dispute as it would have to go to court to be litigated anyway, wasting both the parties' time as well as that of the mediator.

In *Halsey*, the Court of Appeal identified another reason for keeping mediation voluntary: that ordering mediation could involve denying litigants access to court and could therefore contravene Article 6(1) of the European Convention on Human Rights (the right to a fair trial). However, B. Tronson ('Mediation Orders: Do the Arguments against them Make Sense' (2006) 25 CJQ 412) has observed that *Halsey* is a 'paradox' in that the Court of Appeal is (on one hand) denying that the courts have the power to order mediation but is also (on the other hand) threatening to penalise parties that do not mediate (if that refusal is unreasonable). Tronson concludes that, in reality, the Court of Appeal probably has made mediation compulsory because the financial risks of not mediating are simply too great.

In March 2011, the Ministry of Justice published a Consultation Paper entitled 'Solving Disputes in the County Court: Creating a simpler, quicker and more proportionate system'. Amongst other reform ideas, the government proposed making mediation compulsory in some small claims cases, whilst also raising the ceiling for small claims cases, possibly to as high as £25,000. In February 2012, the Ministry of Justice published its official Response to those who responded to the Consultation Paper during that period. In summary, the government is now proposing the following changes:

- Raising the ceiling for small claims from £5,000 to £10,000, with the possibility of raising it again to £15,000 'after full evaluation' of the initial increase to £10,000.

- All small claims to be 'automatically' referred to mediation, but on the basis that 'this is not compulsory mediation', rather 'a requirement to engage with a small claims mediator'.

ⓘ Critical debate

Michael Lind has noted that '[i]n certain US states, mediation is ordered automatically in many cases. However, a call for mediation to become mandatory in the UK would conflict directly with the voluntary nature of mediation' ('ADR and Mediation – Boom or Bust?' (2001) NLJ 1238). Three years later, B. Mahendra pointed out that '*Halsey* brought home the reality to those advocating greater use of ADR. The court explained that to oblige unwilling parties to refer their disputes to mediation would be to impose an unacceptable obstruction on the right of access to the court, and that if the court were to compel parties to enter into mediation when unwilling, that would achieve nothing except to add to the costs, possibly delay matters and damage the perceived effectiveness of ADR' ('Popular but no Panacea' (2004) NLJ 1398).

Compulsory mediation exists in a number of jurisdictions (including Australia and parts of Canada, as well as the USA), begging the question: if it can work there, why not here? The answer, according to commentators such as Lind and Mahendra, is that non-voluntary mediation could be perceived to be an infringement of the litigants' right, enshrined in Article 6(1) of the European Convention of Human Rights, to 'a fair and public hearing...by an independent and impartial tribunal established by law'. It could also be a waste of time and resources – after all, mediation is predicated on the parties' willingness to negotiate their way to a mutually acceptable compromise solution to their dispute, so forcing parties unwillingly into the process is unlikely to lead to a productive outcome.

The counter-arguments were neatly presented by Kent Dreadon, 'Mediation Order' (2005) 149 SJ 12, who argued that '[t]he judgment in *Halsey* is at odds with the accepted view in Australia and the United States and, probably, the view of most experienced mediators in England. Even where a party is initially unwilling to participate, surprising results can be achieved with the aid of a skilful and experienced mediator. Further, mediations can be set up very quickly and parties are free to leave at any time, so concerns about the obstruction of a party's right of access to the court would appear to be misconceived.'

In the light of this, identify the advantages and disadvantages of making mediation compulsory. Are there some areas of dispute resolution that would be more suitable than others for compulsory mediation?

17.4 Other forms of ADR

17.4.1 Adjudication

The construction industry has long been bedevilled by disputes. Arbitration is widely used but to some extent suffers from many of the drawbacks of litigation. Disputes during lengthy construction projects were particularly problematic, as delays to the project were inevitably caused. Section 108(1) of the Housing Grants, Construction and Regeneration Act 1996 introduced another form of ADR: adjudication. The section states that a 'party to a construction contract has the right to refer a dispute arising under the contract for adjudication under a procedure complying with this section'. Adjudication is designed to be quick and to take place during the continuation of the construction contract, rather than leaving resolution of the dispute until after completion of the project. Adjudication, however, does not necessarily finally resolve a dispute. The parties may contractually agree that a dispute adjudicated upon is determined for the remainder of the duration of the construction contract only, and thereafter will be finally resolved by arbitration. In this sense, adjudication can be seen as an interim measure.

17.4.2 Conciliation

This is similar to mediation, except that the conciliator plays a more interventionist role. ACAS, the Advisory, Conciliation and Arbitration Service (**www.acas.org.uk/**) administers a statutory conciliation scheme in collective employment disputes.

17.4.3 Med-arb

This is a hybrid of mediation and arbitration. One weakness of mediation is that there is no guarantee of a successful resolution of the dispute, whereas with arbitration a solution will be reached when the arbitrator imposes his or her decision. 'Med-arb' therefore begins with mediation and the parties try to reach a compromise agreement. If this is achieved then the dispute is resolved. But if mediation is unsuccessful, then the process shifts to arbitration because that will produce a solution. Med-arb is well established in the US and may be set for expansion in this country following its recommendation by the Court of Appeal in the case of *IDA Ltd & Metcalf v Southampton University & Howse* [2006] EWCA Civ 145. The case involved a dispute over who was entitled to a patent for a cockroach trap, originally invented by Professor Philip Howse of Southampton University but subsequently modified following a suggestion made by Colin Metcalfe, of IDA Ltd. In that case, Jacob LJ said (emphasis added):

> Parties to these disputes should realise, that if fully fought, they can be protracted, very very expensive and emotionally draining. On top of that, very often development or exploitation of the invention under dispute will be stultified by the dead hand of unresolved litigation... It will often be better to settle early for a smaller share than you think you are entitled to – a small share of large exploitation is better than a large share of none or little. This sort of dispute is particularly apt for early mediation. Such mediation could well go beyond conventional mediation (where the mediator facilitates a consensual agreement). *I have in mind the process called 'medarb' where a 'mediator' trusted by both sides is given the authority to decide the terms of a binding settlement agreement.*

Thinking point

It was noted earlier that one of the problems with mediation is that, because it involves two parties trying to reach a compromise through negotiation, it does not necessarily follow that any agreement will be reached. Where this happens, the parties are really back to 'square one'. Med-arb avoids this frustrating (non)-outcome by starting with mediation but then switching to arbitration if no agreement can be reached through negotiation. Given this, do you think med-arb should replace mediation? Are there any disadvantages with med-arb?

17.4.4 Early neutral evaluation/expert determination

According to the Centre for Effective Dispute Resolution (CEDR) website (**www.cedr.co.uk/**), early neutral evaluation is 'a preliminary assessment of facts, evidence or legal merits. This process is designed to serve as a basis for further and fuller negotiations or, at the very least, help parties avoid further unnecessary stages in litigation.' Meanwhile, expert determination is:

> a process in which an independent third party, acting as an expert rather than judge or arbitrator, is appointed to decide the dispute. There is no right of appeal and the expert's determination is final and binding on the parties. It is particularly suited to disputes of valuation or a purely technical nature across a range of sectors.

17.4.5 Industry codes of conduct

A number of industries have their own codes of conduct, the aim of which is to provide protection for consumers. The best-known example is probably the travel industry scheme set up by ABTA, the Association of British Travel Agents (**http://abta.com/go-travel/travel-clinic/arbitration-and-mediation**). Their code encourages resolution of any dispute between holiday-makers and travel companies through independent arbitration and/or mediation.

17.5 Court's powers to 'stay' litigation

In many areas of dispute, one party may be more willing to try an alternative form of resolution than the other. In some cases, however, both parties to a commercial contract agree to incorporate a provision into their contract committing themselves to a form of ADR (arbitration, adjudication, mediation, etc.) in the event of a dispute. Are such contractual clauses legally binding? Generally speaking, the answer is 'Yes', and the courts will grant a 'stay' of litigation until the prescribed form of ADR has been attempted.

Section 9(1) of the Arbitration Act 1996 expressly states that:

> A party to an arbitration agreement against whom legal proceedings are brought…in respect of a matter which under the agreement is to be referred to arbitration may…apply to the court in which the proceedings have been brought to stay the proceedings so far as they concern that matter.

This provision is important as it serves to emphasise that if parties have agreed to arbitrate in advance of any dispute arising, and it does subsequently arise, then they cannot renege on that agreement. Section 9(1) was applied by the Court of Appeal in *Inco Europe v First Choice Distribution & Others* [1999] 1 WLR 270. Inco had brought an action against the four defendants claiming a breach of contract. This was despite the fact that Inco had earlier agreed to refer such a dispute to arbitration. One of the defendant companies, Steinweg, applied for a stay under s.9(1). The judge hearing the application ruled that the arbitration agreement was 'null and void or inoperative' and refused the application. On appeal, however, the Court of Appeal reversed this decision and granted the stay.

In *Cable & Wireless PLC v IBM (UK) Ltd* [2002] EWHC 2059, the High Court held that a contractual agreement to go to ADR is analogous to a contractual agreement to arbitrate, and so the same principles applied. A contract between Cable & Wireless and IBM stated that:

> the Parties shall attempt in good faith to resolve any dispute or claim arising out of or relating to this Agreement…through negotiations…If the matter is not resolved

through negotiation, the Parties shall attempt in good faith to resolve the dispute or claim through an Alternative Dispute Resolution (ADR) procedure as recommended to the Parties by the Centre for Dispute Resolution.

Subsequently, a dispute did arise, and a question was then raised regarding the enforceability of the ADR clause. The High Court held that the clause was enforceable, provided that it was

> sufficiently certain. In this case, it was, because of the reference to the Centre for Dispute Resolution being able to recommend a particular procedure. The effect of this ruling is that one of the parties to a contract containing an ADR clause can injunct the other party from pursuing litigation until ADR has at least been attempted – provided the ADR clause is sufficiently certain.

In *DGT Steel & Cladding Ltd v Cubitt Building & Interiors Ltd* [2007] EWHC 1584 (TCC), a case in which the parties had agreed in their contract to refer any future dispute to adjudication, the court again ruled that it had the power to grant a temporary stay to restrain litigation until an adjudication of the underlying dispute had taken place.

17.6 **Problems with court hearings**

Lord Woolf's report, *Access to Justice: Final Report* (July 1996), identified numerous problems with civil litigation, which has arguably contributed to the growth of ADR ever since. In his report Lord Woolf stated:

> The defects I identified in our present system were that it is too expensive in that the costs often exceed the value of the claim; too slow in bringing cases to a conclusion and too unequal: there is a lack of equality between the powerful, wealthy litigant and the under-resourced litigant. It is too uncertain: the difficulty of forecasting what litigation will cost and how long it will last induces the fear of the unknown; and it is incomprehensible to many litigants. Above all, it is too fragmented in the way it is organised since there is no-one with clear overall responsibility for the administration of civil justice; and too adversarial as cases are run by the parties, not by the courts and the rules of court, all too often, are ignored by the parties and not enforced by the court.

See chapter 15, 'The civil process'.

17.6.1 **High cost**

Legal costs can be exorbitant, meaning that those individuals with neither private means nor access to legal aid have little prospect of taking a case to court or, if they do get to court, of taking it to appeal should they lose. For example, it has been estimated that the amount of damages likely to be awarded at a 'typical' libel trial might constitute 'between 2 and 4 per cent of the total costs, or less' (see Shillito 'Mediation in Libel Actions' (2000) NLJ 122; see also G. Webber 'Mediate!' (2000) 144 SJ 654).

17.6.2 **Adversarial procedure**

A trial necessarily involves a winner and a loser and the adversarial process may divide the parties, making them enemies even when they did not start out like that. This is particularly problematic where there is some reason for the parties to maintain a relationship afterwards – e.g. child custody cases. In 1999, the Lord Chancellor's Department (now the Ministry of Justice) published a consultation document, *ADR – a Discussion Paper*, in which the government argued that:

> Typically, a claim for damages proceeds by establishing liability, and then determining an award. It is therefore a process focused on finding the fault; not just adversarial, but antagonistic, with an inherent risk of entrenching positions, and encouraging the nursing of grievances. Characteristically, too, in litigation one side 'wins' and one side 'loses'.

17.6.3 **Inaccessible**

Courts do not sit on weekends or in the evenings, making access very difficult for employed people. The nearest court may also be a considerable distance away, making access very difficult for everybody.

17.6.4 **Inflexible**

Despite the revolution in civil litigation under the Civil Procedure Rules (1998), discussed in chapter 15, courts nevertheless still have to apply rules – both of procedure and of evidence. This may be inappropriate for some cases.

17.6.5 **Publicity**

The majority of court hearings are public. This may be undesirable in some business disputes, where one or both of the parties may prefer not to make public the details of their financial situation or business practices because of potentially damaging publicity. Nor do they want sensitive information becoming available to the public at large, including their competitors. Publicity can also portray celebrity claimants in a less-than-flattering light, even if they are successful in litigation, especially where the defendant is a newspaper or magazine publisher.

17.6.6 **Imposed solutions**

Court judgments impose a solution on the parties which, since it does not involve their consent, may need to be enforced.

17.7 **Advantages of ADR**

The advantages of ADR in general, and mediation in particular, are well known. We can list them as follows:

- it is quick and cost-effective;
- the parties retain control of their dispute;
- its informality and the lack of adversarial procedure helps to preserve the parties' existing relationship; and
- it is confidential.

17.7.1 **Low cost**

With mediation and conciliation, the theory is that neither party will be represented (although in practice this is not always the case). This helps to keep costs down. The lack of specialised facilities – in terms of courtrooms, etc. – also saves cost.

17.7.2 **Speed**

Given its flexibility, ADR is generally much faster. Of course, there are exceptions. If mediation fails to produce a compromise solution, then litigation may be necessary and the time spent in fruitless negotiation has been wasted. Similarly, if one party challenges the award of an arbitrator and the case then has to go to the High Court, the advantages of time-saving are lost.

17.7.3 **Informality**

ADR procedures and locations are usually much less formal, less adversarial, and less stressful as a result. This affords a greater chance of preserving an ongoing relationship than does litigation. This has benefits in just about every possible dispute, from contractual disputes between business partners or corporate organisations, to disputes between neighbours, to matrimonial disputes, particularly where there are children involved. In other words, ADR means that disputes can be more quickly and easily resolved and (as a bonus) the parties have a better chance of maintaining a relationship afterwards. By contrast, litigation, which is formal, and adversarial, will eventually produce an outcome to the dispute, but it will take longer and may perhaps come at a much higher cost in terms of the parties' relationship.

17.7.4 **Accessibility**

Arbitrators and mediators will usually be able to sit on a pre-arranged date and time to suit both parties so minimising time-wasting for all concerned. Virtually all forms of ADR are much more accessible than courts in that they do not have to sit at a specific venue and have been known to sit in places as diverse as local authority buildings, solicitors' offices, church halls, hotels, etc. It has been argued that, 'it must be preferable to take the justice to the people rather than expecting the people to come to the judgment seat' (see J. MacMillan 'Employment Tribunals: Philosophies and Practicalities' (1999) 28 ILJ 33).

17.7.5 **Expertise**

Arbitrators and mediators will usually be specialists in their particular field. For example, disputes in shipping contracts could be referred to specialists in shipping, and disputes between the various parties to a construction contract could be arbitrated by a surveyor, or an architect. The arbitrator or mediator's expertise will allow him or her to grasp the issues in dispute much more quickly, consequently saving time and therefore cost.

17.7.6 **Privacy**

With ADR the proceedings are in private, so that the individuals are not obliged to have their personal circumstances or confidential business secrets broadcast to the general public. This also prevents the taint that disputes can have on reputations. Moreover, the losing party (in arbitration) is not faced with the public ignominy of defeat.

17.7.7 **Agreed solutions (mediation)**

Mediation helps the parties to explore mutually agreeable options for the resolution of their dispute. An agreement reached with the consent of all parties to the dispute is more likely to be adhered to than if it had been imposed by a judge or an arbitrator.

17.7.8 **Eases pressure on the courts**

Sir John Donaldson, in his book *Arbitration for Contractors* (1987) wrote that arbitration was:

> a vitally important alternative to resorting to the courts for the settlement of disputes. If it did not exist, it would have to be invented, because the courts could not possibly handle the sheer volume of disputes which arise in a complex modern society.

These comments also apply, perhaps even more strongly, to other forms of ADR such as mediation. Similarly, in her article, 'The Rise of Mediation in Administrative Law Disputes: Experiences from England, France and Germany' [2006] PL 320, Sophie Boyron writes (about the French legal system, but the arguments do apply to England) that:

There are three main reasons why … courts aspire to pre-trial mediation. First, the case-load is growing at an alarming pace; the workload of many [administrative courts] seems to have reached critical levels and the issue needs to be addressed. Until now the answer had always been to create more courts, to increase the number of chambers in each court and to recruit an ever larger number of judicial personnel. However, it is felt that it is not possible to resort to such solutions forever.

17.8 Disadvantages of ADR

17.8.1 Non-availability of legal aid

Full civil legal aid is available for only a couple of tribunals and for mediation in certain cases. Of course, arbitration and tribunals are designed to dispense with the need for representation – but the hard facts are that in many of them an individual would be faced with a well-resourced and consequently well-represented opponent, be it a government department or an employer. This obviously puts the individual at a disadvantage.

17.8.2 Lack of legal expertise

Where a dispute hinges on difficult points of law, an arbitrator or mediator may not have the required legal expertise to judge. This might generate appeals (bear in mind that the Arbitration Act 1996 specifically allows for appeals to the courts on points of law), generating delays and costs. This problem should not arise, generally speaking, in tribunals, as the chair should be legally qualified. However, there is no requirement that the chair necessarily be qualified in the *relevant* area of law.

Chapter 11, 'Access to justice'.

17.8.3 Imbalance of power

One weakness regarding mediation is its assumption that the parties freely negotiate the terms of their final agreement from a position of equal bargaining strength. This is not necessarily the case and a more powerful party (whether employer, business rival, or ex-partner, husband, or wife) may be able to exploit the weaker party and distort the mediation process to their advantage. Unless the mediator is sufficiently aware of these dangers the weaker party may find the dispute resolved but on very disadvantageous terms to themselves. Arguably, those in a weaker bargaining position should seek the protection of legal representation before the courts rather than risk being exploited in mediation.

Similarly, two-thirds of cases brought to ACAS, the Advisory, Conciliation and Arbitration Service, are either settled by it or withdrawn. This is sometimes taken as an indication of its success; however, this is to ignore the imbalance of power between employer and employee – just because a case has been settled does not mean it was done fairly.

17.8.4 **No system of precedent**

Because each case is judged on its merits and there is no doctrine of precedent, there may be no guidelines for future cases. Tribunals are, however, subject to precedents established by the courts. The competing values of flexibility versus certainty were considered by Sir John Waite, President of the EAT from 1983 to 1985 ('Lawyers and Laymen as Judges in Industry' (1986) 15 ILJ 32):

> A single-minded pursuit of the Franks/Donovan objectives of informality, speed, cheapness and accessibility is bound sooner or later to come into conflict with the aim of certainty. A voice moved wholly by the spirit of Franks and Donovan would say...leave the tribunals to apply their own definition of fairness according to the notions of industrial practice, which it is their unique duty to interpret and apply. The guardian of certainty would be heard to reply that such a course would leave the tribunals navigating in an uncharted sea where they would be at serious risk of collision with each other.

(The reference to 'Franks' is to the Franks Committee Report on Tribunals (1957), and to 'Donovan' is to the Royal Commission Report on Trade Unions and Employers' Associations (1968), known as the Donovan Report.) There is no reason, however, why ADR should not be allowed to create precedents whilst at the same time preserving the hallmarks of privacy and confidentiality that make ADR so attractive in the first place. This could be done by publicising anonymised decisions, which could be referred to in future cases.

Thinking point

Sum up the advantages and disadvantages of litigation when compared to ADR.

17.8.5 **'Legalism' in arbitration and tribunals**

Not all tribunals enjoy the same flexibility and freedom from procedure, however. One obvious example is the Employment Tribunal (previously known as Industrial Tribunals), which has become more formal with more procedural rules. It has also generated a large body of case law. This has attracted plenty of academic and judicial criticism accusing the tribunal of 'legalism'. According to Judge McKee QC ('Legalism in Industrial Tribunals' (1989) ILJ 110):

> Legalism can be defined generally as an inflexible adherence to strict legal formalities and, more particularly, as an undue and an unnecessary reliance on legal authority...There is no place for 'legalism' in Industrial Tribunals. All those involved working in these tribunals must be on their guard to prevent it. 'Legalism' properly so called, is contrary to the principles on which Industrial Tribunals were set up.

Similarly, R. Munday ('Tribunal Lore: Legalism and the Industrial Tribunals' (1981) 10 ILJ 146) has written that 'legalism' refers to the 'unnecessary, narrow-minded formalism' with which the layman associates lawyers. He said that tribunals should 'continue to dispense with the flummery and much of the procedural and evidential paraphernalia of the law courts' but he did acknowledge that, in some respects, tribunals do closely resemble courts.

In *Clay Cross (Quarry Services) Ltd v Fletcher* [1978] 1 WLR 1429, after argument lasting two-and-a-half days, during which a wide selection of Court of Appeal, Employment Appeal Tribunal, European Court of Justice, and various American authorities were cited, Lawton LJ remarked:

> I found all these complications disturbing. Parliament intended that Industrial Tribunals should provide a quick and cheap remedy for what it had decided were injustices in the employment sphere. The procedure was to be such that both employers and employees should present their cases without having to go to lawyers for help. Within a few years, 'legalism' has started to take over. It must be driven back if possible.

Lord Denning, in *Walls Meat Co. Ltd v Khan* (1979) 1 IRLR 499, said that, '[i]f we are not careful, we shall find the Industrial Tribunal bent down under the weight of the law books or, what is worse, asleep under them. Let principles be reported, but not particular instances.' Another area of ADR where there have been accusations of 'legalism' is commercial arbitration. John Flood and Andrew Caiger put forward an argument that ('Lawyers and Arbitration: the Juridification of Construction Disputes' (1993) 56 MLR 412), 'lawyers have been engaged in a struggle to shift the procedures and style of arbitration from the informal to the formal end of the spectrum. That is, their aim is to reproduce the court within the arbitral forum.' In support of this theory, they quote an anonymous 'senior construction solicitor' who commented that 'lawyers tend to overjudicialise the arbitration process', while an engineer observed that 'the lawyers have hijacked arbitration; it's no different from going to court'.

More significantly, they also quote a senior barrister, John Uff QC, who said: 'The whole process of arbitration has become far too legal and complicated.' The reason for this was the fact that many arbitrators in construction disputes were engineers or architects, with little knowledge of building issues. This encouraged both sides to call witnesses, and adopt what he called 'the formal High Court procedure' of examination followed by cross-examination.

Thinking point

Judicial processes must be operated according to rules and 'legalism' in tribunals will occur due to need for the involvement of lawyers, especially in complex areas of law, such as employment law. Is it inevitable that tribunals will suffer from 'legalism'?

➕ Summary

- Tribunals are effectively specialist courts dealing in single issues, for example immigration, housing, social security, tax. Tribunals have similar features to ADR (accessibility, flexibility, informality), with the added quality of specialisation.

- In 2008, the tribunal system in the UK was thoroughly restructured under the Tribunals, Courts and Enforcement Act 2007. Most tribunals have now been relocated to one of the seven chambers in the 'First-tier' Tribunal or one of the four chambers in the Upper Tribunal, although some (such as the Employment and Employment Appeal Tribunals) remain outside of that structure.

- Decisions of the First-tier tribunal can be appealed on points of law to the Upper Tribunal and decisions of the Upper Tribunal can be appealed to the Court of Appeal; tribunal decisions can (in limited circumstances) be subject to judicial review in the High Court, following *Cart & Another* (2011).

- There are several different forms of ADR:
  - arbitration, which is relatively formal and the arbitrator conducts proceedings like a judge and gives a binding decision;
  - mediation, which is much more informal, negotiations with the mediator facilitating a mutually acceptable compromise solution (although this is not guaranteed);
  - conciliation, which is as described earlier, but the conciliator is more pro-active/interventionist; and
  - med-arb, which is a process which starts with mediation but if no compromise agreement is forthcoming, the process changes to arbitration, which guarantees a solution.

- Reasons why ADR exists are essentially the converse of the problems with litigation:
  - cost and time-consuming nature of litigation;
  - accessibility issues;
  - lack of flexibility in courts' procedure/range of outcomes;
  - publicity;
  - formality; and
  - adversarial nature of litigation.

- There is a growing body of case law on 'adverse costs consequences' which was designed to promote mediation/ADR by penalising litigants who failed to respond positively to a suggestion from the other party to enter into mediation (*Cowl, Dunnett v Railtrack*). However, this hard-line approach has since softened and the courts now require the losing party to litigation to prove that the winner's failure to mediate was unreasonable (*Hurst v Leeming*, and *Halsey v Milton Keynes NHS Trust*).

- The courts have no powers to compel mediation or indeed any other form of ADR (*Halsey*), as to do so would create barriers and could even infringe the human rights of the litigants (Article 6 of the ECHR: right to a fair trial). However, courts can and do strongly encourage alternatives to litigation.

? Questions

1 Why is ADR so much cheaper than going to court?

2 Why is ADR so much quicker than going to court?

3 What are the other advantages of ADR?

4 Why is lack of precedent, a typical feature of ADR, a possible disadvantage?

5 What are the other disadvantages of ADR?

✳ Sample question and outline answer

Question

The problems inherent in civil litigation make it imperative that parties are shown the benefit of alternatives to litigation such as arbitration and mediation. It is, therefore, regrettable that the Court of Appeal has taken the step of curtailing the power of courts to penalise parties for not pursuing alternative dispute resolution (ADR) in *Halsey v Milton Keynes Trust*. A return to the firm line taken by the Court in *Dunnet v Railtrack* is required. Discuss.

Outline answer

Begin your answer by explaining the inherent problems of civil litigation – the cost, delays, publicity, formality, inaccessibility (in terms of location and restricted 'opening hours'), how the involvement of lawyers and the adversarial nature of court-based litigation creates antagonism, the limited range of solutions available to the courts, etc.

Explain the alternatives – mediation, arbitration, concilitation, med-arb, etc. Make sure that you differentiate these different forms of ADR from each other. Point out, for example, that arbitration is relatively formal and not necessarily cheaper than litigation but leads to a definite solution. Also point out, for example, that mediation is relatively informal but is dependent on the parties' willingness to negotiate a compromise solution. Perhaps comment that this is a weakness of mediation (the fact that there is no guarantee of an outcome to the dispute) and that med-arb arguably provides a better solution (i.e. if mediation fails, the process switches to arbitration).

Explain how the courts have tried to promote alternatives to litigation in cases such as *Dunnett v Railtrack* (2002) (promotion of mediation) and *IDA* (2006) (promotion of med-arb). In particular, explain how the Court of Appeal in *Dunnett* indicated that a failure by a litigant to respond with sufficient enthusiasm to an offer from the other party to mediate might lead to 'uncomfortable costs consequences', i.e. that even if they were to succeed in court, the winning litigant may be penalised by having to pay the other party's costs.

Then explain how *Dunnett* has been distinguished in subsequent cases such as *Hurst v Leeming* (which decided that costs penalties will only follow where mediation has a realistic prospect of success), effectively limiting *Dunnett* to cases where it was unreasonable to refuse to consider mediation. Explain how, in *Halsey v Milton Keynes NHS Trust* (2004), the Court of Appeal clearly placed the burden of proof on the party asserting that a failure by the other side to respond to an offer to mediate was unreasonable. Explain the factors which Dyson LJ (as he then was) identified as being relevant in determining this issue, i.e. the nature of the dispute; the merits of the case; the extent to which other settlement methods had been attempted; whether the costs of ADR would be disproportionately high; whether any delay in setting up and attending the ADR would have been prejudicial; and whether the ADR had a reasonable prospect of success. Consider the application of the factors in subsequent cases such as *Burchell v Bullard* (2005).

Reach a conclusion. Your conclusion will depend on whether you agree with the hardline approach of the Court of Appeal in *Dunnett* or the more flexible approach of the same court in *Halsey*.

Further reading

- **Boyron, S.** 'The Rise of Mediation in Administrative Law Disputes: Experiences from England, France and Germany' [2006] PL 320
  Examines the use of mediation in the resolution of public law disputes (i.e. those involving public bodies) in three different jurisdictions.

- **Elliott, M.** and **Thomas, R.** 'Tribunal Justice and Proportionate Dispute Resolution' (2012) 71 CLJ 297
  Examines the relationship between tribunals and courts following the Tribunals, Courts and Enforcement Act 2007 and the Supreme Court's ruling in *Cart & Another* (2011).

- **Flood, J.** and **Caiger, A.** 'Lawyers and Arbitration: the Juridification of Construction Disputes' (1993) 56 MLR 412
  Examines the differences between arbitration proceedings in the construction industry conducted with the involvement of lawyers and similar proceedings conducted using subject specialists, e.g. architects, surveyors, etc.

- **Jacobs, E.** 'Something Old, Something New: The New Tribunal System' (2009) 38 ILJ 417
  Examines the changes to the tribunal system under the Tribunals, Courts and Enforcement Act 2007.

- **Shipman, S.** 'Court Approaches to ADR in the Civil Justice System' (2006) 25 CJQ 181
  Examines the Court of Appeal's case law (including *Dunnett* and *Halsey*) on the cost consequences of failure to mediate.

- **Tronson, B.** 'Mediation Orders: Do the Arguments against them Make Sense?' (2006) 25 CJQ 412
  Compares and contrasts the situation in the English legal system (whereby mediation can only be encouraged by the courts) with other jurisdictions, in particular New South Wales in Australia (where the courts have the power to order mediation).

Online Resource Centre

You should now attempt the supporting multiple choice questions available at **www.oxfordtextbooks.co.uk/orc/wilson_els/**.

Index